Paper = Dec 7

HOTEL, RESTAURANT, AND TRAVEL LAW

A Preventive Approach

SIXTH EDITION

NORMAN G. COURNOYER
ANTHONY G. MARSHALL
KAREN L. MORRIS

THOMSON
DELMAR LEARNING

Hotel, Restaurant, and Travel Law: A Preventive Approach, Sixth Edition
by Norman G. Cournoyer, Anthony G. Marshall, Karen L. Morris

Vice President, Career Education
Strategic Business Unit:
Dawn Gerrain

Editorial Director:
Sherry Gomoll

Senior Acquisitions Editor:
Joan M. Gill

Developmental Editor:
Andrea Edwards

Editorial Assistant:
Lisa Flatley

Production Director:
Wendy A. Troeger

Production Manager:
Carolyn Miller

Production Editor:
Matthew J. Williams

Marketing Director:
Donna J. Lewis

Channel Manager:
Wendy E. Mapstone

Cover Design:
Dutton & Sherman Design

For permission to use material from this text or product, contact us by
Tel (800) 730-2214
Fax (800) 730-2215
www.thomsonrights.com

Library of Congress Cataloging-in-Publication Data

Cournoyer, Norman G.
  Hotel, restaurant, and travel law: a preventive approach / Norman G. Cournoyer, Anthony G. Marshall, Karen L. Morris.
    p. cm.
  Includes bibliographical references and index.
  ISBN 0-7668-3599-5
  1. Hotels--Law and legislation--United States. 2. Hospitality industry--Law and legislation--United States. 3. Travel agents--Legal status, laws, etc.--United States. I. Marshall, Anthony G. II. Morris, Karen, 1950- III. Title
  KF951.C62003
  33.73'07864794--21   2003051632

NOTICE TO THE READER

CONTENTS

TABLE OF CASES

PREFACE

Lawsuits are expensive, time-consuming, and damaging to a business's reputation. *Hotel, Restaurant, and Travel Law: A Preventive Approach*, Sixth Edition, focuses on *prevention* as the means to minimize the number of lawsuits a hospitality establishment experiences. While it is true that good hospitality management means satisfying patrons and guests, it also encompasses protecting the business from the kinds of accidents and incidents that can lead to litigation. Indeed, the two concerns of good service and lawsuit prevention overlap substantially. Pleasing guests involves not just comfortable surroundings, a welcoming staff, and good food; an additional component is a safe facility that enables guests to enjoy their time away from home without injury or harm. Most lawsuits can be prevented if management and staff are properly trained to recognize potential pitfalls and guard against them. Throughout the six editions of this book, a primary objective of the authors has been to arm future hospitality industry personnel with the legal knowledge needed to enhance the guest's experience and to prevent lawsuits.

Revised for Clarity and Critical Thinking

This sixth edition has been revised and updated to make Hospitality Law more approachable and understandable for students. We think this edition is a better tool for the development of critical-thinking skills in managers—skills needed to adapt to the contemporary legal environment and its new laws and regulations, high expectations by patrons, and many legal rights for employees. For example, this edition includes the following:

- New **Web site references** offer students the opportunity for expanded exposure to the topics in each chapter.

- The **case study format** has been retained; the book continues to include substantial portions of many court decisions on numerous topics. Utilizing the cases to teach hospitality law sharpens students' skills in understanding the rules and the nuances of the law, both of which are critical competencies in a discipline such as law where the outcome of a case depends on many variables. The case method also helps students learn to decipher important information from large amounts of data. This is a necessary management skill in today's world given that technology has made the amount of accessible information daunting, and the legal environment of business makes the absence of critical information damning.

- The **end-of-chapter material** entitled "Preventive Law Tips for Managers" has been retained and, where appropriate, expanded. This feature provides a concentrated summary of the issues addressed in the chapter.

- The number of **chapters on negligence** has been reduced from three to two. While this topic is of great importance to hospitality managers, the complexities of the legal environment in which hospitality facilities presently do business require significant time on many other competing topics.

- The chapter that previously included both **food and alcohol** has been divided into two chapters to facilitate student learning and to underscore the importance of the laws related to each of these topics.

- The **text** presents *plain-English explanations* of essential legal concepts. Also, each chapter includes many subtopics. The effect of both is to enhance the ability of students to read and comprehend the material.

- Case questions engage readers at the end of most case examples, drawing together practices and principles.

- End-of-chapter questions expand review and discussion of the material and add the challenge of applying legal principles to business situations.

Training Intelligent Management

The goal of this book is to enable managers to understand the law as it relates to the hospitality industry, to appreciate how a legal case proceeds in court, and to engage their lawyers more intelligently. It is important that managers recognize the legal ramifications of the policy and practices of their business and be able to apply legal principles to everyday operations. Without this knowledge and ability, avoidable accidents and illegal conduct will go unabated, resulting in unfortunate and preventable lawsuits and penalties.

This book gives managers a base of expertise on which to build and includes the following:

- **Clearly defined legal terms** help students understand important principles when they are first introduced and apply those principles to factual situations.

- **Preventive Law Tips for Managers** recast the main points of each chapter as review and practical advice.

- **Lessons on risks of injury in a hospitality facility** enable managers to identify hazards and correct them, thereby protecting their guests from harm and their employer from lawsuits.

Profiting from Real-World Experience

This book provides readers with the opportunity to profit from the experience of others through the careful study of real lawsuits that resulted from mistakes of hotel and restaurant managers working in the field.

- **Case examples** detail recent legal situations that led to lawsuits, as well as the outcome of the cases and the reasoning of the courts. Attention is focused on what the facility did wrong and how similar problems can be avoided.

- **Updated coverage** strengthens understanding of technology's impact on the law, liquor liability, legal consequences of foodborne illnesses, employment and discrimination laws including résumé fraud, the Americans with Disabilities Act, civil rights acts, and sexual harassment, plus negligence, and casino operations.

Organization

The sixth edition of *Hotel, Restaurant, and Travel Law* is organized in the following four units:

- Unit 1, Legal Fundamentals for the Hospitality Industry, presents the sources and principles of hospitality law, basic court procedures, civil rights issues, and contract law.

- Unit 2, Negligence, presents the legal principles relevant to this topic and many cases that help define the scope of obligations and liability.

- Unit 3, Relationships with Guests and Other Patrons, explores the special responsibilities that hospitality businesses have to their different publics, and the obligations individuals owe those businesses.

- Unit 4, Special Topics, addresses food and alcohol liability, legal duties of travel agents, airlines and car rental companies, employment matters, franchising, copyrights and trademarks, licensing, and casino law.

Supplementary Materials

The *Instructor's Guide* contains answers to the end-of-chapter questions, answers to in-text case questions, case briefs, and transparency masters. The Web site contains a variety of additional resources to aid the student.

ABOUT THE AUTHORS

Norman G. Cournoyer is a lawyer and Professor Emeritus at University of Massachussets, Amherst. A nationally recognized expert in hospitality law, zoning for service industries, labor management, computer applications, and econometrics for hospitality management, he has ten years experience owning and operating hotels and restaurants.

A widely published writer, Dr. Cournoyer has authored several texts, references, and directories for the hospitality disciplines. He has contributed scholarly journals and has published numerous studies for the Massachussets Department of Commerce and Development.

Dr. Cournoyer is currently president of Applied Econometrics and has served as consultant to Hilton Corporation, Sheraton Corporation, the U.S. Army, and Canadian National Marine Services, Inc.

Dr. Cournoyer holds a Juris Doctorate from American University, and an MBA in financial accounting and a Ph.D. in econometrics from the University of Massachussetts. He resides in Amherst.

Anthony G. Marshall, Dean of the School of Hospitality Management at Florida International University in Miami, Florida, is a nationally recognized expert in Risk Management and Hospitality Law. He is well known by members of the hospitality industry through his speaking engagements and journal publications.

Dr. Marshall serves as a board member of the Commission Scolaire of the Centre International de Glion, Switzerland; a board member of the Greater Miami Convention & Visitors Bureau and vice chair of the Board of Trustees of the Educational Institute of the American Hotel and Motel Association. He is the recipient of the American Hotel and Motel Association's "Lamp of Knowledge" award.

Dr. Marshall authors the column "At Your Risk" (21 issues per year) in Hotel and Motel Management magazine. He is publisher and editorial board member of the Florida International University Hospitality Review; and a member of the editorial board of the International Journal of Hospitality Management.

He earned a Juris Doctorate from the College of Law at Syracuse University and a Bachelor of Science in Hotel Administration from the University of New Hampshire.

Dr. Marshall resides on Key Biscayne, Florida.

Karen L. Morris is a lawyer, judge, and Professor of Law at Monroe Community College in Rochester, New York. She teaches courses including Hotel and Restaurant Law, Business Law, Constitutional Law, Criminal Law and Law 101. As a town judge she presides over criminal and civil cases, including lawsuits brought against hotels, restaurants, and travel agents.

In addition to writing three editions of this textbook, she has published a case-studies book for Business Law and a treatise on Penal Law, as well as articles in various publications on topics of interest to the hospitality industry. She has been honored with several awards including Excellence in Teaching, Golden Pen, and Distinguished Citizen.

Professor Morris is the legal advisor to the New York State Restaurant Association, Rochester Chapter. She has served as President of Text and Academic Authors Association, Dean of Academy of Law, and President of her Faculty Association. She is a past president of the Greater Rochester Association for Women Attorneys. She has also served as president of The Academy of Legal Studies in Business, Northeast Region. Her favorite volunteer activity is being a Big Sister in the Big Brother program.

Before beginning her teaching career, Judge Morris was in-house counsel for a corporation that operates department stores throughout the United States, and thereafter a criminal prosecutor.

She has a Juris Doctor degree from St. John's University and a Masters of Law (LL.M.) in Trade Regulation from New York University.

Acknowledgments

The authors wish to express thier appreciation to the reviewers who enhanced the quality of this book:

G. Michael Harris, Jr.
Bethune-Cookman College
Daytona Beach, Florida

Linda Enghagen, J.D.
University of Massachusetts
Amherst, Massachusetts

Dr. Dan Crafts
Southwest Missouri State University
Springfield, Missouri

Norman G. Cournoyer
Anthony G. Marshall
Karen L. Morris

UNIT I

■

Legal Fundamentals for the Hospitality Industry

CHAPTER 1

■

Introduction to Contemporary Hospitality Law

CHAPTER OUTLINE

■

Introduction

What is Law?

Principles of Hospitality Law

Sources of Law

Attributes of Law

How to Read a Case

INTRODUCTION

You are about to embark on an exciting study. Law is a unique and contemporary discipline with many applications to our everyday lives. You will sometimes applaud a court's decision and at other times you will be perplexed at the outcome. But above all you will be fascinated and engaged as you study hotel, restaurant, and travel law.

This chapter will introduce you to some basic principles of law including its sources, some of its attributes, and important legal definitions. The chapter will also teach you how to read a case.

What is Law?

Law has many definitions, including a "body of rules to which people must conform their conduct"; "a form of social control"; and "a set of rules used by judges in deciding disputes." The common denominator in all of these definitions is that law consists of rules that require people to meet certain standards of conduct and are enforceable in court.

Principles of Hospitality Law

Hospitality law covers a wide range of law applied primarily to restaurants, bars, places that offer lodging to the public (referred to collectively as either hotels or inns), travel agents, and airlines. Much of this body of law also applies to recreational facilities such as casinos, amusement parks, theaters, night clubs, and sports facilities.

Balancing Rights and Duties

As you study hospitality law you will notice that the various lawmaking branches of government try to balance the interests of travelers with those of business proprietors. We will conduct an in-depth study of the legal rights and duties of the hotel guest and restaurant patron, as well as those of the innkeeper and restaurateur. While these rights and obligations are quite complex, at the basic level they require that the hotel or restaurant owner must provide patrons a safe place in which to lodge or eat, and the customer must act within acceptable bounds and pay for the services received. Similarly, the duty of the travel agent is to provide travel services, and the responsibility of the traveler is to pay. Often the interests of the service providers and patrons conflict. As is its function, the law provides an organized set of rules to resolve these conflicts.

History of Hospitality Law

The history of hospitality law is not a proud one. It is based on a very low opinion of innkeepers that was apparently justified by their unethical behavior. In fourteenth- and fifteenth-century England, innkeepers were believed to associate with robbers and even to help thieves steal from guests. To counteract innkeepers' supposed illegal activities, early laws pertaining to inns and taverns were stringent and usually favored the guests.

A quotation from a book by W. C. Firebaugh entitled *The Inns of the Middle Ages* illustrates the need at that time for strict laws to protect guests:

> [I]n the eyes of the law, the innkeeper, the pander and others of like standing were on the same footing. ... In past ages, the tavern and innkeeper have been guide, philosopher, and friend to all the evil reprobates in his neighborhood.

Today, innkeepers are in a different class than their fifteenth-century counterparts and enjoy a respectable reputation.

Another factor that contributed to the harshness of hospitality laws in the early years was the limited number of inns and the resulting monopoly enjoyed by innkeepers. When competition is virtually nonexistent, unscrupulous businesspeople may take advantage of the situation. The law was the guest's primary protection. Today, of course, inns are no longer few and far apart. On the contrary, there is a great deal of competition in most locations.

Sources of Law

Our law comes from four main sources: the Constitution, statutes, common law (also called case law), and administrative law. The following material explains each of these sources.

Constitutional Law

The law embodied in the United States Constitution is called **constitutional law**. It prescribes the organization of the federal government, including the executive, legislative, and judicial branches, and defines the powers of the federal government. As you will recall from your studies of early American history, the states were suspicious of a strong federal government. Having just overthrown England, the states wanted significant limitations on the authority granted to the central government. As a result, its authority is limited to the delegated powers. **Delegated powers** are those expressly allocated to the federal government in the Constitution. All other authority is left to the states. Examples of delegated powers include development of a system of money and regulation of interstate commerce. **Interstate commerce** is business affecting more than one state, as opposed to business done between two parties in the same state.

The process by which the federal government as well as other units of government adopt laws is called the **legislative process**. The Constitution defines the method by which **Congress**, the primary lawmaking body of the federal government, adopts laws. The legislative process is described in greater detail in Chapter 2.

The Constitution establishes important rights such as equal protection under the law, freedom of speech, and freedom of religion. We will study more about civil rights in Chapters 3 and 14.

The Constitution also authorizes the federal government to enter treaties with other countries. Some of these treaties affect travel to locations outside of the United States. We will study one of these treaties in Chapter 13. Another treaty addresses international protection of a copyright, which is the exclusive right to reproduce certain types of works such as art, literature, musical compositions, and software. We will study this treaty in Chapter 15.

Broad Wording

The Constitution declares broad principles of law and provides very little detail. For example, the Constitution states that we have the right of free speech. Does this include the right to publish false information about another person? Does it include the right to yell "fire" in a crowded theater? The Constitution provides no clarification on these issues

The Constitution also provides the right of religious freedom. Suppose you work as a food server afternoons and evenings, Thursday through Sunday. You choose to become an Orthodox Jew and refuse to work on the Sabbath (Friday night and Saturday). If you are terminated from your job because you cannot work on those days, has your right to religious freedom been violated? The Constitution does not answer these questions; instead, it establishes broad, foundational principles of law. We need additional sources of law to provide the details.

Statutory Law

The second source of law in the United States is statutory law. **Statutory law** is law promulgated by legislators and generally agreed to by the executive (president, governor, or mayor). A **legislature** is a lawmaking body consisting of members elected to office by the citizenry. The elected members of the legislature are called **legislators**. We elect legislators at the federal level (members of the House of Representatives and the Senate), the state level (state legislators), and the local level (county legislators and city or town councilmembers). When a federal or state legislature adopts a law it is called a **statute**. When a local legislature adopts a law it is often called an **ordinance**.

Common Law

The third source of law in the United States is **common law**, the legal rules that evolved, not from statutes, but rather from decisions of judges and from custom and practice. Historically, it was called common law because it was intended to be common or uniform for the entire English kingdom. These customs and practices obtained their authority from the test of time. Common law was modified gradually as habits were modified and as new inventions created new wants and conveniences and new methods of doing business.

Precedents

A feature of a common-law system that distinguishes it from other legal systems is its reliance on case decisions. A **case decision** is an interpretation of the law applied by a judge to a set of facts in a given case. The case decision becomes a **precedent**—that is, a basis for deciding future cases. If another judge later must decide a case with a similar issue (a related set of facts and legal questions), the judge will consult the precedent for help in deciding the case. Absent a good reason not to follow precedent, the judge will likely decide the later case consistent with the earlier case. This process of following earlier cases is called "**stare decisis**," which is Latin for "the matter stands decided." The purpose of stare decisis is to give some uniformity to the law. Since judges are expected to follow precedent, you can anticipate that the case law you study today will remain in effect until a court decides that a good reason exists to change it.

Sometimes circumstances suggest that a prior decision is no longer appropriate. Perhaps the judge made a bad decision in the first case, or societal forces have changed suggesting a different outcome would be more in tune with the times. Under these circumstances a judge is not bound by stare decisis to follow the prior judge's decision. Rather, the judge can decide the case differently and may even adopt the opposite position. The new decision then becomes the precedent for subsequent judges addressing the same issue.

For example, the United States Constitution provides that we all have the right to equal protection under the law. What does that mean? In 1896 the highest court in our country, the United States Supreme Court, determined that racial segregation was consistent with the constitutional mandate of equal protection; facilities could be separate provided they were substantially equal. The case was *Plessy v. Ferguson*, 163 U.S. 537 (1896). Applying the doctrine of stare decisis, other courts throughout the country followed that ruling whenever segregation issues arose. Almost sixty years later, in *Brown v. Board of Education*, 347 U.S. 483 (1954), the Supreme Court reversed *Plessy* and held the exact opposite, that the separate-but-equal doctrine is inconsistent with the equal-protection clause of the Constitution. The case was the legal death knell of segregation. Why did the court not follow precedent? It explained in its decision that circumstances and knowledge developed since *Plessy* had established that separate-but-equal worked to deprive black people of the range and quality of opportunities available to whites, and was thus inherently unequal. Therefore, the precedent was no longer acceptable.

In cases where judges are confronted with issues that have not been previously resolved, and thus no precedents exist, they will use their best judgment to determine the case after considering the facts, relevant social factors, other cases that may not be directly on point but are analogous, and any other factors that may be helpful. Thereafter, that decision will be a precedent for subsequent cases.

The common law has survived because, when coupled with stare decisis, it provides consistency to our law and yet its foundations are sufficiently flexible to develop and adapt to changes over time, including social movements and technological advances.

Relationship between Statutes and the Constitution

Occasionally a statute may be found to conflict with the United States Constitution. In these circumstances the statute is declared void, for the Constitution is the supreme law of the United States. For example, in *Roe v. Wade*, a pregnant woman challenged the legality of a statute that prohibited doctors from performing abortions. The woman claimed it violated her constitutional right to privacy. The court agreed and declared the statute to be void. That decision is now precedent in other cases in which a state may seek to adopt a statute restricting access to abortions.

In another case, a town had a statute limiting the number of political signs people can display on their lawn to one. Residents who wished to show their support for more than one candidate objected, claiming the law violated their right to free speech. The court agreed and held the restriction to be unconstitutional and therefore void.

Relationship between Statutes and Common Law

To some extent statutes and common law are intertwined. Sometimes statutes are ambiguously worded. If such a statute is relevant in a lawsuit, the judge in the case will have to interpret the law; that is, the judge will have to determine its meaning. The judge's decision in that case will become precedent for future cases.

For example, a statute in New York makes it a felony to cause physical injury to someone while using a dangerous instrument. The term "dangerous instrument" is defined as an article that, under the circumstances in which it is used, is readily capable of causing death or serious physical injury. A defendant caused injury to his victim by beating him with a cane. The judge had to determine whether a cane was a dangerous instrument. Consistent with stare decisis, the judge first researched to determine if any other cases with the same issue had been previously decided. If so, the judge would have considered following that prior decision. No earlier case existed. Therefore, the judge analyzed all the facts and circumstances, reviewed the statute defining a dangerous instrument, and determined that the cane qualified. This decision will be precedent for subsequent cases that present the same issue.

Sometimes statutes are adopted to modify the common law. For example, common law once imposed absolute liability on innkeepers for all goods of guests. If a guest's property was stolen while the guest was at the inn, the innkeeper was almost always liable. In 1850, Massachusetts became the first state to change the common-law rule with a statute that limited the liability of innkeepers for lost property. New York followed suit in 1853, and all states now have such a statute. We will study these laws in Chapter 9.

Administrative Law

The fourth source of law is administrative law. **Administrative law** refers to laws that define the powers, limitations, and procedures of administrative agencies. An **administrative agency** is a governmental subdivision charged with administering legislation that applies to a particular industry. Administrative agencies have many names, including departments, commissions, bureaus, councils, groups, services, divisions, and agencies. Agencies exist at all levels of government, but are generally part of the executive branch. Examples of administrative agencies include the following:

- The Food and Drug Administration, which oversees food and pharmaceutical businesses
- The Federal Communications Commission, which oversees the communications/broadcasting industry
- The Consumer Product Safety Commission, which polices the safety of consumer products.

Some agencies are authorized to adopt laws relevant to the industry they administer. For example, the Occupational Safety and Health Administration not only investigates and enforces statutes addressing safety in the workplace, but also passes laws on the topic. Laws adopted by administrative agencies are called **regulations** to distinguish them from laws passed by legislators. Unlike legislators, the people who govern administrative agencies are not elected; rather, they are appointed by elected officials.

Attributes of Law

Law is a dynamic discipline, always changing to adjust to societal transformations, yet also striving to remain constant enough not to disrupt the legal order that has developed. Law can be both an exciting and difficult field to study. It is not a discipline with clear-cut rules whose applications to factual situations are easy and obvious. Reasonable people can disagree on how and whether a particular rule of law applies in a given case. Confusion may result from the fact that different judges have decided seemingly similar cases differently. Sometimes the law on a particular topic may be unclear because it is in a developmental stage. For example, the law relating to new technological advances takes time to crystallize. The law is further complicated by the fact that it can vary from state to state. Because of these challenges, the study of law can be both difficult and rewarding.

The Role of the Judge

The role of the judge in our legal system is very significant. As we have seen, the judge both "makes" the law in cases where no precedent or statute exists and interprets the law in cases where a statute applies. We will see that some judges, called appellate judges, also review decisions of other judges. The words *judge* and *court* are frequently used interchangeably.

Civil and Criminal Law

There are numerous classifications of law. One classification is **civil** and another is **criminal**. The differences are as follows:

1. In civil law a wrong usually is done to an individual. In criminal law the wrong is considered to be done to society at large and involves violation of a criminal statute.

2. The objective of a civil lawsuit is compensation for an injury. The objective of a criminal case is punishment of the wrongdoer.

3. The party who commences the lawsuit in a civil case is the injured person. The title of the case includes that person's name and the name of the person being sued. Thus, the title of a civil case involving injury to the female coauthor of this textbook caused by one Mindy Sanders would be *Karen Morris v. Mindy Sanders*. On the other hand, the party who undertakes a criminal case is society-at-large, usually referred to as "The State of ...," "The People of the State of ...," or "The Commonwealth of ...". Thus, a Massachusetts criminal case might be titled *The Commonwealth of Massachusetts v. John Doe*.

4. In a civil case the person who is suing hires and pays for his or her own lawyer. In a criminal case, society (for example, The People of the State of California) is represented by a lawyer paid by the government. The title frequently used for that attorney is district attorney and/or prosecutor.

Examples of Civil Law

The following are examples of civil law:

Contracts

A **contract** is an agreement between two or more parties that is enforceable in court. If one person fails to abide by the agreement, the other can sue for breach of contract. Unlike statutes, which are laws made by legislatures, and unlike common law, which is law made by judges, contracts represent "law" made by individuals. Businesses in the hospitality industry enter numerous contracts on a regular basis, including contracts with guests for hotel rooms and contracts by restaurants with food vendors. We will study more about contracts in Chapter 4.

Torts

A tort is a violation of a legal duty by one person that causes injury to another. (Breaches of contractual duties, however, are not considered torts.) Included among the various torts are the following:

- **Negligence**, which means breach of a legal duty to act reasonably, often defined as carelessness. For example, a hotel is negligent if it fails to fix a broken railing on steps in a prompt manner. We will study negligence in Chapters 5, 6, and 7.
- **Trademark Infringement**, which means use of another company's business name or logo without permission. For example, a restaurant infringes a trademark if it adopts as its name the same name used by another restaurant in the same vicinity without the other restaurant's approval. We will study this tort in Chapter 15.
- **Fraud**, which is an intentionally untruthful statement made to induce reliance by another person. For example, if a resort represents in its advertisements that it has a golf course, but in fact it does not, and a guest opts to stay at the hotel because of the purported golf facilities, this is fraud. We will revisit this tort in a number of contexts throughout the book.

Remedies in Civil Cases

The remedy sought by the injured party in a civil case is **damages**, meaning money. Two main types of damages exist—compensatory and punitive. **Compensatory damages** refers to money given to the plaintiff to compensate for injuries. Compensatory damages include post and future out-of-pocket expenses, such as medical bills, lost wages, and certain other losses. The exact amount awarded to a plaintiff is determined by a jury or, in a nonjury case, the judge. Compensatory damages can also include pain and suffering, meaning physical distress or mental anguish; loss of enjoyment of life, meaning inability by the plaintiff to continue to engage in those activities that brought joy or fulfillment before the injury; loss of consortium, meaning loss of the companionship and sexual relations of a spouse; and loss of services, meaning loss of the aid, assistance, and companionship of another person, such as a parent.

Punitive damages, also called *exemplary damages*, refers to money in excess of compensatory damages. Punitive damages are awarded to a plaintiff, not for reimbursement of a loss, but rather to punish or make an example of the defendant. They are awarded only in cases where the defendant's wrongful acts are aggravated by violence, malice, fraud, or a similar egregious wrong.

Examples of Crimes

Included among the many types of crimes are the following:

- **Theft of services**, which is the use of services like a hotel room without paying and with the intent of avoiding payment. We will study theft of services in Chapter 10.
- **Assault**, which is intentionally causing physical injury to another person. Chapter 7 will discuss the unfortunate circumstance of assaults occurring in hotel rooms as a result of lax security.
- **Rape**, which is forceful sexual intercourse against the victim's will. As with assault, Chapter 7 discusses cases involving rapes occurring in hotel rooms.

Penalties and Remedies in Criminal Cases

The possible penalties for committing a crime include community service, fines, probation, jail, and in some states, death. **Probation** is a system whereby criminal offenders remain out of jail but are supervised by a probation officer. What punishment will be applied in a given case is determined in part by statute and in part by the judge. The applicable statute will provide a range of sentences available to the judge. For example, in New York the range of sentences for theft of services includes a jail sentence of up to one year, a fine up to $1000, probation for up to%three years, and unlimited community service. The judge must decide in each case what sentence within the allowable range is appropriate for the particular defendant. The sentence will vary depending upon the facts of the particular case, the circumstances and criminal record of the perpetrator, and the impact of the crime on the victim.

How to Read a Case

Judges' decisions are customarily written and thereafter recorded in books used for legal research. These written decisions are called **cases**, and the books in which they are published are called **case books**. These cases are part of the common law. You will read many cases in your study of hotel and restaurant law. Although at first they may seem hard to understand, you will soon develop the skill necessary to read them with a high level of comprehension. To understand a case you should attempt to identify four elements as you read it:

1. The facts
2. The issue
3. The judge's decision
4. The reasoning supporting the decision.

The *facts* are those circumstances that gave rise to the lawsuit. The *issue* is the legal question that the parties have asked the judge to resolve. The *decision* is the judge's response to the issue. The *reasoning* is the basis and rationale for the decision. After reading the case, consider its implications vis-a-vis stare decisis; the decision, although involving unknown parties, informs hospitality managers how the law will likely be applied to their own situations. This enables innkeepers and restaurateurs to predict how the law will be interpreted and to prevent legal disputes before they arise. By understanding the implications of cases, the manager or owner can modify company policies and actions to conform to the law.

The following is an example of a case. As you read it, write down the four elements as you come to them. Then compare your findings with the analysis that follows the case.

CASE EXAMPLE 1-1

Immormino v. McDonald's
698 N.E.2d 516 (Ohio, 1998)

Plaintiff Mary Lee Immormino alleges injury due to a hot water spill from a cup served by defendant McDonald's fast food franchise. ... The incident in question occurred on September 24, 1993 in Chesterland, Ohio. Plaintiff and her husband purchased several food products from the drive-thru window at McDonald's, including hot tea for the plaintiff herself. Plaintiff, who was a front-seat passenger, executed a series of maneuvers to steep her tea. As she was replacing the lid on the cup, she spilled the tea on her lap causing injury. Plaintiff's complaint alleges that defendant failed to warn consumers of the temperature of the beverage. ... According to the uncontradicted evidence, the cup contained the following legend: "CAUTION—CONTENTS MAY BE HOT". The warning was printed in two locations on the cup. ...

The court holds that the warnings issued in this case were adequate. The cup in question contained bold warnings cautioning the holder about hot contents. The consumer had ordered hot tea. The Oxford Encyclopedic English Dictionary describes "tea" as follows: "A drink made by infusing tea-leaves in **boiling water.**" This court holds as a matter of law that consumer expectations coupled with warnings on the cup established sufficient warning to the plaintiff that the tea might be too hot for the tongue; that the tea was capable of causing injury to other body parts; and that the consumer should expect potential injury from a spill of hot liquid. ...

The defendant is entitled to judgment as a matter of law.

Now for the analysis of the four elements and the implications. The important *facts* are that Immormino purchased hot tea at a McDonald's drive-thru. She spilled the heated liquid on her lap causing injury. The cup contained warnings that the contents were hot. The *issue* is—Did the restaurant give sufficient warnings to consumers of the temperature of the tea? The *decision* was yes, sufficient notice was provided. The *reasoning* for that conclusion is twofold. First, the cup contained a clear warning alerting plaintiff that the tea was potentially dangerous. Second, plaintiff should have known that the tea was hot because by definition the drink is served with boiling or near-boiling water. The *implications* of the decision are that if restaurants selling hot "to-go" liquids place warnings on the cups and serve the beverage at a temperature within the range anticipated by the customer, the restaurant will not be liable for injuries that may result from a scalding beverage.

Key Terms

administrative agency
administrative law
assault
case books
case decision
cases
civil law
common law
compensatory damages
Congress
constitutional law
contract
criminal law
damages
decision
delegated powers
facts
fraud
interstate commerce

issue
law
legislative process
legislature
legislators
negligence
ordinance
precedents
probation
punitive damages
rape
reasoning
regulations
stare decisis
statute
statutory law
theft of services
trademark infringement

Summary

Law is at once an exciting and challenging study.

Our law comes from four sources—the Constitution, statutes, common law, and administrative law. The rule of stare decisis encourages judges to decide cases consistent with precedent, absent good reason to deviate. The objective of this rule is to achieve consistency in the law.

Numerous classifications of law exist, including civil and criminal. Civil law involves wrongs against individuals whereas criminal law encompasses wrongs against society.

When reading legal cases, the four main elements to identify are the facts, the issue, the decision, and the reasoning. Students should also consider the implications of the case for the hospitality industry.

Review Questions

1. How is law defined?
2. In what country did common law originate?
3. What is a precedent and how is it related to stare decisis?
4. What is a tort? Name two.
5. According to common law, who was liable when a guest's property was stolen from a room at an inn?
6. What changes have been made to the common law concerning liability to a hotel when a guest's property is stolen?
7. What is the difference between common law and statutory law?
8. Name several differences between civil and criminal law.
9. Under what circumstances can a judge deviate from stare decisis?
10. What are the differences among the following: statutes, ordinances, and regulations?
11. When reading a case, what are the four elements to look for?

Discussion Questions

1. Why did the lack of competition between inns in earlier times contribute to the development of laws that favored guests rather than innkeepers?
2. In what way does stare decisis enhance the stability of the law?
3. In what way is the common law able to adapt to changes in society?
4. If no precedent exists in a case, what factors will the judge use to decide the issue presented in the case?
5. Name two roles of a judge, as discussed in this chapter.

Application Questions

1. Natalie, who is married with two children, was injured at a hotel due to its negligence. She broke her leg and suffered a back injury. As a result she was bedridden for five weeks, missed work during that time, and experienced considerable pain. What type(s) of damages should she be able to collect from the hotel? What type will she likely not be able to collect?

2. The defendant in a criminal case has been found guilty of stealing a pack of cigarettes from a hotel store. The applicable statute authorizes the judge to sentence the defendant to a maximum of one year in jail, fine him up to $1,000, and/or place him on probation for one year. The defendant is 23 years old and is unemployed. He has no prior convictions. If you were the judge, what do you think might be an appropriate sentence in this case? Why?

3. A statute defined the crime of disoderly comduct as using profanity in a public place. A defendant, while standing on his porch, yelled odscene comments at a passerby. The defendant was charged with disorderly conduct. He denied that the porch was a public place. What is the issue in this case that the judge must decide? If a precedent exists, what effect will that have on the decision? What do you think the decision should be? Why? If the defendant claims that the statute is unconstitutional because it infringes his right of free speach, who decides that issue?

Web Sites

Web sites that will enhance your understanding of the material in this chapter include:

http://www.uscourts.gov This site is the official site of the federal court system and includes information about the courts, answers to frequently asked questions, and links to other legal sources.

http://www.supremecourtus.gov This is the official site of the United States Supreme Court. It contains profiles of each Supreme Court judge, past and present; an archive of the court's decisions; and the history of the court.

http://www.oyez.com Another site about the United States Supreme Court, this one contains pictures and short biographies of each justice, a virtual tour of the court building, information about recent cases, and descriptions of pending cases.

http://www.hotelbusiness.com This site provides a wealth of business information about recent occurrences in the hotel industry, including openings, sales, and mergers. Among the legal topics covered are franchising and security issues.

CHAPTER 2

■

Legal Procedures: Journey of a Case through the Courts

CHAPTER OUTLINE

■

Introduction

The Parties and Proof

Commencing the Lawsuit

Pretrial Procedure

The Trial

Appeal

Alternative Dispute Resolution

Interpreting a Case Citation

INTRODUCTION

Conflicts can be resolved in a variety of ways. Some will grow into lawsuits and be heard in court. Others will be settled either before or after a lawsuit is begun. In settling a case, the injured party may compromise and accept less than he originally sought. Still other cases are resolved through alternative dispute resolution methods whereby a person other than a judge listens to both parties' positions and then either makes a determination concerning the merits of the case or assists the parties in developing a mutually acceptable solution.

   When a claim is asserted against a hospitality establishment, or if the establishment has a claim against an individual or a business, a decision must be made on how to proceed. A **claim** is a demand for a remedy, usually money, to compensate for a perceived wrong. Should the claim be settled? Should it be pursued in court? Is some form of alternate dispute resolution the best option? In answering these questions the owner or manager of the establishment must consider the merits of the claim, the cost in both time and money required to pursue the case, and the effect of the decision on future, similar cases. The costs include attorney's fees (which may be hundreds of dollars an hour), court fees (charged for the services of the court), expert witness fees, and the time of employees to oversee the case, work with the lawyer, and testify. These expenses are minimized if the case is settled early. Another factor that may impact the decision on how to handle a case is the wishes of the insurance company of the party being sued. Sometimes a hotel or restaurant's insurance coverage authorizes the insurance company to determine whether to settle the case or pursue it.

The decision on how to proceed with the claim will vary from case to case as the relevant factors are weighed. A very small percentage of cases go to trial. Most cases are settled earlier in the process, due in large part to the costs involved. The decision on how to proceed with the claim may be the most important strategic decision in the case.

This chapter will acquaint you with fundamental legal procedure and describe what takes place throughout the various stages of a claim that is pursued in court. The chapter will also explain different methods of alternate dispute resolution. Given the fact that most cases involving hospitality facilities are civil cases and not criminal, the procedural rules discussed in this chapter relate to civil proceedings. The procedural rules applicable to criminal cases are similar in some respects, but differ in others.

The Parties and Proof

Although the procedure for pursuing a case through the courts varies from state to state, certain practices are common. The **parties** to a lawsuit are the individuals engaged in a conflict, also referred to as **litigants**. A party may be a person, a business, or a governmental body. The **plaintiff** is the party who initiates the lawsuit. The plaintiff usually has suffered an injury or loss, and believes the defendant is responsible. The **defendant** is the party that the plaintiff has sued.

To be successful in the lawsuit the plaintiff must prove that

1. The defendant violated the law
2. The plaintiff suffered an injury or loss
3. The cause of plaintiff's injury or loss was the defendant's violation of the law.

The system of justice employed in the United States is an adversary system. It is based on the premise that when a lawsuit develops between two people, it will best be resolved if each party to the dispute vigorously asserts its claim before an independent judge who ultimately determines the outcome.

Commencing the Lawsuit

The lawsuit is begun by serving or filing a complaint and a summons.

The Complaint

The **complaint** is a document issued by the plaintiff that contains **allegations**—that is, unproven statements that when combined constitute a claim against the defendant. The complaint informs the defendant of the basis for the plaintiff's claims. Depending on the law of the state where the case is pursued, lawsuits are commenced by either filing the complaint with the appropriate court and/or serving the complaint on the defendant. A complaint consists of three parts

1. A statement showing the jurisdiction of the court
2. Details about why the plaintiff is suing the defendant
3. A claim for relief.

Figure 2-1 shows a sample complaint.

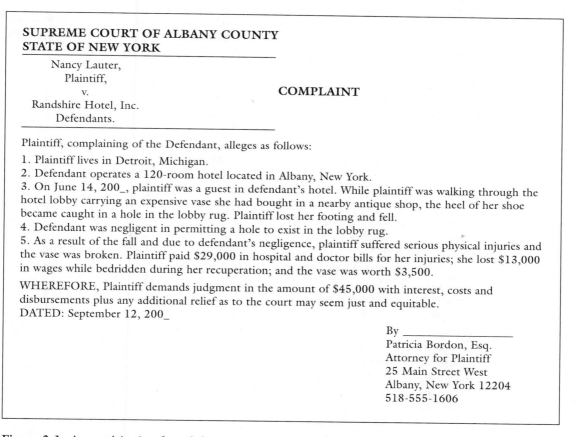

SUPREME COURT OF ALBANY COUNTY
STATE OF NEW YORK

Nancy Lauter,
    Plaintiff,
        v.   **COMPLAINT**
Randshire Hotel, Inc.
    Defendants.

Plaintiff, complaining of the Defendant, alleges as follows:

1. Plaintiff lives in Detroit, Michigan.
2. Defendant operates a 120-room hotel located in Albany, New York.
3. On June 14, 200_, plaintiff was a guest in defendant's hotel. While plaintiff was walking through the hotel lobby carrying an expensive vase she had bought in a nearby antique shop, the heel of her shoe became caught in a hole in the lobby rug. Plaintiff lost her footing and fell.
4. Defendant was negligent in permitting a hole to exist in the lobby rug.
5. As a result of the fall and due to defendant's negligence, plaintiff suffered serious physical injuries and the vase was broken. Plaintiff paid $29,000 in hospital and doctor bills for her injuries; she lost $13,000 in wages while bedridden during her recuperation; and the vase was worth $3,500.

WHEREFORE, Plaintiff demands judgment in the amount of $45,000 with interest, costs and disbursements plus any additional relief as to the court may seem just and equitable.
DATED: September 12, 200_

                                          By _____
                                          Patricia Bordon, Esq.
                                          Attorney for Plaintiff
                                          25 Main Street West
                                          Albany, New York 12204
                                          518-555-1606

Figure 2-1   A complaint is a formal document that details allegations by the plaintiff against the defendant. Those allegations form the basis for the lawsuit.

Statement of Jurisdiction

Jurisdiction is the authority of a court to hear a case. Jurisdiction is determined by the legislature. No single court has the power to decide all kinds of cases. For example, the United States Bankruptcy Courts have the power to decide only cases involving bankruptcy. If a catering patron with a large outstanding bill petitions the court for bankruptcy protection, the Bankruptcy Court will hear and decide the case. The same court does not have the authority to hear such cases as contract disputes between a hotel and its employees or claims that a restaurant supplier sold unhealthy food. The statement of jurisdiction in the complaint must set forth facts that demonstrate that the court designated by the plaintiff has the authority to decide the particular case.

In Personam Jurisdiction

Another type of jurisdiction is **in personam jurisdiction**, which means authority of a court to determine a case against a particular defendant. For a state court to have in personam jurisdiction over the defendant, the latter must either be a resident of the state or have significant contacts with the state. If, for example, a resident of New York sought to sue a restaurant in South Dakota, claiming that the restaurant served the New Yorker rancid food while the latter dined in the restaurant, New York would not have in personam jurisdiction over the restaurant because it has no contacts with the state of New York. To pursue the lawsuit the plaintiff would have to sue in South Dakota.

An example of a sufficient contact to establish jurisdiction would be a tour company with its principal place of business located in one state and a sales office located in another. Both states could exercise in personam jurisdiction over the tour company.

An issue that has arisen with the advent of the Internet is whether a business located in one state that has a Web site accessible by residents of other states is thereby subject to in personam jurisdiction in the other states. For example, in one case a jazz club in New York City sued a jazz club located in Missouri claiming the latter infringed the former's trademark, "The Blue Note." The suit was brought in New York. The Missouri club denied that the New York court had jurisdiction since the club's only involvement with New York was a Web site accessible by New York residents. The site contained general information about the club in Missouri, a calendar of events, and a number to call for charge-by-phone ticket orders available for pick-up at the Missouri club's box office on the night of the performance.

The court held that the Web site alone was insufficient to permit New York to exercise jurisdiction over the Missouri club. Had computer users been able to buy goods from the site that were thereafter shipped into New York, the outcome might have been different. Subsequent cases continue to draw a line between "passive" Web sites that merely provide information and "active" Web sites through which a consumer can purchase items and have them shipped into the state. Only the latter can be the basis for in personam jurisdiction. *Bensusan Restaurant Corporation v. King*, 937 F.Supp. 295 (NY, 1996).

Federal Jurisdiction

Each state, as well as the District of Columbia and Puerto Rico, has its own system or network of courts, as does the federal government. Federal courts have jurisdiction to hear two types of cases: (1) Lawsuits that involve the United States

Constitution, a federal treaty, or a federal law—called collectively, federal questions; and (2) lawsuits that involve diversity of citizenship—that is, the plaintiff and defendant are from different states or one is from a different country and the amount of money in controversy exceeds $75,000. All other types of cases are heard in state court. See Figure 2-2 for an illustration of a typical state court system and Figure 2-3 on page 22 for an illustration of the federal court system.

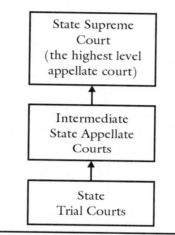

Matters of note:
1. Trial courts are called "courts of original jurisdiction" because they are the first courts to hear and decide a case. Examples of trial courts are city and town courts, county courts, family courts, and surrogate courts.
2. The losing party in a case that has been decided by a state supreme court can seek review by the United States Supreme Court, the highest court in the country.

Figure 2-2 State court systems include courts of original jurisdiction and courts of appeal. This diagram reflects the system adopted in most, but not all, states.

The Basis for the Claim

The complaint must explain to the defendant and the court the circumstances comprising the plaintiff's claim. The complaint contains allegations—unproven statements—detailing the occurrence the plaintiff alleges results in liability of the defendant.

The Claim for Relief

The complaint must tell the defendant and the court what the plaintiff wants the court to do. Plaintiffs in civil cases customarily seek relief in the form of an award of money.

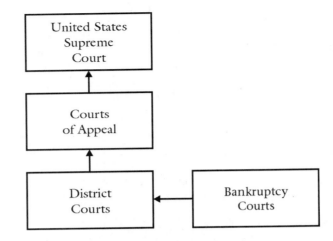

Figure 2-3 Federal courts hear two categories of cases: those dealing with federal questions, and those involving diversity of citizenship and a minimum of $75,000 in controversy.

The Summons

A **summons** is a document ordering the defendant to appear and defend the allegations made against him. It is served with the complaint. Among other things, it informs the defendant of the time within which he or she must respond to the complaint and the consequences of a failure to do so. A sample summons is provided in Figure 2-4.

Service of Process

Delivery of the summons and complaint to the defendant is known as **service of process**. The summons and complaint are collectively called *process*. In most states these documents are filed with the court, after which a specially appointed agent of the court serves them on the defendant. In other states they are served on the defendant before they are filed with the court. If the documents are properly served and the defendant fails to provide a timely response, the defendant loses the case by default. In such circumstances, the plaintiff is entitled to a default judgment—that is, a court order summarily declaring the plaintiff the winner of the lawsuit due to the defendant's failure to defend.

Responses to the Complaint

After being served with the complaint, a nondefaulting defendant must do one of two things in response: either file motions addressed to some defect in the complaint or, if the defendant concludes that no defects exist, file an answer to the complaint.

SUPREME COURT OF ALBANY COUNTY
STATE OF NEW YORK

Nancy Lauter,
Plaintiff,

v.   **SUMMONS**

Randshire Hotel, Inc.,
Defendants.

YOU ARE HEREBY SUMMONED and required to appear in the Supreme Court of Albany County located at 1000 Ridge Road, in the City of Albany, County of Albany, State of New York, by serving an Answer to the annexed Complaint upon Plaintiff's attorney at the address stated below, within thirty days after service of this Summons and Complaint is complete. Upon your failure to so answer, judgment will be taken against you for the relief demanded in the annexed Complaint, together with the cost of this action.

DATED: September 12, 200_

By _____
Patricia Bordon, Esq.
Attorney for Plaintiff
25 Main Street West[
Albany, New York 12204
518-555-1606

Figure 2-4   The summons is delivered to the defendant with the complaint. Transferring the summons and complaint to the defendant is called *service of process.*

Preliminary Motions

A **motion** is a request to a judge for relief that is made while a lawsuit is ongoing. For example, motions may consist of a request for an extension of time, a request to clarify the allegations in the complaint, or a request that the lawsuit be dismissed because the court lacks jurisdiction. Motions are usually made in writing.

After a motion has been filed with the court, attorneys for both the plaintiff and defendant appear at a hearing and argue their respective sides. The judge then either grants or denies the motion. The case proceeds in accordance with the ruling. For example, if the defendant makes a successful motion to dismiss because the court lacks jurisdiction, the case ends. The plaintiff may, however, file the case again in another court that *does* have jurisdiction. If the defendant makes a successful motion for clarification of the complaint, the case will continue, but the plaintiff will have to supplement the complaint with explanatory information.

The Answer

If the case is not dismissed on motion, the defendant must serve an **answer** on the plaintiff and the court within the permissible time period, which is defined by statute and varies from state to state. Failure to serve an answer in a timely manner will result in a default judgment in favor of the plaintiff. Stated differently, the defendant automatically loses due to his inaction. The answer fulfills the following purposes: it admits or denies the allegations made by the plaintiff in the complaint; it sets forth any defenses the defendant may have to the plaintiff's claim; and it states any claims the defendant may have against the plaintiff (a **counterclaim**). A sample answer is provided in Figure 2-5.

SUPREME COURT OF ALBANY COUNTY
STATE OF NEW YORK

Nancy Lauter,
Plaintiff,
v.   **ANSWER**
Randshire Hotel, Inc.
Defendants.

The Defendant, answering the Complaint:

1. Denies knowledge and information sufficient to form a belief as to the allegations contained in paragraph 1.
2. Admits the allegations contained in paragraph 2.
3. Concerning paragraph 3, admits that Plaintiff was a guest in Defendant's hotel on June 14, 200_; and denies each and every other allegation contained therein.
4. Denies each and every allegation contained in paragraph 4.

WHEREFORE, Defendant demands judgment dismissing the complaint against it.

DATED: October 8, 200_

By _____
Mark Fuller, Esq.
Attorney for Defendant
423 Monroe Street
Albany, New York 12210

Figure 2-5 The answer is the defendant's response to the complaint.

Responses to the Answer

Motions Directed to the Answer

After the defendant files an answer, the plaintiff is entitled to make motions relating to it. For example, the plaintiff may move for a more definite statement if the answer is vague or may move to strike all or part of the defendant's answer because the information is redundant or immaterial.

Reply

If and only if the answer contains a counterclaim, the plaintiff must issue a **reply**. This document contains the plaintiff's response to the allegations in the counterclaim.

Summary Judgment

The complaint, the answer, and the reply are known as **pleadings**. Once the pleadings have been filed and all motions relating to the pleadings have been made and ruled on by the judge, either party may make a motion for judgment on the pleadings. Such a motion, called a *motion for summary judgment*, asks the judge to decide the case in favor of the moving party without the need for a trial. This motion asserts that the opposing party's pleading has not raised any genuine issue in the case.

Pretrial Procedure

Once the pleadings have been filed and, if necessary, clarified through use of motions, the parameters of the legal dispute become apparent. Both parties know the general framework of the opponent's position.

To win a lawsuit, a party must convince a jury that her version of the facts is the more probable one. So the second stage of the suit is devoted to the collection of evidence with which to convince the jury.

Discovery

If justice is to be done, all facts and evidence must be equally available to both parties. The law does not permit one party to hoard evidence and surprise his adversary at trial when it may be too late to prepare a response. Rather, the law facilitates each side's obtaining evidence and information available to the other. This is done through **discovery**, the process by which each side obtains evidence known to the other side.

Discovery usually occurs after the filing of the complaint and answer and before the trial. Discovery may take one or more of several forms, such as (1) written or oral questions (interrogatories and depositions, respectively) posed by one party to the other party or to a witness; (2) inspection of physical evidence that may be relevant to a case, such as a hotel elevator that allegedly malfunctioned; (3) review of documents or other evidence held by the adverse party or by a potential witness; and, (4) if the mental or physical condition of one of the parties is in issue, a physical or mental examination of the party concerned.

A plaintiff or defendant who proceeds to trial without undertaking discovery forfeits a valuable opportunity to obtain information about the other party's case and is therefore at a significant disadvantage.

Pretrial Conference

After discovery is completed, the judge and the opposing lawyers meet to prepare for the trial. The judge normally utilizes this opportunity to encourage the parties to reach a **settlement**—that is, a resolution of a dispute without a trial. Usually, when a settlement is attained, the plaintiff agrees to accept less than the amount sought in the complaint and the defendant agrees to pay part of the plaintiff's claim.

Although the parties may settle a case at any time, the period following discovery is particularly advantageous. Through discovery the parties have learned the strengths and weaknesses of their position and that of their adversary and can realistically assess the chances of success at trial. A weak case will often prompt a party to seek a settlement. If the parties do not settle, the case proceeds to trial.

The Trial

After the preliminaries of serving the pleadings and gathering evidence, the attorneys present the case to an impartial tribunal—a judge or jury. This tribunal must weigh the evidence and render a verdict as determined by the evidence and the law. This process, whereby the parties present evidence and the judge or jury decides the issues, is called a **trial**.

Just as laws regulate the pretrial process, rules also regulate the trial. These laws are designed to resolve the dispute in an orderly fashion.

The following trial procedure is generally followed in all states.

1. Selection of the jury
2. Opening statements
3. Plaintiff's case-in-chief
4. Defendant's case-in-chief
5. Plaintiff's case in rebuttal
6. Summation
7. Judge's charge to the jury
8. Jury's deliberations
9. Verdict
10. Judgment

Types of Trials—Jury and Bench

A case may be tried by a jury (called a jury trial) or by the judge (called a bench trial), depending on the wishes of the parties.

In a **criminal case**—one in which the state charges a defendant with a violation of the state's criminal law—the determination of whether or not to have a jury is made exclusively by the defendant. In a **civil** (noncriminal) **case**, if either the plaintiff or the defendant wants a jury, the case will be tried by a jury. Only if neither party desires a jury will the case be tried without one. Factors a party might consider when deciding whether to choose a jury trial include:

1. *Will my case benefit from emotional appeals?* For example, a child who became a paraplegic as a result of a dive in a hotel pool will evoke sympathy. Conventional wisdom suggests a jury is more apt to be swayed by emotional appeals than a judge because jurors are inexperienced in lawsuits whereas judges are exposed daily to difficult and heart-rending cases. A judge is therefore more likely to be objective in evaluating the case.

2. *Will I be presenting technical evidence?* For example, the proof in an embezzlement case against a restaurant manager may include analysis of many checks and financial records. The proof in a case involving injuries caused by a faulty hotel escalator may require extensive evidence about the mechanical aspects of equipment. Jurors may be inexperienced listeners and "tune out" technical testimony. An experienced judge has a lot of opportunity to perfect listening skills and thus is expected to comprehend complicated testimony.

3. *Is there anything about the case that may evoke distaste in a jury for me or my position?* For example, a defendant charged with a gruesome murder in a restaurant parking lot may choose a bench trial on the theory that a jury will likely develop animosity toward him once the testimony is presented.

Jury Selection

If the case is to be tried before a jury, the trial begins with the examination of prospective jurors, a process called **voir dire**. Prior to the date set for trial, a group of people are randomly selected as potential trial jurors from the jury pool. The pool consists of registered voters, utility subscribers, licensed operators of motor vehicles, registered owners of motor vehicles, state and local taxpayers, recent high-school graduates, people who have volunteered to serve as jurors, and other state-specific categories. Those selected are notified that they are to appear at the courthouse on a given day. The trial jurors are chosen from this group.

Most judges start the voir dire by asking jurors general questions, such as whether they know or are acquainted with either the plaintiff or defendant, their attorneys, or the judge. Jurors who answer affirmatively will be questioned as to whether that familiarity will interfere with their ability to decide the case objectively. When the judge has concluded general questioning, the attorneys ask more detailed questions.

Individual jurors' eligibility may be challenged by either attorney **for cause** when, among other reasons, a juror expresses an inability to render an impartial verdict because of prior knowledge of the parties or the facts in the case, bias, or some other reason. If the judge agrees that the juror is not suitable, the juror will be dismissed for cause. The attorneys also can make a limited number of **peremptory challenges**—that is, dismissal of potential jurors without a stated cause.

Opening Statements

The **opening statement** is a presentation to the jury outlining the proof a lawyer expects to present during the trial. Each lawyer has an opportunity to make an opening statement before any evidence is presented. The opening statement is the first exposure the jury has to the specific facts of the case.

The Case-in-Chief

After the opening statements, the plaintiff presents its evidence. Testimony is presented one witness at a time through a process of direct examination and cross-examination. The party who calls a witness questions that person first. This is called **direct examination**. The purpose of direct examination is to elicit pertinent information to help prove the party's claim. Next, opposing counsel questions the same witness, called **cross-examination**. The objective of cross-examination is to discredit the witness. Once cross-examination is concluded, the party who origi-nally called the witness may ask additional questions, called *redirect examination*, after which the opposing party will have an opportunity to recross.

After the plaintiff has called all its witnesses, the defendant presents its **case-in-chief** in the same manner as the plaintiff.

The Plaintiff's Rebuttal Case

When the defendant has concluded its case, the plaintiff can present evidence in **rebuttal**. Suppose, for example, the plaintiff has sued a hotel for injuries sustained when the elevator malfunctioned and claims the hotel failed to inspect it properly. The hotel defends the case by introducing into evidence inspection records that indicate the elevator had been examined and serviced at frequent intervals. The plaintiff, in its rebuttal case, may present evidence showing that the records had been altered and, in fact, the elevator had not been inspected for a long period of time.

Summation

After the cases-in-chief and the plaintiff's rebuttal, the attorneys summarize the case for the jury, called **summations** or closing statements. Summations allow the attorneys to review for the jury the contentions of their respective sides and to demonstrate how the evidence supports those contentions. In many states, the plaintiff presents a summation first, followed by the defendant and concluded by the plaintiff, who gets a last opportunity to respond to the defendant's closing argument. In other states, the defendant gives a summation first, followed by the plaintiff.

Charging the Jury

After the summations, the judge informs the jury of the law applicable to the case. This is called the **charge to the jury**. For example, in a case that involves a question of negligence, the judge will instruct the jury on the law of negligence and explain what that term means. The judge will inform the jurers that unless they find, from the evidence presented in court, that the defendant was negligent within the legal meaning of that word, they cannot return a verdict for the plaintiff. In effect, in the charge the judge gives the jury a short course on the principles of law applicable to the case.

Jury Deliberations

Once the jury has heard the evidence and the applicable law, it retires to a jury room for **deliberations**. The jury first makes findings of fact. Despite contradictory evidence, the jury must determine what happened in the case. For example, a jury may be called upon to determine whether or not the food served at a restaurant caused the plaintiff's illness. As fact finder, the jury has a large degree of discretion in deciding what evidence to believe and what evidence to discredit. When the jury has decided what actually happened, it considers whether, based on the law as relayed to them by the judge in the charge, the defendant has violated the law. For example, if the food served at the restaurant did cause the plaintiff's injuries, does the law impose liability on the restaurant under the particular circumstances of the case? Thus, there are two separate processes that take place during jury deliberations: (1) determination of the facts and (2) determination of how the law applies to the facts in the given case.

The Verdict

The **verdict** is the jury's decision in a case. In most states, to have a verdict the jury must reach a unanimous decision that the defendant is either liable or not liable. In some states agreement by most but not all of the jurors is sufficient for a verdict. If less than the necessary number of jurors are in agreement, the jury is "hung" and the judge will declare a mistrial. In this event the case can be tried again with a new jury at the discretion of the prosecutor.

The Judgment

A **judgment** is the official decision of a judge about the rights and claims of each side in a lawsuit. A verdict is not binding on the losing party until the court has entered judgment on the verdict. Basically, this means that the attorney for the losing party will have a chance to attack the verdict after it is issued by the jury and before the judge issues a judgment. The attorney may pursue any one or more of the following procedures after the verdict and before the judgment:

1. Ask that the jury be polled to ensure that the necessary number of jurors were in agreement.
2. Ask for judgment notwithstanding the verdict—that is, an order from the judge reversing the jury's decision (rarely granted).
3. Ask for a new trial on the grounds of an erroneous ruling of the judge during the trial, a prejudicial statement improperly heard by the jury, or an improper charge by the judge.
4. Ask for a **remittitur**—a ruling that the amount of money awarded by the jury was unreasonable.

If the trial judge denies these motions, a judgment on the verdict is entered.

Appeal

An **appeal** is a complaint made by a litigant to a superior court that a trial judge committed an error and a request that the superior court correct the error.

Grounds for Appeal

Appellate courts have the authority to review the handling and decision of a case tried in a lower court. Many events at a trial occur rapidly. The decisions a judge makes during trial must, by necessity, be made without much time for deliberation. For this reason, mistakes will be made from time to time. These mistakes may entitle a party to an appellate-court review of the proceedings at the trial. Appeals occur in a calm and reflective environment removed from the passions and speed of the trial.

Appellate Courts

An **appellate court** is very different from a trial court. In appellate courts there are no juries. Whereas a trial court consists of one judge, an appellate court may consist of three to nine judges. To reverse the results of a trial, the vote of a majority of these judges is necessary. To appeal, the attorneys first submit **briefs**, or written arguments. Briefs attempt to convince the court that the trial judge was right or wrong, depending on the position of the party submitting the brief. At some point after submission of the briefs the case will be scheduled for oral argument, at which time the attorneys argue their positions in person before the court. The judges have the opportunity to ask questions. The court will thereafter issue its decision in a written opinion justifying its conclusions.

The appellate court can do any of the following

- Affirm the decision of the lower court, in which case the judgment stands
- Reverse the decision of the lower court and order a new trial
- Order that the case be dismissed.

Normally, each party has a right to appeal to at least one appellate court. However, the right to an appeal to the highest appellate court—the state supreme court in most state court systems or the United States Supreme Court in the federal court system—is restricted. The party seeking to appeal must demonstrate that his case falls into one of the limited categories for which appeal to the highest appellate court is permitted by law. Even if this can be demonstrated, the highest appellate court may still decide to refuse review. For example, the United States Supreme Court hears less than one out of every twenty cases seeking that court's review.

Alternative Dispute Resolution

The cost to pursue or defend a lawsuit can be very high due to attorney's fees, court costs, witness fees, and the parties' time away from work. In civil cases, a number of alternatives to trial exist, called **alternative dispute resolution** (ADR). They are usually quicker, less formal, and less expensive than a trial. More and more, litigants are choosing ADR. Some courts are even requiring it.

Methods of ADR include arbitration, mediation, and summary trials. **Arbitration** is a process in which a dispute is submitted for resolution to an *arbitrator*, an objective third party who may or may not be a lawyer. An informal hearing is held at which evidence is presented. After the hearing is completed, the arbitrator will decide who should win the case. With few exceptions, an arbitrator's decision cannot be appealed. The parties pay a fee for the services of the arbitrator.

Mediation is a process in which a *mediator* facilitates discussion and negotiations between the parties to the dispute in an informal setting. Unlike an arbitrator, the mediator does not have the authority to impose a decision; rather, the mediator assists the parties in reaching a settlement of their dispute. The parties pay a fee for the services of the mediator.

Summary jury trials are used in federal courts. The lawyers summarize their arguments and evidence to a jury without using witnesses. The jury renders a nonbinding decision, which is intended to facilitate settlement discussions. The parties thereafter negotiate their dispute. Since no witnesses are used, the process is much faster than a trial. If the negotiations do not result in a settlement, either side can demand a trial.

The high cost of trials in both money and time suggests the trend toward ADR will continue.

Interpreting a Case Citation

Throughout the book you will see case citations. A **citation** is a reference to a legal authority such as a court decision, a statute, or a treatise. A case citation will appear as follows: 99 N.Y.2d 38 (2002). Each part of the citation provides important information to aid the reader in locating the case in a law library. The middle section refers to a set of books that contains case decisions written by judges. In the referenced citation, "N.Y.2d" refers to the second series of a set containing cases from the highest court in New York.

Books in sets are numbered sequentially. The first number in the citation identifies the volume in which the case is located within the set. The second number in the citation identifies the page within the volume on which the cited case begins.

In the citation 99 N.Y.2d 38 (2002), the cited case begins on page 38 of the 99th volume in the New York Second set of books in the library.

The date in parenthesis identifies the year in which the case was decided. Thus, in the referenced example, the case was decided in 2002.

As another example, consider the following federal Court of Appeals citation: 320 F.3d 1052 (9th Cir. 2003). The case begins on page 1052 of the 320th volume of the set of books entitled, *Federal Reporters, 3rd series*. "9th Cir." means Ninth Circuit, which references the geographical location in which the court is located. The United States is divided into twelve circuits for purposes of distinguishing federal district courts. To assist your understanding of the material, throughout this book the authors will include in *Federal Reporter* citations the state in which the case originated rather than the circuit.

Key Terms

allegations
alternative dispute resolution
answer
appeal
appellate court
arbitration
briefs
case-in-chief
charge to the jury
civil case
claim
complaint
counterclaim
criminal case
cross-examination
defendant
deliberations
direct examination
discovery
for cause
in personam jurisdiction

judgment
jurisdiction
litigants
mediation
motion
opening statement
parties
peremptory challenges
plaintiff
pleadings
rebuttal
remittur
reply
service of process
settlement
summary jury trial
summation
summons
trial
verdict
voir dire

Summary

Claims can be resolved by lawsuits, settlement, or alternative dispute resolution. Which method to pursue in a given circumstance is an important question that should be decided only after careful review of the case.

The stages of a lawsuit include the pleadings, pretrial procedures, the trial, and appeals. The purpose of the pleadings is to identify the factual issues in the case. The purpose of pretrial procedures is to eliminate surprises at trial. The objective of the trial is to determine the facts of the case and how the law applies to the facts. The reason for an appeal is to provide an opportunity to correct an erroneous ruling.

The specific steps in a lawsuit are as follows:

COMMENCING THE LAWSUIT
    Complaint
        Statement of jurisdiction
        Basis for the claim
        Claim for relief
    Summons

Service of process
Responses to the complaint
   Preliminary motions
   Answer
Response to the answer
   Motions directed to the answer
   Reply
Summary judgment motion
PRETRIAL PROCEDURE
Discovery
Pretrial conference
THE TRIAL
Selection of the jury
Opening statements
Cases-in-chief
Plaintiff's rebuttal
Summations
Charge to the jury
Jury deliberations
Verdict
Judgment
APPEAL

Alternative dispute resolution methods include arbitration, mediation, and summary trials. These options are quicker and less expensive than lawsuits.

Preventive Law Tips for Managers

If You Are the Plaintiff
- *Involve a lawyer early in the process.* Pursuing a lawsuit involves technical rules of procedure and evidence. A good case can be lost if procedural or evidentiary errors are made. Consult a lawyer as early as possible when planning to commence a lawsuit. He will advise you whether you have a basis to sue and will guide you through the legal maze.

If You Are the Defendant
- *Upon receiving a complaint, contact an attorney immediately.* If the defendant fails to respond he will lose by default, so action is necessary. Once the summons and complaint are served, the defendant's time to answer is limited. The sooner the lawyer is contacted the more time will be available to properly prepare the response.

Concerns for Both Plaintiffs and Defendants

■ *Fully investigate the facts of the case.* Knowledge of all the relevant facts is critical to the success of a lawsuit.

■ *Document the incidents underlying the lawsuit well.* Cases are won or lost on the basis of the available evidence. The more documentary proof a party presents, the greater the likelihood of convincing a jury of the merits of that party's case. Keep good records of the circumstances that constitute the basis for the lawsuit.

■ *When working with your lawyer, be forthcoming with information about the facts of the case.* For the lawyer to best represent a litigant, she needs to know as much about the facts of the case as possible. All reports and evidence should be shared with the attorney.

■ *Avoid unnecessary court and trial costs—consider alternative dispute resolution.* Not every dispute should result in a lawsuit. Court cases are expensive. In appropriate situations, much time and money can be saved by pursuing alternative dispute resolution such as arbitration. When thinking about ADR, consider the type of case involved, the amount of money in issue, and whether the dispute is a factual or legal one. Consider whether your case is better pursued in a more efficient forum than a court.

■ *Avoid an unnecessary trial—settle if appropriate.* In many cases settlement is an appropriate resolution. After discovery is complete, the parties should have a good idea of the strengths and weaknesses of their respective cases and thus the likelihood of success. With the resulting bargaining power that the information gives, make an earnest effort to resolve the case without the considerable expense of trial.

Review Questions

1. How is a lawsuit begun?
2. What is jurisdiction?
3. What is contained in a complaint?
4. What is a counterclaim?
5. What happens if the defendant does not respond to the complaint?
6. What is the name given to the procedure for examination of prospective jurors?
7. What does the judge do when charging a jury?
8. What is a motion? Name two types of motions that might be made during a trial.
9. What is an appellate court?
10. Name two differences between a trial and an appellate court hearing.

Discussion Questions

1. What role do the pleadings play in a lawsuit?
2. What role does discovery play in a lawsuit?
3. Why, in the case of a hung jury, can the case be retried?
4. Why do most states require that the jury be unanimous for a verdict?
5. Why do different courts have different types of jurisdiction?

Application Questions

1. Assume that you live in California and are on vacation, traveling by car from California to Texas. You are injured in a motel room when the bed on which you are sleeping collapses, causing you to fall to the floor. You suffer substantial back and leg injuries, requiring many medical treatments and causing you to miss work for fifteen weeks. Your medical bills total $16,000 and your lost wages $9,000. You intend to sue the owner of the Texas motel. Can you bring your case in federal court? Why or why not?

2. If you were the defendant in the following cases, would you opt for a jury trial or a bench trial? Why?

   A. A 12-year-old guest at a hotel broke her spine and became a quadriplegic as a result of a dive she took into a hotel pool. The plaintiff claims the hotel was at fault for not maintaining the water in the pool at required levels.

   B. A guest at a hotel was injured when an in-room heater exploded. To prove that the hotel was negligent in its maintenance of the device, the plaintiff will present as expert witnesses an engineer and a mechanic who specialize in heating systems. Both will testify concerning the mechanisms that operate the heater and the circumstances surrounding the malfunction at the time plaintiff was injured.

   C. Matt, a state senator, is charged with bribery. He is accused of accepting money from several bars and restaurants in exchange for his promise to vote for a bill that would reduce the drinking age from 21 to 18.

3. What information would you try to obtain through discovery in the following cases? What methods of discovery would you use to obtain that information?

   A. A child was riding on the ferris wheel at an amusement park. Something malfunctioned and the seat in which the child was riding dropped 60 feet to the ground with the child in it. The fall seriously injured the child. Assume you are the child's parent.

   B. Inez is a guest at a hotel. She returns to the hotel after an evening out. While she is walking to her hotel room she trips in the lobby. She claims to have suffered two broken ribs, a painful injury to her back and a broken ankle. She further claims the hotel is at fault and sues for $1,000,000. Assume you are the vice president of the hotel and are responsible for overseeing legal cases.

Web Sites

Web sites that will enhance your understanding of the material in this chapter include:

http://www.courttv.com Court TV maintains this exciting and interactive site. It includes clips of gavel-to-gavel coverage of newsworthy trials and provides information about current legal cases covered by the media.

http://www.findlaw.com This site contains updates on legal news and many links to sites covering a variety of legal topics including how to find a lawyer and mediation.

http://www.adr.org This is the site for the American Arbitration Association, which organizes arbitrations for disputants who wish to utilize this method of alternative dispute resolution.

http://www.lectlaw.com Once on this site, click on "alternative dispute resolution" for a plethora of information about arbitration and mediation.

For additional resources, visit our Web site
www.hospitality-tourism.delmar.com

CHAPTER 3

∎

Civil Rights and Hospitality Businesses

INTRODUCTION

Discrimination, the act of treating some people different from and less favorably than others, is manifested primarily in two circumstances:

1. Access to places of public accommodation
2. Employment.

This chapter addresses the first circumstance, while Chapter 14 addresses discrimination in employment.

According to common law, a hotel with a vacancy cannot refuse accommodations to a guest desiring to stay at the inn (a few exceptions are discussed in Chapter 10, "Rights of Innkeepers"). Because travelers need rooms in which to stay while they are away from home, hotel accommodations are viewed by the law as quasi-public, creating a duty on the part of innkeepers to accept all transients who come seeking accommodations.

Until the 1960s, this common-law rule was largely ignored in southern hotels, which regularly practiced discrimination, particularly against blacks. Most wronged guests were discouraged from bringing lawsuits, in part because of the expense involved.

This common-law rule did not apply to restaurants. Before the advent of civil rights laws (statutes that prohibit discrimination), a restaurant owner could refuse any person, including blacks and other minorities, without violating the law. Many restaurant proprietors did discriminate.

In the aftermath of the Civil War, Congress passed the Civil Rights Act of 1866, which contained certain civil rights protections. The intent was to implement the constitutional mandate of equal protection of the laws. Relevant to hospitality law is section 1981, which reads as follows:

> All persons within the jurisdiction of the United States shall have the same right in every State and Territory to make and enforce contracts, ... and to the full and equal benefit of all laws ... as is enjoyed by white citizens ... .

These early civil rights protections were seldom honored or enforced prior to the passage of the Civil Rights Act of 1964 a century later.

In the 1950s discrimination based on race was, regrettably, prevalent in our country, particularly in the south. Restaurants, hotels, theaters, schools, and many other public places withheld services from blacks; they were not permitted access to facilities available to whites. Blacks were denied the right to vote and were forced to ride in the back of buses and trains. It was not a proud time in the history of the hospitality industry or the United States.

In 1954, the United States Supreme Court decided the landmark case of *Brown v. Board of Education of Topeka, Kansas.* (*Note:* A **landmark decision** sets an important precedent sometimes marking a turning point in the interpretation of law.) The high court declared school segregation unconstitutional. The ruling invalidated the practice of "separate but equal" accommodations, which in practice were rarely equal, and paved the way for integration of institutions open to the public.

Despite the court's ruling in *Brown v. Board of Education*, many public facilities resisted integration. In response, blacks accelerated their enduring struggle to achieve freedom and equality. Some of their methods included freedom marches publicizing the black community's discontent with public facilities disregarding the law mandating integration; sit-ins at lunch counters during which blacks occupied seats reserved for whites; freedom rides in which blacks occupied seats on buses and trains reserved for whites; and voter-registration drives during which blacks were encouraged to challenge the practice of restricting voting rights of minorities.

The Civil Rights Act of 1964

Against this backdrop Congress passed the historic **Civil Rights Act of 1964** (hereafter "the Act").[1] **Civil rights** are the personal rights that derive primarily from the Constitution. These include freedom of speech, freedom of contract, privacy, and due process, to name a few. The Act as originally passed outlawed discrimination on the basis of race, color, religion, and national origin in most

---

[1]42 U.S.C. § 2000a *et seq.*

hotels, restaurants, places of entertainment, and gas stations. A subsequent amendment added gender to the list of protected classes. The general intent and overriding purpose of the Act was to end discrimination in hospitality facilities open to the public, thereby eliminating the unfairness and humiliation of racial bigotry as well as the difficulty and inconvenience discrimination created for blacks who wished to dine out or travel. The Act set the stage for eventual desegregation and a new social order. It was the death knell of Jim Crow, the name given to the unequal treatment of blacks in education, social institutions, and transportation that until the Act was passed had been sanctioned by either law or tradition. No longer could hotel owners refuse to provide rooms to blacks. No longer could a restaurant provide sit-down services for whites and restrict blacks to take-out service. No longer could restaurants set aside a particular room or area and shepherd all black customers to it, keeping them separate from the white customers.

As far-reaching as the Act is, it left some gaps. For example, it did not originally cover discrimination based on gender, and it still does not protect marital status, disability, or sexual orientation. Bars are not expressly covered, nor are stores or schools. To remedy these omissions, most states have passed their own laws extending protection to groups and facilities not covered by the Act. Discrimination based on disability is now prohibited by the Americans with Disabilities Act, a federal law that became effective in 1992.

This chapter will discuss:

- What the 1964 Civil Rights Act covers
- What state statutes cover
- The Americans with Disabilities Act
- Exceptions to civil rights laws (permissible discrimination)
- Implications of these statutes for service-industry managers.

Scope of the Act

The Act outlaws discrimination based on any of five factors:

1. Race
2. Color
3. Religion
4. National origin
5. Gender (since 1991).

To be illegal under the Act, the discrimination must occur in one of four types of establishments, and then only if the establishment is engaged in interstate commerce. The four places covered by the Act are:

1. Lodging facilities for transients
2. Dining facilities
3. Places of entertainment
4. Gasoline stations.

Interstate commerce means business transactions between people or companies from two or more states. This requirement will be explored in more detail later in this chapter. The term *discrimination*, as used by the Act, means denial of access on the same terms as others to goods, services, facilities, and accomodations.

To achieve the goal of ending discrimination, courts construed the Act broadly to include within its reach the maximum number of incidents of discrimination. A single act of illegal discrimination violates the Act; a pattern of discriminatory conduct is not required.[2] The following is a discussion of the places where the Act prohibits discrimination.

Lodging for Transients

Overnight accommodations covered by the Act include, "any inn, hotel, motel, or other establishment which provides lodging to transient guests." Court decisions have determined that the following establishments are included: places that rent rooms not only by the night but also weekly, YMCAs, trailer parks that rent to short-term guests, and cottages at beach resorts. **Transients** are people passing through or by a place for only a brief stay or sojourn.

Dining Facilities

The dining facilities covered by the Act are "any restaurant, cafeteria, lunchroom, lunch counter, soda fountain, or other facility principally engaged in selling food for consumption on the premises ... if its operation affects [interstate] commerce." Court decisions have determined that the following establishments are included: drive-in restaurants, retail-store lunch counters, sandwich shops, lunch counters at golf courses, food facilities at hospitals, and similar establishments. On the other hand, a food store such as 7-11, which sells ready-to-eat food but does not provide facilities for on-premises consumption, is not covered by the Act.

Places of Entertainment

The Act prohibits discrimination in "any motion picture house, theater, concert hall, sports arena, stadium or other place of exhibition or entertainment" that "affects commerce." The catch-all phrase "places of entertainment" includes both establishments that present shows for viewing by an audience, such as an auditorium staging a rock concert, and establishments that provide recreational or other activities in which patrons actively participate, such as bowling alleys. Also included are health spas, golf clubs, and beach clubs.

Jurisdiction Through Interstate Commerce

A hospitality business must affect interstate commerce to be covered by the Act. Why is this so? As we discussed in Chapter 1, when our country was formed the

---

[2] *Hughes v. Marc's Big Boy*, 479 F.Supp. 834 (Wisc. 1979)

states were very jealous of a strong central government. The founding fathers had bad experiences under England's autocratic rule in mind when they crafted the Constitution, so they gave a great deal of lawmaking authority to the states. The only powers given to the federal government were specifically listed in the Constitution. These powers are called the "delegated powers." Congress, the legislative body of the federal government, can pass laws that address delegated powers only. One of these areas of authority designated for Congress is interstate commerce—that is, business done between people or companies from two or more states. Thus, Congress can pass laws dealing with interstate commerce; it does not have the authority to outlaw discrimination in businesses that are purely local. Those establishments are governed by state or local law.

Hotels

Most of the guests at a hotel are travelers and some will undoubtedly be from out of state. Thus, hotels normally satisfy the requirement of affecting interstate commerce.

Restaurants

A restaurant affects interstate commerce if it serves interstate travelers or if a substantial portion of the food it serves was transported from out of state.

Serving Interstate Travelers

Normally, food establishments do not inquire whether their patrons are residents of the state or from another state. The courts have devised certain rules to determine whether a restaurant serves interstate travelers. A dining facility located near a federal highway will be deemed to serve interstate travelers. A coffee shop in a hotel is likewise assumed to serve interstate travelers. If a dining facility advertises in a magazine delivered to hotels and motels for distribution to guests, or advertises on the radio, the facility qualifies because the magazine and radio advertisements reach out-of-state readers and listeners. In one case, a restaurant in Puerto Rico argued that it was not engaged in interstate commerce, noting that it was not located at an airport or on an interstate highway. However, the restaurant was located in a primary tourist area near several large hotels. The court held that the restaurant's location was sufficient evidence that it serves interstate travelers.[3]

Using Food Moved in Interstate Commerce

A dining facility that does not serve interstate travelers will nonetheless be covered by the Act if a substantial portion of the food it serves is imported from another state. Although the Civil Rights Act does not provide a test for determining "substantial," precedents provide guidelines. Cases have held that, where ingredients in three of four food items sold by a snack bar (hot dogs, hamburgers, milk, and

[3]*Bermudex Zeonon v. Restaurant Compostela, Inc.*, 790 F.Supp. 41 (USDC, Puerto Rico, 1992)

soft drinks) were from out of state, the "substantial portion" test was satisfied.[4] In another case the requirement was met because 46 percent of an establishment's purchases consisted of meat bought from a local supplier who purchased it from outside the state.[5] Also qualifying as substantial was the purchase by a snack bar at a beach club of syrup from outside the state that was used in Coca-Cola beverages. Many of the purchases at the snack bar were for cold drinks, and Coca-Cola was the most popular.[6]

Places of Entertainment

A theater or stadium affects interstate commerce if it regularly presents movies, performances, exhibits, athletic teams, or other sources of entertainment that are imported from other states. A theater group importing traveling shows qualifies. Golf courses that purchase out-of-state carts, pro-shop inventory, rental equipment, or related items likewise qualify. Similarly, in one case a youth football association was a covered place of entertainment because it used sports equipment manufactured outside the state.

A bar or lounge qualifies as a place of entertainment if it provides facilities such as a piano, juke box, or television set. If these items are manufactured outside the state, the bar or lounge will be bound by the Act.

Relief

The Act provides limited relief for people who have been denied equality of services in establishments covered by the Act. Money as a remedy is not recoverable. A mistreated plaintiff may qualify for monetary remedies under other anti-discrimination laws.[7] The possible remedies under the Act include:

1. *Injunctive relief*—that is, a court order that requires a party to refrain from doing a particular act. In civil-rights cases, an injunction usually orders the offending person or business to stop discriminating. It is a preventive measure that guards against future injuries rather than affording a remedy for past wrongs.

2. *Reasonable attorney's fees* charged by the attorney for a successful plaintiff. This is unusual in the law; in most lawsuits the parties pay for their own attorneys. Even a successful plaintiff is normally not entitled to collect attorney's fees from the defendant. The reason for allowing attorney's fees in cases involving civil-rights violations is the legislature's recognition of the importance of eradicating discrimination. By eliminating attorney's fees as a deterrent for bringing a civil rights lawsuit, victims of discrimination are more likely to pursue the wrongdoers.

---

[4] *Daniel v. Paul*, 395 U.S. 298, 23 L.Ed.2d 318, 89 S.Ct. 1697 (1969)

[5] *Katzenbach v. McClung*, 379 U.S. 294, 13 L.Ed.2d 290, 85 S.Ct. 377 (1964)

[6] *United States v. Landowne Swim Club*, 894 F.2d 83 (3rd Cir. 1990)

[7] *Wilson v. Waffle House*, 1998 WL 1665880 (Alabama 1998)

Enforcing the Act

Facilities that had discriminated before the passage of the Act did not embrace the new law. Many sought to challenge the Act's legality. Indeed, the constitutionality of the Act was tested immediately after its passage in two landmark cases involving recalcitrant proprietors who resisted the law.

Establishing Jurisdiction

The first landmark case challenging the Act involved a motel. The plaintiff, a 216-room motel in Atlanta, Georgia, did not rent rooms to blacks. When charged with violating the Act, the motel claimed it was not engaged in interstate commerce and therefore application of the Act to its business exceeded congressional power. The evidence established that the motel in question did solicit guests from outside the state of Georgia through various national-advertising media and that it also maintained over fifty billboards and highway signs within the state. The motel accepted convention trade from outside Georgia, and approximately 75 percent of registered guests were from out of state. The court upheld the application of the Act to the motel as constitutional, pointing out that the evidence proved the motel served interstate travelers.[8]

The second test case of the Act's constitutionality involved a family-owned restaurant in Birmingham, Alabama—Ollie's Barbecue—which catered to a family and business trade with only take-out service available for blacks. The restaurant was accused of violating the Act, and in response denied that it was engaged in interstate commerce. The restaurant purchased much of its meat and other products from out of state. The court upheld the application of the statute to the eatery, concluding that Congress acted within its power to protect and foster interstate commerce by extending the coverage of the Civil Rights Act to restaurants that serve either interstate travelers or food purchased from out of state.[9]

The hotel and restaurant involved in these landmark cases both argued that if they were required to serve blacks they would lose a substantial amount of business from whites who did not wish to dine with blacks or stay in a hotel that accommodated them. The district (lower) courts accepted this argument and barred government officials from enforcing the Civil Rights Act against the businesses involved in the two cases. The United States Supreme Court, which granted certiorari in both cases and heard the appeals, rejected loss of business as a justification to avoid the mandates of the Act. The high court noted that enforcement of the Act should increase business by enlarging the potential clientele. Enforcement would also achieve the desirable outcome of expanding interstate commerce. As the court said,

> A comparison of per capita spending by Negroes in restaurants, theatres, and like establishments indicated less spending, after discounting income differences, in

---

[8] *Heart of Atlanta Motel, Inc. v. United States*, 379 U.S. 241, 13 L.Ed.2d 258, 85 S.Ct. 348 (1964)

[9] *Katzenbach v. McClung*, 379 U.S. 294, 13 L.Ed.2d 290, 85 S.Ct. 377 (1964)

areas where discrimination is widely practiced. ... This diminutive spending springing from a refusal to serve Negroes and their total loss as customers has ... a close connection to interstate commerce. The fewer customers a restaurant enjoys the less food it sells and consequently the less it buys. ... Moreover there was an impressive array of testimony that discrimination in restaurants had a direct and highly restrictive effect upon interstate travel by Negroes. This resulted, it was said, because discriminatory practices prevent Negroes from buying prepared food served on the premises while on a trip, except in isolated and unkempt restaurants, and under most unsatisfactory and often unpleasant conditions. This obviously discourages travel and obstructs interstate commerce for one can hardly travel without eating. Likewise, it was said, that discrimination deterred professional, as well as skilled, people from moving into areas where such practices occurred, and thereby caused industry to be reluctant to establish there.

As discussed in the following sections, the Act continues to be vigorously enforced.

Racial Discrimination

Refusing to permit anyone to enter an establishment because of race constitutes a violation of the Act. In a 1996 settlement of a Louisiana case, a Louisiana night-club owner admitted the club discriminated against blacks. The case arose when a white woman, out for the evening with two friends—one black and one white, walked to the entrance of the nightclub to see if it was open. Meanwhile, her two friends waited in the car. When the bouncer advised her the bar was open, she and her friends parked the car and sought entry. They were then advised they would not be admitted because the club was hosting a private party. Later that evening the white woman returned to the club alone and was admitted. After she reported the incident to law enforcement, the government sent two pairs of FBI agents, one white couple and one black couple, to the nightclub. The latter was denied entry while the former was admitted.

In the settlement, the bar owner agreed to stop violating the Civil Rights Act of 1964, train employees in civil-rights law requirements, and advertise that the bar is open to all races. Said a prosecutor involved with the case, "Over three decades ago, Congress spoke for all decent Americans by making it illegal to exclude people from [restaurants and bars] because of their skin color ... America must have zero tolerance for racial discrimination."[10]

In another case, several blacks claimed to have been discriminated against by the admission policies of a well-attended restaurant and nightclub called the Glass Menagerie. The plaintiffs claimed they were kept waiting in line outside the nightclub while white people were admitted ahead of them. Their protests to employees were ignored. Two former doormen testified they had been instructed to discourage black customers from coming to the restaurant and nightclub because the owner believed they did not spend as much money as white customers,

[10]1996 WL 66969 (1996)

they bothered white female patrons, and they were not big tippers. The court, finding that this constituted discrimination, stated,

> The court would like to believe that these discriminatory acts occurred through shortsightedness rather than malice. The court is optimistic that voluntary corrective action will be promptly taken to eliminate all vestiges of discrimination at the Glass Menagerie. Even so, however, and even though the discrimination was sporadic, compelling public interests require the immediate issuance of injunctive relief [a court order prohibiting any further discrimination].[11]

Action by a restaurant manager in refusing to serve a group of racially mixed customers, escorting them out of the restaurant, locking the door behind them, and then allowing other caucasians to enter likewise constitutes illegal discrimination.[12] The Civil Rights Act was violated by a restaurant that required blacks, but not others, to prepay for their meals while the customary practice was for customers to pay after the meal had been consumed.[13] However, requiring *all* customers to prepay for their dinners does not constitute illegal discrimination, even though prepayment is contrary to normal practice.[14]

Caucasions Are Also Protected

In *O'Connor v. 11 West 30th Street Restaurant Corp.*, 1995 WL 354904 (SDNY, 1995), a Korean restaurant refused to seat and serve plaintiff O'Connor, "a male of European descent." When O'Connor sought service, he was advised by the restaurant host that the restaurant was a private club and since O'Connor was not a member he could not enter. O'Connor returned a month later with "another white male" and was again refused service. Thereafter on two occasions of which the plaintiff was aware, Korean males who were nonmembers were seated and served at the restaurant. On other occasions, two white males and a black female sought service and were denied because they were not members.

In response to the plaintiff's lawsuit claiming a violation of various civil-rights laws, the restaurant argued that only members of a racial minority are protected and therefore the white plaintiff could not sue. The court rejected this claim, holding that "a white person, just as a nonwhite," is protected by the statutes. The restaurant's motion to dismiss plaintiff's case was denied.

Poor Customer Service

Case law also teaches that the Civil Rights Act does not remedy all perceived wrongs. Instead, it protects only against discriminatory denial of the right to enter a covered facility and receive service. Certain indignities resulting from inferior service are not covered.

---

[11] *U.S. v. Glass Menagerie, Inc.*, 702 F.Supp. 139, 142 (E.D. Ky. 1988)

[12] *Laroche v. Denny's Inc.*, 62 F. Supp2d 1375 (Fl. 1999)

[13] *Bobbitt v. Rage, Inc.* 19 F. Supp2d 512 (N.C. 1998)

[14] *Stevens v. Steak N Shake, Inc.*, 35 F. Supp.2d 882 (Fl. 1998)

In one case the plaintiff, a black male, entered a Burger King and ordered breakfast. He was the first in line. Several white men entered the line behind him. The employee serving the food stopped waiting on the plaintiff and attended to the others. When the plaintiff complained to the assistant manager, he left his office and prepared the plaintiff's order. Upon receiving his order, the plaintiff paid and left. In this action, the plaintiff claims the delay in his service was the result of racial discrimination.

The court dismissed the plaintiff's case stating, "In the instant case, plaintiff was not denied admittance or service—his service was merely slow. While inconvenient, frustrating, and all too common, the mere fact of slow service in a fast-food restaurant does not, in the eyes of this Court, rise to the level of violating one's civil rights."[15]

In a case involving a car dealership, a black plaintiff claimed he was ignored by salespeople until he requested help while white customers were promptly assisted. The court held that poor staffing and shoddy customer service did not amount to discrimination. However, if inferior service is substantially below the level of assistance provided to others and can be proven to be racially motivated, illegal discrimination may be established.[16]

Proprietor's Discretion on Music Selection

In another case the plaintiff, a black patron of a dance bar, claimed the bar's owner discriminated against blacks by discontinuing rap music and playing rock-and-roll music to induce black patrons to leave. Employees of the restaurant testified that the manager would tell the disc jockeys that it was "too dark in here" when it was thought there were too many blacks in the bar. In response, the disc jockeys allegedly began playing "hard rock-and-roll" music, which was not the favored music of many blacks. The court dismissed the case noting that the manager did not refuse the plaintiff admittance to the bar or service while he was there. Said the court, "A bar's music selection cannot be grounds to find that it engages in discriminatory conduct."[17]

Refusal of Service Because Would-Be Customers Caused a Disturbance Is Not Discrimination

If a customer is refused service for reasons other than race, religion, color, or national origin, the refusal does not violate the Civil Rights Act of 1964. A recent case involved three sisters who were dissatisfied with the service they received at a Burger King. They later returned to the restaurant with their mother to complain to the manager. While doing so the mother became contentious, manifested by yelling, screaming, waiving her arms, and grabbing the manager's arm. To avoid

---

[15] *Robertson v. Burger King., Inc.*, 848 F.Supp. 78 (E.D.La. 1994)

[16] *Callwood v. Dave & Buster's, Inc.*, 98 F. Supp.2d 694 (Md. 2000)

[17] *Sterns v. Baur's Opera House, Inc.*, 788 F.Supp. 375 (C.D. Ill. 1992), dismissed on other grounds, 3F.3d 1142 (1993)

further disturbance the manager called the police and refused to serve them. The mother sued for discrimination but the court rejected the claim. The manager had the right to refuse service because of the disturbance the mother caused.[18]

Religious Discrimination

Similar to racial discrimination, a successful case of religious discrimination requires a showing that service was refused. Where service is offered but a requested accommodation of one's religious practices is refused for good reason, the Act has not been violated.

In *Boyle v. Jerome Country Club*, 883 F.Supp. 1422 (D. Idaho 1995), the plaintiff was a tournament golfer and member of the Church of Jesus Christ of Latter-day Saints. Due to religious beliefs, the plaintiff did not play golf on Sunday. The club's tournaments were customarily played on Saturday and Sunday. He requested an alternate playing schedule, but the club refused. He sued, claiming a violation of the Act. The club claimed that to give the plaintiff an alternate schedule would create complications and expense, making the administration of the tournament more difficult. Among the problems would be an increased work-load for the tournament marshals and umpires, a delay of the public's access to the course, and possible disruption of the practice of the lowest-scoring golfers playing at the end of the tournament, which serves economic purposes.

The court dismissed the plaintiff's action, noting that the club had "legitimate business reasons, completely unrelated to religious considerations, for scheduling its final round of play on Sunday." Further, the club had never denied the plaintiff entry to a tournament or access to the course. The court thus concluded that the club's denial of an alternate tournament date was based on the stated administrative concerns and not on hostility toward his religious beliefs.

Broad Enforcement Through the Unitary Rule

The Act covers only lodging facilities, dining facilities, places of entertainment, and gasoline stations. Other businesses, such as stores, barber shops and beauty parlors, transportation facilities, bars, and colleges are not covered. However, if a covered business is physically located within another facility not otherwise covered by the Act, such as a snack bar in a store or a food car on a train, the food facility and the store or train are *both* covered. Similarly, if a business not covered by the Act is located within a covered business, both are subject to the Act's provisions. For example, a barber shop, which is not covered by the Act, will be bound by its provisions if located within a hotel. This principle is known as the **unitary rule**, which means that if a covered facility is located within a noncovered business, both the covered and noncovered business are subject to the Act.

---

[18] *Wells v. Burger King Corp.*, 40 F. Supp.2d 1366 (Fl. 1998)

Exempt Establishments

The Act excludes from its coverage certain establishments, including bed-and-breakfast operations and private clubs. These businesses are not barred from discriminating by the Act.

"Mrs. Murphy's Boarding House"

The Act exempts tourist homes, known today as bed-and-breakfasts, with five or fewer rooms and occupied by the proprietor. This exception, referred to as the "Mrs. Murphy's boarding house clause," allows proprietors who admit transients into their home to retain discretion and control over who sleeps in their house.

Private Clubs

The Act's ban on discrimination does not apply to "private clubs or other establishments not in fact open to the public." The law recognizes that people customarily affiliate with a private club because of common interests among the membership; the Act supports the perpetuation of those shared agendas. The Act does not clearly define what constitutes a private club, so the courts must interpret the statute when the issue is raised. It usually arises when a club claiming to be private excludes someone on the basis of race, color, religion, or national origin and that person challenges the legality of the exclusion. In considering whether a club is private, the courts examine the following:

1. Is the club selective in choosing its members? A private club usually has a limited number of members. The more selective the club is, the more likely it will qualify as a private club.

2. Are new members sought discretely? If the club publicly advertises for members it most likely is not a private club.

3. Does the club have clearly designated criteria for choosing members and do members participate in the selection process? A private club typically has specific traits it seeks to perpetuate in its members. The more specific the criteria, the more likely the club will qualify as private. Also, by participating in the selection process, members help to ensure that the interests they share with other members will continue to bind the membership in the future.

4. Do members govern and control the club's operations? A private club is usually owned and governed by members. If the "club" is simply a business operated for profit, it will not qualify as a private club.

5. To what extent are club facilities available for use by nonmembers? The more access by nonmembers, the less likely it is a private club.

6. Is the primary purpose of the club social or business? If the primary purpose is business, it likely will not be a private club.

The following two case examples illustrate private clubs.

A bridge club (Bridge is an intricate card game played with a partner; tournaments are held throughout the country) was found to be private in *Baptiste v. Cavendish Club, Inc.*, 670 F.Supp. 108 (N.Y. 1987) for the following reasons:

> [T]he club is dedicated to the promotion of bridge and other games of skill. ... Club facilities are open only to members and their guests, ... Prospective members must be sponsored by a current member and seconded by another member. They are subject to evaluation of their ethical reputation at the bridge table, their skill and knowledge of the game, their standards of dress and deportment, and their ability to meet their financial commitment to the Club. Members are admitted only if they are approved by the Board of Directors.

In *Moose Lodge v. Irvis*, 407 U.S. 163, 92 S. Ct. 1965 (1972), a black man was refused service by Moose Lodge, a local branch of the national fraternal organization. He sued claiming illegal discrimination. The court held the club was private for the following reasons:

> Moose Lodge is a private club ... It is a local chapter of a national fraternal organization having well-defined requirements for membership. It conducts all of its activities in a building that is owned by it. It is not publicly funded. Only members and guests are permitted in any lodge of the order; one may become a guest only by invitation of a member or upon invitation of the house committee.

Many clubs have sought exemption from application of the Act on the basis of being a private club. The issue in many discrimination cases is whether the defendant club is, in fact, private.

Assailing "Private-in-Name-Only" Clubs

If a club claimed by its members to be private is really a place of public entertainment, it will be subject to the restrictions of the Civil Rights Act, as the following decision shows. The case also illustrates the unfortunate practice, following passage of the Civil Rights Act, of groups forming "quickie" private clubs in an attempt to avoid serving blacks and other minorities.

CASE EXAMPLE 3-1

Daniel v. Paul
89 S.Ct. 1697 (1969)

Petitioners, Negro residents of Little Rock, Arkansas, brought this class action to enjoin respondent from denying them admission to a recreational facility called Lake Nixon Club owned and operated by respondent, Euell Paul, and his wife. The complaint alleged that Lake Nixon Club was a "public accommodation" subject to ... the Civil Rights Act of 1964, ... and that respondent violated the act in refusing petitioners admission solely on racial grounds.

After trial, the District Court, although finding that respondent had refused petitioners admission solely because they were Negroes, dismissed the complaint on the ground that Lake Nixon Club was not within any of the [enumerated] "public accommodations" covered by the 1964 Act. ...

Lake Nixon Club, located 12 miles west of Little Rock, is a 232-acre amusement area with swimming, boating, sun bathing, picnicking, miniature golf, dancing facilities, and a snack bar. The Pauls purchased the Lake Nixon site in 1962 and subsequently operated this amusement business there in a racially segregated manner.

... [T]he Civil Rights Act of 1964 enacted a sweeping prohibition of discrimination or segregation on the ground of race, color, religion, or national origin at places of public accommodation whose operations affect commerce. This prohibition does not extend to discrimination or segregation at private clubs. But, as both courts below properly found, Lake Nixon is not a private club. It is simply a business operated for a profit with none of the attributes of self-government and member-ownership traditionally associated with private clubs. It is true that following enactment of the Civil Rights Act of 1964, the Pauls began to refer to the establishment as a private club. They even began to require patrons to pay a 25-cent "membership" fee, which gains a purchaser a "membership" card entitling him to enter the Club's premises for an entire season and, on payment of specified additional fees, to use the swimming, boating, and miniature golf facilities. But this "membership" device seems no more than a subterfuge designed to avoid coverage of the 1964 Act. White persons are routinely provided "membership" cards, and some 100,000 whites visit the establishment each season. Negroes, on the other hand, are uniformly denied "membership" cards, and thus admission, because of the Pauls' fear that integration would "ruin" the "business". The conclusion of the courts below that Lake Nixon is not a private club is plainly correct—indeed, respondent does not challenge that conclusion here.

We, therefore, turn to the question whether Lake Nixon Club is "a place of public accommodation" as defined by ... the 1964 Act, and, if so, whether its operations "affect commerce" within the meaning of ... that Act.

Petitioners argue first that Lake Nixon's snack bar is a covered public accommodation ... and that as such it brings the entire establishment within the coverage. ... Clearly, the snack bar is "principally engaged in selling food for consumption on the premises." Thus, it is a covered public accommodation if "it serves or offers to serve interstate travelers or a substantial portion of the food which it serves ... has moved in commerce." We find that the snack bar is a covered public accommodation under either of these standards.

The Pauls advertise the Lake Nixon Club in a monthly magazine called "Little Rock Today," which is distributed to guests at Little Rock hotels, motels, and restaurants, to acquaint them with available tourist attractions in the area. Regular advertisements for Lake Nixon were also broadcast over two area radio stations. In addition, Lake Nixon has advertised in the "Little Rock Air Force Base," a monthly newspaper. This choice of advertising media leaves no doubt that the Pauls were seeking broad-based patronage from an audience which they knew to include interstate travelers. Thus, the Lake Nixon Club unquestionably offered to serve out-of-state visitors to the Little Rock area. And it would be unrealistic to assume that none of the 100,000 patrons actually served by the Club each season was an interstate traveler. Since the Lake Nixon Club offered to serve and served out-of-state persons, and since the Club's snack bar was established to serve all patrons of the entire facility, we must conclude that the snack bar offered to serve and served out-of-state persons.

The record also demonstrates that a "substantial portion of the food" served by the Lake Nixon Club snack bar has moved in interstate commerce. The snack bar serves a limited fare—hot dogs and hamburgers on buns, soft drinks, and milk. The District Court took judicial notice of the fact that the "principal ingredients going into the bread were produced and processed in other States" and that "certain ingredients [of the soft drinks] were probably obtained ... from out-of-State sources." ... Thus, at the very least, three of the four food items sold at the snack bar contain ingredients originating outside of the State. There can be no serious doubt that a "substantial portion of the food" served at the snack bar has moved in interstate commerce.

The snack bar's status as a covered establishment automatically brings the entire Lake Nixon facility within the gambit of ... [the] Civil Rights Act of 1964.

Petitioners also argue that the Lake Nixon Club is a covered public accommodation under [other provisions of the statute.] ... These sections proscribe discrimination by "any motion picture house, theater, concert hall, sports arena, stadium or other place of exhibition or entertainment" which "customarily presents films, performances, athletic teams, exhibitions, or other sources of entertainment which move in commerce." Under any accepted definition of "entertainment," the Lake Nixon Club would surely qualify as a "place of entertainment." And indeed it advertises itself as such. Respondent argues, however, that ... "place of entertainment" refers only to establishments where patrons are entertained as spectators or listeners rather than those where entertainment takes the form of direct participation in some sport or activity. We find no support in the legislative history for respondent's reading of the statute. The few indications of legislative intent are to the contrary. ...

The remaining question is whether the operations of the Lake Nixon Club "affect commerce." ... We conclude that they do. Lake Nixon's customary "sources of entertainment ... move in commerce." The Club leases 15 paddle boats on a royalty basis from an Oklahoma company. Another boat was purchased from the same company. The Club's juke box was manufactured outside Arkansas and plays records manufactured outside the State. The legislative history indicates that mechanical sources of entertainment such as these were considered by Congress to be "sources of entertainment" within the meaning of [the Act.]

Ruling of the Court: Reversed.

CASE QUESTIONS

1. Summarize the two separate grounds the court used to determine that Lake Nixon was a place of public accommodation and thus covered by the Act.

2. Can you think of any business within the hospitality/entertainment industry that is not covered by the Civil Rights Act?

Scrutinizing Admission Policies

Many cases involve clubs that claim to have sufficiently selective admission policies to qualify as a private club. In these cases the court will carefully review those policies to determine if in fact they are adequately selective.

In a Virginia case, a golf club was accused of violating the Civil Rights Act by ejecting a foursome because one golfer, who was invited to the club by a member, was black. The club defended on the ground that it was a private club and so could discriminate on the basis of race. The club's requirements for membership included a $750 initiation fee, the signature of two members on a written application, and approval of the application by the club's board of directors. The club adopted a membership ceiling of 450. The club did not routinely investigate the background and character of its applicants, nor did it measure applicants against any moral, religious, or social standards. The evidence presented indicated that only four white applicants had been rejected in the previous 15 years. The court ruled that these admission procedures, while "official and formal," were not sufficiently selective to render the club private.

Said the court, "If only four white applicants have been denied membership [in the last fifteen years], the club cannot fairly be described as truly selective about its members."[19]

---

[19] *Brown v. Loudoun Golf & Country Club, Inc.*, 573 F.Supp. 399, 403 (E.D.Va. 1983)

Another case raised the issue of whether the Lions Club, a service organization with a worldwide membership of 313,000, was a private club. The application process for new members was as follows: they had to be sponsored by a current member; they were required to complete an application form; the club was supposed to investigate applicants' backgrounds thoroughly, but customarily no investigation was done; the board of directors then voted on the applicants; if approved by a majority of the board, applicants were asked to join. No proposed member had been rejected in eighteen years. Noting that the screening process for new applicants was "cursory and operates to allow vast numbers of members," the court rejected the club's claim that it was private[20]

A similar case involved the Jaycees, another service organization. The local chapter in question had 430 members. The club did not use any criteria for judging applicants for membership. New members were routinely admitted with no background inquiry. The court denied the club's claim that it was a private club, stating, "[T]he local chapters of the Jaycees are neither small nor selective."[21]

Unlike the service clubs, the Disabled American Veterans Association (DAV) was found to be a private club notwithstanding a national membership that exceeds 1,000,000. One of its primary objectives is to advance the interests and work for the betterment of all wounded, injured, and disabled American veterans. It has national and regional offices that provide services to all veterans, whether or not disabled. While admission is restricted to individuals disabled in the line of duty during war time in service of the United States armed forces or its allies, entry is not otherwise subjected to review. The court weighed against the broad membership criteria and the large number of members the fact that the military experience that admits one to membership is "profoundly meaningful for almost all who go through it. It defines not simply an interest group, but a group for whom a very special social intimacy is possible. Encouragement of such intimacy is among DAV's express purposes."[22]

The following case illustrates the application of the private club rules to a swimming club.

CASE EXAMPLE 3-2

U.S. v. Lansdowne Swim Club
894 F.2d 83 (3rd Cir., 1990)

The Lansdowne Swim Club (LSC), ... a nonprofit corporation, is the only group swimming facility in the Borough of Lansdowne, Pennsylvania. Since its founding in 1957, LSC has granted 1400 full family memberships. Every white applicant has been admitted, although two as limited members only. In that time, however, LSC has had only one nonwhite member.

---

[20] *Rogers v. International Association of Lions Clubs*, 636 F.Supp. 1476 (E.D. Mich. 1986)

[21] *Roberts v. United States Jaycees*, 468 U.S. 609, 82 L.Ed.2d 462 (1984). For a similar holding, see also *Kiwanis International v. Ridgewood Kiwanis Club*, 627 F.Supp. 1381 (D.N.J. 1986).

[22] *Kreate v. Disabled American Veterans*, 33 SW3d 176 (Kentucky 2000)

The uncontroverted experiences of the following Lansdowne residents are significant. In 1976, the Allisons wrote to LSC requesting an application but LSC did not respond. Dr. Allison is black; his three children are part-black. In 1977, the Allisons twice again wrote for an application but LSC did not respond. The following year, the Allisons repeated the procedure with similar results. In 1983, the Allisons filed a timely application and otherwise qualified for membership but were rejected. The following year, the Ryans filed a timely application and otherwise qualified for membership. Nonetheless, they were rejected. Two of the Ryans' adopted children are black. The Ryans then complained to the media and picketed LSC, joined by the Allisons. In 1986, the Iverys, who are black, filed a timely application and otherwise qualified for membership. Nonetheless, they were rejected (as were the Ryans and Allisons who had again applied).

The United States alleges that LSC is a place of public accommodation … which has engaged in a pattern or practice of discrimination by refusing membership to blacks because of their race or color, in violation of [the Civil Rights Act]. …

LSC's first argument is that it is a private club. Under [the Civil Rights Act], "a private club or other establishment not in fact open to the public" is exempt from the statute. … LSC has the burden of proving it is a private club. … Although the statute does not define "private club," cases construing the provision do offer some guidance. The district court distilled eight factors from the case law as relevant to this determination, three of which it found dispositive of LSC's public nature: the genuine selectivity of its membership process, its history, and use of its facilities by nonmembers. LSC disputes these findings.

First, the court concluded that LSC's membership process was not genuinely selective. Essential to this conclusion was the court's finding that "LSC possesses no objective criteria or standards for admission." The court identified four "criteria" for admission to LSC: being interviewed, completing an application, submitting two letters of recommendation and tendering payment of fees. We agree, and LSC apparently concedes, that these criteria were not genuinely selective. Nonetheless, LSC challenges the court's failure to consider membership approval a criterion for admission. … [A] formal procedure requiring nothing more than membership approval is insufficient to show genuine selectivity. … In addition, LSC stipulated that the only information given to the members prior to the membership vote is the applicants' names, addresses, their children's names and ages, and the recommenders' identities. In such a situation, the court was correct to conclude that LSC "provides no information to voting members that is useful in making an informed decision as to whether the applicant and his or her family would be compatible with the existing members." Therefore, even if membership approval were considered a fifth criterion, it would not make the process any more genuinely selective in this case.

The district court also found the yields of the membership process indicative of lack of selectivity. Since 1958, LSC has granted full memberships to at least 1400 families while denying them to only two non-black families. LSC contends that emphasizing the few instances of non-black applicant rejection "misconstru[es] the significance of selectivity. The crucial question should be whether the members exercised their right to be selective rather than the statistical results of the exercise of that right."… [F]ormal membership requirements have little meaning when in fact the club does not follow a selective membership policy. … We find the evidence of lack of selectivity convincing.

CASE QUESTION

1. What would the club need to do differently to qualify as a private club?

In the following case, a country club was found to be private. It developed sufficiently selective membership criteria, limited nonmember use of its facilities, assigned management of the club in its members through the board of trustees, and was organized for social purposes.

The underlying complaint in this case resonates in numerous country clubs throughout the country—female members discontented that their male counterparts receive more favorable services. While this case does not provide any details on the dissimilar opportunities, common complaints are that desirable tee times and days of the week to play are foreclosed to women.

CASE EXAMPLE 3-3

Barry v. Maple Bluff
Country Club, Inc.
629 NW2d 24 (Wisconsin, 2001)

Maple Bluff Country Club is [a] nonprofit organization that provides its members and guests with a clubhouse, pool, tennis courts, golf course and other recreational facilities. Plaintiff is a member of the Club. She alleges that the Club engaged in sex discrimination by providing more advantageous services and opportunities to men than to women club members [no additional details on the alleged disparity of service was provided.] ... The club must be a public place of accommodation or amusement for Barry's claim of discrimination to lie. ...

The Club has a plan that is consistently employed in determining who will obtain membership. First, a prospective member must be proposed and seconded by two members who must vouch for the nominee's moral and financial character. If the prospective member is not a resident of the village in which the Club is located, two letters must be sent to the membership committee supporting the nomination. If the nominee resides in the village, the Club requires one letter. Second, the membership committee interviews all nominees and makes recommendations to the Club's board of directors. Third, no one may be admitted to the membership except through the unanimous vote of the board. ...

The membership owns the Club's property and, through its board which is elected by the membership, it decides what programs and facilities will be provided and the hours of use. The board's control of the Club's facilities is an important factor. ...

Furthermore, the history of the Club shows its purpose has always been that of a private country club established to provide social and recreational services and facilities to its members and guests ... The use that nonmember residents make of the facility is limited ... .

We conclude that the club is a private organization [and therefore it can continue to provide enhanced opportunities and services to male members].

CASE QUESTION

1. What specific facts led the court to hold that the country club was private?

Extending Civil Rights Protection

The Act represented a major step forward in this country's attempt to eliminate discrimination. As we have seen, however, the classes of people protected and the types of facilities covered are limited. Other federal, state and local laws help to fill the gaps.

State Civil Rights Laws

Virtually every state has a civil rights law that, in part, duplicates the Act and, in part, expands its coverage. The differences are as follows:

Coverage

The state laws include within their coverage businesses that are purely intrastate in nature—that is, not involved in interstate commerce. Remember, the Civil Rights Act of 1964 applies only to businesses engaged in interstate commerce.

Covered Facilities

Remember that the Act applies only to lodging facilities, dining facilities, gasoline stations, and "places of entertainment." Most state laws encompass a large number of additional "places of public accommodation," including bars, stores, clinics, hospitals, barber and beauty shops, libraries, schools, colleges, public halls, public elevators, public institutions for the care of neglected or delinquent children, garages, and public transportation.

Thus, if a store refused to sell merchandise to customers because they were Buddhist, Chinese, Hispanic, or black, the store would be in violation of the state (but not federal) civil rights act. However, where a store displayed novelties for sale that demeaned people of Polish extraction, the state civil rights act was not implicated. Said the court, "The novelty items, although offensive and in poor taste, were not communications to the effect that any of the accommodations, advantages, facilities and privileges of the shop would be refused, withheld from or denied to any person on account of national origin."[23]

Protected Classes

As we studied, the protected classes in the Act are race, color, religion, and national origin. The state statutes customarily expand the categories of protected classes and frequently include marital status and disability. Some statutes and local government ordinances also outlaw discrimination on the basis of sexual orientation.

Advertisements

Many state statutes prohibit advertisements that contain statements or suggestions, whether express or implied, that accommodations will be denied because of a protected characteristic, such as race, religion, or gender.

---

[23] *State Division of Human Rights v. McHarris Gift Center*, 419 NYS2d 405 (NY 1979)

This issue arose in a 1974 New York State case in which female plaintiffs objected to the name and exterior sign of a bar because it implied women would not be served. The objectionable name was "Silent Women Tavern" and the exterior sign depicted a headless woman. The owner conceded that the sign and name were intended to attract male patrons. The court refused to require the bar to remove the sign or change its name, and said,

> The law does not prohibit appealing by signs or trade name to one sex or another. Rather, the prohibition is against displaying notice or advertisement to the effect that any of the facilities or privileges will be refused or withheld from or denied a person on account of sex. ... There is nothing about the name or the exterior sign, in the form used here, that would suggest that women would be refused the use of the facilities.[24]

Remedies

Under the federal Act, remedies were limited and included primarily injunctive relief and attorney's fees. The state remedies are more expansive. One important redress available for violation of many state civil rights laws is damages (money), meaning an establishment that wrongfully denies services may be liable to pay money to the would-be patron. In addition, violation of many state civil rights laws is deemed a crime, which can result in jail and fines.

The Americans with Disabilities Act

The **Americans with Disabilities Act**, (hereinafter "Disabilities Act"),[25] a federal law passed by Congress in 1991, is a far-reaching commitment to the rights of the disabled. Its purpose is "(1) to provide a clear and comprehensive national mandate for the elimination of discrimination against individuals with disabilities; and (2) to provide clear, strong, consistent, and enforcible standards addressing discrimination against individuals with disabilities."

The Disabilities Act prohibits places of public accommodation from discriminating against individuals on the basis of disability. The statute defines "discrimination" as including a failure to make reasonable modifications in policies, practices, or procedures when such modifications are necessary to provide goods, services, or accommodations to disabled people.

The Disabilities Act's definition of "places of public accommodation" is significantly broader than the Civil Rights Act of 1964. In addition to the hotels, restaurants, places of entertainment, and service stations covered by the latter Act, the Disabilities Act applies to bars, stores, service establishments such as barber and beauty shops, laundromats, banks, public transportation, and schools and colleges.

---

[24]*Rosenberg v. State Human Rights Appeal Board*, 45 A.D.2d 929, 357 N.Y.S.2d 325 (4th Dept. 1974)
[25]42 U.S.C. § 12101

The Disabilities Act does not apply to private clubs, which are defined in the same manner as under the Civil Rights Act of 1964.

Integrated Settings

A goal of the Act is to ensure that goods, services, and facilities are provided to disabled persons in the most integrated setting possible. Thus, a resort that offers exercise classes could not require a wheelchair-bound patron to attend a separate exercise class for the disabled. Instead the wheelchair-bound guest must be permitted to join the class offered to able-bodied patrons. Similarly, a restaurant cannot place all wheelchair-accessible tables in an isolated corner of the dining room. Instead, they must be placed throughout the dining area.

In a case involving a casino, only one of three bars surrounding the gambling pit was wheelchair accessible. The bars were in close proximity to each other. A wheelchair patron sued claiming a violation of the Disabilities Act. The casino argued that since the three bars were in the same area and one was accessible, the establishment had complied with the statute. The court noted that, although the drinks served at the bars are identical, each bar had a different theme and ambiance. Friends of disabled customers may prefer the atmosphere in one bar over another. Further, the court determined that modification of the bar counter space would not place an undue financial burden on the casino. The court thus held that wheelchair accessibility at each bar is required.[26]

In the same case, the plaintiffs also complained that only six of nine poolside cabanas were accessible. All nine had similar amenities. On this claim the court held for the casino, noting that not all facilities in a place of public accommodation need to be accessible. For another example, not all seats at a stadium are required to accommodate wheelchairs.

A sports arena with 33 wheelchair seats violated the Disabilities Act by locating all 33 on the same level. The Disabilities Act requires that disabled seating be dispersed throughout the stadium.[27]

Mandates No Permitted

The Disabilities Act is violated if the provision of services to people with disabilities is conditional upon requirements that are not imposed on others. For example, a restaurant that requires patrons in wheelchairs to be chaperoned by a companion but seats single, able-bodied customers violates the Disabilities Act.

Modifying Rules to Accommodate the Disabled

Where the policies or practices of a place of public accommodation have the effect of discriminating against people with disabilities, the place of public accommodation must modify its policies or practices unless the modification would fundamentally

---

[26]*Long v. Coast Resorts, Inc.*, 32 F. Supp.2d 1203 (Nev. 1999)

[27]*Independent Living Resources v. Oregon Arena Corporation*, 982 F.Supp. 968 (Or. 1997)

alter the nature of the goods or services provided. For example, a place of public accommodation may have a rule prohibiting pets, but must modify that rule by permitting entrance to a service dog.

Two cases addressed the issues associated with guide dogs for blind customers. In *Johnson v. Spoetzl Brewery*, 116 F3d 1052 (5th Cir. 1997), a brewery that provided public tours of its facilities but refused to permit a guide dog to accompany a blind patron violated the Act. Allowing the animal to accompany its owner would not fundamentally alter the nature of the brewery tour nor jeopardize safety to others. Another case, *Fischer v. Cedar Creek Inn*, 214 F.2d 1115 (9th Cir. 2000), was based on a restaurant's refusal to allow a service dog inside. The parties settled the case with the restaurant agreeing to give full and equal access to blind people with guide dogs, to post the new policy conspicuously throughout the establishment, and to insert the statement into its policy manual for all the restaurant's employees, agents, and representatives.

A bar may have a rule requiring a customer ordering a drink to present a driver's license as proof of age. To accommodate persons with disabilities that prevent them from driving, the bar must modify the rule to accept an alternative form of identification.

In a case against the Professional Golf Association Tours (PGA), the plaintiff was a talented golfer who qualified for the tournament. He had a degenerative circulatory disorder that prevented him from walking golf courses. The PGA sought to enforce its rule requiring competitors to walk the course. The player sought an accommodation enabling him to use a golf cart during the tournaments. The PGA claimed that allowing a golfer to ride a cart fundamentally altered the nature of a PGA tournament. The court rejected this argument noting that the essence of golf is shot-making, not walking. In response to the PGA's concern that walking induces fatigue giving a rider an unfair advantage, the court concluded that the evidence presented established that "fatigue from walking during a tournament cannot be deemed significant." The PGA was thus required to permit the plaintiff to use a cart.[28]

If an accommodation would alter the essential nature of a business, the accommodation is not required. For example, a nightclub that regularly hosts live bands is not required to dispense with the bands to accommodate a hearing-impaired server who requires very low background noise to understand customers' orders.

Providing Auxiliary Aides and Alternative Services

To accommodate disabled individuals, the Disabilities Act requires places of public accommodation to provide auxiliary aides and services where necessary, unless such aides or services would fundamentally alter the nature of the goods or services offered, or would result in an undue burden. For example, while a restaurant is not required to provide braille menus for blind patrons, it will be required to provide someone to read the non-braille menu to the visually-impaired diner. A

---

[28]*PGA Tour, Inc. v. Martin*, 121 S.Ct. 1879 (USSC 2001)

hotel will be required to provide a hearing-impaired guest with a flashing-light device to denote emergencies, since an alarm would not be heard, and an alarm-clock mechanism that causes the bed to vibrate at a designated waking time.

Structural Modifications for Existing Buildings

The Disabilities Act contains requirements concerning accessibility of facilities. Structural obstacles often preclude access by disabled persons to buildings open to the public. For example, a second floor reachable only by steps is not available to a person in a wheelchair. Blind persons may be unable to use an elevator because they cannot determine which button to push. The requirements to remove obstacles vary depending on whether the inaccessible building is an existing one, an existing one that is being altered, or a new one under construction.

For existing buildings not undergoing renovations, the Disabilities Act requires places of public accommodation to undertake the removal of barriers, if doing so is "readily achievable." **Readily achievable** is defined as "easily accomplished without much difficulty or expense." When drafting the Disabilities Act, Congress sought to protect the business community from incurring undue costs. Examples of barrier removal that the Disabilities Act considers readily achievable include:

- Ramping of a few steps (such as those in the entryway of a building or leading to a sunken area of a dining room in a restaurant)
- Lowering of telephones
- Adding raised letters and braille markings on elevator control buttons
- Adding grab bars in bathrooms, provided only routine reinforcement of the wall is required
- Rearranging tables in a restaurant to permit wheelchair passage
- Similar modest corrections.

Where removal of a barrier is readily achievable, failure to remove it constitutes illegal discrimination. If, however, the removal of the barrier is not readily achievable, its continued presence does not violate the Disabilities Act. For example, installation of an elevator for access to a second floor would be quite costly and would therefore not be required for existing buildings by the Disabilities Act.

If removal of a physical barrier is not readily achievable, the obligation to accommodate disabled persons is not eliminated. Instead, the Act requires the facility to make its goods or services available through an alternate method if one is readily achievable. For example, it may not be readily achievable for a restaurant to alter the location of a bar positioned one level above the dining area. To accommodate wheelchair patrons, such a restaurant would be required to modify a house rule requiring customers who want to drink but not order food to sit at the bar. Instead, the restaurant must permit disabled persons to order drinks from a table.

Structural Requirements During Construction

New facilities and buildings undergoing renovation must be constructed in such a way that they can be approached, entered, and utilized easily and conveniently by people with disabilities. New construction and alterations must comply with the Disabilities Act's accessibility guidelines. These regulations contain technical standards for most aspects of a facility, including entryways, door sizes, layout, bathroom construction, and so forth. If, however, the cost to make the new or altered building accessible would be disproportionate to the overall cost and scope of the alteration or construction, alternative methods can be pursued. The Disabilities Act does not mandate that facilities undertake major alterations or new construction. The requirement of barrier removal imposed when making alterations is not triggered by minor repairs such as painting or wallpapering. More extensive modifications are required.

For a new hotel, the Disabilities Act requires the following: all doors and doorways must be designed to allow passage by a wheelchair; bathrooms need to be sufficiently wide to allow use by people in wheelchairs; a percentage of each class of hotel room must be fully accessible, including grab bars in the bathroom and at the toilet; audio loops are required in meeting areas; emergency flashing lights or alarms are needed in hotel guest rooms; braille or raised-letter words and numbers are required on elevators and signs; and handrails must be installed on stairs and ramps.

If a person with a disability needing a fully accessible room makes a reservation without informing the hotel of the need for such a room and, when the person arrives, the needed room is not available, the hotel has not violated the Disabilities Act. While the hotel must make an effort to afford disabled persons accessible rooms, it can rent those rooms to nondisabled persons if an identified disabled person has not sought a reservation and other rooms are occupied.

Transportation and Telecommunications

The Disability Act also requires that businesses offering transportation attempt to make their facilities accessible to the disabled. A hotel that provides a hospitality van must remove barriers to its use provided removal is readily achievable.

The Disabilities Act also requires that companies offering telephone service provide telecommunication devices for the deaf that will permit a hearing-impaired person to communicate with anyone in this country who has a telephone.

Legal Action Directed at Noncompliance

Two types of lawsuits can be brought under the Act for noncompliance. One is a private action by individuals and the other is a lawsuit by the Department of Justice.

A private lawsuit can be brought by a disabled person who is subjected to discrimination on the basis of disability or who has reason to believe that he is about to be subjected to discrimination. For example, construction of a new hotel is being planned, but the specifications are not in compliance with the Disabilities Act. Remedies for a private lawsuit include an injunction requiring compliance with the Disabilities Act, a court order requiring alteration of facilities to comply with the Disabilities Act, or a court order requiring an auxiliary aide or service be provided, a policy be modified, or an alternate method of barrier removal be undertaken. Money as a remedy is not recoverable.

The second type of lawsuit can be brought only by the United States Attorney General, the chief law-enforcement officer of the country. This type of action is pursued against a violator where a pattern or practice of discrimination exists or where the discrimination raises an issue of general public importance (where the discrimination impacts many people). In addition to the remedies available in a private action, a court in a case brought by the Attorney General may award monetary damages. Punitive damages cannot be awarded, although a court may assess a civil penalty not exceeding $50,000 for the first violation and not exceeding $100,000 for any subsequent violation. Like the Civil Rights Act of 1964, the Disabilities Act withstood constitutional challenge early in its history. Just as the courts in the *Heart of Atlanta Motel* and *Ollie's Barbecue* upheld the Civil Rights Act, a court rejected claims by the House of Pancakes that the Disabilities Act was unconstitutional.

In *Pinnock v. International House of Pancakes Franchisee*, 844 F. Supp. 574 (S.D.Cal. 1993) the court rejected the Pancake House's claim that it was not engaged in interstate commerce because the restaurant was located within two miles of two interstate highways, and three hotels were within walking distance of the restaurant. The court likewise rejected the Pancake House's claim that the term *readily achievable*, used as the standard for determining when a modification must be made, was too vague to guide those bound by the Act. The court noted that the statute provides direction by listing examples of what qualifies as readily achievable—including rearranging tables and chairs, installing small ramps, and installing grab bars in restrooms. Further, federal regulations explaining the statute clarify the term.

The Pancake House also claimed that the phrase *most integrated setting appropriate*, used by the statute to describe the goal for accommodating disabled patrons, was too vague to be enforceable. The court rejected this claim noting that the statute contains two pages of examples and explanations, and thus was sufficiently clear.

The following case highlights the Disabilities Act's requirement that restaurants make readily achievable modifications to enable disabled patrons to utilize the establishment's facilities, including the bathrooms.

CASE EXAMPLE 3-4

Boemio v. Love's Restaurant
954 F. Supp. 204 (Cal. 1997)

This is an action based upon claims of discriminatory practices by a public accommodation. ... The allegations surround Mr. Boemio's visit to the Love's Restaurant in San Diego on or about April 19, 1996. Plaintiff suffers from a medical condition which requires that he use a motorized wheelchair. On the date in question, Plaintiff attempted to use the restrooms at the premises owned and operated by Defendant and alleges that he was unable to do so because the restrooms were inaccessible to wheelchair users. As a result of the inaccessibility, Plaintiff alleges that he was forced to urinate in the restaurant parking lot. ...

The issues at trial were whether Plaintiff could access the bathroom facilities at the premises ... Having heard the oral testimony produced by parties, and the argument of counsel, and after reviewing the documentary evidence, the Court now makes the following findings.

1) On or about April 19, 1996 Defendant, Love's Restaurant, operated the restaurant facility in San Diego.

2) On or about April 19, 1996, Defendant's restaurant was a public accommodation as contemplated by law and required to be accessible to physically handicapped persons.

3) On or about April 19, 1996 Plaintiff, Ralph Boemio, was lawfully on the premises of Defendant's restaurant.

4) Plaintiff, Ralph Boemio, is a qualified handicapped individual as provided in the relevant sections of the Americans with Disabilities Act.

5) Plaintiff, Ralph Boemio, suffers from a medical condition which requires that he use a motorized wheelchair.

6) On or about April 19, 1996, while on Defendant's premises, Plaintiff, Ralph Boemio, attempted to use the restroom facilities, but was unable to do so because the restrooms were inaccessible to him.

7) The men's restroom at Love's Restaurant was totally inaccessible to wheelchair patrons.

8) The ladies' restroom was historically used by some disabled individuals with assistance from the restaurant staff.

9) The ladies' restroom entry door from the corridor provided a clear opening of 28 and 1/2 inches and the door from the foyer to the toilet area provided a clear opening of 28 inches, both in violation of the ADA Accessibility Guidelines (32 inches required).

10) The doorway size and configuration and layout of the corridor to the restroom prevented reasonable access to the restroom facilities on Defendant's premises.

11) As a result of the inaccessibility, Plaintiff Ralph Boemio, had to urinate in the parking lot.

12) Plaintiff, Ralph Boemio, suffered actual damages in the form of mental anguish and humiliation as a result of the discrimination associated with the inaccessible bathrooms on Defendant's facility.

13) Plaintiff's actions in the parking lot were unwitnessed by third parties and unaccompanied by any mishap, injury, physical harm or property damage.

The ADA [Americans with Disabilities Act] prohibits discrimination against any individual "on the basis of disability in the full and equal enjoyment of goods, services, facilities, privileges, advantages or accommodations of any place of public accommodation by any person who owns leases or operates a place of public accommodation." A restaurant is clearly a public accommodation under the ADA. ...

The remedies for an ADA violation include injunctive relief and attorney's fees. Monetary damages are not recoverable by private Plaintiffs under the ADA. ...

Based upon the Findings of Fact previously set forth, it is clear that Plaintiff, as a qualified individual, has met his burden of proof with regard to the discrimination experienced in this action. While the operators and employees of Love's Restaurant made attempts to accommodate disabled individuals who needed to use the restroom on the facilities, Plaintiff was denied reasonable access on April 19, 1996 in this case.

While the defense offered that with additional time, patience, and jockeying of the wheelchair, access could have been achieved, this was not reasonable nor consistent with the public policy interest in providing physically handicapped persons with equal access to public facilities and warrants a finding for Plaintiff in this action. The standard cannot be "is access achievable in some manner." We must focus on the quality of access. If a finding that ultimate access could have been achieved provided a defense, the spirit of the law would be defeated. It is clear that the legislative purpose behind these disability access laws would not support such a finding. ...

The restaurant's past practice of rendering assistance to disabled persons also supports the lack of any animus toward disabled individuals in the community. On the night in question, however, the clear violation of access standards, and the practical preclusion of Plaintiff from reasonable access to the restroom facilities is undeniable. The physical location and layout of the restroom interfered with full and equal access to the Plaintiff.

Plaintiff's standard sized wheelchair, and the necessary attachments and configuration are not something that present some atypical anomaly. ...

Judgment is hereby entered in favor of Plaintiff and against Dedendant.

CASE QUESTION

1. Why is "quality of access" a concern of the Disabilities Act?

Also constituting a violation of the Disabilities Act is failing to provide handicapped parking at a restaurant or hotel.[29]

In another case, the plaintiffs complained that the cashier counter at a restaurant did not have a lowered section for wheelchair accessibility. It was the practice for all patrons of the eating facility to pay the server at the table, rather than at the cashier counter. Under these circumstances, the absence of an accessible cashier did not violate the Disabilities Act. Said the court, "The plaintiff's argument that perhaps a wheelchair user might elect to pay the bill directly, rather than to the server, is without merit. The present situation provides wheelchair users the same services as those provided to and utilized by the general public."[30]

In the following case, several restaurant patrons with asthma or lupus claimed that restaurant policies permitting smoking in the building violated the Disabilities Act. The case explores the often difficult question of what is meant by "readily achievable" or "reasonable accommodation," the standard for determining necessary modifications to buildings not under construction and not being substantially altered. Disabled patrons, hoping for the greatest possible access, seek a broad interpretation. Hospitality establishments, keenly aware of the costs for accessibility modifications, often seek a more narrow definition.

CASE EXAMPLE 3-5

Staron v. McDonald's Corp. and Burger King Corp.
51 F.3d 353 (2nd Cir. 1995)

These actions are brought by three children with asthma and a woman with lupus against two popular fast-food restaurant chains: McDonald's Corporation ("McDonald's") and Burger King Corporation ("Burger King").

---

[29] *Boston v. Paul McNally Realty*, 216 F3d 827 (9th Cir. 2000)

[30] *Long v. Coast Resorts, Inc.*, 32 F.Supp.2d 1203 (Nev. 1999)

Plaintiffs claim that defendants' policies of permitting smoking in their restaurants violates the Americans with Disabilities Act (the "ADA" or "Act"). Plaintiffs appeal judgments granting defendants' motions to dismiss plaintiffs' claims. ...

For the reasons stated below, we reverse the judgements and remand the cases [send them back to the court of original jurisdiction] for further proceedings.

Background

The facts alleged in plaintiffs' complaints are rather straightforward. During one week in February, 1993, each plaintiff entered both a McDonald's and a Burger King restaurant in Connecticut. Each plaintiff found the air in each restaurant to be full of tobacco smoke, and because of his or her condition, was unable to enter the restaurant without experiencing breathing problems. Each plaintiff has also encountered similar difficulties at other times in other restaurants owned by McDonald's and Burger King.

After registering complaints with the defendants ... without satisfactory results, plaintiffs filed separate suits against McDonald's and Burger King on March 30, 1993. Their complaints alleged that the defendants' policies of permitting smoking in their restaurants constituted discrimination under the Act. Each complaint requested ... an injunction to rohibit defendants from maintaining any policy which interfered with plaintiffs' rights under the Act, and more specifically to require [defendants and their franchisees] to establish a policy of prohibiting smoking in all of the facilities they own, lease or operate. ...

Discussion

Because we find that plaintiffs' complaints do on their face state a cognizable claim against the defendants under the Americans with Disabilities Act, we reverse the district court's orders of dismissal.

The ADA was promulgated "to provide a clear and comprehensive national mandate for the elimination of discrimination against individuals with disabilities" as well as to establish "clear, strong, consistent, enforceable standards" for scrutinizing such discrimination.

"Discrimination" includes the failure of an owner, operator, lessee, or lessor of public accommodations to make reasonable modifications in policies, practices or procedures, when such modifications are necessary to afford such goods, services [or] facilities ... to individuals with disabilities, unless the entity can demonstrate that making such modifications would fundamentally alter the nature of such goods, services, [or] facilities. ...

[D]efendants do not dispute that the [Act] applies to them as owners and operators of public accommodations. They also concede at this point that plaintiffs qualify as individuals with disabilities under the ADA. ... The principal contention of McDonald's and Burger King on appeal is that a total ban on smoking does not constitute a "reasonable modification" under the ADA.

The ADA and cases interpreting it do not articulate a precise test for determining whether a particular modification is "reasonable" ... [A predecessor statute] stated that "accommodation is not reasonable if it either imposes 'undue financial and administrative burdens' ... or requires 'a fundamental alteration in the nature of the [business].'"

Although neither the ADA nor the courts have defined the precise contours of the test for reasonableness, it is clear that the determination of whether a particular modification is "reasonable" involves a fact-specific, case-by-case inquiry that considers, among other factors, the effectiveness of the modification in light of the nature of the disability in question and the cost to the organization that would implement it.

... [I]n the case before us a fact-specific inquiry was required. None has occurred. The [judge in the court of original jurisdiction] concluded that plaintiff's request for a ban on smoking in all of defendants' restaurants was unreasonable as a matter of law. ...

It is plain to us that Congress did not intend to isolate the effects of smoking from the protections of the ADA. In fact, language of the Act expressly permits a total ban on smoking if a court finds it appropriate under the ADA. We therefore reject any argument by defendants to the contrary ... "The determination as to whether allergies to cigarette smoke ... are disabilities covered by the regulation must be made using the same case-by-case analysis that is applied to all other physical or mental impairments. We see no reason why, under the appropriate circumstances, a ban on smoking could not be a reasonable accommodation. ...

To be sure, the few courts that have addressed the question of reasonable modification for a smoke-sensitive disability have found a total ban unnecessary. Yet these courts only reached this conclusion after making a factual determination that existing accommodations were sufficient. ...

Plaintiffs in this case are entitled to an opportunity to prove that a ban on smoking is a reasonable modification to permit them access to defendants' restaurants. Given that McDonald's has voluntarily banned smoking in all corporate-owned restaurants, the factfinder may conclude that such a ban would fully accommodate plaintiffs' disabilities but impose little or no cost on the defendants. Plaintiffs have alleged that, regardless of the different structural arrangements in various restaurants, the environment in each establishment visited by the plaintiffs contained too much smoke to allow them use of the facilities on an equal basis as other nondisabled patrons. These allegations belie the [lower court] judge's assumption that no-smoking areas offer a sufficient accommodation to plaintiffs. ...

If plaintiffs should fail in their quest for an outright ban on smoking, they may still be able to demonstrate after discovery that modifications short of an outright ban, such as partitions or ventilation systems, are both "reasonable" and "necessary," and plaintiffs should be allowed the opportunity to do so.

Defendants raise another objection. ... They contend that plaintiffs' request for a smoking ban is unreasonable because it applies to all of defendants' restaurants "regardless of whether these four plaintiffs have ever visited, will visit, might visit, or never will visit" the many McDonald's and Burger King restaurants across the country. This objection pertains to the permissible scope of injunctive relieve in this case ... doubts about the scope do not justify dismissal of the complaints where plaintiffs have alleged cognizable claims at least with respect to the restaurants they expect to visit.

We therefore reverse the judgments of the district court and remand for proceedings consistent with this opinion.

CASE QUESTIONS

1. Explain the differences between the decision of the court of original jurisdiction and the decision of the appeals court.

2. What factors in this case suggest that a total ban on smoking in defendants' restaurants would be a reasonable modification? What factors suggest such a ban would be unreasonable?

Language Discrimination

The following case involves discrimination against Spanish-speaking bar patrons. A person's primary language is an important part of and flows from his or her national origin. Therefore, discrimination based on language is often viewed as discrimination based on national origin in violation of the Civil Rights Act of 1964. Since the Act does not cover bars, the court could not rely on the Act to stop the tavern from discriminating. Instead, the court creatively used different federal laws that grant all citizens of the United States equal rights to enter contracts and purchase property. The proprietor in this case violated those laws by limiting the rights of the Spanish-speaking patrons to purchase beer.

CASE EXAMPLE 3-6

Hernandez v. Erlenbusch
368 F.Supp. 752 (Oregon, 1973)

... At trial, a preponderance of the evidence showed the following: The setting for both cases is the same—a community of approximately 8,500 persons in which more than 2,000 Mexican-Americans have been living for at least the last four years. The plaintiffs in these cases are all U.S. citizens, most of them native born. Some two years ago, the defendants, owners of the Taffrail Tavern ("Tavern"), issued these orders to their bartenders:

> You are instructed to observe the following. ...
>
> 11. Do not allow a foreign language to be used at the bar, if it interferes with the regular trade. If there should be a chance of a problem, ask the 'Problem' people to move to a table and turn the juke box up. (Use house money).

The rationale for this policy, as explained by its formulators and enforcers, is that the tavern has many Anglo and Chicano patrons, with attendant friction between the two groups caused by the dislike by some of the local white populace of the "foreigners" in their midst. According to the Erlenbusches, the tavern's owners, the language rule as carried out by them and their employees served everyone's interests by accommodating both Anglo and Chicano customers and ensuring peaceful continuance of the tavern business. The complaints concerning Spanish spoken at the bar allegedly stem from fear on the part of the white clientele that the Chicanos are talking about them. It was in this atmosphere ridden with mistrust and apprehension that the following incidents occurred:

On August 23, 1972, Gilberto Hernandez and Abel and Alfredo Maldonado went to the tavern where defendant Krausnick, the bartender, served them beer. While drinking, the three men began conversing in Spanish, their native tongue. Anglo customers, who were also sitting at the bar, were "irritated" and complained to Krausnick. She advised the Chicanos that if they persisted in speaking Spanish, they would have to go to a booth or leave the premises.

Hernandez and the Maldonados took issue with these orders and an argument ensued.

Krausnick poured out their remaining beer and refused to refund any money. The police were called, the plaintiffs left peacefully.

Two days later, the scene was reenacted with different plaintiffs and an additional three antagonists. Krausnick "pulled" the beers of Gonzalez, Perez and Vasquez who were then followed out of the tavern and assaulted by defendants Salisbury, Dunn, and Clary, three Anglo regular customers. Clary was subsequently tried and convicted in state court for battering Gonzalez over the right eye with a fire extinguisher. (Gonzales was the only plaintiff who was physically struck.)

Defendant Krausnick testified that she agreed with and willingly enforced "Rule 11." Clary, Dunn, and Salisbury concurred, saying they knew of the rule and wholeheartedly endorsed it. John Erlenbusch testified he adopted the policy simply to avoid trouble and to preserve his license.

Conclusions of Law

... In examining the practical effect of the tavern's policy against the speaking of foreign languages at the bar, it is obvious that it amounts to patent racial discrimination against Mexican-Americans who constitute about one-fourth of the tavern's trade, regardless of an occasional visit by a customer able to speak another language. The rule's results are what count; the intent of the framers in these circumstances is irrelevant. ... In the instant case, Rule 11, as intended and applied, deprives Spanish-speaking persons of their rights to buy, drink and enjoy what the tavern has to offer on an equal footing with English-speaking consumers.

Plaintiffs' rights ... to the full and equal benefit of all laws and proceedings for the security of person and property as is enjoyed by white citizens have been violated. Likewise, plaintiffs have been denied their ... guarantee that [a]ll citizens of the United States shall have the same right ... to ... purchase ... personal property. ... Just as the Constitution forbids banishing blacks to the back of the bus so as not to arouse the racial animosity of the preferred white passengers, it also forbids ordering Spanish-speaking patrons to the "back booth or out" to avoid antagonizing English-speaking beer-drinkers.

The lame justification that a discriminatory policy helps preserve the peace is as unacceptable in barrooms as it was in buses. Catering to prejudice out of fear of provoking greater prejudice only perpetuates racism.

Courts faithful to the Fourteenth Amendment will not permit, either by camouflage or cavalier treatment, equal protection so to be profaned.

CASE QUESTION

1. What can the Erlenbusches do legally to address the friction between the Anglo and Chicano patrons?

Age Discrimination

Age is a classification not protected in places of public accommodation by the Act or most state civil rights laws. Thus, it is normally not illegal to treat varying age groups differently in such places. For example, a large discount department store, concerned about the high rate of shoplifting in the CD and audio tape department, barred school-age youths in the store after school hours on weekdays unless accompanied by an adult. Again, although this amounts to treatment of young people differently from others, discrimination on the basis of age is not illegal. Similarly, a skating rink that wishes to promote a Saturday-evening session as an event for teens can exclude from the rink people who are younger or older.

While discrimination on the basis of age in places of public accommodation is generally permissible, discrimination on the basis of age in employment decisions is restricted, as we will discuss in Chapter 14.

Gender Discrimination

Another type of discrimination not outlawed by the Civil Rights Act of 1964 is discrimination based on gender. In a 1968 case, a woman was refused service at an all-male bar operated by a hotel. She was forced to leave although she was sitting quietly and not disturbing other patrons. She sued the bar, challenging its discriminatory policy. The court reiterated that the Civil Rights Act of 1964 did not cover gender discrimination and dismissed the case, suggesting that the plaintiff address her complaint to Congress, which has the authority to change the law, and not to the courts.[31]

Although the Civil Rights Act does not protect women, under some circumstances they can obtain redress for discrimination in places of public accommodation through the Fourteenth Amendment to the Constitution. That amendment states, "[N]or shall any *state* ... deny to any person within its jurisdiction the equal

---

[31]*DeCrow v. Hotel Syracuse Corp.*, 288 F.Supp. 530 (N.Y. 1968)

protection of the *laws*" (emphasis added). The operative word is *state*, meaning the government. The amendment does not prohibit private discrimination. How does a place of public accommodation qualify as the state? It qualifies only if it is subject to considerable supervision and control by the government. Is a bar or restaurant with a liquor license issued by the state subject to the necessary degree of state supervision and control, and therefore bound by the Fourteenth Amendment prohibition against unequal protection of the laws?

That question was answered in the affirmative in *Seidenberg v. McSorley's Old Ale House, Inc.*, 308 F.Supp. 1253 (N.Y. 1969). Two female members of the National Organization of Women (NOW) entered the defendant establishment, a bar primarily engaged in serving beverages. They were told by the bartender that the facility did not serve women and that it had consistently adhered to this practice throughout its 114 years of existence. The two women sued the bar claiming illegal discrimination on the basis of the Act and the Fourteenth Amendment. The court denied their Civil Rights Act claim, noting that Congress did not outlaw discrimination based on gender. Concerning the Fourteenth Amendment claim, the Court noted that a liquor licensee is restricted by state law in who it can sell alcohol to and when it can sell, and the licensee is subject to inspection of its premises by the State Liquor Authority, which can suspend or revoke the license. The court held this to be sufficient supervision and control to qualify the bar as an instrumentality of the state.

Supplementing the Constitution, virtually all states now have state statutes that prohibit discrimination in places of public accommodation based on gender. As we studied, the phrase *place of public accommodation*, as used by state law, customarily covers more establishments than does the federal Act. The phrase includes almost every place open to the public including, for example, stores and schools.

In a case involving the New York statute, a tavern refused to serve women at the bar during certain hours. The plaintiff sought a court order barring the owners from continuing that practice. Based on state law, the court granted plaintiff's request and ordered the bar to cease and desist its discriminatory practice.[32]

In another case involving Michigan's civil rights statute, the court barred the Lion's Club, an all-male service organization, from denying women membership. The club had refused to accept a woman who met all membership requirements except gender.[33]

Like the Civil Rights Act of 1964, most state civil rights acts exempt private clubs. As with the Act, the issue arises whether an establishment is public or private. The right of an allegedly private golf club to refuse to grant membership to women was at issue in *Warfield v. Peninsula Golf & Country Club*, 896 P2d 776 (Cal. 1995). Plaintiff wife and her husband had a family membership at defendant golf club. When they divorced, the plaintiff was awarded the couple's membership. A rule of the club provided that family memberships "shall be issued only in the

---

[32] *Rosenberg v. State Human Rights Appeal Board*, 357 N.Y.S.2d 325 (1974)

[33] *Rogers v. International Association of Lions Club*, 636 F.Supp. 1476 (E.D. Mich. 1986)

name of adult male persons, ... and shall not be approved for females or minors."
The rule further provided that where a family membership was awarded to the wife
in a divorce and the husband failed to purchase it from the wife, the board of
directors of the country club could terminate the membership.

The board cancelled the plaintiff's membership accordingly and the plaintiff
sued based on gender discrimination. The club claimed it was a private club and so
was not bound by the California state statute that prohibited discrimination by
"business establishments" based on gender.

The court rejected the golf club's argument that it was a private club and held
for the plaintiff wife. Pivotal to the decision was the significant use of club facilities
by nonmembers. While as a general rule the club's facilities were open only to
members, notable exceptions existed.

In another case, male bar patrons challenged a "ladies drink free" promotion
that defendant bar sponsored weekly. Defendant also featured a weekly "Men's
Night Out" which offered reduced drink prices and free dart games for male
patrons. On other nights of the week, promotions were offered to all patrons. The
Wisconsin state statute in issue prohibited a place of public accommodation from
giving preferential treatment because of gender. The court held that ladies' night
promotions gave preferential treatment to women on the sole basis of gender,
therefore violating the law. Said the court, "Our interpretation of [the law] does
not prohibit [defendant bar] from offering a wide array of promotions in the form
of reduced or no prices for food, drinks and entertainment. It prohibits only those
promotions that base price differentials on the categories specified in the statute
[which include gender]."[34]

One of the bar's arguments was that, since it gave men promotional benefits
on another night, ladies night was not discriminatory. The court responded,
"Preferential treatment to men on other nights does not correct the violation."
Had female patrons challenged the men's night promotions, the outcome would
have been the same.

Gender discrimination in access to places of public accommodation is less
prevalent today. Such discrimination in employment is more widespread. While the
federal Act does not protect against gender discrimination in places of public
accommodation, it does protect against gender discrimination in employment, as
we will discuss in Chapter 14.

Rights of Proprietors

Discrimination against some categories of people is not prohibited by law. For
example, no law offers protection against discrimination in places of public accommodation to people who are dressed in jeans or males not wearing shirts. Thus, a

---

[34] *Novak v. Madison Motel Associates*, 188 Wis.2d 407, 418–419; 525 N.W.2d 123, 127–128
(Ct. Appls., Wis. 1994)

restaurant's policy of refusing to serve anyone in jeans is legal even though it discriminates against people wearing denim pants.

An interesting case involved a casino's ejection of a patron who was a counter—that is, someone who keeps track in blackjack of what cards have been played. When certain cards that tilt the odds in favor of the player remain to be played, the counter bets the house limits and frequently wins, to the chagrin of the casino.

The expelled counter challenged the casino's right to evict him. The court held the counter was not protected by the Civil Rights Act because his exclusion was not based on race, color, religion, or national origin.[35]

Innkeepers have a common-law obligation to provide accommodations to all who seek them. However, even this rule has exceptions that allow an innkeeper to refuse accommodations to a guest who is unable to prove ability to pay, a guest who is disorderly, or a guest who has a contagious disease. These exceptions and others will be discussed in Chapter 10.

Permissible to Remove a Disorderly Person

Removal of a restaurant patron who is acting disorderly does not violate the civil rights laws. Although the unruly diner may be a member of a protected minority, ejection based on conduct does not violate the Act. The following case, involving a McDonald's restaurant, illustrates this point. As you read the case, note how the customer sought to prove racial discrimination and the reasons why the court rejected that proof.

CASE EXAMPLE 3-7

Alexis v. McDonald's Restaurants of Massachusetts, Inc.
67 F.3d 341 (1st Cir. 1995)

At approximately 10:00 P.M. on July 20, 1990, in Framingham, Massachusetts, Alexis and her family, who are African Americans, entered a McDonald's restaurant, proceeded to the service counter, placed their order, and paid in advance. When the food was placed before them at the service counter, it became apparent that [their server] Alfredo Pascacio, whose native tongue is Spanish, had mistaken their order. During the ensuing exchange between Alexis and Pascacio, defendant-appellee Donna Domina, the "swing manager," intervened on behalf of Pascacio, which prompted

Alexis to say: "[You] take care of the people in front of you. He's taking care of me, and we're sorting this out." Domina nonetheless persisted for several more minutes.

Ultimately, Domina said to Alexis, "I don't have to listen to you." Alexis replied, "[Y]ou're damn right you don't have to listen to me. I was not speaking to you. I was speaking to him." Domina then instructed Pascacio: "just put their stuff in a bag and get them out of here." Turning to Alexis, Domina retorted: "You're not eating here. If you [do] we're going to call the cops." Alexis responded: "Well you do what you have to do because we plan to eat here." Notwithstanding Domina's instructions, Pascacio placed the food order on a service tray, without bagging it. The entire incident at

---

[35] *Uston v. Airport Casino, Inc.*, 564 F.2d 1216 (Cal. 1977)

the service counter had lasted approximately ten minutes.

After the Alexis family went into the dining area, Sherry Toham, a managerial employee, summoned defendant Michael Leporati into the restaurant. Leporati, a uniformed off-duty police sergeant, had been patrolling on foot outside the restaurant by prearrangement with the Town of Framingham, but had witnessed no part of the earlier exchange among Alexis, Pascacio, and Domina.

Upon entering the restaurant, Leporati was informed by Domina that Alexis had been yelling, creating a "scene" and an "unwarranted disturbance" over a mistaken food order, and directing abusive remarks at Pascacio. Domina informed Leporati that Alexis had argued loudly with her and another employee; that she "just wasn't stopping"; and that Alexis was still in the dining area though Domina had "asked her to leave." Finally, Domina told Leporati, "I would like her to leave."

Without further inquiry into the "disturbance" allegedly caused by Alexis, Leporati proceeded to the dining area where Alexis and her family were seated, and informed the entire Alexis family that the manager wanted them to leave and that they would have to do so. Alexis immediately asked why, denied causing any disturbance, and claimed a right to finish eating in the restaurant. When she urged Leporati to ask other restaurant customers whether there had been a disturbance, Leporati simply reiterated that the family would have to leave. ...

Approximately ten minutes later, Officer William Fuer arrived, and Alexis was told by Leporati that she was being placed under arrest. ...

Alexis eventually was charged with criminal trespass, a misdemeanor. Following her acquittal by a jury, Alexis and her family filed the present action ... asserting civil rights claims. ... The district court granted summary judgment for the defendants. ...

Alexis submitted deposition testimony of six witnesses—the five Alexis family members and Karen Stauffer, an eyewitness to the events—each of whom opined, in effect, that had Alexis been a "rich white woman," she would not have been treated in the same manner. The court found that the proffered testimony was "not supported by sufficient factual undergirding" to permit a reasonable inference that either Domina or McDonald's discriminated against Alexis on the basis of her race. ... The six deponents based their inferences of racial animus on their personal observations that Domina reacted "angrily" toward Alexis and with a "negative tone in her voice," was "unfriendly," "uncooperative," "high strung," "impolite," "impatient," and had "no reason" to eject Alexis. Although these observations may be entirely compatible with a race-based animus, there simply is no foundation for an inference that Domina harbored a racial animus toward Alexis or anyone else, absent some probative evidence that Domina's petulance stemmed from something other than a race-neutral reaction to the stressful encounter plainly evidenced in the record, including Alexis's persistence (however justified). ...

As Alexis points to no competent evidence that Domina and McDonald's intentionally discriminated against her on account of her race, the district court correctly ruled that this claim should be dismissed. Disputes generally arise out of mutual misunderstanding, misinterpretation, and overreaction, and without more, such disputes do not give rise to an inference of discrimination. Accordingly, the summary judgment entered in favor of Domina and McDonald's must be affirmed. ...

CASE QUESTION

1. On what basis did the court find that the restaurant was not liable for discrimination?

Reasonable Rules of an Establishment

The management of a service establishment, like any other business enterprise, must have rules to maintain order and express the philosophy of its management. Often these rules result in different treatment of different groups. If the rules are reasonable and do not result in illegal discrimination against protected classes, they are enforceable even though the result may be that some people will be treated differently than others.

In the following case, the management of a restaurant had a rule that excluded any person who was barefoot. A woman, ejected from the restaurant because she had removed her shoes, unsuccessfully challenged the legality of the rule.

CASE EXAMPLE 3-8

Feldt v. Marriott Corporation
322 A.2d 913 (D.C. 1974)

[Appellant], about 26 years of age, and her male escort had attended a dance at a fraternity house and after leaving the dance went to a Junior Hot Shoppe, owned and operated by appellee. They went through a cafeteria line, selected, and paid for some food and then sat at a table and began to eat. The manager of the shop approached the table and told appellant she would have to leave because she was not wearing shoes. [Appellant left her shoes in her escort's automobile parked near the entrance.] No sign to that effect was posted, but the manager said it was the company's policy to serve no one who was not wearing shoes. She replied she would leave as soon a she finished eating. The manager did not offer to refund her money, and she asked for no refund. [There was testimony that the manager offered to get a bag so she could take the food— a hamburger and french fries—with her.] He continued to insist that she leave, and she continued to insist she would leave only when she had finished eating. The argument continued and she finally said to the manager: "Will you, please, go to hell." He walked outside and returned with a police officer. The manager again asked her to leave, and the officer told her she would be violating the unlawful entry statute if she refused to leave after the manager had asked her to leave. She replied she would leave when she had finished eating. The officer took her arm and said unless she left he would arrest her. She arose and walked to the door and then, observing the officer behind her, began struggling with him and hit him.

Appellant was then placed in a patrol wagon, taken to a precinct station, and later taken to the Women's Detention Center. Hours later she was released on her personal recognizance and told to appear in court the next day. When she appeared in court, she was told the charge against her would be dropped and she was free to leave.

It is clear that appellant entered the premises lawfully, but it is also clear that under our unlawful entry statute ... one who lawfully enters may be guilty of a misdemeanor by refusing to leave after being ordered to do so by the person lawfully in charge of the premises. Our question is whether the police officer was justified in arresting appellant when she, in his presence, refused to leave after being ordered to do so by the manager.

At common law, a restaurant owner had the right to arbitrarily refuse service to any guest. Absent constitutional or statutory rights, the common law still controls in this jurisdiction. This is not a case of racial discrimination or violation of civil rights. We do have a statute making it unlawful for a restaurant to refuse service to "any quiet and orderly person" or to exclude anyone on account of race or color; but, as we have said, there was no racial discrimination here and we do not think the requirement to serve any quiet or orderly person prevents a restaurant from having reasonable requirements as to the dress of its customers, such as a requirement that all male customers wear coats and ties, or, as here, that all customers wear shoes. Had the restaurant manager observed that appellant was not wearing shoes when she first entered the restaurant, he could have properly and lawfully refused to serve her and requested her to leave. Our question narrows down to whether the fact that the restaurant had served appellant food and received payment for it prevented the restaurant from ordering appellant to leave when her shoeless condition was observed.

The status of a customer in a restaurant, as far as we can ascertain, has never been precisely declared. It is not the same as a guest at an inn. ...

The nearest analogy we have found in the reported cases to the one here is that of a patron of a theater, racetrack, or other place of public entertainment, who, after having purchased a ticket, is ordered to leave. It has been generally held that such a patron has only a personal license, which may be revoked at any time, leaving him only with a breach of contract claim [against the proprietor].

We think that is the applicable rule here. When appellant was ordered to leave, her license to be on the premises was revoked, whether legally or illegally, and she had no right to remain. Her remedy, if any, was a civil action for breach of contract. ...

Our conclusion is that when appellant, in the presence of the police officer, refused to leave on the demand of the restaurant manager, the officer was justified in arresting her for violation of the unlawful entry statute. ...

Retaliatory Exclusion

Often when a customer sues a hotel or restaurant she is disinclined to return to the establishment for service. In cases where a plaintiff does seek service after commencing the lawsuit, the facility is not obligated to accommodate the would-be patron.

In one case a plaintiff sued a bar claiming illegal discrimination. The grounds for the discrimination was not specified by the court; it might have been, for example, race, color, or national origin. While that case was pending, the plaintiff returned to the defendant's bar intending to purchase drinks. She was denied admission by the doorman and informed that the reason for the exclusion was that she had sued the bar. She filed a second suit, claiming that denial of services because of her lawsuit constituted illegal discrimination. The court dismissed the action on the ground that discrimination based on retaliation for bringing a lawsuit was not a protected class. Said the court, "[A]n exclusion based on a customer's *conduct*, whether or not the customer was a member of a class, was reasonable as a matter of law."[36]

In the following case a restaurant refused service to a repeat patron who sued the establishment relating to its smoking policy.

CASE EXAMPLE 3-9

King v. Hofer
49 Cal. Rptr.2d 719 (1996)

... King's complaint alleges that he was a regular patron of defendant's restaurant, which has a bar area in the same undivided space, where smoking is prohibited by local ordinance during hours in which the restaurant is also open. On the afternoon of April 16, 1994, King was dining in the restaurant when

---

[36] *Gayer v. Guluch, Inc.*, 282 Cal.Rptr. 556 (Ca. 1991)

he noticed tobacco smoke and that patrons of the bar were smoking. This caused him respiratory distress and, upon leaving, he asked an employee working at the restaurant counter why smoking was being permitted. The employee told him that smoking was allowed in the bar during overlapping hours. King complained by letter to the city manager three days later, requesting enforcement of the ordinance, and on April 28 that office sent Hofer [the restaurateur] a letter requiring compliance, along with a copy of King's complaint letter.

On the next day, April 29, King allegedly got two telephone calls from Hofer, who "acted in a retaliatory, hostile, rude and abusive and insulting manner, telling King that if he didn't like smoke he should go somewhere else, that he was no longer welcome in the restaurant, and that he would not be served in the restaurant in the future." [The restaurant's] motion to dismiss urged that King was not a member of any protected class under the state anti-discrimination act, had not been discriminated against on any such basis, ...

Hofer conceded that she told King over the telephone that she had the right to refuse him service and that if he did not like smoking he could go elsewhere. The exclusion was not based on his membership in a group or any of his personal characteristics, but instead it was based on his behavior in writing to the City of Orinda to request enforcement of the ordinance.

King's response urged that the discrimination against him was, by inference, based on his "personal characteristic" of being a non-smoker, making him a protected class member. ...

We find lack of class status for nonsmokers dispositive. Because King's entire claim rests on discrimination for being a nonsmoker, dismissal was proper ...

The anti-discrimination act does not cover business retaliation against patrons who have brought actions against the establishment. King summarizes the act's express categories as being personal characteristics that are either "fixed attributes, unchangeable and inherent to the individual" or "chosen attributes, involving choices changeable though often not changed, based on deep conviction [religious beliefs]." He then offers as to nonsmoker: "Certainly being a nonsmoker is a kind of physical attribute and personal belief, a personal trait, an attribute not readily changed, a life-style and inherent to a person's basic and permanent nature, and usually a personal belief based on deep conviction; nonsmokers are certainly a discrete and significant class within society, who have as a class endured oppression from public smoking and smokers and it is in the public interest to protect non-smokers from the health hazards of smoking, and the consequent cost to society."

The argument is overblown. Nonsmoking might be termed a physical attribute of sorts, but it is not one which is immediately apparent or carries any negative connotation in the usual setting. Also, nonsmokers enjoy solid majority status in our society, and few would regard that lifestyle choice as a "personal belief." For those who do, it is obviously not a belief seriously equatable with religion, the only express "belief" category in the anti-discrimination act. Nor is it an immutable characteristic. As for the wisdom of protecting nonsmokers from the health hazards of smoking, that is a policy matter for health and safety legislation. We are cited no authority or history suggesting that the anti-discrimination act addresses health and safety in public accommodations—only certain forms of discrimination.

CASE QUESTION

1. How might Hofer have better handled the situation upon intitially learning that King had complained to the authorities?

Ejection of Objectionable Persons and Trespass

Patrons who enter the premises despite a warning not to may be guilty of criminal trespass. Even if the patrons enter the premises lawfully, they may be guilty of trespass if they fail to obey a lawful order to leave made by the owner or the owner's designee. To commit this crime, patrons must first be informed they are not welcome on the premises. For example, where an organization's meeting was restricted to members of the Board of Governors (the association's governing body), others could be legally excluded. Removal of an attendee who was not a board member and who failed to leave when asked did not constitute illegal discrimination.[37] What should hoteliers and restaurateurs do if an individual they have asked to leave refuses to go? The best response is to call the police to handle the matter. Ideally, a confrontation like the one described in *Feldt v. Marriott Corp.* will be avoided. The rights of the proprietor in this type of situation will be discussed at more length in Chapter 10.

Key Terms

Americans with Disabilities Act
civil rights
Civil Rights Act of 1964
discrimination
interstate commerce

landmark decision
readily achievable
transients
unitary rule

Summary

Sadly, discrimination was a practice quite prevalent in the hospitality industry before the passage of the Civil Rights Act of 1964. Today, many laws prohibit discrimination. The common law prohibits innkeepers from refusing accommodations to anyone who seeks them, unless certain exceptions apply. The Civil Rights Act of 1964 prevents hotels, restaurants, gas stations, and places of entertainment engaged in interstate commerce from refusing to provide services or accommodations on the basis of race, color, religion, or national origin. The Americans with Disabilities Act prohibits discrimination on the basis of disability and requires various accommodations for handicapped patrons. State civil rights laws fill in the gaps by preventing discrimination within the state in a large class of facilities on the grounds not just of race, color, religion, and national origin, but also gender, marital status, disability and in some locales, sexual orientation.

We have seen in this chapter how the law can be used as a tool to deter discrimination and encourage hospitality facilities to provide their services to all equally.

---

[37] *Miranda v. Resident and Directors of Georgetown College*, 818 F. Supp. 16 (D.C. 1993)

Preventive Law Tips for Managers

■ *Do not refuse a hotel room to anyone on the grounds of membership in a protected class.* Failure to provide a room based on race, color, religion, or nationality violates the Civil Rights Act of 1964 and can result in an injunction and judgment for attorney's fees in favor of the plaintiff. Discrimination based on disability may violate the Americans with Disabilities Act. Refusal to provide a room based on gender or marital status may violate a state civil rights law and subject the innkeeper to criminal penalties. If the hotel is located in a locality that forbids discrimination based on sexual orientation, refusal to provide a room to someone who is homosexual will result in liability. In addition to the legal penalties, discrimination contradicts the basic principle of equal opportunity and treatment upon which our country was founded and violates a basic tenet of the hospitality industry to treat customers well and make them feel comfortable. *Note*: If a legitimate reason exists to refuse accommodations (for example, violation of reasonable house rules, disorderly conduct, or trespassing) the innkeeper can legally decline to provide a room.

■ *Do not refuse a hotel room to anyone who shows ability to pay* unless the innkeeper has a legitimate reason for the refusal (for example, violation of reasonable house rules, disorderly conduct, or trespassing). The common law requires that hotels provide rooms for everyone requesting accommodations. Failure to provide a room to a would-be guest with the financial means to pay can result in liability.

■ *Do not refuse restaurant services to someone on the ground of race, color, religion, or nationality.* The Civil Rights Act of 1964 outlaws discrimination on these grounds. *Note*: If a legitimate reason exists to refuse accommodations (for example, violation of reasonable house rules, disorderly conduct, or trespassing) the restaurateur can legally decline to provide a table.

■ *Do not refuse restaurant services to someone on the grounds of gender, marital status, or disability.* State civil rights laws customarily outlaw discrimination on these grounds, and the federal Americans with Disabilities Act outlaws discrimination against disabled persons. Failure to abide by these laws can result in civil and criminal liability. Also, local ordinances may prohibit discrimination on the basis of sexual orientation. These types of discrimination can be as hurtful to the guest and damaging to the hospitality industry as discrimination based on race, color, religion, and nationality. *Note*: If a legitimate reason exists to refuse accommodations (for example, violation of reasonable house rules, disorderly conduct, or trespassing) the restaurateur can legally decline to provide a table.

■ *Do not refuse access to places of entertainment on the grounds of race, color, religion, or nationality.* The Act prohibits discrimination in places of entertainment based on race, color, religion, or nationality. The word *entertainment*, as used by the Act, includes enterprises such as movie theaters that offer entertainment presentations to a viewing audience, as well as places where the patron actively participates in the activity such as a ranch offering horseback riding.

■ *Do not refuse access to places of entertainment on the grounds of gender, marital status, or disability.* State civil rights laws customarily outlaw discrimination on these grounds, and the federal Americans with Disabilities Act outlaws discrimination against disabled persons. Violation of these laws can result in civil and criminal liability. Also, local ordinances may prohibit discrimination on the basis of sexual orientation. *Note:* If a legitimate reason exists to refuse service, such as violation of reasonable house rules, disorderly conduct, or trespassing, the proprietor can legally deny admission.

■ *If covered by the Americans with Disabilities Act, eliminate barriers to accessibility if the removal is readily achievable.* Places of public accommodation are required to remove hindrances that can be eliminated easily and without a lot of expense. Barrier removal that would be costly or difficult to achieve is not required. If new construction or alterations are undertaken, more extensive obstacle removal will be required. However, accessibility is not required where the cost to remove barriers is out of proportion with the cost or scope of the alteration or construction project.

■ *A private club wishing to retain that status should limit membership, develop clear selection criteria, ensure that control and ownership of the club rests with members, and refrain from widely advertising for members.* The courts have developed rules to determine which clubs are private—and therefore not bound by the Act—and which clubs are not. Unless the rules are followed closely, a club will not be deemed private.

Review Questions

1. According to the common law, to whom can a hotel refuse to provide accommodations?

2. Why did Congress pass the Civil Rights Act of 1964?

3. Who is protected by the Civil Rights Act of 1964?

4. What facilities are covered by the Act?

5. What is interstate commerce and why is it relevant to the Act?

6. What remedies are available to a plaintiff suing for a violation of the Act?

7. Name three types of businesses not covered by the Act.

8. Identify three differences between the Act and state civil rights laws.

9. In addition to prohibiting the denial of a hotel room or restaurant services to certain persons, what conduct is outlawed by state civil rights laws?

10. Identify three tests used by the courts to determine whether or not a club is private.

11. What is a restaurant required to do under the Americans with Disabilities Act to remove barriers to accessibility?

12. Can a restaurant legally require that all wheelchair-bound customers eat in the same area of the restaurant?

Discussion Questions

1. Some localities have laws that require restaurants to seat smokers in an area separate from nonsmokers. Does this constitute illegal discrimination? Why or why not?

2. Why do you think Congress did not include gender as a protected class in the Act?

3. Why is a successful plaintiff in most lawsuits unable to collect attorney's fees from the defendant, while a successful plaintiff suing under the Act can?

4. Why do you think the Act outlaws even single acts of discrimination rather than requiring a pattern of discriminatory conduct?

5. A train station has a snack bar located in it. What additional information would you need to know to determine if the train station is covered by the Act? Why would you need that additional information?

6. Why do you think Congress omitted many bed-and-breakfast operations from the Act (the "Mrs. Murphy's Boarding House" clause)?

7. If you were devising an expansion of the civil rights laws, would you include any additional protected classes? Who and why?

8. What distinguishes the establishments covered by the Americans with Disabilities Act from those covered by the Civil Rights Act of 1964?

Application Questions

1. Devise an operating plan for a private club that would pass muster if its status as private was challenged.

2. A community college, primarily serving residents of the local county, has a candy shop on campus. Of twenty varieties of candies it sells, only one ingredient of one variety was purchased from out of state. Is the college governed by the Act? Why or why not?

3. Identify whether the following is illegal discrimination and explain your reasoning:
   A. A restaurant refuses to serve anyone who is Swiss.
   B. A restaurant refuses to serve someone who arrives for dinner two minutes before the kitchen closes.

C. A restaurant refuses to serve a person in a wheelchair with a service dog because the restaurant does not allow pets in the dining area.

D. A hotel refuses to provide a room to a couple because they are not married.

E. A movie theater refuses to sell a ticket to someone who is carrying a weapon.

F. A private club refuses to admit a couple because they are protestant.

G. A hotel refuses to provide a room to a person who is deaf because he is unable to provide proof of ability to pay.

Web Sites

Web sites that will enhance your understanding of the material in this chapter include:

http://www.ll.georgetown.edu/topics/civil_rights.cfm   This is an excellent site for information about laws that establish our civil rights, government agencies that enforce our civil rights, associations that advance civil rights, and general civil rights information.

http://www.law.cornell.edu/topics/civil_rights.html   This is a good site for explanations about civil rights laws.

For additional resources, visit our Web site
www.hospitality-tourism.delmar.com

CHAPTER 4

■

Contract Law and the Hospitality Industry

CHAPTER OUTLINE

■

INTRODUCTION

A **contract** is an agreement between two or more parties that is enforceable in court. Examples of contracts include the following:

- A hotel agrees to buy new furniture for its lobby and in exchange agrees to pay a specified price.

- A guest agrees to rent a room for a weekend and pay the quoted rate. In exchange, the hotel agrees to reserve the room for the guest and not rent it to anyone else.

- An association agrees to hold its annual convention at a hotel and pay the specified costs. In exchange, the hotel agrees to provide rooms, banquet facilities, food, and related services.

Failure to perform the terms of a contract constitutes **breach of contract**, which in turn results in liability. In a case involving the purchase of a sports bar and restaurant called "Cheerleaders," sellers helped to finance the purchase; in other words, buyers borrowed money for the transaction from the sellers, giving promissory notes for payment of the debt. The buyers had no experience or training in the restaurant/bar industry and were unable to operate the facility profitably. Eventually buyers closed the eatery and stopped paying on the promissory notes they had issued the seller. Although the restaurant failed, the contractual obligation to pay the debt remained in effect. Remember the definition of a contract—an agreement between two or more people that is enforceable in court.[1]

A contract can be in writing and signed, or it can be oral. It can even be implied, which means it can come into existence without a word ever being written or spoken. For example, on your way to an 8:00 A.M. class you stop at the cleaners with a pair of slacks. You are in a hurry to get to class, and the attendant is in the back of the store reading the morning paper. He hears you enter and looks up. You put the slacks on the counter and wave. He waves back and resumes reading. The two of you have not exchanged a word; nevertheless, a contract exists obligating the cleaning company to clean your slacks and obligating you to pay the going rate.

Contracts can also be created on the Internet. Cyberspace is an increasingly popular forum for the development of business agreements.

The Elements of a Contract

Regardless of whether the contract is written, oral, or implied, certain essential elements must exist for the contract to be **valid**, meaning enforceable in court. These elements are

- Contractual capacity
- Mutuality
- Legality
- Consideration
- Proper form
- Genuine assent.

Capacity to Contract

For a valid contract, the parties must have legal **capacity to contract**—that is, the ability both to understand the terms of the contract and appreciate that failure to perform its terms can lead to legal liability, including a lawsuit. According to law,

---

[1] *Del-Rena, Inc. v. KFM, Inc.,* 789 So.2d 397, 2002 WL 575139 (Fla. 2001)

the following groups of people lack contractual capacity: minors (people under age 18 in some states, under 19 or 21 in others); the very intoxicated; and the mentally incompetent. Their contracts are voidable.

A **voidable contract** is one that may be canceled at the option of one party (in this case, the person with the disability). This right to cancel, also called the right to *avoid* or *disaffirm*, applies while the disability exists and for a reasonable time after it disappears—that is, after the minor reaches 18 (or 19 or 21 depending on the state), the very intoxicated person becomes sober, or the mentally incompetent person becomes competent. Thus, a 17-year-old girl who purchases a car can return it if she changes her mind about the purchase within certain time limits. She can do so anytime before she turns 18 and for a reasonable period of time thereafter. Depending on the state, she will receive a refund of all or some of the price she paid. The explanation for allowing a reasonable time after removal of the disability is to permit the previously incapacitated person to rethink the appropriateness of a contract with the benefit of new-found capability.

Certain exceptions exist to the right to cancel, the most significant being contracts for the purchase of necessities. A minor who enters a contract for necessities can disaffirm the contract, but remains liable for the reasonable value of the necessities he received. Necessities include food, shelter, clothing, and depending on the minor's circumstances, possibly other items such as a car or education. A minor who decides after enjoying a full meal at a restaurant that he wants to avoid the contract will be liable to the restaurant for the reasonable value of the meal. The main reason for this rule is concern for the well-being of the minor. If minors could avoid payment for necessities, sellers would be reluctant to contract with even those minors who are in need of the basics.

Mutuality: Offer and Acceptance

Mutuality means that all parties to the contract are interested in its terms and intend to enter an agreement to which they will be legally bound. Mutuality is sometimes called a *meeting of the minds*. Mutuality is established by one party making an offer and the other party accepting that offer.

An **offer** is a proposal to do or give something of value in exchange for something else. For example, "We have a room we can provide to you for the night for $65," or, "We can cater your dinner party for fifteen people with the menu you requested for $25 per person." An **offeror** is the person who makes an offer; an **offeree** is the person to whom the offer is made.

The Offer Must Be Definite

The terms of an offer must be definite. If the terms are vague a contract may not result, either because the lack of clarity may evidence a lack of commitment to enter a contract or because the terms are too indefinite to obligate the parties to do anything sufficiently specific. For example, the following statements are too general and vague to constitute offers: "The rooms in this hotel range from $42 to $95 a night" or "We cater parties of all sizes." Rather than offers, these statements constitute what the law calls **invitations to negotiate**, which means they open discussions that may or may not lead to an offer.

Responses to an Offer

When an offer is made, the offeree has two options: accept the offer or reject it. An **acceptance** is an expression of agreement by the offeree to the terms of the offer. If the offeree accepts the offer, mutuality is achieved. If the other essential elements needed for a contract are present, an enforceable contract will exist. If, however, the offeree rejects the offer, the parties have not mutually agreed upon the terms and so no contract exists.

Sometimes the offeree is interested in the offer but wants to change a few terms. In such a case the offeree makes a **counteroffer**, a response to an offer that modifies one or more of its provisions. A counteroffer is not an acceptance. Rather, the counteroffer is treated as a new offer. The original offeror then has the option of accepting the counteroffer, rejecting it, or making yet another counteroffer. For example, a hotel makes an offer to an association to host its annual three-day conference—including guest rooms, meeting rooms, and meals—for $465 per person based on a specified minimum number of reservations. The organization likes the location and layout of the hotel, but thinks the price is high. It responds by saying it will hold its conference at the hotel if the hotel lowers the price to $425 per person. This is a counteroffer and no contract exists unless the hotel accepts the counteroffer or unless the hotel makes another counteroffer that is accepted by the association.

Legality

To be enforceable, a contract must have a legal objective. If what the parties obligate themselves to do is illegal, the contract is not just voidable but rather void. A **void contract** is one that is unenforceable in court. For example, we will study in Chapter 15 that it is illegal for competing hotels to agree among themselves to each charge a specified amount for a room in exchange for the others agreeing to charge the same amount, and it is likewise illegal for competing restaurants to agree to charge the same price for meals. This is called price-fixing and violates **antitrust laws**, laws that restrict limitations on competition, because such agreements guarantee that competitors will not undersell each other and deprive consumers of the benefits of competition. If one hotel that is a party to such a contract deviates from the agreed price and the other hotels attempt to sue for the first hotel's failure to abide by the contract, the court will summarily dismiss the case without hearing the merits because the contract is illegal and therefore void.

Consideration

For an agreement to be binding and enforceable in court there must be consideration. The word *consideration*, as used in the legal sense, means something quite different from the definition of consideration in normal parlance. In connection with contracts, **consideration** means something of value exchanged for something else of value. For example, a guest in a hotel gives the innkeeper money and in return receives the right to occupy a room. The consideration for the guest's payment is the right to occupy the room; the consideration for the hotel's providing the room is the guest's money.

Another way to understand consideration is to recognize it as the phenomenon that distinguishes a contract from a gift. A gift transaction is one-sided; one person gives something to the other and receives nothing in return. With a contract, each person gives something and each person receives something. That which is received is the consideration.

Consideration can take one of three forms:

1. A tangible item of value or a promise to give such an item (such as food or money)
2. Performance or a promise to perform (such as cleaning a swimming pool, working as a front-desk clerk or waiting on tables)
3. **Forbearance**—agreeing to refrain from doing something you have a legal right to do—or a promise to forbear. For example, if you are injured while at a restaurant, you might promise not to sue the restaurant for your injuries if the owner agrees to pay you a satisfactory sum of money.

Parties to a contract may exchange one form of consideration for the same form of consideration, such as when a restaurant patron buys dinner. The customer gives money (something tangible with value) and the restaurant gives food (something tangible with value). The parties can also mix two different forms of consideration in the same contract, such as when an employee contracts to work for a hotel. The employee gives services (performance) and the hotel gives money (a tangible item of value).

Illusory Contracts

Sometimes the terms of the contract do not contain a firm commitment. If an apparent commitment is so indefinite that the party has not in fact promised to do anything, the promise is said to be **illusory**. An illusory promise does not constitute consideration and will not give rise to a contract. In the following case, the court found that an alleged contract was illusory; an association scheduling its annual convention did not, in fact, agree to rent any rooms from the plaintiff hotel.

CASE EXAMPLE 4-1

Lederman Enterprises, Inc.
v.
Allied Social Science Associates
709 P.2d 1 (Colo. App. 1985)

The defendant, Allied Social Science Association (ASSA) ... an unincorporated group of associations which meet together annually, contacted the Denver Convention and Visitors' Bureau in 1975 when ASSA was considering holding its 1980 convention in Denver. The Visitors' Bureau wrote to several Denver hotels, including The Regency, asking that the hotels commit to hold open a block of rooms in order to attract the ASSA convention to Denver. The Regency responded to the Visitors' Bureau, indicating it would hold 375 rooms open. This information was conveyed by the Bureau to ASSA. Thereafter, ASSA and The Regency corresponded and, on March 19, 1980, the parties signed a document prepared by The Regency, entitled "Regency Inn-Meeting/Convention Contract." In May of 1980, ASSA mailed preregistration forms to its members informing them of the different Denver hotels available, and requesting the members to list their preferences. When the forms were returned by the members to ASSA, they were forwarded to the Visitors' Bureau which then assigned members of ASSA to the hotels in accordance with the preferences of the members.

Few of the 2,500 members who registered for the convention listed The Regency on their preference list, and none selected it as their first choice. Therefore, the Visitors' Bureau did not assign any members to The Regency. On July 21, 1980, realizing that no members would be making reservations at the Regency, the convention coordinator for ASSA wrote to the Regency stating that: "There is no need to continue to hold rooms for us. ..."

The Regency filed suit against ASSA and its convention coordinator. ...

We agree with ASSA that The Regency's form "contract" entitled "Regency Inn-Meeting/Convention Contract" did not, as a matter of law, constitute a reservation of rooms by ASSA. ...

The "contract" between the parties specified that reservation cards had to be returned by August 4, 1980, and then stated:

> The Regency's cut-off policy calls for all unreserved rooms within your block to be released for sale 30 days prior to arrival. All reservations received thereafter will be accepted on a space available basis only. Should you wish to guarantee any unreserved rooms past the cut-off date, please advise us in writing ...

[Payment of] one night's deposit with each guest room reservation [is requested]. All reservations and agreements are made upon, and are subject to the rules and regulations of the Regency, and the following conditions: ...

We require a non-refundable deposit of first night's room rate with reservation, unless your organization guarantees payment for any "no shows" in your group.

The gist of this "contract" is that, for an ASSA member to make a reservation at The Regency, a reservation card had to be used and had to be returned to the reservation manager of The Regency by August 4, 1980, accompanied by a deposit. To say that the document itself made reservations [which is what the Regency asserts in this breach of contract case] would make meaningless the need to return reservation cards.

Other provisions in the "contract" are also inconsistent with an interpretation that it constituted a reservation of rooms at The Regency. The several references to "unreserved rooms" within the block of rooms held by The Regency would be rendered meaningless by so holding. The provision that "all unreserved rooms within your block ... [will] be released 30 days prior to arrival" demonstrates that the rooms within the block had not been reserved merely by ASSA's agreement to the contract's terms.

In our view, the "contract" merely imposed upon The Regency the obligation to make available, under certain conditions, a number of rooms to ASSA; it did not obligate ASSA to reserve any rooms. ASSA's only obligation was to mention The Regency as one of the hotels where members could obtain rooms. Only if further steps were taken by the members would rooms actually be reserved.

There being no reservation of rooms under the "contract" ... [ASSA did not breach the contract and therefore is not liable to The Regency].

CASE QUESTION

1. How might the wording of the Regency's "contract" have been changed so as to obligate ASSA to rent rooms from The Regency?

Proper Form

Is an oral contract enforceable? The general rule is yes, oral contracts are enforceable. Such contracts may, however, be difficult to prove. For example, Mrs. Gordon called the Townhouse Hotel and made a reservation for the following weekend. In contract terms, she agreed to pay for a room in consideration of the hotel agreeing to reserve one for her use and to make it available to her on the specified dates. Neither the hotel nor Mrs. Gordon reduced the contract to writing. Nevertheless, the contract is valid and enforceable. If, when Mrs. Gordon arrives at the hotel, the reservation clerk informs her that the hotel has no available rooms, the hotel will be liable to Mrs. Gordon for breach of contract. The fact that the contract was not in writing is of no consequence.

Now assume a different set of facts. Mrs. Gordon arrives at the hotel and requests her room. The hotel not only has no room for her but denies ever making a reservation in her name. Despite Mrs. Gordon's protests, the hotel holds firm to its position. In this situation Mrs. Gordon will have a difficult time proving the hotel agreed to reserve a room for her. As this scenario indicates, a good practice is to put all contracts in writing and thereby avoid the "proof problem." But an oral contract is enforceable if it can be proved.

Contracts that Must Be in Writing: The Statute of Frauds

The rule that oral contracts are enforceable is a general rule; several exceptions exist. Certain types of contracts are not enforceable unless they are in writing. For these contracts *only*, oral agreements are *not* enforceable. The primary law that requires a writing for these contracts is called the **Statute of Frauds**. The name derives from the statute's objective of preventing the perpetuation of a fraud by someone claiming a contract exists when in fact none does. The statute might better be named the "Statute to Prevent Frauds."

Among the types of contracts within the Statute of Frauds that must be in writing to be enforceable are the following:

- Contracts for the purchase and sale of real property, which includes land and buildings. An example is a contract to purchase a hotel. Also included within the definition of real property is an easement, which is the right of one person to use another person's land for some particular, limited purpose. A case example involves a restaurant owner who needed additional parking space for customers. He allegedly entered an oral agreement with an adjacent land owner in which the latter consented to allow restaurant customers to utilize his parking lot, thereby constituting an easement. Thereafter, disputes arose and the adjoining property owner installed a fence to keep restaurant patrons out. The restaurant owner sued to enforce the oral agreement. The court held the Statute of Frauds rendered the contract unenforceable because the agreement involved an interest in real property and it was not in writing.[2]

---

[2] *Payne v. Edmonson*, 1999 WL 350928 (Tex. 1999)

- Contracts that cannot be completed within one year from when they are made. An example is a two-year employment contract for a restaurant manager.

- Contracts to pay another person's debt if that person fails to pay. For example, a hotel guest, when registering, presents the credit card of a small out-of-town company as the means for payment of the hotel bill. The hotel, uncertain of the financial well-being of the company, may require that the guest agree to pay the hotel bill if the company fails to do so. This commitment by the guest must be in writing to be enforceable.

- Contracts for the sale of goods (moveable, tangible objects, not services) in excess of $500. An example is a contract between a hotel and a furniture store for the purchase of a $1200 couch for the hotel lobby.

An exception exists to the need for a writing with a contract for the sale of goods valued in excess of $500. In two situations, a writing is not required: (1) the seller has delivered the goods and the buyer has accepted them or (2) the buyer paid for the goods and the seller accepted the payment. In both these circumstances each party to the contract evidenced the existence of the contract by their actions. In such circumstances a written agreement to prove its existence is needless. The first of these exceptions to the Statute of Frauds is illustrated in the following case.

CASE EXAMPLE 4-2

Adams v. H&H Meat Products, Inc.
41 SW3d 762 (Tex. 2001)

Norwick Adams ("Adams") is employed by and is the director general and a minority shareholder of Whataburger Mexico. H&H Meat Products, Inc. ("H&H") is a company that sells meat products to Whataburger franchises in the United States. Sometime in 1991 or 1992, Liborio Hinojosa ("Hinojosa"), the president and CEO of H&H, met with Adams to set up a procedure so that meat products could be sent to Mexico for Whataburger Mexico.

The procedure was as follows. Adams or an associate ordered meat products from H&H by fax or telephone. Adams instructed H&H to ship the ordered meat products to SR Forwarding, a forwarding agent (a company that would arrange for the meat to be shipped across the US-Mexico border) in Laredo, Texas. Adams also instructed H&H to invoice the meat products in the name of Proveedora de Alimentos Constratados ("PAC") because PAC had a permit to import meat products into Mexico, and Adams did not. PAC would then sell the meat to Whataburger Mexico.

This case stems from three unpaid shipments of meat that were delivered by H&H to SR Forwarding, pursuant to Adams' instructions. ... H&H sued Adams for breach of contract. The trial court found in favor of Adams. ...

On appeal Adams asserts that recovery by H&H is barred by the statute of frauds. Specifically, Adams contends that a contract for the sale of goods for more than $500 must be in writing, and the transactions at issue, although more than $500, were not in writing.

[Texas law provides:]

"[A] contract for the sale of goods for the price of $500 or more is not enforceable unless there is some writing sufficient to indicate that a contract for sale has been made between the parties and signed by the party against whom enforcement is sought ... A contract which does not satisfy the [writing] requirement is nonetheless enforceable with respect to goods for which payment has been made and accepted or which have been received and accepted. ...

[In reference to the three deliveries in issue, the evidence established that Adams, or someone associated with Adams, ordered meat products from H&H; the meat products were delivered to SR Forwarding per Adams' instructions; and Adams received the meat products and accepted them.]

Based on these facts we hold the contract between Adams and H&H is an exception to the statute of frauds [and thus a written agreement between the parties is not required]. Judgment for H&H is affirmed.

CASE QUESTION

1. Why does the Statute of Frauds dispense with the need for a writing where the seller has delivered and the buyer has accepted them?

The Nature of the Writing

The required writing need not be a formal contract. Notes, a letter, or memorandum are sufficient. The writing should specify the essential terms of the agreement and must be signed by the party who is the defendant in a lawsuit to enforce the contract. Initials will suffice in lieu of a full signature.

Part Performance Exception

An exception to the writing requirement of the Statute of Frauds is the doctrine of part performance. Where the party asserting the absence of a writing as a defense has partly performed the contract, the court may construe therefrom both the existence of the contract and its terms. The need for a writing is thus eliminated.

The doctrine of part performance was illustrated in a case in which a chef was hired by a restaurant on favorable terms with a three-year contract. The parties prepared a written contract, but neither signed it. The chef nonetheless went to work for the restaurant and was paid pursuant to the terms of the agreement. Three months later the chef was terminated. He sued the restaurant claiming breach of the three-year commitment. The restaurant's defense was the Statute of Frauds (the agreement could not be completed within a year from its making) and the absence of a signed writing. The court held that the restaurant had partly performed consistent with the written but unsigned agreement. The court concluded that the parties had a contract consisting of the terms of the writing and held the restaurant liable for breach of contract.[3]

Parol Evidence Rule

Often in the course of negotiating a contract, many terms are added and later dropped before the final agreement is reached. If the final contract is reduced to

---

[3] *Schneider v. Carlisle Corporation*, 2001 WL 400387 (Tenn. 2001)

writing and is complete on its face (it addresses all of the terms that parties to that type of contract are likely to include), the parties usually intend the writing to document their full agreement. Any terms not included in the writing are viewed by the law as intentionally abandoned by the parties.

One party may later try to claim that one of the terms abandoned in the negotiation process was intended by the parties to survive the writing. The parol evidence rule will preclude that term from becoming part of the contract. **Parol** means oral. The **parol evidence rule** prevents the parties from modifying a written contract with evidence of oral agreements made prior to signing the writing. For example, assume you are negotiating to purchase a motel. In the rear of the property is an unsightly storage shed. You ask the seller to remove it and she agrees. Thereafter you prepare a written contract containing the terms of your purchase agreement, and it is signed by you and the seller. The writing does not mention the seller's agreement to remove the shed. You want it removed and remind the seller of the agreement but she refuses. In this case the parol evidence rule supports the seller; she need not remove the shed. Since the agreement about removal of the shed was reached prior to signing the contract, and since the promise to remove the shed was not included in the writing, the parol evidence rule bars the buyer from enforcing the seller's commitment to remove the shed. To avoid a similar outcome, be sure to include in your written contracts *all* of the terms of your aggreement!

The parol evidence rule does not apply to agreements made *after* a contract is signed. Therefore, a written contract can be modified by agreements made after parties sign a contract, even if those agreements vary or modify the written contract.

Genuine Assent

Another requirement for a valid contract is **genuine assent**, meaning that the parties must genuinely agree to the contract terms. If, for example, one party enters a contract, not because he truly consents to its terms, but because he was subjected to **duress** (threats of harm if he did not sign), the contract is voidable and can be disaffirmed by the party who was threatened.

Fraud and Misrepresentation

A person who enters a contract due to fraud or innocent misrepresentation can avoid the contract. **Fraud** is an intentionally untruthful statement made for the purpose of misleading someone, usually for the fraudulent party's gain. For example, you make a reservation at a hotel because the reservation clerk, under pressure to increase sales, informed you that the hotel is air conditioned. The clerk knows that the hotel is not. When you arrive in the heat of the summer you discover the hotel is not air conditioned. You are the victim of fraud and can cancel the reservation without liability.

The following case illustrates another example of fraud.

CASE EXAMPLE 4-3

Filet Menu, Inc.
v.
C.C.L. & G., Inc.
94 Cal. Rptr.2d (Ca. 2000)

... Filet Menu, Inc. ("FMI") was in the printing and design business catering to the food service industry. C.C.L.&G. ("CCLG") owned and operated two restaurants of a five restaurant chain of Mexican restaurants, the other three of which were owned by Salazar, an officer of CCLG. In the middle of 1992, FMI's salesman, Michael Klein ("Klein") made a sales solicitation call on Salazar. ...

In February, 1993 Salazar signed numerous purchase orders with FMI, one to purchase 4,000 menus at $4 each, one to purchase 5 million place mats at $0.39 cents each, one to purchase 5 million dinner napkins at $0.39 each and one to purchase 5 million cocktail napkins at $0.09 each, the latter three items to be delivered 250,000 at a time, every 90 days.

The facts presented to the jury revealed an elaborate, fraudulent scheme. Klein testified that he handled the CCLG account while he was with FMI. He admitted that he dealt with CCLG and Salazar "with intent to defraud them purposefully." He acknowledged making numerous misrepresentations to Salazar. When Klein first solicited Salazar in August, 1992, Klein represented to Salazar, "per Mr. LeVine's [Klein's boss'] instructions on how to sell, that we were able to go into a restaurant and design a menu for them and accompanying products, that would guarantee a specified increase to the bottom line, a percentage of their bottom line." [Klein guaranteed CCLG a 20 to 40 percent increase.]

Klein also told Salazar that Klein could sell him colored napkins for "a little bit more" than the white napkins they were using, though he knew he could not. [Apparently the cost for colored napkins was substantially more than for white ones.] As per instructions from LeVine, Klein told Salazar that the application Salazar signed was "a mere credit application and nothing more" needed to check references, though Klein had been told that it was more than a credit application. It was a credit application and a purchase order designed to bind the customer to terms in the ultimate transaction. The purpose of getting the customer to sign the application document was to "hook them" into the transaction. Klein was instructed by LeVine never to leave a copy of this document with the customer. Klein was also instructed by LeVine to make certain that there were distractions when the application was being signed so that the customers "don't really understand what they're signing and know what they're signing." Salazar was induced to sign the application.

With respect to the purchase of menus, Salazar said that he did not want to spend more than $4 per menu and wanted to purchase no more than 3000 menus. LeVine told Salazar at a meeting that he could work within that budget knowing that the menus would cost $7.00 to $8.88, at a minimum, but failing to disclose that to Salazar. There were numerous other misrepresentations and sharp practices employed by FMI and LeVine during the course of the transaction, elaborated upon in the trial testimony.

The jury returned a verdict which found that the contract for FMI to supply menus, place mats, dinner napkins and cocktail napkins was entered with CCLG but that CCLG's consent was induced by fraudulent misrepresentations by FMI. ... The jury also found that FMI and LeVine's misconduct was engaged in with the intent to defraud CCLG and Salazar. ...

[The evidence supports the jury's verdict in favor of CCLG.] The judgment is affirmed.

CASE QUESTION

1. Identify four fraudulent statements made by Klein and LeVine and two fraudulent practices they perpetrated.

Innocent misrepresentation is an untruthful statement that the speaker believes to be accurate. For example, you arrive at a hotel on a hot summer day and find the temperature in the lobby uncomfortably warm. You ask the manager if the air conditioning is working properly. The repair person had worked on it that afternoon and informed the manager that it was fixed. Based on that statement, the manager answers your question in the affirmative. Relying on the manager's statement, you contract for a room. In fact, the air conditioner is not working, as you discover a short time later when the temperature fails to cool. The manager made an innocent mistake; you can cancel your contract for the room and go elsewhere. The law allows the buyer to avoid the contract in both fraud and innocent-misrepresentation cases because in both the buyer has been misled.

Mistakes

Parties to a contract may make various types of mistakes in the process of negotiating and agreeing to the contract. Some of those mistakes have legal significance and others do not. Mistakes made by a buyer as to value or quality of a good being purchased will not affect the validity of the contract. For example, the manager of a restaurant purchases a desk for the receptionist, believing it is an antique made with expensive wood. Here, the manager's belief is based on her own assessment of the desk and not on any representations made by the seller. Later the manager learns that the desk is an imitation of an antique and worth significantly less than the amount paid. The manager in this case has made a mistake in judgment as to the value or quality of the good. The contract is not affected by this mistake; the manager cannot cancel the contract. The manager should have investigated the value of the desk more carefully before completing the purchase.

Mistakes as to facts, aside from value or quality, may affect the validity of the contract. Two types of factual mistakes exist—unilateral and mutual. A **unilateral mistake** is an error made by only one party to the contract as to the terms or performance expected. A **mutual mistake** is one made by both parties.

Generally, a unilateral mistake is not a basis to avoid a contract. Thus, when only one party makes a mistake as to a fact involved with the contract, that party cannot cancel the contract on the basis of the mistake. For example, in *Freeman v. Kiamesha Concord Inc.*, 351 N.Y.S.2d 541 (1974), a guest at a resort hotel misread an advertisement concerning the Memorial Day weekend entertainment and so believed that a popular entertainer would be performing for three nights during the weekend rather than just one. Upon learning the truth he sought to cancel part of his three-day reservation. The court held that his mistake was unilateral and therefore did not support a cancellation of his reservation. Although he departed the resort before the end of the three-day weekend, he remained obligated to pay his hotel bill for the full three days.

Unlike unilateral mistakes, mutual mistakes involving an important fact will enable either party to avoid the contract. For example, Theresa owns two hotels. She contracts to sell one of them to Jeff. Theresa thinks she is selling the hotel on East Main Street. Jeff thinks he is purchasing the one on Dewey Street. The parties in this example made a mutual mistake as to an important fact, the identity of the hotel. Since the parties never had a meeting of the minds, either can cancel the contract without liability.

Ambiguous Terms/Trade Usage

It is important for contracting parties to state the terms of their agreement clearly and without ambiguity. If the terms are vague or confusing, the parties may end up in court disputing the meaning. Careful drafting can avoid such lawsuits. Unfortunately for the parties in the following case, the language in their contract left room for argument as to its meaning. Thus, time and money had to be spent on a lawsuit that could easily have been avoided.

CASE EXAMPLE 4-4

Lire, Inc. v. Bob's Pizza Inn Restaurants, Inc.
541 N.W.2d 432 (N.D. 1995)

In 1989 Lire, Inc. purchased Bob's Pizza Inn Restaurant in Rugby, North Dakota, from the Schmidts for $400,000. A July 3, 1989, "offer to purchase" said: "Seller to agree to a noncompetition agreement for the selling of Italian type foods for a period of 5 years and within a radius of 60 miles of Rugby." The Schmidts accepted the offer on July 10, 1989. No other documents to the transaction mentioned a noncompetition agreement.

In May 1993 the Schmidts opened Bob's Pizza Inn Restaurant and Lounge in Rugby. Lire sued the Schmidts for breach of contract, seeking damages and injunctive relief. The Schmidts contended the language in the offer to purchase did not create an enforceable noncompetition agreement. [The Schmidts argued that the statement in the offer—"seller to agree"— anticipated a noncompetition agreement in the future that never was entered into.] ...

The dispositive issue in this appeal is the interpretation of the parties' written contract, specifically the noncompetition language. ...

Contracts are construed to give effect to the mutual intention of the parties at the time of contracting. ... Unless used by the parties in a technical sense, words in a contract are construed in their ordinary and popular sense, rather than ... their strict legal meaning. ...

To create an enforceable contract, there must be a mutual intent to create a legal obligation. ...

The phrase "seller to agree" was part of a July 3, 1989 written offer to purchase, which was accepted by the Schmidts on July 10, 1989. The remaining noncompetition language was definite and certain as to its terms—"a noncompetition agreement for the selling of Italian type foods for a period of 5 years and within a radius of 60 miles of Rugby." Those terms completely describe the type of business restriction, the duration of the restriction, and the geographic limitation for the restriction. ... When this noncompetition language is read as a whole and as part of a subsequently accepted offer to purchase, we believe the ordinary and popular understanding of the phrase "seller to agree" objectively evidences the parties' mutual intent to create an enforceable noncompetition agreement at the time of the Schmidts' acceptance. We conclude the written noncompetition language ... creates an enforceable noncompetition agreement for Rugby.

Because the parties' written contract unambiguously created an enforceable noncompetition agreement in Rugby, Lire was entitled to judgment. ...

CASE QUESTION

1. How might the parties have drafted the noncompetition clause to avoid the ambiguity that led to this lawsuit?

In another case, a landscaping company agreed to plant and maintain a large number of trees and shrubs over a two-year period on a parcel of land. The contract required the landscaper to replace any trees that died within one year of planting, but excluded from the guarantee damages resulting from "extreme acts of nature, such as tornadoes, or excess amounts of wind." A cold wave occurred during the first year of the contract, one of the coldest ever recorded in the state. For six consecutive days the average low temperature was colder than 30 degrees below zero. 115 trees with a replacement value of $52,760 were killed. The landowner claimed the landscaper was obligated to replace them. The landscaper argued that the cold wave was an extreme act of nature and thus relieved him from liability. The court determined that the contract reference to "extreme acts of nature" included only sudden and unforeseeable disasters "such as tornadoes and excess amounts of wind" and not an unexpected cold spell. The landscaper was thus required to replace the trees.[4] Had the language been clearer, the landscaper might have avoided liability.

Sometimes when contract terms are ambiguous the court will use "trade usage" to clarify the ambiguity. **Trade usage** means practices or modes of dealing generally adhered to in a particular industry, such that an expectation arises that they will be honored in a given transaction. For example, in *Frigaliment Importing Co., Ltd. v. B.N.S. International Sales Corp.*, 190 F.Supp. 116 (N.Y. 1960), the contracting parties were unable to agree on the meaning of the word *chicken*. Their contract required the seller to deliver a specified quantity of chicken to the buyer. The seller delivered stewing chickens, the least-expensive poultry. The buyer objected, claiming the word *chicken*, as used in the contract, required a higher grade of chicken. The dispute ended up in court. Experts in the poultry field testified (an additional expense for the seller) that various grades of chicken exist and that each is identified by a different name, except for the lowest grade that simply is called *chicken*. The court thus determined the seller had fulfilled its contractual obligation by delivering the bottom-of-the-line stewing chickens. This case underscores the importance of careful drafting of a contract. Use of more exacting language on the part of the buyer could have resulted in purchase of the product he intended, thus saving considerable money in attorney fees and litigation expenses.

The following case provides another example of the application of trade usage as an aid to interpretation of a contract. Note how the court relies almost exclusively on trade usage to clarify an ambiguity or fill in a gap left by the parties. A novice who does business in an industry without knowing its customs and practices does so at considerable risk.

Conditions

In most contracts, the promises of the parties to perform their contractual obligations are **absolute**, meaning they must be performed or the promising party will be in breach of contract. Occasionally a contractual duty is not certain, but rather

---

[4] *Tandem Properties v. Lawn and Landscape*, 1999 WL 185204 (Minn. 1999)

is contingent upon the occurrence or nonoccurrence of a specified event. That event is called a **condition**. If the condition occurs, the contractual duty remains in effect. If the condition does not occur, the contract is discharged and the parties are not obligated to perform.

CASE EXAMPLE 4-5

Pennyrile Tours, Inc. v. Country Inns, USA, Inc.
559 F.Supp. 15 (Tenn. 1982)

... In December 1981 the defendant, Country Inns, mailed a brochure to the plaintiff, Pennyrile Tours, advertising that defendant [hotel which was under construction] was accepting reservations. ...

Subsequent to receipt of the brochure, plaintiff orally contracted for various group room reservations with the defendant by telephone and was required to pay advance deposits totalling $10,720. Defendant represented that its facilities would be completed well before May 1982, the opening day of the 1982 World's Fair. At this time there was no discussion between the parties of a cancellation policy. Plaintiff's first reservations were for May 16 and May 17, 1982.

Subsequent to the telephone conversation between the parties, plaintiff received written confirmation of room reservations on the dates requested. Subsequent to the receipt of confirmation of room reservations, the plaintiff mailed checks at various times which totalled $10,720 to the defendant as deposits for room reservations.

The Court is convinced from the testimony that there is an industry-wide custom and standard used in the motel business for a refund of reservation deposits. [According to this custom,] a refund is made if reservations are canceled at least 30 days prior to the reserved dates.

On or about March 27, 1982, representatives of plaintiff inspected the facilities advertised by the defendant. The facilities were not near completion as of that date, as the defendant had previously represented they would be. ...

On or about April 16, 1982, plaintiff's representatives returned to Knoxville to again inspect defendant's facilities. The facilities remained far from completion and serious doubts were raised as to whether the facilities would ever be completed. ... [T]he plaintiff, by letter dated April 18, 1982, canceled its reservations with the defendant and demanded full refund of all deposits.

By letter dated April 23, 1982, the defendant refused to refund any deposits made by the plaintiff because of company policy. Mrs. Miller, representative of plaintiff, testified that she never received the company policy until she canceled the reservations. She says that the letter of April 23, 1982, was the first knowledge that she had of any cancellation policy contrary to the industry-wide standard. ...

The plaintiff has not received any refund of the deposits in the amount of $10,720 from the defendant.

The parties agree that they had a valid oral contract. Defendant promised to provide motel accommodations in exchange for plaintiff's promise to pay for the accommodations. The Court has found that the parties did not discuss the terms for cancellation of the contract and that there was no written provision relating to refunds of deposits. We must therefore look to the intention of the parties for the fair and reasonable construction [of the contract] under the circumstances. ...

[U]sages of trade may be considered in determining the intentions of the parties. ... A usage of trade is defined as:

[A]ny practice or method of dealing having such regularity of observance in a place, vocation or trade as to justify an expectation that it will be observed with respect to the transaction in question.

The practice of refunding deposits if reservations are canceled thirty days prior to the scheduled arrival date is a regular method of dealing in the tourist business. Exceptions to the usual practice are made known during initial negotiations between the parties. Plaintiff relied on defendant's silence and the customary practice in this case. ...

Accordingly, it is ORDERED [that defendant must return plaintiff's deposit and] that judgment be entered in favor of plaintiff in the amount of $10,720.

CASE QUESTIONS

1. Why did the Court apply the industry-wide cancellation practice to the contract between Pennyrile Tours and Country Inns?

2. What could Country Inns have done to avoid the application of the industry practice to its contract with Pennyrile?

For example, a person hired to repair a hotel pool may promise to complete the work within a week, provided that a drain pump ordered from out of town arrives before the end of the week. The timely delivery of the pump is a condition. If the part is delivered before the week is over, the pool repairs must be completed within a week from when the contract was made. If the part is delivered late, the repairer is not obligated to conclude the work within a week.

The following case provides another illustration of a condition and its effect on a contractual duty.

CASE EXAMPLE 4-6

Casino Resorts
v.
Monarch Casinos, Inc.
1997 WL 793134 (Minn. 1997)

Casino Resorts, Inc. [hereinafter Casino Resorts] and Monarch Casinos, Inc. [hereinafter Monarch], executed a letter of intent in July 1993. In the letter of intent, Casino Resorts expressed an interest in acquiring certain gaming-related assets held by Monarch. The document specifically states that the contemplated transaction is subject to three conditions precedent: (1) a definitive and mutually satisfactory purchase agreement, (2) shareholder approval of the purchase agreement, and (3) approval by respective counsel. Monarch agreed that after acceptance of the letter of intent and prior to the closing date, neither Monarch nor its agent would directly or indirectly initiate or solicit any discussions or negotiations with any third party.

No purchase agreement was ever prepared or executed, and Casino Resorts never held a shareholder's meeting.

In March, 1994, approximately eight months after the execution of the letter of intent, Monarch negotiated a preliminary agreement with the Tribal Chairman of the Pokagon Band of Potawatomi Indians to provide management of its proposed gaming activities. ...

[Thereafter Monarch entered into a contract with another business to sell the gaming-related assets.] Casino Resorts sued Monarch for breach of contract. ...

A condition precedent is one that must be performed before the agreement of the parties becomes operative. If the event required by the condition does not occur, there is no breach of contract because the contract is unenforceable. ...

It is undisputed that none of the conditions precedent were performed; Monarch and Casino Resorts did not obtain the approval of their respective counsel, a purchase agreement was never drafted, Casino Resorts did not seek or obtain the approval of its shareholders, and a closing never occurred. ...

The parties' actions constituted [nonoccurrence of a condition], which ... results in a discharged contract.

Contracts Formed on the Internet

The Internet is playing a growing role in all aspects of business. Virtually every type of commercial deal can be and is pursued via the Internet, including hotel reservations, airline reservations, and purchase of restaurant supplies. Major hotel chains report that their on-line business as of the year 2001 constituted approximately five percent of their total room sales, a figure that had more than doubled over the prior year.

How valid are these contracts? This question was baffling to lawyers and judges when the Web first became a popular means of doing business because the law relevant to the Internet had not yet developed. Since then legislatures and judges have strived to provide clear rules to guide Internet users. Today, as a general rule, contracts reached on line are as enforceable as their "land-based" counterparts. The on-line versions are subject to similar rules of contract law.

Many of the problems that arise with computer-generated contracts are identical to problems with traditional contracts. An example is ambiguous language, which can wreak the same havoc in an on-line contract as we saw it produce in standard contracts.

An issue that was undetermined in the early days of the Internet was the legal effect of a "click-on acceptance." Often an Internet user is directed to indicate consent to an offer relayed on line by clicking on an acceptance icon. More and more courts are recognizing these click-on acceptances as a valid means of creating a contract.

As time passes and the uses of the Web in business continue to grow, new legal issues will be confronted and legislatures and judges will address them. A savvy business person will keep informed of changes in the law by reading industry journals, newspapers of general circulation, and trade-association newsletters.

Breach of Contract

Failure to perform as required by a contract constitutes **breach of contract**, a civil wrong, not a criminal one. An example of a breach of contract is provided by a case involving the purchase of a motel. The sales agreement "detailed that the motel contained 23 units … and that the air-conditioning system as well as other mechanical systems were in good operating condition and repair." A list of assets annexed to the contract included a telephone console. After the closing, the buyers discovered that four of the 23 rooms were not rentable, the phone console was leased by sellers, and the air-conditioning system was leaking Freon and had a defective compressor. Evidence established that the sellers were informed by their repair technician two years prior to the sale that the air conditioner had a Freon leak and a broken timer on the lead compressor. Based on this the court said, "Defendants [sellers] were aware, at the time of conveyance, that the system was not in good operating condition and repair." These circumstances clearly constituted breach of contract by the seller.[5]

---

5 *Cheng Sing Liang v. Chwen Jen Huang*, (3rd Dept. 1998)

A nonbreaching party may be entitled to a remedy of either **damages** meaning money to compensate for resulting loss, or **specific performance**, meaning performance of the contract terms.

Compensatory Damages

The breaching party may be required to pay compensatory damages to the other contracting party (the nonbreaching party). **Compensatory damages** refers to the sum of money necessary to cover loss incurred by the nonbreaching party as a result of the breach. Stated differently, the nonbreaching party is entitled to the "benefit of the bargain," meaning the breaching party must put the nonbreaching party in the position the latter would have been in had the contract been fully performed. The nonbreaching party is generally not entitled to pain and suffering—that is, compensation for physical pain, mental anguish, stress, or other similar injury resulting from breach of contract. Pain and suffering as an element of damages is limited to cases involving negligence and other torts. We will discuss pain and suffering in more detail in Chapter 5, "Principles of Negligence."

Requirement of Foreseeability

A plaintiff seeking to collect damages for breach of contract must prove that the damages were foreseeable to the breaching party. If the latter could not anticipate the loss, the plaintiff will not be awarded compensation therefor.

Requirement of Reasonable Certainty

The plaintiff in a breach of contract case must prove to a reasonable certainty that she suffered a loss as a result of the breach. Some states also require that the plaintiff prove the *amount* of the loss to a reasonable certainty. For example, a resort hotel hired an unknown singer to perform in the nightclub. Due to low reservations, the hotel canceled the show. Unbeknownst to the hotel, the singer had arranged for a talent scout to attend the show. When the hotel breached the contract, the singer sued for loss of income that might have resulted had the scout liked the performance and agreed to promote the singer. The singer will lose the lawsuit for two reasons: (1) inability to prove reasonable certainty of the fact or amount of damages and (2) inability to prove the hotel could have foreseen those damages.

In the following case the plaintiff was unable to establish any damages from defendant's breach of contract. If a plaintiff cannot prove a loss, it will not be entitled to collect damages.

CASE EXAMPLE 4-7

Casino Resorts, Inc.
v.
Monarch Casinos, Inc.
1997 WL 793134 (Minn. 1997)

[The facts of this case were presented in the previous discussion of conditions. Reread the facts to refresh your memory.]

... [J]udgment in favor of Monarch was also appropriate because Casino Resorts failed to demonstrate damages. The controlling principle is that damages that are speculative, remote or conjectural are not recoverable ... . Uncertainty as to the amount of damages is not fatal to recovery, but a claim cannot be maintained when it is uncertain that there are any damages at all.

The general rule is that damages for lost future profits of a new business are not recoverable, because the evidence is inherently too speculative. ...

Casino Resorts projects its losses based on the assumption that the letter of intent would have allowed them to develop the Pokagon Band's gaming operation. But even if that opportunity were considered a part of the agreement, the damages are still speculative. The development of any casino facilities by the Pokagon Band requires [per federal law] governmental authorizations, including a compact approved by the Governor of Michigan and ratified by the Michigan legislature. A compact was approved by the Governor of Michigan in early 1996, but the Michigan legislature failed to ratify it. ... Even if the necessary state approvals are obtained, additional federal approvals, which may take as long as two years, are necessary.

Casino Resorts has failed to establish that it has sustained any loss, much less a loss that could be reasonably measured. The district court correctly concluded that the damages were too speculative, and, because proof of damages is required for the Casino Resorts' claim, [judgment for Monarch] on all claims was appropriate. ... Affirmed.

CASE QUESTION

1. What facts were cited by the court as proof that the damages claim was too speculative to support a recovery?

The following case also involves the issue of recovery of damages when a new enterprise is forced out of business because of another party's breach of contract. Unlike Case Example 4-7, the court in this case finds that the existence and amount of damages are sufficiently certain to be recoverable. As you read the case, identify what facts differentiate it from *Casino Resorts* that may have resulted in the varying outcomes.

CASE EXAMPLE 4-8

Cardinal Consulting Company
v.
Circo Resorts, Inc.
297 N.W.2d 260 (Minn. 1980)

Cardinal Consulting was established by William O'Neill and Wayne Haas in August 1974 to operate one-stop charter tours to Las Vegas and other holiday areas. ... The defendant was Circo Resorts, a Nevada corporation that operates the Circus Circus Hotel in Las Vegas. Jay Valentine was the sales manager for Circus Circus Hotel and had made the original contract with Cardinal Consulting.

Valentine verbally agreed that Circus Circus would set aside fifty rooms at a price of $16 per night for Cardinal, and if rooms had to be canceled later, it would pose no problem because that period was traditionally slow in Las Vegas.

In November 1975, the management of Circus Circus was reorganized under the leadership of Mel Larson, ... In an attempt to make the operation of the hotel more efficient and to ensure that all rooms were full, Larson decided to draft formal contracts to govern Circus Circus's relations with all tour operators using its facilities. ...

On December 10, 1975, Valentine called Cardinal from Las Vegas to set up a meeting in Minneapolis for December 13. Haas told Valentine then and on December 13 that Cardinal was canceling the first three tours. Valentine then told him to put it in writing, which he did in his letter of December 16.

At their meeting, Valentine presented Haas with the proposed written contract between Cardinal and Circus Circus, which Haas refused to sign because it did not represent their agreement. Although Valentine agreed to take it back and get it redrafted, Larson refused to alter the contract and took the position that without the signature of O'Neill and Haas, there was no agreement.

On January 5, 1976, Cardinal received a letter from Circus Circus canceling the rooms that had been reserved by Cardinal for the entire 1976 season. O'Neill and Haas immediately called Las Vegas, and Larson told them that since they had refused to sign the agreement, they had no rooms. ...

After Circo's cancellation, O'Neill and Haas attempted to salvage their tour package. They contacted numerous Las Vegas hotels, and, finally, ... they learned that the Marina Hotel, which had just opened, still had rooms available ... they were able to salvage eight tours that operated at 100 percent capacity, although not back-to-back. [Therefore] they had to use the money they would have earned from these tours to cover the charges of bringing back empty planes, [and so] Cardinal never made a profit.

The disastrous nature of the 1976 season ruined Cardinal Consulting Company, although in subsequent years the one-stop charter business from the Upper Midwest to Las Vegas flourished. ...

Circo contends that Cardinal's claim for lost profits should have been dismissed because Cardinal was not an established business and could not prove its lost profits with the requisite degree of certainty to support recovery. It attacks [Cardinal's claimed right to damages] on [the following] grounds: (1) that Cardinal did not prove the fact of lost profits because it could show no past or future profitability;

(2) that Cardinal did not prove causation because other factors, such as its undercapitalization and lack of advertising, more plausibly explained its failure; ...

The general rule is that damages in the form of lost profits may be recovered where they are shown to be the natural and probable consequences of the act or omission complained of and their amount is shown with a reasonable degree of certainty and exactness. ... This rule does not call for absolute certainty.

The controlling principle is that speculative, remote, or conjectural damages are not recoverable. ... Although the law recognizes that it is more difficult to prove loss of prospective profits to a new business than to an established one, the law does not hold that it may not be done. ... Uncertainty as to the fact of whether any damages were sustained at all is fatal to recovery, but uncertainty as to the amount is not. ...

We agree with Circo that the evidence relating to lost profits that was presented by Cardinal lacks precision. Nevertheless, we cannot say that it was unreasonable for the jury to award lost profits to Cardinal, given the unusual circumstances of this particular enterprise and the devastating effect of Circo's breach.

Although Cardinal was able to demonstrate no past or future profitability, one of several substitutes was available in the evidence presented at trial. Haas and O'Neill were portrayed as persons with extensive experience in arranging tours who were also familiar with Las Vegas. They entered the one-stop charter market early with packages that others, such as retail agencies or social clubs, would be selling for them. Moreover, the market they chose was a fertile one. Las Vegas was very popular with the people from the Upper Midwest, and the small cities on which they were concentrating offered an untapped source of tour participants. ... [T]hey were planning to operate their tours during the peak tourist period. ... This same market and time period have been extremely profitable for those travel agencies who began one-stop charter packages the following year. ...

Similarly, the evidence, although weak, supports the inference that, were it not for the cancellation by Circo, Cardinal would have been able to fill all its flights except the first three. ...

Cardinal sold out the eight trips it actually ran, which could not have been accomplished but for the energy and skill of Haas and O'Neill, and the significant unmet demand for a travel service of this kind. That they were able to do so well on such short notice is persuasive to us, particularly because the substituted hotel, being new, lacked the appeal that the better known and advertised Circus Circus Hotel would have had for prospective customers. ... As the wrongdoer, Circo should not be per-mitted to evade its liability just because its wrongful cancellation involved a new business rather than an established one. ...

Moreover, although Cardinal's capital was limited, the business depended more on the character and personality of the entrepreneurs than on the amount available either for investment or advertising. ...

Ruling of the Court: [Cardinal is entitled to collect lost profits from Circus.]

CASE QUESTIONS

1. Why is reasonable certainty as to damages a prerequisite for a nonbreaching party to collect damages?

2. Why did Cardinal have difficulty proving its damages to a reasonable certainty?

3. What facts convinced the court that the breach by Circus Circus resulted in damages to Cardinal that could be proved to a reasonable certainty?

Duty to Mitigate

A plaintiff seeking to collect damages for breach of contract must prove that it attempted to mitigate its loss. **Mitigate** means to reduce or lessen. If the plaintiff takes no steps to contain the damages and instead ignores the possibility of reducing them, plaintiff will not be able to recover any of its loss from the breaching defendant. The reason for this rule is the law's objective to avoid economic waste—that is, an unnecessary loss. Assume a motel has a contract with a snow-plower to plow the motel's driveway. Following a big storm the plower does not plow and the motel is unable to contact her. If the motel takes no steps to call another plower, guests might cancel reservations because they are unable to drive into the motel's parking lot. The motel may be able to avoid this loss of income by locating another plower to do the job. If the motel does not attempt to mitigate its loss, it will not be able to collect its lost profits from the plower. If the motel makes a good-faith effort to hire a substitute, but is unable to find someone available to plow, the original plower will be liable for the motel's lost profits.

Punitive Damages

As we have learned, punitive damages are a sum of money sometimes awarded to a plaintiff in excess of compensatory damages, the purpose of which is to punish the defendant. Punitive damages are awarded only if the defendant's actions are wanton or malicious. This type of damage is not often awarded in a breach of contract case.

Specific Performance

Another remedy for breach of contract is specific performance, which is a court order requiring the defendant to perform the act promised in the contract. Specific performance is applicable only to contracts involving the sale of unique, one-of-a-kind items such as a particular restaurant or a famous painting. If the seller fails to execute the sale, the buyer can sue for specific performance.

Contracting for a Room

As with all contracts, a contract for a room between an innkeeper and a guest must satisfy the essential elements—contractual capacity, mutuality, legality, consideration, proper form, and genuine consent.

Most contracts for hotel rooms begin with an invitation to negotiate from a would-be guest who inquires as to room availability and price. An offer is often thereafter made by the hotel or guest. If it is accepted, the necessary mutuality exits.

As we have seen, if the hotel and guest are savvy, they will put their agreement in writing. Misunderstandings as to dates, duration of stay, and special needs of the guest are thereby avoided.

Overbooking and Breach of Reservation Contract

Wise travelers will make advance hotel reservations at their destination and at places along the route of their itinerary. The hotel reservation, once made and confirmed, constitutes a contract and binds the hotel to provide accommodations. Nonetheless, hotels sometimes overbook; in other words, they confirm more reservations than the number of rooms they have available. Experience proves that a certain percentage of confirmed guests will not use their reservations. Hotels that overbook "play the odds"—that is, they overbook by a number approximately equal to the number of people with confirmed reservations who, based on the hotel's experience, are expected not to show. If the numbers work out, everyone with a reservation who comes to the hotel will have a room. However, if the expected no-shows do appear, the hotel will not be able to accommodate everyone. For those the hotel cannot house, it will be in breach of contract and liable for damages.

For example, in *Brown v. Hilton Hotels Corporation*, 211 S.E.2d 125 (Ga. 1974), the hotel failed to honor the plaintiffs' confirmed reservation. The plaintiffs were unable to find other accommodations and so were forced to fly home. The plaintiffs sought and received damages for breach of contract.

Damages Allowed for Overbooking

Like any nonbreaching party, the would-be guest who is denied a room because the hotel has overbooked is entitled to collect compensatory damages. This typically includes travel expenses associated with seeking and finding alternate lodging, telephone calls necessitated by the move to let family and friends know of the changed location, and other costs that may be incurred in a particular case. The overbooked hotel is well-advised to assist the guest in finding a room at a second hotel. This was done by the hotel in the following case and may have saved it from liability for punitive damages.

CASE EXAMPLE 4-9

Dold v. Outrigger Hotel
501 P.2d 368 (Ha. 1972)

[The issue before the court was whether the plaintiff was entitled to punitive damages.] ... Upon arrival at the Outrigger on February 18, 1968, the plaintiffs were refused accommodations and were transferred by the Outrigger to another hotel of lesser quality because the Outrigger lacked available space. On February 19 and 20, the plaintiffs again demanded that the defendants honor their reservations, but they were again refused.

Though the exact nature of the plaintiffs' reservations is in dispute, the defendants claim that since the plaintiffs made no cash deposit, their reservations were not "confirmed" and, for that reason, the defendants justifiably dishonored the reservations. Plaintiffs contend that the reservations were "confirmed," as the American Express Company had guaranteed to Outrigger a first night's payment in the event that the plaintiffs did not show up. Further, the plaintiffs claim that this guarantee was in fact the same thing as a cash deposit. Thus, plaintiffs argue that the defendants were under a duty to honor the confirmed reservations. ...

An examination of the record ... shows the following: ...

3. In lieu of a cash deposit, the Outrigger accepted American Express Company's guarantee that it would pay the first night's deposit for the plaintiffs.

4. On February 18, 1968, the Outrigger referred twenty-nine parties holding reservations at the Outrigger to the Pagoda Hotel, which deemed these referrals "overflows."

5. On February 18, 1968, the Outrigger had sixteen guests who stayed beyond their scheduled date of departure.

6. From February 15 to 17 and 19 to 22, 1968, the Outrigger also had more reservations than

it could accommodate. Plaintiff's exhibits ... indicate the number of overflows and referrals ... made by the Outrigger to the Pagoda Hotel on the following dates:

February	15	20	referrals
"	16	20	"
"	17	32	"
"	19	44	"
"	20	9	"
"	21	9	"
"	22	20	"

7. Evidence was adduced that the Outrigger made a profit from its referrals to the Pagoda Hotel. Upon advance payment for the rooms to American Express, who in turn paid Outrigger, the plaintiffs were issued coupons representing the prepayment for the accommodations at the Outrigger. On the referral by the Outrigger, the Pagoda Hotel's practice was to accept the coupons [from the guests in full payment of the room] and bill the Outrigger for the actual cost of the rooms provided [which was less than the Outrigger's rate]. The difference between the coupon's value and the actual value of the accommodations was retained by the Outrigger.

The plaintiffs prevented a profit from being made by the Outrigger by refusing to use the coupons and paying in cash for the less expensive accommodations.

May Plaintiffs Recover Punitive Damages for Breach of Contract? The question of whether punitive damages are properly recoverable in an action for breach of contract has not been resolved in this jurisdiction. ...

We are of the opinion that the facts of this case do not warrant punitive damages. ... It has long been recognized that an innkeeper, holding himself out to the public to provide hotel accommodations, is obligated, in the absence of reasonable grounds for refusal, to provide accommodations to all persons upon proper request. ... However, where the innkeeper's accommodations had been exhausted, the innkeeper could justly refuse to receive an applicant. ...

We are not aware of any jurisdiction that renders an innkeeper liable on his common law duty to accommodate under the circumstances of this case. Consequently, plaintiffs are not entitled to ... punitive damages. ...

CASE QUESTIONS

1. Why did the court not impose punitive damages?

2. Under what circumstances do you think a court might impose punitive damages where a hotel overbooked?

The following case includes factual material about the scope and causes of overbooking. The reader should not conclude from the court's decision that a hotel can overbook with virtual impunity. Not all courts will be as sympathetic to the hotel as the court in this case seems to have been. As you read this case, take note of the following: (1) the different types of losses suffered by the plaintiff and (2) which types of damages the plaintiff was able to recover for and which the plaintiff was not.

CASE EXAMPLE 4-10

Vern Wells et al. v. Holiday Inns, Inc.
522 F.Supp. 1023 (W.D. Mo. 1981)

This case arose out of the events which occurred when the individual plaintiffs, Vernon Lee Wells and Robert K. Hughes, traveled to San Francisco, California in July of 1976 for a convention of the National Office Machine Dealers Association (NOMDA). At that time, Wells [and Hughes were co-owners] of the corporate plaintiff, Central Office Machines. Wells planned the trip as both a business undertaking relating to the convention and as a vacation, taking his wife and son with him. The Wells family, Hughes and another co-owner of the corporation had reservations at defendant's Union Square Holiday Inn for three nights commencing July 15, 1976.

The reservations were made through the NOMDA travel coordinator in Bridgeport, Connecticut, to whom the check to cover the entire travel package cost was sent. ... Although the check to cover costs included the hotel, reservation confirmation slips sent to

plaintiff's by the Housing Bureau ... indicated that no deposit had been received and that the confirmation would not be held after 6:00 P.M. unless the hotel is notified of late arrival. The Holiday Inn also sent its own confirmation slip to plaintiffs, which did not specifically indicate whether a deposit had been received but did state that these were "6 P.M. only" reservations.

On July 15, 1976, after a flight delay of approximately an hour, the plaintiffs' party arrived in the lobby of the Union Square Holiday Inn at around 3:00 in the afternoon to find a crowd waiting to check in to the hotel. After a considerable wait, and inquiries with various hotel personnel, plaintiffs were informed that no rooms were available for that night and that arrangements would be made with another hotel for one night. They were referred to the Jack Tarr Hotel, and vouchers for taxi fares to the Jack Tarr and for the return trip to the Holiday Inn were provided. Plaintiff Hughes used the vouchers but plaintiff Wells did not. Hughes returned and stayed at the

Holiday Inn on July 16; Wells did not, but remained at the Jack Tarr that night and moved to the Hyatt Regency for the night of July 17, 1976.

The Inn Operations Manual of defendant contains provisions for procedures for defendant's personnel to follow in the event reservations are dishonored. These include arranging substitute accommodations and paying the difference in cost if that of the substitute is higher, providing taxi fare, and other incidental expenses necessitated by the change, such as the cost of telephone calls to notify family members of a change. Such procedures appear to have been followed in plaintiffs' case. Plaintiffs received a refund of all payment made to the NOMDA convention group which was to have been applied to lodging at Holiday Inn for the nights when it was not actually used, a total of $268.40. Because Hughes and the other business associate went to Las Vegas for the last scheduled night of the San Francisco trip, plaintiffs paid, overall, $41.95 less than the amount which had been anticipated by them as payment for lodging prior to the trip. Plaintiff Wells was required to pay $16.00 for parking when he removed his rental car from the Holiday Inn garage which he would not have been charged had he been registered at the Holiday Inn, and testimony indicated that some taxi fares expended would not have been necessary if the plaintiffs had stayed at Holiday Inn.[1]

Plaintiffs contend that the dishonoring of the reservations by Holiday Inn gives rise to a claim for fraud or misrepresentation and for breach of contract. They seek actual damages in very substantial amounts, asserting (1) business losses from failure to acquire equipment at the convention for which they had a ready market, and, as to Wells (2) the triggering of a series of excruciating cluster headaches which continued for approximately two months. Punitive damages are sought under the fraud claims.

Absent a showing that defendant knowingly or willfully misrepresented a material fact to plaintiffs or intended not to reserve a room, there is no fraud. The failure to perform a contract cannot be transmuted into fraud or misrepresentation absent that intent. Although there may be a duty to disclose material facts, concealment of a remote possibility of non-performance does not seem to be considered deceitful at common law. ...

Expert testimony indicated that overbooking to some extent is a recognized and accepted practice within the hotel industry. The day that plaintiffs were refused their rooms there was a dishonor rate at that Holiday Inn of almost four percent (4%). However, the hotel's average dishonor rate was much lower, or about half the national average of one-half of one percent. Moreover, the dishonor rate is not completely attributable to the practice of overbooking, but also is affected by such unknowns as unexpected "stay-overs." ...

Further, the television commercials aired by defendant, which plaintiffs testified they viewed and took into account before making the reservations, add nothing to the claim for fraud or misrepresentation. The most pertinent commercial, on the general theme "The Best Surprise Is No Surprise" depicts a traveler being rejected at the front desk of another hotel or motel by a desk clerk who denies receipt of a reservation. The message most obviously derived from the scene is that Holiday Inns are comparatively reliable in their reservation practices. There is no evidence in this case to the contrary. The reservation system described by the witnesses, particularly the "Holidex," appears to be generally efficient. The overbooking practice of Holiday Inns is fairly conservative compared with the general industry, and any slight exaggeration of the extent of reliability contained in the commercial falls within the category of mere "puffing" [an expression of opinion not made as a statement of fact and not legally binding as a promise or warranty] which is not actionable.

As a general rule, the measure of damages for breach of contract is that "compensation should be equal to the injuries subject to the condition that the damages be confined to those naturally and approximately resulting from the breach and be not uncertain or speculative." [R]ecovery for breach of contract [is limited] to those damages which could reasonably be supposed to have been within the

---

1The additional fares total $22.00 as to Wells and $4.00 as to Hughes for a trip to Chinatown (within walking distance of the Holiday Inn).

contemplation of the parties at the time they entered into the contract. The rule generally precludes such special, consequential damages as lost profits from transactions not known to the party charged with breach, in addition to barring recovery for disappointment, mental distress, and similar claims, because such items are not normally predictable by the party breaking a contract. ...

[T]he Court finds that plaintiffs have failed in their proof of causation. Proof as to lost business opportunities is not adequate to support an assessment of damages with reasonable certainty. A claim for loss of anticipated profits of a commercial business may be too remote, speculative and too dependent upon changes of circumstances to warrant judgment for recovery. The Court is satisfied that a considerable amount of business is conducted at the trade show in question, and that plaintiffs had a ready market in Kansas City for various items of business equipment. However, the proof is not satisfactory as to the critical nature of the room reservation at the Holiday Inn-Union Square to acquisition of the necessary items, or that the lost room reservation seriously impeded the business activities ... Plaintiff Hughes and the third co-owner lost no appreciable time in attempting to locate desirable equipment. Plaintiff Wells appears to have been more interested in litigating than in buying. He voluntarily took time off to confer with a lawyer about the prospects of litigation. ...

The Court must also be skeptical of the theory that plaintiffs could not reasonably have located suitable equipment except at the convention. Trade shows are doubtless the most convenient times to negotiate sales agreements, but it is likely that any solid prospects would have been followed up before or after the convention closed, and no showing was made why acquisitions could not be made from Kansas City after the convention, in time to satisfy the needs of the potential purchasers. The purchasers waited months and even years before buying substitute equipment. The frustrations of the trip are thus not shown to have foreclosed the market. Skepticism as to the critical nature of the NOMDA convention is increased by Wells' failure to attend the shows in 1977, 1978, or 1980.

The Court does not discount the very serious nature of Mr. Wells' problem of cluster headaches. The evidence is convincing that he suffered intermittent excruciating pain, so severe that it caused him to pace the floor at night, occasionally rolling weeping on the floor or making other attempts to block the pain, such as striking his head against the wall. Cluster headaches were shown (as the name indicates) to occur in series, the onset of which has been observed in Mr. Wells' case to be closely associated with stress, such as business pressures or overwork. ... Shortly after midnight on Friday night, July 16, Wells experienced the first in what became a new cluster of headaches. ... [T]he Court concludes that this is not recoverable under present legal standards.

It is accordingly hereby

ORDERED that judgment shall be entered in favor of plaintiff Vernon L. Wells and against defendant in the amount of Thirty-eight dollars ($38). ... It is further

ORDERED that judgment shall be entered in favor of plaintiff Robert K. Hughes and against defendant in the amount of Four dollars ($4). ...

CASE QUESTIONS

1. Why was Wells able to collect for the cab fares to Chinatown but not for the business losses from failure to acquire the desired equipment at the convention?

2. Why did the court refuse to award damages for Wells' cluster headaches?

3. The court referenced a reservation system utilized by Holiday Inns. What impact did this system have on the outcome of the case?

Damage to Goodwill

If the plaintiff in an overbooking case is not an individual but rather a tour operator, it may suffer cancellations and loss of future business as a result of a hotel not honoring reservations. The tour operator thus may suffer substantial damages from loss of goodwill. **Goodwill** is a favorable reputation producing an expectation of future business. For example, assume you contract with a tour company for a cruise that is advertised to include a particular, upscale ship. When you arrive at the dock you discover that the boat you will be traveling on is inferior to the advertised ship. It is smaller, has fewer amenities, and is not as nicely decorated or designed. The cause of the switch was that the ship had overbooked and so your tour was bumped, through no fault of your tour operator. When you return from your trip you are not likely to recommend the tour company to your friends and, upon hearing about your experience, your friends will likely decline from utilizing the company in the future. The tour company has suffered injury to its goodwill.

The amount of loss that a company will experience as a result of damage to its goodwill is hard to prove. Before a court will grant compensation it must be satisfied that damages are proven to a reasonable certainty. Note how the court in the following case addresses this issue.

CASE EXAMPLE 4-11

Rainbow Travel Services, Inc.
v.
Hilton Hotels, Corp.
896 F.2d 1233 (10th Cir. 1990)

... [P]laintiff Rainbow Travel Service [Rainbow] won a jury verdict against the defendants for breach of contract and fraud. ... The Fontainebleu Hilton is a deluxe resort hotel in Miami Beach, Florida. The hotel is operated by the defendant Hilton Hotels, Inc. ("Hilton"), ... Plaintiff Rainbow is a travel agency ...

In the spring of 1986, Rainbow began organizing several tour packages for Oklahoma football fans who wanted to attend a University of Oklahoma versus University of Miami football game. The game was scheduled for September 26, 1986, in Miami, Florida. Rainbow initially contacted the Fontainebleu concerning the possibility of reserving hotel rooms for Rainbow's groups. After telephone calls and correspondence between the parties, the Fontainebleu sent Rainbow two contracts which called for the hotel to reserve one hundred and five rooms for Rainbow on the weekend of September 27, 1986. The second of

these contracts, which is at issue in this case, provided that forty-five rooms were to be reserved for Rainbow on September 26, 1986. Rainbow executed the agreements and returned them to the Fontainebleu. In June of 1986, the Fontainebleu confirmed Rainbow's reservation by mail and requested prepayment for one night for Rainbow's groups. In response, Rainbow sent a partial payment of over $6,000. The Fontainebleu sent another confirmation in August and requested the remainder of the payment. The payments were made by checks drawn on Rainbow's account in Oklahoma.

Rainbow's president, A.J. Musgrove, went to Miami on September 24, 1986, to make sure that all arrangements had been made for his groups' stay at the Fontainebleu. One group from Rainbow arrived on September 25 and was accommodated as planned. Musgrove met with the hotel's tour representative, Livia Cohen, on September 24, twice on September 25, and again on the morning of September 26. Ms. Cohen assured Mr. Musgrove that everything was fine and that all of the reserved rooms would be available. When the Rainbow group arrived at the hotel on the afternoon of September 26, however, they were told by Hilton representatives that no rooms were available at the Fontainebleu. Hilton made arrangements for the group to stay at the Seacoast Towers, a hotel/apartment complex located about ten blocks away from the Fontainebleu. Rainbow subsequently filed this action. ...

The jury found that Rainbow had sustained $37,500 in damages to its good will. Rainbow's primary witness on this issue was its president, A.J. Musgrove, who testified that he was familiar with the value of Rainbow's goodwill from his history with the company and from reviewing Rainbow's financial statements. Mr. Musgrove estimated that the incident at the Fontainebleu damaged Rainbow's goodwill in the amount of $250,000. His opinion was based in part on his observation that when customers are dissatisfied they tell others about it, meaning that a bad incident such as this one has a "rippling effect" on a business' reputation. He indicated that this is particularly true for the travel agency because it relies heavily on its reputation in the community. Additionally, Rainbow presented the testimony of witnesses who had traveled to Miami on the Rainbow tour. These witnesses stated that they were dissatisfied with Rainbow because of the hotel incident and stated they probably would not choose Rainbow again as a travel agent.

Viewing this evidence in the light most favorable to the plaintiff, we find that there was substantial evidence reasonably tending to support the jury's verdict. ... Appellants argue nonetheless that the amount of damages to goodwill was so uncertain as to be speculative. The rule in Oklahoma, however, is that the prohibition against recovery of damages because the loss is uncertain or too speculative in nature applies to the fact of damages, not to the amount.

Rainbow presented evidence that Hilton accepted reservations for more rooms than were available on September 26, 1986. Hilton admitted that its policy was to book the Fontainebleu up to one hundred and fifteen per cent of its capacity, but argued that it did so based on a historic fifteen per cent "no-show" rate for guests with reservations. Hilton insisted that this policy allowed the hotel to honor almost all of its reservations. Although Hilton showed that an exceedingly high percentage of reservations were in fact honored over the course of the year, Rainbow presented evidence showing that on fifty per cent of those occasions when the hotel was operating at capacity the hotel had to dishonor reservations. Additionally, Rainbow presented evidence tending to show that Hilton was aware of a substantial likelihood that Rainbow's reservation might be dishonored. Rainbow showed that Hilton knew at least one month in advance that a large number of rooms would be closed for maintenance during September of 1986. ... Additionally, Rainbow showed that on the date in question Hilton gave a block of rooms to a group from the University of Oklahoma even though the group had not reserved the rooms. ...

Hilton argued strenuously ... that the overbooking situation was due to factors beyond its control, such as guests extending their stay at the Fontainebleu and rooms being out of order for repairs. These explanations may have sounded rather hollow to the jury, however, in light of a portion of the Fontainebleu's policy manual which read:

> Overbooked
> We never tell a guest we "overbooked." If an overbook situation arises, it is due to the fact that something occurred that the hotel could not prevent.
>
> Examples:
> 1. Scheduled departures do not vacate their rooms.
> 2. Engineering problems with a room (pipe busted, thus water leaks, air conditioning, heating out of commission, broken glass, etc.)
> Always remain calm and as pleasant as possible.

In addition to the foregoing, the record contains much circumstantial evidence showing that Hilton had knowledge of a likelihood of dishonoring reservations at the time in question. The Fontainebleu was extremely busy during the week of Rainbow's visit. On September 22 and 23 for instance, the hotel was completely sold out and the Fontainebleu had to dishonor reservations. Although there were some vacant rooms on September 24 and 25, the number of vacancies was very few. Also, the "no-show" rate for reservations was much less during this period than the fifteen per cent annual average used by Hilton. Although Hilton's agent indicated to Mr. Musgrove on the morning of September 26 that his rooms would be available, the Night Clerk Summary for September 25 indicated that the hotel would be short of rooms even if fifteen per cent of the reservations for the 26th failed to show.

Some of the testimony at trial raised questions about the candor of Hilton's explanation concerning its treatment of Rainbow's reservations. Hilton said that it only became aware of a shortage of rooms after Mr. Musgrove had gone to the airport to pick up his group, yet when the group arrived back at the hotel they had already been assigned specific rooms at the Seacoast Towers. ... [W]e find substantial evidence in the record that Hilton was aware of having overbooked the hotel to such an extent as to create a substantial likelihood that Rainbow's reservation would be dishonored. Despite this, Hilton repeatedly told Rainbow that its rooms would be available and did not tell Rainbow that the group might be "bumped." Based on this and all of the evidence in the record before us, we find that a reasonable juror could find by clear and convincing evidence that Hilton recklessly made statements without knowledge of their truth, that Hilton did so with the intention that plaintiff rely on them, and that plaintiff relied on the statements to its detriment. ...

[Plaintiffs were entitled to recover $37,500 as compensatory damages for injury to its reputation.]

CASE QUESTIONS

1. Why is the potential for damages great when a hotel dishonors the reservations of a tour group?

2. How can a hotel damage its own goodwill by overbooking?

In another case involving damage to goodwill, the issue of proof to a reasonable certainty was likewise raised. The plaintiff operated a restaurant for six years, leasing space from a mall landlord. Thereafter the premises were damaged extensively by fire. The parties negotiated a new five-year lease with an option to renew and the landlord began to rebuild. Due to construction disagreements, the landlord canceled the new lease and the plaintiff successfully sued for breach of contract. Concerning lost future profits, the accountant who prepared the restaurant's financial statements testified that the business had always turned a profit. He expressed the opinion that the restaurant had a good reputation and a good location, and therefore profits could be expected in the future. Said the court, '[W]hile the claimant must demonstrate a reasonable probability of future profits, ... mathematical precision is neither required nor possible. There was ample evidence here that [the restaurant] could expect profitable operations for the term of the lease." The plaintiff was thus entitled to collect lost future profits.[6]

Another Goodwill Issue—Agreements Not to Compete

When an owner of a restaurant or hotel sells the business, the sales contract customarily includes an **agreement not to compete**, which is a provision barring the seller from competing in the same geographical area for a specified period of

[6] *Joe Garavelli's Restaurant, Inc. v. Colonial Square Associates*, 21 SW3d 149 (Mo. 2000)

time. This type of agreement attempts to preserve for the buyer the business's goodwill—that is, the expectation that the firm's established customers will continue to patronize the purchased business. If the seller reenters the market and competes with the buyer for the same customers, the buyer is denied part of what was sold to him. The agreement, called a *noncompetition clause* or an *agreement not to compete*, is generally enforceable provided the time and territory within which competition is restricted is reasonable in duration and area.

In a case involving the sale of a restaurant, the seller, in a typical noncompetition clause, agreed not to "engage either directly or indirectly as an employee, owner, partner, or agent, shareholder, director or officer of a corporation in a similar restaurant business which is directly in competition with the type of business [seller sold to buyer] within a five mile radius" of the restaurant. Had the seller become a part owner of a competing restaurant or worked there as a chef, manager, or server, the agreement not to compete would clearly have been violated. In the referenced case the seller only did landscaping work for a competing restaurant and gave directions to another laborer at the restaurant regarding work to be done inside the building. The buyer sued, claiming breach of contract. The court ruled that because the restaurant was not in the landscaping or construction business, the seller's work did not harm the buyer's goodwill and therefore did not breach the noncompetition clause.[7]

Breach by a Guest

Sometimes the party who fails to perform in a hotel reservation case is not the hotel but rather the guest; for example, when the latter cancels a reservation. The hotel may have a cancelation policy that permits the guest to cancel without liability until a specified number of days prior to the date of the reservation. If such a policy is not applicable, a guest who cancels a reservation may be liable for damages for breach of contract. In such a case, the same legal rules concerning remedies apply to the hotel as applied to the guest when the hotel breaches: the hotel as the nonbreaching party must attempt to mitigate the loss by renting the room to another guest. If the hotel is unable to re-let the room, it is entitled to collect compensatory damages from the guest, which is commonly the agreed price for the room.

The next case illustrates a situation where the guest breached the contract and the hotel was entitled to damages.

CASE EXAMPLE 4-12

Freeman v. Kiamesha Concord, Inc.
351 N.Y.S.2d 541 (1974)

... Plaintiff, a lawyer, has commenced this action against the defendant, the operator of the Concord Hotel (Concord), one of the most opulent of the resort hotels in the Catskill Mountains resort area, to recover the ... rate for a day charged and not refunded after he and his wife checked out before the

---

[7]*Kladis v. Nick's Patio, Inc.*, 735 N.E.2d 1216 (Ind. 2000)

commencement of the third day of a reserved three-day Memorial Day weekend. ...

The testimony adduced at trial reveals that in early May 1973, after seeing an advertisement in the New York Times indicating that Joel Gray would perform at the [Concord] during the forthcoming Memorial Day weekend, plaintiff contacted a travel agent and solicited a reservation for his wife and himself at the hotel. In response, he received an offer of a reservation for a "three-night minimum stay" that contained a request for a $20 deposit. He forwarded the money confirming the reservation, which was deposited by the defendant.

While driving to the hotel, the plaintiff observed a billboard, located about twenty miles from his destination, that indicated that Joel Gray would perform at the Concord only on the Sunday of the holiday weekend. The plaintiff was disturbed because he had understood the advertisement to mean that the entertainer would be performing on each day of the weekend. He checked into the hotel, notwithstanding this disconcerting information, claiming that he did not wish to turn back and ruin a long-anticipated weekend vacation. The plaintiff later discovered that two subsequent New York Times advertisements, not seen by him before checking in, specified that Gray would perform [only] on the Sunday of that weekend.

After staying at the hotel for two days, the plaintiff advised the management that he wished to check out because of his dissatisfaction with the entertainment. He claims to have told them that he had made his reservation in reliance upon what he understood to be a representation in the advertisement to the effect that Joel Gray would perform throughout the holiday weekend. The management suggested that since Gray was to perform that evening, he should remain. The plaintiff refused and again asserted his claim that the advertisement constituted a misrepresentation. The defendant insisted upon full payment for the entire three-day guaranteed weekend in accordance with the reservation. Plaintiff then told the defendant's employees that he was an attorney, and that they had no right to charge him for the third day of the reserved period if he checked out. ... The plaintiff was finally offered a one-day credit for a future stay if he made full payment. He refused, paid the full charges under protest, and advised the defendant of his intention to sue them. ... This is that action.

I find that the advertisement relied upon by the plaintiff did not contain a false representation. It announced that Joel Gray would perform at the hotel during the Memorial Day weekend. Gray did actually appear during that weekend. ...

The advertisement contained no false statement. It neither represented nor suggested that Gray would perform throughout the holiday weekend. The defendant cannot be found liable because the plaintiff misunderstood its advertisement. ...

It must be noted that the plaintiff checked into the defendant's hotel pursuant to a valid, enforceable contract for a three-day stay. The solicitation of a reservation, the making of a reservation by the transmittal of a deposit, and the acceptance of the deposit constituted a binding contract in accordance with traditional contract principles of offer and acceptance. Unquestionably the defendant would have been liable to the plaintiff had it not had an accommodation for plaintiff upon his arrival. The plaintiff is equally bound under the contract for the agreed minimum period.

The testimony reveals that the defendant was ready, willing, and able to provide all of the services contracted for, but that plaintiff refused to accept them for the third day of the three-day contract period. These services included lodging, meals, and the use of the defendant's recreational and entertainment facilities. ...

Hotels such as the one operated by the defendant have developed techniques to provide full utilization of their facilities during periods of peak demand. One such method is the guaranteed minimum one week or weekend stay that has gained widespread public acceptance. Almost all of these enterprises have offered their facilities for minimum guaranteed periods during certain times of the year by contracting with willing guests who also seek to fully utilize their available vacation time. These minimum period agreements have become essential to the economic survival and well-being of the recreational hotel industry. The public is generally aware of the necessity for them to do so and accepts the practice. ...

A hotel such as the defendant's services thousands of guests at a single time. The maintenance of its facilities entails a continuing large overhead expenditure. It must have some means to legitimately ensure itself the income that its guests have contracted to pay for the use of its facilities. The minimum period reservation contract is such a device. The rooms are contracted for in advance and are held available while other potential guests are turned away. A guest who terminates his contractual obligations prior to the expiration of the contract period will usually deprive the hotel of anticipated income if that guest cannot be held financially accountable upon

his contract. At that point, replacement income is virtually impossible. ...

The defendant has contracted to supply the plaintiff with a room, three meals a day, and access to the use of its varied sports, recreational, or entertainment facilities. As long as these are available to the plaintiff, the defendant has fulfilled its contractual commitment. ...

Ruling of the Court: Judgment is accordingly awarded to the defendant. ...

CASE QUESTIONS

1. What is the meaning of the court's statement in the third-to-last paragraph, "At that point, replacement income is virtually impossible"?

2. Would the decision have been different if the hotel could have rented the room to someone else? Why?

3. Why could the plaintiff not avoid the contract based on his mistake concerning when Joel Gray would perform?

If the hotel is able to re-let the room for the same or higher price than the breaching guest had contracted to pay, the hotel cannot collect the agreed price for the room from the breaching guest, nor can it retain a deposit the guest might have made. Otherwise the hotel would recover twice and profit from the breach, neither of which is permitted. The hotel in the following case tried unsuccessfully to retain an advance payment although it had re-let the room.

CASE EXAMPLE 4-13

2625 Building Corp. (Mariott Hotel)
v.
Deutsch
385 N.E.2d 1189 (Ind. 1979)

... [O]n December 7, 1972, Deutsch, a resident of Connecticut, made reservations by telephone for six rooms at the Mariott for the 1973 "500" Mile Race weekend (May 27, 28, 29). Mariott requested advance payment for the rooms. Deutsch complied with Mariott's demand and paid by check in the amount of $1,008 in full for the reserved rooms. At the end of March, or the beginning of April, 1973, Deutsch, by telephone, canceled the reserva-

tions and requested the return of his advance payment. Mariott refused his demand. Deutsch did not use the rooms and later brought action against Mariott to recover the $1,008 advance payment, alleging the above facts and, in addition, that Mariott had relet the rooms and was not harmed by the cancellation...

The Mariott cites *Freeman v. Kiamesha Concord, Inc.* in support of its position that it had a right to refuse to refund $1,008 to Deutsch when he canceled his reservations. However, we find the facts in the case at hand to be clearly distinguishable. In *Freeman* the guest had checked into the hotel pursuant to the contract, whereas in this case Deutsch had not. Moreover, *Freeman* involved a "last minute" checkout prior to the end of the contract period, whereas Deutsch gave the Mariott approximately two months' advance notice of his cancellation.

We do not disagree with the reasoning in *Freeman* as applied to the facts therein, and such reasoning is certainly applicable in "last minute" cancellation cases, especially at resort-type hotels. Thus, we recognize there may be instances when a guest's cancellation of reservations would not justify a refund of an advance payment. ... [T]he making and acceptance of the reservation in this case constituted a binding contract. Upon Deutsch's breach, Mariott was entitled to actual damages in accordance with traditional contract principles. ...

The evidence in the record reveals that Deutsch made reservations, tendered full payment for the use of the rooms in advance, and approximately two months prior to Marriott's time for performance, canceled the reservations and demanded refund, which demand was refused. In addition, we take judicial notice that the Indianapolis "500" Mile Race has the largest attendance of any single, one-day, arena-type sporting event in the world. The influx of dedicated racing fans to the Indianapolis metropolitan area in order to witness this spectacle of racing is legend. Attendant with this influx is the overwhelming demand for, and shortage of, hotel accommodations.

Therefore, we find that the facts of this case justified the trial court's conclusion that assessing Deutsch for the full amount of his room payments would cause him to suffer a loss that was wholly disproportionate to any injury sustained by Mariott. Since Mariott sustained no damage, [it is not entitled to retain any of plaintiff's money].

CASE QUESTION

1. Do you agree with the distinction made by the court between this case and *Freeman v. Kiamesha Concord, Inc.*? Why or why not?

Cancellation Clause for Organization Reserving a Large Block of Rooms

When the party canceling hotel reservations is an association that had reserved many rooms—sometimes 100s or even 1000s—for a conference, the hotel may face a substantial loss. As is the duty of any nonbreaching party, the hotel must mitigate its loss by attempting to sell the available rooms.

Many contracts between associations and hotels have a cancelation provision that identifies the obligations of each party in the event of termination of the contract. Those terms vary from contract to contract and control the liability of the canceling organization. Some cancelation provisions require that the association pay the full amount of lost revenue experienced by the hotel (the number of unsold rooms multiplied by the established group rate).[8] Other contract terms may require payment of a lesser amount such as the established group rate for only two nights, although the canceled reservations were for three,[9] or damages "equal to one night's anticipated room revenue based on single occupancy."

---

[8]See, for example, *Opryland Hotel v. Millbrook Distribution Services, Inc.*, 1999 WL 767816 (Tenn. 1999)

[9]*Princess Hotels International, Inc. v. Delaware State Bar Association*, 1998 WL 283465 (Del. 1998)

The specific terms of cancelation clauses for organizations reserving blocks of rooms are subject to negotiations between the association and the hotel.

Attrition Clause for Organizations that Do Not Utilize All Rooms on Hold

Customarily, with a conference reservation the hotel holds rooms for conventioneers and members make reservations directly with the hotel. Occasionally, the group's estimate is significantly above the actual number of rooms rented by organization members. An **attrition clause** addresses this situation. It is a contract provision that obligates the organization to compensate the hotel if less than the contractual number of rooms are rented by conventioneers. The terms of the contract will control the liability of the association.

In a case involving the Women's International Bowling Conference (WIBC) and a Hyatt Regency Hotel, significantly fewer rooms were rented than were being held by the hotel for the tournament. The hotel claimed the WIBC was liable to pay for the extra rooms. The contract between the hotel and the WIBC did not contain an attrition clause. The issue had been addressed in correspondence from the WIBC to the Hyatt, which stated, "From past experience we estimate the following number of rooms will be picked up [reserved] from your block [the rooms the Hyatt was holding for WIBC] as headquarters hotel." The court held that the word *estimate* denotes that the number of rooms to be held aside by the hotel in the block was not intended as a firm commitment, but rather an approximate figure. Further, the phrase *picked up* evidences that some further action—that is, the making of a reservation by an attendee—was needed before any of the rooms held in the block would be occupied by a convention attendee. Therefore WIBC was not contractually bound to pay for rooms held by the hotel and not rented.[10]

No-Cause Termination Clause

Some contracts have a **no-cause termination clause**, which is a contract provision permitting either party to terminate the contract for any reason or for no reason at all. If the terms of the contract permit termination, ending the contractual relationship is not a breach of contract.

An example is provided in a case involving a contract between United Airlines and a catering company for the purchase of in-flight meals. After the contract was signed, the catering company invested almost one million dollars to expand its facilities to accommodate the airline's need. The contract included a no-cause termination clause that read as follows, "The term of this Agreement shall commence on May 1, 1988, and shall continue for a period of three years; provided, however, either party may terminate this Agreement upon ninety (90) days' prior written notice." After one year, the airline gave ninety days notice and thereafter terminated the contract. The catering company sued for breach. The court dismissed the case saying that the meaning of the termination clause was clear

---

[10]*Hyatt Regency v. Women's International Bowling Congress, Inc.*, 80 F.Supp2d 88 (1999)

and unambiguous, no-cause termination clauses are widely utilized, and the airline abided by the terms of the provision giving ninety days written notice.[11]

Guaranteed Reservations

Some hotel reservations are guaranteed and others are not. With a nonguaranteed reservation, the hotel is obligated to provide a room for a guest provided the guest arrives by a specified hour. If the guest does not arrive by that time, the hotel can assign the room to someone else and will not be in breach to the late guest, even if no vacancy exists. If the guest never arrives, perhaps because of a change in plans, the hotel cannot charge the guest for the room, even if the hotel was not able to sell it to someone else.

A guaranteed reservation requires the hotel to hold a room for the guest no matter how late the guest arrives. If the hotel does not have a room available for the late arriver, it will be in breach. In return for this guarantee on the hotel's part, the guest agrees to pay for the room even if she fails to arrive at all.

Sometimes hotels will include the commitment to provide a room at the hotel "or its equivalent" in their guaranteed reservation contracts. This provision would excuse a hotel from breach if it could not provide a room but secures accomodations for that person at a nearby hotel with similar amenities.

Intentional Interference with Contractual Relations

Breach of contract can also give rise to the tort of intentional interference with contractual relations. A **tort** is noncriminal conduct done by one person that causes injury or financial loss to another. We will discuss torts in detail in Chapter 5. To commit the tort of intentional interference with contractual relations, three elements are necessary:

1. A valid contract must exist between two parties
2. A third party must be aware of the existence of the contract
3. The third party must intentionally cause or induce one of the contracting parties to break the contract and do business instead with the third party.

The third party inducing the breach will be liable in damages to the contracting party who did not breach.

For example, if a particular cola company has a two-year contract to be the exclusive supplier of soda for a fast-food chain, and a competing cola company that is aware of the contract induces the chain to break the contract and purchase its beverage instead, the competing company has committed the tort; the original cola company can sue it for damages. Note that a breach of contract is inherent in interference with contractual relations cases. For example, in the example involving the competing cola companies, the fast-food chain breached the contract with the original cola company by terminating the agreement prematurely to do business with the second company.

---

[11] *United Airlines, Inc. v. Good Taste, Inc.*, 982 P.2d 1259 (Ala. 1999)

The following case vividly illustrates the tort of intentional interference with contractual relations.

CASE EXAMPLE 4-14

Melo-Tone Vending, Inc.
v.
Sherry, Inc.
656 N.E.2d 312 (1995)

... Melo-Tone Vending, Inc., the plaintiff (Melo-Tone), is in the business of installing coin-operated vending machines (e.g., cigarette machines, jukeboxes, games, amusements, and pay telephones) in locations such as barrooms and restaurants. Among its accounts was Bentley's Steak House, an establishment owned by Sherry, Inc. (Sherry). ... On June 22, 1989, Melo-Tone and Sherry entered a contract under which Melo-Tone was to install at Bentley's a jukebox and two pool tables, in addition to a cigarette machine already in place. Sherry was to receive a "commission" of 22.75% on each package of cigarettes sold and 50% of the net yield from the jukebox and pool tables. For a term of eight years (i.e., until June 21, 1997), Melo-Tone would have the "sole and exclusive right" to operate vending machines in ... Sherry's premises. Melo-Tone identified its machines by large green labels, bearing its name and telephone number, that were placed on the fronts of the machines.

Business between Melo-Tone and Sherry was uneventful until January, 1992, when Sherry was approached on behalf of James Indelicato, proprietor of Park Square Vending (Park Square), with a proposition about making Bentley's over into a sports bar, for which—not incidentally—Park Square's machines would replace Melo-Tone's. Sherry ... gave the word to Park Square's advance man that there was a small matter of a contract with Melo-Tone, but that did not derail the sports bar project. Late in January or early in February 1992 Melo-Tone's principal officer, Jack D. Kerner, got wind that Park Square was going to install an air hockey game at Bentley's. Kerner called Park Square and mailed to Park Square a copy of his "exclusive" contract with Sherry. Nevertheless, on February 11, 1992, Park Square moved its air hockey game machine onto the Sherry premises.

By letter dated February 18, 1992, Melo-Tone's lawyer informed Park Square that it had exclusive rights to place vending machines at Sherry's establishment and demanded immediate removal of Park Square's air hockey machine. Park Square instead added two pool tables and a cigarette machine, as well as some other machines, at Sherry's place of business. Space was a problem that Park Square solved by furnishing funds to Sherry to move Melo-Tone's machines out. On March 6, 1992, Melo-Tone brought an action against Indelicato [for wrongful interference with contractual relations], and Sherry [for breach of contract] ...

As to the defendant Sherry, the plaintiff Melo-Tone stipulated dismissal well before trial. There had been a reconciliation; Melo-Tone was back in and Park Square was out. Melo-Tone's [claim for wrongful interference with contractual relations] was tried to a jury. The jury returned a verdict that the defendant Indelicato had intentionally interfered with the contractual relationship between Melo-Tone and Sherry; ... The jury set the damages at $21,000 ... Indelicato has appealed. ...

To make out a case of intentional interference with a contract, a plaintiff must prove that: 1) he had a contract with a third party; 2) the defendant knowingly induced the third party to break that contract; 3) the defendant's interference, in addition to being intentional, was improper in motive or means; and 4) the plaintiff was harmed by the defendant's actions. ...

[T]here was more than sufficient evidence to permit the jury to find that: 1) Sherry had entered into an eight-year contract with Melo-Tone to have Melo-Tone operate vending machines on Sherry's premises; 2) Indelicato had induced Sherry to get vending machines from him and to push Melo-Tone's out the door; and 3) Melo-Tone lost profits while its machines were excluded from Sherry's place. ...

Indelicato argues that his motives were competitive and financial, not to harm Melo-Tone, and that his conduct was not improper. ... For competition and for the rough and tumble of the world of commerce, there is tolerance ... .

It is one thing to lure a customer away from someone with whom it has been doing business by means of better product, service, or prices, but quite another to abet the repudiation of solemn contractual obligations of which the party interfering is well aware. Indelicato not only knew Melo-Tone's contract with Sherry still had five years to run, but also received a copy of it. Indelicato went beyond inducing Sherry to commit a breach of contract, itself sufficient to make out the tort; he abetted the breach by paying to have his competitor's machines unlawfully moved from Sherry's premises. ... The means were improper and spoke eloquently to Indelicato's purpose, although it is enough to prove either improper means or motive.

CASE QUESTIONS

1. Could Melo-Tone have won the case against Indelicato for breach of contract? Why or why not?

2. In what way could Indelicato legally compete with Melo-Tone for Sherry's business?

3. In the penultimate paragraph we learn that one of Indelicato's defenses was "the rough and tumble of the world of commerce." What is meant by this expression?

Catering and Convention Contracts

Restaurants and hotels should exercise great care when entering a catering contract to ensure the parties are in agreement on all the terms. Mistakes made at banquets or other catered affairs can cause very unhappy customers.

Given the many details involved when planning a catered event, there is virtually no excuse for not having a written contract. The items that should be included in the writing are identified in Figure 4-1 on page 118.

Leaving any of these terms undecided or unclear can result in a displeased patron, lost opportunity for repeat business, and a lawsuit for breach of contract. By putting the agreement in writing and including in it the parties' understandings on all terms, the restaurant is protected against unjustified complaints from the customer. If, for example, the customer complains because no ham is included on the cold-cut trays and the restaurant can point to a contract provision that lists the meats to be included and ham is not among them, the customer cannot reasonably continue to complain. The written contract goes a long way to ensuring a successful event, goodwill with the patron, and avoidance of litigation.

Another type of contract that requires much planning and involves many details is a convention contract—that is, a contract between an organization planning a conference and the hotel at which the conference will be held. Typically, conventions held at hotels are annual gatherings of an organization's members who come from a wide geographical area. The organization might be a professional association such as accountants, or a group with a common interest such as religion, athletics, or a hobby.

CATERING CONTRACT

The following subjects should be addressed in a catering contract:

1. Names and addresses of the restaurant and the customer.
2. The date of the affair.
3. The location at which the food will be served (for example, the customer's home, a park lodge, or a specific room in the restaurant). If in the restaurant, the time limit on the use of the room, if any.
4. The shape and arrangement of the tables.
5. The type of flatware to be used—paper plates, china, or other types.
6. If the food is to be served away from the restaurant, what kitchen/cooking facilities will be available for the restaurant staff and when they will be available.
7. If the location is away from the restaurant, whose dishes will be used—the restaurant's or the customer's?
8. The type of service ordered (buffet or sit-down).
9. The menu in its entirety.
10. If hors d'oeuvres are ordered, whether they will be served on a table, carried by servers, or a combination of both.
11. Whether the restaurant will provide liquor, and if so, what types? Will there be an open bar (guests pay no fee for drinks) or cash bar (guests pay for their own drinks)?
12. Will the restaurant provide bartenders, and if so, how many?
13. Decorations, color scheme, and theme.
14. Arrangements for a head table, if applicable.
15. Whether the restaurant will provide a musician or other entertainer.
16. The number of people expected; a minimum guaranteed number, if applicable; the date when the final count must be relayed to the caterer.
17. Price; amount of deposit; when payment is due; policy on gratuities.
18. Circumstances under which the price might be adjusted; for example, an increase in the costs of food, beverage, or labor between when the contract was entered and the date of the affair.
19. Equipment to be provided by caterer.
20. Attire of servers.
21. Parking arrangements (for example, whether valet services will be provided).
22. Circumstances under which the caterer will be excused from performance, such as labor troubles, accidents, restrictions on availability of food or beverage, or other causes beyond the caterer's control.
23. Cancelation policy, including any penalties that will be charged.
24. Any other terms relevant to the particular event.

Figure 4-1 Recommended subjects for a catering contract

The services offered to conventioneers by a hotel are many and varied. In addition to rooms, they can include food, banquet facilities, recreational facilities, entertainment, meeting rooms, presentation equipment such as overhead projectors, and tourist information about the area. The particular services to be provided at a given convention are subject to agreement between the sponsoring organization and the hotel. Some conventions are elaborate affairs while others are low-cost operations. The hotel and the association must discuss what services the organization desires and can afford, and what services the hotel is willing and able to provide. Customarily, a representative from the organization will negotiate with the hotel on these matters.

The parties should prepare a written contract embodying their agreement. The terms in the contract should be specific and unambiguous to avoid later disputes.

A thorough contract will contribute greatly to a smooth flow of events during the convention. The written contract should include the terms identified in Figure 4-2.

CONVENTION CONTRACT

The following subjects should be addressed in a convention contract:

1. The name and address of the hotel, organization, and person(s) authorized to act on behalf of the organization.
2. The dates of the convention.
3. The number of guest rooms the hotel will hold for the organization's members and whether the association will be liable if all the reserved rooms are not rented by members.
4. The type of rooms (luxury, medium-priced, budget).
5. The location of the rooms (for example, main building or a wing).
6. The deadline for convention-goers to make reservations.
7. The method for convention-goers to reserve rooms.
8. Check-in and check-out procedures.
9. The number of meals to be provided by the hotel.
10. All the applicable terms identified in Figure 4-1 for catering contracts.
11. Number and location of meeting and exhibit rooms.
12. The arrangement of tables and/or chairs in meeting rooms.
13. The type of equipment to be provided in meeting rooms (for example, audio/visual equipment, including computer hook-ups).
14. Cancellation deadline and terms.
15. Restrictions on posting signs and announcements in the hotel, if any.
16. Any other special services to be provided by the hotel, such as food for coffee breaks, a hospitality suite, complimentary rooms, or entertainment.
17. Any other terms relevant to the particular event.

Figure 4-2 Recommended subjects for a convention contract

Key Terms

absolute	contract
acceptance	counteroffer
agreement not to compete	damages
antitrust laws	duress
attrition clause	forbearance
breach of contract	fraud
capacity to contract	genuine assent
compensatory damages	goodwill
condition	illusory
consideration	innocent misrepresentation

invitations to negotiate
mitigate
mutuality
mutual mistake
no-cause termination clause
offer
offeree
offeror
parol

parol evidence rule
specific performance
Statute of Frauds
tort
trade usage
unilateral mistake
valid
voidable contract
void contract

Summary

By using contracts, a hotel or restaurant can create legally binding obligations. To be enforceable, a contract must satisfy the following essential elements: contractual capacity, mutuality, legality, consideration, proper form, and genuine assent.

Failure to perform a contractual obligation constitutes breach of contract. Overbooking by a hotel resulting in cancellation of reservations constitutes breach of contract, as does cancellation by a guest.

A party breaching a valid contract will be liable to compensate the nonbreaching party for its resulting loss. The nonbreaching party must be able to prove the damages to a reasonable certainty and must attempt to mitigate the loss.

While most oral contracts are enforceable, they may be difficult to prove. Whenever possible, contracts should be reduced to writing. This is particularly important for catering and convention contracts because of the many details involved. Well-written contracts will help achieve and maintain good relationships with patrons and avoid lawsuits.

Preventive Law Tips for Managers

- *Be sure your contracts contain the six essential elements.* To be enforceable, a contract must have six essential elements: legality, proper form, contractual capacity, mutuality, consideration, and genuine assent. If even one is missing, the enforceability of the contract is in jeopardy.

- *Do not enter an illegal contract.* Contracts that are illegal are unenforceable. If you enter an illegal contract, you will not be able to sue for damages or enforce the contract. Assume your business generates toxic wastes. The law requires specific procedures be followed for their disposal. To save money, you contract with a company to dispose of those wastes illegally. You pay the company but it fails to discard the wastes. You will not be able to regain your money; because you were a party to an illegal contract, the courts will not come to your aid.

- *For contracts covered by the Statute of Frauds, be sure to generate a writing signed by the other contracting party.* Contracts covered by the Statute of Frauds are unenforceable without a writing. The writing must be signed by the defendant party, which means your concern is to get the other party's signature. Without the signed writing, you will not be able to pursue a breach of contract case. Contracts required to be in writing include: contracts for the purchase and sale of real estate; contracts that cannot be completed within one year from when they are made; contracts to pay another's debts; and contracts for the sale $500 or more of goods.

■ *Reduce all your contracts to writing even if they are not covered by the Statute of Frauds.* A party can easily prove the existence and terms of a written contract. The writing indisputably establishes the terms. An oral contract is difficult to prove. The only evidence is your word and that of the other contracting party. In a disagreement, you lack documentation to prove the truthfulness of your position. If the dispute goes to court, a judge or jury will determine which party is telling the truth. The process is cumbersome, and the wrong person could win. A written contract avoids these problems and facilitates easy resolution of contract disputes.

■ *Include in written contracts all the agreed-upon terms.* A written contract should contain the entire agreement between the parties. The parol evidence rule prevents parties from modifying a written contract with evidence of additional terms agreed upon by the parties but not included in the writing. Failure to include a term in the writing will result in that provision being unenforceable. Review your contracts carefully before signing them to ensure they are complete.

■ *Use clear and unambiguous language in your contracts. Know the meaning of the contract terms.* When contract terms are unclear and a dispute results, their meaning may be determined by reference to trade usage. The application of trade usage may or may not result in terms the parties intended when they entered the contract. It is best to use clear language. Also, before working in an industry you should familiarize yourself with the jargon. Use of terms with double meanings—one from normal parlance and the other from industry usage—can produce unexpected and unwanted results. If your contracts contain a cancellation, attrition, or no-cause cancellation clause, be sure the wording is intelligible so as to achieve your objective. If the contract is unclear, the provisions may not be enforceable.

■ *Keep good records of information that might be helpful in proving the amount of damages suffered from a breach of a contract.* To recover damages for breach of contract, the nonbreaching party must prove the amount of the loss to a reasonable certainty. Maintaining good records of such matters as sales figures, occupancy rates, and cost of supplies can enhance your ability to prove a loss.

■ *Mitigate damages resulting from breach of contract.* To collect damages for breach of contract, the nonbreaching party must mitigate its loss. Failing to attempt to reduce the loss may negate the right to obtain damages for a breach. Whenever someone breaches a contract with you, consider what you might reasonably do to avoid or reduce the loss, and do it.

■ *If you have overbooked and cannot accommodate would-be guests with reservations, assist in locating alternate accommodations, and be sure your staff is courteous.* If you are unable to provide accommodations to a guest with reservations, you are in breach of contract. To assist the customer and defuse a lawsuit, be as helpful to the would-be guest as possible. At a minimum, help arrange alternate accommodations; pay for transportation to the second hotel; if the second room costs more, pay the difference; and pay for phone calls necessitated by the move, such as calls by the guest to home or office to inform relatives or colleagues of the new location. Additional courtesies may be in order; for example, a gift certificate for a discounted rate at a later time. Keep good records to establish the cause for the overbooking.

■ *If requiring a minimum stay at the hotel, be sure your contract with the guest clearly states the number of days required.* If your hotel is offering a special rate or event requiring a minimum stay, you will want to collect for the full period of the minimum stay, even in the event a guest departs early. To preclude the guests from arguing that they were unaware of the minimum stay and therefore should not have to pay, the contract should clearly state the minimum number of days required and the liability of guests to pay for those days even if they leave before the end of the minimum period.

■ *Draft detailed contracts for catering engagements.* Catering contracts involve numerous details, many of which are very important to your customer, the host of the event. To avoid misunderstandings and mix-ups, prepare a writing containing the agreement and all the details. Review the agreement prior to the affair to ensure that you provide all the contracted services and menu items.

■ *Draft detailed contracts for convention agreements.* Convention contracts also involve many details and an ongoing relationship while the convention progresses from planning to execution, often a lengthy period. To avoid disputes and unnecessary ill will, document all decisions and agreements relating to every aspect of the convention. Review the agreement prior to the convention to ensure that you provide all the contracted services. Failure to utilize and review written contracts can foreseeably lead to dissatisfaction with the hotel's service, thus jeopardizing future business opportunities with the organization. An avoidable lawsuit might also result.

■ *Be watchful for developments in the law of contracts pertaining to the Internet.* Changes in the law are to be anticipated given the growing popularity of the Internet as a means to transact business. Keep abreast by reading industry journals, trade-association newsletters, and newspapers of general circulation.

Review Questions

1. What are the six essential elements of a contract?
2. What categories of people lack contractual capacity?
3. What is meant by mutuality?

4. What is the legal effect of an illegal contract?

5. Name three types of contracts that are unenforceable unless they are in writing.

6. Which of the following types of damages will a plaintiff in a breach of contract case be able to recover?
   A. Lost profits
   B. Pain and suffering
   C. Punitive damages

7. If a guest cancels her reservation with a hotel, how can the hotel mitigate its loss?

8. If a plaintiff in a breach of contract case is unable to determine the amount of its loss, is it entitled to recover any damages?

9. List eight items that should be included in a catering contract.

10. List eight items that should be included in a convention contract. Do not include any of the items you listed in response to question 9.

11. What is an agreement not to compete?

12. What is an attrition clause?

13. What is a no-cause termination clause?

14. What are the elements of a claim for interference with contractual relations?

15. As a general rule, are contracts entered into on the Internet valid?

Discussion Questions

1. Identify whether each of the following is an offer or an invitation to negotiate.
   A. Three pounds of fresh shrimp will cost $23.50.
   B. I will play the piano at your restaurant from 5:30 until 9:00 P.M. every night during October for $50 a night.
   C. I have gourmet ice cream for sale.
   D. I am thinking about selling my motel.
   E. Private swimming lessons are available at the hotel pool for $25 per half hour.

2. Why, in a breach of contract case, must the amount of the plaintiff's damages be proven to a reasonable certainty?

3. If a contract term is ambiguous, how will a court decide its meaning? How can parties to a contract avoid ambiguity?

4. Which of the following contracts must be in writing to be enforceable?
   A. A contract to hire a banquet manager for three years.
   B. A promise made by a casino patron to cover the betting debts of his friend.
   C. A contract to hire a musical trio to play for three weekends at a restaurant for a total of $1200.
   D. A contract to purchase three acres of land on which the buyer intends to build a restaurant.

5. Why does the law require a nonbreaching party to mitigate damages?

6. Why, as a practical matter, should all contracts be in writing?

7. What determines the obligations owed to a hotel when a person or organization with a hotel reservation cancels the reservation?

8. To successfully pursue a case for interference with contractual relations the plaintiff must prove, in addition to other elements, that the defendant was aware of the existence of the contract between the plaintiff and a third person. What is the policy reason for making this a necessary element?

Application Questions

1. In a telephone conversation with a sales representative of a linen company, the manager of a hotel ordered $1000 worth of sheets. Following the conversation he wrote a memo to file documenting the agreement, initialed it, and sent a copy to the sales representative. A dispute arose between the parties and the linen company sued the hotel. Does the parol-evidence rule bar the lawsuit? Why or why not?

2. Laurie is planning a reception for her parents' fiftieth wedding anniversary. She and her parents keep kosher, which means they follow dietary laws prescribed by the Jewish religion. She decided to hold the anniversary party at the Westside Party House because the manager, under pressure to increase sales, told Laurie the Party House serves kosher food. Laurie later discovers that the Party House does not serve kosher food. If she cancels her contract with the Party House and holds the party elsewhere, will she be liable to the Party House for breach of contract? Why or why not?

3. A restaurant ordered 20 cases of champagne for New Year's Eve. Delivery was due on December 29, but the seller failed to deliver. As a result the restaurant was unable to offer its New Year's Eve patrons a midnight champagne toast. The hotel sued the seller for breach of contract, claiming lost profits from the midnight toast and from future parties the angry patrons would be discouraged from hosting at the restaurant. Discuss the restaurant's chances for success in this lawsuit.

4. A contract for laundry services between a hotel and a linen company contains an ambiguous term. A dispute arose concerning the term and the parties to the contract interpreted it differently. A lawsuit resulted. What rules of contract interpretation will the court use to determine the meaning of the unclear term?

5. Tyshawn sold a bar he owned to Nicolette. A provision in the contract precluded Tyshawn from opening another food or beverage establishment within ten miles of the bar for a two-year period. If Tyshawn bought and operated a Motel Six franchise within the ten-mile radius of the bar and within one year after the sale, would he be in violation of the contract? Why or why not?

Web Sites

Web sites that will enhance your understanding of the material in this chapter include:

http://www.findlaw.com This site contains a great deal of legal information, including good material on contracts.

http://www.nolo.com/lawcenter/faqs Once on this site, click on *Consumer & Travel*, then scroll down to *Hotels and Other Accommodations FAQ*. Several questions and answers address legal issues associated with various hotel contracts, including room reservations and breach of contract by the hotel for providing lower-quality facilities than advertised.

UNIT II

■

Negligence

■

CHAPTER 5

■

Principles of Negligence

CHAPTER OUTLINE

■

Introduction	Negligence Doctrines Generall Favoring the Plaintiff
Negligence	Negligence Doctrines Generally Favoring the Defendant

INTRODUCTION

Guests at a hotel or restaurant can injure themselves in many ways. One might trip in the dining room. Another might suffer burns from scalding water in a shower. Yet another might drown in the pool. This chapter answers the question, When is the hotel or restaurant liable for guests' injuries? Stated differently, must the hospitality facility compensate patrons for injuries they suffer while at the restaurant or hotel?

The answer depends on whether the establishment violated a legal duty. The hotel or restaurant is not an insurer of guests' safety. This means the hotel is not liable for all injuries that occur while guests are on the premises. With few exceptions, the hotel or restaurant will only be liable when it does something wrong— that is, when the hotel or restaurant commits a tort. The term *tort* refers to many types of noncriminal wrongs done by one person that injure another, but not to breaches of contract. If the guest who tripped in the dining room did so because the heel on her shoe broke due to shoddy workmanship, the restaurant did not do anything wrong and therefore will not be liable. Similarly, if the scalding water in the shower occurred because the guest carelessly left the knob turned to hot, the hotel will not be obligated to compensate the guest. If, however, the patron tripped on a hole in the dining-room rug, or the hot water resulted from a defective plumbing system, the restaurant or hotel may indeed be liable to the guest.

Negligence

As was mentioned in Chapter 1, **negligence** is the breach of a legal duty to act reasonably that is the direct (or proximate) cause of injury to another. In nonlegal language, negligence is carelessness that causes harm. Assume the hole in the restaurant rug had been there for two weeks. Failure to fix the hole is careless; the restaurant could anticipate that someone would be injured by it. As a result, the restaurant will be liable for the customer's injury.

Assume the hotel had received several complaints about excessively hot water during the week before the accident, yet the hotel had not called a plumber or taken any steps to fix the problem. Failure to investigate and correct the water problem was careless; the hotel could anticipate that someone would be harmed. As a result, the hotel will be liable to the injured guest.

The law requires that people and businesses act reasonably in attempting to prevent injuries. When someone acts unreasonably or carelessly, that person is negligent. A reasonable restaurant employee, seeing a hole in the dining-room rug, would repair it to avoid an accident. A reasonable hotel employee who had been alerted about hot-water problems in the hotel would investigate and correct the problem. Failure to make the necessary repairs in these examples constitutes negligence.

If the cause of a hotel guest's injury was the carelessness of an employee, the hotel will be liable to the guest. Managers and employees of restaurants and hotels should strive to act reasonably in the way they perform their duties to avoid liability for negligence. The cases in this chapter and in Chapter 6 will illustrate some of the countless injuries that can occur at a restaurant or hotel that may result in liability. By reading these cases, future hospitality managers will begin to appreciate situations that can cause injuries and will cultivate a keener eye with which to survey hotels and restaurants to ensure they are in suitable condition for customers and guests.

Elements of a Negligence Case

A plaintiff suing in negligence must prove four elements; failure to prove any one of them is fatal to the plaintiff's case. The four elements are

1. The existence of a legal duty to act reasonably owed by the defendant to the plaintiff
2. A breach of that duty
3. Injury to the plaintiff
4. Proximate cause.

This last element means the breach of duty must be the direct cause of the injury and no intervening cause exists. Let us examine each element individually.

Existence of a Duty to Act Reasonably

Surprisingly, we do not owe *everyone* the duty to act reasonably. We owe the duty only to those people who would foreseeably be injured by our actions. A restaurant can foresee that if the leg of a chair is broken, a patron will sit on the chair and fall. Therefore, the restaurant owes a duty to its guests to repair the chair. If a restaurant or hotel cannot foresee a particular type of injury, it does not owe a duty to protect patrons against that injury even though someone is in fact injured.

In the following case, the court concluded that hotel guests could not have foreseen that their son would sexually assault a housekeeper. Therefore, the parents owed no duty to closely monitor their son's activities.

CASE EXAMPLE 5-1

Ordonez v. Gillespie
2001 WL 294553 (Tex. 2001)

... Ordonez alleged that on or about March 9, 1996 she was working as a housekeeper at a Dallas hotel. The Gillespies had rented adjoining rooms 1224 and 1225. While cleaning room 1224, Ordonez alleged she was sexually assaulted by seventeen-year-old Jason Gillespie, who is mentally challenged. Ordonez alleged the Gillespies acted negligently "by violating the duty which they owed her to exercise ordinary care in the care of their mentally challenged son, a minor." More specifically, Ordonez asserted the Gillespies failed to properly supervise their son, which included failing to ensure Jason would not be left alone with unfamiliar people. ... The Gillespies asserted that Jason's alleged conduct was not foreseeable to his parents ... The trial court granted summary judgment for the Gillespies. ...

Ordonez contends a duty existed because Jason's alleged sexual assault [was] a foreseeable result of the Gillespies' negligently leaving him alone in a hotel room.

Negligence consists of three essential elements: (1) a legal duty owed by one person to another; (2) a breach of that duty; and (3) damages proximately resulting from the breach. Duty is the threshold inquiry. It is the function of several interrelated factors, the foremost and dominant consideration being foreseeability of the risk. A parent's duty to protect third parties from acts of the parent's minor

child depends on whether the injury to the third party is reasonably foreseeable. Foreseeability means the [defendant], as a person of ordinary intelligence, should have anticipated the dangers his negligent act created for others. ...

Ordonez relies on a copy of the Gillespies' hotel reservation for room 1225 which includes the notation that the Gillespies needed to be connected to their mentally handicapped son. [Evidence also indicates that] at school Jason "disrupted the class" and "got into a lot of trouble". The Gillespies put Jason in a boarding school in Massachusetts "for kids with psychological or school problems." After six or eight months he was asked to leave the facility because he had run away a couple of times and smoked in the high school. He got his GED when he was sixteen.

... Jason had never been detained for any type of criminal activity.

It was Ordonez' burden to present some evidence that Jason's conduct was foreseeable to his parents. We conclude she failed to do so. Evidence that Jason did not like school and disrupted class is no evidence that his parents should have foreseen the possibility that he was capable of assaultive conduct. Likewise, evidence that Jason's parents considered him to be mentally handicapped is no evidence that it was foreseeable he might be a danger to others. The trial court properly granted the Gillespies' motion for summary judgment.

CASE QUESTION

1. What changes in the facts might have resulted in the Gillespies being liable?

In another case, a bridesmaid was injured at the wedding reception when several party-goers, participating in a "wheelbarrow race" (where one person walks on his hands and his partner runs and steers from behind by holding the legs of the first person) ran into her from behind. She sued the restaurant at which the reception was held, claiming it had not adequately protected her safety. The court, noting that the race was "spontaneous and inappropriate," found the restaurant could not have anticipated the contest and thus owed no duty to protect the plaintiff from it.[1]

The owner of an amusement park has no duty to protect patrons against unforeseeable and unexpected assaults. Thus, where a patron who had just exited the roller coaster was attacked spontaneously and unexpectedly, the park was not liable for failing to prevent the assault.[2]

Similarly, a restaurant owed no duty to protect patrons from a firecracker that was unexpectedly thrown into the establishment by an unknown person. The firecracker shattered a glass picture frame propelling shards of glass that hit a diner and caused permanent injury. The restaurant could not reasonably foresee this type of injury, and so it had no duty to protect customers against it.[3]

Where the presence of bees could not be foreseen, an inn hosting a fiftieth-wedding-anniversary party did not owe a duty to protect the guests from being stung. A guest was stung resulting in anaphylactic shock and cardiac arrest causing permanent quadriplegia. The circumstances included the following: In the 20 years prior to this incident no other guest had been stung; at the time of the sting the bee was isolated and not in a swarm; no hive or nest was found on the premises; and the inn was maintained in a similar manner.[4]

In all of these cases, since no duty was owed, the lawsuits were dismissed.

Breach of Duty

For a defendant to be liable for negligence, the defendant must not only owe a duty to the plaintiff to act reasonably, but must also breach that duty. A restaurant owes a duty to its customers not to serve rancid food because customers who eat it will foreseeably become ill. If the restaurant serves spoiled food, it thereby breaches that duty.

Failure by a private club to maintain floors in its building in a safe condition constitutes a breach of duty to those who utilize the premises. Another example of a breach of duty involves an Elks Club (an organization that exists to foster fellowship among its members and to provide services to the community) that maintained a building with a dining room and kitchen. A portion of the kitchen floor had sunk and split resulting in a crack in excess of four to six inches between lateral floor joists. The plaintiff, wife of an Elks member, was helping to set up for a dinner. She fell on the crack, which had been covered by a mat, and sued the club. She was able to prove that the Elks had been aware of the problem for at least

---

[1] *Lee v. Durow's Restaurant, Inc.*, 656 N.Y.S.2d 321 (App. Div. 2nd Dept. 1997)

[2] *Scotti v. W.M. Amusements*, 266 A.D.2d 522, 640 N.Y.S.2d 617 (2nd Dept. 1996)

[3] *Mee-Hsiang Lee v. 69 Mott Street Corporation*, 638 N.Y.S.2d 261 (N.Y. 1999)

[4] *Febesh v. Hollow Inn*, 157 A.D.2d 102, 555 N.Y.S.2d 46 (N.Y. 1990)

two years. The club had investigated repairs but failed to take any remedial action. The Elks use of a mat to cover up the crack makes it unlikely a person using the kitchen would see the hole. The appeals court affirmed a judgment entered for the plaintiff by the trial court.[5]

A hotel owes its guests and the occupants of adjacent buildings a duty to maintain fire extinguishers in operable condition. Failure to do so will forseeably cause injury in the event of a fire and so constitutes a breach of duty. In a case where a hotel fire spread to and destroyed an adjacent saloon, hotel guests had attempted to put out the fire. These efforts were unsuccessful because of a faulty and nonserviceable fire extinguisher. The hotel thus breached its duty to take reasonable measures to prevent the spread of fire and was liable to the bar for its loss.[6]

Determining if the defendant acted reasonably is not always easy. The law provides a standard to help judge whether a defendant's actions were or were not within the bounds of the law. Though difficult to apply in some cases, it is a helpful guide. The standard is a mythical "reasonable person of ordinary prudence." The issue in each case is whether the defendant acted as a reasonable person of ordinary prudence would have acted under similar circumstances.

Sometimes this imaginary person is described in cases by judges not only as "reasonable" and "prudent" but also as "a person of average prudence," or even as "a person of ordinary sense using ordinary care and skill." All these phrases mean much the same thing. This reasonable person does not have bad days; he is always up to standard, a personification of a community ideal of reasonable behavior. What constitutes reasonable behavior in a given situation is determined by a jury or, in a bench trial, by the judge.

If the defendant in a lawsuit has not breached a duty, the defendant is not liable. The plaintiff has the burden of proving the defendant's wrongdoing. If the plaintiff is unable to prove that the defendant breached a duty, the plaintiff will not be able to recover.

This principle is evidenced in a case in which a plaintiff fell while dancing at the defendant's restaurant. Testimony established that servers carried beverages onto the dance floor on the night in question. The court denied the plaintiff a recovery, saying it would be "sheer speculation" to conclude that the liquid substance that caused the plaintiff's fall was spillage from a beverage carried by a server as opposed to a dancer or other customer.[7]

In another case the plaintiff was a model in a fashion show at the defendant's hotel. While she was exiting the stage after one of her walks down the runway, she tripped and fell on something "liquidy." She did not know what caused the liquid. She testified that there was a dishwasher room that opened into the hallway used by the models and that the defendant's employees washed dishes during the fashion show. The hallway was not in close proximity to the stage. Further, the plaintiff was uncertain if she in fact stepped in any substance when she fell, she did not pay attention to whether there was any water on the stage or the stairs, and she did

---

[5] *White v. Waterbury*, 2001 WL 477381 (Conn. 2001)

[6] *Bartelli v. O'Brien*, 718 N.E.2d 344 (Ill. 1999)

[7] *Funt v. Saul Rubinstein Trust*, 686 N.Y.S.2d 111 (1999)

not notice any substance on her shoes after the fall. The court said the plaintiff was merely speculating as to the cause of her fall and awarded judgment for the hotel.[8]

The following case also illustrates that a plaintiff in a negligence case must prove that the cause of injury was the defendant's carelessness. The plaintiff was injured when someone fell on her at a hotel restaurant. She sued both the hotel and the person who fell on her.

CASE EXAMPLE 5-2

Shadburn v. Whitlow
533 S.E.2d 765 (Ga. 2000)

... [T]he record shows that Shadburn, Whitlow, and Jewel Palmer were on their way to Ormond Beach, Florida. En route, they stopped at New Perry Hotel to eat lunch. The three proceeded up a flight of stairs to the hotel restaurant. Palmer proceeded first, followed by Shadburn. Whitlow, an elderly woman who had impaired vision due to cataracts, followed last. Palmer was waiting in line at the restaurant when she heard a noise. Turning, she saw Whitlow, who had reached the top of the stairs, fall into Shadburn who was standing in the lobby area. Shadburn was injured.

Palmer and Shadburn believed Whitlow's fall was caused by loose carpeting which they noticed at the top of the stairwell the evening after the fall; however, all three ladies testified that they were not actually certain what caused Whitlow to fall. Palmer also averred in her affidavit that Whitlow may have tripped because she may have been inebriated after sipping an unknown beverage from a cup during the trip to Perry.

The trial court properly granted summary judgment to New Perry Hotel because Shadburn failed to present any evidence that a condition on the stairs, the loose carpeting, caused Whitlow to fall. The speculation that Whitlow may have tripped on loose carpeting does not sufficiently establish causation.

On the issue of causation, as on other issues essential to a cause of action for negligence, the plaintiff, in general, has the burden of proof. The plaintiff must introduce evidence which affords a reasonable basis for the conclusion that it is more likely than not that the conduct of the defendant was a cause in fact of the result. A mere possibility of such causation is not enough; and when the matter remains one of pure speculation or conjecture, or the probabilities are at least evenly balanced, it becomes the duty of the court to grant summary judgment for the defendant.

Similarly, the trial court also properly granted summary judgment to Whitlow because there is not evidence that Shadburn's injuries were caused by an act or omission of Whitlow. There is no evidence in the record of the cause of Whitlow's fall. Shadburn can point only to speculation that Whitlow may have tripped and fallen because she was inebriated.

CASE QUESTION

1. What more would the plaintiff need to prove to establish that the defendant in this case breached a duty?

Proximate Cause

The **proximate cause** of an injury refers to its direct and immediate cause. The requirement of proximate cause means that the injury must have been caused by

---

[8] *Thomas v. Grand Hyatt Hotel*, 749 F.Supp. 313 (D.C. 1990)

the breach of duty; in other words, there must be a cause-and-effect relationship between the injury and the unreasonable conduct. The connection also must be direct or immediate, so that a reasonable person could foresee the potential danger of the careless act.

For example, assume a hotel van driver was adjusting the radio while driving and not watching the road. He carelessly swerved up and over a curb and came to a stop near the sidewalk. A rollerblader was skating on the sidewalk near the van and was looking up at a low-flying plane. She thus failed to see an uneven spot in the cement slabs. She fell due to the jagged edges of the sidewalk. In this example, the hotel employee was negligent and the blader was injured. But the negligence was not the cause of the injury, so the hotel will not be liable.

In another example, shampoo was spilled in a hotel stairwell on the landing and the right side of the first step. The spillage had not been cleaned for more than a day, constituting negligence. A guest using the stairs slipped and was injured as she descended along the right side of the stairway on the third step below the landing. The cause of her fall was a break in the heel of her shoe. Although the hotel was negligent in not cleaning the shampoo, and although the guest was injured, the guest did not trip on the shampoo and thus her injuries were not the proximate cause of the hotel's negligence. The hotel was therefore not liable. For a case with similar facts, see *Munno v. State of New York*, 698 N.Y.S.2d 107 (1999).

If injuries suffered by a plaintiff who falls constitute a **preexisting condition** (a physical impairment suffered prior to the fall), the fall would not be a proximate cause of the injury. In this circumstance the hotel would not be liable for the pre-existing injury, even if the fall was the result of the hotel's negligence.[9] (*Note*: If the hotel's negligence aggravated an existing injury, the hotel will be liable for the additional injuries it caused.)

Events independent of and occurring after the defendant's alleged negligence may be the direct cause of the injury, rather than the defendant's negligence. Such an event is called an *intervening* or *superseding occurrence* and has the effect of breaking the chain of causation between the defendant's negligence and the plaintif's injury. In the following case, an intervening occurrence and not the hotel's negligence was determined to be the cause of the plaintiff's injury.

CASE EXAMPLE 5-3

Smith v. West Rochelle Travel Agency, Inc.
656 N.Y.S.2d 340 (2nd Dept. 1997)

... The plaintiffs commenced an action against all the parties who had any connection with a 1993 spring break vacation trip to the Bahamas in which their 17-year-old son, Thomas Smith, Jr. (hereinafter the decedent), participated. ... During the vacation, the decedent purchased a ticket for a "booze cruise", a sunset cruise in international waters where alcoholic beverages were sold to anyone, regardless of their age. The decedent voluntarily leapt overboard and was killed when he came in contact with the cruise vessel's propellers. The evidence

---

[9] *Hines v. KMart Corporation*, 2001 WL 709515 (Mich. 2001)

indicated that the vessel was not owned or operated by the defendant ... Wyndham Hotel Co., Ltd.

The parents sued Wyndham, the hotel at which the decedent was registered, arguing that since the groundhandler promoted the "booze cruise" on the hotel premises during an "orientation party" at which alcoholic beverages were served, the hotel bore some liability for facilitating the sale of tickets to the cruise. ...

[T]he court correctly determined that, as a matter of law, the decedent's action of voluntarily jumping off a moving vessel in open waters was a superseding event which severed whatever causal connection there may have been between the occurrence of the accident and Wyndham's alleged negligence three days earlier in permitting alcohol to be served on its premises during the orientation party. ...

In another case illustrating a superseding occurrence, a valet parking attendant at a nightclub negligently facilitated the theft of a patron's car. Later the same night a police officer observed the stolen car and attempted to stop it. The thief fled, first in the car and then on foot. The officer fell and was injured. He sued the nightclub for negligence. The case was dismissed because the club's negligence was not the direct cause of the injury. "The conduct of the thief was an intervening cause which the defendant was not bound to anticipate and guard against."[10]

Another example of a superseding cause of injury is provided by a case involving storage in a vat of used restaurant cooking oil pending pick-up by an oil retrieval company. The vat had malfunctioned and the restaurant called for service. The repair company failed to respond in a timely manner. The restaurant continued to use the vat. A restaurant employee was injured while pouring oil into the container. He was not wearing protective clothing and he used a "greasy and wobbly" ladder to reach the top of the vat. He sued the service company for negligence due to their delay in repairing the vat. The court dismissed the case, ruling that the negligence of the repair company was not the proximate cause of the employee's injuries. Instead, his own negligence was the cause.[11]

In *Messina v. Sheraton Corporation of America*, 291 So.2d 829 (La. 1974), the plaintiff was the promoter of a boxing match that was to feature one Beau Jaynes. The night before the fight, Jaynes injured his hand in his room at a Sheraton Hotel when a venetian blind collapsed as he was adjusting it. The boxing commission canceled the fight and the promoter sued the Sheraton to recover lost revenue. The court said that while Jaynes might have a good lawsuit against the hotel, the promoter did not. It is a basic principle of tort law that a wrongdoer is responsible only for the direct and proximate injuries resulting from its acts. When a third person such as a boxing promoter suffers damage because of a contractual relationship he has with the injured party, such damage is too remote and indirect to hold the wrongdoer liable.

---

[10] *Poskos v. Lombardo's of Randolph, Inc.*, 423 Mass. 637, 670 N.E.2d 383 (Mass. 1997)
[11] *Griffin Industries, Inc. v. Foodmaker, Inc.*, 2000 WL 714604 (Tex. 2000)

Injury

To win a lawsuit, a plaintiff must have been injured as a result of the defendant's breach of duty. The injury might be bodily harm (the legal term for this is "personal injury"), such as a broken arm or a head wound. The injury could also be property damage, such as a dented car, or it could be emotional suffering or monetary loss.

Summary of the Elements of Negligence

Remember, before a hotel or restaurant will be liable to a plaintiff for negligence, all four elements must be present: (1) the existence of a duty; (2) breach of that duty; (3) proximate cause; and (4) injury. If any element is missing, the hotel or restaurant is not liable.

Legal Status of Plaintiff

The duty of care owed by a hotel or restaurant for the safety of its patrons depends, in many states, on the legal status of the person injured. He may be an invitee, a licensee, or a trespasser. The greatest degree of care is owed to an invitee, the next greatest to a licensee, and the least to a trespasser.

Duty Owed to Invitees

In the hospitality industry, an **invitee** is someone who comes to an establishment for the purpose for which the business is open to the public, or for a purpose directly or indirectly connected with that business. For a hotel, invitees include guests and visitors of guests. If the hotel has stores or a theater-ticket service in the lobby and a nonguest enters the hotel to patronize the store or purchase tickets, that person also qualifies as an invitee. For a restaurant, diners are invitees. For a bar, patrons are invitees. For all three types of establishments, employees are invitees, as is a delivery person delivering some item necessary for the business such as food or alcohol.

The hotel or restaurant owes a duty to its invitees to reasonably inspect the premises for dangerous conditions and to exercise reasonable care to eliminate them. Liability may result if and only if the business (1) knows, or by the exercise of reasonable care would discover, a dangerous condition that presents an unreasonable risk of harm to invitees; and (2) should expect that invitees will not discover or realize the danger or will fail to protect themselves against it; and (3) fails to exercise reasonable care to protect its invitees against the danger. The necessary reasonable care (lack of negligence) encompasses both repair of and warning about the dangerous condition.

Assume that on a rainy night the floor in the entrance to a restaurant is wet and slippery. A patron entering the restaurant falls and is injured. Is the food establishment liable? The customer is an invitee, so the restaurant owes the duty to make a reasonable effort to discover the condition and eliminate it by mopping frequently, or at the very least, to warn of its presence. Failure to do so will result in liability. To determine if the restaurant is liable, we need to know how frequently it mopped the entrance. If it mopped regularly, the eatery may not be liable even though the guest fell. The duty is to exercise reasonable care, not to be right there the moment a drop of water gathers.

The duty to mop on a rainy day would require greater frequency than on a dry evening.

Active Vigilance Required

Note that ignorance on the part of the restaurant of the presence of the water on the floor and resulting slipperiness normally will not relieve the restaurant of liability. The restaurant has a duty to inspect for and discover the wetness, and then to protect guests from resulting risks. The following case illustrates this point.

CASE EXAMPLE 5-4

Montes v. Betcher
480 F.2d 1129 (8th Cir. 1973)

On the warm Sunday afternoon of July 13, 1968, 35 year old Fernando Montes, a citizen of Nebraska, took a running dive off a short dock which served the Appellants' resort, one of the many enhancing Minnesota's beautiful lakes. He surfaced with a severely lacerated scalp and a vertebral fracture. Shortly after the incident, a jagged piece of concrete was recovered from the lake floor in the general area where plaintiff had entered the water. The concrete piece resembled the home-made boat anchors constructed by Appellants to use in the boats which frequented the boat dock.

Plaintiff, Montes, a proficient swimmer and diver, claims that he executed a flat, "racing" dive because he knew he was plunging into shallow water. The water depth was variously described to be from 27 inches to waist level. Montes testified, however, that his ultimate purpose was to grab the ankles of a friend who was standing in the water 15 feet from the end of the dock, a purpose which would require either a deep dive or a subsequent submergence.

Montes was very familiar with the swimming area, and had executed dives from the boat dock on numerous previous occasions. Never before had he encountered rocks or blocks in the water.

The Appellants, Mr. and Mrs. Betcher, citizens of Minnesota, had owned the resort since 1963. They charged $10 per day for cabin accommodations. Although the area surrounding the boat dock was perennially in use by Appellants' swimmer-patrons and although Mr. Betcher had seen swimmers jump off the boat dock, he testified that he had never made any special attempt to inspect the lake bottom for debris nor had he ever "raked" the shoreline lake bottom. Never had he erected signs warning of the dangers of diving in the shallow water or the possible presence of debris in the swimming area. Never had he placed floats in the water to discourage the intrusion of boats into the swimming and diving area; in fact there was no segregation whatsoever of swimming waters from boating waters. ...

Appellants ... first contend that a riparian owner [an owner of waterfront property] is not responsible for the safe maintenance of property beyond the ... line ... that marks the boundary between Appellants' shoreline land and submerged land which belongs to the state. But even if Appellants are held responsible for the maintenance of submerged lands, Appellants contend, that responsibility extends only to the remedy of dangerous conditions known to Appellants or of which they could have acquired knowledge had they ... exercised reasonable care. Since there was no evidence that Appellants knew of the presence of the cement block nor that it had been there long enough to mandate ... constructive knowledge, Appellants contend [they breached no duty]. ...

[This argument was properly rejected.] ... A resort owner who avails himself of the advantages of riparian ownership for resort purposes owes to his patrons a duty of reasonable care which includes "active vigilance" in their protection from foreseeable risks. ...

The jury was perfectly justified in determining that Appellants had violated this duty in any one or more of three respects: (1) their failure to warn of the dangers of diving off the boat dock; (2) their failure to periodically "rake" the swimming-diving area in search of dangerous obstructions; and (3) their failure to segregate swimming areas from boating areas.

CASE QUESTIONS

1. What is meant by *constructive notice*, as used in the fifth paragraph?

2. We are told that Montes had two or three drinks the afternoon of the accident. What effect do you think that should have on the outcome of the case?

This case clearly establishes that, for a resort to satisfy its obligation to an invitee, it is not enough to correct dangerous conditions of which the resort is aware. The business must also regularly inspect the premises to locate and identify dangerous conditions, correcting any that are found. If the hotel fails to inspect, it will be liable to invitees for injuries caused by conditions that an inspection would have revealed.

Invitees must also exercise some care in protecting themselves. Generally a hotel or restaurant will not be liable for injuries caused by a condition that is "open and obvious," meaning that the dangers are so obvious that the invitee can reasonably be expected to discover them. If the hazard is open and obvious, invitees are expected to protect themselves. For example, a patron of a Wendy's restaurant exited the restaurant via a concrete ramp, part of which was cracked. She tripped and fell on the cracked portion. The court denied her claim against the restaurant stating, "[I]t was a discrete hazard in an otherwise safe walkway which plaintiff could have easily avoided by stepping over it or walking around it. Because plaintiff tripped over a defect which was an open and obvious condition that could easily have been avoided, no interpretation of the evidence could render that defect an unreasonable hazard."[12] When sued for negligence, hotels and restaurants need to be alert to the possible defense that the condition was open and obvious.

Duty Owed to Licensees

A **licensee** is someone who has been given permission by the owner or occupier of a facility to enter or remain on the property, but his presence does not further the defendant's business. An example of a licensee is a waitress or front-desk clerk who,

---

[12] *Boyd v. Warren Restaurants, Inc.*, 2001 WL 753886 (Mich. 2001)

on a day off, goes to the place of employment to pick up a paycheck. At that time the employee is not advancing the employer's business interests, but nonetheless is on the premises with the employer's consent. Similarly, a former employee who enters the premises to meet with a current employee is a licensee.[13]

States define the duty owned to licensees differently. In a majority of the states, the duty owed is twofold

1. Refrain from willfully or wantonly injuring the licensee or acting in a manner to increase peril

2. Warn of any latent dangers on the premises of which the property owner has knowledge.

In some states, the duty owed to licensees is merely to refrain from willful or wanton injury.

Note that, for the invitee, the hotel or restaurant must inspect for dangerous conditions and either repair them or warn the invitee about them. For the licensee, the duty is less. The hotel or restaurant can dispense with the inspection. According to the majority rule, the hotel or restaurant's only duty is to warn of those dangers about which it knows. Thus, the hotel or restaurant must disclose known defects but need not make any effort to determine what defects exist. Had the plaintiff in *Montes v. Betcher*, Case Example 5-4, been a licensee rather than an invitee, the resort would have satisfied its obligation and the plaintiff would have lost the case.

In states where the minority rule applies, the hospitality facility does not even owe a duty to disclose and warn of known dangers.

The following case explores the circumstances under which a visitor of a hotel guest qualifies as an invitee and when he is treated as a licensee.

CASE EXAMPLE 5-5

Steinberg v. Irwin Operating Co.
90 So.2d 460 (Fla. 1956)

... Appellant, Essie Steinberg, accompanied two friends to the Cadillac Hotel operated by appellee. The purpose of the mission was to enable one of the friends to deliver a message to a registered guest at the hotel. Inquiry at the desk revealed that the registered guest was not in. Thereupon, Mrs. Steinberg and her friends decided to explore various lounges and other rooms adjacent to the lobby. This was done for their own diversion. They first went into a "TV Room." They didn't like the program then showing. They then apparently attempted to enter an adjoining "Movie Room." This room was dark except for the light cast by the movie screen and projector. The floor level of the "Movie Room" was four inches lower than the floor level of the "TV Room." Claiming that she did not see the difference in level, Mrs. Steinberg fell and suffered injuries. She filed a complaint seeking compensation for damages resulting from the alleged negligence of appellee. The alleged negligence was the difference in the floor level. ...

Appellant contends that at the time of the alleged injury, Mrs. Steinberg was an invitee of the hotel. They seek recovery on the theory that the hotel was obligated to furnish its invitees with reasonably safe premises.

---

[13]*Mutual Life Insurance Co. v. Churchwell*, 221 Ga. App. 312, 471 S.E.2d 267 (Ga. 1996)

Appellee contends that Mrs. Steinberg was merely a licensee. They assert that the only duty owed to her was to refrain from willfully or wantonly injuring her.

There is no doubt that a registered guest of a hotel is a business invitee and is entitled to receive the degree of care applicable to invitees. We are of the view that one entering a hotel to communicate with a registered guest is entitled to receive and enjoy the same degree of care. This rule is subject to the limitations hereafter expressed. ... [B]y the very nature of the business, the operator of the hotel is bound to anticipate that a registered guest is apt to have business and social callers. The invitation to such callers arises by operation of law out of the relationship between the hotel and its registered guests. The operator of the hotel should provide reasonably safe ways of ingress and egress for those legally entering and leaving the place pursuant to the implied invitation implicit in the relationship between hotel operator and registered guests.

However, this implied invitation is not without its limits. The invitation to enter the hotel to visit a guest is circumscribed by the rule that it extends only to appropriate usage of the means of ingress and egress, such as the lobby, elevator, hallways, and room area rented to the guest.

It would be stretching the doctrine of implied invitation beyond justifiable limits to hold that such invitation extends to all of the private or semi-public rooms of the hotel. When the visitor crosses the boundaries of the invitation, he ceases to be an invitee. His status then changes to that of a licensee or even a trespasser. He is entitled to the status of an invitee only to the extent justified by the implied invitation.

In this case, it is perfectly clear that Mrs. Steinberg enjoyed the status of an implied invitee when she entered the hotel lobby. This status continued so long as she used the facilities of the hotel reasonably included within the invitation. When, for her own pleasure and convenience, she crossed the bounds of the invitation on her own initiative, sought entertainment in the "TV Room," and later in the "Movie Room," she became at most a licensee. While she was in this status, the hotel owed to her only the duty to refrain from willfully or wantonly injuring her. The record is clear that there was no willful or wanton injury.

Ruling of the court: The judgment [for the hotel operator] is affirmed.

CASE QUESTIONS

1. What change of facts would be necessary to make Mrs. Steinberg an invitee at the time of her injury?

2. If Mrs. Steinberg was an invitee, what duty would the hotel have owed to her?

A Tennessee court dealt with the issue of the status of a guest's visitor in the case of *Kandrach v. Chrisman*, 473 S.W.2d 193 (Tenn. 1971). A young man drowned while he was visiting his fiance, who was a guest at the defendant's motel. Neither could swim. They entered the motel pool together at a time when no one else was in it. He was either walking or standing in the water when he suddenly started to struggle and sank beneath the surface. His survivors sued the hotel for negligence.

The case hinged on whether the deceased was an invitee. A sign at the end of the pool read, "Motel Guests Only." The lower court held that the visitor ceased to be an invitee upon entering the pool and that the motel from that time on owed him only the minimum duty owed to a trespasser. The appellate court reversed, saying that a visitor of a hotel guest is in fact an invitee of the hotel provided the visitor has not exceeded the bounds of the invitation to visit extended by the guest. In this case the visitor was invited by the guest to join her in the pool; thus, the hotel owed the deceased a duty to exercise reasonable care in the maintenance of the pool. Contrast this situation to the case where the hotel guest invites a visitor to lunch and when the meal is through bids him farewell. On his own initiative and unaccompanied by the hotel guest, he utilizes the pool. While in the pool, this visitor is beyond the parameters of the invitation to visit extended by the hotel guest and therefore is not an invitee of the hotel.

In a case discussed earlier in this chapter, the Elks (a service club) requested that the wife of the newly elected Exalted Ruler (the equivalent of president) come to the organization's headquarters to assist in the preparations for her husband's installation dinner. While helping to set the tables, she entered the kitchen seeking matching china. While there, she fell due to a sizeable crack in the floor and suffered substantial injuries. In her lawsuit against the association, the question arose as to whether she was an invitee or a licensee when she entered the kitchen. The court first addressed her status when she entered the building. Since she had been invited to the premises by Elks members, she qualified as an invitee. She remained an invitee when she walked into the kitchen since "it was reasonable to expect as part of her functions that day that she would need to go into the kitchen."[14]

Duty Owed to Trespassers

The least duty is owed to a **trespasser**—a person who enters a place without the permission of the owner or occupier. If an employee who has been fired and ordered not to return to the hotel nonetheless enters the premises, he is a trespasser. Someone who enters a restaurant after it is closed for the night without the owner's permission is a trespasser. A landowner or possessor does not owe a duty to safeguard a trespasser from injury caused by conditions on the land. Some states impose a duty not to willfully or randomly injure a trespasser, and other states impose this duty only when the trespasser's presence is known or reasonably foreseeable. For example, a trespasser's presence would be known or foreseeable where neighborhood children regularly use vacant land for snowmobiling that is located adjacent to, and owned by, a hotel and the hotel is aware of this use.

The following case illustrates the application of the rule for trespassers.

CASE EXAMPLE 5-6

David Hanson v. Hyatt Corp.
196 Ill.3d 618, 554 N.E.2d 394 (1990)

[P]laintiff was not a registered guest at defendant's hotel. He entered the pool area sometime after 9:30 P.M. through a gap/hole in a fence surrounding the pool. It was dark, and the lights around the pool area were off. ...

[H]e dove into Hyatt's pool and sustained injuries which rendered him a quadriplegic; he was 19 years old at the time of the accident. ...

---

[14] *White v. Waterbury Lodge*, 2001 WL 477381 (Conn. 2001)

Hanson argues that he properly alleged the element of duty ... based upon Hyatt's "implied invitation" to him to enter upon its premises "for the purpose of inspection and use of its restaurant, gift shop, meeting rooms, lobbies, and swimming pool," as a licensee or invitee. The implied invitation concerning his use of Hyatt's swimming pool is specifically based on the allegation that the pool "was not fully enclosed and was open to access by the public at large."...

Hanson was required to allege facts to support a relationship which imposed a duty on Hyatt to protect him from his injury. ...

A [business operator] has a duty to exercise reasonable care for the safety of an invitee. The duty owed to a licensee or trespasser is not to willfully and wantonly injure him and to use ordinary care to avoid injuring him after he is discovered in a place of danger.

Hanson ... appears to define an implied invitation as a failure by Hyatt to take reasonable steps to secure access to the pool area, presumably by closing up a hole in the fence through which he entered on the date of the accident ... We find this argument without merit. ... [T]o be upon premises by an implied invitation means that the person is there for a purpose connected with the business in which the owner of the premises is engaged. Here, Hanson simply failed to allege facts to support a position that he was using Hyatt's swimming pool for a reason connected with Hyatt's business ... Plaintiff is a trespasser. Judgment for the hotel.

CASE QUESTION

1. Why do you think the duty imposed on businesses vis-a-vis trespassers is significantly less than for invitees?

In another case, a plaintiff was hungry late one night and left his house to walk to Hardee's Restaurant. He took a shortcut through a parking lot of a then-closed Burger King. After arriving at Hardee's, he discovered he had forgotten his wallet. On this return trip he decided to see if there was any food in the Burger King dumpster. It was shielded on three sides by brick walls that were close to eight-feet tall, and on the fourth by a set of wooden hinged gates. In an attempt to enter the dumpster area, the plaintiff jumped up on one of the brick walls, which then collapsed, severely injuring him. Unbeknownst to the plaintiff, the wall had been damaged a month earlier by a trash truck and had not been repaired. Employees had been alerted not to touch the wall. The plaintiff sued Burger King, which in turn argued that the plaintiff was a trespasser and therefore Burger King owed him no duty to keep the wall safe. Agreeing with Burger King, the court stated, "[A] trespasser ... assumes the risk of injury from the condition of the premises. ... While a possessor of land may not intentionally set booby traps with the design of causing injury, the possessor owes no duty to adult trespassers for conditions on the premises."[15]

Minority Position

Some states have abolished the distinction between licensees, invitees, and trespassers and the duties owed to each. Instead, in those states the occupier of land

---

[15] *Cochran v. Burger King Corp.*, 937 S.W.2d 358 (Mo. Crt. App. 1996)

owes a duty of care to all three. However, even in these states the standard of reasonable care may vary with the circumstances of the visitor's entry on the premises.

No Special Duty Owed to Others

What about people who do not qualify as invitee, licensee, or trespasser? In most cases, no duty is owed. In the following case, the innkeeper had no relationship with the injured party and therefore owed no duty of care.

CASE EXAMPLE 5-7

Callender v. MCO Properties
885 P.2d 123 (Ariz. 1994)

... On March 26, 1988, appellant John Scott Callender was boating with friends on Lake Havasu. ... They steered the boat toward the beach at the Crazy Horse Campground. Two women occupants of the boat got out to retrieve an inflatable raft they had left at the beach. The young women attempted to row the raft out into the water. When Callender saw that they were having difficulty, he dived from the boat into the water to assist them. During the dive, however, he struck his head on the bottom of the lake, broke his neck, and was rendered a quadriplegic.

At the time of Callender's accident, the State of Arizona owned the land along the Lake Havasu shore where the Crazy Horse Campground was located. The federal government owned and controlled the lake itself. ... Appellees Ray and Marie Totah ... operated the Crazy Horse Campground. Callender filed a civil action ... alleging that the defendants failed to adequately warn that it was unsafe to dive in the water near the Crazy Horse Campground. ... In response, the Totahs pointed out that Callender's accident occurred between twenty and fifty feet offshore from the campground premises, Callender had not been a guest of the campground, nor had he ever been on the premises nor docked at the campground. Finally, they argued that the lake's

waters and subsurface were owned by the United States Department of the Interior and that Crazy Horse had no legal interest in those waters. The Totahs thus argued that they had no duty to Callender.

Callender argued in response that because the Totahs reasonably could foresee that patrons of the campground and nonpatrons in the company of patrons would approach the Crazy Horse beach by boat and might dive from the boats, the Totahs had a duty to act reasonably to warn people of the risk of diving. ...

The campground was a business enterprise. A business invitee "is a person who is invited to enter or remain on the land for a purpose directly or indirectly connected with business dealings with the possessor of the land." ... Callender was not an invitee of the Totahs. He did not enter the campground before the accident nor did he use any of the campground services or its dock. He was not attempting to enter the campground at the time of the injury. There simply was no relationship between Callender and the campground that would have imposed a duty of care on the Totahs for his benefit. ...

The trial court correctly granted summary judgment for the Totahs after finding they had no duty to warn Callender of the dangers of diving in waters offshore from the campground. We therefore affirm the trial court judgment in favor of the Totahs.

CASE QUESTION

1. How would the liability of the Totahs for the accident have been different if Callender had been a camper at the campground and had been within the campground's beach area at the time of his diving accident? Why would the liability have been different?

In another case, a motel owner rented a room to the owner of a used-car lot located next door. In the middle of the night, the motel owner was awakened by noises from two unauthorized men on the used-car lot. The motel owner called the used-car lot owner and informed him of the intruders. The lot owner shot at the intruders from the motel room. One intruder was killed; the other was wounded. The intruders sued the motel owner, among others. The motel owner contested liability. Since the intruders were not guests of the motel or otherwise connected with it, the court found no duty was owed and entered judgment for the motel.[16]

No Duty Owed on Property Not Owned or Maintained by the Hospitality Facility

A hotel or restaurant is generally not liable for injuries that occur to patrons on property not owned or maintained by it, even if the property is near the hotel or restaurant's facility. Thus, a restaurant was not liable to diners who were assaulted in a parking lot located behind the restaurant but not owned or maintained by it. The court specifically noted that the restaurant did not own, pave, snowplow, clear, or patrol the area where the assault occurred.[17]

Negligence Doctrines Generally Favoring the Plaintiff

Numerous legal doctrines are associated with negligence. In any negligence case one or more of these doctrines may apply and affect the outcome. Some doctrines favor the plaintiff by making the plaintiff's case easier to prove. Others benefit the defendant. We will examine first those that benefit the plaintiff, and then those that favor the defendant.

Res Ipsa Loquitur

In many negligence cases, the plaintiff has difficulty proving the necessary elements. Evidence to prove that the defendant was negligent does not always exist, even though the facts of the case may strongly suggest the defendant was negligent. The legal doctrine of res ipsa loquitur aids the plaintiff in such situations. It applies to cases in which the circumstances suggest the defendant was negligent but no proof of specific acts of negligence exists. In such cases, the doctrine of **res ipsa loquitur**, which means "the thing speaks for itself," frees the plaintiff from the burden of proving the specific breach of duty committed by the defendant.

In a classic example of res ipsa loquitur, the plaintiff was walking by a flour factory when, for an unexplained reason, a barrel of flour fell out of a window and injured the plaintiff. Because he was not inside the factory at the time of the incident, the plaintiff cannot prove why the barrel fell from the window. Nevertheless,

---

[16] *Fedie v. Travelodge Intern, Inc.*, 782 P.2d 739 (Ariz. 1989)

[17] *Mankowski v. Denny's, Inc.*, 1997 WL 525083 (Oh. 1997)

the occurrence is such that it likely would not have happened without negligence on the part of someone inside the factory. In such a case, the doctrine of res ipsa loquitur creates an inference that the defendant was negligent and allows the plaintiff to proceed with the lawsuit without having to prove through witnesses or otherwise the specific negligent acts of the defendant.

Elements

To use the doctrine of res ipsa loquitur, the plaintiff must prove the following three elements:

1. The plaintiff's injury was caused by an accident that would not normally have happened without negligence
2. The thing causing the injury (in the referenced case, the barrel of flour) was within the exclusive control of the defendant
3. The plaintiff did not provoke the accident.

Opportunity to Rebut

Where the doctrine applies, the defendant does not automatically lose. Rather, the defendant has an opportunity to rebut the inference that it was negligent. If the defendant can prove that the cause of the accident was some factor other than its own negligence, the defendant will not be liable.

Accident Suggestive of Negligence

The first element of res ipsa loquitur, that the accident would not normally have happened without negligence, was missing in the following case involving an object in a meatball.

CASE EXAMPLE 5-8

Jones v. GMRI, Inc.
2001 WL 747812 (N.C. 2001)

On 11 November, 1994 Loretta Jones was injured when she bit into a meatball at an Olive Garden Restaurant owned by GMRI, Inc. ("defendant") in Pineville, North Carolina. Plaintiff filed a complaint on 10 November 1997 against defendant and Rich Products Corporation which allegedly supplied or manufactured the meatball asserting claims of negligence ... .

[P]laintiff presented the testimony of a friend who was present at the restaurant the day of the incident, themselves, and three physicians. Plaintiffs' evidence tended to show that when plaintiff Loretta Jones attempted to take her first bite of the meatball, she bit down into an unidentified metal object. At that time, she experienced an "incredible stabbing pain in her tooth and her jaw" caused by a broken tooth. Because she was startled, she "sucked in and immediately sucked down the food" and the object. On cross-examination, plaintiff testified that she cut the meatball into eight pieces prior to taking the bite, and that she did not detect any foreign object in the meatball at that time.

Defendant presented evidence tending to show that most of the restaurant's meatballs come into the store frozen and in sealed bags.

The restaurant does a visual inspection of the sealed bags of meatballs and sends back those that do not meet the inspection. The meatballs are put into the freezer at the restaurant until needed, then put into a plastic holding container and placed in a refrigerator. The meatballs, which are slightly larger than a golf ball, are then mixed with a tomato sauce, heated, and served whole. Restaurant personnel testified that they do not poke or slice the meatballs, other than to check the temperature with a probe. ...

The defendant presented the following evidence on the issue of whether it exercised due care: (1) the restaurant removes whole, already formed, meatballs from the sealed bags, defrosts and reheats them, (2) the restaurant does not slice or cut into the meatballs because that would alter the nature of the dish, but (3) the restaurant does probe some of the meatballs with a thermometer to check the temperature. The evidence also showed that plaintiff cut the meatball into eight pieces prior to eating it and did not discover the object. ...

The jury awarded plaintiff no recovery. ...

Plaintiff's evidence at trial established that she was injured after biting into a piece of meatball. She offered no evidence showing defendant's breach of a duty or standard of care. [The evidence suggests if anyone may have been negligent it would be the manufacturer and not the restaurant. Thus, this was not the type of incident that would not happen without the negligence of the restaurant. Therefore,] the doctrine of res ipsa does not apply.

Exclusive Control of Defendant

The second element of res ipsa loquitur is that the instrumentality causing the injury must have been in the exclusive control of the defendant prior to the accident. If exclusive control is missing, the party who was careless in the maintenance of the item causing the injury may not have been the defendant, but rather someone else with access to the instrumentality.

This element of exclusive control can be difficult to establish. A diner at a restaurant was injured when the chair she was seated in collapsed, causing her to fall to the ground. The court rejected her attempt to utilize res ipsa loquitur because the element of exclusive control was lacking. Said the court, "Defendant's customers had continuous access to the chair. Defendant's control was not sufficiently exclusive."[18] The same result for the same reason occurred in a case involving an injury occasioned when a stool at a casino slid out from under the plaintiff as she was attempting to mount it.[19]

Another case with a similar holding involved a customer at a Pizza Hut who was injured while using the ladies room. As she entered the room, the door came off its hinges and struck her in the head. Since patrons regularly utilize the bathroom, the court held the restaurant did not have sufficient exclusive control of the door to apply the doctrine of res ipsa loquitur.[20]

---

[18] *Chini v. Wencentral Corporation, Inc.*, 692 N.Y.S.2d 533 (N.Y. 1999)

[19] *Nickel v. Hollywood Casino*, 730 N.E.2d 1212 (Ill. 2000)

[20] *Thompson v. Pizza Hut of America, Inc.*, 691 N.Y.S.2d 99 (N.Y. 1999)

In another case, the plaintiffs were sleeping in a double bed in a room in the defendant's hotel when plaster fell from the ceiling and injured them. The plaintiffs sued the hotel, but were unable to prove exactly how the hotel was negligent. The court held that the doctrine of res ipsa loquitur applied because ceilings do not normally fall and the maintenance of the ceiling was under the exclusive control of the hotel.[21] Likewise, where a plaintiff was injured when a ceiling fan fell on her at a Ground Round Restaurant, res ipsa could apply.[22]

Plaintiff Did Not Provoke the Accident

The third element requires that the plaintiff did not provoke or cause the accident. Revisiting the barrel-of-flour case, if the plaintiff had been throwing rocks up to the window from which the flour fell and the rocks had dislodged the barrel, causing it to fall, the plaintiff would not be able to use res ipsa loquitur.

In a case involving a health club located on the second floor of a building in New York City, the plaintiff had completed a set of repetitions on a leg-curl machine and stepped back to tie his shoe. In doing so his buttocks "brushed against" a large, five-foot glass window, which simultaneously exploded, causing him to fall to the street. The court held the window likely failed because it was brushed by the plaintiff's derriere. The plaintiff, having thus provoked the glass to break, could not benefit from res ipsa loquitur.[23]

Children and the Reasonable Person Test

Children do not comprehend dangers obvious to more mature persons. Nor are children able to weigh cause and effect accurately. Unlike an adult, children cannot be expected to recognize risks and take appropriate precautions. This impacts the duty imposed by law *on* young people as well as the duty owed by adults *to* children. The law excuses a young child from negligent acts; a person injured by a young person's conduct is not entitled to compensation. Similarly, the duty imposed on adults to act reasonably is usually greater when young children are involved.

For example, a hotel was liable to a six-year-old child who was injured when she inadvertently ran into glass panels that constituted a major portion of a wall in her hotel room. Although the glass panels were properly installed, "those who invite children to go upon their premises are required to exercise a relatively higher degree of care for their safety than to adults." To avoid liability, the hotel should have placed markings on the glass to indicate its presence or constructed guards around the panels.[24]

Another case reaffirms the heightened duty owed to children. A hotel was negligent when a youngster was struck by a car as he ran onto a public highway

[21] *Day v. Sheehan*, 2001 WL 577178 (Conn. 2001)

[22] *Pappalardo v. NY Health & Racquet Club*, 718 N.Y.S.2d 287 (N.Y. 2000)

[23] *McCleod v. Nel-Co Corp.*, 112 N.E.2d 501 (Ill. 1953)

[24] *Waugh v. Duke Corporation*, 248 F.Supp. 626 (N.C. 1966)

that separated two parts of the hotel. Because of the inn's layout, a guest who wanted to use all of the facilities would be required to cross the highway. The hotel attracted a significant number of Orthodox Jews and, to accommodate their needs, transformed the game room into a place for services on Sabbath mornings. The plaintiff, age five, and his Orthodox Jewish family were assigned a room on the opposite side of the highway as the game room. After services one Saturday, the boy "darted" onto the highway where he was hit by a passing car. The court noted that "The risk of injury to young children crossing the road is entirely foreseeable under these circumstances." Thus, the defendant had a duty to take reasonable steps to alleviate that risk.[25]

While a proprietor of a hospitality facility owes an enhanced duty to protect the safety of children, some young people may have a duty to act reasonably to protect themselves from harm. The existence and extent of that duty depends on the age and circumstances of the child and on the relevant facts. The following case discusses these issues in relation to a ten-year-old boy who was injured in a restaurant.

CASE EXAMPLE 5-9

Frelow v. St. Paul Fire & Marine Insurance Co.
631 So.2d 632 (La. 1994)

On December 30, 1990, a Sunday afternoon at about 2:00 P.M., James Papillion, ten years old, was having lunch at Western Sizzlin Steakhouse in Lake Charles with his mother, brothers, and sisters. James had just been to the salad bar with his mother and sister and was carrying his salad plate back to his family's table. His sister was right behind him. James's mother, Carolyn Frelow, had already returned to the table.

James and his sister chose the most direct route between the tables back to their own table, a fairly straight path. This route took them past a recently vacated booth which was being cleaned by Michael Bruce, a busboy. On the other side of the aisle was an occupied table. As James proceeded to pass this point, at a fast walk, he tripped over Bruce's foot, which was sticking into the aisle as he leaned into the booth he was cleaning. James reeled and hit his back on the corner of a table, then fell onto the floor face down. His salad plate fell on the back of his head. ... His mother had previously admonished James for running in

the restaurant, before they had gone to the salad bar. ...

Carolyn Frelow, James's mother, testified at trial that James complained of headaches and a backache for a week after the accident. Carolyn gave him Tylenol® for the headaches. Then, the following Sunday, James developed a severe headache during church which caused him to break into a cold sweat. ... [He was treated by a chiropractor for three months,] at which time he was asymptomatic.

The trial judge found James Papillion was negligent for walking too fast and Bruce was negligent for obstructing James's path after he saw James approaching. The court apportioned 40 percent fault to James and 60 percent to Bruce [See the discussion on comparative negligence later in this chapter]. ...

An owner of a business who permits the public to enter his establishment has a duty to exercise reasonable care to protect them. This duty extends to keeping the premises safe from unreasonable risks of harm or warning persons of known dangers. When the presence of small children is expected, the duty increases. ...

[W]e find that Bruce did have a duty to Western Sizzlin customers to use reasonable care

---

[25] *Kellner v. Lowney*, 761 A2d 421 (N.H. 2000)

not to obstruct the aisles so that customers could travel freely between the food service stations and the tables. A reasonable man would realize that he may trip someone if he extends his leg into an aisle in a self-service restaurant. ...

A patron is charged with using reasonable care for his own safety and must see and avoid obvious hazards. However, a child is not held to the same standard of care as that of an adult; rather, the test is whether the child, considering his age, background, and inherent intelligence, indulged in gross disregard of his own safety in the face of known, understood, and perceived danger.

It is well settled that a child of nine or ten years of age may be capable of negligence. However, in determining the negligence of a child, the actions of the child must be judged by his maturity and capacity to evaluate circumstances. The degree of caution expected of a nine- or ten-year-old boy varies with the circumstances of each case.

In the case before us, an apparently normal, average ten-year-old boy was carrying a plate of salad through a restaurant to the table where his family was sitting. The testimony of all eye witnesses, including Michael Bruce, the busboy, was that James was walking fast, but not running.

The defendants would have us assess 100 percent fault to James for walking too fast, for not watching where he was going, and for not taking a different route to his table. However, we are discussing a ten-year-old boy who was trying to carry a plate of salad from the salad bar to his table without spilling it. We do not believe that a ten-year-old child generally has sufficient experience to discern the best possible route by which to negotiate a crowded self-service restaurant while carrying a plate of food; many adults find this difficult. The route he did take led directly to his family's table. The trial judge found this was a reasonable route and we agree.

However, we do not believe that the danger inherent in walking too fast in a self-service restaurant while carrying a plate of food is beyond the understanding of a normal ten-year-old boy. Moreover, James had already been admonished by his mother not to run in the restaurant. The trial judge found that James's conduct was negligent. We cannot say the trial judge was clearly wrong.

CASE QUESTIONS

1. What is the standard of care an adult must exercise for his own safety? How does that differ from the standard of care a child is expected to exercise?

2. The judge noted that the restaurant was self-service. What impact does this have on Bruce's negligence?

3. Do you agree with the court's apportionment of liability (40 percent to James and 60 percent to Bruce)? Why or why not?

Room Furnishings

A hotel must anticipate dangers and use reasonable care to protect against them when furnishing a room that will be occupied by children. In *Seelbach, Inc. v. Cadick*, 405 S.W.2d 745 (Ky. 1966), the court upheld a jury award of $56,000 to an eight-month-old infant who fell from an adult bed against hot radiator pipes in a hotel room where no baby crib was furnished. The hotel had at least one crib available when the family arrived at the hotel, but the clerk did not offer or give it to the plaintiffs. The court ruled that the jury could properly hold a hotel negligent for failing to provide a baby bed while maintaining exposed hot radiator pipes in the hotel room. The court said that a hotel owes its guests a "duty to provide articles of furniture that may be used by them in the ordinary and reasonable way without danger." The negligence in the facts of this case was not in the exposed pipe in the room but rather the failure of the hotel to provide a bed suitable for the infant given the existence of the exposed pipe.

Attractive Nuisance Doctrine

As we have discussed, a landowner generally owes no duty to a trespasser other than to refrain from causing him willful injury. There is an exception to this rule for child trespassers called the *attractive nuisance doctrine*.

This doctrine is an outgrowth of youngsters' limited capability to detect danger and protect themselves from risk. An **attractive nuisance** is a potentially dangerous object or condition of exceptional interest to young people, such as a swimming pool, a large empty box, a snow pile suitable for sliding created by a plow, and equipment or ditches at a construction site. If an attractive nuisance exists on the property, the owner or occupier is required to exercise reasonable care to protect a child from associated risks. Thus, a hotel with a pool would be well advised to install a tall fence with a lock to prevent children from using the pool when it is closed or unattended. A restaurant that purchased a new refrigerator should discard the box only after removing all tacks and other sharp items and flattening it.

The elements of an attractive nuisance are the following:

1. A condition exists that is attractive to children and is likely to cause them injury
2. The owner or occupier of the land knows or should know of the condition
3. Due to the child's immaturity, he does not appreciate the danger.

In such a case, the owner or occupier must take reasonable steps to eliminate the danger.

Some states have abolished the concept of attractive nuisance in circumstances where the risk should be obvious to the child. These states hold that certain risks are so obvious that even children are expected to exercise caution when confronting them, relieving the property owner from liability.

In *Daniels v. Byington*, 707 P.2d 476 (Id. 1985), a six-year-old boy fell four feet to the ground from the deck of a stationary boat used as a playhouse on the defendants' property. His parents sued the property owners to recover for the child's broken arm. The court held for the defendants on the ground that the fall was not caused by a hidden defect in the boat and that the danger of falling should have been apparent to the boy. Said the court,

> From the time they are born, all children realize the danger of falling and instinctively clutch at something when they feel that danger is near. While the instinct to climb is practically universal, and it is carried on in a venturesome spirit, a consciousness of the risk of falling is always present.

Negligence Per Se Doctrine

Negligence per se describes conduct that violates a law or ordinance designed to protect the safety of the public. Under the majority view, such acts are treated as negligence without any need for further proof of breach of duty. When applicable, this doctrine is of great help to the plaintiff because he does not have to prove that the defendant failed to act as a reasonable person. Instead, the only facts the plaintiff needs to prove are the existence of the law or ordinance, the defendant's violation of it, the extent of the injury, and proximate cause between the violation and the injury.

Under the minority view, noncompliance with the safety law or ordinance is not conclusive on the issue of the defendant's breach of duty, but is some evidence of such a breach. In some states, such noncompliance is **prima facie** evidence of negligence, which means it alone is sufficient evidence if unrebutted to support a judgment for the plaintiff.

The reasoning supporting the negligence per se doctrine is that the proprietor of an establishment has a duty always to comply with legal mandates designed to protect patrons. This legal duty applies even when the owner is unaware of the existence of the safety laws. Innkeepers and restaurateurs are expected to stay current on both new laws applicable to their business and changes in existing laws. Sources of this information include trade journals and presentations at trade-association meetings. In addition, a business can request a lawyer to perform a legal audit in which the attorney will examine the business and its compliance with applicable laws and advise the owner of any deficiencies.

The following case illustrates the application of the majority view of negligence per se in a case against a hotel that was woefully deficient in its compliance with safety laws relating to swimming pools.

CASE EXAMPLE 5-10

First Overseas Investment Corp.
v.
Cotton
491 So.2d 293 (Fla. 1986)

... Cleophus Cotton and his wife were guests at the Monte Carlo Hotel (hotel). Mr. Cotton went swimming in the shallow end of the hotel pool. The pool water was extremely cloudy as the pool attendant had that morning dumped a bucketful of soda ash into it to "sweeten" the PH. The pool attendant testified that the pool's soda ash feeder was inoperable, hence his practice of dumping the soda ash directly into the pool. Expert testimony was offered that soda ash should never be dumped directly into a pool and that a bucketful was ten to twelve times more than is needed. Soda ash increases turbidity [muddiness, thickness, darkness] and makes the water cloudy until completely filtered. The pool attendant testified that he had no training in first aid or in the use of lifesaving apparatus. He further testified that the pool's filtration system was inoperable. The pool did not have lifesaving apparatus such as a shepherd's hook, an elevated lifeguard's chair, or first aid equipment.

Michael Wolfe testified that he observed Mr. Cotton swimming in the shallow end of the pool. Mr. Wolfe turned away from the pool for about 60 seconds and when he looked back, Mr. Cotton was gone. Mr. Wolfe went to the side of the pool and looked for Mr. Cotton, but did not see him. He asked another hotel guest,

Daniel Jones, if he had seen Mr. Cotton. Mr. Jones indicated that he had not seen him. Mr. Wolfe told the pool attendant that he thought Mr. Cotton was in the pool. The pool attendant and Mr. Wolfe stood at the edge of the pool and looked for Mr. Cotton, but still did not see him. Subsequently, Mr. Wolfe and Mr. Jones began swimming the length of the pool at the bottom, looking for Mr. Cotton. They testified that they did not find Mr. Cotton on the bottom until they were practically on top of him. They then brought him up to the side of the pool. Mr. Jones ran down the beach to get a lifeguard. A lifeguard was located by Mr. Jones. The lifeguard attempted to resuscitate Mr. Cotton, but his efforts were unsuccessful, as were the efforts of a fire rescue squad which arrived at the scene shortly after the lifeguard.

Mr. Wolfe testified that twelve to twenty minutes elapsed between the time he first started looking for Mr. Cotton and the time resuscitation efforts were first made. According to expert testimony, there was a high probability of Mr. Cotton's survival if he had been rescued within four to five minutes after disappearing. It was plaintiff's contention that Mr. Cotton would have been rescued within four to five minutes and would not have drowned if the hotel had complied with the following Florida Department of Health and Rehabilitative Services (HRS) rules:

Rule 10D-5.66(3)

All items of equipment designed for recirculation, filtration, disinfection, and pool water treatment, shall be kept in service at all times and shall be properly maintained to perform the functions of the units and protect the swimming pool water from contamination.

Rule 10D-5.68(6)

Clearness—At all times the pool water shall be sufficiently clear so that the main drain or drains are clearly defined when viewed from the pool deck.

Rule 10D-5.81(1)

All owners, managers, and/or other attendants in charge of a public swimming pool shall be responsible for supervision and safety of the pool. The attendant, if provided, shall be in full charge of bathing, shall have authority to enforce all rules, and shall be trained in first aid and the use of lifesaving apparatus.

Rule 10D-5.81(2)

Lifesaving apparatus—All swimming pools shall be provided with a shepherd's hook securely attached to a one piece pole not less than sixteen (16) feet in length, and at least one (1) eighteen (18) inch diameter lifesaving ring with sufficient rope attached to reach all parts of the pool from the pool deck. Lifesaving apparatus shall be mounted in a conspicuous place and be readily available for use. Pools greater than fifty (50) feet in length shall have multiple units with at least one (1) shepherd's hook and one (1) lifesaving ring located along each of the longer sides of the pool.

Rule 10D-5.81(3)

Lifesaving chairs—One elevated lifeguard chair ... platform shall be provided for pools having over two thousand (2,000) square feet up to four thousand (4,000) square feet of pool water surface area. One additional lifeguard chair or platform shall be provided for each two thousand (2,000) square feet, or major fraction thereof, of pool water surface area above four thousand (4,000) square feet. The lifeguard chair(s) or platform(s) shall be located to allow a clear and unobstructed view of the pool bottom in the area of surveillance.

Rule 10D-5.81(6)

First aid equipment and materials—Each pool shall have available first aid equipment and materials sufficient for use in connection with injuries which may occur in the pool or on the pool deck.

Plaintiff contended that Mr. Cotton would not have drowned if the pool's filtration system had been operating properly; the water in the pool had been clear; an elevated lifeguard chair had been in place affording a clear and unobstructed view of the pool; there had been lifesaving apparatus and first aid equipment available and the pool attendant had been trained in the use of lifesaving apparatus and first aid. ...

The well established rule is that it is "negligence per se" for a defendant to violate a statute which establishes a duty to protect a particular class of persons from a particular type of injury. This applies to violations of HRS rules as well. ... We find that all of the HRS rules at issue obligated the hotel to protect a particular class of persons (guests using the pool), from a particular type of harm (drowning). All of the rules were designed to ensure a clear view of swimmers in distress and/or the capability of saving them from drowning. ...

[Judgment for plaintiff.]

CASE QUESTIONS

1. What class of persons were the pool maintenance laws designed to protect? Why do these people need protection?

2. How did the plaintiff prove proximate cause in this case?

A building owner that fails to comply with elevator safety and inspection rules will face liability for negligence per se if the elevator malfunctions and people are injured. A plaintiff was injured when an elevator dropped past the ground floor (despite buttons pushed for lobby exit) struck bottom, and rebounded to the third floor. The building elevators experienced numerous malfunctions in the days leading to the incident. State statutes required building owners to maintain elevators in a safe condition. The court held negligence per se applied to this circumstance.[26]

Another application of negligence per se involves a restaurant and bar that permitted loud music to emanate from the restaurant. This caused excessive noise and vibration to permeate the plaintiff's condominium located directly above the restaurant. Extensive testimony at trial by police officers and experts established that noise-level readings were taken in the plaintiff's unit and they substantially violated the allowable limits of an ordinance in the zoning district in which the plaintiff's condominium was located. The jury's verdict for the plaintiff based on negligence per se was upheld on appeal.[27]

For a restaurant or hotel to be liable under negligence per se, it is not enough that the establishment violated the law. In addition, the violation must be the proximate cause of the plaintiff's injury. If it is not, the hotel or restaurant will not be liable. In *Truett v. Morgan*, 266 S.E.2d 557 (Ga. 1980), Sanders and Truett, both guests at a hotel, had an altercation. Shortly after the fight Sanders went to Truett's room and knocked on the door. When Truett opened it, Sanders shot him. Contrary to statute, the door opened outward instead of inward. Truett sued the hotel, claiming negligence per se. The court rejected the claim because no connection existed between the direction in which the door opened and the injury.

Obligations Beyond Regulation

Suppose a hotel fully complies with a statute but the requirements of the law are inadequate to protect the guests. Can that hotel be found negligent for failing to

---

[26] *Golden Shoreline Limited Partnership v. McGowan*, 2001 WL 387737 (Fl. 2001)

[27] *Peck v. Rattlesnake Ventures, Inc.*, 1998 WL 846100 (Conn. 1998)

do more than the law requires? The answer is yes. The hotel has a duty to exercise reasonable care to protect guests from injury. If satisfying the law falls short of reasonable care, the hotel must do more than what the statute requires. Failure to provide that added measure of safety will result in liability for negligence, not negligence per se. Thus, where a hotel complied with the local fire-safety codes that did not require smoke alarms, and guests were seriously injured in a fire due in part to the absence of the alarms, the hotel was liable for negligence. Said the court, "Compliance with the appropriate regulations is not conclusive evidence of due care. If the defendants knew or should have known of some risk that would be prevented by reasonable measures not required by the law, they were negligent if they did not take such measures."[28]

How does an innkeeper or restaurateur know what is required to satisfy the due care obligation if compliance with statutory mandates is not enough? The level of care required will be determined in part by standards followed in the industry as well as technological advances. Proprietors must stay abreast of new and state-of-the-art products and techniques, and should always be asking, "What new practice or procedure can I be performing to enhance the safety of my patrons?"

Strict or Absolute Liability

Normally defendants are not liable unless they do something wrong. If a patron trips and falls in a restaurant solely because the heel on her shoe broke, the restaurant will not be liable for any injuries sustained in the fall. Since the restaurant was not negligent it did not breach any duty owed to the customer.

One exception does exist. If applicable, a defendant will be liable even though she violated no duty and did nothing wrong. That exception is sometimes called *strict liability* and sometimes *absolute liability*. Strict liability imposes liability for injury resulting from an ultrahazardous activity upon those who engage in it. Such activities might include keeping wild animals or using explosives. This doctrine imposes liability for resulting injuries even if the defendant took every precaution and was not negligent. The principle supporting this rule is that the ultrahazardous activity could be outlawed because of the danger it creates. Sometimes the ultrahazardous activity has, despite its danger, a useful purpose. In such circumstances, in lieu of outlawing the activity, the law may impose liability for the activity on the party who engages in it, without regard to fault.

Suppose Jake purchases an old office building in the downtown section of a sizeable city intending to destroy the building with dynamite and build a ten-story luxury hotel. He plans the dynamiting for a Sunday morning when very few people are downtown. He constructs a tall barricade-like fence around the building to prevent people from entering the site and to protect against any debris hitting a passerby. Nonetheless, following the explosion, a small piece of the building is propelled over the fence and hits a pedestrian. Under normal negligence rules, Jake would not be liable; he satisfied the duty to exercise reasonable care to prevent

---

[28]*Miller v. Warren*, 390 S.B.2d 207 (W.Va. 1990)

injury. But under strict liability, freedom from negligence is not a defense. Because dynamiting is a very hazardous undertaking, he will be liable to the injured passerby.

Strict Products Liability

In recent times, the doctrine of strict liability has been extended significantly to sellers of defective products. This application of strict liability is called **strict products liability** and imposes liability on the seller of a defective product without regard to negligence. A product is defective for this purpose if it is designed or manufactured improperly or if it contains inadequate warnings of the dangers it presents. For example, suppose a chef buys a toaster for a restaurant. When he plugs it in and turns it on it explodes, causing injury. The store that sold the toaster is strictly liable; the chef does not have to prove negligence. If the toaster was defective when the manufacturer sold the toaster, it too will be liable in strict products liability. The chef need only prove that the toaster was defective when it was sold. Liability in these circumstances is a matter of social policy and based on three objectives. First, consumers are often powerless to protect themselves from defective products, so the responsibility for consequences of those products is more fairly placed on the manufacturers who design them. The producers are in the best position to prevent defects. The second goal is to encourage manufacturers to develop safe products. The third goal justifies holding not only the manufacturer, but also the retail seller strictly liable. The objective is to spread the cost of losses suffered by individuals from defective products. The expenses associated with an injury may be an overwhelming burden to an individual, whereas manufacturers and retailers can purchase insurance and allocate the cost over all its sales.[29]

Note that the product causing the injury must be defective for strict products liability to apply. Sometimes a product malfunctions for reasons other than a product flaw. An example is provided by an employee of Wendy's who picked up a glass coffeepot that had not been sitting on a warmer and filled it with hot water from a water machine to pour into containers on the Superbar. The carafe broke, causing scalding water to spill on her right foot and left leg. Among her injuries were third-degree burns to her right foot that required a skin graft. She sued the seller and manufacturer of the pot in strict products liability, but lost the case. The court determined that the plaintiff did not prove the coffeepot was defective, saying, "It is common knowledge that a characteristic of glass is it will break when subjected to sudden extreme temperature differences. We therefore hold that the coffeepot was not [defective] … because an ordinary user or handler of the product would contemplate this potentially dangerous characteristic of glass."[30]

[29]*Jiminez v. TM Cobb Company*, 98 Cal.Rptr.2d 587 (Ca. 2000)
[30]*Myles v. Cain's Coffee Co, Inc.*, 756 So.2d 632 (La. 2000)

Restaurants and hotels can both benefit and be hurt by strict products liability. If they buy products that are defective and incur a loss as a result, they can sue the seller without the need to prove negligence. Thus, where a Hunan restaurant sustained significant damage from a fire because the fire-suppression system it had purchased malfunctioned and failed to extinguish the fire, the manufacturer of the system may be liable in strict products liability.[31] Similarly, the manufacturer of a deep-fat fryer that did not adequately provide protection against boiling oil spills may be liable in strict products liability to a scalded restaurant employee.[32]

Restaurants and hotels can also be sued in strict products liability if they sell defective products, such as rancid tuna salad in the dining room or an exploding hair dryer in the gift shop. If the product was defective when it was sold to the hospitality facility, the restaurant or hotel can sue the manufacturer when the hotel or restaurant is sued by a customer or guest.

Respondeat Superior

Hotels and restaurants employ many people. In general, an employer is liable for the acts of its employees done in furtherance of their jobs. Thus, employers are liable to their customers, guests, and other invitees for the negligence of their employees. If a bellhop negligently drops a heavy suitcase on a guest's foot, the innkeeper will be liable for the resulting injuries. If a waiter carelessly spills hot coffee on a customer causing burns, the restaurant will be liable.

This liability of the employer for the acts of its employees is called **respondeat superior**, which means "let the master (employer) answer." The doctrine is founded on the theory that an employee is an agent of the employer; whenever an employee is performing the duties of his job, he is acting on behalf of the employer. The law in effect renders acts of the employee those of the employer. Stated differently, the employer is vicariously (through a substitute) liable for the employee's wrongful conduct.

Several explanations exist for this doctrine. It encourages employers to exercise caution and care in the selection and training of employees. This liability should have the desirable effect of limiting the number of injuries occurring from employee wrongdoing. Another rationale for the doctrine is that it increases the injured party's chances of receiving compensation, as the employer usually has more resources than does the employee.

An employer is not liable for every negligent act of its employee. It is not liable for negligent acts committed by the employee at home or school during the employee's off-duty hours. The employer is liable only if the employee's negligent act occurred **within the scope of employment**, which means in furtherance of duties performed for the employer.

In the following case, the negligence clearly occurred while the employee was acting within the scope of his employment.

---

[31] *Chiang v. Pyro Chemical, Inc.*, 1997 WL 330622 (Conn. 1997)

[32] *Bullock, Inc. v. Thorpe*, 353 S.E.2d 340 (Ga. 1987)

CASE EXAMPLE 5-11

Scott v. Salerno and GNOC, Corp., d/b/a Bally's Grand Hotel & Casino 297 N.J. Super. 437, 688 A.2d 614 (N.J. 1997)

On June 14, 1993, Salerno, while operating an automobile owned by Pauline N. Marchese (Marchese), was involved in an accident with an automobile owned and operated by plaintiff Denise Rae Bishop Scott (Scott) in Atlantic City, New Jersey. At the time of the accident,

Salerno was valet parking automobiles for Bally's as an employee. ...

Bally's was legally responsible for the acts or omissions of Salerno. ... Marchese gave Bally's permission to park her automobile. At the time of the accident, the automobile was being driven by Salerno, as agent for Bally's, for the very purpose for which it was given to Bally's. Bally's was responsible for the acts of Salerno. ...

CASE QUESTION

1. Can you think of a circumstance where an employee, while on duty, acts outside the scope of employment?

Acting Outside the Scope of Employment

Several assault cases illustrate the situation in which an employee is not acting within the scope of employment. A McDonald's employee, either on a break or at the end of his shift, cut in the customer line to order a drink. An argument ensued between the employee and a customer who objected. It escalated into a fistfight in which the customer was injured. He sued the McDonald's restaurant, asserting respondeat superior. The restaurant denied that the employee was acting within the scope of his employment. The court agreed and dismissed the case stating, "When the altercation occurred, [the employee] was in the process of ordering a drink for himself. He was not cleaning, nor was he performing any of his job duties, or in the process of performing any task for his employer. ... Standing in line and placing an order was not one of his job duties ... even if he was 'on the clock' when the fight started."[33]

A similar outcome occurred in another case involving a McDonald's dispute. The grill worker was apparently quite unhappy when a customer threw a straw wrapper into a garbage can that was being used to hold Happy Meal toys. The cook emerged from the rear of the restaurant and assaulted the customer, who thereafter sued the eatery based on respondeat superior. The court dismissed the charges, finding that a grill worker's job responsibilities do not include any contact with customers.[34]

In another fight case, several members of a Steak & Ale Restaurant kitchen staff came to the aid of a woman who was believed to be a victim of abuse by her boyfriend. The kitchen workers attacked the boyfriend in the restaurant parking

---

[33] *Montgomery v. McDonald's Corporation*, 2001 WL 705520 (Ill. 2001)

[34] *Yono v. Coolidge #1, Inc.*, 2001 WL 716928 (Mich. 2001)

lot. He sued the restaurant, relying on respondeat superior. Denying the claim, the court said, "[T]he duties of the kitchen staff were limited to activities within the kitchen, and they had no authorization to employ physical force against any party for any reason. Furthermore, the kitchen staff had no duties to maintain security on the premises. ... The test of liability is not whether the act was done during the existence of the employment, but whether it was done within the scope of the actual transaction of the master's business for accomplishing the ends of his employment."[35]

Depending on the facts, a fight may be included within an employee's scope of employment. A Burger King supervisory employee was attempting to resolve a refund request from a customer complaining about her order. During the discussion, the customer accused the worker of harassing her son in school, a matter unrelated to the food complaint. The employee became angered and swung his fists into a stack of trays. One of the trays rebounded and hit the customer in the face. She sued Burger King, which denied that the employee was acting within the scope of his employment. The court noted that although the actions may have been mingled with personal motives, they occurred during a discussion involving work responsibilities. The court referred the matter for a jury trial to address whether the fight occurred within the scope of the employee's job.[36]

In another case, a housekeeper for an Adam's Mark Hotel was given keys for the supply rooms at the beginning of each shift and was required to return them at the end. One day he forgot to return the keys, which fact he did not realize until after arriving home from work. He drove back to the hotel to return the keys. On his return home he negligently caused an accident, seriously injuring the plaintiff who suffered permanent brain damage. The jury awarded damages and determined the housekeeper was not acting in the course of his employment. As a result, the hotel was not liable to pay any of the damages. The court referenced the rule that generally an employee is not within the course of his employment while driving his own car to and from his place of work. Further, a hotel supervisor testified that employees occasionally went home with the keys by mistake. Such action had never resulted in an "advisory" (a warning) or in other disciplinary action. The court thus affirmed the jury's determination that the housekeeper was not acting within the scope of his employment at the time of the accident.[37]

Independent Contractors

While an employer is liable for the acts of its employees committed in the scope of employment, a company is generally not liable for the acts of any independent contractors it hires to do various jobs. An **independent contractor** is someone who contracts to do one or more specific projects for someone else and maintains control of the method for doing the work. In *Robinson v. Jiffy Executive Limousine*

---

[35] *Waters v. Steak & Ale of Georgia, Inc.*, 527 S.E.2d 592 (Ga. 2000)
[36] *Reynolds v. L&L Management, Inc.*, 492 S.E.2d 347 (Ga. 1997)
[37] *Soto v. Adam's Mark Hotel*, 2000 WL 1508820 (Tex. 2000)

Co., 4 F.3d 237 (3rd Cir. 1993), a casino called a limousine service to transport a patron. While en route to the patron's destination, the limousine driver caused a car accident that resulted in serious injuries to the patron. The patron sued the casino for his damages. The court determined that the limousine service was an independent contractor and therefore the casino was not liable.

A nightclub was sued by a patron who was injured when a member of the band playing that night broke a beer bottle on the customer's face. The case was dismissed because the band member was an independent contractor and therefore the bar was not liable for his actions.[38]

Determining whether a worker is an employee or independent contractor is often not easy. There exists no definitive rule for determining the status of a worker. Additional factors to consider are provided by the *Restatement Second of Agency*, a compilation of recommended rules of agency law. Those additional factors include: who as between the employer and worker supplies the tools and the place of work (if the employer, the worker is more likely to be considered an employee); the length of time for which a person is hired (the longer the engagement, the more likely the worker will be considered an employee); the method of payment—whether by time or by the job (if by time, it is more likely the worker will be considered an employee); whether or not the work being performed is part of the regular business of the employer (if so, the more likely the worker will be considered an employee); and the intentions and beliefs of the parties concerning their relationship.

Nondelegable Duties

An exception exists to the general rule that an employer is not liable for the acts of an independent contractor. Normally, the duty imposed on a hospitality facility to keep the premises reasonably safe for guests is **nondelegable**, meaning it cannot be transferred (or delegated) to another. For policy reasons, the employer is not permitted to avoid liability on the ground that an independent contractor failed to properly perform the work. The rule is intended to motivate the hotel or restaurant to monitor carefully the work of the independent contractors it hires. Thus, a hotel may be liable to a guest who slips and falls on the sidewalk due to the failure of a snow-removal service hired by the hotel to sufficiently clear the snow.[39] Similarly, a hotel that hires an independent contracting service to provide security for its premises remains liable to a guest who was criminally attacked because the security service was negligent in the performance of its duties.[40]

Another nondelegable duty for a hotel is the obligation to use effective pest-control methods. If a licensed pest-control company is hired by a hotel, the inn will be liable if the service fails to exterminate properly and a guest is bitten, even though the company is an independent contractor. A Days Inn guest who was

---

[38] *Stevens v. Spec, Inc.*, 224 A.D.2d 811, 637 N.Y.S.2d 979 (3rd Dept. 1996)

[39] *Wood v. Chalet Susse International*, 1995 WL 317058 (Conn. 1995)

[40] *Security Services Corp. v. Ramada Inn., Inc.*, 665 So.2d 268 (Fl. 1996)

bitten by a brown recluse spider while she slept would be entitled to recover against the hotel if she can prove the extermination contractor was negligent.[41]

Where liability is imposed due to a nondelegable duty, the responsible hotel or restaurant may be able to seek compensation from the negligent independent contractor.

Duty to Aid a Person in Distress

If someone in need calls out to you for help, are you legally obligated to offer assistance? If you fail to respond, will you be liable for resulting injuries to the person in trouble? The answer to both questions is generally *no*. The law does not impose a legal duty on individuals to rescue someone in trouble. Indeed, courts have denied damage claims in the following situations:

- A man who watched while a young woman drowned, even though he could easily have gone to her aid
- A man who failed to warn a neighbor's child he saw hammering on a tube of gunpowder.

In each case, the moral duty was plain enough, but the courts agreed that moral duties are a matter of conscience and not of law.

If a person does come to the aid of another, the law imposes a duty on the rescuer to exercise reasonable care. While no liability would have resulted had the rescuer chosen to do nothing, liability will result if a rescue attempt is done negligently. The reason for this rule is the expectation that, had the rescuer not attempted to help, someone else with requisite skills would likely have offered to assist. Once others observe that a person in need is being tended to, they are less likely to come forward to help.

An application of these principles is found in a case involving Gimbels Department Store. A shopper fainted on the floor of the store. Employees moved her to the ladies room and there mishandled her injuries. She sued the store for negligence. The court stated that the store management owed no duty to come to her rescue "even if death resulted." However, by removing her to the ladies room the store precluded other potential rescuers from coming to her aid and so owed her a duty to act reasonably in caring for her.[42]

Duty to Invitees in Danger

The law in a growing number of states requires business owners to lend a hand under certain circumstances. These include situations where the proprietor's lack of care would aggravate the harm. For example, in one case a bar customer fell down an open stairway and died. His wife alleged that the bar operator and employees failed to obtain medical assistance for over an hour after they became aware of his fall. The bar denied that it owed any duty to help the customer and

---

[41] *Copeland v. The Lodge Enterprises, Inc.*, 4 P.3d 695 (Ok. 2000)

[42] *Zelenko v. Gimbel Bros.*, 287 N.Y.Supp. 134 (1935)

asked the court to dismiss the case. Refusing to do so, the court agreed that, while at common law there is no general duty to aid a person who is in peril,

> under some circumstances, moral and humanitarian considerations may require one to render assistance to another who has been injured, even though the injury was not due to negligence on his part and may have been caused by the negligence of the injured person. Failure to render assistance in such a situation may constitute actionable negligence if the injury is aggravated through lack of due care. ... There may be a legal obligation [on one who invites others to his premises] to take positive or affirmative steps to effect the rescue of a person who is helpless and in a situation of peril ... or when the injury resulted from use of an instrumentality under the control of the defendant.[43]

Thus, in many states a business open to the public owes a duty to its patrons to aid them if they are in danger while on the premises. The rationale for this duty is that the store owner is deriving some economic benefit from the presence of the customer, and ensuring that invitees are safe is a cost of doing business. In the following case, this duty was breached.

CASE EXAMPLE 5-12

Starling v. Fisherman's Pier, Inc.
401 So.2d 1136 (Fl. 1981)

... The complaint charged a corporation, which operated a commercial fishing pier, with negligence for failure to safeguard a passed-out drunk customer who was left lying near the ocean on the pier, by himself, in the early hours of the morning, and who rolled over into the water and drowned.

The above facts involve gross conduct on the part of the man who drowned, perhaps exacerbated by the fact that his consumption of the alcoholic beverage, which he brought with him to the pier, was in violation of a municipal ordinance. ... The question here presented is: when an invitee comes upon the commercial premises of another and passes out cold on the floor, whether through illness, injury, or drunkenness, can the owner or operator of the premises ignore the inert figure lying in a dangerous place or does that owner or operator have an affirmative duty to make at least some

minimal steps to safeguard the inert figure? We believe the owner or operator does have such a duty. ...

The pier operator cites us to [a legal encyclopedia] for the proposition that there is "no general duty to come to the assistance of a person who is so ill or intoxicated as to be unable to look out for himself." However, that section appears to be concerning itself with the level of duty owed by a chance bystander or neighbor, and there is no discussion on whether the quoted statement would apply to a customer found on commercial premises. ...

A proprietor simply cannot ignore and step over an unconscious customer lying in a dangerous place upon his premises, and he must take some minimal steps to safeguard any customer upon his premises from extreme danger, even though the customer has allowed himself to be exposed to that danger in the first place. ...

The complaint thus stated a cause of action and should not have been dismissed.

CASE QUESTION

1. What could the pier operator have done in this circumstance to avoid liability?

[43]*Palace Bar, Inc. v. Fearnot,* 376 N.E.2d 1159 (Ind. 1978)

In another case, an intruder entered a hotel room and bound, gagged, and raped the guest. He then left, threatening to return and kill her. Still bound, she managed to kick the phone receiver off the hook and call the front desk. The operator was slow to respond and waited a while before calling the police. The court ruled the hotel was negligent for failing promptly to respond to the guest's call for help.[44]

Limitation on Duty to Invitees

If the guest who is in danger is being cared for by others who appear competent to render the necessary assistance, the hotel or restaurant does not have a duty to offer aid. The following case illustrates this point.

CASE EXAMPLE 5-13

Fish v. Paul, d/b/a Horseshoe Motel 574 A.2d 1365 (Me. 1990)

Gretchen Fish, individually and as personal representative of the estate of her son, Mark Colvin ... argues that [defendant motel owners] are liable for their failure to help Colvin, a guest who became ill at their motel. ...

The plaintiff alleges the following: On August 13, 1987, Colvin, who was 18 at the time, travelled with two companions, Steven Fahsel and Frederick Wood, from Bangor to Old Orchard Beach to attend a concert. After the concert, the three rented a room in Saco at the Horseshoe Motel, owned by the Pauls. During the night the three drank a substantial quantity of alcohol. The next morning an employee of the motel saw Fahsel and Wood carrying Colvin, who was semiconscious, to a waiting car. After placing Colvin in the rear seat, Fahsel and Wood started back toward Bangor. On I-95 near Etna, the car overheated and stopped. A police officer stopped and called an ambulance for Colvin, but he was pronounced dead on arrival at St. Joseph's Hospital in Bangor. The complaint sought compensatory damages. ...

We have recognized the general duty of a business proprietor to exercise reasonable care to prevent injury to business invitees. ... We also recognize that in certain circumstances the relationship between a guest and an innkeeper may give rise to a duty to render aid in case of illness or injury. ... [H]owever, ... the innkeeper "is not required to give any aid to one who is in the hands of apparently competent persons who have taken charge of him, or whose friends are present and apparently in a position to give him all necessary assistance." The defendants contend that ... the presence of Colvin's friends already rendering aid relieves the motel of any obligation to do so. ... We find the defendants' argument persuasive. ... We conclude that the facts alleged are not sufficient to state a claim against the [motel owners].

CASE QUESTION

1. Why in the previous case, Case Example 5-12, did the proprietor owe a duty to aid a customer in distress while in this case the proprietor was relieved of that duty?

---

[44]*Boles v. La Quinta Motor Inns*, 680 F.2d 1077 (Tex. 1982)

Statutory Protection for Good Samaritans

While requiring rescuers to act reasonably, the law also recognizes that the conditions available to the rescuer in an emergency may be far from ideal and often even crude. For example, roadside treatment immediately following a car accident involves conditions drastically different from the sterile environment of an operating room. The law affords the rescuer protection from liability resulting from these less-than-ideal conditions. This is accomplished through **Good Samaritan Statutes**, which are laws that protect a person who reacts in an emergency situation by trying to help a sick or injured person or someone in peril. According to these statutes, the rescuer will not be liable for any injuries caused in the attempt to render assistance if the means used were reasonable in relation to the emergency conditions at the time. Many such statutes further provide that the rescuer is not liable for ordinary negligence, but only for gross negligence (excessive negligence). The purpose of these statutes is to encourage voluntary aid to persons in danger by removing the rescuer's fear of potential liability.

A related principle, called the **rescue doctrine**, benefits a rescuer who is injured while administering aid. It provides that a person who negligently creates a peril and thereby endangers another person is liable for injuries to a rescuer who comes forward to offer assistance to the person in need.

This principal is demonstrated in *Altamuro v. Milner Hotel, Inc.*, 540 F.Supp 870 (Pa. 1982). A defective television set in a guest room caused fire to a hotel. The defect in the set was known to a hotel employee. Leaving the set plugged in was negligent. A guest at the hotel repeatedly reentered the hotel during the fire, rescuing other guests each time. He did not return from his final rescue attempt. His family sued the hotel. The court ruled the inn was liable based on the rescue doctrine. Explained the court, "Danger invited rescue. ... The wrong that imperils life is a wrong to the imperiled victim; it is a wrong also to his rescuer."

Rule in Choking Situations

A classic emergency at a restaurant occurs when a piece of food becomes lodged in a person's airway, blocking off all air to the lungs. Such a situation presents a grave condition because a person with a blocked airway will become unconscious in about one minute, will suffer irreversible brain damage in about four to five minutes, and will die usually within a few minutes of the onset of brain damage. These situations occur with sufficient frequency as to be recognized as a real problem in the restaurant industry.

At least for the present, it appears that the law throughout the country does not require a restaurant to administer first aid to a choking patron. Instead, a restaurant whose employees summon medical assistance for the hapless diner will be free from liability. If a restaurant comes to the aid of a choking patron, but does so negligently, the restaurant will be liable in many states.

To encourage restaurants to attempt to save the afflicted person's life, some states have enacted statutes that both encourage restaurants to be ready to offer aid in the event of a choking incident and also protect restaurants from liability when employees do offer first aid. A typical law requires that every restaurant and cafeteria in the state display prominently a poster showing the proper first-aid procedures to use in assisting a person who has a blocked airway and is choking. This procedure is called the Heimlich Maneuver and is a relatively simple method of first aid that requires no apparatus or medical knowledge. The legislation does not require anyone to administer this procedure; no duty exists upon restaurateurs or their employees to render assistance to the choking victim other than to call 911 or an ambulance. If restaurant owners, their employees, or patrons assist the choking person in accordance with the instructions on the poster, they will not be liable if the choking person is injured, except in cases of gross negligence. If the rescuer deviates from the poster's directions, liability may result. The statutes also provide that the restaurant cannot be held liable for injuries to or the death of the choke victim if the poster is not displayed.

The following case illustrates an application of the law concerning the duty of a restaurant to aid a choking victim.

CASE EXAMPLE 5-14

Lee v. Golden Nugget Hotel and Casino
22 P.3d 209 (Nev. 2001)

... The decedent, Bobby Lee Sturms, and a companion were having dinner at a restaurant located within the Golden Nugget Hotel and Casino in Las Vegas. ...

Sturms' companion observed that Sturms, after only a few bites of his meal, appeared nauseated and seemed to be "getting sick." Shortly thereafter, Sturms vomited in his lap and on the floor, slumped over in his chair and closed his eyes. At this point, Strums' companion believed that Sturms had blacked out. Sturms' companion summoned a waitress and security personnel. They arrived within sixty seconds, immediately checked Sturms' vital signs and noted that Sturms' pulse was "strong." At no time did Sturms choke or cough, or exhibit any other signs that an object was obstructing his breathing. Soon thereafter, Sturms' pulse began to slow. Immediately security personnel radioed the hotel dispatcher and requested the assistance of the Las Vegas Fire Department paramedics. While waiting for paramedics to arrive, security personnel obtained an oxygen tank, laid Sturms on the floor and began CPR procedures.

Upon arrival, the paramedics took over the efforts to resuscitate Sturms. Their attempts to clear Sturms' airway proved unsuccessful. Sturms was then transported to the University Medical Center. At the emergency room, doctors attempted to clear Sturms' airway, but these efforts were also unsuccessful. At 10:10 P.M. doctors announced Sturms dead.

An autopsy was performed the next day. In the examining doctor's view, Sturms had choked to death when food became lodged in his airway. ...

Sturms' estranged wife, Ahiliya Lee, personally and on behalf of their minor son, brought this action claiming negligence on the part of the restaurant. The eatery argued that it fulfilled its duty to Sturms when its employees promptly summoned emergency medical assistance. Lee argued that the restaurant's duty encompassed not merely summoning emergency medical assistance, but also administering the Heimlich maneuver to the decedent. ...

In Nevada, as under the common law, strangers are generally under no duty to aid those in peril. However, where a special relationship exists between the parties, such as innkeeper-guest or restauranteur-patron, an affirmative duty to aid others in peril is imposed by law. ...

The issue in this case is the nature and extent of the restaurant's duty to Sturms and whether that duty was breached. ... Lee contends that the restaurant's duty under the circumstances of this case required the restaurant to administer the Heimlich maneuver to Sturms because a choking victim may only have minutes before serious injury or death results, and because the Heimlich maneuver is relatively simple to perform. ...

[The court referenced precedents in California, Florida, Illinois, and Wyoming that hold that a restaurant satisfies its duty to exercise reasonable care in choking situations where its employees promptly summon medical assistance.]

In this case the restaurant employees examined and assessed Sturms' condition immediately upon being summoned by his dining companion. The employees diligently continued to monitor Sturms' condition until his condition worsened. Upon realizing that his condition was deteriorating, restaurant employees summoned professional medical assistance. We cannot say that the behavior of the restaurant employees under these circumstances was anything other than reasonable. We perceive no breach of the duty owed to Sturms in failing to perform the Heimlich maneuver. ...

We affirm the trial court's grant of summary judgment in favor of the restaurant.

CASE QUESTION

1. Under what circumstance might the restaurant have been liable?

Courts recognize that restaurants would be strapped with a considerable burden if required to train employees to provide medical assistance or first aid. The courts seem intent on not imposing that responsibility. Said a Wyoming court,

"We are concerned that a specific requirement of first aid, rather than aid in the form of a timely call for professional medical assistance, would place undue burdens on food servers and other business-invitors. ... Courses in first aid techniques require both time and money. Annual recertification classes are required in CPR and the Heimlich maneuver. Because employee turnover in the food service industry is high, continual training efforts might be required to provide a staff capable of providing first aid. This duty would apply to every food server, regardless of size. ... The only persons expected to perform rescue techniques regardless of circumstances are the professional medical responders called for just that purpose. Whether that call is made within a reasonable time is the appropriate factual issue for jury consideration.[45]

Negligence Doctrines Generally Favoring the Defendant

The following doctrines benefit the defendant by shifting some or all of the responsibility for an injury to the plaintiff.

Contributory Negligence and Comparative Negligence

In some situations where a plaintiff is injured, not only is the defendant negligent but the plaintiff is as well. For example, assume that a plaintiff who trips on a hole

---

[45] *Drew v. Lejay's Sportsmen's Cafe, Inc.*, 806 P.2d 301 (Wy. 1991)

in a restaurant's rug was wearing a high-heeled shoe she knew had a loose heel. The plaintiff fell due to both the loose heel and the hole. What effect does the plaintiff's negligence in wearing the shoe have on the lawsuit against the restaurant? Does the restaurant's duty to keep the premises reasonably safe give the plaintiff immunity from the consequences of her own inattention?

The impact on the lawsuit of the plaintiff's negligence depends on the applicable state's law. Each state follows either the rule of contributory negligence or the rule of comparative negligence.

Contributory Negligence

According to the rule of **contributory negligence**, if the plaintiff's carelessness contributed to the injury, the plaintiff cannot successfully sue a negligent defendant. Instead, the case will be dismissed. The defendant will not be liable for the plaintiff's damages and the plaintiff must absorb the full loss associated with the injuries. This is true regardless of how slight or insignificant the plaintiff's negligence may have been. While contributory negligence used to be the rule in most states, today only a few follow it—Alabama, Maryland, North Carolina, Virginia, and the District of Columbia.

An example of the application of this rule involves a girl-scout leader who escorted four scouts to McDonald's. The leader directed the girls to sit at a table and she alone placed the order. While in line, she noticed a low, unpainted, wooden platform positioned partially beneath the counter overhang. The platform was a bridge that allowed young customers to climb to a level where they could be seen and served by the cashier. When the scout leader's order was ready, she picked up the tray and as she turned to walk to the dining area she tripped over the wooden structure and fell, hitting her hip and shoulder. Her resulting lawsuit was dismissed based on contributory negligence. Said the court, "Although an argument may be made that defendant was negligent in placing the platform so that it was partially hidden by the counter overhang, plaintiff's contributory negligence [in failing to avoid the structure after having observed it] would necessarily defeat any verdict in her favor."[46]

The reason for the trend away from the contributory negligence role is that the all-or-nothing effect of this rule is considered unduly harsh to the plaintiff.

Comparative Negligence

According to the rule of **comparative negligence**, a plaintiff's negligence will not defeat the lawsuit. Instead, the jury will allocate the liability between the plaintiff and the defendant depending on their relative degree of culpability. For example, the jury might find that the restaurant patron who knew her heel was broken was 30 percent responsible and the restaurant that failed to repair the hole in the rug was 70 percent responsible. The plaintiff collects from the defendant a percentage of the damages equal to the percentage of liability attributed to the defendant. In

---

[46]*Allsup v. McVille, Inc.*, 533 S.E.2d 823 (N.C. 2000)

the example, the plaintiff must absorb 30 percent of the loss but can collect 70 percent from the defendant.

In another example, a hotel guest was raped by an intruder to her room. She had fastened the chain lock on the door, but failed to activate the doorknob lock. The hotel had improperly installed the chain lock so that, once the door was unlocked and cracked open slightly, the chain lock could easily be lifted out of its slot and the door opened. The attacker was thus able to enter the plaintiff's room. The guest sued the hotel for her damages. The court concluded that each was partially responsible for the incident and allocated liability between them. The case did not report the exact percentages attributed to each.[47]

In another case, the plaintiff entered a restaurant, saw that all the tables were occupied, noticed a couple vacating a table in an adjacent room, and began proceeding toward that table, watching it as she walked. Her attention was so diverted that she did not see a chair in the aisle in which she was walking. She tripped over it and suffered injuries. A manager came to her aid. Upon learning the cause of her fall, he said he had instructed servers "an hour ago to move this damn chair." In plaintiff's lawsuit the court found she was negligent for failing to watch where she was walking and the restaurant was also negligent for failing for an hour to remove the chair from a passageway. The court found the plaintiff and the restaurant each 50 percent responsible.[48]

Another comparative negligence case involved a restaurant disc jockey who spun records from an elevated platform. Upon leaving for the night, and with his arms loaded with 45 to 50 pounds of equipment, he stepped across a 19-inch gap to a set of stairs leading to the back door. Unbeknownst to the disc jockey, the stairs were moveable. As he placed his foot on the top step, the stairs went out from under him, causing him to fall and suffer a back injury. At trial his expert witness testified that the steps should have been either fixed or of a sufficient weight to prevent their easy movement—approximately 120 pounds. The actual weight of the moveable steps was only 40 pounds. The court found the disc jockey was negligent for being so heavily loaded with equipment and the restaurant was negligent for using such lightweight moveable steps. The court allocated 40 percent of the negligence to the plaintiff and 60 percent to the restaurant. The disc jockey was thus able to collect only 60 percent of his loss.[49]

In a "pure system" of comparative negligence, the plaintiff will collect the appropriate share of his damages regardless of the percentage of fault attributed to him. Some states that follow the comparative negligence rule provide that, for the plaintiff to recover, the percentage of liability allocated to the plaintiff must be less than that assigned to the defendant (i.e., a maximum of 49 percent assigned to the plaintiff). This is known as the "less-than" rule. Other states allow the defendant to recover if his percentage of fault is equal to or less than the defendant's (i.e., a maximum of 50 percent assigned to the plaintiff). A few states follow a

---

[47] *Ledbetter v. Concord General Corp.*, 665 So.2d 1166 (La. 1996)

[48] *Morace v. Melvyn's Restaurant, Inc.*, 719 So.2d 139 (La. 1998)

[49] *Michalopoulos v. C&D Restaurant*, 764 A.2d 121 (R.I. 2001)

"slight-gross" system in which the plaintiff can recover only if his share of the fault is slight and the defendant's share is gross.

The Doctrine of Last Clear Chance

While the contributory negligence doctrine greatly benefits defendants by barring plaintiffs from suing, in certain circumstances plaintiffs can use the doctrine of **last clear chance** to support their cases. Ordinarily, a plaintiff who is negligent in a state that follows the contributory negligence rule will be denied recovery against a negligent defendant. But if the last clear chance doctrine applies, the defendant will be liable for failing to prevent the injury even if negligent acts of the plaintiff initially put the plaintiff in peril.

The doctrine, alternatively called the subsequent negligence rule, requires exactly what its name implies: that the defendant actually had a last clear chance following the plaintiff's negligent act to avoid infliction of an injury on the plaintiff.

Four elements must be established before the doctrine will come into play:

1. The plaintiff has been negligent.
2. As the result of this negligence, the plaintiff is in a position of peril that cannot be escaped by the exercise of ordinary care.
3. The defendant knew or should have known of the plaintiff's peril.
4. The defendant had a clear chance, by the exercise of ordinary care, to avoid the injury to the plaintiff, but failed to do so.

For example, a plaintiff seeking to retrieve her parked car in the rain ignored a crosswalk and ran across four lanes of road, dodging traffic while jaywalking. The defendant was a motorist in the fifth lane of traffic. He observed the plaintiff traversing the road, but nonetheless hit her. The plaintiff admitted her negligence, but asserted that the defendant had ample time to take reasonable steps to avoid the accident. The plaintiff claimed the defendant was thus liable under the last clear chance doctrine. The jury agreed and awarded a verdict to the plaintiff which was upheld on appeal.[50]

If any one of the four elements is absent, the doctrine of last clear chance will not apply.

Most states that have adopted the comparative negligence rule have abolished the last clear chance doctrine. The reason is as follows: "To give continued life to [last clear chance] would defeat the very purpose of the comparative negligence rule—the apportionment of damages according to the degree of mutual fault."[51]

Assumption of Risk

Another legal doctrine with an application that has changed considerably in those states that follow the rule of comparative negligence is **assumption of risk**. Historically, and currently in states that follow the contributory negligence rule, the

---

[50]*Zaharavich v. Clingerman*, 529 So.2d 978 (Ala. 1988)

[51]*Spahn v. Town of Port Royal*, 486 S.E.2d 507 (S.C. 1997)

doctrine benefits the defendant and applies in cases where the plaintiff voluntarily engages in conduct known to present a risk of injury. If the plaintiff is injured as a result of that risk, the plaintiff, according to the doctrine, cannot successfully sue for the loss. Instead, the plaintiff is said to have assumed the risk—that is, accepted the chance that injury might occur and impliedly agreed not to sue if it does.

To establish assumption of risk, the defendant must show that the plaintiff

- Had knowledge of the risk
- Understood the risk
- Had a choice of either avoiding the risk or engaging in conduct that confronted the risk
- Voluntarily chose to take the risk.

The following case illustrates an application of the assumption of risk doctrine.

CASE EXAMPLE 5-15

Ball v. Hilton Hotels, Inc.
290 N.E.2d 859 (Ohio 1972)

It appears from the record that the plaintiff, a resident of Michigan, went to Cincinnati, Ohio, on May 27, 1967, with a reservation to stay at the defendant's hostelry, known as the Terrace Hilton Hotel.

Upon arrival at the hotel, she was informed by the defendant's doorman that there was a downtown area electric power failure and there was no lighting or elevator service in the hotel. The hotel lobby and registration desk were on the eighth floor of the hotel building. The plaintiff checked her baggage with the doorman and then inquired about the use of restroom facilities.

In response to her request, the doorman advised plaintiff the restroom was downstairs; that it would be quite dark on the staircase due to the electric power failure; that plaintiff would not be able to see the doors to the restrooms; and that the doors to the restrooms were located to the right at the bottom of the stairway. The doorman gave the plaintiff a small lighted candle, and she proceeded down the darkened stairway, moving slowly and carefully groping along the handrail.

After arriving at the platform portion of the stairway [apparently the halfway point of the flight of stairs], plaintiff [apparently believing she had reached the bottom of the stairs] began to grope about for the restroom door and, while so doing, she fell to the bottom of the stair steps and received personal injuries.

In her complaint against the hotel, plaintiff alleges that her personal injuries and resulting damage were directly and proximately caused by the negligence of the defendant in inducing her to enter a hazardous, darkened area of the hotel facility. ...

Before the defendant would be entitled to a judgment on the theory of assumption of the risk, it must be proven that plaintiff had full knowledge of a condition; that the condition was patently dangerous; and that she voluntarily exposed herself to the hazard created. ...

[P]laintiff was told that the electric power in the downtown area had failed and there was no light or electric power in the defendant's hotel; that it was dark in the stairway leading to the hotel restrooms; that plaintiff had full knowledge of the darkness when she walked down the stairway with a small lighted candle; and that she moved slowly and carefully as she descended the stairway.

Since it appears there is no genuine issue of any material fact, the trial court correctly determined the plaintiff assumed the risk of her injury and damage when she proceeded into the darkened area of the premises in question. ...

Ruling of the Court: Judgment affirmed for defendant.

CASE QUESTION

1. Identify the elements of assumption of risk and state the particular fact(s) in *Ball* that satisfy each element.

Participants in sporting activities are considered to assume the obvious and inherent risks associated with the sport. In *Coleman v. Ramada Hotel Operating Co.*, 933 F.2d 470 (7th Cir. 1991), the plaintiff was injured while participating in a timed obstacle course at a company picnic held at a resort owned by defendant Ramada. The first obstacle of the course was mounting a slide backwards. In the process the plaintiff fell from the ladder portion of the slide. The court held for Ramada, as the dangers associated with the activity were obvious and therefore the plaintiff assumed the risk. If, however, the reason the plaintiff fell was because a step on the ladder had rotted and weakened, Ramada would be liable because this was not a normal risk of the activity and the plaintiff therefore did not assume it.

Comparative Negligence and Assumption of Risk

Most states that have adopted the comparative negligence rule have abolished assumption of risk as a total bar to recovery in tort lawsuits. Instead, assumption of risk is treated as another factor for the trier of fact (jury or judge) to consider when making a comparative negligence allocation of liability. Thus, in some cases where assumption of risk fits the facts, the defendant's negligence may nonetheless be a partial cause of the injury. In such a case, an apportionment of fault between the plaintiff and defendant will be made. "Thus, there is no arbitrary bar to recovery and no sweeping exemption from duty accorded a defendant."[52]

In the following case, rowdy crowds spurred the plaintiff to expose himself voluntarily to significant risks. The assumption of risk rule was applied and the doctrine constituted a total bar to the plaintiff's recovery. As you read the case, consider whether the outcome would be different under the newer rule of comparative negligence.

CASE EXAMPLE 5-16

Eldridge v. Downtowner Hotel
492 So.2d 64 (La. 1986)

[O]n February 7, 1978, Mardi Gras day, plaintiff was the guest of a patron of the Downtowner in the French Quarter. While on the second floor balcony of the hotel, he observed various individuals on other balconies toying with the crowds below by exposing their breasts or "mooning" the crowds by exposing their bare buttocks. Spurred on by the wild atmosphere in the Quarter, plaintiff climbed on the balcony railing and mooned the crowd. While on the railing plaintiff fell to the street below and was seriously injured.

Plaintiff filed suit for 1.75 million dollars arguing that Downtowner was negligent in failing to have a protective screen or a uniformed guard on the balcony to prevent just such accidents as occurred herein. ...

---

[52]*Auckenthaler v. Grundmeyer*, 877 P.2d 1039 (Nev. 1994)

The record reflects that plaintiff's fall resulted solely from his own conduct. Plaintiff was not pushed off the railing, and he was neither enticed nor encouraged by defendant to sit on the railing. Moreover, the railing was not defective. It is clear, therefore, that plaintiff's fall was in fact caused by his own want of skill, that is, exercising bad judgment by sitting on the railing and in losing his balance. Thus, the question becomes whether Downtowner had a duty to protect plaintiff from his own conduct.

[A] "visitor assumes the obvious, normal or ordinary risks attendant on the use of the premises and owners are not liable for injuries to a visitor when those injuries result from a danger which he should have observed in the exercise of reasonable care."

Here the risk of harm was that of falling while sitting on a railing on a second floor balcony.

Such a risk is an obvious and reasonable risk of harm which the defendant had no duty to protect against.

But plaintiff argues that because of the wild atmosphere of Mardi Gras and the fact that traditionally women would expose themselves from the balconies, defendant should have foreseen that an accident was likely and was under an obligation to protect plaintiff from himself. We find no merit in this argument. ... [A]bsolutely no evidence was offered at trial demonstrating that anyone had ever fallen from the balcony during Mardi Gras or even that people sat on the balcony railings. ...

For these reasons we hold that the trial court was not required to charge the jury that the defendant had a duty to protect patrons from the type of conduct engaged in by the plaintiff herein. ...

CASE QUESTIONS

1. What was the particular risk of injury that the plaintiff assumed in this case?

2. The plaintiff claimed the hotel owed him a duty to provide either a protective screen or a uniformed guard on the balcony. Do you agree? Why or why not?

Ignorance of Risk Negates Application of Assumption of Risk

The assumption of risk doctrine will not apply if the plaintiff is unaware of the risk. For example, a newly hired bartender at a restaurant was assigned the duty of stocking the bar. This task required that he bring beer and liquor up to the first floor from the basement. A co-worker suggested he use the dumbwaiter. The bartender had never used the device before and had not been instructed on its use. Believing it would facilitate the stocking process, he employed it. The bartender loaded the dumbwaiter, closed the door and pressed the start button. He then went upstairs to meet it. He waited several minutes, but there was no indication it had arrived. Deciding to investigate, he opened a service access panel into the dumbwaiter shaft. He saw moving cables and believed the dumbwaiter was descending from the first floor to the basement. He put his head sideways into the panel to look into the shaft. Only then did he realize that the dumbwaiter's path continued up to the second floor and it was then above him. Before he could pull his head out, the dumbwaiter struck his face and jaw. He sued the restaurant, which asserted the defense of assumption of risk. The court refused to apply it

[53] *Lang v. The Red Parrot, Inc.*, 746 A.2d 142 (R.I. 2000)

noting that the plaintiff was a new employee, had never used the dumbwaiter before, and had not been given any instructions. When he put his head in the shaft, he was not aware that it extended up to the second floor.[53]

Key Terms

assumption of risk
attractive nuisance
comparative negligence
contributory negligence
Good Samaritan Statutes
independent contractor
invitee
last clear chance
licensee
negligence
negligence per se

nondelegable duties
preexisting condition
prima facie
proximate cause
rescue doctrine
res ipsa loquitur
respondeat superior
strict liability
strict products liability
trespasser
within the scope of employment

Summary

Hotels and restaurants face substantial liability for negligence. If a customer is injured by a restaurant or hotel's failure to act reasonably, the business will be obligated to compensate the customer.

For a successful negligence case, a plaintiff must prove four elements: (1) the existence of a duty owed by the hotel or restaurant to the plaintiff to act reasonably; (2) a breach of that duty; (3) injury to the plaintiff; and (4) proximate cause, meaning the plaintiff's injury was caused by defendant's breach of duty.

To avoid liability for negligence, hotels and restaurants must constantly be vigilant to ensure they are exercising reasonable care to protect the safety of their patrons. In states that continue to recognize varying standards of duty depending on the status of the injured party, for invitees the hospitality facility must inspect the premises, remove any risks of injury that exist, and make the premises reasonably safe. For licensees, the facility must disclose any known defects and refrain from causing willful or wanton injury. For trespassers, the facility must refrain from causing willful or wanton injury. In states that no longer recognize the differences between an invitee, licensee, or trespasser, a varying duty of care is owed to all three.

Various legal doctrines are associated with negligence. Those that aid the plaintiff are:

- *Res ipsa loquitur*, which means "the thing speaks for itself" and relieves the plaintiff of the need to prove specific acts of negligence

- *Higher duty of care owed to children* because of their relative lack of judgment and experience

- The *attractive nuisance doctrine*, which obligates occupiers of land to exercise reasonable care to protect trespassing children
- *Negligence per se*, which in most states eliminates the need for a plaintiff to prove negligence where the defendant violated a safety law
- *Strict liability*, which renders a defendant liable without fault under limited circumstances
- *Respondeat superior*, which obligates an employer to compensate persons injured by the negligent acts of its employees
- The *doctrine of last clear chance*, which applies in states that follow the contributory negligence rule and holds that, even if a plaintiff is negligent, a defendant may be liable if he knew of the plaintiff's peril and had an opportunity to prevent the injury but failed to do so.

The legal doctrines related to negligence that aid the defendant include:

- *Assumption of risk*, which, in contributory negligence states, relieves a defendant from liability for injuries incurred by a plaintiff when the plaintiff voluntarily engages in conduct known to present risks of injury
- *Contributory negligence*, which relieves a defendant from liability if the plaintiff is at all negligent
- *Comparative negligence*, which relieves a defendant from complete liability if the plaintiff is negligent and instead results in partial liability on the defendant
- *Good Samaritan Statutes*, which restrict exposure to liability for rescuers
- *Choking laws*, which relieve a restaurant from liability for failing to perform the Heimlich procedure on a chocking patron.

Preventive Law Tips for Managers

- *Always anticipate dangers that may exist at a hotel or restaurant and take the necessary action to eliminate the risks.* Hotels and restaurants are obligated to use reasonable care to protect their patrons from injury. Failure to do so will result in liability. Managers and employees should always be alert to conditions that may present risks. Upon discovery of any such conditions, fix them promptly. If removal of the condition is not immediately feasible, warning notices should be conspicuously posted.
- *Make frequent inspections of the premises so that dangerous conditions can be detected.* Undetected and uncorrected dangers increase the risk of injury to patrons. The purpose of regular and thorough inspections is to discover problems before they lead to injury. Once uncovered, they can be corrected and injury avoided.
- *Promptly repair dangerous conditions.* Elimination of dangerous conditions decreases the chances that guests will be injured. Reasonable care should

be taken to ensure that the repair process does not itself generate injury. For example, while washing a floor, housekeeping should post a sign cautioning passersby that the floor may be slippery.

■ *Train employees on how to detect dangerous conditions, and include inspections and reporting in their job responsibilities.* The better trained employees are, the more likely they will uncover unsafe conditions. The more employees are responsible for identifying safety risks, the less likely accidents are to occur.

■ *Carefully examine facilities used by children.* The duty of care owed to youngsters takes into consideration their lack of judgment and thus requires more on the part of the hotel or restaurant than the duty owed to adults. Since children cannot be expected to take precautions for their own safety, hotels and restaurants must be especially careful to ensure facilities likely to be used by them are suitable. Play areas, toys, pinball machines, highchairs, cribs, and similar items must be maintained in a condition safe for youngsters.

■ *Be alert to attractive nuisances, and take precautions to protect youngsters from related dangers.* An attractive nuisance is a condition on property that is appealing to children and likely to attract them, even though the property owner or occupier does not invite them. While hotels and restaurants do not ordinarily owe a duty to trespassers, if businesses tolerate a condition that is likely to attract children, they must maintain that condition in a way that neutralizes associated dangers. Failure to do so may result in liability.

■ *Stay current on laws that relate to your business and comply with them.* Failure to abide by applicable safety laws may result in liability based on negligence per se. In such cases, proof of negligence is not required. Instead, the plaintiff need only prove the existing law and the defendant's failure to comply (plus proximate cause). To avoid overlooking statutes that apply to the hospitality industry, diligently read trade journals, regularly consult with a knowledgeable attorney, and become active in trade associations.

■ *Do not rely on compliance with statutes alone to protect your business from lawsuits; in addition, exercise reasonable care to protect patrons from injury.* Compliance with statutes alone may not relieve the hotel from liability. Instead, compliance with laws may be only the beginning of what is required to avoid liability. Analyze risks associated with the establishment and determine what action, in addition to that required by statute, is necessary to eliminate those risks.

■ *Carefully choose the suppliers of goods that your hotel or restaurant resells, such as food and gift-shop inventory.* The rule of strict products liability enables a buyer of defective goods to sue the seller without regard to negligence. All the plaintiff must prove is that the product was defective when sold and the defect caused injury. To minimize the number of incidents of rancid food in restaurants and defective products in shops, be discriminating in the supplier's from whom inventory is purchased. Check references and reputation, inspect the merchandise when it is delivered, and verify the supplier's financial viability. If you are sued, you may be able to pursue the supplier in strict liability. A supplier who is no longer in business will be of little value in this regard.

- *Select employees carefully and train them well.* An employer may be liable for the acts of its employees based on the rule of respondeat superior. Much potential liability can be avoided by conducting thorough background checks on employees to ensure their suitability, by verifying their qualifications for the job, and by providing in-depth training to secure their compliance with company rules, policies, and expectations.

- *Aid patrons in need of assistance.* Many states now require a hotel or restaurant to come to the aid of a guest in need. If a hotel guest calls the front desk seeking help for an illness or assault, respond quickly. Delay in reaction time can result in liability. Train front-desk personnel on how to handle emergency phone calls. Instruct restaurant and hotel employees on first aid and who to call in the event of an emergency.

- *Prominently display the required poster showing first-aid procedures, including the Heimlich Maneuver.* The Heimlich Maneuver is a procedure that can dislodge food on which a diner is choking. Posters that illustrate the maneuver and contain directions on how to administer it are available, and in some states are required. By prominently displaying the poster, the information needed to assist a patron in trouble is readily available whenever needed. However, in most states, statutes relieve a restaurant from a duty to apply the Heimlich Maneuver. Promptly summoning medical assistance may be sufficient legally as a response to a choking patron.

Review Questions

1. What does *negligence* mean?
2. Who or what is the reasonable person?
3. Identify the four elements of a negligence case.
4. Which two elements of a negligence case must have a cause-and-effect relationship?
5. What is res ipsa loquitur?
6. If the assumption of risk doctrine applies in a case, who wins—the plaintiff or the defendant?
7. What is the difference between comparative negligence and contributory negligence?
8. What duty of care is owed by innkeepers to guests who are children? Does the duty differ at all from the duty owed to adults? If so, how does it differ?
9. What is an attractive nuisance?
10. What differentiates negligence per se from ordinary negligence?
11. What is the difference between an invitee, a licensee, and a trespasser?

Discussion Questions

1. In which of the following cases would res ipsa loquitur apply? Why?
   A. The plaintiff was driving his car on hotel property and hit an obstacle in the road.
   B. The plaintiff was sitting at the desk in her hotel room writing postcards when the ceiling light fixture fell on her head and injured her.
   C. The plaintiff tripped in a restaurant.

2. The plaintiff was a guest at a hotel with a baseball field. While playing on the field he tripped on a large hole in the ground and was injured.
   A. Did the plaintiff assume the risk? Why or why not?
   B. What is the effect of the assumption of risk doctrine in a state that has adopted the rule of comparative negligence? Why?

3. You are a manager at a restaurant. Your restaurant is sued by a customer who fell while at your establishment. What does the element of proximate cause require the plaintiff to establish? How might you dispute proximate cause?

4. Under what circumstances does a hotel or restaurant have strict liability? What can a business do to protect itself against this type of liability?

5. What is the significance of the doctrine of respondeat superior to a hotel or restaurant?

6. How might the duty of care owed by a hotel or restaurant differ depending on whether the plaintiff is an invitee, a licensee, or a trespasser? How might the outcome of a case vary depending on the status of the plaintiff? What is the rationale for such different results?

Application Questions

1. The plaintiff, while about to descend a flight of stairs from a second-story restaurant, was engaged in conversation with a companion and failed to survey the steps. An obstacle on the second step caused her to slip and fall, resulting in injuries. The state in which the restaurant was located adopted the rule of comparative negligence. What impact will her negligence have on her lawsuit against the restaurant? Explain fully.

2. Assume in question 1 that the applicable state rule was contributory negligence rather than comparative negligence. What impact would that have on the outcome of the case?

3. A customer at a pizza parlor ate a piece of pizza with a tack in it. Did the customer assume the risk of the tack's presence? Why or why not? What other negligence doctrine(s) might apply?

4. The Drumlin Hotel has a pond on its property. During the winter the pond freezes and neighborhood children come to play on it. One day in late March

the ice was thin and a child fell through and suffered from exposure and frost-bite. Will the hotel be liable for the child's injuries? Why or why not? Discuss the issues thoroughly.

5. At a bowling banquet one of the diners started to choke on a steak. He was assisted to the bathroom by several of his bowling friends and in the process passed by you as manager. You do not assist him personally, but you do call the police and an ambulance. They respond in three minutes. The choking diner is taken to a hospital, where he dies. His wife is now suing your restaurant for $1 million. What defenses are available to the restaurant?

6. Identify the legal status (invitee, licensee, or trespasser) of each of the following.
   A. A hotel guest.
   B. A person who comes to the hotel to meet a friend who is a guest of the hotel.
   C. A person who enters the hotel restaurant only to use the bathroom.
   D. A person who enters the hotel to attend a meeting being held in a room rented for the day by her employer.
   E. A person who enters the hotel to buy a gift in the lobby gift shop.
   F. A person who enters the hotel to take a shortcut through the building.
   G. A person who enters the hotel to rob a guest.
   H. A patron of a restaurant who left his coat and returns the next day to retrieve it.

Web Sites

Web sites that will enhance your understanding of the material in this chapter include:

http://www.findlaw.com   This site contains updates on legal news and many links to sites covering a variety of legal topics, including personal injury (negligence) cases.

http://www.nolo.com   This site provides articles and information on numerous legal topics relevant to this chapter, including personal injury and independent contractors. Once on the homepage, click on the desired topic from the list down the left side of the screen.

http://www.expertpages.com   This site provides listings of expert witnesses and consultants on a large variety of topics, including accidents and injuries, food and restaurant industries, lighting and illumination, premises liability, casinos, amusement parks, and many more.

For additional resources, visit our Web site
www.hospitality-tourism.delmar.com

CHAPTER 6

Negligence and Hospitality Practices

INTRODUCTION

In Chapter 5 we learned what types of conduct constitute negligence. We also learned about various legal doctrines that apply to negligence cases. In this chapter we will examine a variety of cases in which an injured plaintiff claimed a hospitality facility acted negligently. In some of the cases the plaintiff was able to prove that the hotel or restaurant was liable; in others, the facility won.

We know that a business owner owes invitees a duty of reasonable care, including the duty to inspect the premises, discover dangerous conditions such as a hole in the lobby rug, and correct them. This, however, does not make a hospitality business an **insurer**, one who is generally obligated to compensate another for all losses. Hotels and restaurants are liable only when they are negligent.

This chapter discusses the precautions the proprietor must take regarding the following areas and items in hotels and restaurants: the lobby, guest rooms, furniture, windows, bathroom appliances, elevators, doors, hallways, stairways, dining rooms, grounds, sporting facilities, and swimming pools. Also addressed are legal issues associated with security, fires, and medical service.

Duty Owed Guests in Hotel Rooms

Numerous circumstances in guest rooms can lead to liability if a hotel fails to exercise reasonable care. These circumstances include the level of cleanliness; the condition of the furniture, windows, lighting, and heating; bathroom appliances; and the presence of insects or animals.

Cleanliness of Hotel Rooms

Guests expect a clean room when they register. If a guest room is not cleaned well, liability can result. In *Nelson v. Ritz Carlton Restaurant and Hotel Co.*, 157 A. 133 (N.J. 1931), the plaintiff was assigned to a hotel room that recently had been vacated by other guests. The room was very messy. Wastebaskets had not been emptied and the floor was covered with lint and cigarette ashes. The plaintiff reported the condition to the front desk and then left for a few hours to allow housekeeping time to clean. When the plaintiff returned, the bed linens had been changed and clean towels placed in the bathroom, but the other problems had not been remedied. The plaintiff retired for the night. In the morning while answering a knock on the door she stepped on a needle that snapped after breaking the skin. She received medical attention but her foot became infected. The plaintiff sued the hotel for negligence and was awarded $2,500 compensation. The court stated that the proprietor of a hotel is required to use due care to have rooms thoroughly cleaned before reassignment. Because the hotelkeeper failed in the performance of this duty, the hotel was liable for resulting injuries.

Beds, Chairs, and Other Seats

Courts have generally permitted recovery for injuries caused by defective beds and furniture. In an early case, the hotel room was equipped with a bed that would fold up so as to leave the bed in an upright position when not in use (a "Murphy bed"). The top of the bed was heavy, weighing about 300 pounds. After sleeping in the bed all night, and as the plaintiff was about to leave it in the morning, "the top or upright portion of the bed fell forward upon him, crushing his head down upon his breast and inflicting severe injury." The plaintiff sued the hotel. The testimony presented by the plaintiff stopped short of identifying the exact defect in the bed that caused it to fall down and entrap him. He was able to use res ipsa loquitur and won the case.[1] Murphy beds are sometimes used today to enhance

---

[1] *Lyttle v. Denny*, 71 A. 841 (Pa. 1909)

the size of a room during the day when the bed is not needed for sleeping. The mechanisms should be inspected regularly to ensure proper functioning.

In *Nettles v. Forbes Motel, Inc.*, 182 So.2d 572 (La. 1966) the thermostat for the air conditioner in a motel room was located 6'9" above the floor. Plaintiff, a 5'2" woman, used the dressing-table stool to reach the knob to adjust the temperature. As she was standing on the stool it collapsed, causing her to fall and suffer injuries. She sued the motel for negligence. It denied liability and argued that the plaintiff knew the stool was not intended for that use. The court rejected this defense and held for the plaintiff, saying the hotel should have foreseen the particular misuse involved here given the height of the air-conditioner control. Further, the testimony revealed that the stool had been improperly assembled by the hotel and the legs on several other stools at the hotel had come loose necessitating repairs. Despite this reoccurring problem, the hotel had failed to inspect the remaining stools for soundness.

Furniture used by guests is sometimes abused or just wears out. To what extent should a hotel be liable when such furniture breaks and a guest is hurt? The cases hold that the hotel or restaurant must regularly inspect the furniture and discard any that is no longer suitable. Failure to do so will result in liability.

In *Gary Hotel Courts, Inc. v. Perry*, 251 S.E.2d 37 (Ga. 1978), the webbing on a chair seat was missing. The hotel covered the seat with a cushion. When a guest sat on the chair the cushion collapsed, causing him injury. The court held the hotel was liable to the guest because it breached its duty to provide the guest with premises that are reasonably safe for use and occupancy. The same result was obtained in *Palagano v. Georgian Terrace Hotel Co.*, 181 S.E.2d 512 (Ga. 1971), where injury was sustained when a bed in the defendant's hotel collapsed while the plaintiff was sitting on it with one foot raised removing his socks. The court said, "There was evidence from which a jury might find that the bed was defective and that such defect could, or should, have been discovered by a reasonable inspection." In another case, *Gresham v. Stouffer Corp.*, 241 S.E.2d 451 (Ga. 1978), the plaintiff was seated in the defendant's restaurant attending a meeting when his chair collapsed, injuring him. The court held the restaurant was negligent for failing to properly maintain the chair.

A casino escaped liability for a collapsing bar stool used by a patron to play video poker. Immediately prior to the fall the plaintiff, who weighed 350 pounds, was leaning back on the stool so that two of the four stool legs were off the ground. An expert witness testified that the reason for the fall was the plaintiff's leaning back on the stool. The jury held for the casino, finding that it was not negligent. The verdict was upheld on appeal.[2]

A casino stool was also involved in another case in which a slot-machine player attempted to mount the seat. In the process the stool slipped, causing the player to fall and sustain injuries. The player sued the casino and attempted to benefit from res ipsa loquitur. The court, however, refused to apply the doctrine reasoning that the casino did not have exclusive control of the chair. Rather, many customers

---

[2] *Hagenet v. Jackson Furniture*, 746 So.2d 912 (Miss. 1999)

use it nightly. The plaintiff could proceed with his lawsuit but could not use res ipsa loquitur.[3]

In a case involving a sports bar, the plaintiff was injured when metal bleachers he was sitting on collapsed. The bleachers had been installed four months earlier for use by patrons while watching sporting events on a big-screen television. Testimony established that the bleacher manufacturer's assembly instructions called for metal cross-bracing to be installed across the back of the bleachers in an *X*. Instead, the metal supports had been fastened in a vertical position. The cause of the bleachers' collapse was the improper installation. Although the bar had hired an independent contractor to install the bleachers, the duty to install them safely was a nondelegable duty. Therefore, the bar was liable for the resulting injuries.[4]

In another case involving a Kentucky Fried Chicken restaurant, a diner, attempting to sit at a table while holding his tray, fell and injured himself when the bench collapsed. Expert testimony suggested that the cause of the collapse was either faulty construction of the bench by the restaurant in using inappropriate, inflexible screws to attach the bench to its frame or failure to occasionally check for loosening bolts that would have been evident by simply jiggling the bench with one's hands. Summary judgment entered by the trial court in favor of the Kentucky Fried Chicken restaurant was therefore reversed on appeal and a trial ordered.[5]

Regular inspections for broken or defective furniture will help reduce these types of incidents. Catering and other departments regularly handle portable chairs and tables that are exposed to much wear and tear, making loose screws, nuts, bolts and brackets predictable. Setup crews should watch for needed repairs and carry a screwdriver and wrench. When an item of furniture needing repair is discovered, it should be immediately removed from service until the repairs are completed.

Windows, Window Fixtures, and Screens

The same duty to inspect for defects and remedy them exists in regard to windows and screens. A plaintiff on a riverboat casino was knocked to the floor by fallen decorative woodwork that framed a window. The woodwork and window had been negligently maintained. In these circumstances, the casino would be liable.[6] In *Rue v. Warner Hotel Co.*, 186 So. 625 (1939), the plaintiff-guest in the defendant hotel was trying to close a window when it shattered, injuring her arm. Testimony showed that the putty around the window pane was old and decayed, a defect that could have been ascertained by reasonable inspection. The hotel was liable for the oversight. In another case, a window shade fell on a guest and injured her, resulting in the application of res ipsa loquitur and liability on the hotel.[7]

---

[3] *Nickel v. Hollywood Casino*, 730 N.E.2d 1212 (Ill. 2000)

[4] *Otero v. Jordan Restaurant Enterprises*, 922 P.2d 569 (N.M. 1996)

[5] *Bishop v. KFC National Management Co., Inc.*, 473 S.E.2d 218 (Ga. 1996)

[6] *Morris v. Players Lake Charles, Inc.*, 2000 WL 349039 (La. 2000)

[7] *Hotel Dempsey Company v. Teel*, 128 F.2d 673 (5th Cir. 1942)

Maintaining appropriate fixtures in good condition can protect a hotel from liability. In *Schlemmer v. Stokes*, 117 P.2d 396 (1941), a child pushed through a window screen in a hotel room and fell out. The evidence showed no visible defect in the screen and, despite inspection, neither the plaintiff nor the defendant had found any defects in the screen before the accident. The hotel was therefore not liable to the injured child. Remember, a hotel is not an insurer of its guests' safety; it is only liable when it fails to exercise reasonable care.

Electrical and Heating Hazards

Electrical and heating devices must be maintained in good working order. The early case of *Reid v. Ehr*, 174 N.W. 71 (N.D. 1919), has not been modified through the years. In that case, the plaintiff suffered a shock when she turned on an electric light in her hotel room. The court held that the injury was occasioned by the hotel's lack of reasonable care in maintaining and inspecting the electrical equipment in the room, and so the hotel was liable.

Failure to furnish safe heating can result in an injured guest recovering damages. In *Wilson v. Benoit*, 231 S.W.2d 916 (1950), the court held that the proprietor of tourist cabins was liable when a guest was killed by a gas explosion in his cabin caused by a defective hose connection on the gas heater. The court said the fact that the plaintiff was drunk had no causal connection with the explosion and ruled out a verdict of contributory negligence.

Animals and Insects

The duty of reasonable care owed by hotels and restaurants to their customers applies also to injuries from animals or insects. If a guest is injured by an animal or insect and the hotel or restaurant's negligence led to its presence, liability will result.

The plaintiff in *Williams v. Milner Hotel Co.*, 36 A.2d 20 (Conn. 1944), was bitten by a rat while lying in bed at a hotel. Evidence showed that numerous rat holes existed in the baseboard of the room prior to this event. The defendant claimed that it had taken all necessary precautions by employing a cleaner and a competent exterminator, and by routinely inspecting the room. The jury held for the plaintiff, apparently relying on the failure of the hotel to discover and remove the rat holes.

The following case addresses the equally unpleasant thought of spiders in a hotel room. To help you understand this case, let us review the concept of summary judgment. Once a case is begun defendants often move for summary judgment, claiming that the plaintiff has failed to raise any factual issues on which the defendant could be held liable. If there are no issues, there would be nothing for a jury to decide, and so the judge dismisses the case without the need for a trial. Summary judgment represents a substantial victory for the defendant and a total loss for the plaintiff. In the following case the court was determining whether or not to grant summary judgment.

CASE EXAMPLE 6-1

Copeland v. The Lodge Enterprises, Inc.
4 P.3d 695 (Ok. 2000)

In November of 1992, Joyce Kathleen Copeland ("Copeland") was working as a pharmaceutical sales representative. While on a business trip, she spent the night as a paying guest at the Days Inn Motel in Muskogee, Oklahoma, a roadside hotel owned by the Lodge Enterprises, Inc., and operated by Sharon Andrews ("defendants"). Sometime during the night, she was allegedly bitten by a brown recluse spider. Copeland alleged the spider bite caused her to suffer severe, permanent, and disfiguring injuries. ... The plaintiff and her husband bring this action alleging that defendants were negligent in failing to provide Copeland with a safe premises, free of "varmints, critters and harmful insects" or in the alternative, to warn of their presence. Copeland sought damages for injuries, and her husband for loss of services, society, companionship and consortium.

Defendant moved for summary judgment, arguing that (1) they fulfilled their duty of care owed to invitees to maintain the premises in a reasonably safe and suitable condition, (2) their duty of care did not encompass protecting Copeland from injury from the bite of a brown recluse spider because the particular risk of harm from the presence of a brown recluse spider was not foreseeable; (3) they were not the insurers of the safety of motel guests; and (4) their conduct did not create or worsen any risk of harm, but rather prevented or lessened any such risk.

In support of their motion, defendants submitted copies of monthly invoices from Admiral Pest Control Co ("Admiral") showing a continuous program of pest control services at the Days Inn from August 1989 through February 1993, including the time period in which Copeland suffered her injury. Defendants also tendered portions of Sharon Andrews' deposition. Andrews, who was the Days Inn manager at the time of Copeland's injury, testified that she was trained in motel management, including pest control, she had engaged Admiral to spray the motel premises for insects and other pests, she had given Admiral oral instructions

that all pests were to be eliminated from the property, she sometimes personally watched as the pest control chemical was applied, she had terminated the services of the previous extermination company because it had failed to eradicate a roach infestation, she had never had to call Admiral because of a problem with any type of spider, and she had never received any complaints from customers other than Copeland about the presence of spiders.

Andrews also testified in her deposition that on Monday or Tuesday morning after Copeland's incident the previous Wednesday, she and Admiral's exterminator searched for spiders in the room in which Copeland had stayed as well as several other rooms. Although no spiders were found, they nonetheless sprayed the rooms. According to her deposition, the Days Inn received two or three annual, unannounced inspections by the Oklahoma Department of Health and had not been cited for any deficiencies during her tenure as manager.

In response, plaintiffs offered an affidavit from a licensed, experienced exterminator, who stated that (1) brown recluse spiders are common and indigenous to eastern Oklahoma and (2) if reasonable care were exercised in the pest control treatment of a facility, brown recluse spiders would be eradicated. Plaintiffs also tendered a letter of apology from defendant Andrews *acknowledging that Oklahoma is known for spiders*. Finally, plaintiffs offered copies of certain rules of the Oklahoma State Department of Health pertaining to lodging establishments, which condition licensure to operate a motel on compliance with the state's health and safety regulations.

On this record, the trial court entered summary judgment for the defendants, and plaintiffs appealed. ... We now reverse.

... The elements of negligence are: (1) a duty owed by the defendant to protect the plaintiff from injury, (2) a failure properly to exercise or perform that duty, and (3) an injury to plaintiff proximately caused by the defendant's breach of that duty. Plaintiff's licensed exterminator's affidavit speaks to the elements of duty and breach of duty by raising an issue of material fact as to the liability of defendants for the alleged negligence of their extermination contractor. This provides a sufficient evidentiary basis to defeat defendants' quest for summary judgment.

An innkeeper in Oklahoma continues to have a status-based, common-law duty of care to a guest. This duty remains unaltered by inspection and licensing statutes enacted under the police power of the state. The owner or operator of a motel is not an insurer of his guests' personal safety. Often described as a duty to maintain the premises in a reasonably safe and suitable condition, the innkeeper's common-law responsibility applies only to defects or conditions which are in the nature of hidden dangers, traps, snares, pitfalls, and the like—things which are not readily observable. The duty is fulfilled when reasonable care is taken to prevent the invitee's exposure to dangers which are more or less hidden, not obvious.

Although a hirer ordinarily cannot be held liable for the negligence of an independent contractor, the rule of non-liability does not apply where the hirer contracts for the performance of a duty imposed by law. Hence, while an innkeeper may hire an independent contractor to perform the former's nondelegable duty, he may not pass off to an independent contractor the ultimate legal responsibility for the proper performance of that duty. Under the nondelegable duty rule, an innkeeper may be held vicariously liable for an independent contractor's failure to exercise reasonable care *even if the innkeeper has himself exercised due care*.

The duty of an innkeeper to provide a reasonably safe premises encompasses the duty to use effective measures of pest control. ... The improper or ineffective application of pest control agents creates a foreseeable risk of harm to motel guests from the presence of what may otherwise be eradicable pests. Insects, arachnids, and other undesirable creatures in a motel room ... can pose a hidden, unexpected danger to unsuspecting motel guests.

Because the innkeeper's duty of care to invitees is nondelegable, the duty to use effective measures of pest control encompasses not only the motel's own actions or missions, but also those of an independent contractor/exterminator with whom the motel contracts to perform the services.

The affidavit of the licensed exterminator offered by plaintiffs in the case under review raises a disputed fact issue as to whether the Days Inn's extermination contractor might have been negligent in the performance of the pest control services. Where a genuine disputed issue of material (on the merits) exists, disposition of a case by summary judgment is erroneous. Plaintiffs are entitled to a jury's consideration of this dispositive issue.

CASE QUESTIONS

1. What is meant by the following statement in the beginning of the eighth paragraph: "An innkeeper in Oklahoma continues to have a status-based, common-law duty of care to a guest."

2. What facts presented in the case might establish that the hotel used reasonable care to keep spiders and insects out of the hotel?

3. What facts presented in the case will favor the plaintiff's argument that the hotel failed to exercise reasonable care to keep spiders out?

In *Cunningham v. Neil House Hotel Co.*, 33 N.E.2d 859 (Ohio 1940), the plaintiff-guest at the defendant hotel was awakened by a burning and stinging sensation on her right arm caused by an insect bite. The critter that stung or bit the plaintiff was not known or identified, nor was it known where the bug came from, how long it had been in the room, or the conditions under which it had entered. The plaintiff claimed res ipsa loquitur applied, but the court disagreed, stating that to permit the jury in this situation to draw an inference of lack of due care on the part of the hotel would have been mere conjecture. Only if the plaintiff can prove lack of due care on the part of the hotel, and proximate cause between that negligence and the inset bite, will the hotel will be liable.

In *Brasseaux v. Stand-By Corp. d/b/a Plantation Inn*, 402 So.2d 140 (La. 1981), the plaintiff-guest was stung by bees while showering, causing him to fall and injure his left wrist. Beehives were located outside the window of the room. The plaintiff sued the hotel. The manager admitted knowing of the existence of the hives but had not received reports of bees inside any rooms. The court held that if a hotel is on notice of the existence of beehives on or near its building, it should foresee that bees might enter the premises and sting a guest. The hotel was negligent for failing to remove the hives and for failing to warn guests of the bees' presence. The hotel was thus liable for the plaintiff's injuries.

Sometimes insect or animal bites occur despite careful action on the part of the hotel. If the inn was not negligent, it will not be liable. In Chapter 5 we studied *Febesh v. Elcejay Inn Corp.*, in which the court held a restaurant was not liable to a guest who suffered a bee sting at an outdoor reception, where no prior incidents of bee stings occurred at the eatery and the outdoor area was sprayed for bees at least once a day.

Bathroom Appliances and Hot Shower Water

Many problems including bathroom fixtures and plumbing can be avoided if housekeeping personnel are instructed to examine the bathroom fixtures routinely, and turn on the water in the shower and sink and let it run a bit. If fixtures appear cracked or broken, or if the water temperature rises substantially, maintenance should be called to inspect.

Water Faucets

Several cases have originated in hotel bathrooms involving defective appliances and plumbing systems. The same rules of negligence apply. *In Brown Hotel Company v. Marx*, 411 S.W.2d 911 (Ky. 1967), the guest, while turning on the water faucet in his hotel room, cut his hand when the porcelain faucet broke into pieces. The guest sued the hotel and used the doctrine of res ipsa loquitur, eliminating the need to prove the manner in which the defendant was negligent. The evidence established that the hotel failed to make regular inspections of the plumbing fixtures, and the hotel had "mysteriously" lost the shattered faucet fragments. Therefore, the hotel was unable to rebut the inference of negligence and so lost the case.

In another lawsuit, the plaintiff was injured by the faucet on a bathroom sink when the spigot "spun around and came back very quickly and with extreme force" hitting the plaintiff's fingers, causing injury. The force of the impact was such that a diamond and emerald on the plaintiff's ring were knocked out of their setting. The parties were unable to determine the cause of the incident. The facts did not suggest that the defect could have been discovered by inspections of the sink's hardware; therefore, the building owner was not liable to the plaintiff for her injuries.[8]

---

[8] *Lonsdale v. Joseph Horne Co.*, 587 A.2d 810 (Pa. 1991)

Showers

In addition to bathroom sinks, showers can malfunction leading to injuries. Excessively hot water has generated a number of negligence cases, one of which is *Wolfe v. Chateau Renaissance*, 357 A.2d 282 (N.J. 1976). The plaintiff, a hotel guest, turned on the shower water and set it at a comfortable temperature before entering. While he was in the shower and rinsing off, and without touching the controls again, very hot water came gushing out unexpectedly. The plaintiff jumped back, hit the back of the tub, and fell, suffering injuries. The court applied res ipsa loquitur and held for the plaintiff, noting that the sudden gush of water suggested a malfunction and negligence on the part of the hotel, which had exclusive control of the heating plant, pipes, and plumbing devices.

As illustrated in the following case, routine inspections can save the hotel from liability. In *Bearse v. Fowler*, 196 N.E.2d 910 (Mass. 1969), a guest sustained injuries when she slipped and fell in her bathroom at the defendant's motel while trying to shut off the hot water on a shower fixture. The knob failed to respond. The evidence established that the fixture was brand new; the motel owner inspected the shower handles daily and had no difficulty in turning them. The owner was thus unaware of any defect in the fixture and in the exercise of due care would not have discovered any defect. As you should expect given these circumstances, the court held the motel was not negligent.

Hand Bars and Grips

Proper maintenance of a bathroom requires inspection and repairs of hand railings and other grip devices. Lack of attention to these mechanisms can result in liability.

The following case illustrates an example of liability that can result from failing to properly care for hand bars.

CASE EXAMPLE 6-2

Sheridan Holiday Inn v. Poletis
954 P.2d 1353 (Wy. 1998)

Andrew Poletis sued the owner of the Sheridan Holiday Inn, John Q. Hammons, Inc., for injuries Poletis sustained while a guest at the hotel. Following a jury verdict in favor of Poletis, the Holiday Inn moved for a judgment notwithstanding the verdict. Holiday Inn now appeals the court's denial of its motion. We affirm. ...

Poletis and his family, on vacation from their home in Michigan, checked into the Sheridan Holiday Inn on the night of July 25, 1993. The next morning when Poletis was showering, he grasped the hand bar to lower himself into the bathtub. As he lowered himself, the bar came out of the wall and Poletis fell, hitting his lower back on the tub. ... Dr. Meengs examined Poletis and reviewed his spine x-ray. Dr. Meengs concluded that Poletis suffered from a low back strain or contusion as a result of the fall, and he instructed Poletis to work on a gentle exercise program to stretch and strengthen the area. Poletis visited Dr. Meengs two other times due to continuing back pain and discomfort. Both times Dr. Meengs advised Poletis to continue his stretching and strengthening program as long as the pain and discomfort continued, and to use anti-inflammatories to keep any pain under control.

Poletis brought suit against Holiday Inn, alleging the hotel's negligence resulted in injuries to his back. The case was tried to a six-person jury. The jury found in favor of Poletis and awarded him $75,000.

An innkeeper must use ordinary care to keep the property in a reasonably safe condition for the purpose for which the property was reasonably intended. It was for the jury to determine, based on the evidence presented and with the background of ordinary human experience, whether Holiday Inn exercised ordinary care to keep the property in a reasonably safe condition.

Negligence and proximate cause are never presumed from the happening of an accident, and mere conjecture cannot form the basis of liability.

Poletis testified at trial that the bar came out of the wall when he put his weight on it. He stated that the wall where the bar came out was "punky soft" and that there was mold. Mrs. Poletis testified that when she came into the bathroom she saw Poletis lying in the tub, with the bar in his hand, with the screw still in it. She stated that the "crumbled wall was all over the place" and tiles were missing. She described the wall where the bar detached as being "crumbly and rotted" and "mushy." Holiday Inn maintains that because there was no evidence of Holiday Inn's failure to maintain or inspect the bar, or that the bar was improperly installed or the wall improperly constructed, Poletis did not show that Holiday Inn violated its duty.

The mere fact that the bar came out of the wall, causing Poletis to fall, is not sufficient to show that Holiday Inn breached its duty to keep the hotel room in a reasonably safe condition. However, Poletis and his wife both testified that the wall was mushy, crumbly and rotted where the bar came out. From this testimony, a jury could reasonably infer that the condition of the wall had occurred over a significantly long period of time and that Holiday Inn, in the exercise of reasonable diligence, should have discovered and fixed the problem. ... The jury could infer, based on common knowledge and ordinary human experience, that moisture had to have been accumulating behind the tiles for more than a short time for the wall to assume that appearance. ...

Damages

The jury awarded Poletis $75,000 in compensatory damages. Holiday Inn contends that the verdict is grossly excessive arguing that Poletis only showed $400 in medical expenses actually incurred, no past or future wage loss, no future medical expenses, and very little evidence of pain and suffering.

... [T]he amount of money to be awarded rests almost totally within the discretion of the jury. Appellate courts are reluctant to interfere with the jury's decision unless the award, by its excessiveness or inadequacy, denotes passion, prejudice, bias or some erroneous basis.

At trial the jury heard testimony from Poletis and his wife of the ongoing effects of the injury. Poletis testified that he experiences a great deal of pain in his back and legs when he sits for long periods in the car or stands for several hours, both of which are requirements for his job as a salesman. He testified that he can no longer run without aggravating his back. Mrs. Poletis testified that her husband is not able to walk with the family anymore because he gets sore. She stated that when he rides his bike it alleviates the pain, but that activity takes time away from the family. She also testified that he must sometimes rearrange his work schedule to avoid long-distance driving if his back is too achy or sore.

The jury also heard Dr. Meengs' deposition testimony that Poletis could perform normal functions of daily living, but had to curtail more strenuous physical and recreational activities which he enjoyed. Dr. Meengs testified that, in his opinion, Poletis' pain was real, not feigned. Dr. Meengs also stated that although exercise alleviated the symptoms, Poletis was likely to continue to experience pain and discomfort.

Taken together, the evidence amply supports the $75,000 awarded by the jury, and we find no evidence that passion or prejudice influenced the award.

CASE QUESTIONS

1. The court stated, "the mere fact that the bar came out of the wall, causing Poletis to fall, is not sufficient to show that Holiday Inn breached its duty to keep the hotel room in a reasonably safe condition." Why not? What more is needed?

2. How does a jury determine the appropriate amount of damages?

Bathroom Doors

Bathroom doors can create problems if their maintenance is overlooked. Broken hinges can cause a door to fall on a patron. Broken latches or locks can result in accidents. In one case, a plaintiff entered the only available stall in a store bathroom layed out like many bathrooms in the public areas of hotels. She discovered that the latch to lock the door was missing. She closed the door and placed her pocketbook on the floor of the stall in front of the door so that anyone looking at the outside of the stall would see that it was occupied. "She was in the process of rearranging her clothing when a woman opened the door to the stall forcefully and caused it to hit plaintiff's head." As a result, the plaintiff suffered injuries and sued the store. The maintenance manager established that this store cleaned and restocked the restroom daily and performed more comprehensive cleanings weekly that would have revealed the broken latch. There had been no prior broken latches at the store. The court held that, given the store's reasonable maintenance schedule and the lack of similar incidents, the store could not have foreseen the risk and therefore was not liable for the plaintiff's injuries.[9] Had the store been less vigilant, it likely would have been liable.

In-Room Hot Tubs and Whirlpools

Some hotel rooms sport hot tubs or whirlpools for guests' pleasure. Like all appliances, if not properly maintained and utilized, they can cause accidents and injuries. However, most guests are aware that hot water can cause burning and scalding and they must take precautions to avoid such injuries.

A couple, who became plaintiffs, were celebrating a birthday and reserved a hotel room with a whirlpool. They began the celebration with some friends at the hotel lounge. During the course of the evening, two of the celebrants went to the plaintiffs' hotel room and filled the whirlpool bathtub with hot water. They covered the whirlpool with balloons and returned to the lounge to continue the party. Later when the plaintiffs returned to their room they stepped into the whirlpool without testing the temperature of the water. Due to its heat they suffered burns over portions of their bodies requiring hospital treatment.

---

[9] *Parks-Nietzold v. J.C. Penney, Inc.*, 490 S.E.2d 133 (Ga. 1977)

In the lawsuit the hotel proved that the heaters in the whirlpool complied with applicable temperature specifications and warnings set by the American National Standards Institute. The plaintiffs each acknowledged that they were aware that hot bath water could cause scalding. That acknowledgment renders the risks open and obvious, eliminating any duty on the part of the hotel to warn guests. Instead, the plaintiffs needed to take precautions to protect themselves against scalding, which they failed to do. The court thus held for the hotel.[10]

Duty Owed Guests and Others in Public Areas

This section deals with a hotel's public areas, such as the lobby, stairs, elevators, bars, doors, and dining rooms. These cases also apply to restaurants, most areas of which are public.

Lobby

Because the lobby is the most frequently used public area of a hotel, special precautions should be taken. Frequent and regular inspections should be made to ensure the walkways are not blocked by suitcases or similar items, the rugs have no bumps or holes on which people might trip and fall, the furniture is in good condition and able to hold anticipated weight, no intruders are bothering guests, debris is picked up and everything else is generally in good order. When hotel employees are repairing or cleaning the lobby floors or furniture, they should place barriers around the work area to protect invitees from related harm.

Elevators

Elevators are an indispensable part of most hotels. Guest rooms are usually located on upper floors. Hotels often position restaurants and bars above the lower floors to take advantage of the view or for efficiency of space utilization. As a result, elevators are in great demand and accidents occasionally occur. The type of accidents range from failing to level the elevator with the floor when a guest is exiting, to malfunctioning elevators that plunge down the shaft out of control.

In general, a hotelkeeper who operates an elevator is obligated to use at least ordinary care in its maintenance and operation. In some states, a high degree of care is required.

Self-Service Elevators

Automatic elevators, also called self-service elevators, are those designed to operate by buttons controlled by passengers without a full-time operator. Guests of all

---

[10]*Severn v. Fifth Season Inn*, 1998 WL 254444 (Tex. 1998)

ages and aptitudes who may have little familiarity with elevators use them. The manufacturer or contractor installing an automatic elevator, as well as the owner and those under contract to service or inspect it, must act with care.

A hotel guest stumbled while exiting an automatic elevator because the car stopped below the floor level. The guest sued. At trial the guest presented an expert witness who testified that the cause of the misleveling was carbon dust buildup in the elevator's motor generator. The jury determined the hotel was negligent in its maintenance of the elevator and the verdict was upheld on appeal.[11] We learn from this case that businesses with elevators should ensure that their maintenance programs includes regular cleaning of the system components.

Where an elevator headed for the ground floor dropped past that floor, struck bottom, and rebounded to the third floor causing injuries, a lawsuit resulted. The plaintiffs, patrons in the elevator at the time of the incident, proved that the elevator had a history of recent malfunctions. Within the preceding six days the service company was called three times and the day before the accident, the elevator had been stuck between floors trapping people inside. Although a service call had been made just hours prior to the rebound incident, an award of summary judgment for the building owner was reversed and the case was referred to a jury to determine liability.[12]

Elevator Maintenance Is a Nondelegable Duty

The duty to maintain an elevator in reasonably safe condition is a nondelegable duty. Thus, if a hotel hires a maintenance company and it negligently overlooks a problem that leads to an accident and injury, the hotel will be liable to injured guests although the negligent party was the elevator service company.

A woman entered a self-service elevator on the building's third floor intending to go to the ground floor. When the doors shut the elevator plummeted and came to an abrupt stop below the first floor, causing injuries to the passenger. The building owner will be liable if the cause of the injury can be traced to the owner's negligence or to negligence on the part of a repair or maintenance company it may have hired. Liability for the latter would be based on the owner's nondelegable duty to keep the premises safe.[13]

Freight Elevators

Freight elevators are customarily maintained at a lower level than are elevators used by guests. This circumstance not only creates added risks to employees who use the freight elevators, but may also result in injury to guests who somehow find their way to the service elevators. Care should be taken to maintain freight elevators in a safe condition.

---

[11]*Dowden v. Otis Elevator Company*, 2001 WL 824406 (Mich. 2001)

[12]*Golden Shoreline v. McGowan*, 787 So.2d 109 (Fl. 2001)

[13]*Gaffney v. EQK Realty Investors*, 445 S.E.2d 771 (Ga. 1994)

Supervision of Maintenance

Safety risks result when elevators are being repaired. Precautions must be taken. For example, when an innkeeper leaves the door to an elevator open or unlocked, which sometimes happens when an elevator is undergoing repairs, a guest might fall into the well and suffer injury. This type of accident will likely result in a finding of negligence against the hotel. It could easily be avoided by roping off the area around the elevator and displaying warning signs.

Escalators

Like stairs, escalators need maintenance attention. Injury can result if an escalator is not working properly or is overcrowded; if running or horseplay is permitted while riding; or if dents, holes, or other damage to the steps develop and go unattended.

Two recent escalator cases, both involving casinos, are instructive on the factual circumstances that can lead to accidents. In one, the escalator stopped suddenly, throwing the plaintiff forward causing injuries. The apparent problem was defective installation.[14] In another case, the plaintiff fell and injured her knee while on an allegedly overcrowded escalator. The plaintiff was unable to prove any previous problems involving pushing or tripping on the device. No one had reported any problems with the escalator in the period preceding the incident. Based on these facts, the court dismissed the case, holding that the plaintiff failed to show the defendant was negligent.[15]

Likewise, an escalator's railings and access areas must be inspected and any dangerous conditions removed. A restaurant may be liable where it failed to remove a screw protruding one inch from the railing of an escalator, causing injury to a patron.[16]

Doors

The duty of restaurateurs and innkeepers to exercise reasonable, ordinary due care to keep the premises reasonably safe also applies to doors. Development of and adherence to a maintenance plan can save a hospitality facility from liability. A plaintiff in the ladies room of a Pizza Hut was struck in the head and upper body by a door to a stall that came off its hinges as she pulled it toward her to close it. The eatery sought summary judgment, claiming that the plaintiff could not establish that it had actual or constructive notice of the defective condition of the door. Said the court, Pizza Hut "failed to demonstrate reasonable maintenance of the bathroom facility" and thus failed to establish a lack of constructive notice of the unsafe condition of the door.[17]

---

[14] *Lupkus v. Otis Elevator Co,* 2000 WL 486936 (Conn. 2000)

[15] *Hilton Hotels v. Fleming,* 774 So.2d 174 (La. 2000)

[16] *Anderson v. Market Street Developers, Ltd.,* 944 S.W.2d 776 (Tex. 1997)

[17] *Thompson v. Pizza Hut,* 691 N.Y.S.2d 99 (N.Y. 1999)

Crowded Doorways

In *Schubert v. Hotel Astor, Inc.*, 5 N.Y.S.2d 203 (1938), the court stated that under ordinary circumstances hotels and restaurants need not have a door attendant; but, if they are aware that an extraordinary crowd will be gathering, a duty exists to employ an attendant to ensure the safety of patrons entering and leaving. In that case the Hotel Astor was the traditional Army team headquarters on the day of the Army-Notre Dame football game, an event that attracts a lot of people. In the early evening, not surprisingly, the hotel lobby was congested with people in a "gay, hilarious and carousing mood." The plaintiff, a sixty-three-year-old woman, entered the hotel through the revolving door on her way to a banquet hosted by the hotel and sponsored by the Danish Society. As she had almost completed her entrance, suddenly "there was an awful rush" and several "young fellows" chasing each other inside the hotel lobby ran into the same compartment of the revolving door the plaintiff was in and gave it a hard push. As a result, she was struck by a part of the door and suffered a fractured hip and other injuries.

The hotel was held liable because it should have foreseen the large, rowdy crowd generated by the football game; thus, it should have provided a door attendant to help control the crowd's ingress and egress. If an unruly crowd is not foreseeable, an innkeeper or restaurateur cannot be held liable for the unexpected conduct of its patrons.

Automatic Doors

Automatic doors are very common, providing the public ingress and egress to an abundance of facilities on a daily basis. Malfunctioning automatic doors can injure an unsuspecting patron in a variety of ways. To avoid these kinds of injury, hospitality facilities should make regular examinations of the doors' mechanisms and promptly repair any defect discovered.

A ninety-four-year-old woman attempting to enter a hotel in Las Vegas was partly through the doorway when the automatic doors unexpectedly closed on her, knocking her down and causing injury. The plaintiff's expert witness testified that automatic doors should receive thorough mechanical inspections at least every six months, and they should be inspected weekly to determine if they are working properly. The hotel's chief engineer testified that the hotel did not have a regular maintenance or inspection program for the doors. A jury found the hotel liable and the verdict was upheld on appeal.[18]

Note that the plaintiff in this case was ninety-four years old and therefore arguably would take more time than the average person to get through the door. She might also be more susceptible than the average person to serious injury in this type of accident. Do these facts lessen the hotel's liability? The answer is no. Hotels and restaurants invite people of all ages and circumstances to their establishments and must anticipate that some guests are more injury-prone than others. Hospitality facilities owe a duty to exercise reasonable care to protect the safety and well-being of *all* their patrons, regardless of frailties.

[18]*Landmark Hotel & Casino, Inc. v. Moore*, 757 P.2d 361 (Nev. 1988)

Sliding-Glass Doors

Another popular door used in many hotels and restaurants is the sliding-glass door. Without careful maintenance, the glass can shatter, causing injury to those nearby. The following case illustrates this scenario.

CASE EXAMPLE 6-3

Sheppard v. Crow-Barker-Paul
968 P.2d 612 (Ariz. 1998)

... Tarik Sheppard ("Tarik")—then fifteen years old—was playing in a basketball tournament in Scottsdale, Arizona. The members and coaches of Tarik's team were registered guests at the Safari Hotel. Tarik was injured on the hotel premises when his teammate, Melvin Johnson, closed the sliding glass door to his hotel room, number 249, as Tarik was about to enter. The parties ... do not dispute that the door shattered into pieces of glass, severely lacerating Tarik's arms.

Tariks' father, Daniel Sheppard ("Sheppard"), brought this suit against Safari. Because Tarik was a minor at the time, Sheppard asserted Tarik's claim for personal injuries and his own claim for the cost of necessary medical treatment for his son.

Safari denied liability and alleged Tarik's comparative fault. The case proceeded to a trial by jury and concluded in a $445,000 verdict in Sheppard's favor; the jury assigned Safari 100% of the fault. ...

As background, in 1956, when the Safari Hotel was built, the Arizona laws neither required safety glass nor proscribed plate glass in hotel sliding doors. As of July 1, 1974, the Arizona Legislature made it unlawful to install any form of glass other than safety glass in hazardous locations in public buildings, including hotel and motel sliding doors. The statute does not impose a statutory duty to retrofit pre-1974 installations with safety glass. [The glass on Tarik's door was annealed (plate) and not safety glass.] ...

Safari had a common-law duty to avoid subjecting its guests to a foreseeable and unreasonable risk of harm. The trial court defined this duty to the jury in the following instructions:

> The duty of a hotel like defendant to its guests is to maintain its premises in a reason-

ably safe condition. Defendant is required to use ordinary care to inspect for, warn of, safeguard against or remedy a dangerous condition of which Defendant has notice.

Safari seeks judgment notwithstanding the verdict contending that Sheppard introduced no evidence that Safari had pre-accident notice of any unreasonably dangerous condition in Tarik's room. We disagree.

Actual knowledge of the dangerous condition is not required. The duty to inspect arises when the owner has reason to suspect a defect.

Sheppard introduced substantial evidence to establish that Safari had reason to suspect a defect. Arthur Freedman, Sheppard's expert witness, testified from a review of hotel records that the glass doors in the east building [where Tarik's room was located] were breaking with regularity and that Safari had already replaced eleven of the fifty-eight door panes in that building in the twenty-one months before Tarik's accident. The jury could reasonably have inferred that, in the course of Safari's clean-up and replacement effort, the Safari management had abundant opportunity to discover that its guests were exposed to the danger of annealed glass doors.

Moreover it was undisputed that Tarik's friend Melvin Johnson had reported a malfunction of the door in the Room 249. This testimony, coupled with Freedman's testimony, permitted the jury to conclude that Safari should have known before the accident that a door containing annealed glass was unstable within its track. That door was the single entrance and exit for Room 249. Upon such evidence the jury could properly have concluded that Safari had reason to suspect a dangerous condition and that it breached its common-law duty to use ordinary care to inspect for, warn of, safeguard against, or remedy that condition.

CASE QUESTIONS

1. What maintenance procedures should be followed for sliding glass doors?

2. How might the hotel have avoided liability in this case?

3. In 1974, when the legislature imposed the duty of safety glass, why do you think the law-makers did not require immediate replacement of non-safety glass doors?

Hallways

Hallways are often heavily traveled. Improper maintenance of these spaces can result in liability for negligence. An alert manager will inspect to ensure they are properly cleaned, warning signs are utilized during repairs and cleaning, and rugs are free from holes.

A hole in the rug can trap a shoe heel and result in someone falling. A bulge in a carpet can easily lead to a trip-and-fall accident resulting in injuries and liability.[19]

Is a casino liable when a guest is hurt from a fall in a hallway caused by overcrowding? A plaintiff was walking through a crowded walkway in the midst of numerous gaming tables. Unexpectedly, someone extended his leg and the plaintiff tripped over it. She sued the casino for failing to safely manage the crowds. The court, holding for the casino, differentiated between the facts of this case and a circumstance in which there is only one available route and it is congested. In the latter circumstance, the premises owner may be liable if it fails to protect the customer. However, in a more open setting such as a restaurant, casino, or mall where many hallways and aisles exist, the patron has some responsibility to ensure a safe route. Said the court, "[A]ny one avenue of travel available to a customer may at any moment become temporarily congested so as to require the patron to change his route or to slow his movement to the point of stopping altogether as a precaution against unexpected collisions with other customers." The plaintiff thus lost the case.[20]

Stairways, Steps, and Their Coverings

Guests are entitled to assume that steps and passageways are clear of dangerous impediments and otherwise reasonably safe. Because stairways in a hotel or restaurant constitute a potential danger to guests, hotelkeepers must do all of the following to avoid liability: see that steps are properly constructed; keep them in good repair; install railings; avoid leaving items on the steps; provide adequate lighting; if the step is located in an unexpected place, use some means to alert patrons of the step's presence (e.g., different color carpet or a strip of white paint at the end of the step); and if the step is carpeted, maintain the carpets in good and safe condition.

---

[19] *Carrasquillo v. Holiday Carpet Service, Inc.*, 615 So.2d 862 (Fl. 1993)

[20] *Green v. Harrah's Casino*, 774 So.2d 1174 (La. 2000)

Building codes provide numerous safety specifications for stairways. Deviations that result in injury to guests will likely result in liability. Examples of code mandates are requirements of uniform height for all steps in a stairway and a maximum permissible height. When the elevation is inconsistent, unsuspecting users may trip and fall. In a case involving a woman who fell on steps that were of various heights, including one that exceeded the code's maximum, the building owner was denied summary judgment.[21]

Poor construction of steps can result in liability. For example, the layout of a bar required that customers use a ramp to reach the back room where the bathroom was located. The ramp was made of wood that, per an expert witness, was likely to shrink, crack, and move over time. A patron fell on her way to the lavatory when her high-heeled shoe became stuck in a gap in the plywood ramp, causing serious knee and back injuries. The jury decided the case in favor of the plaintiff, and the verdict was affirmed on appeal.[22]

Another case involved a staple embedded in the carpeting in a hotel conference room. A disc jockey, hired to play for a wedding reception being held in the room, hurt her knee while kneeling to plug electrical cords for her equipment into an outlet. The staple pierced her left knee through the cartilage down to the bone. She sued the hotel claiming it was negligent in the maintenance of the carpet. The hotel night janitor testified that during the week leading up to the injury, he had discovered numerous staples while vacuuming because they made a "clinking noise" in the appliance. He attributed them to construction done for a "Queen of the Universe" pageant held in the room a week earlier. Each night since that event he picked up fewer and fewer staples. He was eventually satisfied that he had picked up all the staples in the room because he no longer heard the clinking noise. The court determined the hotel used reasonable care to remove the staples and dismissed the case.[23]

Another issue with stairs that can result in liability for negligence is inadequate lighting. A plaintiff was attending a concert and needed to use the bathroom, requiring that she descend a flight of stairs from the balcony. There was "no light whatsoever," causing the plaintiff to fall and break a leg and shoulder. The concert hall's motion for summary judgment was denied. The court ruled that a jury might well determine that the concert hall was negligent.[24]

In *Orlick v. Granit Hotel & Country Club*, 331 N.Y.S.2d 651 (1971), the plaintiff tripped on a short flight of four steps leading to her room. The hotel was negligent on several grounds: no handrail existed; no warning of the stairs' existence was provided; the lighting was poor; and the use of the same carpeting on the foyer, stairway, and corridor created an illusion of one level and no stairs. The fact that no previous accident had occurred during the four years since the hotel was built did not constitute a defense.

In the following case, the plaintiff's heel became wedged in a gap on a step that the hotel should have discovered and corrected.

---

[21] *Murray v. West Building*, 534 S.E.2d 204 (Ga. 2000)

[22] *Tannehill v. Joguyro, Inc.*, 712 So.2d 238 (La. 1998)

[23] *Richardson v. Sport Shinko*, 880 P.2d 169 (Ha. 1994)

[24] *McGowan v. St. Antoninus Church*, 2001 WL 331931 (Oh. 2001)

CASE EXAMPLE 6-4

Fields v. Robert Chappell Association, Inc.
256 S.E.2d 259 (N.C. 1979)

... Plaintiff was a registered guest in defendant's motel. She left her room intending to go to the motel office. It was necessary for her to turn to her right and go down a flight of steps. She looked down the steps and saw nothing unusual, except that she saw that the left side was obstructed by the protruding metal handle of a hook that is used to clean swimming pools. She, consequently, did not hold the handrail but moved more to her right towards the wall. There was no handrail on the right side of the step. She fell forward but did not fall all the way down the flight of steps because her foot was caught. She had to pull her shoe loose from the step to get up. There was a deep gash in her leg. She yelled for assistance, and some of the other motel guests gave her first aid before she was taken to a hospital emergency room. After she had been taken to the hospital, another guest went to the stairs where plaintiff had fallen. The stairs were concrete with a metal strip along the front edge of the step. This guest testified that the steps were bloody. She found a piece of plaintiff's shoe heel, the heel cap, wedged between the metal strip and the concrete part of the step. There was a gap between the metal strip and the concrete. Part of the concrete was missing. The witness described it as "a crumbling or an erosion as opposed to a crack." There were similar gaps on several of the steps but on the step where plaintiff's shoe heel had been lodged, the gap was somewhat larger. There was also an eroded area on the top of that step about four inches long that extended back about two inches. It was easier to observe this defect from below than when one looked down the steps from the top. The guest took plaintiff's shoe heel to the motel office and explained what had happened.

Defendant called only one witness, the motel manager. She testified that she was not present on the day the accident occurred. She further testified that the stairs were thirteen years old at the time plaintiff fell and that no repairs had been made after the accident. The motel, including the stairs, was regularly inspected every three months. She had participated in these inspections and had not observed any defects in the steps "prior to the time Mrs. Fields fell, nothing that would be noticeable enough to think you would fall, you know, you might see a crack here or there." She admitted, nonetheless, that the cracks were wide enough to receive the heel of a shoe. ...

The legal principles that arise on the evidence may ... be simply stated. The defendant motel operator was not an insurer of the safety of plaintiff, its invited guest. It was, however, required to exercise due care to keep the premises in a reasonably safe condition so as not to expose plaintiff unnecessarily to danger, and to warn her of any hidden perils. It is liable to plaintiff for any injury proximately caused by a breach of that duty. ...

The evidence all but compels the conclusion that plaintiff fell on defendant's stairs because the heel of her shoe unexpectedly became wedged in a crevice near the front edge of one of the stairsteps. Plaintiff was proceeding in a careful and prudent manner, and the crevice was almost imperceptible to one proceeding down the steps. The wearing away of the concrete and resulting gap between the metal strip and the rest of the step did not occur suddenly. Defendant knew of the condition, should have known that it was dangerous, and yet allowed it to continue to exist without doing anything to warn its guests of the danger. Defendant, thereby, unnecessarily and unreasonably exposed plaintiff and its other guests to a danger that resulted in injury to plaintiff.

[Judgment for plaintiff.]

CASE QUESTION

1. How could the hotel have avoided the injury and liability in this case?

Moveable Steps

A hotel or party house will likely have one or more sets of moveable steps to provide access to platforms and stages. Like other steps, the moveable variety must also comply with relevant safety codes and be properly maintained.

A restaurant disc jockey, after completing his evening's work, sought to dismount the elevated platform that constituted his work station. While carrying approximately forty-five pounds of equipment, he stepped across some nineteen inches from the platform to a set of stairs leading to the back door. As he placed his right foot on the top step, the stairs moved out from under him. He landed on the floor and struck his back against the elevated platform. Before he fell he was unaware that the stairs were moveable. They weighed thirty-five to fifty pounds and were not affixed to the wall or the floor. The smooth, wooden base of the stairs sat on a smooth, wooden floor with a polyurethane finish. The disc jockey sued the restaurant. His expert witness testified that the unattached and moveable stairs violated the building code because the regulations require that stairs be either fixed or, if moveable, weigh approximately 120 pounds. Also, the elevated platform where the disc jockey sat was in violation because it lacked a permanent stair or step. The restaurant, having failed to provide the disc jockey with a reasonably safe means to exit the elevated platform, was negligent and therefore liable for a portion of the injuries (comparative negligence applied).[25]

Duty Owed Guests in Restaurants and Dining Rooms

Restaurateurs and hotels with restaurants have a duty to exercise reasonable care to avoid conditions relevant to restaurants that can result in injury. Those conditions include slippery floors, foreign substances on floors, overcrowding of tables and chairs, hanging mirrors, and flambé dishes.

Slippery Floors

Accidents caused by slippery floors are not infrequent in dining rooms, banquet halls, and bars.

Highly polished and waxed floors are the cause of many slippery-floor cases. For example, in *Mitchell v. Baker Hotel of Dallas, Inc.*, 523 S.W.2d 216 (Tex. 1975), the plaintiff slipped while walking on a polished floor at a banquet. The hotel proved that the floor was waxed only twice a year, the latest being three months before the accident, and the floor was inspected on the day of the banquet and the morning after by the banquet director and found not to have been overwaxed, not unduly slick, and in its normal condition. The court held for the hotel; the plaintiff failed to prove the hotel was negligent.

---

[25]*Michalopoulos v. C&D Restaurant*, 764 A.2d 121 (R.I. 2001)

Before wax or polish is applied to a floor, be sure the type being used is appropriate for the particular floor and be certain it is applied consistent with the directions that accompany the product.

Other conditions will also result in slippery floors and possible liability. A seventeen-year-old guest of the defendant hotel was severely injured when she slipped on a wet spot on a wooden walkway at the rear of the lobby. The evidence established that the floor where the fall occurred was dangerously worn, smooth, and therefore slippery, and the entire area was inadequately lighted. This, according to the court, was ample evidence that the hotel had negligently maintained the premises.[26]

Some floor materials are inherently slippery, such as marble. Use of these materials does not create liability when a patron trips on them unless the floor was improperly constructed or is out of repair.[27]

Foreign Substances on the Floor

Many slippery-floor accidents in a dining room, restaurant, or snack bar result from a foreign substance on the floor. As with all negligence cases, the restaurant is not liable unless it failed to exercise reasonable care.

On a rainy day a restaurant patron, who admitted that he was not watching where he was going, slipped on water near the entrance. An employee had repeatedly mopped the floor in the foyer area to combat the effects of patrons dripping rain water. The court held that the restaurant was not negligent. It had diligently cleaned the front entrance area throughout the day and the plaintiff failed to pay attention to his surroundings.[28]

Often key in these cases is whether the defendant was aware or should have been aware of the existence of the substance on the floor.

Sometimes proof that the restaurant was aware of the problem is easy. Where an unsafe condition is reoccurring, the restaurant is on notice. For example, a restaurant that served jello shots in paper cups was aware that customers routinely discard the cups on the floor. A customer who slipped on one of the cups while dancing sued the restaurant for her injuries. The court held the defendant was 80% responsible for failing to correct a known dangerous condition is negligent.[29]

Even if the existence of an unsafe condition is known to the restaurant, if the circumstance is open and obvious and customers can be expected to observe the condition and take precautions, the restaurant will not be liable. Lone Star Steakhouse restaurants serve peanuts to patrons and encourage them to throw the shells on the floor. A diner tripped on the shells while exiting a restaurant and was injured. The restaurant here was not liable. The court held the presence of peanut

---

[26] *194th St. Hotel Corp. v. Hopf*, 383 So.2d 739 (Fla. 1980)

[27] *Portanova v. Trump Taj Mahal*, 704 N.Y.S.2d 380 (N.Y. 2000)

[28] *Sivira v. Midtown Restaurants, Corp.*, 753 So.2d 492 (Miss. 1999)

[29] *Endres v. Mingles Restaurant, Ltc.*, 706 N.Y.S.2d 32 (N.Y. 2000)

shells on the floor was open and obvious, and the eatery had no reason to anticipate that the customer would not see them.[30]

Query: Why was the plaintiff allowed to collect in the jello-shot case and not in the peanut-shell case, given that both involved obvious debris on the floor?

Answer: In the jello-shot case, the dirtied floor was used for dancing, an activity during which patrons' attention is diverted from the condition and circumstances of their surroundings.

Sometimes a plaintiff cannot prove that the restaurant had actual notice of a condition. In such cases, the plaintiff can nonetheless win the case if she can show that the facility should have known of the problem, called **constructive notice**. A restaurant or hotel has constructive notice of a problem when the condition has existed for a sufficiently long period of time, such that the facility should have discovered the problem in the ordinary course of monitoring the premises.

How long is long enough? There is no definitive time period. Remember that a restaurant is not an insurer of diners' safety. It is not responsible for wiping up fallen food the moment it drops. Such would not be feasible. Rather, the restaurant is liable only if it fails to exercise reasonable care. If the restaurant regularly inspects the floor for spilled or dropped substances and cleans the floor when such substances are found, the eatery will not be liable, even though someone trips and falls. The cases are instructive in defining what is reasonable.

A plaintiff who slipped on a scoop of ice cream dropped by another customer two to four minutes prior to the fall was unsuccessful in her lawsuit against the proprietor for damages because there was insufficient time to discover the unsafe condition.[31]

While dining in a Burger King, a plaintiff slipped on a puddle of water three to four feet away from the self-service beverage center. The restaurant proved that ten minutes prior to the accident an employee had inspected the area and found no water on the floor. The court determined that inspections in ten-minute intervals constitutes sufficient frequency to combat liability for negligence. Summary judgment was granted in favor of the restaurant.[32]

Where a person slips on ice, the size of ice at the time of the fall may be a tell-tale sign of the amount of time water has been allowed to remain on the floor without being wiped up.

CASE EXAMPLE 6-5

Demaille v. Trump Castle Associates
725 N.Y.S.2d 40 (N.Y. 2001)

Plaintiff brings this action to recover for personal injuries sustained on October 2, 1994, when she slipped and fell on one of several puddles of partially melted ice on a marble floor in Trump Plaza Hotel in Atlantic City.

To constitute constructive notice, a defect must be visible and apparent and it must exist for a sufficient length of time prior to the

---

[30] *Johnson v. Lone Star Steakhouse & Saloon*, 997 S.W.2d 490 (Ky. 1999)

[31] *Schnuphase v. Storehouse Markets*, 918 P.2d 476 (Utah 1996)

[32] *Dwoskin v. Burger King Corp.*, 671 N.Y.S.2d 494 (N.Y. 1998)

accident to permit defendant's employees to discover and remedy it. The evidence established that plaintiff fell when she and a friend walked from their room into the elevator lobby, which had a marble floor and was adjacent to the room where the ice machine was located. Circumstantial evidence of defendant's constructive notice of a dangerous condition was provided by the uncontroverted trial testimony of plaintiff and her friend regarding the size of the puddles and the size of the partially-melted ice cubes, relative to the size of those produced by the ice machine, as well as by the deposition testimony of an individual who entered the elevator lobby shortly after plaintiff fell.

The circumstantial evidence was sufficient to permit the jury to draw the necessary inference that the ice had been spilled a sufficient length of time prior to the accident such that defendant's employees should have discovered and remedied the condition.

In another circumstantial evidence case, *Wal-Mart Stores, Inc. v. Gonzalez*, 968 S.W.2d 934 (Tex. 1998), the outcome was different. A plaintiff was in a Wal-Mart store walking in a busy aisle near the cafeteria. She slipped and fell on a piece of macaroni. She testified the macaroni had mayonnaise in it and was contaminated with a lot of dirt, including footprints and cart trackmarks. The court refused to find the store negligent, holding instead that soiled macaroni on the floor of a heavily traveled aisle is not evidence of the length of time it was on the floor. The court noted that no analysis was done of the dirt on the pasta to determine if it was dried or otherwise evidenced the food's presence on the floor for a notable length of time.

In another case with a similar issue, *Colon v. Outback Steakhouse of Florida, Inc.*, 721 So.2d 769 (Fl. 1998), the judge ruled more liberally. A plaintiff who fell at an Outback Steakhouse on dirty mashed potatoes was entitled to present her case to a jury. The court in this case said, "The soil on the potatoes may have been caused by plaintiff stepping on them when she fell, or by them being on the floor for a period of time sufficient to create constructive notice," establishing a factual issue for a jury. These cases are hard to reconcile. Sometimes different results merely reflect varying opinions of different judges on how the law should be applied to particular facts.

Importance of Enforcing a Policy of Frequent Floor Cleaning

A restaurant may be able to establish that it exercised reasonable care and thus was not negligent where it enforces a policy of frequent inspections of the floor to ensure it is free from spilled foods or beverages. A restaurant was saved from liability for a diner's fall on a lasagna noodle because of the restaurant's cleaning policy. The owner testified that the restaurant had adopted and strictly follows a comprehensive cleaning policy. Employees are required to sweep and clean the floor after ever meal and mop with a sterilizing solution at night. All employees are trained and required to watch for objects on the floor at all times and remove any found. Based on these procedures, the court found no basis to assume that the restaurant had constructive notice of the fallen food.[33]

---

[33] *Solomon v. Monjuni's Restaurant*, 768 So.2d 799 (La. 2000)

Similarly, judgment was entered against a plaintiff who fell in a restaurant on a lemon peel because of the restaurant's policy and practice that all waiters inspect for foreign substances on the floor and, if any are found, their servers pick them up. In addition a busboy was always assigned to constantly check for debris during meal periods.[34] Similarly, in *Ochlockonee Banks Restaurant, Inc. v. Colvin*, 700 So.2d 1229 (Fl. 1997), a country and western dancer slipped and fell at a restaurant while "spinning and twirling around the dance floor," resulting in a broken ankle. Testimony from the restaurant established that it had a strictly enforced policy that drinks were not allowed on the dance floor, employees monitored the dance area to ensure patrons did not enter it with drinks, and any spills that did occur were immediately cleaned. This testimony contributed to the appellate court's reversal of a jury verdict in favor of the plaintiff.

To help avoid liability, hospitality facilities should develop floor maintenance policies designed to achieve floors that are safe for customers' use. But a policy alone will not suffice to avoid liability. Strict adherence to the policy is necessary for a hotel or restaurant to establish it exercised reasonable care when sued by a guest who trips on a foreign object on the floor. Where a restaurant has a policy of floor-cleaning procedures that ensures safe, nonslippery floors, but the restaurant fails to adhere to that policy, an inference may be drawn that the restaurant was negligent.[35]

Miscellaneous Matters Relating to Floors

Other circumstances involving a restaurant floor can cause injury. A couple was dancing in the pavilion area of a casino. The dance area was designated by ropes and a row of potted plants on saucers placed just inside the ropes. While slow dancing, the plaintiff tripped on one of the saucers and broke her wrist. In her lawsuit against the casino she was able to rebut its defense that the condition was open and obvious. The saucers were the same color as the carpet and thus not easily visible.[36]

Placement of Chairs and Tables

Overcrowding in a restaurant or banquet hall can create a dangerous condition.

If tables in a dining room are so close together that walking between them is difficult, a diner may foreseeably be injured. While exceeding the maximum number of diners that can comfortably be accommodated in a restaurant may be appealing from a profit vantage point, it can lead to damages that easily negate any additional money the extra diners might generate. The next case helps answer the question: How close is too close to place the tables? Note also the discussion about **expert witnesses**—that is, witnesses with superior knowledge about a subject due to education and/or experience.

[34] *Kauffmann v. Royal Orleans, Inc.*, 216 So.2d 394 (La. 1968)
[35] *BBB Service Co. v. Glass*, 491 S.E.2d 870 (Ga. 1997)
[36] *Creel v. St. Charles Gaming Co*, 707 So.2d 475 (La. 1998)

CASE EXAMPLE 6-6

LaPlante v. Radisson Hotel Co.
292 F.Supp. 705 (Mich. 1968)

... Simply stated, the question is whether a jury may find a hotel negligent where the hotel, in hiring itself out to stage a banquet for 1,200 paying guests in one of its banquet rooms, allegedly set the banquet tables so close to each other as to leave inadequate aisles and room between seated guests, causing the plaintiff to trip over a chair when attempting to leave the room and thereby injuring herself.

[T]he plaintiff, a semiretired school teacher, sixty-seven years of age, was a guest at the defendant's hotel for the purpose of attending the national convention of a professional education sorority of which she was a member. The convention meetings and related banquets were all held at the defendant hotel.

On August 10, 1967, the convention staged its final banquet, and the plaintiff was in attendance. ...

Long tables, seating twelve to eighteen persons each, were placed at preset distances apart, which the defendant claims was forty-two inches though the jury could find from evidence the plaintiff introduced that the actual distance between tables was somewhat less. Further, there was evidence that at least at some of the tables, the chairs were back to back to those at the next table. ...

There was testimony that waitresses were unable to move down the aisles between the long tables, and at the table at which the plaintiff was seated, the plates of food were passed down by the waitresses from person to person from the end of the table. The hotel manager testified this was not a good practice, and he did not permit it, if discovered. ...

The banquet began at 8:00 P.M., and the plaintiff came to the hall and selected a seat about in the middle of one of the long tables.

Several hours later, at approximately 11:15 P.M., before the banquet program was over and while the lights were dimmed, with a spotlight on the head table ... the plaintiff decided to leave the banquet hall to meet her son-in-law as prearranged. Moving sideways, she negotiated a path between chairs as the vari-

ous people moved in toward the table to accommodate her. The jury could find that not realizing the position of the final chair, and believing she had negotiated herself to the main aisle, plaintiff caught her foot on the leg of that last chair and tripped and fell, injuring herself. Based on this evidence and the medical testimony as to the extent of her injuries, the jury awarded plaintiff the sum of $3,500. ...

The defendant contends that since there was no violation of any statute or ordinance pleaded nor proved, the burden was on the plaintiff to show by expert testimony or otherwise the standard of care to which the defendant's conduct should have conformed. ...

The issue becomes one of whether a jury should be permitted, without expert testimony, to draw upon their own knowledge, background, and common experience to determine what the standard of care should be and, hence, whether any departure therefrom occurred.

Certainly the nature of the case is not scientifically complicated nor technical. While some training and experience in catering and hotel management may be a necessary prerequisite to the handling of a banquet for 1,200 people, the court is of the view that such training or background is not [indispensable] to the ability to determine what is unreasonable crowding and what is not. The lay juror, knowing no more than the next person about catering procedures, could determine from the evidence in this case whether or not the tables were too close for safety. ... The rule of evidence applied in determining the appropriateness of opinion "expert testimony" is whether the subject involved is so distinctively related to some science, profession, business, or occupation as to be beyond the ken of the average layman. Here the court is not convinced that expert testimony was required or would necessarily have been helpful to the jury. ...

The jury could find that the hotel reasonably could foresee that during a banquet commencing at 8:00 P.M. and lasting until after 11:00 P.M., a number of people would leave the hall to go to the restrooms or for other purposes; that with a program in progress, the lights might well be dimmed and vision made more difficult; and that with the crowded or overcrowded conditions, such a fall as occurred might be anticipated. ...

Ruling of the Court: ... Judgment for plaintiff.

CASE QUESTIONS

1. Do you agree that the injuries in this case were foreseeable by the hotel? Why or why not?

2. Do you agree that an expert witness was not necessary in this case? Why or why not?

Hanging Mirrors in Dining Rooms

Large plate-glass mirrors in a dining room are another factor that can cause injury. A restaurant must be vigilant to ensure such mirrors remain securely attached. In *Deming Hotel Company v. Prox*, 236 N.E.2d 613 (Ind. 1968), a wall mirror measuring 3.5 × 7 feet fell on a guest and severely injured her. She sued the restaurant claiming res ipsa loquitur. The court upheld the application of that doctrine to this case because the mirror was under the restaurant's exclusive control and the injury would not have occurred if proper maintenance of the mirrors had been exercised.

Ceilings

Improperly built or supported ceilings is another condition that can cause significant injuries and give rise to liability. The following case illustrates this point.

CASE EXAMPLE 6-7

Bank of New York

v.

Ansonia Associates
656 N.Y.S.2d 813 (Sup. Crt. 1997)

... On May 12, 1990, the ceiling collapsed in the croissant shop located in a West Side [of New York City] landmark building. One patron, Miriam Rosa Toigo was killed, and a number of others were injured; thirteen plaintiffs in all have commenced suit. The defendants included owners of the premises, architects, contractors, builders and others. ...

Evidence established, and both sides' experts agreed that the ceiling which caused the plaintiffs' injuries was a disaster waiting to happen. This is because suspended from the plaster ceiling above the croissant shop were ducts weighing 600 pounds, air conditioners weighing over 200 pounds, a sprinkler system weighing over 1000 pounds, and a hung accoustical tile ceiling, none of which were attached to any structural support other than the plaster ceiling. There was testimony from which it could be found that the owners had numerous opportunities to discover and remedy this dangerous condition over the years. There was also testimony of warning signs such as falling chunks of plaster, and falling debris.

There was more than ample evidence supporting the jury's finding of negligence. ...

Menu Boards on Ledges

Restaurants are well advised not to place items on ledges near tables where customers sit. The risks created by such circumstances are illustrated by a case involving a wood-framed chalkboard menu. The restaurant rested the menu board on a ledge immediately above one of the seats at a table. When the server approached the table, he removed the board from the shelf and walked around the table to show each customer the board. The waiter then returned the board to the ledge. While the diners were waiting for their meal to be served, the chalkboard fell and struck the plaintiff in the head. The court, noting that the restaurant controlled the placement of the menu board and the tables and chairs, held that a jury could reasonably determine that the restaurant failed to meet its duty to use reasonable care.[37]

Hanging Televisions

Sports bars and some restaurants display televisions for patrons' entertainment. One restaurant installed a set in all four corners of the dining area, each resting on a platform hung from the ceiling and supported on all four corners by a plastic link chain. A server was hit while cleaning a corner table when one of the televisions fell. He sued the restaurant's builder for negligent construction. The plaintiff's expert witness, a mechanical engineer, testified that the platforms holding the T.V.s were not properly supported, noting that the plastic chains were clearly marked with warnings by the manufacturer that they were not to be used for hanging overhead loads. The jury determined that the restaurant was negligent.[38]

Serving Flambé Foods

Flaming dishes such as cherries jubilee and baked Alaska add an element of excitement to a menu and a dining room. As the next case tragically illustrates, they also add an element of danger and must be handled with great care. Particularly note the facts that constituted the server's negligence and, in the latter part of the decision, the court's discussion on calculating damages.

CASE EXAMPLE 6-8

Young v. Caribbean Associates, Inc.
358 F.Supp. 1220 (V.I. 1973)

This is a tort and breach of warranty action tried by the court without a jury. [*Breach of warranty* means that a guaranty made by a seller of goods has been broken.] A father and his ten-year-old son seek recovery for mental

anguish suffered by the father and bodily injuries suffered by the son brought about in unusual circumstances. The son, Francis Howard Young, was staying with his parents at the defendant, Caribbean Beach Hotel. On New Year's Eve, 1969, the family was having dinner in the hotel dining room. At the end of the meal, the son volunteered to go through the dessert serving line to bring a cherries

---

[37] *Everett v. Peter's La Cuisine*, 739 So.2d 1015 (Fl. 1999)

[38] *Ross v. Paddy*, 532 S.E.2d 612 (S.C. 2000)

jubilee for his father. As the son reached the head of the serving line, the waiter in charge of flaming and serving the cherries jubilee found it necessary to kindle the flames by adding more rum to the chafing pan. He took a bottle of hundred-and-fifty-one proof rum, which was stoppered with a narrow "slow pour" spout, and proceeded to pour the rum directly into the pan. As he did so, the spout either dropped out or was popped out by an internal combustion in the rum bottle, and a quantity of volatile rum gushed out. An abnormally high flame resulted that reached out to touch the boy, setting his shirt on fire. The boy suffered severe burns and has undergone considerable treatment for skin and flesh grafts and plastic surgery. The ... complaint requests $200,000 compensatory damages for the son and $19,912 medical expenses for the father. The complaint [bases] recovery principally upon negligence of all defendants [the hotel, the serving waiter, and Sears, Roebuck & Company which sold plaintiff the shirt he was wearing], but the breach of warranty ... allegations were aimed primarily at Sears, Roebuck & Company, the vendor of the allegedly highly flammable boy's shirt. ...

The father's right to recover his expenditures for medical expenses and the son's right to recover compensatory damages for his bodily injuries are clear. The hotel is, at the very least, accountable for its serving waiter's negligence in using an improperly stoppered bottle, which permitted the "slow pour" spout either to fall out or pop out, thereby discharging a large quantity of volatile rum. Moreover, as the evidence tended to show, the hotel's serving waiter was negligent in the first place in pouring the rum directly from the bottle and not from an intermediary bowl or pitcher. An experienced maitre d'hotel and chef testified that to pour directly from a bottle was to invite the flame to catch onto the stream of rum and leap from the chafing pan to ignite the vaporous gases inside the bottle, blowing out the cork and turning the bottle into a veritable "flame thrower" or "blowtorch," capable of throwing a flame ten to fifteen feet. Although I need not decide that this in fact did happen, I do find that it was negligent to pour directly from the bottle and not from an intervening bowl or wide mouth pitcher. ...

I further find that the negligence of the hotel and its serving waiter was the sole and proximate cause of plaintiff's injuries. The hotel for a time relied in part on the theory that the boy's shirt was itself highly flammable as evidenced by the vigor with which it burned, and that this was an important intervening cause of the holocaust that developed. With this theory in mind, ... the hotel [sued] Sears, Roebuck & Company. ... At the trial, however, a written statement of the waiter was produced that indicated that a substantial quantity of the rum had gushed directly onto the boy's shirt. This itself would be more than enough to support the combustion, no matter what the flammability of the shirt fabric might be. [The alleged flammability of the shirt was thus not the proximate cause of the plaintiff's injury.] The ... complaint against Sears was therefore dismissed. ... The action then proceeded against the serving waiter and the hotel alone. I also find that the boy was not guilty of contributory negligence. Although there was some testimony indicating that he was warned to stand back, the warning would have been, at the very best, an insufficient caution to a normal boy of plaintiff's age.

With the question of liability settled, I must now address myself to the matter of damages. The father's medical expenses, and reasonably related outlays, have totaled some $12,352.08 to date. In addition, some further surgery will be needed in order to minimize the burn scars on the boy's face and body. Although it is difficult for the medical experts to estimate the costs of these future contemplated operations, the uncontroverted estimate given at trial of $6,000 appears reasonable. The father's total [medical] damages would therefore come to approximately $18,352.08.

The most important and troublesome issue of damages is the award of compensable damages that must be granted to the son for his pain, suffering, permanent disfigurement, and the effect thereof upon his psyche and social adjustment. That his pain was considerable is unquestioned. The boy was on fire for more than several seconds before any one of the astonished bystanders came to his rescue. Before falling to the floor, he tried desperately to tear his shirt off. Finally, after perhaps a full half minute of time, one of the waiters came to his rescue with a tablecloth to snuff out the fire. An ambulance was called and soon the boy and his father were taken to the hospital emergency room. ...

At the Washington Hospital Center, several skin grafts were performed by Dr. Fry. On June 17, the boy was again admitted to the hospital for several injections of steroids into the hypertrophic scarred areas. Hypertrophic scarred areas are scars that are thickened and raised from the healthy, normal skin. There was hospitalization again in October 1970 for further operations to improve the scarred areas.

From my personal observations of the boy's scars, I would say that the scars on his right cheek and beneath his chin are unsightly, as are the scars on his chest and on the backs of both hands. The scar underneath the chin is actually a keloid [a thick scar resulting from excessive growth of fibrous tissue] and is red in color. There are two keloid formations on the chest. There was an attempt to remove one by excision, but the result was a scar worse than the one removed.

The doctor obtained skin for the skin grafts from the boy's left and right thighs. These areas are approximately six inches long and two and-a-half inches wide. These are called "donor sites" that will eventually become less noticeable, but ... they may always appear as "patches."

The medical testimony was generally that the boy received second and third degree burns over 30 percent of his body's surface. The boy has no injuries to his organs, nor to his eyes. He can make a fist and move his fingers in the normal way. In sum, he has no physical disabilities. The doctors are of the opinion that the scars and keloid on the face and chest areas can be further improved by a combination of excision and injections. One doctor opined that surgery can make noticeable improvements and improve the boy cosmetically. However, there would have to be between three and five hospitalizations to achieve this improvement. The medical consensus is that time alone will show improvement on the scarred areas and that within a few years much of the scars should become less noticeable. ...

It is no easy undertaking to make a judicial pronouncement that a certain damage award will fully compensate the boy for his pain, suffering and disfigurement. ... I award the boy $80,000 and the father $18,352.08. ...

CASE QUESTION

1. How might the result have been different if the plaintiff were an adult rather than a ten-year-old boy?

A restaurant that serves flambé dishes or does any type of tableside cooking with a flame must carefully train its employees on how to prepare the food safely, how to use the related cooking devices, and what to do in the event of a fire.

Serving Hot Liquids

A number of recent cases have involved circumstances where hot tea or coffee purchased with a take-out order spilled and injured someone. Given that we all expect tea and coffee to be served hot, the question becomes how hot is too hot? In a widely-publicized case, *Liebeck v. McDonald's Restraunts, P.T.S, Inc.*, 1995 WL 360309 (N.M 1994) a woman was burned when coffee she purchased from McDonald's drive-through window spilled from its cup, which she had placed between her legs. The accident occurred while she was adding cream and sugar to the beverage in a parked car. She received a sizeable damage recovery, which likely prompted many of the similar subsequent cases. A critical factor in her case was that the coffee she purchased was served at a higher temperature than the industry standard.

The coffee industry has determined that the optimum temperature needed to release the flavor from coffee beans is 170–175 degrees Fahrenheit. This standard has been accepted by the restaurant industry and is the temperature at which customers anticipate receiving their coffee.[39]

In another case, a woman spilled in her lap coffee she purchased from E-Z Serve. The store established that the coffee was served at the industry standard temperature. The court, noting that "plaintiff clearly intended to purchase hot coffee, not tepid," and that plaintiff frequently drank coffee and so was familiar with the liquid's temperature, found that the store was not negligent and dismissed the complaint.

In another case, the plaintiff spilled on her lap hot tea she had purchased at the drive-through window of a McDonald's. She claimed the restaurant did not give sufficient warning of the risks of spilled tea. The cup in which her drink was served included the following notice in two places, "CAUTION: CONTENTS MAY BE HOT." Said the court, "The cup in question contained bold warnings cautioning the holder about hot contents. In the case at hand, the consumer had ordered hot tea. The *Oxford Encyclopedic English Dictionary* describes teas as, 'A drink made by infusing tea-leaves in boiling water.' This court holds that consumer expectations coupled with warnings on the cup established red lights to the plaintiff that the tea might be too hot for the tongue, … also society is thoroughly aware from childhood of the dangers of a hot liquid spill."[40]

In situations where a diner eats in the restaurant, wait personnel need to be careful as they pour hot beverages. Negligence in serving these hot drinks can result in liability. An example involved a woman who was scalded while eating in a Chinese restaurant. A teapot containing hot tea fell on her lap from the lazy susan where the waitress had placed it. The woman claimed the restaurant was aware of at least one prior similar incident and so should have put the teapot on the tabletop and not the lazy susan. A jury entered a verdict in favor of the injured plaintiff. That verdict was upheld on appeal.[41]

From these cases we learn the importance of not overheating coffee, tea, hot chocolate, and other drinks that are customarily served hot. Heating should be done consistent with industry standards. Warnings on cups that the liquid inside is hot can assist in avoiding liability. Wait personnel should handle hot beverages with care and avoid spilling on customers.

Duty Owed Guests Outside

A variety of conditions outside a hotel or restaurant can lead to liability if reasonable care is not exercised. These include, among others, valet service, sidewalks, handicap ramps, outdoor sporting facilities, and outdoor lighting.

---

[39] *Oubre v. E-Z Serve Corporation*, 713 So.2d 818 (La. 1998)

[40] *Immormino v. McDonald's*, 698 N.E.2d 516 (Ohio 1998)

[41] *Babich v. Hunan Szechwann Inn, Inc.*, 1997 WL 410720 (Ohio 1997)

Outside Door Service

When guests arrive at a hotel by car or taxi, they often stop in front of the establishment, where the door attendant takes their luggage and a valet parks the car. A hotel or restaurant is not, absent foreseeably rowdy circumstances, required to furnish door attendants or valets. If it does, however, the hotel or restaurant may be liable if these employees are negligent. This rule is illustrated by the following case.

CASE EXAMPLE 6-9

**Kurzweg v. Hotel St. Regis Corp.
309 F.2d 746 (N.Y. 1962)**

Plaintiff, descending from a cab stopped in the second lane from the sidewalk in front of the Hotel St. Regis, was injured when a car nearer the curb backed up. She sued the owners of both vehicles and the hotel owner, alleging against the latter negligence of the hotel doorman. The hotel owner moved to dismiss the complaint for failure to state a claim on which relief could be granted. ...

It is the hotel's contention that it was under no duty by New York law to furnish a doorman, and that therefore failure of the doorman to act cannot bring an action against it. But New York has held liable a person under no duty to act who voluntarily undertakes to act and causes injury through his negligent act. ... [T]he complaint states a claim upon which relief can be granted. ...

Grounds

When invitees use the sidewalk of a hotel or restaurant, they have the responsibility to exercise care where they walk. If they trip and fall due to an obvious obstruction or defect, the hotel or restaurant will not be responsible. For example, one case involved a wheelchair-bound restaurant patron who tried to maneuver around a trash barrel situated near the restaurant sidewalk. She recognized passage would be "at best, a tight squeeze." Because she was aware of the risk created by the barrel she was unable to recover for injuries she suffered when it forced her to fall.[42] If, however, a defect is not obvious to patrons and the restaurateur is aware of the problem, the restaurant will be liable, as illustrated in the following case.

CASE EXAMPLE 6-10

**Eisnaugle v. McDonald's
2000 WL 33226184 (Ohio 2000)**

... On a rainy morning Jill Eisnaugle, then fifteen, and her father stopped at the McDonald's restaurant in Jackson for breakfast. Jill walked across the parking lot and stepped up onto the tile sidewalk in front of the side entrance. Upon stepping onto the tile, Jill immediately fell. Jill twisted and broke the neck of her femur. Resetting the bone required surgery and the

---

[42] *Spagnuolo v. McDonald's*, 561 N.W.2d 500 (Mi. 1997)

implantation of surgical screws. ... Her doctor did not release her to full activity until nearly nineteen months after the accident.

The Eisnaugles filed a lawsuit against the restaurant alleging that the McDonald's negligently permitted an unsafe condition to exist. They sought damages for Jill's medical expenses, her pain and suffering, and her parents' loss of Jill's company and services.

At trial the testimony revealed that defendant franchisee leases the land and the building, and is responsible for its upkeep and remodeling. In 1990 defendant opted to change the type of sidewalk outside the restaurant from exposed aggregate (a type of sidewalk material) to tile. The franchise owner testified that he selected the tile sidewalk because it is easier and cheaper to maintain than aggregate. The Eisnaugles' expert witness tested the tile and determined that it did not comply with the Ohio Building Code, the Life Safety Code, or Americans with Disabilities Act standards for safe, slip-resistant outdoor walkways. ...

The jury deliberated and determined that defendant was negligent and that defendant's negligence proximately caused Jill's accident and the resulting injuries. ...

On appeal the judgment affirmed.

Case Question

1. Why was the defect in the tile sidewalk not considered obvious and open?

Another pavement problem is the occasional step located in an unexpected place. Unsuspecting pedestrians may fail to see the step and trip unless its existence is highlighted in some way.

For example, plaintiff who had just exited a restaurant where she had eaten lunch failed to see a single step that was embedded in the sidewalk "two-thirds of the way down a long walk, and not at the entrance to any building or to a parking area or another sidewalk." No sign or warning of the step existed. She fell and severely injured her hip. The walkway was terra cotta (reddish) and was "glaring bright" in the afternoon sun on the day in question. A single white strip one-and-one-half inches wide had been painted on the top of the step to catch the attention of passersby. However, the white strip was nearly worn off and was barely discernable. The restaurant sought summary judgment claiming the existence of the step was open and obvious and thus should have been visible to the guest. The court refused to grant summary judgment and instead referred to a jury the issue of whether the establishment used reasonable care in protecting its customers.[43]

The jury in this case will likely find the restaurant negligent. To avoid liability in a circumstance with an unexpected step, the facility should consider a number of precautions: paint the different levels of the step different colors; install a warning sign; and apply a strip of paint of contrasting color at the top of the step and repaint whenever necessary to avoid fading.

Holes in Sidewalks

Often sidewalks and paved areas deteriorate over time. Numerous cases result from guests tripping on depressions in walkways or uneven sidewalk slabs. The law in many states allows some tolerance of such defects, calling small depressions too

[43]*Sherman v. Arno*, 383 P.2d 741 (Ariz. 1963)

trivial to give rise to liability. The cases give some guidance on the size of a hole that will and will not result in liability.

A ski-lodge patron fell on a crack in the sundeck pavement that had a depth of one-half inch. The court held this was too trivial a defect to impose liability.[44] In another case, a ramp located at the exit of a restaurant was elevated one-half to three-quarters of an inch above the adjacent surface. A diner tripped on the uneven portion of the ramp and was injured. The court refused to hold the restaurant liable due to the limited elevation.[45] A South Carolina court held that a depression in the sidewalk of one and three-fifths inches violated the building code, but nonetheless was too insignificant to raise an inference of negligence. A lawsuit filed by a woman who fell on the hole while walking to her car from a restaurant where she had just eaten was thus dismissed.[46]

In a case with a somewhat different holding, a plaintiff tripped on an elevation differential in the pavement of an amusement park measuring one-half to one and one-half inches. The court refused to grant summary judgment for the park and instead referred the matter to trial for a jury to decide whether the park should be liable.[47]

In summary, where a patron falls on a hole in the pavement, the size of the hole and the law of the particular state in which the fall occurred will determine whether the facility can avoid liability. An advisable practice for hotels and restaurants is to repair pavement problems when they first appear to avoid injury to guests. If, however, an accident occurs and a lawsuit is commenced, the facility should measure the depression and consider if a defense of triviality might be availing.

Ramps and Parking Lots

Other areas of concern on the grounds of a hotel or restaurant include ramps and parking lots. The establishment should inspect these areas regularly. If obstructions such as stones, woodchips, or debris are found, they should be removed immediately. Cracks and holes should be repaired. Other unsafe conditions should be eliminated.

A design defect in a handicap ramp at a hotel resulted in a dropoff of an unspecified size between the end of the ramp and the road. A guest tripped and fell on the ramp while walking to the parking lot due to the dropoff. The court declined to find that the defect was open and obvious and thus refused to dismiss the case on the hotel's motion for summary judgment.[48]

---

[44] *Sullivan v. State of NY*, 2000 WL 1598934 (N.Y. 2000)

[45] *Boyd v. Country Boy Deli Delights*, 2001 WL 753886 (Mich. 2001)

[46] *Desmond v. City of Charlotte*, 544 S.E.2d 269 (N.C. 2001)

[47] *Schatz v. Herco*, 708 N.Y.S.2d 435 (N.Y. 2000)

[48] *Anderson v. Turton Development*, 483 S.E.2d 597 (Ga. 1997)

Outdoor Sporting Facilities

Many resorts owe their popularity to outside activities and sports they offer. Are such resorts liable for injuries sustained by a guest while using the sporting facilities? The hotel owes to its guests a duty of reasonable care in the maintenance of all its sporting facilities. Even in states that continue to follow the rule of assumption of risk (see discussion on that doctrine in Chapter 5), a guest does not assume the risk that the resort will fail to maintain the sporting facility in a condition that makes it reasonably safe for the guest. Such failure on the part of the hotel will result in liability.

Resort hotels often offer bicycles for their guests' use. Precautions are necessary. Regular periodic inspections should be done to ensure the bikes are in good working order. Bikes should not be issued to a child unless accompanied by a responsible adult. The bikes should be equipped with horns, reflectors, and, if used at night, lights. Any other equipment mandated by state or local law should also be provided. No more than one person should be permitted to ride the bike at once.

Play areas may also be provided by a hotel or restaurant. Injuries and liability can result from careless selection of equipment, faulty assembly, haphazard placement, and infrequent inspection.

Tournaments

Resort hotels are becoming a common site for sports competitions such as tennis and golf tournaments and boxing matches. Large and potentially unruly crowds can be anticipated for these events. The facility owes a duty to its patrons to address the risks and provide the necessary crowd control and security to avoid injury. An unruly crowd at a boxing match at the MGM Grand Hotel in Las Vegas resulted in injury to several spectators and a lawsuit for the hotel.[49]

Amusement Rides

Midway rides present potential risks that operators must address. The duty owed by the proprietor of an amusement place to patrons is to use reasonable care to inspect and maintain the rides in a reasonably safe condition. Given that carnival rides attract children, operators must adhere to an exacting vigilance. Liability resulted in a case of a fourteen year old injured on a ride called the Swinger when the operator disregarded manufacturer's warnings by failing to use seatbelts for users and failed to immediately stop the ride when a child exhibited potentially dangerous horseplay during the ride.[50]

Outdoor Lighting Requirements

The high cost of energy makes it easy to understand why a hotel or restaurant might be tempted to reduce outdoor lighting. Yet even when only a few rooms are

---

[49] *Castro v. MGM Grand Hotel, Inc.*, 8 S.W.3d 403 (Tex. 1999)

[50] *Harvey v. Sons Rides, Inc.*, 2000 WL 862821 (La. 2000)

rented, the motel itself and any area used by patrons must be properly lighted. An attempt to save a few dollars on lighting can lead to a guest's injury and liability. An example is the case of *Bowling v. Lewis*, 261 F.2d 311 (4th Cir. 1958). The facts were simple. As stated by the court,

> The ... plaintiff, who was vacationing with his wife and two small children at an ocean front motel, arrived on a Sunday afternoon and used the walk [between the parking lot and the hotel] several times until the following Tuesday, when he and his family spent the early evening in an amusement area and returned to the motel when it was very dark and the walk was unlighted. The plaintiff had ... 18 years' experience driving buses and had very good night vision. He remained in his car with the headlights on to illuminate the walk for his wife and children, and when they had reached the room, he turned off the headlights, waited momentarily to give his eyes an opportunity to adjust to the dark, and proceeded very cautiously along the walk but, nevertheless, tripped over a 10-inch stone in the walk.

Was the guest contributorily negligent by going to his room in the dark? The court ruled that

> A guest or lodger is deemed guilty of contributory negligence in using a dark or unlighted stairway or in using a dark or unlighted passageway, as in instances where lighted stairways, or the means of providing light, are available to him. On the other hand, ... a guest cannot be charged with contributory negligence or assumption of risk merely because he uses a darkened stairway where the elevator is out of commission and the stairway is the only means available for passing between the room and the ground floor, or where, on instructions from an employee, he uses an insufficiently lighted hallway, but exercises care; ...

The plaintiff in this case was not negligent. He was using the only available means of ingress to his room. There was no one present from whom he could have requested help. He was familiar with the concrete walkway and knew its location; he and his family had used it as a means of ingress and egress several times since their arrival. He had good night vision. His wife and the children had safely proceeded along this walkway immediately before the accident. The plaintiff thus had good reason to believe that he could safely negotiate it.

The case of *Rappaport v. Days Inn of America Corp.*, 250 S.E.2d 245 (N.C. 1979), also addresses the duty of a hospitality facility to properly illuminate parking lots. The plaintiff, an eighty-two-year-old woman, fell in the defendant's parking-lot as she attempted to go to her room in the dark. She tripped because she failed to see a six- or seven-inch step up to the walk from the parking-lot surface, which was not illuminated in any way. The jury found for the plaintiff. An innkeeper is under a duty to keep the premises, including the parking lot, in a reasonably safe condition so as not to unnecessarily expose guests to danger.

Outdoor light fixtures should be inspected daily. If they are not in good working order, they should be repaired without delay.

Many facilities use electronic timers that control exterior lighting. These must be reset when daylight savings time begins and ends. If clocks are not adjusted immediately, the timing of the lights will be off by an hour and guests may not have adequate light.

Duty Owed Guests in Swimming Areas

Countless millions of Americans swim, and many hotels and motels have pools or breach area. A swimming pool presents hoteliers with a difficult dilemma. It helps to attract business, but it has high maintenance, energy, and labor costs and it exposes the hotel to another area of potential liability. Many states regulate swimming pools extensively. These requirements relate to lifeguards, required safety equipment, chemicals used for sanitation, and maintenance of the pool. Failure to abide by these laws can result in liability for pool accidents based on negligence per se. Likewise, negligence in tending to a pool or waterfront area can lead to liability.

Swimming-pool accidents can be caused by wet floors, unsafe diving boards, inadequate safety equipment, horseplay, inadequate supervision, and a variety of other factors.

Exercise Reasonable Care

Consistent with general principles of negligence, a hotel is not an insurer of guests' safety in and around a hotel pool. The hotel is only liable if it fails to exercise reasonable care. In *McKeever v. Phoenix Jewish Community Center*, 374 P.2d 875 (Ariz. 1962), the ten-year-old daughter of the plaintiff drowned while playing in a pool with her siblings. The shallow area was roped off, but the children jumped into the deep end and scurried back to the shallow area several times while playing. The deceased had been left by her father for roughly five minutes when the accident occurred. The trained lifeguard on duty did everything in his power to effect her rescue. All necessary and required safety devices for swimmers were on hand. Given these facts, the plaintiff was unable to prove that the defendant was negligent. The operator of a pool must keep it in a safe condition, have safety equipment available, and, depending on the circumstances and state or local law, have qualified personnel on hand; the defendant did all of this.

An example of a facility ignoring pool safety precautions is provided in the following case. As it illustrates, disregard of basic safety requirements can result in serious injury or death to a guest and liability to the hospitality facility.

CASE EXAMPLE 6-11

Turner v. Holiday Inn Holidome
721 So.2d 64 (La. 1999)

Krystal Turner was the 12-year-old daughter of Ms. Eliza Turner. Chosen to be a member of the Jefferson Parish Recreation Department's All-Star girl's basketball team, Krystal was taken to the Holidome in Houma [Louisiana] to participate in a basketball tournament. While there she went swimming in the Holidome's pool and drowned. ...

At check-in at the Holidome, Frey [the team's coach] was not informed of any rules or regulations regarding the children's use of the swimming pool. After the tournament game on Saturday, which finished at 7:00 P.M., the group went to eat. They finished at around 8:30 P.M., arriving back at the hotel at around 9:00 P.M. The pool closed at 10:00 P.M. Most of the kids went in the pool. There were a lot of people in the pool at that time, somewhere between 30 and 50. ...

Frey first realized there was a problem when someone yelled for him; he turned and saw Krystal in the arms of another player. Someone began to administer CPR; Frey ran to call 911. ...

There was no lifeguard at the pool, nor were there any buoys or lifelines. ...

Holidome has had biddy basketball teams come to stay for several years, and the manager knew there would be children using the pool. He knew there would be eight or nine groups of children from southeastern Louisiana on that particular weekend. Holidome had no regulation as to the number of people who could use the pool at one time.

The manager knew that the pool rope, or life line at the deep end [which separates the shallow and deep sections of the pool and alerts swimmers that the depth is changing] had broken, but he could not remember when it happened. He knew that the pool became cloudy when subjected to heavy use, and if employees could not see the bottom, they were instructed to close the pool. Safety devices included a "shepherd's hook" (a long pole with a hook on the end), and a life ring located on the wall adjacent to the pool.

A security guard employed on the night of the accident testified that there were forty or fifty children in the pool on that night and about one hundred people around the decking, at the tables, etc. There were problems with some children running and diving. The pool water started to get cloudy, and he could not quite see the bottom of the pool. There were no life lines in the pool. Both of the security guards on duty and the manager were called to different parts of the hotel for different reasons; when he returned to the pool area, the accident had taken place. ...

Mr. Doky, the brother of one of the team players testified that he swam to retrieve a ball and when walking back he stepped on something and assumed it was a toy. He looked down to see what it was but could not see to the bottom. A few seconds later, he again went to get the ball, at which time he decided to see what was in the water. At that time he found Krystal's body. This was at about six-foot depth level. He swam back to the top of the pool and because it was so loud, he had to scream a few times to get the attention of the coaches. He went back under and brought the body up, pushing her to the side of the pool. ...

[Krystal's mother sued the Holidome for negligence.]

We find that Holidome acted unreasonably by maintaining its pool in an unsafe manner. The testimony establishes that Holidome never employed a lifeguard. The management of the hotel knew that a number of teams of children ages 10–12 would be staying that weekend for the tournament, and had the authority to request a temporary lifeguard, yet failed to do so. Furthermore, there was no one with water safety training assigned to monitor the safety and security of the swimmers. Management was aware from previous experience that these young guests usually use the pool area. There [were] no rules relative to pool capacity, and the pool was, by all accounts, very crowded in the evening. The surrounding area was also extremely crowded and very noisy, making it unlikely that a swimmer in distress would be readily observed. The pool had no safety rope or lifeline at the deep end of the pool, and the rope had been missing for some time. Depth markers inside the pool did not display the pool depth at seven and one-half feet, and the deck marker of that depth [located on the outside of the pool] was difficult to see from inside the pool. Lack of these markers and safety ropes were violative of the Louisiana Sanitary Code.

Testimony also established that the water in the pool was cloudy by the time Krystal drowned, to the extent that the bottom of the pool was obscured. The effect of this is obvious because when Mr. Doby touched Krystal's body with his foot, he did not know that he stepped on the body of a child, perhaps at that point still viable [able to be resuscitated], but thought he had touched a toy. No one could see Krystal at the bottom of the pool ... The whole purpose of maintaining clear water, providing a lifeguard, guarding against overcrowding, providing a safety rope and depth markers, is to insure that there are not accidents in the pool, specifically drownings. In summary, Holidome had a duty to act in a reasonable manner, which duty is breached.

CASE QUESTIONS

1. What should the hotel have done to avoid the problems that led to liability?

2. Was the hotel liable for negligence per se? Why or why not?

The lesson from this case is that a hotel needs to monitor carefully the use of its swimming pool to ensure safety precautions are taken. If the hotel can anticipate high use of the pool, sufficient lifeguards are important. Rules concerning maximum capacity should be developed and honored. A rule should be adopted and followed requiring closing the pool when the water's clarity is compromised. Safety devices, such as the presence of a rope delineating the shallow and deep ends, should be in good working order whenever the pool is being used.

In another drowning case, the plaintiff sought to establish the hotel's negligence by the fact that no lifeguard was on duty at the time of the accident. Signs were prominently posted around the pool warning swimmers of the absence of a lifeguard. A friend who had been swimming with the deceased had seen the signs and was aware no lifeguard was on duty. The applicable law did not require a lifeguard for a pool the size of the hotel's. Rescue equipment was provided poolside. The court held that, in these circumstances, the absence of a lifeguard was obvious and apparent to the deceased and thus the hotel was not liable.[51]

Remove Hazards

A hotel may be liable for leaving maintenance equipment in the vicinity of the pool. In the case of *Tucker v. Dixon*, 355 P.2d 79 (Colo. 1960), the owners permitted pool-cleaning equipment, including large, heavy floats, to remain beside the pool. The evidence showed that the floats were sometimes used as playthings in the pool. The eleven-year-old plaintiff-guest went swimming upon her arrival at the motel. When surfacing from a dive, she hit one of the floats and was injured. In her lawsuit against the hotel the court held for the plaintiff. The motel was negligent for failing to move the cleaning equipment to a place where it would not be easily accessible to swimmers.

Comply with Statutory Requirements

Failure to comply with safety requirements imposed by statutes on pool operators can result in liability under the doctrine of negligence per se.

Diving Boards

Local governments often issue regulations applicable to pool diving boards. Failure to comply with these laws can lead to terrible consequences for both a patron who is injured and for the hotel. In one case, a hotel installed a high-performance

---

[51]*Kemp v. Charter House Inn*, 2000 WL 23180 (Ohio 2000)

aluminum "Duraflex" board. This type of diving board propels divers a significant distance farther forward than other materials. The plaintiff used the board, was catapulted into the shallow area, and struck his head on the pool bottom. As a result of his injuries he was rendered quadriplegic. The court held the hotel liable based on negligence.[52]

An additional risk associated with diving boards and also pool slides is that the divers or sliders will collide with a swimmer in the pool when they hit the water. People injured in this way often sue the hotel, claiming negligent supervision of the guests using the pool.[53]

To avoid risks associated with diving boards and pool slides, many hotels have eliminated them.

Safety Equipment

Hotels with pools must maintain necessary safety equipment to rescue a swimmer experiencing difficulty in remaining afloat. A hotel was found liable for a guest's drowning where it provided a straight pole, but not one with a hook at the end that is needed to help raise a submerged swimmer to the surface. In *Harris v. Laquinta-Redbird Joint Venture*, 522 S.W.2d 232 (Tex. 1975), a swimmer at a hotel pool sank to the bottom. A rescuer, using the available pole that had no hook, was thus unable to lift the submerged swimmer from the water. Instead, the rescuer was limited to the slower process of pushing the victim to the shallow area. The swimmer was dead by the time the rescue was completed. A city ordinance required that all pools be equipped with a hooked pole. The hotel was found liable based on the doctrine of negligence per se. To avoid liability for this type of negligence, a business must carefully study applicable laws and regulations and do what is necessary to comply. If a hotel or restaurant is uncertain as to the meaning of a statute, clarification should be sought from an appropriate source such as the director of the governmental department responsible for enforcing the particular law or the hotel's attorney.

Control Boisterous Conduct of Guests

When boisterous conduct and horseplay are allowed in a pool area, accidents may occur. In *Gordon v. Hotel Seville, Inc.*, 105 So.2d 175 (Fla. 1958), the plaintiff, while swimming face down in the defendant hotel's pool, was hit when another swimmer was thrown into the pool by a group of rowdy boys and landed on her. The hotel denied liability. The court ruled that the defendant, as an operator of a swimming pool, owed its invitees the duty to use reasonable care to eliminate unsafe conditions. If there is horseplay in the pool, the hotel could be liable to the plaintiff for failing to halt the disorderly conduct. If, however, prior to the accident, no one in the pool was acting disorderly, the hotel will not be liable. In *Cohen v. Suburban Sidney-Hill, Inc.*, 178 N.E.2d 19 (Mass. 1961), a twelve-year-

---

[52] *Hooks v. Washington Sheraton Corporation*, 578 F.2d 313 (D.C. Cir. 1977)

[53] *Casey v. Treasure Island Corporation*, 745 A.2d 743 (R.I. 2000)

old youth fell backward off the ladder leading to the diving board at a country club and was injured. He claimed that other children were clamoring up the ladder while he was ascending it, causing the fall. Three lifeguards were on duty and none had observed any horseplay. The court noted that the cause of the fall was as likely to be that the plaintiff lost his foothold as that supervision was lax. Therefore, the plaintiff failed to prove a breach of duty on the part of the club and the court held for the defendant.

Inspect for Glass in Pool Area

Glass and other debris in swimming and wading areas pose a significant risk to pool users. In *Bristol v. Ernst*, 27 N.Y.S.2d 119 (1941), the plaintiff's foot was severely cut on a piece of glass at the bottom of a hotel wading pool. If the glass was dropped or placed in the pool just prior to the injury, it would not have been detected nor could its presence have been prevented in the exercise of ordinary care. In such a circumstance, the hotel would not be liable. However, if the plaintiff can prove the glass had been in the pool for awhile, the hotel will have breached its duty to inspect the property for risks at reasonable intervals.

Waterfront Properties

Many hotels are adjacent to public beaches that front on oceans. These bodies of water present numerous potential dangers that can and do cause injury and death. The risks include heavy surf, riptides, underwater tows, and man-eating animals. In the cases that result from those related deaths or injuries, the plaintiffs argue that the hotel breached a duty to warn of risks and protect guests from them. Most cases hold that hotels, which neither own nor control the ocean, have no duty to warn, correct, or safeguard guests from naturally occurring, even if hidden, dangers common to waters.

A hotel guest drowned when caught in a riptide in the ocean off a public beach adjacent to the hotel. A second guest attempted to rescue the swimmer and also drowned. The survivors of both guests sued the hotel and the case was dismissed. The court held that the hotel did not owe the guests a duty to warn of the riptide or to protect them from it.[54]

Off-Premises Beaches

In a similar case a hotel, physically separated from a public beach only by a four-lane highway, marketed its proximity to the beach and encouraged guests to use the waterfront. The hotel provided beach chairs, umbrellas, towels, and a security escort service. The hotel also furnished guests with pamphlets warning about sun exposure and crime on the beach. A guest drowned in a riptide while swimming there. His survivors sued, claiming that the hotel had a duty to disclose dangerous surf conditions. The court dismissed the complaint, holding that an

---

[54] *Poleyeff v. Seville Beach Hotel*, 782 So.2d 422 (Fl. 2001)

innkeeper owes no duty to a guest injured or endangered while away from the premises. Providing beach accessories and warning of some risks did not create a duty to warn against hazards of the sea. The court noted "it may well have been good practice [to provide warnings] but it was not required."[55]

Given that a goal of hospitality facilities is not just to avoid liability, but also to protect guests' well-being and provide a fun, healthy getaway, a hotel near a beach should keep apprised of related risks and alert their patrons to danger.

A minority of states require a hotel to warn of risks at off-premises facilities that the innkeeper reasonably can foresee that guests will visit. A guest suffered a paralyzing injury while swimming in an ocean near his hotel. The injury ultimately caused his death. The court held the hotel could be liable if it failed to warn of known risks and if it could anticipate that the guest would visit the beach. Proof on the second point will be facilitated at trial by a brochure issued by the hotel touting its location "overlooking the golden sands of Kamaole Beach Park."[56]

Waterfront Risks Created by a Hotel

If a hotel with waterfront property erects an entertainment facility for guests utilizing the water, it must warn of any related risks and prohibit inappropriate use. In the following case, failure to warn resulted in liability.

CASE EXAMPLE 6-12

Mihill v. Ger-Am Inc.
651 N.Y.S.2d 746 (N.Y. 1997)

Plaintiff Michael Mihill (hereinafter plaintiff) and his parents seek to recover for serious injuries sustained by plaintiff when he jumped or fell into Mirror Lake from a swing located on defendant's property. The swings were on the shore of the lake, approximately three to six feet from the water's edge, and were intended for use by patrons of defendant's hotel. According to defendant's president, the swings were posted with a sign stating, "Do not jump from swings." [The existence of the signs was disputed by several other witnesses.] Despite the claims of defendant's president and night manager that they did not tolerate such activities, there is evidence in the record that neighborhood children used the swings to jump into the lake on a fairly regular basis. Although the water was shallow close to the shore, there was evidently a sharp dropoff 10 to 15 feet out, such that if one swung high enough before jumping, he or she would arc past the shallow area and land safely in the deeper water.

On the evening of the accident, plaintiff, then age 17, and his friend, Chad Flyte, were ... on the hotel premises for the purpose of swimming in the lake. Flyte had successfully jumped from the swing into the lake, and plaintiff, who had never swum in that area before and was unaware of the depth of the water or the contour of the lake bed, had begun to swing with the same end in mind. Whether he actually jumped or—as he avers—"chickened out", and was slowing the swing to dismount when his foot caught on the ground, causing him to "flop off" the swing and into the water, is the subject of conflicting deposition testimony. Unfortunately, he apparently entered the water head first, and suffered several injuries rendering him a quadriplegic.

---

[55] *Darby v. Meridien Hotels, Inc.*, 2001 WL 630158 (N.Y. 2001)

[56] *Rygg v. County of Maui*, 98 F.Supp.2d 1129 (Ha. 1999)

... [Given that a dispute existed as to the presence of warning signs near the swings, and the testimony that defendants tolerated children on the swings despite the known danger, defendant's motion for summary judgment is denied.]

CASE QUESTION

1. What should the hotel have done to avoid liability in this case?

Restrict Use or Warn of Hazards in the Water

Another potential danger for swimmers is errant surfboards and other sporting equipment. In *Landrum Mills Hotel Corp. v. Ferhatovic*, 317 F.2d 76 (1st Cir. 1963), a hotel provided surfboards for its guests. A guest completing his ocean swim and about to leave the water was hit in the face with one of the surfboards. The court determined that the hotel acted negligently by failing to either restrict the area in which surfboards were allowed or warn bathers that surfboards were in use.

Inspect Lake Bottoms for Hazards

If a hotel invites its guests to swim in a natural body of water, the inn's duty of reasonable care requires it to inspect the bottom for dangerous objects and, if any are found, remove them. The facility should also prevent the cause of the dangerous objects—such as boats—from using the swimming area.

In *Montes v. Betcher*, 480 F.2d 1128 (1973), presented in full in Chapter 5, the plaintiff, an experienced diver, dived off a pier at the defendant's lake resort. The plaintiff had dived there many times before. On the day in question he hit a jagged piece of concrete and suffered injuries to his scalp and vertebrae. The area was regularly used by both swimmers and boaters. The concrete obstruction was recovered, and it resembled a boat anchor. The defendant never inspected the lake bottom for debris, never raked the bottom, did not erect a warning sign to swimmers, and did nothing to discourage boaters from entering the swimming area. The jury found these omissions to be negligent.

Access to the Water

A hotel with waterfront property may provide a walkway, bridge, or boardwalk between the hotel and the beach. The duty of care owed to guests includes maintaining any such walkway in a reasonably safe condition. A steel catwalk leading from the shore to a marina that collapsed without warning could result in liability if the breakdown was due to shoddy construction or maintenance.[57]

---

[57] *Howell v. Buck Creek State Park*, 2001 WL 710113 (Ohio 2001)

Special Duties

A hotel or restaurant's duty to exercise reasonable care to provide for guests' safety applies in the important circumstances of fire, security, and medical treatment.

Injuries Caused by Fire

Fires present very serious risks to hotels and their guests. Liability can result from inadequate fire safety equipment, delays in notifying the fire department and guests about a fire, and failing to train employees on what to do in the event a fire breaks out.

Innkeepers' concern about fire is heightened as a result of three substantial fires in large hotels in the 1980s that led to many deaths and injuries, much property damage, and many lawsuits. In 1981, fire broke out in the MGM Grand Hotel in Las Vegas, Nevada. Eighty-four people died, almost 700 were injured, and approximately 900 lawsuits were brought against the hotel. Many of the cases were settled for considerable sums of money. In 1982, a fire occurred in the Stouffer's Inn in White Plains, New York, killing twenty-six people. The DuPont Plaza Hotel was the site of a fire in 1986, killing and injuring almost 240. The death toll was due in part to locked exits, obstructed passageways, and inaccessible fire alarms.

Maintain Fire Safety Equipment

Most states and many localities have passed statutes and building codes listing equipment that all hotels and restaurants are required to have for fire protection. Failure to provide the mandated equipment constitutes negligence per se, resulting in automatic liability. Required apparatus include fire extinguishers, sprinkler systems, smoke detectors, fire alarms, smoke and fire dampers, voice-communication systems in guest rooms and other public rooms, exit illumination, posted maps showing exit routes in case of fire, emergency lighting, evacuation plans, employee training, and fire escapes. To accommodate guests who are hearing impaired, alarm systems should include a visual component. Failure to provide required fire safety devices can lead to liability.

In *Pirtle's Administratrix v. Hargis Bank & Trust Company*, 44 S.W.2d 541 (Ky. 1931), the deceased was a guest in the Combs Hotel and died when the hotel was destroyed by fire. The deceased's survivors charged that the defendant innkeeper negligently failed to provide the hotel with either an iron stairway as a fire escape on the outside of the building or fire-fighting equipment, although both were required by statute. The court held for the survivors, stating that it is a firmly fixed rule that one injured by a violation of a statute may recover from a defendant for any damages sustained, based on negligence per se.

Remember, compliance with statutory safety requirements does not guarantee freedom from liability. Rather, these laws set only the minimum standards for fire safety. Innkeepers should view the safety codes as only a starting point and work up from there. For example, since the fire at the MGM Grand in Nevada, the hotel has installed many fire safety devices not required by law, including a computerized alarm system and monitoring mechanisms. Despite significant cost for these initiatives, the potential loss from fire renders the cost a worthwhile investment.

In addition to liability concerns, another reason exists to comply with fire-safety laws. Many states permit an official, often called a fire marshal, to inspect premises for violations. If warranted, the marshal is typically authorized to direct that certain remedial action be taken. If the hotel thereafter fails to act, the marshal can obtain an injunction (a court order) requiring the innkeeper to make certain repairs. See for example, *Crazy Water Retirement Hotel v. State of Texas*, 2001 WL 799946 (Tex. 2001).

Train Staff on How to Respond to a Fire

When a hotel fire breaks out, the hotel has a continuing duty to exercise reasonable care to protect the safety of its guests. A hotel was found negligent where the night clerk, upon learning of a fire in the hotel, first went to the second floor to look for the fire and only after finding it called the fire department. He then returned to the lobby and attempted to turn on the fire alarm, but discovered that it did not work. Further, he testified he had not been instructed on how to use the fire alarm. An occupant of one of the rooms died in the fire. His estate sued the hotel and won. The hotel was negligent for failing to notify the fire department immediately, failing to properly maintain the alarm, and failing to train the night clerk on how to use it.[58]

In another case where an employee failed to respond properly, *Burrows v. Knots*, 482 S.W.2d 385 (Tex. 1972), the night clerk, upon learning of a fire, properly called the fire department first. However, rather than notifying guests, he then went outside to remove his truck from in front of the hotel. The family of a guest who had died in the fire sued the hotel based on a statement in the death certificate that stated the guest had survived for ten minuets after the fire began. The jury found for the plaintiff and the verdict was upheld on appeal.

Liability to Adjacent Premises

Once a fire starts, it is likely to spread if not contained. Neighboring properties are at risk. If the business where the fire originated was negligent in causing the blaze, that business may be liable to the owner of an abutting property that is damaged by the fire. A hairdresser was determined to have been negligent in causing a fire at her salon. The fire caused significant water, smoke, and fire damage to adjoining businesses, including a restaurant located next to the shopping center in which the beauty parlor was located. The salon was liable to the nearby businesses.[59]

In a similar case, a fire began in the defendant hotel and grew quickly. Hotel patrons attempted to extinguish the blaze, but were unable to do so because

---

[58] *Parker v. Kirkwood*, 8 P.2d 340 (Kan. 1932)

[59] *Deardorff Associates, Inc. v. Brown c/b/a HAIR*, 2000 WL 1211078 (Del. 2000)

of "faulty and nonserviceable fire extinguishers." The fire spread to the plaintiff's saloon located next door. As a result of damage the plaintiff was unable to operate the business for seven months and incurred loss of revenue. The court, refusing to grant the defendant's motion for summary judgment, said, "It is foreseeable that, in a hotel where there are inadequate or inoperative smoke detectors and fire extinguishers, a fire could move unchecked throughout the structure to the point where it would spread to buildings immediately adjacent to it."[60]

Security

Appropriately, a primary concern of hoteliers, restaurateurs, and travelers today is security. An examination of the various cases and media accounts dealing with attacks, robberies, and rapes of guests in hotel rooms or on restaurant premises accentuates this concern. Personal injury, loss of life, and loss of property suffered as the result of criminal activity has cost the hospitality industry many millions of dollars in damage payments.

How much security does a hotel, motel, or restaurant owe to guests in the buildings or on the grounds? Is a hotel liable if an intruder attacks a guest in a guest room?

Any business that invites the public onto its premises must take reasonable steps to guard against risk of assaultive behavior. Nevertheless, this duty does not extend to unforeseeable or unexpected criminal acts by third persons. Thus, a business with reason to anticipate the occurrence of a criminal act has a duty to protect patrons. A business is charged with knowing criminal activity will occur where the perpetrator, prior to the criminal act, was abusive or disorderly, or where there existed a pattern of prior criminal activity that made similar or related conduct foreseeable. Thus, foreseeability is an important element in determining whether a hospitality defendant had a duty to protect patrons from criminal acts of third parties.

Foreseeability of Criminal Activity

Under what circumstances is criminal activity reasonably foreseeable, thereby creating a duty on the part of the restaurant or hotel to provide reasonable protection to customers? If the facility is in a high-crime area, or if the facility or its customers have been the victim of criminal activity, the restaurant or hotel should, for the purpose of defining its legal duty, anticipate additional criminal activity. In one case, a plaintiff was robbed and raped in a Wellesley Inn. The hotel had been the site of fifty-six crimes, including robberies, within a two-and-a-half-year period. The jury determined that the hotel was negligent for not providing

[60] *Bartelli v. O'Brien*, 718 N.E.2d 344 (Ill. 1999)
[61] *Simms v. Prime Hospitality Corp.*, 700 So.2d 167 (Fl. 1997)

sufficient security and the verdict was upheld on appeal.[61] *Note:* The hotel in this case had been the victim of many crimes. The duty to anticipate criminal activity and provide against it may be triggered by even one or a few prior incidents.

Another circumstance that alerts a facility that criminal activity may occur is the presence of rowdy or abusive customers. In a case involving a Burger King, a family observed a group of seven teenagers who were "rowdy, obnoxious, loud, abusive, and using foul language." The conduct continued while they all ordered and then when they proceeded into the dining area. The father of the family approached the group, identified himself as an off-duty police officer, and requested that they desist. One of the group hit him, knocking him to the ground, and then struck him in the head with a chair. At the resulting trial, the Burger King manager, arguing that an assault had not been foreseeable, testified that he had worked at the restaurant for three years and had never seen an incident where one customer hit another. "We hold the teenagers' unruly behavior could reasonably have been anticipated to escalate into acts that would expose patrons to an unreasonable risk of injury. ... [T]he teenagers' behavior in the restaurant created a foreseeable risk of harm that the defendant unreasonably failed."[62]

An auditorium that housed a rock concert should have foreseen the increased potential for security problems when many patrons of the concert were unruly and openly drinking alcohol, the floor was littered with liquor bottles and pieces of glass, some patrons were smoking marijuana, and the band performed songs that encouraged the use of drugs and alcohol. A concert-goer who was struck and injured by a bottle thrown from the balcony sued the city that owned the auditorium. The jury's verdict for the plaintiff was upheld on appeal. The court ruled that the city had created an unreasonable risk of harm to those who attended the performance.[63]

If an attack occurs unexpectedly with no reason to anticipate it, the facility owes no duty to the patron to offer protection against the incident. A man was robbed and killed while leaving the drive-through area of a Church's Fried Chicken. His family sued the eatery claiming insufficient security measures. There had been no suspicious conduct by the perpetrator prior to the crime. In the previous five years, the time during which the eatery was owned by the current proprietor, no robbery had ever occurred, nor had there been any reason to summon police. The restaurant and surrounding area were well lighted. Said the court, the crime was a "random and unforeseeable event which could not have been prevented." Therefore the case was dismissed.[64]

Similarly, an attendee at an outdoor concert was struck in the face with a whiskey bottle by a "long-haired gentleman" after an argument arose over a blanket. The long-haired man had originally walked away after a verbal dispute, but then returned within a few seconds and struck the plaintiff with the bottle. The

---

[62] *Iannelli v. Burger King Corp.*, 761 A.2d 417 (N.H. 2000)

[63] *Greenville Memorial Auditorium v. Martin*, 391 S.E.2d 546 (S.C. 1990)

[64] *Oberling v. Jacobs*, 730 So.2d 990 (La. 1999)

court held there was insufficient time for security personnel to be put on notice of the long-haired man's violent propensities.[65]

To review, a hospitality facility has a duty to provide reasonable protection to invitees if it can reasonably anticipate the occurrence of criminal activity. We next explore the amount of security that is required.

Matching Security to Circumstances

Reasonable care is the duty of care required by an innkeeper for guests' safety. It is not a static, clearly defined concept. One definition will not fit all hotels in all locations at all times. The type of security that would constitute ordinary care in a relatively quiet and tranquil location with a low crime rate might be considered grossly inadequate and therefore negligent if employed in a high-crime area with a history of muggings and unauthorized entries into guests' rooms. Security thus becomes a relative concept. The precautions necessary must be determined for each individual hotel.

Factors that are examined to determine if an establishment has provided adequate security include the number and type of security incidents occurring at the facility within the last few years, the community crime rate, crime rate in the immediate area and in similar businesses, industry standards, and any particular security problems posed by the establishment's layout, such as multiple buildings. The very basic measures with which all rooms should be equipped are deadbolts, chain locks or other lock or safety device on the doors, and a peephole. Some hotels dispense with safety chains because they hinder management's entry into rooms in emergencies. If safety chains are used, the chain should be strong. The chain locks and deadbolts should be designed so they are easy for the guest to use. They should be inspected regularly to verify good working order. The peephole, or one-way viewer, enables the guest to determine who is at the door before opening it. This simple device can protect guests from unknown intruders. The placement of the peephole on the door should be eye level for persons of average height. The glass should be properly installed so that the person inside the guest room can look out and not vice versa.

Each door or entranceway to the room should be suitably secured. In *Garzelli v. Howard Johnson's Motor Lodges, Inc.*, 419 F.Supp. 1210 (N.Y. 1976), singer Connie Francis was raped at knifepoint in a Long Island Howard Johnson's Motor Lodge. Her assailant gained access to the room through a sliding-glass door. Said the court, "The doors gave the appearance of being locked but the testimony showed they were capable of being unsecured from the outside without much difficulty." She recovered $2.5 million in damages for her inability to continue her lucrative music career based on the hotel's failure to provide a "safe and secure room."

The court in the following case refused to grant summary judgment in favor of the defendant, finding that a jury could determine that the hotel's security precautions were insufficient.

---

[65] *Hudson v. Riverport Performance Arts Centre*, 37 S.W.3d 261 (Mo. 2000)

CASE EXAMPLE 6-13

Cyzio v. Rihga International USA, Inc. 660 N.Y.S.2d 271 (N.Y. 1997)

Plaintiff Chester T. Cyzio ("Cyzio") sues defendant Rihga International USA, Inc. ("Rihga") hotel located near Times Square in midtown Manhattan. The complaint alleges that on November 21, 1991, Cyzio registered as a guest at the hotel and that in the middle of the night on November 30th he was viciously and violently assaulted in his room as a result of defendant's negligence in maintaining its hotel security system. Defendant now moves for summary judgment arguing that as plaintiff cannot demonstrate how the assailant gained entry into the building, the plaintiff cannot establish that the alleged failure to provide adequate security was the proximate cause of the attack upon the plaintiff.

In opposing summary judgment, plaintiff relies upon an affidavit from a security expert stating that heightened security is warranted at the Rihga due to its location in a high-crime area and to the ninety-two (92) reported crimes in the eleven months prior to the incident. The expert affidavit also states that the policy described by Rihga's security supervisor at his deposition whereby persons entering the hotel in the middle of the night are not stopped and questioned, even if security personnel did not know whether the person was a guest, is inadequate. The expert also stated that the misplacing of the vincard computer readout showing entries into the plaintiff's room as well as other alleged discrepancies in the security team's handling of the incident are further indications of an inadequate security system. ...

In a commercial setting such as a hotel, a landlord has a duty to exercise and use reasonable care to protect guests or tenants, while on the premises, against injuries at the hands of third persons who are not employees of the hotel ... and is required to take reasonable protective measures, including providing adequate security, to protect guests against third party criminal acts ... particularly where the occurrence of criminal activity on the premises was reasonably foreseeable. ... [A] plaintiff who is assaulted in a commercial building need not demonstrate the manner of the assailant's entry, but need only create questions of fact as to whether the landlord breached its duty to maintain minimal security measures, related to the specific building itself, in the face of foreseeable criminal intrusion upon tenants.

In this case, the deposition testimony of Cyzio himself coupled with the expert's affidavit create issues of fact as to whether the hotel security system was appropriate for this particular hotel, particularly in the middle of the night. The Court also is troubled by the loss of video tapes that defendant claims show the plaintiff entering the hotel and riding in the elevator with an invited guest. Defendant claimed that its security personnel turned the tape over to the police without receiving a police receipt in return. The police, however, have conducted a search and have informed the Court that they do not have such a tape. Plaintiff's expert states that he is familiar with hotel security measures and that it is not standard procedure to turn such tapes over to the police without a receipt. Defendant's security chief, Mr. Higgins, testified that the hotel's security policy is not to question guests or other persons entering the hotel if they are "well dressed or properly dressed and appear to know where they are going; the policy is to question a person entering the hotel only if the person is behaving suspiciously." Plaintiff's expert states that following such a procedure in the late night or early morning "is tantamount to inviting well-dressed intruders." As questions of fact exist as to the liability of the hotel for plaintiff's loss and injuries, summary judgment [for the hotel] is denied.

CASE QUESTIONS

1. The video tape, if it existed, would be an important piece of evidence for the hotel. How might it have better protected the tape from loss?

2. What policy should the hotel have adopted concerning people who seek to access guest rooms at night?

A bar in a high-crime area promoted an "End of Summer Bash" on a local radio station that broadcast from the tavern's parking lot, thereby attempting to attract a large crowd. The establishment did not provide a doorman or other security measures such as bouncers or wait staff. This was insufficient protection under the circumstances. The facility was therefore liable to a patron who was hit by another customer.[66]

Likewise, a crew of fourteen security guards at a rock concert attended by 6000 people was insufficient to manage the crowd.[67]

In another case, the court determined that a hotel did not meet its duty to provide reasonable protection where front-desk personnel failed to notify police promptly when a guest called to report a crime in progress within the hotel. Once alerted to a security incident, hotel staff are expected to respond quickly.[68] The ruling in that case also held that, for a hotel with 1200 rooms and hosting a large ball, having on duty only one security officer, one room clerk, and one bellboy was insufficient to satisfy the inn's duty to provide reasonable safety precautions.

In another case, the plaintiff, after registering at a 300-room motel, went to her car to retrieve some papers. She was attacked by a stranger she had seen by the front desk when she registered. The guest was brutally sodomized and left with serious physical and psychological injuries. Management was aware of approximately thirty criminal incidents occurring on the premises during the six months prior to the attack, yet the hotel employed only one security guard "from time to time on a sporadic basis." The plaintiff won the case. Given the prior criminal incidents at the motel, more security precautions clearly were needed.[69]

Adequate Security Can Eliminate Liability

If a hotel or restaurant takes adequate security precautions and a guest is nonetheless attacked, the facility will not be liable. Thus, a case was dismissed against a hotel at which the plaintiff was the victim of a vicious assault, robbery and rape on her honeymoon.[70] Said the court

[I]t would be incorrect for this court to say the mere fact of a rape is conclusive evidence that security at the Inn was unreasonable. To do such would be to hold the Inn as an insurer of its guests' safety.

... There can be no doubt that armed guards in every building, twenty-four hours a day, would have provided the guests with more protection than the security system employed by Islander Inn. However, it must be remembered that the Inn's function was as a luxury island motel, not a prison. In considering the reasonableness of the security, the court must take into account the purpose and function of the business.

Based on the lack of criminal activity on the premises in the past, one uniformed guard during the nighttime hours is reasonable security for a guest

---

[66] *Jeffords v. Lesesne*, 541 S.E.2d 847 (S.C. 2000)

[67] *Greenville Memorial Auditorium v. Martin*, 391 S.E.2d 546 (S.C. 1990)

[68] *Nordmann v. National Hotel Co.*, 425 F.2d 1103 (La. 1970)

[69] *Orlando Executive Park v. PDR*, 402 So.2d 442 (Fl. 1981)

[70] *Courtney v. Remler*, 566 F.Supp 1225 (S.C. 1983)

at the motel. The motel is relatively small with 190 total guest rooms. One trained guard could adequately patrol the premises. ...

The Islander Inn, as a whole, was operated and supervised reasonably. The Inn obviously felt a need to protect its guests from criminal attacks by third person, and measures were taken to ensure their safety. The measures were reasonable. The rape incident was a truly unfortunate and horrible experience, but the defendants cannot be held responsible. For this court to hold otherwise would be equivalent to making all motels the insurer of their guests' safety. Therefore, it is

ORDERED, that this action be dismissed.

Security Personnel and Firearms

Should security personnel in a hotel carry weapons? This is a difficult question and there is no easy answer. A gun in the hands of even a well-trained guard can present dangers. If the guard is attacked and subdued, the attacker will have easy access to the firearm and may misuse it. A gun can be a very dangerous instrument in the hands of someone not well trained in its use. An unarmed security guard may be of only limited help in the event of an attack, and the hotel or restaurant that employs the guard risks civil liability for any injuries the guard incurs. Each facility needs to develop a policy that suits its circumstances.

Medical Care

A hotel is not required to offer its guests medical services. To avoid potential liability if a doctor malpractices, most hotels today will not recommend a particular doctor. Instead, the hotel might provide a list of available physicians and require the guest to select.

If a hotel chooses to offer health services, it must exercise reasonable care in the selection of medical personnel and in the provision of the services.

If the hotel provides or recommends a doctor or nurse, at the minimum the person should be licensed. A guest at a Hilton Hotel fell backward in his hotel room while dressing and hit his head against the wall. He became nauseous and complained to his travel companion of a headache. The latter called hotel management for a doctor and was advised that "some help" would be sent. A woman arrived within a half hour and identified herself as a nurse. After ascertaining the circumstances she recommended the guest remain in bed for twelve hours. By the next day he was in a comatose state. He was taken by ambulance to the hospital where surgery was immediately performed. He suffered permanent brain damage. In fact, the woman who had come to his hotel room was not a licensed nurse. While the hotel had a medical department, a physician was not on call during the evenings. Instead, the woman responded to medical calls "with the full knowledge and consent of the hotel management." Expert testimony established the following: When the woman visited the guest's room the guest was exhibiting classic symptoms of a blood clot in the brain; a licensed nurse would have identified the symptoms; a nurse would have sought immediate treatment; prompt medical care would have averted the brain damage. The court stated that, while the hotel did not owe a duty to its guests to provide medical services, if it undertakes to do so, it must send a doctor "or at the very least a nurse." Judgment was rendered against the hotel.[71]

Clearly, a physician who cannot understand the language of her patients cannot properly treat them. If a hotel opts to recommend medical personnel, it should ensure that the doctors are qualified in all respects, including language compatibility with the guest/patient. A plaintiff and two friends, all English speaking, traveled to the Dominican Republic on vacation. The plaintiff was a "well-controlled, insulin-dependent diabetic." While in the Dominican Republic, she became ill. She sought assistance from the front desk. A hotel representative "put her in touch with" a clinic. The doctor, whose native language was Spanish but who could communicate in English, did not understand the words *diabetic* or *diabetes*. The plaintiff ultimately died as a result of inadequate treatment. The hotel is now subject to a lawsuit. Recommending unqualified medical personnel may lead to liability.[72]

Another case involving medical care illustrates proper conduct on the part of a hospitality facility when confronted with a medical emergency. A casino patron/plaintiff had a heart attack while gambling at a blackjack table. The dealer immediately summoned security who responded quickly and, upon assessing the circumstances, called the casino medical station. A nurse from the medical station arrived at the scene within minutes and immediately instructed security to call an ambulance. She assisted three other patrons in providing CPR. When the ambulance arrived, the attendants intubated plaintiff (a procedure in which a tube is inserted into the trachea to help restore the ability to breathe), which caused him to regain a pulse. In the resulting lawsuit, the plaintiff claimed the casino violated its duty of care to him because the nurse did not intubate him prior to the arrival of the ambulance, as a result of which his heart attack was prolonged. The court held that the casino's duty was to summon aid and, until aid arrived, provide "such first aid as the [facility's] employees are reasonably capable of giving." The casino's duty did not require it to provide medical equipment to perform an intubation.[73]

Negligence was found where a hotel failed to call an ambulance for a guest asking for medical help. Instead, the front desk attendant called a cab to take the guest to the hospital. The guest had explained to the attendant that he was not feeling well and asked for a medical facility on site. He was pale, sweating, and flushed white. Upon learning that the hotel lacked medical care, he decided to go to a hospital emergency room. The guest died soon after reaching the hospital. The hotel's failure to summon emergency medical help resulted in liability.[74]

Sometimes hotel staff may try to diagnose a guest's problem and suggest home remedies. Personnel should be trained not to do this. A guest whose injury is made worse by such advise may sue and is likely to win.

---

[71] *Stahlin v. Hilton Hotels Corp.*, 484 F.2d 580 (Ill. 1973)

[72] *Gianocostas v. Riu Hotels*, 2001 WL 758695 (Ma. 2001)

[73] *Lundy v. Trop World*, 34 F.3d 1173 (N.J. 1994)

[74] *Gingeleskie v. Westin Hotel Co*, 145 F.3d 1337 (Ariz. 1998)

Key Terms

constructive notice   insurer
expert witness

Summary

The potential liability faced by a hotel or restaurant for negligent acts encompasses virtually every part of the facility. To avoid liability, hotels and restaurants must be diligent in maintaining their premises in a safe condition. Liability can result from unclean rooms, broken furniture, poorly maintained windows, and unsafe electrical systems. Also exposing hotels and restaurants to lawsuits are uncontrolled rodents, deteriorated bathroom appliances, unsafe elevators, broken doors, improperly maintained ceilings, dangerous steps and escalators, slippery floors, out-of-control flambé dishes, and excessively hot drinks. Likewise, hospitality establishments will be liable for failing to properly maintain sidewalks and sporting facilities on the premises and for inadequate lighting inside and outside of the buildings. A hotel offering swimming facilities must use reasonable care to protect the safety of guests who use these amenities. Similarly, precautions must be taken to avoid fire and, if fire does break out, to minimize injury to guests. Security measures consistent with the foreseeable risks are required.

If a hotel chooses to offer medical services, it must ensure that the caregiver is qualified and has proper credentials. If a guest complains of illness and expresses a need for immediate medical care, the hotel or restaurant should quickly call an ambulance.

Preventive Law Tips for Managers

- *Be sure guest rooms are thoroughly cleaned after each guest leaves and before the next guest is allowed access.* A guest has a legal right to expect the room to be in a clean and safe condition. Failure to clean it before the room is reassigned can result in injuries to the incoming guest, as in the case where the guest stepped on a discarded needle. Inadequate cleaning constitutes negligence and will likely result in liability on the hotel for any resulting injuries.
- *Regularly inspect the furniture in guest rooms, the lobby, and other public rooms to verify they are in good repair and able to withstand expected use.* A hotel may be liable for injuries resulting from collapsing beds and chairs, unsturdy stools, wobbly legs on desks or tables, and other furniture flaws that create risk of injury. These problems should be discovered during frequent inspections, and disabled furniture should be removed from service. Failure to detect and either remove or repair the broken items constitutes negligence.
- *Anticipate likely misuses of furniture and protect against them either by providing written warnings to guests or taking other action appropriate under the*

circumstances. We read about a case in which a hotel was liable when a guest fell while standing on an unsteady dressing-table stool to adjust the air-conditioner knob. While the stool was not meant for standing on, this use was foreseeable given the location of the knob almost seven feet from the floor. Be alert to similar foreseeable misuses and take appropriate steps to prevent them.

■ *If furniture is purchased unassembled, be sure the assembly is done correctly and no lose screws or other dangerous conditions result*. Furniture assembly requires a certain expertise. Be sure the assembly is done properly and consistent with accompanying instructions so that harm will not result. If an injury occurs, determine what the problem was, inspect all other like furniture still in service, and correct any similar problems.

■ *Inspect windows to ensure the glass is not broken and is securely attached, fittings are in good working order, and screens, blinds, and curtains are securely affixed.* A hotel must ensure that the window fixtures in guest rooms and other public rooms are safe. The hotel can foresee that guests will be injured if window glass or fixtures are loose or otherwise unsafe. A regular regime of inspection and repair is necessary to avoid liability.

■ *Maintain the heating and electrical systems in a hotel or restaurant in good repair.* The potential injuries from defects in these systems are devastating. These systems require special attention. In-house employees may not have the required skills. Frequent maintenance and check-ups by a business specializing in heating and electricity may be required.

■ *Develop a plan to minimize the presence of insects, rodents and other objectionable animals on the premises.* The plan should include: (1) regular inspections for rat holes, beehives, and other telltale signs of unwanted critters; (2) hiring exterminators if needed; and (3) additional precautions required by the particular circumstances of the establishment.

■ *Regularly examine the bathroom appliances and plumbing system to ensure they are in good working order.* Numerous accidents occur in the bathroom. These can result from deteriorating faucets, poorly maintained toilet seats or stall doors, and faulty plumbing systems. Frequent inspections will alert management to unsafe conditions that need repair or replacement. Failure to detect defects and repair them will lead to liability for the hotel or restaurant.

■ *Regularly inspect the lobby and other public rooms for unsafe conditions such as walkways blocked by luggage, bumps in rugs, intruders bothering guests, and repairs in progress.* Many people regularly use the lobby. Unsafe conditions can easily cause injury. Precautions must be taken to reduce risks of injury from circumstances in the lobby and other public rooms.

■ *Develop a maintenance plan for elevators including regular inspections by both in-house employees and a company specializing in elevator maintenance.* Virtually everyone in a sizeable hotel uses the elevators. A faulty elevator is likely to cause injury. As with the electricity and heating systems, the hotel or restaurant may not have the required expertise in house. The elevator maintenance plan should include regular and frequent inspections by a company with the necessary skill to keep the elevators in good working order. Maintenance is required, not just for the elevators used by guests, but also for service elevators.

■ *Access to service elevators should be strictly limited.* Often a service elevator requires training for use and lacks amenities available in elevators used by guests. Access to the service elevators should be restricted to those employees who have received the necessary training. Precautions should be taken to prevent guests and customers from using the service elevators.

■ *Inspect automatic doors regularly to ensure they are working properly.* Malfunctioning automatic doors will foreseeably cause injury. They should be inspected regularly and any operational problems corrected.

■ *If a large, rowdy crowd is expected, increase security by the front door and in the lobby.* A boisterous crowd is likely to push, shove, and run, causing injury to others in the vicinity. If such a crowd can be anticipated, the hotel should undertake crowd-control efforts. Failure to do so will lead to liability if someone is injured by the unruly crowd.

■ *Check stairs for conditions that can cause injury, including deterioration, obstructions, poor lighting, lack of railings, unexpected location, and inappropriate warning.* Countless accidents occur on steps, many of them avoidable. Frequent assessment of the safety of steps in the establishment can greatly decrease the number of incidents.

■ *Inspect floors for dangerous conditions, including excessive polish or wax, worn spots, and spilled food or beverages.* Failure to detect and correct these conditions will foreseeably lead to injury and liability. Dining-room floors should be inspected before an event or meal. Service personnel should be alerted to inspect the floor for fallen food or debris throughout the meal and while diners are leaving. Regarding construction of floors, consider the slipperiness of the tile or covering when selecting and purchasing materials.

■ *Do not overbook your dining room or other facilities.* Overbooking leads to crowded, unsafe conditions in which guests and patrons may trip and be injured. If your facilities cannot comfortably accommodate an event, do not accept the booking. Clearly inform event planners of limitations on the number of attendees and hold firm to your maximum numbers.

■ *Do not serve flambé dishes unless the proper serving utensils are used, emergency equipment is readily available, and your employees have been thoroughly trained on how to control and handle the flames and what to do in an emergency.* Flambé dishes, if not strictly controlled, can lead to serious injury and significant property destruction by fire. Precautions will reduce the chance of injury. Consider avoiding the problem by exploring alternatives to flambé dishes being flamed in the dining room.

■ *Do not serve hot liquids that are so hot as to cause burns.* While customers expect—indeed demand—their tea, coffee, and like drinks hot, remember that customers may spill their drinks on themselves or others nearby. The temperature at which such beverages are sold should be no hotter than industry standards.

- *Instruct valets how to protect patrons from dangers presented by arriving and departing vehicles.* The unloading area of hotels and restaurants often becomes congested with people and several lanes of traffic. A car pulling out, pulling in, or backing up could foreseeably hit an arriving or departing guest. The valet and other employees who greet arriving patrons at their cars must be alert to the risks and guide both pedestrian and vehicular traffic to avoid accidents.

- *Adequately illuminate all areas in a hotel or restaurant, and be particularly watchful of parking lots and stairs.* Many accidents occur because customers are unable to see where they are walking. Areas particularly prone to accidents due to insufficient lighting are parking lots and stairways. Once adequate lighting is installed, examine it regularly to ensure the fixtures and bulbs are fully operable.

- *Be sure sporting facilities are designed safely and maintained properly.* Poorly designed and inadequately maintained facilities increase the risk of injury to users. A hotel owes its guests the duty to exercise reasonable care to keep the facilities in a safe condition. While guests assume the ordinary risks associated with a sport, they do not assume the risk that the facilities are hazardous.

- *Hotels with swimming pools must provide rescue equipment including, without limitation, ropes, rings, poles, and shepherd's hooks.* Failure to provide lifesaving devices can result in a drowning that was avoidable. The equipment should be kept very close to the pool and readily accessible. It should be examined regularly to ensure freedom from defects.

- *Conspicuously display the depth of the pool.* Clearly posting the depth of pool water can prevent accidents caused by guests diving in water that is too shallow, and by guests proceeding into water that is too deep for their abilities. The depth should be painted in large numbers and bright colors along the perimeter of the pool. Regularly verify that the depth of the water is consistent with the postings. For pools with unusual depths, such as a pool that has no deep end, prominent signage should also be used to alert unsuspecting swimmers.

- *Provide every possible safety precaution in the pool area.* Always rope off the shallow area to alert swimmers when they are entering the deep end. Demand a life-saving certificate from lifeguards. Install a telephone close to the pool so that help can be summmoned quickly in an emergency. Be intolerant of horseplay in and around the pool. Prevent the water from becoming cloudy by maintaining the filtration system in good repair and by use of appropriate chemicals. Use underwater lights in the evening and keep them operable. Verify that the diving board is made from appropriate material and is the proper length. Do not let the water in the pool become low, thereby rendering the depth markings inaccurate. Alert guests if a lifeguard is not provided. Use material that is slip-resistant for the floor of the area around the pool. Clean regularly around and in the pool to remove objects that might cause injury to bare feet.

- *Check the statutes in your state and locality that mandate pool safety features and strictly comply.* Failure to abide by safety laws constitutes negligence per se. The laws in different states and localities vary. Review the applicable laws with a lawyer and make arrangements to comply.

- *Take every possible safety precaution in beach areas.* Rake the sand along the beach to protect barefoot strollers from foot injuries. Rake the bottom of the water where swimmers walk and dive to remove objects a swimmer might hit. Restrict the areas in which surfboards and like paraphernalia can be used to avoid swimmers being hit by them. Post signs warning of unusual water conditions such as a strong undertow.

- *Check state and local fire-safety laws and strictly comply.* Failure to abide by fire-safety laws constitutes negligence per se. Such laws often require that equipment such as fire extinguishers be maintained in good condition on the premises and that fire escapes be provided. They also mandate specifications in the construction of new buildings and additions. The laws in different states and localities vary. Review the applicable laws with a lawyer and make arrangements to conform

- *Train employees thoroughly on what to do in case of fire.* Many lawsuits requiring hotels to compensate guests injured in fires result from employees who fail to call the fire department or alert the guests in a timely manner. This problem can be remedied by thorough training and practice drills. Employees should be instructed to call the fire department immediately when a fire is reported. Their next step should be to alert guests in a manner consistent with hotel facilities and policies.

- *Exercise reasonable care to protect guests from criminal activity.* Make an assessment of the security risks at the establishment and implement a plan to address them. The assessment should include a review of recent security incidents at the hotel or restaurant and in the vicinity, as well as particular risks presented by the particular facilities such as multibuilding layouts and outdoor access to guest rooms. The plan could include such security devices as: security guards; enhanced lighting in the parking lot, in hallways, and in other appropriate places; TV-type monitors; automatic locks on doors; chain or safety locks; special doorknobs that deter picking of locks; peepholes; door construction designed to prevent unauthorized entry; and computerized keys that change with each guest. The business should also develop an alliance with the local police for advice and back-up help.

- *Instruct employees on how to handle a phone call announcing an emergency.* In the event of an emergency, time is of the essence. If an employee receiving an emergency call does not respond timely and adequately, a patron may be severely injured and the hotel or restaurant may be liable. Adequate training of employees and prompt summoning of police can mitigate many would-be security incidents.

- *Be alert to suspicious circumstances on the premises.* Employees should be trained to watch for unusual circumstances or suspicious people on the premises, such as an ex-employee who enters the premises late at night or a person in the lobby who approaches guests for no apparent reason. Depending on the circumstances, the person should be observed until the suspicion fades, the person should be asked to leave, or the police should be called.

■ *If a hotel provides medical services, verify the credentials and capability of the caregiver.* A hotel will be liable if it represents to a guest that a doctor or nurse will be provided when the supposed professional is not certified. A hotel should have referral information on local doctors readily available to give to inquiring guests. Before referring a guest to a particular local doctor, the hotel should confirm the physician's qualifications and standing in the medical community. If a guest complains of illness and expresses a need for immediate medical care, call an ambulance immediately.

Review Questions

1. In what rooms of a hotel does the innkeeper's duty to exercise reasonable care apply?
2. What responsibility, if any, does an innkeeper have to maintain self-service elevators in a safe condition?
3. What risks are associated with flaming foods? What precautions should a restaurant take when serving them?
4. What precautions should a restaurant take when serving hot beverages?
5. For what safety concerns should a valet be watchful?
6. What responsibility, if any, does an innkeeper have to maintain sporting facilities in a safe condition?
7. Name four causes of swimming-pool accidents and state how they can be avoided.
8. Must all hotels have security guards to protect guests' safety?
9. Must a hotel have medical personnel on duty at all times?

Discussion Questions

1. Identify several circumstances in which liability can result to a restaurant for failing to inspect and maintain the furniture in the dining-room properly. State how the liability could be avoided.
2. Identify several circumstances in which liability can result to a hotel for failing to inspect and maintain the windows, screens, and doors properly. State how the liability could be avoided.

3. Identify several circumstances in which liability can result to a restaurant for failing to inspect for and contain rodents, bugs, and animals properly. State how the liability could be avoided.

4. Identify several circumstances in which liability can result to a hotel for failing to inspect and maintain the bathrooms properly. State how the liability could be avoided.

5. Identify five circumstances in which liability can result to a hotel for failing to maintain its sporting facilities properly. State how the liability could be avoided.

6. Identify five circumstances in which liability can result to a hotel for failing to maintain its swimming pool properly. State how the liability could be avoided.

7. Identify five circumstances in which liability can result to a hotel for failing to provide adequate security. State how the liability can be avoided.

8. How should the front desk personnel at a hotel respond when a guest calls stating, "This is an emergency"?

9. What response is appropriate if a guest says "There is a fire on the second floor"?

10. What safeguards should a hotel or restaurant take to minimize liability for fires?

Application Questions

1. You are the banquet manager at a party house. The guests for a large wedding reception will start to arrive in twenty minutes. You are inspecting the premises to ensure everything is in order. What should you be looking for?

2. Jan was a guest at the Hideaway Hotel. As she was walking from her room to the hotel's restaurant for breakfast, a maintenance worker was washing the floor. Jan tripped on the wet floor and fell. What additional information do you need to know to determine if the hotel should be liable?

3. One night Joshua fell in a restaurant parking lot because the lights were dim. At the time he was on his way to attend the anniversary reception of a close friend, which was being held in the restaurant. The hotel argued that Joshua was negligent for exiting his car in the dark. Was Joshua negligent in this case?

4. While swimming at the pool at the Browninger Resort, Ursala, age thirty-one, was hit on the head by Tom, another swimmer, age eleven, who had been engaged in horseplay with two friends for a half hour. The lifeguard had twice requested that Tom and his friends settle down but to no avail. If Ursala sues the resort for negligence, what is the likelihood she will win? Why?

5. Juan was sitting in the bar in a restaurant waiting to be seated for dinner. A man he had never seen before mistook him for someone else and, without warning, hit Juan in the face. He was injured and sued the bar for negligence because it failed to prevent the assault. Will the hotel be liable under these circumstances? What additional facts would you like to know before deciding?

6. The Charming Motel, located in a medium-crime area, was the site of a rape eight months ago. As a result, the hotel installed monitors covering the front and back entrances and the elevators, and requested that the police increase their normal surveillance of the building during the night. Tyrone, a guest at the motel, was assaulted in his room in the middle of the night by two attackers who broke a window to gain entry. Tyrone suffered a broken jaw and the theft of $1000. No crimes had occurred at the motel during the eight months before the inital rape and none after it until the assault of Tyrone. Is Charming Motel liable for his injuries? Explain.

7. In one episode of the once popular television show "L.A. Law," the door to an elevator on an upper floor at the law firm was left open while the elevator was grounded and undergoing repairs on the first floor. No warning sign was posted. One of the characters, not realizing the elevator was not waiting at the door, stepped into the shaft and fell to her death. Should the law firm be liable? Why or why not? Does it matter whether or not the law firm owns the building? Why or why not?

Web Sites

Web sites that will enhance your understanding of the material in this chapter include:

http://www.findlaw.com   This site contains updates on legal news and many links to sites covering a variety of legal topics including personal injury (negligence) cases.

http://www.experts.com   This site contains a listing of available expert witnesses and their field of expertise.

http://www.hotelbusiness.com   This site provides a wealth of business information about recent news in the hotel industry, including security issues.

http://www.ahma.com   This is the site of the American Hotel and Lodging Association, a trade organization for the hotel and lodging industry. The site addresses numerous topics of interest to the hotel industry, including guest safety.

http://www.nolo.com/lawcenter/faqs   Once on this site, click on *Consumer & Travel*, then scroll down to *Hotels and Other Accommodations FAQ*. Numerous questions and answers on this site address legal issues associated with guests who have fallen and hurt themselves at a hotel.

UNIT III

■

Relationships with Guests and Other Patrons

■

CHAPTER 7

■

Guests and Other Patrons

INTRODUCTION

An innkeeper owes certain duties to those who use the hotel's facilities. Those duties vary depending on whether the patron fits the legal definition of a *guest*. Not everyone who utilizes or seeks to utilize the facilities of a hotel or inn becomes a guest in the legal sense. Instead, they may be shoppers, restaurant customers, special event-goers, tenants, or trespassers. The list goes on. Whether or not a person qualifies as a guest has legal significance. For example, if property is stolen from a hotel, the extent of the hotel's liability depends on whether or not the property owner is a guest. We will study this in Chapter 8. A hotel owes certain duties to guests but not to others; for example, to refrain from insulting or humiliating them. We will study this obligation in Chapter 10. As we saw in Chapter 5, a hotel owes to invitees a duty to act reasonably. Guests are invitees. Thus, the outcome of many negligence lawsuits turns on whether or not the plaintiff is a guest.

This chapter explains who qualifies as a guest and discusses the other types of relationships that exist between a hotel and the people who use its various facilities.

Who Qualifies as a Guest?

For a person visiting an inn to qualify as a guest, the visit must be for the primary purpose for which an inn operates—rental of rooms suitable for overnight stay. As a general rule, people are not guests unless they require overnight accommodations. People who register at the hotel for rooms are guests. People in the hotel for some other reason do not qualify. For example, a passerby who enters the hotel to shop in a lobby store is not a guest. A person who comes to the hotel for the sole purpose of attending a banquet or reception and does not register for a room is likewise not a guest.[1] Similarly, a person attending a seminar at a hotel who does not register for a room is not a guest.[2]

In the following case, a patron in a hotel cocktail lounge who was not a registered guest in the hotel claimed he was shortchanged by the waiter, and then was insulted, humiliated, and embarrassed. The liability of the hotel turned on whether the patron qualified as a guest. As we will study in Chapter 11, a hotel but not a restaurant owes a legal duty to treat its customers respectfully and without insult. The hotel in this case will be liable if the patron is a guest; it will not be liable if he is not a guest. As you read this case, you should be able to anticipate how the court ruled.

CASE EXAMPLE 7-1

Wallace v. Shoreham Hotel Corp.
49 A.2d 81 (D.C. 1946)

... The substance of the complaint is that plaintiff, in company with his wife and four friends, was a guest at the cocktail lounge of defendant's hotel; that, in payment of the check rendered, plaintiff gave the waiter a $20 bill but received change for only $10; that the waiter insisted he had received from plaintiff a $10 bill and stated publicly for all in the lounge to hear: "We have had people try this before"; that in fact plaintiff had tendered a $20 bill, which fact was later admitted by representatives of the hotel and proper change given plaintiff; that the language of the waiter indicated to those present in the lounge that plaintiff was underhanded and of low character and that his demand for change was illegal and comparable to that of a cheat or other person whose reputation for honesty is open to question;

that by reason thereof plaintiff was "insulted, humiliated, and otherwise embarrassed." The plaintiff sought judgment for punitive damages of $3,000.

... The question thus presented is whether a patron of a cocktail lounge has a cause of action for humiliation and embarrassment resulting from insulting words of a waiter.

It has been held that an innkeeper owes a duty extending to a guest of respectful and decent treatment, and that the innkeeper is liable to a guest for insulting words or conduct. ... Such duty, however, rests on the peculiar relationship between innkeeper and guest. ... In the instant case the defendant is an innkeeper. The complaint alleges plaintiff was a "guest" at the cocktail lounge and not a registered guest of the hotel. ... One who is merely a customer at a bar, a restaurant, a barber shop or newsstand operated by a hotel does not thereby establish the relationship of

---

[1] *Ross v. Kirkeby Hotels*, 160 N.Y.S.2d 978 (1957)

[2] *Augustine v. Marriott Hotel*, 503 N.Y.S.2d 498 (1986)

innkeeper and guest. ... The situation, as we see it, is the same as if the plaintiff had been the customer of any restaurant or tavern where drinks are served [and not one that happened to be affiliated with a hotel].

[Judgment, therefore, was for the defendant.]

CASE QUESTION

1. What one fact in this case, if changed, would have resulted in the plaintiff winning the lawsuit?

Intent of Parties

The innkeeper-guest relationship is a contractual one—the parties exchange the exclusive use of a guest's room for money. An essential element of all contracts is an intention by the parties to enter a contract. Guest status can arise once the intention is formulated, even before the contract is entered. Thus, a transient becomes a guest upon entering a hotel intending to procure overnight accommodations where the innkeeper has a room available. It is not essential that the guest be registered yet.

How does one determine whether the parties have formulated an intention to enter a contract? The actions of the parties usually provide the needed evidence. A request for a room or an advance reservation is sufficient to evidence intent on the part of a would-be patron to become a guest; of course, if the innkeeper indicates a willingness to register the traveler and provide a room, this is sufficient evidence of intent on the innkeeper's part to form an innkeeper-guest relationship. A trickier issue arises when registration has not occurred or is incomplete. These issues are decided on a case-by-case basis and are determined by the facts.

Registration

While registration clearly evidences intent on both the guest's and innkeeper's part to develop an innkeeper-guest relationship, registration is not essential for the relationship to exist. In the following case, two young males registered for a hotel room. A question arose as to whether the innkeeper intended to contract with two minor females who did not register and who, unknown to the innkeeper, accompanied the two males. One of the females was injured due to the hotel's negligence. If the females qualified as guests, the hotel would be liable for the injuries. If, on the other hand, an innkeeper-guest relationship did not exist, the girls would in these circumstances be trespassers and the innkeeper would not be liable.

CASE EXAMPLE 7-2

Langford v. Vandaveer
254 S.W.2d 498 (Ky. 1953)

[Ruth Vandaveer] was severely burned in the explosion of a butane or propane gas heater in a cabin of a motor court operated by the appellant, Clyde B. Langford. ... Our present inquiry is whether the young lady was a guest.

On Sunday afternoon of January 22, 1950, four young people, C. P. Howe, Bill Nash, Ruth Vandaveer, and Myna Walker, drove to Henderson, Kentucky, from Albion, Illinois, a distance of sixty miles or more. Miss Vandaveer, ... 17 years old, and Miss Walker, about 15, were students in the high school at Albion and the young men worked in the oil fields near Henderson. The men went into a hotel where Howe's brother was staying, but could not procure accommodations. The party then drove to Langford's Motor Court, a short distance from the city. This was about 8:30 o'clock. The car was stopped in a well lighted place near the entrance of the office and restaurant. Howe met Langford at the door and asked for rooms for four oil men, saying that one of them was then at work but would return early enough to get some rest before checking out time. Langford showed the cabins to the two men, lighted the heaters and explained to them how the valves worked. He and Howe returned to the office and Howe filled out a registration card, giving his address and an automobile license number and signed it "C.P. Howe and party." He filled in the figure "4," showing the number of people in the party and paid $6 for the two rooms. Neither Howe nor Miss Walker testified. Miss Vandaveer and Nash testified he stood by the side of the automobile at all times. It is undisputed that Langford passed twice within ten or fifteen feet of the parked automobile. He says he looked at the car and could have seen anyone in it but saw no one. As the car started over to the cabins he noted that the license number was not the same as that registered and he entered the correct number on the card. (It appears that Howe had given the number of his own car instead of Nash's which he was driving.) Miss Vandaveer testified that when Langford passed the automobile she was sitting on the edge of the back seat looking into the small mirror in front, combing her hair, and Miss Walker was on the front seat doing the same thing. Both were erect and could be easily seen.

According to Miss Vandaveer and Nash, the party entered one of the cabins and then the other where they spent some time together. Then the boys left about ten o'clock to go to work. They planned to return early enough to drive the girls back to Albion in time for school. After they had gone, she and Myna concluded to occupy separate cabins. She took No. 4 and retired about eleven o'clock. Neither had any baggage. On the contrary, Langford and his sister testified that about 11:15 Howe came to the restaurant, ate a sandwich, drank a cup of coffee and then left with three colas. Nash testified he and Howe left the motor court about ten o'clock and worked until seven the next morning. However, there is evidence that immediately following the explosion Howe was there. A man in or about the cabin was heard to say, "I told you not to do that." One of these witnesses, according to Langford, first told him of the presence of the girls on the premises.

The relation of innkeeper and guest is a mutual contractual one, and the existence of intention by both parties is an essential element. It is an exceptional case where that requisite is not clearly established, usually by implication. Ordinarily, where one holds himself out to the public as an innkeeper, and is accustomed to receive all who apply and a transient goes to the [inn] to procure accommodation and receives [same], the relationship is created. But ... it is not essential that the guest shall have registered ... though it may be an important circumstance in determining the status.

In the case at bar, the intention of the young lady to become a guest in the legal sense is apparent. The question is whether or not she was intentionally or knowingly *received* as such by the proprietor of the motor court. (Emphasis added.)

[A] person may not impose himself upon the proprietor and become a guest without [the proprietor's] knowledge or intention to receive [that person]. One becomes a guest only if he is received to be treated as a guest and the intention to become such must be communicated to the innkeeper or his agent. [As stated in a prior case,] ... "a mere guest of the registered occupant of a room at a hotel, who shares such room with its occupant without the knowledge or consent of the hotel management, would not be a guest of the hotel, as there would be no contractual relations in such case between such third person and the hotel proprietor."...

Here we have the acceptance of four men as guests when there were in fact two men and two women. ... According to the innkeeper's testimony, the young lady slipped into the cabin and occupied the room for the night without the proprietor's knowledge or consent. ... [In another case,] where a registered guest, without permission from anyone representing the hotel, transferred a room to a woman, she had no right to its possession [and did not qualify as a guest]. ...

There is no dispute in the evidence that Howe procured the two rooms for four men. But if the proprietor of the motor court saw the young women in the car under the circumstances described and could reasonably have anticipated or understood that they would occupy the cabin, then the jury could find he accepted her as a guest and assumed the legal responsibility owing in such relationship. ... Ruling of the [appeals] court: [The trial court should not have determined Vandaveer was a guest as a matter of law. Rather, the issue turns on a question of fact and should have been submitted to a jury for determination. Trial ordered.]

CASE QUESTION

1. Assume you are on the jury in this case. Based on the information available, would you hold that the plaintiff was a guest? Why or why not?

Delivery of Property

As the court in *Langford* stated, registration at the hotel is not essential for an innkeeper-guest relationship to exist. Some cases hold that a person who intends to register but has not yet done so becomes a guest by delivering luggage to a hotel employee. In such circumstances, the soon-to-be guest evidences an intent to become a guest by giving possession to the hotel employee. The hotel's intent is evidenced by its acceptance of the suitcase. In these situations, the responsibility of the proprietor as innkeeper starts at the moment of the delivery and acceptance of the suitcase.

In one lawsuit a jewelry salesman, upon arrival at the MGM Grand Hotel in Las Vegas, checked his luggage and jewelry samples with the bellhop at the door. Thereafter he registered, went to his room, and waited for his luggage. When it arrived he discovered that some of the jewelry samples were missing. The liability of the hotel depended on whether the salesman was a guest when he gave his baggage to the bellhop. The court held the salesman became a guest at the time he made use of the hotel's luggage check service, since that service was provided specifically for guests.[3] Similarly, the innkeeper-guest relationship can begin when the traveler alights from a taxi in front of the hotel and gives the bellhop a suitcase, or steps into a hotel van or car at the airport and gives the driver the luggage, assuming a room is available at the hotel and the traveler intends to register.

In the next case, the plaintiff left her luggage at the defendant hotel, although her room reservation did not begin until the next day. Jewelry was stolen from her suitcase. The issue was whether the parties' intention to enter a contract on the following day was sufficient to render the plaintiff a guest on the day the baggage was checked. The court held it was.

[3] *Pachinger v. MGM Grand Hotel-Las Vegas, Inc.*, 802 F.2d 362 (9th Cir. 1986)

CASE EXAMPLE 7-3

Adler v. Savoy Plaza Inc.
108 N.Y.S.2d 80 (1951)

This is an action for the loss of jewelry and personal effects contained in a suitcase which was delivered by plaintiff to defendant for safe-keeping. The claimed value of the jewelry was something over $20,000 and the claimed value of the personal effects about $3,300.

The facts are as follows: The plaintiff was accustomed to staying at the defendant's hotel whenever she visited New York and had been a guest of the hotel many times. She and her husband had requested reservations for May 15, 1946. Upon their arrival at 10 o'clock that morning, they were advised that their reservation was for the following day, but that the hotel would try to accommodate them, so they registered, hoping that a room might be assigned during the day. At the same time, they delivered their luggage to the bell captain, and it was deposited in a section of the lobby set aside for the luggage of arriving and departing guests. Plaintiff's husband attended to business during the day while plaintiff was in and out of the hotel. When both returned to the hotel in the afternoon, they found that a room was still not available, so they whiled away some time in the lounge bar and had dinner in the room of a friend who was a guest of the hotel.

All during the day defendant's manager was seeking accommodations for the couple but was unable to locate any in the hotel. He finally secured accommodations for them for the night at the Sherry Netherlands Hotel where they registered at about 8:00 P.M., taking with them two suitcases and a cosmetic case, and leaving the suitcase with the valuables and two matching cases at defendant's hotel.

When plaintiff returned to defendant's hotel the next morning to take up residence for two or three weeks and requested delivery of her luggage, the large suitcase was missing. During the night the suitcase had been delivered by the night manager of the hotel to an imposter. The circumstances of this delivery are not altogether clear as the night manager was deceased at the time of the trial. Whether there was some complicity on the part of one or more of the hotel employees, as plaintiff suggests, we are not called upon to surmise.

[One of] the questions as to the [hotel's liability for the lost] jewelry, was whether plaintiff was a guest of the hotel.

… We are prepared to rule as a matter of law on the admitted facts that plaintiff was a guest.

CASE QUESTIONS

1. Why do you think the court ruled that the plaintiff was a guest?

2. What role did her intent to rent a room play in the determination that she was a guest?

3. Suppose the plaintiff did not have reservations and the hotel was full, but she was allowed to leave her bags for the day while she looked for a room elsewhere. Would the plaintiff qualify as a guest?

If, when people deliver baggage to the hotel porter, they do not intend to become guests of the hotel, an innkeeper-guest relationship does not exist. In *Blakemore v. Coleman*, 701 F.2d 967 (D.C. 1983), the plaintiffs had come to Washington, D.C. to celebrate President Reagan's inauguration. Before returning home, and after checking out of their hotel, they decided to have lunch at the Jockey Club, an elegant restaurant that was part of the Fairfax Hotel, which was not the hotel in which they had stayed. When they arrived at the restaurant, they checked a briefcase and a small carry-on bag with the hotel doorman. After lunch they retrieved their bags from the doorman and discovered a jewelry pouch was missing. The liability of the hotel turned on whether the plaintiffs qualified as guests. The court held they were not, stating, "One who is merely a customer at a bar, a restaurant, a barber shop or newsstand operated by a hotel does not thereby establish the relationship of innkeeper and guest."

Even a person who has not yet decided whether to rent a room may, under certain circumstances, be considered a guest. The key issue is whether that person came to the hotel for the purpose of benefiting from the various services offered by the hotel to guests. This rule of law is illustrated in the following case. The plaintiff, a traveling salesman who frequently stayed at the defendant's hotel, had not yet registered for a room on the date in issue, but was considering doing so. In the meantime he placed his property in a hotel safe deposit box. The property was stolen from the box. Since the innkeeper's liability in such cases turns on whether the property owner is a guest, the court had to determine whether the plaintiff qualified. As you read the case, note that the plaintiff's prior business with the hotel was an important factor in the court's decision.

CASE EXAMPLE 7-4

Freudenheim v. Eppley
88 F.2d 280 (Pa. 1937)

... [F]reudenheim was the traveling salesman of his diamond firm, and ... he was accustomed to visiting Buffalo, Detroit, Cleveland, Toledo, Chicago, Indianapolis, Cincinnati, and Pittsburgh. That if trade justified, he stayed at hotels which had vaults for the deposit of valuables and he left his bag containing diamonds in their vaults. ... Prior to 1930 he came to Pittsburgh eight or nine times a year and stayed at the William Penn [Hotel] two, three, or four days at a time, depending on trade conditions. In 1933 he was twice in Pittsburgh, received his mail at the hotel, but did not stay overnight. On every one of his trips to Pittsburgh he used the vault at the William Penn. On the morning of December 5, 1933, after visiting other cities, he arrived in Pittsburgh from Cincinnati before 7:00 A.M. After checking his personal bag at the railroad station, he went to the hotel. [He testified]: "I intended to stay here as long as I could do business here." He arrived at the hotel around 7:00 A.M., but the cashier's office, where the hotel had vaults, was not open, and the cashier, Schaller, had not arrived.

His testimony was: "I waited around the lobby until about seven-thirty and around seven-thirty I went back to the cashier's office and saw Mr. Schaller there and he greeted me. I told him I wanted a box, or he said, 'I suppose you want a box. ...' Whether he knew me by name, I don't know, but he knew me quite well." Continuing, the witness said: "Mr. Schaller came out of the cage, which is controlled by a wire door—grill—there, and he brought out a couple of keys and a tag. He tore off part of the tag and gave me the bottom of it, and asked me to sign the upper part, which I did and returned it to him, and he gave me this stub bearing the same number as appears on the part bearing my signature which I gave to him. He then gave me two keys, which were attached to this little ring bearing a metal disc on which is noted the letter 'C.' He then inserted the key which was attached to this ring and opened the box—opened the door—and I put my brief case in which my merchandise had been placed right inside that box. I closed the door and I went downstairs."

In the first place, we have the fact that Freudenheim was known to the hotel as a past guest and that there was the possibility of his lodging at the hotel if trade warranted such stay. There was, therefore, in the mind of both parties that the hotel would have Freudenheim as a guest. He was recognized by the cashier; inquiry was made whether he wanted a box; he was given the box; his merchandise was deposited; ... This was a service or accommodation which the hotel had extended before and Freudenheim had enjoyed before.

Now it is clear that vault service for valuables is a customary hotel accommodation, and that it was the intention of both parties that Freudenheim should have that accommodation, ... The responsibility of an innkeeper for the safety of a traveler's property begins at the moment when the relation of guest and host arises, and that relation arises as soon as the traveler enters the inn with the intention of using it as an inn, and is so received by the host. It does not matter that no food or lodging has been supplied or found up to this time of the loss. It is sufficient if the circumstances show an intention on the one hand to provide and on the other hand to accept such accommodation.

Moreover, later on, and before he left, Freudenheim, who was busy with his customers all morning and into the afternoon and took no lunch, did take his dinner in the general dining room of the hotel. It is true he did not take a room and register, but his omission to do so does not put him out of guest protection. ... It is not necessary that a traveler shall register at an inn as a guest in order to become such, but it is sufficient if he visits the inn for the purpose of receiving [customary services and receives them]. ...

CASE QUESTION

1. How does this case expand our definition of a guest?

Checking Out

The status of guest is not instantaneously terminated upon check-out, but rather continues for a reasonable period of time while the guest remains on the hotel premises.[4]

Guests' Illegal Acts

A question arises concerning the status of a would-be guest who registers at a hotel giving false information. In one case, the plaintiffs sought damages for personal injuries allegedly sustained when they attempted to escape a fire in the lodging house where they were staying. They had registered as husband and wife, but were not in fact married. The defendant lodging house argued that by reason of the plaintiffs' misrepresentation, they were trespassers and not guests. Therefore, the argument went, the lodging house owed them no duty to exercise reasonable care.

The court, however, stated that without a demonstration that the plaintiffs' illegal act directly contributed to their injuries, neither false registration nor an illegal or immoral purpose in occupying a room would change their status as guests to whom the defendant owed the duty of reasonable care. Therefore, the plaintiffs

[4] *Moog v. Hilton Hotels Corp.*, 882 F.Supp. 1392 (N.Y. 1995)

qualified as guests and could pursue the case against the lodging house notwithstanding the false registration.[5]

In an older case, dated by its facts but not by the legal ruling, an unlicensed peddler staying at an inn stored his peddler's cart in the hotel stable overnight. Goods were stolen from the cart while the peddler slept. In the peddler's lawsuit against the hotel, the innkeeper denied liability on the ground that the peddler, by selling without a license, was engaged in illegal activity. In this case, too, the court held the fact that the peddler was unlicensed was not a bar to the lawsuit because the illegal act of selling without a license did not directly contribute to the theft.[6]

Termination of a Guest-Innkeeper Relationship

The innkeeper-guest relationship ends when any of the following occurs:

1. The contracted time for the room has elapsed and it has not been extended
2. The bill is not paid when due
3. Proper notice is given to vacate the hotel
4. A reasonable amount of time has passed since checkout
5. The bill has been settled and paid.

Guests are allowed a reasonable time after vacating the room to remove their luggage and check out of the hotel, during which they continue to qualify as guests. The length of this period (one-half hour, one hour, or longer) depends on the facts of each case.

Landlord-Tenant Relationship

A person who rents a room at a hotel on a long-term basis may have the legal status of a tenant, rather than a guest. The innkeeper's responsibilities to a tenant differ from those owed to a guest.

To be a guest, a person must be a transient; that is, his stay at the inn is temporary. If the person is staying on a permanent basis, he is a tenant. Whether a hotel patron is a tenant or a guest is determined from a number of factors, including:

■ The terms of the contract between the parties. For example, use of the terminology *landlord* and *tenant* rather than *innkeeper* and *guest* suggest the customer is a tenant.

■ The extent of control or supervision of the patron's room maintained by the proprietor. The more control and supervision retained by the hotel, the more likely the patron is a guest.

---

[5] *Cramer v. Tarr*, 165 F.Supp. 130 (Me. 1958)
[6] *Kimbel's Case* 168 A. 871 (1929)

- The rental rate interval; for example, daily, weekly, or monthly. The shorter the interval, the more likely the patron is a guest.
- Length of occupancy. The longer the occupancy, the greater the suggestion the patron is a tenant.
- Incidental services offered. For example, frequent housekeeping and room services are often associated with guests but not tenants.
- Whether the room has cooking facilities. Those are more frequently associated with a landlord-tenant relationship than innkeeper-guest.
- The kind of furnishings in the room and who owns them. Whereas hotel rooms virtually always are furnished, rooms intended as apartments are less likely to be furnished.

None of these factors alone determines the legal relationship; the more the circumstances resemble a landlord-tenant relationship, the less likely an innkeeper-guest relationship exists.

Two cases help explain how these factors are applied. In the first, a plaintiff had an eleven-month, written lease for a room at a hotel. His rent included housekeeping and telephone switchboard services. He was a tenant and not a guest.[7]

In the second case, a patron at a licensed hotel occupied a room that was 12' × 15' and contained a bed and sink. Toilet and bathing facilities were located down the hall and shared with others. Cooking facilities were not provided. Rent was paid weekly. The patron occupied the room for three-and-one-half months, during which time he had no other residence. When he registered, he was required to sign a hotel registration card. He did not make any special arrangements with the hotel concerning the duration of his occupancy. The issue of whether he was a guest or a tenant arose when he was two weeks late with his rent. The legal method of evicting a guest is different from and easier than that for tenants, as is discussed in Chapter 9. The hotel used the easier method applicable to guests. The patron argued that he was a tenant, and therefore the eviction was invalid. The court determined the relationship was innkeeper and guest, stating,

[A]ny unilateral intention on the part of the plaintiff to remain at the hotel indefinitely or to make it his home of which [the hotel] had no reasonable notice, would not be determinative in ascertaining what contractual arrangements existed between the parties. ...

The three month duration of plaintiff's occupancy of the room was not so extended that the trial court was obliged to view it as "permanent". In conjunction with ... the operation of the premises as a licensed hotel, the rudimentary nature of the accommodations furnished, without cooking, bathing or toilet facilities in the room, is some indication that only a temporary living arrangement was intended.[8]

---

[7] *Chawla v. Horch d/b/a Master Hotel*, 333 N.Y.S.2d 531 (N.Y. 1972)

[8] *Bourque v. Morris*, 460 A.2d 1251 (Conn. 1983)

Summary

The legal duties owed by an innkeeper to guests are different from those owed to nonguests. A threshold issue in many lawsuits against hotels is whether the plaintiff was a guest in the legal sense. The outcome of the case may depend on the resolution of that issue.

The easiest-to-identify guest is one who has registered for a room on a temporary basis. By registering, the guest has evidenced an intention to utilize overnight accommodations and the hotel has evidenced an intention to provide the guest a room. The definition of *guest* has been expanded to include people who mistakenly come to the hotel a day earlier than the first day of their reservations and utilize baggage-check services in the interim; people who are in the process of checking in or out; and regular overnight patrons who, on a day in question, utilize the hotel safe although unsure if they will stay in town overnight, but who intend to stay at the hotel if they do decide to remain. While the class of guests has expanded, still necessary is an intention by the guest to use the hotel's accommodations and intention by the hotel to provide the guest a room on a temporary basis.

A hotel guest should be distinguished from a tenant, whose use of a room is of a longer duration than a guest's. The obligations of an innkeeper to a guest differ from those of a landlord to a tenant.

Preventive Law Tips for Managers

- *Recognize that the innkeeper has special obligations to guests.* For this reason, know who qualifies as a guest and who does not.
- *Keep in mind that the following categories of people may qualify as guests:*
  - A person who arrives at the hotel and registers for a room.
  - A person who arrives at a hotel, intends to register, and gives luggage to the bellhop who accepts it, assuming the person has a reservation or the hotel has rooms available.
  - A person who arrives at the airport, enters a hotel courtesy van, and gives the driver the luggage, which is accepted, assuming the person intends to register and the hotel has a room available.
  - A person who arrives at the inn, has reservations for the following day, intends to register as soon as a room is available, and leaves luggage with the bellhop who accepts delivery of it.
  - A regular guest of the hotel who arrives without reservations and, as per prior dealings with the inn, intends to stay the night if business warrants it.
- *Illegal activity on the part of the guests may not affect their status as guests.* A person injured at a hotel who registers using false information or engages in illegal activity in the room is not thereby any less a guest for purposes of

obligations owed by the innkeeper, unless the illegality was the direct cause of the injury that underlies a lawsuit.

■ *The innkeeper-guest relationship terminates when certain events occur.* Those events include that the contracted time for the room has elapsed; the bill is not paid when due; proper notice is given to vacate the hotel; or a reasonable time has passed following check-out.

■ *A tenant is not a guest.* The circumstances of a tenant vary from those of a guest in numerous ways, including that the duration of a tenant's stay usually exceeds that of a guest's; the proprietor's right to enter the room of a guest to clean or otherwise tend to the room usually exceeds that for a tenant; the room rates of a guest are usually based on a daily or weekly amount, whereas the rates of a tenant are usually weekly or monthly; and a tenant's room will customarily have kitchen facilities included, whereas a guest's room is less likely to have them.

Review Questions

1. What role does registration play in the formation of the innkeeper-guest relationship?

2. Under what circumstances can a person who has not registered at a hotel be considered a guest?

3. What is the significance of someone qualifying as a guest?

4. Does a person who is attending a half-day seminar at a hotel without registering for a guest room qualify as a guest?

5. When does an innkeeper-guest relationship terminate?

6. What are some factors that distinguish a guest from a tenant?

Discussion Questions

1. Which of the following qualify as guests?
   A. A patron of a hotel beauty shop who works in an office nearby.
   B. A person who has a reservation at a hotel and enters the hotel's hospitality van at the airport, handing her luggage to the driver, who accepts it.
   C. A person who registers for a room for two weeks.
   D. A resident of the area in which a hotel/resort is located who takes tennis lessons twice a week from the professional on the hotel premises.

2. What is the significance of someone qualifying as a guest?

3. Under what circumstances might a guest's illegal activity on hotel premises affect the liability of the hotel for injuries to that guest?

4. The Mandarin Hotel provided rooms on a nightly, weekly, and monthly basis. Jim rents a room by the week. What additional information would you need to determine whether Jim is a guest or a tenant?

5. At what point in the hotel check-in process do you think a person should first be deemed a guest? Why? How does your answer compare to the decisions in the cases in this chapter?

Application Questions

1. Sarah is having her wedding reception at the local Holiday Inn. Her parents contracted with the hotel for the use of a banquet room and catering facilities. Sarah and her then-husband will leave immediately after the reception for their honeymoon in another state. Some out-of-town guests will be staying at the hotel overnight. Who is a guest of the hotel? Why do the others not qualify?

2. Fran flew from her home in Butte, Montana, to New York City. She planned to meet a friend at the airport for dinner. While waiting for the friend, she noticed a hospitality van from the hotel at which she had reservations for that evening. She gave her luggage to the driver so she would not have to worry about her suitcase during dinner. Does Fran qualify as a guest?

3. Mindy had reservations to stay at the Islander Inn for a week. After she was there for three nights, she received a call advising that her father was quite ill. She immediately left the Inn and returned home. For what period of time was Mindy a guest? When did she cease being a guest?

4. Jerry made reservations at the Snowway Motel near a ski center. Before the trip, he hurt his foot working out on a stairmaster machine and was unable to ski. He told his friend, who decided to go skiing in Jerry's stead. When the friend arrived at the hotel, he explained the circumstances to the motel proprietor, who agreed to rent the room to the friend. Was Jerry ever a guest of the motel? Why or why not? Does the friend qualify as a guest? Why or why not?

For additional resources, visit our Web site
www.hospitality-tourism.delmar.com

CHAPTER 8

Protecting Patrons' Property

INTRODUCTION

Hotel guests bring a variety of personal property to hotels, including money, jewelry, clothing, sports equipment, and cars. Business travelers may bring merchandise samples or inventory for sale. Hotels often provide safes for such property, but guests may choose not to use them. Sometimes property may be left in a guest's car (parked in a hotel parking lot) or in the lobby, a restaurant, the pool area, or other rooms in the hotel. Occasionally, guests' property is stolen. This chapter will discuss the liability of a hotel or restaurant when property disappears.

Risks to Property in the Hotel

Hotel theft is a problem the hospitality industry has not fully solved. The liability of the innkeeper for losses has lessened over time.

Hotel Theft

Unfortunately, hotel thefts are not rare. Hotel crime is an industry-wide problem. Most hotel thieves are professionals seeking money, jewels, and credit cards. They often register as guests in the hotel they plan to burglarize. The many tricks of the hotel thief include acquiring confidential information from maids, bartenders, or other hotel personnel. These thieves generally do not carry a weapon; if surprised in the act, they may convincingly feign drunkenness.

Hotels have developed numerous strategies to stem the increase of hotel thefts, including increasing the number of security personnel; hiring trained professionals; warning guests to lock their rooms and put their valuables in a hotel safe; installing closed-circuit televisions to monitor hallways; installing electronic lock devices for guest rooms that are changed for each guest using the room, preventing access by retained keys; instituting tighter security checks on employees; and, in small hotels, installing electronic lobby doors that can be opened only by the desk clerk when a guest is recognized.

Alliances between the police and hotel security staff can enhance efforts to reduce crime. For example, the New York City Police Department has a hotel unit that concentrates on crimes committed at city hotels. The members of the unit and the security forces at hotels meet regularly to share information and alert each other to potential problems. Issues discussed include new methods of break-ins, security occurrences, and the latest in detection techniques and prevention devises.

Keycards and Keys

Most hotels today have abandoned the use of keys and instead use electronic keycards, also called punch-cards, which have a magnetic strip. These devices allow the hotel to change the code that opens the door every time a new guest occupies the room.

The keycard system, which has gained wide acceptance in the hotel industry in the last fifteen years, was inspired by problems associated with the more traditional keys. Some hotel guest-room keys could easily be duplicated. Guests often checked out of a hotel and failed to return the key, fueling an underground market among thieves for hotel keys. A hotel in Kentucky with 227 guest rooms had an average of 50 keys a month carried away, only about one-third of which were eventually returned. A would-be thief is often willing to pay a good price for guaranteed easy-entrance to hotel rooms.

To help avoid these problems, hotels that still use keys should avoid printing the name and address of the hotel or the room number on the key. Many hotels cross-code keys so that the number on the keys is not the room number.

Guests' Insurance Does Not Protect Hotels

Many people are not personally insured against the loss of their valuables. Therefore, if their property is stolen while they are at the hotel, they are likely to sue the hotel seeking compensation. If a traveler whose property disappears does have insurance coverage and recovers the loss from the insurance company, the hotel is not relieved from liability. Normally the insurance policy provides that the insurance company is subrogated (substituted) to the rights of the guest. This means that the insurance company can sue the hotel to recover the money the insurance company paid to the guest.

Absolute Liability for Guests' Goods

In prior times and according to common law, hotelkeepers were liable for any loss of guests' property occurring on hotel premises. This doctrine was called **infra hospitium**, literally meaning "within the inn." Thus, if property was stolen or otherwise disappeared from the hotel, the innkeeper was liable to reimburse the guest. This strict rule originated several centuries ago when inns were not always safe and the innkeeper was often the culprit. The rule contributed in no small measure to an increase in the level of safety associated with travel. The hotel industry has changed substantially since those early days. We will see shortly that the rule of absolute liability has likewise been modified.

Exceptions to the Absolute Liability Rule

Almost every rule of law has exceptions, and the outdated rule that held the innkeeper absolutely liable for guests' goods was tempered by three exceptions

1. The loss was attributed to what the law calls an **act of God**, which includes earthquakes, lightning, snowstorms, tornadoes and floods

2. Loss caused by a **public enemy**, which includes war time and terrorists activities

3. Negligence by the guest, such as leaving luggage unattended in the lobby.

Prima Facie Liability Rule—Minority View

Six states have adopted a rule that modified the common law absolute liability rule as follows. Hotelkeepers are liable for property loss only if the loss occurs through their negligence; if the innkeeper can prove that the loss resulted from some other cause, for example, if the goods are stolen by robbers without the aid or negligence of the innkeeper, the innkeeper is not liable. This is called the **prima facie liability rule**. If, however, the innkeeper cannot prove that it is free from negligence, the innkeeper will be liable for the loss. The six states that have adopted this rule are Illinois, Indiana, Maryland, Texas, Vermont, and Washington. Justification for the rule was stated in an early case from Indiana:

> Innkeepers, on grounds of public policy, are held to a strict accountability for the goods of their guests. The interests of the public, we think, are sufficiently [served] by holding the innkeeper prima facie liable for the loss or injury of the

goods of their guests; thus throwing the burden of proof upon [the innkeeper], to show that the injury or loss happened without any default whatever on his part, and that he exercised reasonable care and diligence.[1]

Limited Liability—Modern Limitations to the Absolute Liability Rule

As hotels grew in size and the number of travelers increased, the difficulty of safeguarding property increased. Current law recognizes that the absolute liability rule is unnecessarily burdensome to modern-day hotels and innkeepers. All state legislatures have adopted statutes to limit significantly hotelkeepers' liability for guests' property losses, provided the hotels follow specific procedures. The result of these "limiting liability statutes" is that a hotel that complies with the mandated rules will face liability of only a few hundred dollars, although guests' property valued at many thousands of dollars or more is stolen.

While the details of these statutes vary from state to state, certain common provisions exist, as follows:

- The hotel must provide a safe for use by guests to protect their property.
- The hotel must post notices announcing to guests the availability of the safes.
- The hotel must post notices announcing that the hotel's liability for guests' property is limited.
- The maximum recovery allowed to a guest for stolen or lost property is prescribed by statute and is usually substantially less than the value of the missing property. For example, a statute may specify that the maximum liability will be $1,000 regardless of the value of the lost property. If a hotel complies with the statute and a guest's $50,000 ring is stolen, the hotel will be liable to the guest for only $1,000.

In essence, limited liability statutes provide that if a hotel proprietor provides a safe or safe deposit box for the storage of valuables and posts conspicuous notice that a safe is available, a hotel guest who fails to use the safe or safe deposit box cannot hold the hotel responsible if his valuables are later lost or stolen. Alternatively, if the guest utilizes the safe, the hotel owner will be liable only for the limited amount provided in the statute. In a case where a guest left several thousand dollars in cash and checks in his hotel room and they were stolen while he was at dinner and the hotel had properly posted notices that safes were available, the guest could not recover from the hotel for the loss because he had failed to store the items in the safe.[2] If the guest had locked the items in the safe and they were stolen, the hotel would have been liable to the guest, but only for a limited amount of money.

To qualify for the reduced liability, the hotel must strictly comply with the statute's mandates. Courts interpret them very strictly. If the innkeeper deviates

---

[1] *Laird v. Eichold*, 10 Ind. 212 (1858)

[2] *Beam v. Marriott Corp.*, 655 N.Y.S.2d 566 (N.Y. 1997)

from the requirements of the statute in any manner, the common law rule will apply and the innkeeper will have unlimited liability. Thus, innkeepers must be careful to provide the mandated safe, post the necessary notices in the required places, and otherwise strictly comply with the applicable state statute.

In this chapter, the laws that restrict innkeepers' liability will be called **limiting liability statutes** or **limiting statutes**. Each of the requirements for limited liability outlined above will be discussed separately.

Providing a Safe

Almost invariably, the limiting liability statutes require that the innkeeper provide a "proper safe" for guests' valuables. In the past, hotels uniformly provided a safe or safe deposit boxes in a central location, usually in the vicinity of the front desk. A growing trend is for hotels to provide individual safes in each guest room.

In the following case, the hotel provided a central safe but it was not available late in the evening when the plaintiff sought to deposit two diamond rings. What impact do you think that fact had on the hotel's liability? See if your answer agrees with the judge's decision.

CASE EXAMPLE 8-1

Zaldin v. Concord Hotel
421 N.Y.S.2d 858 (1979)

Plaintiffs, registered guests, bring suit on a theory of absolute liability for the loss of two valuable diamond rings that disappeared from their hotel room. In its answer, the defendant hotel pleaded [New York's limiting liability statute] by way of defense. Asserting that the hotel's vault was not available to guests at the time they attempted to place the jewelry there for safekeeping, plaintiffs moved for ... judgment. ... [W]e hold that a hotel may not claim the limitations on liability afforded it by [the limiting liability statute] at times when it fails to make a safe available to its guests.

[The limiting liability statute] reads: "Whenever the proprietor or manager of any hotel shall provide a safe ... for the safekeeping of any money, jewels, ornaments, bank notes, bonds, negotiable securities, or precious stones, belonging to the guests ... and shall notify the guests or travelers thereof by posting a notice stating the fact that such safe is provided ... in a public and conspicuous place and manner in the office and public rooms ... and if such guest or traveler shall neglect to deliver such property ... for deposit in such safe, the proprietor or manager ... shall not be liable for any loss of such property, sustained by such guest or traveler by theft or otherwise." ... The statute goes on to limit a hotel's liability for property so deposited with it, whether the loss is sustained "by theft or otherwise," to a sum not exceeding $500.

... It is agreed that on Friday afternoon, the plaintiffs William and Shelby Modell, accompanied by their daughter [Anna Zaldin] and son-in-law, checked into the defendant's large resort hotel. No one disputes but that the hotel provided a safe-deposit vault for the use of its guests and that shortly after the plaintiffs' arrival, the daughter requested and was assigned one of its boxes. Plaintiffs allege that she then placed two diamond rings belonging to her mother in the box and that late the following afternoon, she withdrew them from the box for her mother to wear while attending the Saturday evening festivities sponsored by the hotel.

Sometime after midnight, however, upon the conclusion of the hotel's nightclub performance and before retiring, when the Modells and their daughter attempted to redeposit the jewelry, a hotel desk clerk informed them that the vault was closed and that they would have to retain possession of their valuables until it was opened in the morning. The defendant concedes that it would not allow guests access to the vault between the hours of eleven in the evening and eight in the morning. The Modells claim they thereupon secreted the jewelry in their room only to find, upon arising at about 9:00 A.M., that the chain lock with which they had secured the room had been cut from the outside and the rings were missing. They promptly notified the hotel and police of what they took to be a theft.

In now applying the statute to this factual framework, we first remark on the obvious: The statute's wording is plain. ... [W]hen, as here, a statute is free from ambiguity ... we must do no more and no less than apply the language as it is written.

Thus read, the statute offers the innkeeper an option: "Provide" a safe for your guests and sharply restrict your liability; or, feel free to do absolutely nothing about a safe and continue the risk of exposure to open-ended common law liability. But, whichever choice you make, since the statute is in derogation of [deviates from] the common law rule, to obtain the benefit of the more circumscribed liability ... you must conform strictly with its conditions.

The statute fixes no time when a safe may or must be provided. Nor does it mandate availability around the clock. ... These matters are left entirely up to the hotel. The statute makes no effort to evaluate cost or convenience. Neither does it distinguish between large and small inns, between those that cater to the large convention and those that cater to the individual patron, between those that come alive at night and those that do so in the day, between those that have a wealthy clientele and those that do not. The legislative formula is uncomplicated. It says, straightforwardly, that "whenever" a safe is provided, the liability limitations shall be applicable. Conversely, at those times when an innkeeper chooses not to provide a safe for the use of its guest, he cannot claim the statutory protection. ...

More specifically, nowhere does [the limiting liability statute] suggest that an innkeeper may provide a safe part of the time and yet gain the benefit of the exemption all the time. ...

[Judgment for plaintiffs.]

CASE QUESTIONS

1. Did the hotel violate any law by closing the safe during the night?

2. What was the consequence of failing to make the safe available at all hours?

In a Louisiana case, several guests wanting to deposit jewelry in the hotel safe waited for the night clerk for up to forty minutes in the early morning hours. Without success they went to bed, taking their valuables with them. Following a theft that night from their room they sued the hotel. The court held the hotel was liable for the full loss because the front desk was unattended and therefore access to the safe was unavailable.[3]

Another issue involving limiting liability statutes is the theft-resistant qualities of the safe. If a safe is not adequate to withstand theft or fire, the hotel may not be able to benefit from the limiting statutes. Innkeepers are well-advised not to scrimp on the purchase of safes.

[3] *Durandy v. Fairmont Roosevelt Hotel, Inc.*, 523 F.Supp. 1382 (La. 1981)

Posting Notice of Availability of Safe

Virtually all limiting statutes require posting of one kind or another. "Posting" means displaying a sign that calls the guests' attention to the availability of a safe and the fact that, by law, the hotel's liability for valuables is limited. Each state's statute identifies the places where the notice must be posted and what the notice must state. The required locations and contents vary from state to state. Typically, notice must be posted at the registration desk, on the check-in form, and in guest rooms.

Strict Interpretation of Posting Requirements

Failure by a hotel to comply strictly with the posting requirements will result in loss of the limited liability. The law applied in such a case will be absolute liability as imposed by common law. If the relevant state statute mandates posting in three locations, compliance with two out of the three is not good enough. This principle is illustrated in the following case.

CASE EXAMPLE 8-2

Searcy v. La Quinta Motor Inns, Inc.
676 So.2d 1137 (La. 1996)

Plaintiff checked into the La Quinta Inn. ... She left the room and returned 45 minutes to one hour later, unlocked the door, and found her suitcase practically empty, with some of her things scattered around the room. ...

A notice was posted by the hotel in the registration area which read, "This property is privately owned and operated. The management reserves the right to refuse service to anyone for lawful and legitimate reasons. Safety deposit boxes are available at the front desk and money, jewelry and documents or other articles of value should be deposited for safekeeping. Unless deposited, the motel assumes no responsibility for any loss or injury to such articles." The writing was very small. ...

[The relevant Louisiana statute states that the hotel is liable for $500 if the guest is informed of a safe, uses the safe, and a guest's property disappears. The statute also states that the guest has the right to negotiate with the hotel manager a special written agreement in which the hotel would have greater liability.]

The notice posted in the registration area clearly only advises guests that the hotel is not responsible for the protection of personal property. This notice is totally inadequate. It does not contain either the complete text of the applicable Louisiana statute or the gist of the text. The correct notice was posted in the guest room and apparently was also contained on the check-in slip. However literal compliance with the statute requires that the notice also be placed in the registration area. The hotel did not comply with the statute. ... Judgment is rendered in favor of the plaintiffs in the amount of $4,938.95.

In a similar case, liability for $35,000 worth of jewelry was at stake. The limiting liability statute required the hotel to post notices "in the office and public rooms," and in the guest rooms. Although the hotel properly posted in the guest rooms, it failed to post in all of the public rooms. Therefore, the hotel was strictly liable and forced to pay the $35,000.[4]

While strict compliance is required in most states, a few states are more forgiving. For example, Kentucky has enacted a statute that provides,

[A]ll statutes of this state shall be liberally construed with a view to promote their objective and carry out the intent of the legislature, ...

Kentucky's limiting statute requires hotels to post notice in the office and public rooms of the inn. A hotel posted only on the doors in each of the guest rooms; it failed to post in the hotel office or public rooms. The Kentucky court held the innkeeper had sufficiently complied with the statute. This decision was based on the quoted statute.[5]

Conspicuous Posting

Most limiting liability statutes require that the posted notice be **conspicuous**, meaning that the notice must be displayed in such a way that people are likely to see it. If, for example, the posted notice in a lobby is obscured by the branches of a decorative tree or a banner announcing a special event, the notice would not be conspicuous. If the print is not easily readable, the notice likewise is not conspicuous. In one case, the hotel placed the notice under the glass on a dresser table in the hotel room. The notice was two and one-half inches square and was displayed among promotions describing the hotel and its features. In determining the notice was not conspicuous, the court stated that a guest who glanced at the total display of printed material on the dresser would likely assume its general import was advertising.[6]

In another case, a court strongly suggested (but did not decide) that posting notice on the inside of the closet in a motel room was not conspicuous.[7]

Some hotels print the information required to be posted on registration cards or on the register in which arriving guests sign their names. This is generally not a permissible substitute for mandated posting elsewhere.

If the only notice of limited liability is posted near the room-key drop off, where guests would see it only after their stay was completed, the conspicuous posting requirement likely has not been met.[8]

Posting Notice of Hotel's Limited Liability

It is not enough for a hotel to post conspicuously the availability of a safe. Virtually every state's limiting statute requires that the posted notice also inform guests that the hotel's liability is limited. Without that notice, guests are led to believe that if valuables are deposited in the safe, the guest will be protected for the full

---

[4] *Insurance Co. v. Holiday Inns, Inc.*, 337 N.Y.S.2d 68 (N.Y. 1972)

[5] *Roth v. Investment Properties*, 560 S.W.2d 831 (Mo. 1978)

[6] *North River Insurance Company v. Tisch Management, Inc.*, 166 A.2d 169 (N.J. 1960)

[7] *Fennema v. Howard Johnson Co.*, 559 So.2d 1231 (Fla. App. 1990)

[8] *Moog v. Hilton Waldorf-Astoria*, 882 F.Supp. 1392 (N.Y. 1995)

value of the deposited items. Absent notice of limited liability, the common law rule will apply and the hotel will be fully liable.

This principle is illustrated in a case in which a Days Inn hotel was sued for $142,834.00—the value of jewelry stolen from a safe located in a guest's room. A sign was located on the front check-in desk that read, "Because We Care: For your safety and convenience, a SAFEKEEPER is provided for you in the privacy of your room to secure and protect your valuables." Also located at the front desk was another posted sign that stated, "The hotel is not responsible for loss of valuables left unprotected. A personal safe with contents insurance in case of forced entry is located in each room." When the plaintiff returned to her room one night she observed that the SAFEKEEPER had been forcibly removed from the wall and floor. In the ensuing lawsuit, the court held the hotel liable for the full value of the jewelry—$142,834.00, because the inn failed to inform the guest of limits to its liability.[9]

In another case, $10,000 of a guest's money stored in a hotel safe was stolen. The posted notices said, "We have safe-deposit boxes that are available for you without charge. We will appreciate your cooperation." A note on the registration card read, "Money, jewels and other valuables must be placed in the safe in the office, otherwise the management will not be responsible for any loss." The hotel sought the benefits of limited liability. The court held that the notices led guests to believe that if they deposited their valuables in the safe, no limitation of liability applied. The hotel was ordered to pay the full $10,000 loss.[10]

Languages Other than English

If a hotel can anticipate guests who speak languages other than English, the hotel is well advised to post notices written in those other languages in addition to English. By so doing, the hotel avoids an argument by non-English speaking guests that they had not been provided notice of the availability of a safe or of the hotel's limited liability.

What Property Belongs in the Safe?

Not all property brought to a hotel by a guest is appropriate for a safe. If it is not and the property is stolen, the hotel may have no liability. Most state statutes require the following property to be deposited in the safe: money; jewels; ornaments; bank notes; bonds; negotiable securities; and precious stones. Ambiguities exist. For instance, are cufflinks ornaments? How much money may guests keep in their rooms? Must they put a watch in the safe?

In *Federal Insurance Co. v. Waldorf Astoria Hotel*, 303 N.Y.S.2d 297 (1969), the court ruled that cufflinks valued at $175 were not ornaments. The court also held that a watch is neither a jewel nor an ornament; it is instead a timepiece, an article of ordinary wear used daily by most travelers of every social class. A gold money clip was likewise found not to be jewelry in *Chase v. Hilton Hotel Corp.*, 682 F.Supp. 316 (E.D. La. 1988).

---

[9] *Days Inn v. Tobias Jewelry, Ltd.*, 751 So.2d 711 (Fl. 2000)

[10] *Depaemelaere v. Davis*, 351 N.Y.S.2d 808 (N.Y. 1973)

However, in a case in the state of Washington involving an expensive watch, the court treated it as more than a timepiece and the result was otherwise. The guest left his $3,685 watch on a nightstand and went out to dinner. When he returned, the watch was gone. The court ruled that the watch should have been deposited in the safe. Since it was not, the hotel was relieved of all liability.[11]

Theft During Check-Out

Consider the circumstances where a guest is in the process of checking out of the hotel. She has already retrieved her valuables from the safe and, while settling her account with the hotel, her jewelry is stolen. In a case addressing this circumstance, the court held that the hotel would not be liable. Said the court, "A hotel guest who fails to use the safe deposit box cannot hold the hotel responsible if his or her valuables are later lost or stolen. ... The hotel's freedom from liability is not altered by the fact that the loss occurred as the guest was preparing to leave the hotel."[12]

Hotel Guest in Hotel Restaurant

An interesting case involved a hotel guest whose purse was stolen in the hotel restaurant. In the purse were cash and valuables. The guest sued the hotel and lost because, said the court, even in the restaurant she retained her status as guest since the eatery was owned and operated by the hotel. The limiting statute precluded the guest from recovering for lost cash and valuables that were not placed in the safe.[13]

Door Locks and Window Fastenings

Some states' limiting statutes require a hotel seeking to benefit from limited liability to maintain suitable locks and bolts on doors and fastenings on windows. The reason for this requirement is that these devices help deter in-room thefts.

Clothes and Other Personal Property

What about property not required to be placed in a safe, such as clothes, sporting equipment, inexpensive watches, or merchandise samples? Does a hotel have unlimited liability as to those items? The generally applicable answer is no. Most states have a statute that limits the hotel's liability for these types of property.

The typical limiting statute restricts a hotel's liability for damage or loss of a guest's apparel and other personal property such as a camera, to a specified maximum, for example, $500. The amount may vary from the hotel's maximum

---

[11] *Walls v. Cosmopolitan Hotels, Inc.*, 534 P.2d 1373 (Wa. 1975)

[12] *Moog v. Waldorf-Astoria*, 882 F.Supp. 1392 (N.Y. 1995)

[13] *Summer v. Hyatt Corp.*, 266 S.E.2d 333 (Ga. 1980)

liability for lost money and jewels required to be in the safe. Where, however, the loss or damage to clothes and other personal property is caused by negligence on the part of the hotel, in most states the hotel is not entitled to the benefit of the limiting statute and will be liable for the full amount of the guest's loss.

The limiting liability statute in Florida treats clothes and personal property a bit differently. Florida's statute relieves the hotel from any liability for loss caused to guests' clothes and personal property unless the hotel was negligent. If it is negligent, the hotel's liability is limited to $500. The application of this provision is illustrated by a case in which two guests sharing a hotel room in Florida discovered that the lock on the door to their room was broken. They called the front desk and requested it be repaired. The hotel sent a repairman, but he negligently went to the wrong room. The room of the guests' with the broken lock was burglarized and property was stolen. In the lawsuit that followed, the guests sought reimbursement for the full value of their loss, which significantly exceeded $500 each. The court held the hotel was negligent and so it had some liability to the plaintiff-guests. Based on the Florida limiting statute the maximum liability was $500 for each plaintiff.[14]

Checkrooms

Some states' limiting statutes differentiate between clothing lost or damaged in the lobby, hallways, and guestrooms, on the one hand, and property lost in a checkroom. While many provisions of limiting statutes may apply only to hotels, those that have a separate section for checkrooms may also cover restaurants because both hotels and restaurants typically have a coat-check area. Later in this chapter we will look closer at the rules applicable to checkrooms.

Baggage Room

Most states' limiting statutes restrict a hotel's liability for loss or damage caused to guests' property while stored in a baggage or storage room. The hotel's liability will be limited to a specified maximum amount, such as $100. If, however, the loss or damage to property stored in the baggage room is caused by negligence on the part of the hotel, the statutes customarily provide that the hotel is liable for the full amount of the guest's loss.

Merchandise Samples

The term **merchandise samples** refers to goods for sale brought to a hotel by a salesperson-guest. Even in common law days, the strict liability rule governing an innkeeper's liability for guests' property recognized a distinction between property brought to the hotel for personal use and property brought for commercial purposes. The unlimited liability rule applied only to the former and not the latter.

---

[14]*Southernmost Affiliates v. Alonzo*, 654 So.2d 1066 (1995)

In an early United States Supreme Court case, a salesman sued a hotel to recover for the theft of his samples. The court held for the hotel, saying:

Although Fisher [the salesman] was received by the defendants into their hotel as a guest, with knowledge that his trunks contained articles having no connection with his comfort or convenience as a mere traveler or wayfarer, but which, at his request, were to be placed on exhibition or for sale in a room assigned to him for that purpose, [the innkeeper] would not, under the doctrines at common law, be held to the same degree of care and responsibility, in respect to the safety of such articles, as is required in reference to baggage or other personal property carried by travelers. The defendants, being owners or managers of the hotel, were at liberty to permit the use of one of the rooms by Fisher for such business purposes, but they would not, for that reason and without other circumstances, be held to have undertaken to hold and safely keep them.[15]

Many limiting liability statutes provide that innkeepers have no liability for damage to or loss of merchandise samples unless the innkeeper receives written notice that the samples are in the hotel and acknowledges in writing that a guest has such property and its value. If the guest gives the necessary notice and the hotel makes the required written acknowledgment, the statutes customarily limit the hotel's liability. Strict compliance with the statute is mandatory if the guest seeks to hold the hotel liable, as evidenced in *Associated Mills, Inc., v. Drake Hotel, Inc.*, 334 N.E.2d 746 (Ill. 1975). The plaintiff had manufactured a prototype (working model) of a new product and used the prototype to demonstrate the benefits to be offered by the finished product. The plaintiff rented a room at the defendant's hotel for display of the model to potential customers. The hotel had orally agreed to "plug and seal" the room where the model was being displayed to prevent overnight entry and removal of the model. The hotel had also orally agreed that it would order its employees not to enter or clean the room during the night. The next morning the plaintiff discovered the room had not been plugged, sealed, or locked; it had been cleaned, and the model was missing.

The plaintiff claimed the hotel was liable for $87,000, the value of the prototype, because the hotel had breached its agreement with him. The hotel denied liability, arguing that the prototype was a merchandise sample within the meaning of the limiting statute and the plaintiff failed to give written notice of the presence of the model. The court agreed with the hotel; the plaintiff lost the case.

Some states' limiting statutes require that a guest who keeps merchandise samples in his room declare to (inform) the hotel of the value of the merchandise. Without that notification, the hotel is not liable if the property is stolen. For example, a dealer in the business of buying and selling baseball cards attended a baseball card show. He took with him five briefcases full of cards. While out to dinner one night, he left the cards in his room at a Marriott hotel. When he returned he discovered that all of his inventory had been stolen. In the resulting case against the hotel, the evidence was undisputed that the dealer failed to declare to any employee of the hotel the value of the cards. Therefore, the hotel was not liable.[16]

---

[15] *Fisher v. Kelsey*, 121 U.S. 383 (1887)

[16] *Beam v. Marriott Corp.*, 655 N.Y.S.2d 566 (N.Y. 1997)

Property in Transit

Occasionally, hotel personnel will take possession of guests' suitcases or other property before arriving at a hotel. For example, a guest arriving at the airport may take the hotel shuttle bus to the hotel and give the driver his luggage. Without a limiting statute, the hotel would have unlimited liability in this circumstance. In a New York case predating that state's limiting statute, a bellhop was sent to pick up a guest's trunk at the railroad station. He made a stop while returning from the station and left the bag unattended. The trunk was stolen, along with its contents, which consisted of expensive furs and dresses valued at $10,000. The guest sued the hotel for the full value of the lost property and won, based on common law unlimited liability.[17]

Today, most states have limiting statutes that restrict a hotel's liability for guests' property while in transit. For example, currently in New York liability in this circumstance is limited to $250. These statutes customarily provide that if the loss is due to the hotel's negligence, the hotel's liability is unlimited.

Property Not Covered by Limiting Liability Statutes

The limiting liability statutes do not cover all property that might be stolen or disappear in or around a hotel. These statutes apply only to property of hotel guests; they do not cover property of nonguests. The limiting statutes also do not apply to cars.

The liability of a hotel or restaurant for cars, property of nonguests, and property of restaurant patrons is based primarily on the law of bailments, discussed in detail later in this chapter.

Fire

Just as the innkeeper was liable at common law for virtually all losses to guests' property occurring at the hotel, the innkeeper was likewise liable where the loss was caused by fire. This was true even if the innkeeper was not responsible for starting the fire.

Consistent with the statutory limitations on innkeepers' liability that we have been studying in this chapter, most states have passed laws limiting or eliminating the hotel's liability for damage caused by fire where the fire was not the result of the hotel's negligence. If, however, a fire is caused by the hotel's failure to exercise reasonable care, the hotel will be fully liable for the resulting loss.

Estoppel: Loss of Limited Liability

Hoteliers or their agents may make comments to a guest that result in the hotel losing the benefits of a limiting liability statute. This is known as the doctrine of

---

[17] *Davidson v. Madison Corp.*, 177 N.E. 393 (N.Y. 1931)

equitable estoppel, a legal principle that precludes a person from claiming a right or benefit because that person made a false representation to another person who relied on the statement to his detriment.

Implying Greater Liability

An example of estoppel is the following. A desk clerk at a hotel tells a guest that the hotel maintains safe deposit boxes that she can use free of charge to safeguard her valuables. The clerk further tells the guest that if she deposits the jewelry in one of the boxes, there will be no limit on the hotel's liability if the jewelry is stolen. As a direct result of the clerk's statement, the guest places her jewelry in a safe deposit box. The jewelry disappears without explanation. The guest sues the hotel for the full value of the jewelry; the hotel asserts the limiting liability statute as a defense. The guest claims that the desk clerk orally modified the terms of the statute and that the guest incurred the loss only because she relied on the desk clerk's representation. The hotel will likely be estopped from denying liability for the full loss.

Now assume one change of the facts in this scenario. When the hotel clerk informs the guest about the safes, the clerk tells the guest that if the jewelry is stolen from the safe, the hotel's liability will be limited according to statute. Under these circumstances, the hotel will be entitled to the benefit of limited liability.

Misrepresenting Risk

The principle of estoppel will also be imposed if the innkeeper or an employee misleads a guest into believing that property can be left safely at a particular place in the inn, causing the guest to disregard posted directions for safekeeping property. The hotel in the following case was estopped for this reason.

CASE EXAMPLE 8-3

Fennema v. Howard Johnson Co.
559 So.2d 1231 (Fla. 1990)

The material facts of this case are undisputed. In August, 1985, plaintiffs Robert J. Fennema and his wife Kimberly A. Fennema came to Dade County, Florida from the state of Washington so that Robert Fennema could become a university professor at Florida International University. They travelled to Dade County in a Chevrolet Camaro and a rented twenty-four foot U-Haul truck which, in turn, towed their 1970 Toyota Land Cruiser; they placed all their possessions in the U-Haul truck. Mr. Fennema drove the U-Haul truck, and Mrs. Fennema

drove the Camaro. Upon their arrival in Dade County, they stopped at a Howard Johnson Motor Lodge located at 1430 South Dixie Highway, Coral Gables, Florida, at approximately 6:00 P.M. on August 10, 1985. This lodge was owned and operated by defendants H. William Prahl, Jr. and Robert A. Prahl, under a franchise from the defendants Howard Johnson Company.

Mrs. Fennema went into the motel office and registered for her and her husband. She specifically advised the registration clerk that they had a Toyota Land Cruiser towed by a large U-Haul truck with nearly all their personal belongs in it; she asked where would be a safe place to park this vehicle. The clerk directed her to park the vehicle in a particular area of the motel parking lot behind a building where presumably it would be safe from vandalism or theft. Mrs. Fennema conveyed this information to Mr. Fennema who, in turn, parked the vehicle in the place designated by the clerk. Although there had been numerous incidents of criminal activity including motor vehicle thefts on or about the grounds and parking lot of this motel, the plaintiffs were not provided with this information nor warned of the risks of leaving their vehicle in the lot. The Fennemas thereafter spent the night in the motel without incident, and, the following day, went for a drive in the Camaro. When they returned to the motel at 3:00 P.M. that afternoon, they discovered that the U-Haul truck with all of its contents and the attached Toyota Land Cruiser had been stolen by unknown third parties from the place in the parking lot where the clerk had told them to park it for safekeeping.

Plaintiffs brought a negligence action ... against defendant innkeepers for the property loss sustained as a result of the above theft in the amount of $177,000. They alleged that the defendants were negligent in failing to warn the plaintiffs that there had been criminal activity in the motel parking lot, and that defendants failed to take other steps to warn their guests and/or to prevent criminal activity from occurring in the parking lot. Plaintiffs also claimed that defendant Howard Johnson, as owner, departed from a standard of care nationally advertised by it, that all defendants knew the parking lot was dangerous, and that, as owners, lessees and operators of the motel, they had an obligation at a minimum to warn their guests. Defendant filed an answer denying any liability for the theft loss and setting up various affirmative defenses, including that plaintiffs' recovery was limited by ... Florida's limited liability statute. ...

Plaintiffs [argue that] ... the statute had no application to their vehicle and its contents under the circumstances of this case. ...

It is settled in Florida that "[a]n innkeeper owes the duty of reasonable care for the safety of his guest" (person and property) ... and that an innkeeper's knowledge, as here, of prior criminal activity on or around the grounds of his inn imposes a duty to take adequate security precautions for the safety of his

guests and their property. ... With respect to any damage to or loss of a guest's property, however, an innkeeper's negligence liability is specifically limited by ... [Florida's limiting liability statute]—provided a copy of that statute is posted "in the office, hall, or lobby or another prominent place of such public lodging ... establishment." ...

It does not follow, however, that an innkeeper may, under all circumstances, rely on the ... statute to limit his liability even if the statute is properly posted at the inn. [W]e conclude that an innkeeper is estopped to rely on the innkeeper's limitation of liability statute if he personally misleads his guest into believing that the latter's property may be safely placed at a particular location in the inn, as this causes a guest to disregard whatever posted statutory procedures there might be for safeguarding a guest's property generally. ...

[I]n our view, the defendant innkeepers are estopped to invoke whatever protection ... [the limiting liability statute] may afford. This is so because the defendant's motel clerk affirmatively misled the plaintiffs into believing that their motor vehicle and its valuable contents were safe if parked at a particular location in the motel parking lot. Mrs. Fennema specifically informed the motel registration clerk concerning the valuable contents of the plaintiffs' motor vehicle and asked where would be a safe place to park the vehicle; the clerk, in turn, directed the Fennemas to park their vehicle at a particular spot in the motel guest parking lot behind a building where presumably the vehicle would be safe. Plaintiffs had every right to believe and did believe that their vehicle would be safe at that location; they parked their vehicle in the exact spot as directed and later the vehicle was stolen from the spot.

Having affirmatively misled the plaintiffs that it was, in effect, safe to leave their vehicle and its contents at this location in the motel parking lot, the defendant innkeepers are in no position to claim the limited liability protection. ... Plaintiffs had every right to rely on defendant's affirmative assurance of safety for their property and to believe that these personal assurances of safety overrode whatever statutory procedures might exist for safeguarding guests' property generally. ... [T]he defendants, by their conduct, are estopped to rely on the protection of the subject statute because they, in effect, misled the plaintiffs into disregarding the procedure stated in the posted statute as being unnecessary, given the motel's personal directive which they followed for safeguarding their property. ...

CASE QUESTIONS

1. What was the representation made by the hotel that enabled the guest to invoke the doctrine of estoppel?

2. What was meant by the court's statement, "Plaintiffs also claimed that the defendant Howard Johnson, as owner, departed from a standard of care nationally advertised by it." What was the significance of that statement on the outcome of the case?

The court in a case with similar facts likewise held that a hotel, whose clerk affirmatively misled a guest into believing his belongings would be safe in the car, would be estopped from seeking the protection of a limited liability statute.[18]

Hotel's Negligence

As we have learned, most limiting statutes do not protect an innkeeper in situations where the loss of guests' property is due to the hotel's negligence. The following case illustrates this principle.

CASE EXAMPLE 8-4

Bhattal v. Grand Hyatt-New York
563 F.Supp. 277 (N.Y. 1983)

... Plaintiffs, residents and citizens of India, registered as guests in defendant's Grand Hyatt Hotel in Midtown Manhattan on July 19, 1981 and were assigned Room 2946. Following the customary practice in first class hotels in this City of the sort operated by defendant, plaintiffs turned over to the bell captain various pieces of personal luggage, which are now said to have contained valuables of great significance, and this luggage was duly transferred by defendant's employees to plaintiffs' assigned hotel room.

Plaintiffs did not request that any of their valuables be placed in the safe depository provided by the hotel. ...

Shortly after arriving at their room with the luggage, plaintiffs left the hotel for luncheon with friends, locking their door with a key provided by defendant. On returning [early] the same evening, plaintiffs discovered that their luggage and the contents thereof were missing. ...

Apparently defendant's front desk relies heavily on computer support, and as a result of computer error, employees of defendant transported plaintiffs' luggage from plaintiffs' room to JFK International Airport, along with the luggage of aircraft crew members of Saudi

---

[18] *David v. Prime Hospitality Corp.*, 676 So.2d 1049 (Fl. 1996)

Arabian nationality, who had previously occupied Room 2946. In other words, the computer omitted to notice that the room had been vacated and relet to plaintiffs, and hotel employees responding to computer direction, included plaintiffs' luggage along with the other luggage of the departing prior guests. This is not to suggest that the Grand Hyatt-New York is a hotbed house, but apparently it was operating at 100 percent occupancy with no lost time between the departure of the Saudi Arabian aircraft crew members who had previously occupied the room, and the arrival of plaintiffs.

Needless to say, plaintiffs' luggage departed for Saudi Arabia and has not since been seen. A missing pearl is always a pearl of the finest water, and accordingly plaintiffs demand damages in the amount of $150,000. ...

The [case] presents the question of whether [the limiting liability] statutes limit the liability of an innkeeper in a case where the innkeeper, by his own agents, intentionally and without justification, took custody and control of plaintiffs' luggage and contents, without plaintiffs' authorization, and intentionally, although inadvertently, caused the luggage to be transported to Saudi Arabia. The Court concludes that the statutes do not extend so far as to protect the innkeeper under these facts. ...

Here, defendant's employees entered plaintiffs' locked room, without plaintiffs' permission or knowledge, and removed their luggage, commingled it with the luggage of the Saudi Arabian aircraft crew members and placed it on a bus headed for Kennedy Airport. The Court infers that if the luggage was not stolen at Kennedy Airport, it arrived in Saudi Arabia and was eventually stolen by a Saudi thief who still had the use of at least one good hand. In this instance, the intentional acts of the defendant clearly constituted conversion [unauthorized exercise of ownership over goods] under New York law.

... New York [limiting liability laws] were adopted in the middle of the nineteenth century to relieve an innkeeper from his liability at common law as an insurer of property of a guest lost by theft, caused without negligence or fault of the guest. ... These statutes and the cases cited thereunder by the defendant extend to the situation where there is a mysterious disappearance of valuable property, either as a result of a theft by an employee of the hotel—or a trespass or theft by an unrelated party, for whose acts the innkeeper is not responsible. The statutes are also intended to protect the innkeeper from the danger of fraud on the part of a guest in a situation where the property said to have disappeared never existed at all, or was taken or stolen by or with the privity of the guest.

The reason for limiting a hotel's liability ... is to protect against just such a situation. When a hotel room is let to a guest, the innkeeper has lost a large measure of control and supervision over the hotel room and its contents. While housekeeping and security staff can enter the room at reasonable hours and on notice to any persons present therein, essentially, for most of the time at least, property of a guest which is present in a hotel room can be said to be under the exclusive dominion and control of the hotel guest, rather than the innkeeper.

... In this case ... employees of defendant, acting within the scope of their employment and relying on the accuracy of the employer's computer, intentionally converted the luggage of the plaintiffs by removing it from plaintiff's room and delivering it to an aircraft bound for Saudi Arabia. [The limiting statute does not limit the liability of the hotel in this case. Rather, the hotel is liable for the full value of the loss.]

CASE QUESTION

1. What would have been the outcome of the case if the luggage had been stolen by a thief through no fault of the hotel?

Comparative Negligence

Consider a circumstance when the hotel and the guest are both negligent and the guest's loss is due to the combined negligence. What liability does the hotel have? According to *Vasilios Nicholaides v. University Hotel Associates*, 568 A.2d 219 (Pa. 1990), at least in states that adopted the comparative negligence rule, the hotel's liability will be reduced by the extent of responsibility for the loss attributed to the guest. In that case, the plaintiff brought to the defendant's hotel a coin collection valued at $34,973. The plaintiff placed the collection in a dresser drawer in his guest room under some garments. Two days later, he discovered the collection missing. The jury determined, without explanation, that both the hotel and the guest were negligent. It allocated to the guest 49 percent of the responsibility for the loss. The guest recovered only 51 percent of his damages.

Nevada's Limiting Statute

Nevada is very protective of its innkeepers. The state's limiting liability statute is quite different from that found in most other states. Its limitation of liability (maximum $750) applies even if the hotel is not only negligent, but grossly negligent.

Liability During Check-In and Check-Out

Should there be a period of time while guests are checking in and out of a hotel that the statute does not apply? When guests first enter a hotel and have not yet completed the registration process, they have not had time to access the safe. When they are packing and preparing to check out, they will likely remove their valuables from the hotel safe. Generally, when goods are stolen or disappear during check-in or check-out, the courts have found the limiting statutes applicable and the hotel not liable for the full loss.

Guest Status

If the person whose property disappears during check-in or check-out is a hotel guest at the time of the loss, the limiting statute applies. In most of the following cases, the owner of the missing property was found to be a guest; thus, recovery was limited.

A guest of the Hilton Hotel in New Orleans left two rings in her hotel room after washing her hands. She checked out of the hotel that day and did not realize the rings were missing until she was partway home. She immediately called the hotel and an investigation was made. The rings, valued at $10,000, were never found. Like most limiting statutes, Louisiana's applied only to guests. The owner of the rings sued the hotel for their value, claiming the innkeeper-guest relationship had terminated before the loss occurred and thus the hotel should be liable for the full value of the jewelry. The court ruled the loss occurred when she left the rings in the room, which happened while she was still a guest. Therefore, the hotel was only responsible for $500, the maximum provided by the applicable limiting statute.[19]

In another case, a jewelry salesman had been a guest at the hotel for several days. On the last day of his stay he attended a sales presentation to which he took $150,000 worth of diamonds. After the presentation, he returned to his room to pack and took the diamonds with him. A few minutes before leaving his room, he was beaten and robbed of all the diamonds. He sued the hotel, claiming the limiting statute should not apply since, at the time of the theft, he was about to leave. The court disagreed and ruled the statute was applicable. The salesman should have deposited the diamonds in the safe before he went to his room to pack.[20]

In another case, a jewelry salesman, upon arrival at the MGM Grand Hotel in Las Vegas, checked his luggage and jewelry samples with the bellhop at the door. He told the bellhop that the samples were valuable. After checking in and going to his room, his luggage was delivered, but one case of jewelry samples worth $19,000 was missing. The salesman sued the hotel for the value of the jewelry. The plaintiff argued that he was not a guest at the time he gave the luggage to the bellhop since he had not yet checked in and therefore the limiting liability statute should not apply. The court held that the innkeeper-guest relationship was established when the plaintiff checked his luggage with the bellhop. Therefore, the salesman could only recover the limited statutory amount—$750.[21]

Liability after Check-Out

In many cases, guests retain their status after check-out, and limiting liability statutes still apply. In *Nagashima v. Hyatt Wilshire Corp.*, 279 Cal.Rptr. 265 (Cal. App. 1991), the plaintiff was in the hotel lobby in the check-out line, having just removed from the hotel safe her jewelry valued at $72,000. While she waited for her turn to check out, someone grabbed the jewelry from her possession and it was never recovered. The court held the limiting statute applied, and so her recovery was restricted to $500. In response to the plaintiff's argument that application of the statute in her case was unjust, the court suggested she address her argument to the legislature, which alone has the power to change the statute.

In the following case, the court held that guests who had checked out of a hotel retained their status as guests for purposes of the limiting statute where they left their luggage in the hotel's luggage room while they went shopping for the day.

[19] *O'Rourke v. Hilton Hotels Corp.*, 560 So.2d 76 (La. 1990)

[20] *Pacific Diamond Co., Inc. v. Hilton Hotels Corp.*, 149 Cal.Rptr. 813 (Ca. 1978)

[21] *Pachinger v. MGM Grand Hotel-Las Vegas, Inc.*, 802 F.2d 362 (Nev. 1986)

CASE EXAMPLE 8-5

Salisbury v. St. Regis-Sheraton Hotel
490 F.Supp. 449 (N.Y. 1980)

On the morning of November 22, 1978, Mr. and Mrs. Roger Salisbury concluded a three-day stay at the St. Regis-Sheraton Hotel in New York. While Mr. Salisbury paid the bill and surrendered their room key, Mrs. Salisbury checked their luggage with a bellhop in the lobby. The couple was to spend the day in town and return for the luggage that afternoon. Mrs. Salisbury did not inform the hotel when she checked the luggage that one of their pieces, a cosmetic case, contained jewelry and cosmetics worth over $60,000 and did not ask that the case be kept in the hotel's safe. ...

When the Salisburys returned to the hotel to retrieve their luggage at about 4:30 that afternoon, the cosmetic case containing the jewelry was missing. Mrs. Salisbury sued to recover the value of the case and its contents.

It is undisputed that posted conspicuously in the public areas of the hotel was a notice informing guests that the hotel provided a safe for the safekeeping of their valuables, and

notifying them of the provisions of the [limiting liability statute] of the New York General Business Law. ...

The question, then, is whether Mrs. Salisbury ceased to be a "guest" within the meaning of the limiting liability statute when she checked out of the hotel, even though she arranged to have the hotel hold her luggage for the day. ... The lost luggage was not stored with the hotel for a lengthy period, but simply held for the day as an accommodation to departing guests. ...

It is not uncommon for a hotel to hold luggage for a few hours after guests check out as an accommodation to them. This would appear to be one of the services that a hotel performs for its guests in the normal course of its business, and there is no reason why it should be deemed to alter the otherwise existing legal relationship between them. Accordingly, we conclude that the limiting liability statutes are fully applicable in the circumstances of this case and preclude any recovery against the hotel for the loss of Mrs. Salisbury's jewelry and limits any recovery for the loss of the case and its other contents to $100.

CASE QUESTION

1. On what basis did the court determine that the plaintiffs were still guests at the time of the loss?

At what point in the check-out process does a guest cease to be a guest for purposes of a limiting liability statute? According to the next case, a guest is no longer considered a guest if she has checked out of the hotel and given luggage to a bellhop to place in a vehicle in which the guest will depart the hotel.

CASE EXAMPLE 8-6

Spiller v. Barclay Hotel
327 N.Y.S.2d 426 (1972)

Plaintiff, a guest of the Barclay Hotel, sued for the value of the property, primarily wearing

apparel and jewelry, lost on the steps of the hotel while she was in the process of leaving.

Plaintiff testified that after her two bags were brought to the lobby floor, she asked a bellboy to take them to the cab area and to watch them while she checked out. When she came to the cab area, only one of her bags was there and the bellboy was not present. A search failed to disclose the missing bag or its contents.

No directly contradictory testimony was presented. A representative of the hotel did testify to a telephone conversation in which plaintiff allegedly gave a different version of the event and described the personal property as business samples. However, I accept as substantially accurate plaintiff's trial testimony as to the property that was lost and the manner in which it was lost. ...

The claim for the items of lost jewelry presents a troublesome problem. [New York's limiting liability statute] excludes recovery by a hotel guest for loss of, among other categories enumerated, jewels, ornaments, and precious stones where the hotel provides a safe for such items, gives appropriate notice of that fact, and the guest does not use that facility. It was conceded that the hotel maintained such a safe and had posted the required notice. ...

What seems to me decisive here is that [New York's statute] was not designed to apply to a loss occurring under the circumstances of this case. [New York's statute] clearly contemplates a procedure for safeguarding the specified categories of property during a guest's stay at a hotel. Its provisions do not seem to me to be reasonably applied to a loss that takes place when a guest is about to leave, has gathered together her property preparatory to an imminent departure, and is arranging for the transfer of luggage to a vehicle for transportation.

Although that situation presents some conceptual difficulties, I am satisfied that the sensible and fair approach is to consider a loss occurring at that point in time neither in terms of the provisions of [New York's limiting statute], nor in terms of the traditional common law liability of innkeepers, but rather on the basis of the presence or absence of actual negligence. ...

Having found that the loss here resulted from the negligence of a hotel employee, acting within the scope of his employment, I hold that plaintiff is entitled to recover the value of the lost jewelry. ...

CASE QUESTIONS

1. On what ground did the court find the hotel liable for the full value of the jewelry?

2. If the missing property had been merchandise samples, what would the outcome of the case likely have been?

Bailment

Another basis of potential liability for a hotel when a guest's property is lost or stolen is the law of bailment. A **bailment** is a transfer of possession of personal property from one person to another, with the understanding that the property will be returned. The person giving possession of the property is called the **bailor**; the person receiving possession is the **bailee**. For example, if a guest leaves a shirt with room service for ironing, the guest is the bailor, the hotel is the bailee, and the arrangement is a bailment. Other examples of bailment include hotel guests who give their car and keys to a valet (the guest is the bailor and the hotel is the bailee); a hotel that rents projection equipment from a rental company for use by conference attendees (the rental company is the bailor and the hotel is the bailee); and a diner at a restaurant who leaves her coat with a coatroom attendant (the diner is the bailor and the restaurant is the bailee).

The essential elements of a bailment are:

1. *Personal property.* Bailments involve only moveable, tangible objects such as cars, clothing, sporting equipment, and the like. Bailment does not apply to real property (land and buildings).

2. *Delivery of possession.* Possession of the personal property must be transferred to the bailee.

3. *Acceptance of possession by the bailee.* The bailee must knowingly accept possession of the bailed property.

4. *Bailment agreement.* Part of every bailment is an agreement, express or implied, by the bailee to return the bailed goods to the bailor.

Assume a hotel lent its hospitality van to another hotel during a week when the first hotel was closed for renovations and the second hotel expected a high demand for van services. The parties agreed that the second hotel would return the van at the end of the week. A bailment was thus created. Assume further that the second hotel/bailee thereafter sold the van rendering return of it impossible. The bailee thereby breached the bailment agreement and will be liable to the bailor for the value of the trailer. For similar facts, see *Hickman v. Cole*, 1999 WL 254379 (Oh. 1999).

Suppose a restaurant patron leaves her coat with a hat-check person. Does a bailment exist? The answer is yes. The coat is personal property; possession has been given to the attendant; and an implied agreement exists that the hat-check attendant will return the coat when the patron (bailor) is ready to leave.

Let us change the facts a bit. Suppose the patron enters the restaurant, removes her coat, and hangs it on an unattended coat rack near the table where she is sitting. Does a bailment exist? The answer is no. Although the coat is personal property, the restaurant has not accepted possession since no one physically took possession of the coat on behalf of the restaurant.

Does a bailment exist when you park your car at a parking lot? The answer is— it depends. A critical factor is whether or not you leave your key with a parking-lot attendant. In most circumstances, if you park the car and take the key with you, you have not delivered possession. If, however, you leave the key with the attendant, that person has the ability to move the car and therefore has possession of it. In this latter case a bailment exists.

Effect of Bailment on Liability

The existence or nonexistence of a bailment directly affects liability. If no bailment exists, neither does liability. For example, if you leave your coat on an unattended coat rack in a restaurant and it is stolen during your meal, the restaurant is not liable. Because the restaurant was not a bailee, it is not responsible for the coat. The following case illustrates this point. Also note the court's determination that the limiting liability statute was not applicable to the property involved in this case.

CASE EXAMPLE 8-7

Augustine v. Marriott Hotel
503 N.Y.S.2d 498 (1986)

Plaintiff attended, for a fee, a dental seminar at the Marriott Hotel. The seminar sponsor rented a banquet room, furnished with seats, from defendant.

At the request of the sponsor, defendant furnished a movable coat rack, placing it outside the [seminar] room, in the public lobby.

Plaintiff placed his coat on the rack before entering the seminar. At the noon recess, plaintiff exited the seminar room, but found that the rack had been moved a distance down the lobby and around a corner, near an exit.

Unfortunately, his cashmere coat was missing. He then commenced this action in the Small Claims Part of this court.

Under the common law an innkeeper was an insurer of property, infra hospitium [within the hotel facility], of his guests, and liable for the loss thereof or damage thereto unless the loss was caused by negligence of the guest, act of God, or the public enemy.

By statute, such liability has been limited. ...

The relationship of guest on the part of plaintiff, and that of hotel keeper on the part of defendant, vis-a-vis each other never arose. The occupancy by plaintiff of a private [guest] room was never contemplated by the parties.

Plaintiff was a patron of the seminar sponsor, who rented facilities from defendant. The status of plaintiff was like that of a wedding guest of individuals who rent banquet facilities from a hotel. ...

Therefore, the New York limiting statutes is in no way applicable to the facts presented here.

The relationship of bailor and bailee never came into existence because plaintiff did not entrust his coat to defendant. Not only was there never a delivery to defendant, but defendant never was in actual nor constructive custody of plaintiff's coat.

The sole question remaining is whether defendant owed a duty to plaintiff to provide a guard for the coat rack. Defendant placed the rack in a position near the door to the seminar room, at the request of the seminar sponsor. This created not only an opportunity but an implied invitation on the part of the sponsor, to patrons of the seminar to use the rack.

However, there was no evidence to indicate that users of the rack were led to believe either by the sponsor or by defendant that there would be a guard for the rack. Under the circumstances presented, it was clear that there was merely a rack available for those who wished to use it. Defendant did not lull plaintiff into a sense of security, by which there was created a duty to provide a guard.

There being no duty on the part of defendant, there can be found no breach of duty upon which to underpin a finding of [liability].

Furthermore, a reasonable man would have wondered about the safety of his coat which he hung on a rack in a public lobby of a hotel ...

The claim must be dismissed.

CASE QUESTIONS

1. Why was the limiting liability statute not applicable in this case?

2. Why did the court determine a bailment had not been created?

This case illustrates the principle that if no bailment exists, no liability exists. If, on the other hand, a bailment for property not subject to limiting liability statutes does exist, the bailee is not automatically liable. A bailee is liable only if it fails to exercise the amount of care required by law in tending to the bailed goods. The requisite care varies depending upon the type of bailment. Bailments are classified into three types:

1. For the sole benefit of the bailor

2. For the sole benefit of the bailee
3. Mutual benefit.

The required level of care differs for each classification.

Bailment for the Sole Benefit of the Bailor

A **bailment for the sole benefit of the bailor** exists when the bailee receives no benefit from the bailment. For example, a Caribbean hotel is located on the predicted path of a hurricane. Hoping to avoid damage to its computers, the hotel removes them and stores them with another hotel located outside the expected course of the hurricane. Under the circumstances, the second hotel does not charge a fee to hold the items. The first hotel, the bailor, benefits from this arrangement. The second hotel, the bailee, does not.

In a bailment such as this, entered into for the sole benefit of the bailor, the bailee is obligated to exercise only a slight degree of care over the bailed goods. Stated differently, the bailee is liable only for gross (extreme) negligence.

Bailment for the Sole Benefit of the Bailee

A **bailment for the sole benefit of the bailee** exists where the bailor lends property to the bailee and receives nothing in return. For example, assume that your restaurant is catering four parties this weekend. You are in need of extra serving dishes. A friend of yours owns a restaurant in the business district that is closed on weekends. She agrees to lend you serving dishes for the weekend at no cost. You benefit from this arrangement, but your friend, the bailor, does not.

In this type of bailment—for the sole benefit of the bailee—the bailee is required to take great care of the property and exercise a degree of care higher than a reasonable person ordinarily exercises in connection with her own property. To avoid liability, you should ensure the serving dishes are utilized only by trained wait staff to avoid breakage and that they are securely stored when not in use to avoid theft.

Mutual-Benefit Bailment

A **mutual-benefit bailment**, also called a *bailment for hire*, is one in which both parties receive some benefit from the bailment. Examples of this type of bailment include a traveler renting a car, or a restaurant leasing a tent in which to stage a wedding reception. In the first example, the traveler (bailee) receives the use of the car, and the car rental company (bailor) receives money. In the second example, the restaurant (bailee) receives the use of the tent, and the leasing company that owns the tent (bailor) receives money. In mutual-benefit bailments, the bailee's duty is to exercise *ordinary care* over the bailed goods. The difference in the duty owed in a mutual-benefit bailment and a bailment for the sole benefit of the bailor is illustrated in the following case.

CASE EXAMPLE 8-8

First American Bank v. District of Columbia
583 A.2d 993 (D.C. 1990)

... First American Bank employed Ronald Armstead as a courier whose duties included making deliveries between the bank's various branch offices and the main office. One afternoon, at approximately 4:20 P.M., Armstead parked the bank's station wagon near the entrance of Branch 13 on 7th Street, N.W., in violation of "No Parking Rush Hour Zone" signs, which were in clear view of Armstead. Four locked bank dispatch bags, marked as such, which Armstead had just picked up from four different branches, were in the rear luggage compartment of the station wagon and in plain view of anyone looking into the vehicle. The dispatch bags contained checks and other valuable documents.

Armstead had received tickets for illegal parking at this particular spot on at least five prior occasions and had been warned against future violations by traffic enforcement personnel. Traffic enforcement personnel had counseled Armstead to park across the street during rush hour to avoid being ticketed or towed. Armstead, who had received numerous parking tickets during his employment with the bank, would simply give the parking tickets to a supervisor for payment. The bank did not reprimand or discipline Armstead, nor did it dock his pay, for the parking tickets.

Within a short time after Armstead entered Branch 13, a parking control aide approached the bank's station wagon and began writing up a ticket for illegal parking. Almost immediately thereafter, a tow truck owned by Transportation Management, Inc. (TMI) arrived at the scene. While the parking control aide was completing the ticket and the tow truck operator was simultaneously preparing to tow the car, one of the employees at Branch 13 alerted Armstead that the bank's vehicle was being towed. Armstead, carrying a dispatch bag, ran out to the vehicle and told the tow truck operator that, as the driver of the vehicle, he was prepared to drive the vehicle away immediately. When the tow truck operator ignored his request to return the vehicle, Armstead asked that he be allowed at least to remove the

dispatch bags from the vehicle. The tow truck operator, however, also ignored this latter request, and instead entered the truck and began to drive away with the bank's vehicle in tow. The ... form filled out by the tow truck operator indicated that the doors, trunk, and window of the bank's station wagon were locked when it was towed from 7th Street. When the tow truck operator arrived at the Brentwood impoundment lot at 4:45 P.M., the dispatch bags were still inside the luggage compartment of the vehicle. The tow truck operator observed the District's lot attendant test all the doors and the rear gate of the vehicle. The lot attendant found them all locked and so certified on the same form.

One and a half hours later, the bank's supervisor of mailroom couriers paid for the vehicle's release and retrieved it from the impoundment lot. The bank supervisor found the driver's door unlocked and one dispatch bag missing. There were no signs of forced entry, nor were there signs of the tape which is customarily affixed to car doors at the impoundment lot. The dispatch bag was never found, nor have the police identified or apprehended anyone who may have removed it from the vehicle. The value of the checks and other papers contained in the dispatch bag was determined to be $107,561. ... First American brought suit against the District of Columbia and TMI for breach of bailment ...

The trial court ruled that the District and TMI were gratuitous bailees [bailment for the sole benefit of the bailor] and therefore liable only for gross negligence. The trial court further ruled that First American [was not] grossly negligent. ... We reverse on the bailment issue.

There is no dispute here that TMI and the District had sufficient possession and control of the bank's vehicle to establish a type of bailment. ... The question we must resolve is whether the bailment was gratuitous or for hire. A bailee that takes possession of goods solely for the benefit of the owner is a gratuitous bailee and liable only for gross negligence, willful acts or fraud. ... In contrast, a bailee that receives compensation for its services is held to a standard of ordinary care. ...

A bailment for hire [mutual benefit bailment] relationship may be created even in the absence of an explicit agreement. ... All that is required is the existence of a mutual benefit. ...

The District and TMI actively took possession of the bank's vehicle with the expectation of deriving benefit therefrom. In addition to furthering its interest in insuring the smooth flow of traffic, the District tows and stores illegally parked vehicles for compensation. Likewise, TMI is under contract with the District for the purpose of towing illegally parked vehicles to impoundment lots. Owners of vehicles, on the other hand, receive the direct benefit of having their vehicles safeguarded in the city's impoundment lot until they are ready to retrieve them. As users of the District's roads and highways, they also benefit indirectly from the District's practice of towing illegally parked vehicles that impede the flow of traffic. ...

We hold, therefore, that the District and TMI are held to the standard of ordinary care when they tow and impound illegally parked vehicles. ...

In view of the foregoing, we remand this case [for a trial] for a determination of whether the city and TMI exercised ordinary care in safeguarding the bank's vehicle and its contents.

Duty of Bailor in Mutual-Benefit Bailment

In a mutual-benefit bailment, the bailor has responsibilities as well as the bailee. The bailor is obligated to warn the bailee of any defects in the bailed property that might result in injury to the bailee or interfere with use of the property. This is a form of strict liability; the bailor is liable for failing to disclose defects even if it is unaware of their existence. For example, Jerry rented a car for one day. While he was driving the vehicle, the steering gear broke, causing an accident in which he was injured. Jerry had not been warned by the bailor that the steering mechanism was defective and he sued for injuries. The bailor responded that it did not know of the defect. Notwithstanding the bailor's lack of knowledge, it is responsible for any loss or injury suffered by the bailee as a result of a defect in the bailed goods. A company in the business of leasing goods, such as a car-rental company, should make regular and frequent inspections of its inventory. To avoid liability it must correct any problems discovered or alert the bailee of potential risks.

The case of *Gulf American v. Airco Industrial Gases*, 573 So.2d 481 (La. 1990) is illustrative. It involved the rental of a freezer that was represented as having the capacity to quick-freeze a specified number of shrimp per hour. Gulf American, a processor of shrimp, leased the freezer and discovered it could not process the advertised number of shrimp. Instead, it malfunctioned and the frozen shrimp were "extremely dehydrated, white and sometimes came out in clumps of two or three." Gulf American sued the lessor of the freezer for damages. The court held that the lessor, by failing to disclose the freezer's defects, breached its duty as bailor. It was liable to Gulf American for its damages.

Proof of Negligence in Bailment Cases

A bailor does not usually monitor the bailee while the latter is in possession of the bailed goods. Therefore, when the goods are lost or stolen, a bailor would typically have difficulty in proving that the bailee failed to exercise the required degree of care. Because of this, bailment law does not require the bailor to prove that the bailee was negligent. Instead, a bailor need only prove delivery of the bailed property to the bailee, acceptance by the bailee, and either a failure on the part of the bailee to return the bailed property, or return of the property in a damaged condition. Such proof establishes a **prima facie** case, that is, a case sufficient to warrant a judgment for the plaintiff if the defendant does not contradict it with other evidence. With such proof, a presumption arises that the bailee was negligent (failed to use reasonable care); the bailee will lose the case unless it presents evidence to dispute the presumption of negligence or proves that the loss or damage occurred from a cause other than its own negligence. If the bailee can establish either of those circumstances, it will not be liable for the loss. Application of the presumption and an example of a successful rebuttal is illustrated in the following case.

CASE EXAMPLE 8-9

Value Rent-A-Car, Inc. v. Collection Chevrolet, Inc.
570 So.2d 1376 (Fla. 1990)

Value Rent-A-Car (Value), ... left its car in Collection Chevrolet, Inc.'s (Collection) care for repairs. When Value returned to pick up the car, the car and its keys had disappeared. Collection reported the car's disappearance to the police. The police subsequently recovered the car, stripped and heavily damaged.

Value brought suit against Collection for negligence arising from the disappearance of its car. Collection denied having been negligent. ... Value rested its negligent bailment case upon the stipulation of the parties that: (1) Value delivered the car to Collection; (2) Collection had exclusive possession and control of the car; and (3) Collection failed to return the car to Value. Collection presented testimony about the extensive security measures that existed at the area from where the car was taken. No witness for Collection was able to explain how the car and its keys were removed from Collection's lot. [Value seeks a] verdict based on the general rule that a bailee who has sole, actual, and exclusive possession of the goods is presumed to be negligent if he cannot explain the loss or disappearance of the goods. The trial court [held that] Collection had established due care in its storing of

the car, that the evidentiary presumption of negligence had vanished, and that the burden of establishing Collection's negligence had shifted to Value. ...

Value contends the trial court erred in ruling that the presumption of Collection's negligence, as bailee of the car, vanished, where Collection was unable to explain the loss or disappearance of the car. Collection asserts that proof of its due care overcame the presumption of negligence. Collection further argues that theft of the car was the only logical explanation for its disappearance because the car had been recovered by the police, stripped and vandalized.

As Value correctly argues, and Collection agrees, the well-settled rule in bailment cases is that:

[A] bailee who has the sole, actual, and exclusive possession of goods is presumed to be negligent if he cannot explain the loss or disappearance of the goods, and the law imposes on him the burden of showing that he exercised the degree of care required by the nature of the bailment. ...

This presumption, however, is a vanishing presumption. Once the bailee introduces evidence of its due care, the presumption of negligence vanishes and the case is decided by the trier of fact [jury] without regard to the presumption. ...

In this case, the presumption, which was enveloped in a protective bubble, burst, when Collection presented evidence of its due care, that is, its extensive security measures, and the only logical inference from the evidence presented was that the car had been stolen. ...

A ruling that the presumption continues even though the bailee has presented evidence of its due care, would effectively result in the bailee becoming the insurer of the bailed goods. This is not the rule in Florida. Florida agrees with the weight of authority that a bailee is not an insurer of the bailed goods and if the bailee is not negligent or at fault, the risk of loss by theft is on the bailor. ...

Accordingly, the ... judgment [for Collection] is affirmed.]

CASE QUESTION

1. On what basis did Collection Chevrolet rebut the presumption of evidence?

If the bailee is unable to prove it acted reasonably in caring for the bailed property, the bailee will be liable for any resulting loss or damage. An application of the presumption is illustrated in a case involving valet parking. The plaintiff gave the key to his car to a hotel bellboy to park in the hotel parking lot. After going off duty, the bellboy returned to the lot and, without authorization, took the car out for a joyride. Unfortunately, he was in an accident and the car was destroyed. The court held that the hotel was liable for the damage. When the car was originally delivered to the bellboy, a mutual-benefit bailment was created between the plaintiff and the hotel. The hotel was required to return the property to the bailor (plaintiff) when he requested it. Since the hotel was unable to do that, a presumption arose that the hotel was negligent. The presumption arose even though the plaintiff did not prove negligence on the part of the hotel. Had the hotel been able to prove that it exercised reasonable care, it would not have been liable. However, it was not able to prove freedom from negligence. Therefore, the court ordered the hotel to reimburse the plaintiff for his loss.[22]

The next case illustrates another circumstance where a bailee was unable to prove it acted reasonably.

CASE EXAMPLE 8-10

Proliance Insurance Co. v. Acura
2001 WL 766894 (Oh. 2001)

... [O]n June 13, 1999, Gallagher delivered a car to Lindsay Acura to have repairs or maintenance performed on it, thereby creating a bailment contract. Contrary to the bailment, Lindsay Acura failed to return the car to Gallagher in an undamaged condition at the termination of the bailment. Instead, the vehicle was stolen and damaged in an amount approximately $6,700. Without his car, Gallagher was required to rent a replacement car at a cost

---

[22] *Dispeker v. The New Southern Hotel Co.,* 373 S.W.2d 904 (Tenn. 1963)

of $500. The cost to repair the vehicle was $6,600.26. Proliance, Plaintiff's insurance company, paid plaintiff the amount of his loss and sued Acura for reimbursement. ...

William Lytle, Lindsay Acura's service manager, [had] considerable familiarity with the typical operation of a dealership's service/parts department, including the one at Lindsay Acura.

Lytle stated that he was aware that on or about June 13, 1999 Kevin Gallagher's 1998 Acura automobile was stolen from the Lindsay Acura dealership lot. Gallagher left his vehicle when the dealership was closed by using what is commonly referred to as the "night drop" or "early bird" drop. He parked his vehicle on the dealership lot and would have placed the keys to his car in an envelope that would have been dropped in the "early bird" slot.

... [E]very new car dealership had a similar procedure and Lindsay Acura's is the same or similar in construction to those used at other dealerships. Lytle also stated that before the incident with Gallagher, Lindsay Acura never had a similar problem with a car left by a customer in that manner. ...

In describing the premises, Lytle stated the lot was fully lighted and the level of security taken by Lindsay Acura in its "early bird" service is commensurate with the level of security customarily employed by new car dealerships in the area. ...

Proliance responded to Lytle with Kevin Gallagher who stated ... When he returned to Lindsay Acura the next day, he observed that the door "which held the slot for the early bird drop off was about one inch above the floor. Keys are placed in envelopes and dropped into the slot and land on the floor. "When my car was finally recovered, the envelope which had contained the keys to my car was inside the car."

The parties had a mutual benefit bailment. Lindsay Acura failed to return the car in an undamaged condition. Accordingly, the burden shifted to Lindsay Acura to set forth evidence explaining its failure to redeliver the bailed property. Lytle claims that although the car was stolen from the lot, the theft happened despite Lindsay Acura providing all the typical security found in new car dealerships throughout the area.

Proliance responds by asserting that the theft occurred because a gap in Lindsay Acura's door negligently allowed the thief to pull the envelope from under the door and steal the vehicle. Proliance thus has come forward with evidence that counters Lindsay Acura's evidence and allows an inference of Lindsay Acura's negligence in the theft of Gallagher's car. ...

In the final analysis, Proliance met its initial burden of making a prima facie case for failed bailment. Lindsay Acura claimed it exercised ordinary care as required by its obligations as a mutual-benefit bailee. Proliance responded with evidence which, if believed, identifies the negligence of Lindsay Acura that allowed the theft. Accordingly the trial court improperly granted summary judgment to Lindsay Acura.

CASE QUESTION

1. Why was Lindsay Acura's rebuttal of the inference of negligence not sufficient to save it from liability?

In another bailment case, an employer operated a service garage for cars and large machines. It required that employees furnish their own tools. For the convenience of the employees and employer, the latter allowed workers to leave their toolboxes at the garage. Two employees' tools were stolen from the employer's storage area. The court found the employer accepted the plaintiff's tools for storage, and thus a bailment occurred. The failure of the employer to return the tools to the workers constituted a prima facie case of breach of the bailment agreement. The burden of proof then shifted to the bailee to establish that it exercised reasonable care. There was testimony that the office door had a dead-bolt lock, the garage door had a lock placed in the roller guide track so that the door could not be lifted, and some windows were covered with security bars. However, the window broken on the night of the theft did not have bars. That window measured four feet by eight feet in size and was four feet from the ground in an unlighted area. Further, the premises had no security system. The court ruled in favor of the employees stating, "Although there was evidence that appellant exercised some care, it was reasonable to conclude that appellant failed to exercise due care.[23]

Items Inside Bailed Property

Is a bailee liable when valuable property is located inside the bailed property and its presence is unknown to the bailee? For example, suppose you put a valuable ring in the pocket of your leather coat, which you leave with a hat-check attendant at a restaurant. You do not inform the attendant of the presence of the ring. The attendant took a coffee break, during which the coats were unattended. While the attendant was gone your coat was stolen. The restaurant will be liable for the value of the coat because it was negligent for leaving the garments unattended. Will the restaurant also be liable for the value of the lost ring?

The answer becomes obvious if you apply the elements necessary for a bailment. The bailee must knowingly accept possession of the property. In this example the hat-check attendant knowingly accepted possession of the coat. But did he knowingly accept possession of the ring? The answer, of course, is no; he did not even know of its existence. Therefore, the restaurant was not a bailee of the ring and will not be liable for its loss.

Similarly, when you park your car in a parking lot and leave the key with an attendant, if you fail to inform him of a valuable camera in the trunk, no bailment exists as to the camera. If the car is stolen due to the attendant's negligence, the parking lot will be liable to you for the value of the car. The outcome is quite different for the camera. Since no bailment of the camera existed, the parking lot is not liable for its loss.

In the case of *Dumlao v. Atlantic Garage, Inc.*, 259 A.2d 360 (D.C. 1969), the plaintiff checked into a hotel, removed clothing from the back seat of the car, and then delivered the car and key to an employee of the hotel for parking. The bell captain had observed the guest remove a cosmetic case from the trunk and from where he was positioned could not see anything else in the trunk. He asked if there was any more personal property in the car, but the guest did not respond. The car was then parked by a hotel employee in a nearby garage. A few days later when the plaintiff checked out, the hotel was unable to deliver his car or its contents, nor could it account for its disappearance. The car was located some time later, but drums claimed by the plaintiff to have been in the trunk were missing. The plaintiff sued the hotel for the loss, claiming the hotel was liable to him as a bailee.

---

[23] *Templeton v. DiPaolo Truck Services, Inc.*, 2001 WL 584310 (Oh. 2001)

The court determined a bailment existed between the plaintiff and the hotel as to both the car and any contents the hotel employees knew about. An employee would be aware of property in a car if the guest pointed it out or it was in plain view. Here, there was no evidence to show the hotel employee knew that drums were in the trunk. Therefore, there was no bailment of the drums, and the hotel was not liable.

One exception applies. Most cases hold that, although a bailee may not have known of specific property in a car, a bailment of that property will nonetheless exist if the bailee could reasonably anticipate that the property would be in the vehicle. For example, a country-club bailee should reasonably anticipate that the trunk of a car might contain golf clubs, tennis rackets, and sportswear.[24] Likewise, a bailee should reasonably expect that the trunk of a car might contain spare tires and jacks, but not massage equipment such as a portable massage-therapy table, massage oils, a portable cassette player, massage-therapy tapes, and sheets and towels.[25]

Rules Particular to Bailment of Cars

A hotelkeeper or restaurateur who takes care of a patron's car assumes a great responsibility. The value of an automobile can range from as low as a few hundred dollars to over $100,000. The limiting statutes do not apply to cars. Public parking lots often attempt to limit their liability for stolen or damaged cars by claiming on signs and parking receipts that they are not liable. Because of the quasi-public nature of the accommodations industry, hoteliers are not allowed to limit their liability for loss or damage to bailed property caused by their own negligence. Therefore, such disclaimers of liability on signs or receipts are not effective. The following case clearly illustrates this point.

CASE EXAMPLE 8-11

Ellerman v. Atlanta American Motor Hotel Corp.
191 S.E.2d 295 (Ga. 1972)

Plaintiff, a guest at a motor hotel operated by the defendant, placed his automobile in the defendant's parking facility. He was required by the defendant to leave the ignition key with the defendant's employee, and the latter parked the vehicle in an area unknown to plaintiff. At the time, plaintiff was given a claim check which plaintiff admitted reading. It provided in part as follows: "Liability. Cars parked at owner's risk. Articles left in car at owner's risk. We reserve privilege of moving car to other section of lot. No attendant after regular closing hours." Prior to delivering the ignition key and the car to the attendant, the plaintiff removed a raincoat from the interior, placed it in the trunk of the car, and kept the trunk key. When plaintiff checked out of the hotel, his car was found missing. The car and its contents have never been recovered.

---

[24] *Jack Bowles Services, Inc. v. Stavely*, 906 S.W.2d 185 (Tex. 1995)

[25] *Klonis v. Carroll*, 1991 WL 188693 (Tex. 1991)

Plaintiff's suit sought to recover the value of the items of personality contained in the trunk that he alleged were allowed to be stolen through the defendant's negligence. Plaintiff had been paid by his insurance company for the loss of the automobile. ...

The defendant contends that the depositing of the automobile with the defendant's attendant under these circumstances does not give rise to a bailment relationship because of the disclaimer of liability printed on the claim check given to plaintiff. He relies upon our decision in [a previous case] as controlling. As we view this issue, [that case] is not in point. [It] dealt with an ordinary parking lot. This case involves a parking facility operated by a motel as a part of its service, and this creates the relationship of innkeeper and guest. ...

It is recognized that an ordinary bailee by contract may limit or completely exculpate himself from any liability for loss or damage to the bailed property as a result of his own simple negligence.

However, an innkeeper is not an "ordinary" bailee. Many courts and texts have described an innkeeper as a "professional" bailee. ... Unlike an "ordinary" bailee, the "professional" bailee is often precluded from limiting by contract liability for his own negligence as violative of public policy. The reasoning utilized is that the public, in dealing with innkeepers, lacks a practical equality of bargaining power and may be coerced to accede to the contractual conditions sought by the innkeeper or else be denied the needed services. We think that both the principle precluding the limitation of liability and the reasoning underlying it are sound ... [A]ny ... contract purporting to ... exculpate the innkeeper is contrary to the public interest and policy and cannot be enforced.

CASE QUESTION

1. The court distinguishes between a hotel parking facility and a public parking lot. Why does the court make this differentiation?

A hotel with a parking lot or garage that takes possession of guests' car keys must establish effective security procedures and systems to avoid liability. The high cost of cars dictates the importance of proper management and planning.

An example of negligence on the part of a hotel when acting as bailee is leaving the ignition key in a parked, unattended car, unless the parking lot is carefully monitored at all times. Also, leaving in a place easily accessible to patrons a board or other device on which car keys are kept constitutes negligence. Easy access to car keys facilitates the thief's job. A much better practice is to place all the keys in a specified location accessible only to authorized employees.

We have discussed car bailments as involving transfer of the key. Customarily, if a person parks a car in a lot and retains the key, in the eyes of the law he has not delivered possession of the vehicle to the lot owner and therefore no bailment exists.

A case in Tennessee expanded, at least in that state, the circumstances under which leaving a car in a parking lot will be viewed as a bailment. A guest at a Hyatt Regency parked his car in the hotel parking garage, taking with him his key and a ticket received when he entered the garage. Upon his return, he discovered the car was missing. It has never been recovered. The owner sued the hotel for his loss. Without a bailment, the hotel would not be liable. Although the driver did not leave the key with the attendant, the court determined a bailment existed based on the particular facts of the case.

Entrance to the garage in question was made via a single entryway controlled by a ticket machine. A lone exit was controlled by an attendant in a booth located just opposite the entrance and in full view therefrom. The hotel hired security guards, two of whom were on duty most of the time. They wore a distinctive uniform so as to be easily identifiable and patrolled the hotel buildings and grounds. The guards were instructed to make rounds through the garage, although not at specified intervals. Finding from the facts that a bailment existed, the court said, "Appellee's vehicle was not driven into an unattended or open parking area. Rather is was driven into an enclosed, indoor, attended commercial garage which not only had an attendant controlling the exit but regular security personnel to patrol the premises for safety."[26]

This case is not widely followed by other states. Most cases involving parking lots require a transfer of the car key to the lot attendant for a bailment to exist.

Liability for a Patron's Property in a Restaurant, Bar, or Cloakroom

The only portion of many limiting liability statutes that apply to a restaurant or bar covers no-fee checkrooms where the customer is given a receipt for the checked property. In all other circumstances, the only basis for liability for lost property in a restaurant or bar is bailment. As the next case illustrates, if a bailment does not exist and the patron did not receive a receipt, the bar is not liable.

CASE EXAMPLE 8-12

Kuchinsky v. Empire Lounge, Inc.
134 N.W.2d 436 (Wis. 1965)

Kuchinsky entered the Empire Lounge as a customer and hung his coat on a clothes tree near his table. His coat was stolen while he ate. ...

The rule ... is that before a restaurant keeper will be held liable for the loss of an overcoat of a customer while such customer takes a meal or refreshments, it must appear ... that the overcoat was placed in the physical custody of the keeper of the restaurant or his servants, in which cases there is an actual bailment. ...

In [another case], the plaintiff was a guest at a luncheon held at the defendant's hotel. She hung her mink jacket in an unattended cloak-room on the main floor across from the lobby desk. After the luncheon and ensuing party, the plaintiff went to the cloakroom to retrieve her jacket and discovered it was gone. The court held that no negligence had been established against the defendant and stated: "... In any event, we do not feel that it is incumbent upon a hotel or restaurant owner to keep an attendant in charge of a free cloakroom for luncheon or dinner guests or otherwise face liability for loss of articles placed therein. The maintenance of such rooms without attendants is a common practice, and where the proprietor had not accepted control and custody of articles placed therein, no duty rests upon him to exercise any special degree of care with respect thereto. ..."

Ruling of the Court: [Complaint dismissed]

---

[26]*Allen v. Hyatt Regency-Nashville Hotel*, 668 S.W.2d 286 (Tenn. 1984)

In another case, a diner whose coat had fallen off his chair was directed by the waitress to hang it in an unattended cloak room. The coat was stolen from the room and the patron sued. The court held the restaurant was not liable because the coat had not been delivered to or accepted by the restaurant and so a bailment was never created.[27]

If a bailment does exist, the hotel or restaurant will be liable if it fails to exercise the necessary care. In the following case, the restaurant learned this rule of law the hard way. The case also illustrates a **constructive bailment**, which is a bailment created by law as a result of special circumstances rather than by agreement between the parties. A constructive bailment, like a mutual-benefit bailment, requires the bailee to exercise reasonable care of the bailed goods. In this case, a constructive bailment was created where a restaurant patron mistakenly left her pocketbook by her table when she departed and it was found by an employee.

CASE EXAMPLE 8-13

Shamrock Hilton Hotel v. Caranas
488 S.W.2d 151 (Tex. 1972)

... Plaintiffs, husband and wife, were lodging as paying guests at the Shamrock Hilton Hotel in Houston on the evening of September 4, 1966, when they took their dinner in the hotel restaurant. After completing the meal, Mr. and Mrs. Caranas, plaintiffs, departed the dining area leaving her purse behind. The purse was found by the hotel busboy who, pursuant to the instructions of the hotel, dutifully delivered the forgotten item to the restaurant cashier, a Mrs. Luster. The testimony indicates that some short time thereafter, the cashier gave the purse to a man other than Mr. Caranas who came to claim it. There is no testimony on the question of whether identification was sought by the cashier. The purse allegedly contained $5.00 in cash, some credit cards, and ten pieces of jewelry said to be worth $13,062. The misplacement of the purse was realized the following morning, at which time plaintiffs notified the hotel authorities of the loss.

Plaintiffs filed suit, alleging negligent delivery of the purse to an unknown person and seeking a recovery for the value of the purse and its contents. ...

[W]e find that there was indeed a constructive bailment of the purse. The delivery and acceptance were evidenced in the acts of Mrs. Caranas' unintentionally leaving her purse behind in the hotel restaurant and the busboy, a hotel employee, picking it up and taking it to the cashier, who accepted the purse as a lost or misplaced item. The delivery need not be knowingly intended on the part of Mrs. Caranas if it is apparent that were she ... aware of the circumstances (here the purse being misplaced), she would have desired the person finding the article to have kept it safely for its subsequent return to her.

As stated above, the evidence conclusively showed facts from which there was established a bailment with the Caranases as bailors and the hotel as bailee. The evidence also showed that the hotel, as bailee, had received Mrs. Caranas' purse and had not returned it on demand. Such evidence raised a presumption that the hotel had failed to exercise ordinary care in protecting the appellees' property. When the hotel failed to come forward with any evidence to the effect that it had exercised ordinary care ... the appellees' proof ripened into proof by which the hotel's primary liability was established as a matter of law.

Further, this bailment was one for the mutual benefit of both parties. Appellees were paying guests in the hotel and in its dining room. Appellant hotel's practice of keeping patrons'

---

[27] *Black Beret Lounge and Restaurant v. Meisnere*, 336 A.2d 532 (D.C. 1975)

lost personal items until they could be returned to their rightful owners, as reflected in the testimony, is certainly evidence of its being incidental to its business, as we would think it would be for almost any commercial enterprise that caters to the general public. Though no direct charge is made for this service, there is indirect benefit to be had in the continued patronage of the hotel by customers who have lost chattels and who have been able to claim them from the management.

Having found this to have been a bailment for the mutual benefit of the parties, we hold that the appellants owed the appellees the duty of reasonable care in the return of the purse and jewelry, and the hotel is therefore liable for its ordinary negligence.

Ruling of the Court: [J]udgment for plaintiff.

In another case also ostensibly involving forgotten property, the plaintiff guest placed in his room a paper bag filled with $9,000 in cash and left the hotel temporarily. The housekeeper found the money while cleaning the room. Seeing no personal effects of the guests in the room, she wrongly assumed he had checked out. Consistent with hotel procedure for lost property, she gave the money to her immediate supervisor, who in turn gave it to the general supervisor. He absconded with the money, which was never recovered. The general supervisor had been employed by the hotel for three years and had in that time been given items of value to turn into the office on several occasions. He had consistently done so until the time in question. The guest sued the hotel; it denied liability for the full $9,000, based on the limiting statute. The plaintiff argued the hotel should be liable, notwithstanding the statute, on a bailment theory since it took possession of the money for safekeeping. The court hedged on whether the law of bailment should supersede the limiting statute, but stated that even if bailment law applied, the hotel was not negligent and therefore would not be liable because the housekeeper and her supervisor gave the money to the proper person and that person had always acted responsibly with regard to guests' valuables in the past. The court further held the hotel was not liable for the general supervisor's theft of the money on a respondeat superior theory since, when he stole the money, he was acting outside the scope of his employment. Instead, the hotel's liability was limited by the statute.[28] A significant factual difference between this case and *Shamrock* is that in *Shamrock* the bailee of the purse was negligent; in this case the court held the bailee was not.

Checkrooms

Many hotels, restaurants, clubs, concert halls, museums, and other public businesses have checkrooms available to safeguard guests' valuables. A bailment between the customer who leaves property with a checkroom attendant and the facility is created. The attendant on duty accepts patrons' garments or other property and issues a receipt as proof that the property was delivered. In many states,

---

[28] *Gordon v. Day's Inn*, 395 S.E.2d 876 (Ga. 1990)

the limiting liability laws cover attended checkrooms and baggage rooms and limit the restaurant or hotel's liability for losses occurring there. In New York, for example, the maximum liability for a checked item is $200.

If the coatroom is unattended, the limited liability statute is not applicable. Since typically no bailment arises when a coatroom is unattended, the hotel or restaurant will customarily have no liability for property lost or stolen there.

The following case involves Studio 54, a once-famous upscale New York City disco. (A movie about the club was produced in 1999.) The case addresses three issues: (1) the liability of a discotheque when a coat is missing from the coatroom; (2) the effect of a sign in a coatroom purporting to limit liability for lost articles; and (3) the method for calculating damages when a coat is missing. The case addresses many of the issues we have studied—bailments, limiting liability statutes, and conspicuous notice. This case again highlights the courts' restrictive reading of limited liability statutes. As we have seen repeatedly in this chapter, unless all the terms of the statute are satisfied, the limitation of liability is not applicable.

CASE EXAMPLE 8-14

Conboy v. Studio 54, Inc.
449 N.Y.S.2d 391 (1982)

The issue that I must decide is whether the [New York limiting liability statute] provides a monetary haven for a discotheque. ...

On January 23, 1982, the claimant, his wife and a group of friends convened for a party at Studio 54 (Studio) in Manhattan. Studio, licensed by the New York City Department of Consumer Affairs as a cabaret, is a discotheque, where patrons dance to recorded music usually played continuously on high fidelity equipment. ... Often a psychedelic light show accompanies the music and provides background and impetus for the free-spirited patrons who pay $18 per person to dance to the deafening and often overwhelming disco music played continuously on the sophisticated sound system. ...

No food is sold or served here—not even a single peanut or pretzel to accompany the alcoholic and soft drinks available for purchase.

The Conboy party checked their coats, 14 in all, with the coatroom attendant. They received 7 check stubs after paying the 75¢ charge per coat. A bailment of the coats was created.

After their evening of revelry, they attempted to reclaim their coats. Mr. Conboy's one-month old, $1,350 leather coat was missing. It has not been found and accordingly, he has sued Studio for $1,350.

Under traditional bailment law, once the goods were delivered, the failure of the bailee (Studio) to return them on demand created a *prima facie* case of negligence. The burden of coming forward with evidence tending to show due care shifted to Studio. Studio did not come forward with any evidence to meet this burden. Mr. Conboy is entitled to a judgment.

Studio, relying on [New York's limiting liability statute], contends that its liability is limited to $75. Its argument is incorrect ...

The statute offers innkeepers and restaurant proprietors who comply with it a reduction of the innkeeper's common law insurer-liability as to guest's property deposited with them.

That being said, it need only be noted that the statute offers its protection to restaurants, hotels and motels, not discotheques which appear to be modern-day versions of dance halls.

Simply put, a discotheque may qualify as a restaurant but there is no logic in giving it that classification unless one of its principal activities is the furnishing of meals. Certainly, Studio should not be classified as a restaurant, because it serves no food. ...

The limitations on liability set forth in the statute are therefore not applicable here. ...

Studio claims however that their liability may nevertheless be limited by the posting of a sign in the coatroom. The sign states: "Liability for lost property in this coat/check room is limited to $100 per loss of misplaced article."...

[T]he posting of the sign [is not] a useless act, for it may still function as a common law disclaimer. To bind Conboy to this limitation, I must find however that he had notice of the terms of the disclaimer and agreed to it. Studio did not establish that the sign was posted in a conspicuous manner. I hold that Conboy is not bound by the posted disclaimer of liability.

As to damages, Conboy is entitled to the "real value" of the coat. Real value, especially with respect to used clothing or household furnishings that are lost or damaged is not necessarily its market value which presumably would reflect a deduction for depreciation. In fact, the real value may be measured by the price paid when new for the lost or damaged goods.

One commentator has offered a reason that the strict market value approach is not favored:

> No judge buys his clothing second hand and none would expect any owner to replace his clothing in a second hand store. Hence no judge expects to limit the cost of replacing clothing to a market no one should be expected to use.

I therefore hold that Conboy may be compensated on a basis that will permit him to replace the very same coat purchased new— $1,350.

Judgment for claimant in the sum of $1,350.

CASE QUESTIONS

1. Why did the limiting liability statute not apply in this case?

2. Why did the disclaimer sign hung by Studio 54 not relieve the discotheque from liability?

3. If Conboy's coat was three years old rather than one month, do you think the court would have awarded him its full value of $1,350? Why or Why not?

Concessionaires

Often a hotel or perhaps a restaurant will contract with a **concessionaire** (an independent contractor) to operate the checking facilities (luggage and coats). Usually the concessionaire pays the hotel a fee in exchange for the business opportunity. Such an arrangement saves the hotel from having to manage and staff the checking operations. Several plaintiffs whose checked property was not returned from concessionaires have argued that the concessionaire is not entitled to the benefits of the limiting statutes because those statutes were designed to protect only innkeepers and restaurateurs. Courts have accepted this argument and denied the concessionaire limited liability in *Aldrich v. Waldorf Astoria Hotel, Inc.*, 343 N.Y.S.2d 830 (1973) and *Jacobson v. Belplaza Corp.*, 80 F.Supp. 917 (N.Y. 1949).

Key Terms

act of God
bailee
bailment
bailment for the sole benefit of
   the bailee
bailment for the sole benefit of
   the bailor
bailor
concessionaire
conspicuous

constructive bailment
equitable estoppel
infra hospitium
limiting liability statute
merchandise samples
mutual-benefit bailment
prima facie evidence
prima facie liability rule
public enemy

Summary

The liability of hotels and restaurants for their guests' and patrons' property has appropriately changed over time. The common law imposed unlimited liability on inns and food establishments. Most states have since passed limiting statutes that significantly reduce this liability.

For money, jewels, and securities, limiting statutes typically require that hotels provide safes and post notices in prescribed places announcing the availability of the safes and the hotel's limited liability. The specifics of these statutes vary from state to state. Only if the hotel strictly complies with the statutory requirements will it benefit from limited liability.

For other property a guest brings to a hotel, such as clothes or sporting equipment, limiting statutes provide limited liability for hotels unless the loss is caused by the hotel's negligence. If it is, the hotel will typically be liable for the full value of the missing property. An exception is the state of Nevada, which limits the liability of innkeepers even when they are negligent.

For property not covered by the limiting statutes, the liability of a hotel or restaurant is based on laws regarding bailment. If no bailment exists, the business is not liable for loss or theft of property. If a bailment does exist, the hotel or restaurant will be liable for the loss only if it failed to exercise the requisite degree of care for the bailed goods. The level of care required varies depending on whether the bailment is for the sole benefit of the bailor, the sole benefit of the bailee, or a mutual-benefit bailment. If the hotel or restaurant renders the care required, the establishment will be free from liability even though property is stolen or otherwise disappears.

Preventive Law Tips for Managers

■ *Identify the specific requirements of your state's limiting liability statute and follow them exactingly.* The limiting statutes relieve a hotel from common law strict liability. The statutes are generally not applicable unless the hotel follows their mandates exactly. Most states' statutes require that the hotel provide a safe and post notice conspicuously in specified places announcing the availability of the safe and the hotel's limited liability. To qualify under the statutes, a hotel safe must be secure and capable of withstanding burglary attempts. It should be available to guests twenty-four hours a day. Anything less jeopardizes the relief from full liability provided by the statutes.

The posted notices must not only inform the guest of the safe's availability, but must also state that if goods are lost or stolen from the safe, the hotel's liability will be limited. The notices must be posted each and every place the statute requires. For example, if the statute mandates posting by the registration desk, in the lobby, and in guest rooms, posting in less than all three locations is inadequate in most states and will not protect the hotel from unlimited liability. The notice must also be conspicuous, meaning easily seen and easy to read. A notice hidden behind lobby furniture or in a nonobvious place in the guest room will not satisfy the statute. In these circumstances, the hotel will be liable for the full value of the lost property.

Individual states may have additional requirements. For example, some states require "suitable" locks or bolts on the doors of guest rooms and "suitable" fastenings on windows and transoms. Check your state statute carefully and make sure your establishment is in full compliance. Loss through inadvertence or carelessness of the very significant benefit offered by these statutes is inexcusable.

■ *Train appropriate employees how to use the safe.* If a guest is unable to place valuables in the safe because staff does not know how to operate it, the safe is not "available" to the guest as required by statute and the hotel will have unlimited liability. Employees should be well trained on use of the safe and the importance of its being available around the clock. If an employee does not correctly operate the safe or fails to follow hotel procedures for its use, thefts may be facilitated.

■ *Instruct employees about the hotel's limited liability and the importance of their not overstating that liability.* The consequence of an employee exaggerating a hotel's liability for property stored in a safe may be that the hotel has unlimited liability. The only way to avoid the principle of estoppel from curtailing the limiting statutes' applicability is by ensuring your employees do not misstate the hotel's liability. Training and frequent reminders about the benefits of the statutes and what constitutes appropriate comments to guests about liability should minimize this potential problem.

■ *Adopt procedures to limit thefts of property from the safe.* While the limiting liability statutes remove much of the liability a hotel would otherwise have when property is missing from a safe, such losses are costly to the hotel in terms of good customer relations. Efforts should be made to minimize this loss. Security measures concerning the safes should be reviewed and updated regularly. The number of employees with access to the safes should be limited (but not too limited because guests must have access around the clock for limited liability to apply). Tight control should be maintained of keys to the safe and records that identify contents of the safe. Other security measures appropriate to the particular circumstances of your establishment should be instituted.

■ *Regularly review procedures followed in checkrooms to minimize chances of theft.* Many thefts in hotels and restaurants occur in the baggage checkroom or the coat-check area. Access to these rooms should be limited. Attendants should be instructed not to leave unless another attendant is available. They should be trained always to require a receipt or other proof of ownership before returning goods. The checkrooms should be equipped with security devices to enable attendants to notify security unobtrusively if a theft is in progress.

■ *Develop and strictly enforce procedures for parking guests' cars.* Employees assigned to parking customers' cars should be screened for driving abilities and criminal records for theft or crimes relating to driving, such as driving while intoxicated and reckless driving. Their training should stress the importance of driving patrons' cars carefully. The establishment should have procedures for handling car keys designed to avoid loss or theft. The hotel should maintain adequate insurance to cover its potential liability for violation of a bailee's responsibilities.

■ *If the coat room is unattended, hang a sign stating the hotel is not liable.* The sign alerts the customer that the establishment will not cover the loss; instead, the patron leaves the goods at his or her own risk. This may motivate the patron to take extra precautions to avoid the disappointment of a loss.

■ *Adopt procedures enabling the hotel or restaurant, when acting as bailee, to prove reasonable care.* The law of bailment creates a presumption of negligence on the part of the bailee if the bailor can prove delivery of property, acceptance by the bailee, and damage to or loss of the property. The bailee can rebut the presumption of negligence by showing it used reasonable care while in possession of the goods. Procedures for ensuring safekeeping should be developed and enforced so that the hotel can prove it exercised reasonable care.

■ *If a concessionaire operates the checkrooms, the contract should require safety procedures be utilized and insurance be obtained.* A concessionaire can damage a restaurant or hotel's reputation. A guest is hardly ever aware that a service is being offered by someone other than the hotel or restaurant. When a guest's property is stolen, the guest views the wrongdoer as the hotel, not the concessionaire. The hotel thus has a public relations interest in ensuring that concessionaires do not engage in conduct likely to alienate patrons. The hotel should be vigilant to ensure the concessionaire's practices maximize security and minimize theft. The contract should require that specified security procedures be followed and also that the concessionaire purchase insurance to cover its unlimited liability.

Review Questions

1. According to common law, what is the innkeeper's liability for a guest's lost or stolen property?

2. What is a limiting liability statute?

3. What two key facts must be included in a notice posted pursuant to most limiting liability statutes?

4. Which of the following types of property are covered by limiting liability statutes that require hotels to maintain a safe?

   A. Jewelry

   B. Cash

   C. A laptop (portable) computer

   D. Diamond cufflinks

   E. Expensive sporting equipment

   F. Clothes

5. What is the consequence of a guest failing to put valuables in a safe?

6. What is estoppel? What is its relevance to a hotel's liability for lost property?

7. At what point in the check-in process does a limiting liability statute become effective?

8. What is a bailment?

9. What is the difference between a bailment for the sole benefit of the bailor and a bailment for the sole benefit of the bailee?

10. What is the difference between a mutual-benefit bailment and a bailment for hire?

11. If you leave a watch with the jeweler to be repaired, who is the bailor and who is the bailee?

12. Does a bailment exist between a hotel and a guest when the guest goes out for the evening and leaves property in her room?

Discussion Questions

1. Describe two possible circumstances in which a hotel that provides a safe to its guests fails to satisfy the statutory requirements for a safe.

2. The Mandan Hotel posts the notice required by the limiting statute in the bathroom of guest rooms on the inside door of the medicine cabinet. Has the hotel posted the notice conspicuously? Why or why not? Suppose the notice is placed inside the top dresser drawer near free hotel stationery. Is this conspicuous posting? Why or why not?

3. Jan ate dinner at the Demrich Restaurant. After dinner she paid the cashier and went home without realizing she had left her purse at the restaurant. What liability does the restaurant have if the cashier does not notice the purse and it is stolen? What liability does the restaurant have if the cashier takes possession of the purse intending to notify Jan that it is at the restaurant?

4. Compare the liability of a hotel and a concessionaire for coats checked in a cloakroom.

5. Demitri left his coat with an attendant in the coat-check area of a restaurant. In his coat pocket was a lotto ticket. Does a bailment exist for the lotto ticket? Why or why not?

Application Questions

1. A limiting statute requires that a hotel post the necessary notice in the registration area, in the hotel lobby, and in the guest rooms. If a hotel posts the notice in the registration area and in guest rooms but fails to post in the lobby, will the hotel be entitled to limited liability? Why or why not?

2. A guest arrives at a hotel and informs the desk clerk that she has with her a large amount of cash. She expresses concern for its safety, and the clerk recommends she place it in a hotel safe deposit box. When she hesitates, he assures her that the money will be protected and further, even if it does become lost the hotel will be fully liable. Relying on this assurance, she deposits the money in the safe deposit box. When she sought to retrieve the money it had disappeared and has not been recovered. Is the hotel entitled to limited liability under these circumstances? Why or why not?

3. Terry is a law-book salesperson. She is attending a conference of lawyers and has brought with her approximately $5,000 worth of book samples. What must she do vis-a-vis the hotel to obtain maximum protection for the books? What if she fails to do so?

4. Sandra is talking to the front-desk clerk and is in the process of checking out. While she is reviewing the bill, someone steals her briefcase, which was on the ground near her feet. The briefcase had in it various documents she needed for work, a spare pair of glasses, and a necklace with diamonds in it. Will the hotel be liable for the loss of any of these items? Why or why not?

Web Sites

Web sites that will enhance your understanding of the material in this chapter include:

http://www.nolo.com/lawcenter/faqs Once on this site, click on *Consumer & Travel*, then scroll down to *Hotels and Other Accommodations FAQ*. Several questions and answers address legal issues associated with guests whose property was stolen from a hotel or whose car was damaged while parked at a hotel.

http://www.palmersecurity.com This is one of numerous vendor sites that promote hotel safes for installation in guest rooms.

For additional resources, visit our Web site
www.hospitality-tourism.delmar.com

CHAPTER 9

■

Rights of Innkeepers

CHAPTER OUTLINE

■

INTRODUCTION

This chapter focuses on the innkeeper's rights including room selection; entry into guests' rooms; eviction of guests; and pursuing a nonpaying guest.

While patrons are the lifeblood of hotels and restaurants, an unruly or belligerent customer can interfere with the enjoyment of other patrons and damage the reputation of the business. Hotels and restaurants may not want to serve such people.

In this chapter we will explore the circumstances under which a hotelkeeper or restaurateur can refuse a would-be customer accommodations or a meal or evict a guest. The chapter also discusses how to evict and how not to evict. Overzealous action can lead to a lawsuit accusing the proprietor of assault, false arrest, slander, or false imprisonment.

Occasionally guests are discontent with their room. We will learn in this chapter that the innkeeper owes no legal duty to guests to accommodate their room preferences. Sometimes patrons do not pay their bill or pay by fraudulent means. The law arms hospitality proprietors with various methods to secure payment, including the innkeeper's lien and criminal charges of theft of services, possession of stolen property, forgery, or issuing a bad check. This chapter discusses these legal rights and remedies.

As you read the cases you will likely note that many are relatively old. This is because many of the issues in this chapter have not been the subject of recent lawsuits. The older cases remain viable precedents.

Right to Exclude Nonguests

Generally, innkeepers and restaurateurs extend an implied invitation or license to all, including nonguests, to enter their facility. Therefore, the public's presence on the premises does not constitute **trespass**, which is a legal wrong consisting of entering or remaining unlawfully on a premises. This implied license for nonguests can be revoked by the innkeeper at any time. Persons entering a hotel who are not guests and do not intend to become one are required to leave the premises if asked. Similarly, a restaurateur can ask a person to leave who is not intending to eat or drink, but rather is just lingering, loitering, or otherwise "hanging out." A person who has been requested to leave and fails to do so after being given a reasonable opportunity becomes a trespasser.

The operator may use reasonable force to evict a trespasser, but only after the trespasser has been asked to leave and refuses. The amount of force that can be used is limited by law. Only that amount of force that is reasonably necessary to remove the trespasser from the premises is permitted. **Excessive force** will subject the hotelier or restaurateur to liability; the trespasser will be able to sue the business for injuries that result.

When ejecting troublesome customers, the best practice, if time permits, is to call the police. Officers are trained in how to effectuate the removal of a troublesome patron. In the following case, the defendants were charged with the criminal violation of disorderly conduct for proselytizing door-to-door at a hotel. The innkeeper wisely sought the assistance of the police to remove the defendants.

CASE EXAMPLE 9-1

People v. Thorpe
101 N.Y.S.2d 986 (1950)

Defendants are charged with the offense of disorderly conduct in violation of ... the Penal Law. They are members of a religious group known as Jehovah's Witnesses. Each of these defendants asserts that he is a minister of the gospel and preaches from door to door under the direction of the Watchtower Bible and Tract Society, Inc., a corporation established by law for religious purposes.

Defendants entered the Endicott Hotel located at 81st Street and Columbus Avenue, New York City, at 10:30 A.M. on Saturday morning, February 4, 1950. Defendant Thorpe proceeded to the second floor and defendant VanDyk to the top floor of the hotel. Each went from door to door down the hotel corridors, knocking to gain the attention of the hotel guests, and, upon the door being opened, sought to impart to each person thus approached the religious doctrines advocated by the Jehovah's Witnesses. Literature was tendered by the defendants consisting of a book, booklet, and magazine. Contributions, if not actively solicited, were certainly encouraged and, in any event, were admittedly accepted.

Defendants continued their mission until halted by the hotel manager. They conducted their activities as quietly as possible and seemingly without undue annoyance of the hotel residents. When the hotel manager learned of their presence, he asked defendants summarily to desist. The defendant Thorpe explained that he considered it his constitutional right to preach from door to door, which was, he claimed, established as an appropriate method of preaching in accordance with the tenets of his faith. Defendants refused to leave the hotel, whereupon a police officer was summoned who, upon arrival, informed defendant Thorpe that the hotel management had a right to insist that the defendants' activities stop and that they forthwith leave the hotel. Defendant replied that he had a right to stay there and, admittedly, told the officer then in uniform, "If I was to leave, he would have to put me under arrest."

In the meantime, the hotel manager located defendant VanDyk pursuing his activities on one of the upper floors. He was requested to leave the hotel. Defendant VanDyk thereupon went down to the hotel lobby with the manager, the police officer, and defendant Thorpe, who had been escorted by the policeman to the street. The hotel manager admonished defendants that they could not return to the hotel. ... Defendants insisted that it was their right to preach in the hotel and, admittedly, "returned shortly to the hotel with the intention of resuming their preaching activity."...

It is urged that a conviction will result in abridgement of the liberties of press and worship guaranteed by the United States Constitution.

It was long ago held that "from the very nature of the business, it is inevitable" that a hotel owner "must, at all reasonable times and for all proper purposes" have "control over every part" of the hotel, "even though separate parts thereof may be occupied by guests for hire." ... The hotel management rightfully may exercise control designed to serve the convenience, comfort, or safety of guests and their property. A person who is not a guest "has in general no legal right to enter or remain" in the hotel against the will of the management.

The hotel management may guard against the possible dangers and annoyances of trespassers or unsolicited visits, and to that end it may, and it is common knowledge that it usually does, exclude all uninvited visitors from the private hotel corridors and from gaining access to the private accommodations of the hotel guests, regardless of whether the one excluded is actually engaged in an otherwise lawful mission, be it commercial, political, or religious.

It was entirely proper for the hotel management to enforce that policy here. That some or even many of the hotel guests may not have found the preaching activities of the defendants objectionable did not deprive the hotel manager of the right to compel observances of such policy. ...

Greater vigilance is normally demanded and expected of a hotel in the adoption of measures designed to serve the comfort, convenience, and especially the privacy of its guests, as well as their safety and the safety of their property.

The hotel manager, hence, rightfully halted the defendants' preaching activities and justifiably summoned police aid in ejecting them from the hotel. After they were ejected, and notwithstanding that they were admonished not to return to the hotel by the police officer, the defendants, nonetheless, did return for the express purpose of proceeding with their activities, announcing that they proposed to do so unless arrested. ... Defendants' conduct, "at the very least, was such that it tended to disturb the public peace and quiet and to occasion a breach of the peace. That, under our cases, is sufficient."...

Ruling of the Court: The defendants are found guilty.

Since the decision in the *Thorpe* case in 1950, Congress has enacted the Civil Rights Act of 1964, which we studied in Chapter 3. The Act renders hotels and restaurants places of "public accommodation" and as such they cannot discriminate against persons because of race, color, religion, or national origin. Could Thorpe successfully argue today that he was denied equal access to the hotel because of religion in violation of the Civil Rights Act? The answer would be no, provided the hotel barred all door-to-door solicitors and not just religious proselytizers. The reason the hotel evicted Thorpe was not his religion, but rather his action of engaging in door-to-door solicitations. Excluding all persons who seek to solicit a hotel's guests does not constitute illegal discrimination.

Refusing a Guest Lodging

A general rule is that a hotel cannot refuse accommodations to anyone seeking them. A hotel with vacancies must provide accommodations for all who seek them with limited exceptions. This is true regardless of the hour of the guest's arrival. The exceptions that allow an inn to refuse to provide a room include criminals, would-be guests who are intoxicated and disorderly, those who are unclean and unkempt, and people with easily-spread contagious diseases.

Some states impose by statute a fine for refusing a room to a would-be guest. The reason for this rule is steeped in history. In olden days, the means of travel was horse and buggy, the number of hotels was very limited, and thieves were prevalent along the roads in the night. If a traveler was refused accommodations at one hotel, he might not arrive at the next hotel until very late or be forced to travel throughout the night. He would thus be exposed to considerable risk.

Several exceptions to the general rule exist, in which circumstances a hotelkeeper can legitimately refuse to provide lodging. If a hotel has no vacancies it may refuse a would-be guest. "No vacancies" can exist even though some rooms are not occupied, provided those rooms are legitimately out of service, as where they are being painted, refurbished, or repaired or the unoccupied rooms are being held for reservations. A hotel that refuses accommodations to someone seeking a room and later the same day accepts a different guest will have to explain its actions if challenged by the person who was turned away or by a governmental agency that enforces the civil rights laws. Without a good explanation, the hotel may be liable for violation of its general duty to provide accommodations to all who seek them or for discrimination.

The hotelkeeper can also refuse persons who are criminals, intoxicated, disorderly, unclean (not bathed), or suffering from a contagious disease. The explanation for the innkeeper's right to exclude these categories of people is the hotelier's duty to protect the well-being of its guests. Would-be guests who meet the descriptions may cause existing guests disruption, injury, or disease. The courts have also allowed innkeepers to refuse known persons of bad reputation because of the effect such guests may have on the stature of the hotel. Likewise, the innkeeper can deny a room to a prospective guest who is not able or willing to pay in advance a reasonable price for a room for the duration of the intended stay. If the person seeks an available room for five days, but can only prove ability to pay for one, the innkeeper must provide him with a room for one night. If the would-be guest cannot show means to pay for even one night, the innkeeper can legally refuse to provide that person a room.

A hotel can also refuse to accommodate guests with firearms, explosives, or pets. In recent years, all states have adopted statutes that forbid refusing services to a person with a seeing-eye dog. Many of these statutes have been expanded to include service animals that aid sighted but otherwise disabled people. The Americans with Disabilities Act, a federal law discussed in Chapter 3, likewise requires a hotel to accommodate seeing-eye dogs and other service animals.

The Consequences of Wrongful Refusal

What are the consequences of wrongfully refusing a guest? The excluded guest can sue the hotel for damages, which may include additional expenses of staying elsewhere. If the refusal is based on race, color, religion, sex, or disability, most state statutes have penalty clauses requiring the hotel to pay a fine for the wrongful exclusion in addition to any damages suffered by the would-be guest. The remedy under the federal civil rights law is an injunction barring further illegal discrimination.

Age

Age is not a protected class in places of public accommodation under federal civil rights laws or most state laws. Therefore, restaurateurs can refuse to serve a young person if they are so inclined. While most restaurants would have little motivation to refuse service to a child accompanied by an adult, they may be less willing to serve a table full of young people, perhaps because of concern for rowdiness or inability to pay. A few jurisdictions have statutes prohibiting discrimination against young people in places of public accommodation. An example is Washington, D.C. (D.C. Code § 2-1402.31).

The innkeeper is in a situation different from the restaurateur. The innkeeper has a common law duty to provide accommodations to anyone seeking them, except people within the exceptions just discussed in the section of this chapter entitled "Refusing a Guest Lodging." Thus, a young person is entitled to hotel accommodations unless an exception applies.

In Chapter 4 we learned that a minor can cancel a contract and, in many states, avoid partial or even full payment. Is an innkeeper at risk for not being paid when a room is rented to a minor? The answer is no, for two reasons. First, as we studied, although minors may cancel their contracts, they remain liable for the reasonable value of necessities they receive. Food and shelter are normally considered necessities. Further, parents are liable for necessities furnished to their minor children. Thus, if the minor refuses to pay, the hotel can pursue the minor's parents.

Selecting Accommodations for a Guest

The determination of which room will be assigned to a guest has always been the innkeeper's prerogative. All hotel rooms are different from each other, even though they may be furnished identically and be of the same or similar size. In many instances, the room location is important to a guest—its view, proximity to the lobby, the floor it is on, or other factors affect its appeal. While a hotel might be well-advised to accommodate guest preferences for purposes of customer satisfaction, guests have no legal recourse if denied their preference. The following case illustrates this rule.

CASE EXAMPLE 9-2

Nixon v. Royal Coach Inn of Houston
464 S.W.2d 900 (Tex. 1971)

... On December 4, 1968, Virginia Key Nixon was twenty-eight years of age, married, and in the employ of General Electric Company of Dallas as a systems analyst. On this particular day her work required her to come to Houston. She drove her automobile from Dallas to Houston and, arriving after it was dark, checked in the Royal Coach Inn alone at approximately 8:30 P.M. A motel employee directed her to the room to which she was assigned, which was some distance away from the main desk. After depositing her luggage in her room, she left the hotel to eat outside the motel area. Approximately one hour later, she returned to the motel, parked her car in the parking lot in the rear of the motel, and entered the building. She ascended the stairs and, while in the process of unlocking the door to her room, was attacked by an unknown assailant. She testified that though she did not lose consciousness, everything went black, and then she started screaming. It was at this time that she saw an unidentified man running down the hall in the direction of the main desk. Her screams brought no assistance, but she was able to reach the office switchboard through the phone in her room. Individuals came to her assistance in response to her phone call.

In her original petition, appellant [Nixon] alleged that appellee [the motel] was negligent [for] ..."(1) billeting a single woman in a remote room in a desolate area of the motel."

An innkeeper is not an insurer of the safety of its guests. An innkeeper's responsibility to his guests is limited to the exercise of ordinary or reasonable care. We are cited to no authority that requires an innkeeper to assign any guest to a particular room or to any particular part of a hotel or motel. Nor has our attention been directed to any part of the record that would indicate that the appellant was in fact billeted in a remote or desolate area of the motel. ...

Ruling of the Court: The judgment of the trial court is affirmed for the defendant.

Good customer relations may influence room-assignment decisions. For example, some guests are superstitious and wish to avoid the 13th floor. Others may request an ocean view. If a guest asks for a particular floor or view, the hotel is not under any legal obligation to honor the request, but may seek to do so in an effort to please the patron. If a guest's request is based on a disability, such as a desire to be in a room near an elevator because of difficulty walking, the Americans with Disability Act, studied in Chapter 3, requires the hotel to make reasonable efforts to accommodate the guest.

Changing a Guest's Accommodations

Once a room is assigned to a guest, can an innkeeper require the guest to change rooms? Only two cases have been reported on this issue and both allow the innkeeper to change the room. In an early Canadian case, *Doyle v. Walker*, 26 U.C.Q.B. 502 (1867), the plaintiff-guest sued the defendant hotel for trespassing and taking his goods from the room he was originally assigned and moving them to another room. The court said the hotelkeeper has the right to select the room for the guest and, if expedient, to change it. This ruling was followed in *Hervey v. Hart*, 42 So. 1013 (Ala. 1906), in which the court held that an innkeeper would not be liable for moving a guest "if he offered plaintiff proper accommodations in lieu of the room previously assigned to him." Further, the hotelkeeper does not become a trespasser while transferring the guest's belongings.

It is not good policy to change a room or move a guest's possessions without notice and permission. Recognizing that room changes are disruptive to the guest, they should be avoided unless the reasons are compelling. If a switch cannot be prevented, the preferred approach would be to inform the guest of the impending change and provide an explanation.

Entering a Guest's Room

Most courts hold that when guests are assigned a room, they are to be the sole occupants during their stay. The innkeeper retains the right of access only for such reasonable purposes as may be necessary in the conduct of the hotel such as normal maintenance and repair, imminent danger, nonpayment, and when entry is requested by the guest (for example, room service).

When imminent danger exists, an innkeeper or the police may enter a guest's room to address the emergency circumstance.[1] Indeed, emergency conditions, if known to the innkeeper, impose a duty to enter a guest's room to eliminate the danger. Failure to do so can result in liability.

We saw in Chapter 6 that, where an innkeeper is aware of a rape or assault occurring in a hotel room, the hotelier has a duty to enter the room and provide aid to the guest. Likewise, in *Connolly v. Nicollet Hotel*, 95 N.W.2d 657 (1959), guests were throwing water-filled pillow cases and laundry bags out of the window of their room, causing injury to pedestrians below. The hotel had a duty to stop the offending conduct and had the right to enter the guestroom if necessary to stop the behavior.

---

[1] *People v. Love*, 84 N.Y.2d 917, 620 N.Y.S.2d 809 (N.Y. 1994)

Evicting a Guest

Under certain circumstances an innkeeper has the right to withdraw hotel privileges and evict a guest, provided no more force is used than is necessary. To **evict** means to remove someone from property. The following are grounds for eviction.

Failure to Pay the Hotel Bill

Failure to pay one's hotel bill is grounds for eviction. The eviction is ordinarily carried out by asking the guest for the amount due and requesting the guest to leave by a certain hour if the bill is not paid. If the guest fails to pay after such a demand, the hotel may evict. Thus, a hotel was entitled to remove a guest who had occupied her room for some time, was delinquent in payment for the room, meals, and telephone calls, and who refused to pay after the request was duly made.[2] The reason the law gives the hotel this remedy is to allow the innkeeper to rent the room to someone else who has the ability to pay, thereby producing income for the inn.[3]

In the following case, the guest refused to pay for food he received at the hotel restaurant. In response, the hotel thereafter refused to serve him food, which action was upheld by the court.

CASE EXAMPLE 9-3

Morningstar v. Lafayette Hotel Co. 211 N.Y. 465 (1914)

The plaintiff was a guest at the Lafayette Hotel in the city of Buffalo. ... He ... purchased some spareribs, which he presented to the hotel chef with a request that they be cooked for him and brought to his room. This was done, but with the welcome ... [food] there came the unwelcome addition of a bill or check for $1, which he was asked to sign. He refused to do so, claiming that the charge was excessive. [Remember, the year was 1914. A dollar was worth much more then.] That evening he dined at the [hotel] cafe, and was again asked to sign for the extra service, and again declined. The following morning, Sunday, when he presented himself at the breakfast table, he was told that he would not be served. ... He remained at the hotel till Tuesday, taking his meals elsewhere, and he then left. [He then sued the hotel claiming it wrongfully refused to serve him.] An innkeeper is not required to entertain a guest who has refused to pay a lawful charge. ...

Overstaying

Occupying a room beyond the agreed time is grounds for eviction. The contract for a room is for a definite time, be it one or several days, a week, or longer. When the period is over, the hotel has met its obligation under the contract with the

---

[2] *Sawyer v. Congress Square Hotel, Co.*, 170 A.2d 645 (Me. 1961)

[3] *People v. Lerhinan*, 455 N.Y.S.2d 822 (N.Y. 1982)

guest to rent the room and, if requested by the hotel, the guest must leave. If the guest fails to depart, the contract is breached and the guest becomes a trespasser. The hotel can then do one of two things: either assume that a new contract exists on a day-to-day basis obligating the guest to pay the cost of the room, or, if the hotel has made other commitments for the room, evict the guest. A good practice that most innkeepers have adopted when the vacancy rate is low is to print or stamp the date of departure on the registration card and on a copy given to the guest with an oral reaffirmation of the departure date. This helps to ensure that both the hotel and guest have the same understanding of the duration of their relationship.

Three states—Hawaii, Louisiana, and North Carolina—as well as Puerto Rico have passed statutes that codify this common law position and make a holdover guest a trespasser. For example, Hawaii's statute specifies: "Any guest who intentionally continues to occupy an assigned bedroom beyond the scheduled departure without the prior written approval of the keeper shall be deemed a trespasser." This modifies the common law slightly in that the statute does not require the innkeeper to request overstaying guests to leave prior to evicting them.

North Carolina's statute requires the innkeeper to issue a written statement specifying the time period during which the guest may occupy a room and to have the guest initial it. At the end of the period specified, the innkeeper automatically has the right to lock the former guest out of the room. The statute denies the former guest the right to enter to reclaim any personal property and permits the innkeeper to remove it. The statute also authorizes the innkeeper to use reasonable force in preventing the lodger from reentering the room.

Puerto Rico requires the innkeeper to call the police to physically remove a holdover.

In the states that do not have statutes specifically covering the rights of innkeepers with regard to overstays, innkeepers should proceed with caution when evicting the guest so as to reduce the possibility of lawsuits. Later in this chapter we will examine preferred methods to execute an eviction and the possible grounds for lawsuits that can develop if the ejection is done improperly.

Persons of Ill Repute

In the following case, decided in 1923, the court upheld a hotel's right to evict a guest because she was a prostitute. Read carefully the description of the method used by the hotel for the eviction and the court's decision on the acceptability of that method.

CASE EXAMPLE 9-4

Raider v. Dixie Inn
248 S.W. 229 (Ky. 1923)

Appellant, Thelma Raider, applied to the Dixie Inn, at Richmond, for entertainment, and paid her board and lodging for a week in advance, saying that her home was in Estill county and she had come to Richmond, at the expense of her mother, to take treatments from a physician. At the end of the week she paid in advance for another week, and so on until the end of a month, when she went downtown, and on returning was informed by the proprietor and his wife, who are appellees in this case, that she no longer had a room at that hotel, and remarked to her that no explanation was due her as to why they had requested or forced her removal. Alleging that she was mortified and humiliated by the words and conduct of the proprietors of the hotel, appellant, Raider, brought this action to recover damages in the sum of $5,000. Appellees answered, and denied ... harsh or improper conduct on the part of the proprietors of the hotel, but admitted that they had required appellant to vacate her room and to leave the hotel, and gave as their reason for so doing that she was a woman of bad character, recently an inmate of a house of prostitution in the city of Richmond, and had been such for many years next before she came to the Inn, and was in said city a notoriously immoral character, but that appellees did not know her when she applied for entertainment at their hotel, but immediately upon learning who she was and her manner of life had moved her belongings out of the room into the lobby of the hotel, and kindly, quietly, and respectfully asked her to leave; that they had in their hotel several ladies of good reputation who were embarrassed by the presence of appellant in the hotel and who declined to associate with her and were about to withdraw from the hotel if she continued to lodge there; that appellant had not been of good behavior since she had become a patron of the hotel.

Plaintiff says that she is advised that these defendants (the Dixie Inn) had a legal right to remove her, and that she does not question that right, but that she was removed as a guest for hire from said Dixie Inn at a time that was improper and in a manner that was unduly disrespectful and insulting, and that she was greatly mortified and humiliated thereby, and suffered indignity because of the wrongful manner in which she was removed from said Dixie Inn as herein set out and complained of.

... As a general rule a guest who has been admitted to an inn may afterwards be excluded therefrom by the innkeeper if the guest refuses to pay his bill, or if he becomes obnoxious to the guests by his own fault, is a person of general bad reputation. ...

It appears, therefore, fully settled that an innkeeper may lawfully refuse to entertain objectionable characters, if to do so is calculated to injure his business or to place himself, business, or guests in a hazardous, uncomfortable, or dangerous situation. The innkeeper need not accept any one as a guest who is calculated to and will injure his business. ... A prize fighter who has been guilty of law breaking may be excluded. ... Neither is an innkeeper required to entertain ... persons of bad reputation ... drunken and disorderly persons; ... one who commits a trespass by breaking in the door; ... one who is filthy or who subjects the guests to annoyance. ...

It therefore appears that the managers of the Dixie Inn had the right to exclude appellant from their hotel upon several grounds without becoming liable therefor, unless the means employed to remove her were unlawful. ...

[T]he only remaining question is: Did they do so in a proper manner, or did they employ unlawful means to exclude her? The averments of the petition show she was not present at the time they took charge of her room and placed her belongings in the lobby of the hotel, where they were easily accessible to her; that when she came in they quietly told her that they had taken charge of her room, but gave no reason for doing so. We must believe from the averments of the petition that very little was said, and that the whole proceeding was very quiet and orderly. As they had a right to exclude her from the hotel, they were guilty of no wrong in telling her so, even though there [may have been] other persons present in the lobby at the time they gave her such information, which is denied.

The averments of the petition as amended "that appellees removed appellant from the hotel in an improper manner and were unduly disrespectful and insulting" are mere conclusions of the pleader, and are not supported by the statement of facts found elsewhere in the petition.

The petition ... did not state a cause of action in favor of appellant against appellees.

Judgment [in favor of the hotel] affirmed.

What constitutes an objectionable character is a debatable question, and the hotelier relying on this ground for eviction should proceed carefully. The decision in *Raider v. Dixie* upholding the innkeeper's right to remove a prostitute probably would not be followed today unless the guest was practicing the illegal trade in the hotel or otherwise disturbing other guests.

Intoxication and Disorderly Conduct

Intoxication alone is not an adequate reason in most states for eviction. However, a hotel has the right to evict a person who is intoxicated and disturbing other guests.[4] There must be a disturbance of the peace, disorderly conduct, threat to other guests, damage to the room, or the like. In some circumstances, not only does the hotel have the right to remove a guest, but it may violate a duty to other guests if it does not do so. For example, if the intoxicated person threatens the well-being of other guests, a hotel may be negligent if it fails to remove the disorderly person.

Disorderly Conduct

A sober person engaged in disorderly conduct can likewise be evicted. An interesting example involving unusual disorderly conduct concerns a television station that sent a camera crew to a restaurant that had been cited for health-code violations. The instructions given the camera crew were to enter unannounced "with cameras rolling," apparently in an effort to catch on camera unsanitary practices. The television crew entered as directed with bright lights glaring. Some diners hid under the table, others left without paying their bills, and those waiting to be seated left without purchasing a meal. The restaurant ordered the crew to leave and sued for damages on the grounds of trespass. A verdict in the restaurant's favor for $1200 was upheld on appeal.[5]

Contagiously Ill Guests

According to common law, hotel operators have the right to evict a guest who contracts a contagious disease that is easily spread. When doing so, the innkeeper should use extreme care to avoid aggravating the guest's condition, which generally means the innkeeper should summon the assistance of a doctor or an ambulance if the condition warrants.

According to the Americans with Disabilities Act (ADA), which became effective in 1992 and was discussed in Chapter 3, a debilitating contagious disease may constitute a disability. The Act bars innkeepers and restaurateurs from withholding their services if a reasonable modification can be made to accommodate the disability. Arguably, if the disability is a contagious disease, the innkeeper

[4] *Poroznoff v. Alberti*, 401 A.2d 1124 (N.J. 1979)

[5] *Le Mistral, Inc. v. Columbia Broadcasting System*, 402 N.Y.S.2d 815 (N.Y. 1978)

can continue to exclude would-be guests nothwithstanding the ADA because to provide them a room would expose many others to the illness, violating the innkeeper's duty of reasonable care for guests' well-being. In ADA terms, providing accommodations to a guest with a contagious disease that is easily spread would likely fall outside the realm of a reasonable accommodation.

Breaking House Rules

Hotels are entitled to adopt reasonable rules to ensure order and safety on the premises and to prevent misconduct that can offend guests or bring the hotel into disrepute. These rules, often called house rules, might for example include prohibitions against walking in the lobby in a wet bathing suit, wearing shorts in the lobby after 6:00 P.M., or having pets in guest rooms (other than seeing-eye dogs or service animals, which must be allowed by statute). An innkeeper can evict a guest for failing to comply with a house rule.[6] Such rules should be posted in conspicuous places, including guest rooms. All house rules concerning the use of a pool should also be displayed poolside.

Persons Not Registered

When a person is not or has never been a guest of the hotel, the innkeeper can evict that person for violating house rules or even without cause. In the next case, a hotel had a rule prohibiting unregistered guests in the building above the lobby. A nonguest was ordered to leave the hotel because she was suspected of engaging in prostitution in guests' rooms, which were located on floors above the lobby. She challenged the hotel's right to evict her. The court upheld the hotel's authority to prohibit on the premise of those people who fail to abide by its rules.

CASE EXAMPLE 9-5

Kelly v. United States
348 A.2d 884 (D.C. 1975)

... Between the months of January and March 1974, appellant was seen by the chief of security at the Statler Hilton Hotel on approximately five occasions. He first noticed her in the hotel bar speaking with a guest with whom she later went upstairs. On one occasion when she was in the lobby all night, a police officer assigned to the vice squad told the hotel's security officer that appellant was a prostitute and showed him a copy of her criminal record and her mug shot.

On March 18, hotel security officers again noticed appellant in the hotel. At that time she was once more observed going upstairs with a guest. After about an hour in the guest's room, she came out of the room alone. She was stopped by the hotel security officers and informed of the hotel policy of not allowing any unregistered guests above the lobby. She was also told of the conversation with the police vice squad officer and was read a "barring notice." [That is, a notice that orders someone to remain off the premises. Disregard of the barring notice constitutes the crime of unlawful entry which is the equivalent of trespass. The

---

[6]*McClean v. University Club*, 97 N.B.2d 174 (Mass. 1951)

notice said: You are hereby notified that you are not permitted entry in the Statler Hilton Hotel, 1001 Sixteenth Street, Northwest. In the future, if you return to the Statler Hilton Hotel and gain entry, you may be subject to criminal prosecution for unauthorized entry.] Furthermore, she was told that if she returned to the hotel, she would be arrested and charged with unlawful entry.

On August 19, security officers were called to the fifth floor of the hotel. They waited outside one of the rooms until appellant emerged with two male companions. She was then placed under arrest.

Appellant ... argued that the [unlawful entry] statute [quoted below] was not applicable to a hotel and accordingly a hotel could not issue a valid barring notice. ...

It is a general rule that: ...

[Where a person does] not enter the hotel as a guest nor with the intention of becoming one, [it is] his duty to leave peaceably when ordered by the [innkeeper] to do so, and in case of his refusal to leave on request, [the innkeeper] was entitled to use such force as was reasonably necessary to remove him. ...

It necessarily follows that if a hotel has the right to exclude someone, and he or she receives appropriate notice of his exclusion, that person's subsequent presence in the hotel is without lawful authority. Thus he or she is subject to arrest for the crime of unlawful entry. The unlawful entry statute of Washington, D.C. provides:

Any person who ... being [in or on any public or private buildings] without lawful authority to remain therein or thereon shall refuse to quit the same on the demand of ... the person lawfully in charge thereof, shall be deemed guilty of a misdemeanor.

In the instant case, appellant concedes that she was warned not to return to the hotel. She also admits that she was in the hotel on the evening of August 19, 1974. Consequently, under the authorities cited above, with which we agree, her entrance into the hotel was unlawful...

Appellant's other grounds for reversal, namely that the hotel policy was unreasonably and discriminatorily applied and that the government's evidence was insufficient, are without substance.

Ruling of the Court: ... judgment ... for the defendant.

As illustrated in the next case, the rights of a guest are not assignable—that is, they cannot be transferred; therefore, a registered guest cannot give another person the status of guest.

CASE EXAMPLE 9-6

Hennig v. Goldberg
68 N.Y.S.2d 698 (1947)

... Defendants were innkeepers, and plaintiff occupied a room in their hotel. ... [D]efendants, in [plaintiff's] absence, changed the lock of the room which she occupied, so that upon her arrival at the hotel in the early morning of February 20, 1946 and again in the early afternoon of February 25, 1946 she was unable to gain admittance. [She sued the hotel for forcible entry.]

... Furthermore, I find that plaintiff occupied the room—which had been assigned to one Bihovsky, who had dwelt in it for some time and had paid the February 1946 rent in advance in full—without permission from defendant or any one representing the hotel, that she had not registered as a guest, and that the permission to use the room which she had obtained from the guest Bihovsky gave her no lawful right to the room and did not even put her in possession inasmuch as Bihovsky's rights as a guest were not assignable or transferable.

... Obviously [the relevant statute] was never intended to make it necessary for an innkeeper to resort to court proceedings ... to remove from his inn, or from a room in his inn, one who came in without his permission, express or implied. This is simply a case in which defendants found plaintiff in a room in which she did not belong and changed the lock so that she could not again gain access to that room.

In so doing defendants were within their strict legal right, although I think it probable that they acted as they did because they wished to rent the room to someone who would pay a daily rather than a monthly rate. ... [Defendants] acted lawfully and are not answerable in damages to plaintiff.

Judgment may be entered in favor of defendants dismissing the complaint. ...

Persons Without Baggage

In times past, a hotel could refuse to provide a room to a would-be guest who did not have any luggage. The concern was that the would-be guest was not a traveler in need of a room but rather a person intending to use the room for prostitution or some other illegal purpose. Today such a rule would likely not be sustained by a court. The mere absence of luggage does not in itself indicate an illegal intent. Reference is nonetheless still made in some statutes to the idea that a person arriving at an inn without luggage might be refused. For example, in Alabama's statute defining criminal fraud against hotels and restaurants, included as illegal is the obtaining of accommodations by the "false or fictitious show or pretense of any baggage."[7]

Business Competitors

If a business competitor comes to a hotel seeking accommodations, they cannot be refused. But a business competitor who comes to a hotel to solicit customers can be enjoined, meaning the hotel can obtain a court order barring competitors from continuing such solicitations. In *Champie v. Castle Hot Water Springs Co.*, 233 P. 1107 (Ariz. 1925), the hotel maintained a livery business supplying its guests with horses. The defendant, a competitor in the livery business, likewise supplied horses to the hotel's guests using the hotel's property to make its business arrangements with the guests. The hotel sued and the court granted an injunction prohibiting defendant from taking any of its horses onto the plaintiff's property. Said the court,

> Has an innkeeper the right to refuse a competitor access to his premises, for the purpose of competition, when the presence of the latter is requested by one of the former's guests? ... [I]t has never been held that they must furnish their private facilities for the use of a competitor in business. Cases involving the same general principles as the one at bar have frequently arisen, and it has been held almost invariably that the owner of the premises is within his rights in excluding a competitor therefrom.

---

[7]Code of Alabama, § 34-15-19

Suppose a hotel offers food and room services and a guest orders food to be delivered to the hotel by a competitor. Can the hotel refuse admittance to the competitor, making the delivery impossible? The answer seems to be yes.

If the hotel chooses to grant permission to the competitor to carry on business at the inn and allow the competitor access to the hotel's guests, the hotel can charge a fee for that privilege.

Suppose the hotel does not offer food. Can the inn select one or a few exclusive food preparers and exclude others from doing business on the premises? The answer is yes. The hotel has a legitimate interest in protecting the level of service provided. As we have studied, the hotel has a duty to exercise reasonable care for the well-being of its guests. The hotel also has a rightful interest in maintaining its reputation, which could be adversely affected by allowing unknown or substandard food providers on the premises.

The Process of Eviction

Evicting someone from a hotel or restaurant for cause is proper. It should be carried out considerately; no harsh words or force should be used unless absolutely necessary. A wrongful eviction can result in liability, not only for physical injuries, but also for mental and emotional distress.[8]

How to Evict

Ideally, physical force and harsh words can be avoided when an eviction is made. Good practice requires the innkeeper or restaurateur in the first instance to inform the person being evicted that she is no longer welcome on the premises and should leave. If that person asks the basis for the eviction, she should be told. If the person declines to leave, the innkeeper or restaurateur should repeat that the person's license to remain on the premises has been withdrawn and a second request to leave should be made.

If the person still refuses to leave, the hotel may have only two choices: call the police or use force. If time permits, the preferable method is to call the police. If force is used, the person may become agitated and injury may result to an employee of the hotel or to patrons. The police are specially trained to handle such situations. If the person is out of control and delay until police arrive is not feasible, the courts have consistently held that the hotelkeeper may forcibly remove the guest, provided that no more force is used than is necessary. The question often becomes—How much force is necessary? What is the right amount of force? Only reasonable force may be used; that is, only the amount of force as is reasonably necessary to remove the person or to counter force used by the person.

The eviction of a hotel guest must be for one of the previously stipulated reasons—nonpayment, overstaying, intoxication coupled with disorderly conduct, contagious illness, or breaking house rules. If an eviction from a hotel is prompted by personal animus, or race, color, national origin, religion, gender, disability, or marital status, the hotel may be held liable for wrongful eviction.

---

[8] *Lopez v. City of New York*, 357 N.Y.S.2d 659 (N.Y. 1974)

Hotel and restaurant employees should be carefully instructed on how to evict a guest. Remember, an employee's actions are attributed to the employer per the legal principal of respondeat superior. In all situations, forceful eviction should be a last resort. Efforts to convince the person to leave peaceably should always be attempted first.

Excessive Force

Unnecessary force in the course of an eviction can lead to liability for the torts of assault or battery. In tort law, **assault** means intentionally putting someone in fear of harmful physical contact, such as making a fist in a way suggestive of an imminent punch. The tort of **battery** means causing harmful physical contact to a person. Intentionally hitting someone in the face is an example of the tort of battery. Battery occurs where a hotel or restaurant owner or employee grabs a patron and pushes him or her out of the premises without good cause, resulting in injury.[9]

In the following case, the hotel owner was liable to a patron for battery based on action taken in the course of a wrongful eviction.

CASE EXAMPLE 9-7

Hopp v. Thompson
38 N.W.2d 133 (S.D. 1949)

This is an action to recover damages for assault and battery. Defendant [Appellant] owns and manages the Thompson Hotel in Sisseton. On the evening of June 21, 1946, plaintiff [Respondent] entered the hotel and a fracas occurred in which both parties were injured. Plaintiff brought the action to recover his damages and defendant filed an answer denying liability. Defendant also pleaded a counterclaim for the damages which he claims were sustained by him. The jury returned a verdict for plaintiff in the sum of $10,249 upon which judgment was entered and defendant appealed.

The first question presented is the sufficiency of the evidence to justify the verdict of the jury. Respondent testified that he entered the hotel in response to the invitation of a guest; that appellant, without just cause, ordered him to leave the hotel; that he started to leave, as ordered, when appellant assaulted and beat him with a piece of iron pipe thereby causing unconsciousness, severe cuts and

bruises on his scalp and body, and injuries to his brain. His claim to damages consists of hospital and physicians' expense, loss of time, pain and suffering, both present and future, besides exemplary and punitive damages.

Appellant denied all of these contentions of respondent. He testified that respondent was a stranger to him and was not a guest at the hotel. That when respondent entered the hotel it was about 11 o'clock in the evening which was closing time; that respondent started to go upstairs and as he did so appellant repeatedly asked him who he was and what he wanted to which respondent made no reply; that appellant then told respondent to come down and go home; that respondent still refused to go and thereupon appellant tapped him lightly on the shoulder and told him to get out; that respondent did not leave as ordered and that appellant told him that appellant would call an officer; that when appellant picked up the telephone receiver respondent assaulted him and took the receiver from him. At this time appellant says he picked up a short piece of pipe, tapped respondent on the shoulder with it and again ordered him to

---

[9] *Jones v. City of Boston*, 738 F.Supp. 604 (Mass. 1990)

leave and that respondent still refused to go; that a scuffle ensued in which appellant hit respondent on the shoulder and respondent grabbed appellant by the neck with both hands; that during this time appellant struck respondent on the back of the head with the pipe; that the parties were on the floor part of the time; that appellant called for help, which came, and then the struggle ended. Appellant contends that he struck respondent only to subdue him and that he used no more force than he thought was necessary for that purpose.

It is the general rule that an innkeeper gives a general license to all persons to enter his hotel. Consequently, it is not a trespass to enter an inn without a previous actual invitation, but, where persons enter a hotel or inn, not as guests, but intent on pleasure or profit to be derived from intercourse with its inmates, they are there, not of right, but under an implied license that the landlord may revoke at any time. ... The respondent did not enter the hotel as a guest nor with the intention of becoming one and it was his duty to leave peaceably when ordered by the landlord to do so, and in case of his refusal to leave on request appellant was entitled to use such force as was reasonably necessary to remove him. ...

Here respondent denies that he refused to leave when ordered to do so. He also denies that he knowingly assaulted or beat appellant. He testified that he walked toward the desk, then turned to go out, and that the next thing he remembered he was standing outside on the street covered with blood. This record presents a substantial conflict in the evidence. The jurors are the exclusive judges of the weight of the evidence and the credibility of the witnesses and therefore this court could not substitute its judgment for the verdict. ...

The judgment [in favor of Respondent/Plaintiff] is affirmed.

CASE QUESTIONS

1. The jury believed the guest's version of the facts. Based on that version, what did the hotel manager do wrong? How should he have handled the situation?

2. Why did the Appellate Court refuse to substitute its own opinion for that of the jurors?

Verbal Abuse

Evictions can be carried out verbally without the use of force, or statements by hotel employees may accompany forceful eviction. In either circumstance, untruthful comments can lead to liability. In *Milner Hotels, Inc., v. Brent*, 43 So.2d 654 (Miss. 1949), an eviction for cause was handled very badly. The plaintiff-guest paid the room rent for her husband, daughter, and herself weekly. The rent was current for one more day when the plaintiff tried to pay for an additional week. Her money was refused and she was told to vacate her room by the manager, who said in an angry voice, loud enough for others in the lobby to hear, "We do not want you here." The plaintiff was also locked out of her room. She was embarrassed and distressed over the alleged damage to her reputation.

The plaintiff had recently been a witness in a case against the corporation that owned the hotel. The manager of the hotel later admitted to the plaintiff that he had been ordered to evict her because of her involvement in that case.

The plaintiff sought punitive damages which, as the court said, are only awarded if the defendant committed a wrongful act, intentionally, willfully, and with gross disregard of the plaintiff's rights. The court determined that the manager spoke to the plaintiff, as quoted above, with intentional malice and in gross disregard of the plaintiff's rights, and awarded the plaintiff punitive damages.

As this case illustrates, statements made about the person being evicted can lead to a lawsuit, not only for wrongful conviction, but also for defamation or slander. **Defamation** is the tort of making false and demeaning statements about a person to a third person. **Libel** refers to oral defamatory sttements; **slander** refers to written defamatory statements.

The cases involving both excessive force and verbal abuse underscore the importance of affecting an eviction properly.

Evicting a Hotel Tenant

When considering an eviction, a hotel must distinguish between a guest and a tenant (see Chapter 7 for the distinction). While a guest can be removed for the reasons identified in this chapter, a tenant cannot be evicted without a court proceeding. Due to the relative longevity of a tenant's occupancy of an apartment, a tenant is considered by law to have a greater interest in the apartment than a guest has in a hotel room. That greater interest prevents a hotel/ landlord from evicting the tenant without a court order. The law provides a summary proceeding (a quick legal procedure) for this purpose that enables the landlord to obtain the eviction order within a few weeks, provided grounds for eviction can be proven in court.

Refusing a Diner

A restaurant not associated with a hotel has more leeway than a hotel to exclude people. Under common law, a restaurant, unless it was part of an inn, had the right to select its customers and to refuse any person. Today, absent a state statute that changes the common law, the restaurant has the right to accept some customers and reject others. However, federal and state civil rights laws prohibit discrimination on the basis of race, color, national origin, religion, gender, marital status, and disability. Thus, a restaurant cannot refuse service on these grounds but *can* refuse service on other grounds.

In the case of *Drew v. United States*, 292 A.2d 164 (D.C. 1972), the appellant entered a restaurant at which he had previously worked, sat at a table to have dinner with his friends, and was conducting himself in a proper manner when he was notified by the night manager that he would have to leave because his name was on a list of undesirables. The appellant failed to leave. The police were called and the appellant was arrested for trespass. He defended on the ground that the restaurant was open to the public and so he had a right to be there. The court rejected his defense in favor of the restaurant's common law right to refuse service to a guest even "arbitrarily."

Although a restaurant can refuse service, it cannot in the process use excessive force. In the following case, an overzealous bouncer at a club was found liable for battery.

CASE EXAMPLE 9-8

Durand v. Moore
879 S.W.2d 196 (Tex. 1994)

... Lewis was a doorman at Durand's nightclub when he assaulted a customer waiting to enter the club. Durand complains that Lewis was not acting in the course and scope of his employment when the assault occurred [and therefore Durand is not liable under respondeat superior]. ...

On April 19, 1991, Craig Lewis, an employee of Durand, was assigned to the front door of the club. His job included checking IDs, enforcing the dress code, and coordinating the admission of customers into the club.

That night or early morning April 20, Michael Moore and Lawrence Ward went to the club. The club was filled to capacity, and both men waited in line for customers to leave. However, doorman Lewis did not admit customers into the club in waiting-line order. Instead, he selected several persons from the line behind Moore and Ward. Ward, and then Moore, left the line and complained to Lewis. Ward turned away and walked toward his car, but Moore remained and continued the discussion with Lewis. There was conflicting testimony whether Moore and Ward were loud and abusive and whether Durand personally quieted them down just before the assault.

Without provocation, Lewis grabbed a tall cocktail glass filled with a drink and struck Moore on the side of the head shattering the glass. While Moore struggled to restrain Lewis and ward off further attack, Lewis struck Moore several more times with a flashlight. Ward returned and attempted to break up the struggle, but Lewis struck him in the face with the flashlight, breaking Ward's nose. Ward retreated as Durand and others pulled Lewis and Moore apart. Ward called the police. An ambulance arrived, and Moore and Ward received first aid. Ward was later treated at a hospital. Moore declined treatment. Moore sued Durand and Lewis. Lewis defaulted. After a bench trial, the court found Durand liable under respondeat superior. Durand appeals.

In general, to impose liability upon an employer for the tort of his employee under the doctrine of respondeat superior, the act of the employee must fall within the scope of the general authority of the employee in furtherance of the employer's business and for the accomplishment of the objective for which the employee is hired. ...

When an employee commits an assault, it is for the trier of fact to determine whether the employee ceased to act as an employee and acted instead upon his own responsibility. ...

It is not ordinarily within the scope of a servant's authority to commit an assault on a third person. ...

The nature of the employment may be such as necessarily to involve at times the use of force as where the employee's duty is to guard the employer's property and to protect it from trespassers so that the act of using force may be in furtherance of the employer's business, making him liable even when greater force is used than is necessary.

The master who puts the servant in a place of trust or responsibility, or commits to him the management of his business or the care of his property, is justly held responsible when the servant through lack of judgment or discretion, or from infirmity of temper, or under the influence of passion aroused by the circumstances and the occasion, goes beyond the strict line of his duty or authority and inflicts an unjustifiable injury on a third person. ...

[T]here was evidence that Lewis had the responsibility to control the admittance of customers into the club. There was evidence that Lewis admitted, ahead of Moore and Ward, two spendthrift customers who had "paid the light bill last month." Lewis' assault of Moore immediately followed their discussion of why Lewis was giving preferential treatment to certain customers. We find that this evidence was probative that Lewis' assault of Moore was overzealous enforcement of the criteria and procedures used to select waiting customers for admittance into the club. ...

[The evidence was sufficient to support the verdict against Durand. Judgment affirmed.]

In another case involving assault by a bouncer at a club, the plaintiff patron had too much to drink and was evicted. The bouncer escorted the plaintiff to the front door, took from him the drink he had just purchased, and discarded it. The plaintiff attempted to push the bouncer away, but was seized by two other employees who pushed the plaintiff out the front door. While the plaintiff's arms were pinned by the two men, a third employee, the head doorman, repeatedly hit the plaintiff in the face with his fists. A jury found the employees used excessive force and were acting within the course of their employment. A verdict was issued in the plaintiff's favor against the club. The decision was affirmed on appeal.[10]

In another case, the court interpreted the tort of battery broadly. The manager of a restaurant snatched a black patron's dinner plate just as the latter reached the buffet because the manager refused to serve African-Americans. The patron chose to sue the restaurant for battery rather than discrimination. The jury found that the manager "forcibly dispossessed plaintiff of his diner plate" and "shouted in a loud and offensive manner." The court ruled that this conduct constituted battery stating, "Under the facts of this case, we have no difficulty in holding that the intentional grabbing of plaintiff's plate constituted a battery. The intentional snatching of an object from one's hand is as clearly an offensive invasion of his person as would be an actual contact with the body."[11]

In this case, the plaintiff also could have sued for discrimination on the basis of race in violation of the federal Civil Rights Act of 1964 and state anti-discrimination laws. Why did the plaintiff sue for the tort of battery, rather than violation of civil rights laws? One reason may be that the remedy for a violation of the federal civil rights law is not monetary; it is instead an injunction that prevents the wrongdoer from continuing the discrimination. The remedy for a battery case is compensation for the resulting injuries.

A customer with a reservation has a legal right to be served. A restaurant that fails to honor a reservation may face liability for breach of contract. In *Harder v. Auberge Des Fougeres*, 338 N.Y.S.2d 356 (1972), the court upheld the plaintiffs' right to sue a restaurant where, for unspecified reasons, the restaurant refused to seat them even though they had reservations. This case suggests a reservation creates a binding obligation on a restaurant to seat and serve the patron.

Suppose a would-be diner arrives at the restaurant significantly later than the time of the reservation. Must the restaurant honor the reservation? The answer is no. A patron has an obligation to arrive in a timely manner. A significantly late arrival will release the restaurant from its duty to provide service.

Statutory Protection for the Hotelkeeper

Statutes in most states provide protection to the innkeeper and restaurateurs against patrons who seek to avoid payment. The hotel lien gives an innkeeper the

---

[10] *Country Road, Inc. v. Witt*, 737 S.W.2d 362 (Tex. 1987)

[11] *Fisher v. Carrousel Motor Hotel, Inc.*, 424 S.W.2d 627 (Tex. 1968)

right to retain the personal property of a nonpaying guest. Fraud statutes authorize innkeepers and restaurateurs to pursue criminal charges against those patrons who receive services but intentionally fail to pay. The innkeeper's lien and fraud statutes are discussed in more detail in the next few sections.

The Innkeeper's Lien

A **lien** is a security interest in the property of someone who owes money. The lien entitles the creditor to take possession of the debtor's property, sell it, and apply the proceeds to the unpaid debt. For example, if you borrowed money from a bank to buy a car, the bank probably has a security interest (lien) on your car. If you fail to repay the loan in a timely manner, the bank will likely enforce its lien by repossessing your car, selling it, and applying the proceeds to reduce the outstanding balance on your loan.

The innkeeper's lien originated in early common law when credit cards were not yet invented. The lien's purpose was to protect innkeepers from dishonest guests who failed to pay their bills. The lien authorizes the innkeeper to sell a guest's property that is at the hotel and apply the proceeds toward the unpaid bill. At common law, the innkeeper could sell the property without first obtaining a court order. Today many states require by statute that the hotel obtain a court ruling that the guest is in fact delinquent in payment prior to enforcing the lien.

In the age of credit cards, the lien has only limited application. Currently, most hotels require guests to leave an imprint of their credit card upon check-in. If the guest later departs without settling the bill, the hotel will charge the bill to the credit card; thereby, the hotel is assured of payment. Some states, such as New York, have repealed the innkeeper's lien.

Applicable Property

To what property does the lien apply? Courts have held that most property a guest brings to the hotel is covered by the lien. Innkeepers' liens have been held valid on such diverse items as a portable piano, valuables in a safe deposit box, and cars.[12] Covered property is not limited to articles necessary for travel; merchandise samples of traveling salespeople may be subject to the lien. It does not, however, extend to a person's necessary apparel and certain personal jewelry such as wedding rings. Those items are exempt and the guest is entitled to retain them. The goods of one's spouse are not subject to the innkeeper's lien when the indebtedness is solely that of the other spouse.[13]

When innkeepers have a lien on the personal property of their guest, the innkeeper's right to possession is superior in the law to that of the guest. If the guest attempts to take the property, he can be charged with theft.

---

[12] *Chesham Auto Supply v. Beresford Hotel*, 29 Times L.R. 584 (1913)

[13] *Geobel v. United Railways. Co. of St. Louis*, 181 S.W. 1051 (Mo. 1915)

Applicable Charges

Items on a guest's bill to which the lien applies include the guestroom charge, service charges for delivery of a guest's baggage to and from the hotel, valet service, room service, C.O.D. charges, and the like. However, the innkeeper cannot enforce the lien where the services were rendered by an independent contractor, such as a doctor or the owner of one of the shops in the building. Nor can the independent contractor enforce the lien; it is particular to the innkeeper.

Termination of the Lien by Payment or Sale

An innkeeper's lien terminates when the bill is paid. The hotelkeeper must then return any property seized pursuant to the lien. If payment is not made, the innkeeper can sell the property and use the proceeds to satisfy the bill, as well as expenses associated with the sale, including advertising and storage of the goods pending sale. Many states mandate the procedure to be followed when goods subject to the lien are sold. The objective of these statutes is to ensure, for the benefit of the guest, that the sale generates the most money possible. A typical statute requires the innkeeper to publish notice of the sale in a local newspaper at least two weeks prior to the sale date, including a description of the goods to be sold. The goal is to notify as many people as possible and stimulate their interest in purchasing by the description of the goods. The innkeeper is further required to send notice of the sale to the nonpaying guest. This allows the guest one last opportunity to pay the bill and retrieve the possessions before the sale occurs.

Following the sale, the innkeeper can retain from the proceeds the amount of the unpaid bill and expenses incurred in arranging and advertising the sale. Any surplus must be paid to the guest. If the innkeeper cannot locate the guest, the surplus money can be paid to a designated public official, such as the chief fiscal officer of the city in which the sale occurred. That officer is required to hold the money until the guest retrieves it. The hotel is thus saved from having to keep track of the excess money indefinitely.

Defrauding the Hotelkeeper or Restaurateur

All states and the District of Columbia have passed criminal statutes that seek to protect the innkeeper and restaurateur from guests who attempt to **defraud** by leaving without paying. These statutes criminalize nonpayment where the perpetrator sought services with the intention of avoiding payment. The name given to the crime varies from state to state and includes theft of services, larceny, and fraud. Many of the statutes provide varying penalties depending upon the amount and value of the goods or services received by the absconder. For example, in Massachusetts, a defendant who receives food, entertainment, or accommodations in excess of $100 faces a maximum jail sentence of two years. In New York, theft of services from a hotel or restaurant is punishable by imprisonment up to one year and a fine up to $1,000 without regard to the value of the services stolen. As evidenced by the penalties, states regard this type of crime quite seriously.

Intent to Defraud

Remember that a criminal case is quite different from a civil case, as discussed in Chapter 1. In a civil case, the plaintiff seeks compensation. Inadvertent or unintended action by the defendant can lead to liability if the plaintiff thereby suffers a loss. A criminal case can result in a variety of penalties, including jail time and the resulting loss of freedom. To justify penalizing the defendant requires that he act with a criminal mental state, which usually means "intentionally." A person acts intentionally when his conscious objective is to engage in the illegal conduct.

For example, a defendant planned a surprise party for his wife at a restaurant. As required by the contract he prepaid the bill, using a check for payment. He asked the proprietor to wait five days before cashing it because the defendant anticipated a paycheck in the interim, and the owner agreed. Two days after giving the check and one day before the party, the defendant stopped payment. The party was held and approximately fifty to seventy guests attended. Finding the defendant guilty of the *crime* of defrauding a restaurant, the court said his intent to deceive was established by his accepting the entertainment while concealing the fact that he had stopped payment on the check written to cover the cost.[14]

Likewise, a patron was guilty of theft of services where he ate at a restaurant and signed the bill with a false name, thereby charging the meal to an account on which he did not have authorization to sign.[15]

Consider the circumstances of a restaurant patron who places her purse on the floor while dining and it is stolen. Assume she has no other money with her and will be unable to pay her bill. She is not guilty of a crime because her inability to pay was not by design. However, she remains liable to the restaurant for the cost of her dinner. If she fails to pay once her financial situation is settled, the restaurant could bring a civil action to collect the funds.

To establish a defendant's guilt of a crime such as theft of services, the prosecutor must prove two elements at trial: (1) the defendant obtained food or lodging without paying for it and (2) the defendant intended to avoid payment. Proving a defendant's intentions is often difficult, as illustrated in the following case.

CASE EXAMPLE 9-9

State of Utah v. Leonard
707 P.2d 650 (Utah 1985)

The defendant, Steven Charles Leonard, appeals from his jury conviction of theft of services. ... He argues that the evidence was insufficient to support the verdict; ...

On February 10, 1981, the defendant checked into the Tri-Arc Travel Lodge in Salt Lake City. ... He paid for the first night's lodging in cash. On February 11, 1981, he again paid his full hotel bill in cash. After the payment on the 11th, no more payments were made. By February 14th, the accumulated bill for the defendant's room was over $100. When

---

[14] *Morton v. Commonwealth*, 1999 WL 1129728 (Va. 1999)

[15] *Minkler v. Chumley*, 747 So.2d 720 (La. 1999)

the defendant did not respond to the hotel's requests for him to contact the desk to pay the accumulated bill, his hotel room was locked. On February 15th, the defendant and another male, James Borland, reported to the front desk supervisor that they were locked out of their room. Defendant promised to pay the outstanding $352.40 owed on the hotel and restaurant bills that were in his name the following day when he could go to his credit union for the necessary money. The defendant was let back into his room.

The following day the resident hotel manager called the defendant's room. The person who answered the phone responded to the defendant's name and promised to pay the bill. Instead the defendant and Borland vacated the room. The defendant was arrested shortly thereafter and charged with theft of services. ...

The defendant was convicted of obtaining services by deception. ... [The relevant statute] provides: "A person commits theft if he obtains services which he knows are available only for compensation by deception, threat, force, or by any means designed to avoid the due payment therefore."

Fraudulent intent is the gravamen of the offense of theft of services. Without [the requirement of] proof of a criminal state of mind, the law would imprison people for mere failure to pay a debt, a practice not sanctioned in this or any other state of this nation. ... The rule is that a person who in good faith accepts the benefit of services for which he plans to pay later cannot be convicted of theft even though he subsequently does not recompense the provider of services. The remedy in such case is a civil suit for breach of contract. Obviously, however, a defendant's denial of a fraudulent intent at the time of receiving the services is not binding. As is often the case, circumstantial evidence may speak louder than words.

The defendant made an implied promise to pay for the lodging and services provided the nights of February 12th, 13th, and 14th. However, the implied promise to pay and the subsequent failure to pay the bill, standing alone, are legally insufficient to show the elements of deception ... the prosecution must prove fraudulent intent by more than just a mere failure to pay. Some additional evidence is required to sustain a finding of fraudulent intent. In short, a conviction cannot be sustained merely on proof that a person acquired lodging and failed to pay for it.

Numerous types of circumstantial evidence may show fraudulent intent. For example, circumstantial evidence that a defendant had no money and no prospect of acquiring sufficient money when it was time to pay might be sufficient, as would express false promises, or deception as to the identity of the renter. However, evidence that establishes no more than a breach of an express or implied contract is not sufficient to prove the crime of theft of services, and a jury should be so instructed.

[Reversed and remanded.]

CASE QUESTIONS

1. Why is failure to pay an outstanding bill not sufficient, standing alone, to establish fraudulent or criminal intent?

2. What additional evidence is necessary to establish a fraudulent or criminal intent?

In *State v. Croy*, 145 N.W.2d 118 (Wis. 1966), the court reached a different result for good cause. The defendant had secretly left the hotel without informing the management of his departure. He left his luggage in the room in an apparent attempt to mislead the hotel about his status. When he left he owed the bills that had accumulated for room, board, long-distance telephone calls, and related items. The statute in Wisconsin provides that a crime is committed if a person who "had obtained food, lodgings or accommodations at any hotel, motel, ... intentionally absconds without paying for it." The defendant was found guilty at trial. The appellate court found sufficient evidence to support defendant's conviction. The defendant's attempts to mislead the innkeeper plus the extent of the bills strongly suggested the defendant intended to avoid payment.

To aid the prosecutor, the criminal law in many states creates a presumption of an intent not to pay when a hotel or restaurant customer leaves without paying. In these states, once the prosecutor proves that the defendant received food or accommodations without paying, a presumption arises that the defendant intended to avoid payment. The defendant is given an opportunity to present evidence to rebut the presumption. If the defendant fails to do so, the evidence of nonpayment together with the presumption is sufficient for conviction.

Evidence rebutting such a presumption was present in *Manley v. State*, 633 S.W.2d 881 (Tex. 1982). The appellant and his three children were diners in the Grubsteak Restaurant. Two of the children's spaghetti was cold and sticking together. The appellant and the other child complained about their food as well. The waitress had the dinners recooked but they still were not satisfactory. When the bill was brought to the table, the appellant requested an adjustment. The waitress left to talk to the cook and did not immediately return. Appellant, apparently exasperated, left his card at the cash register with the following note on the back. "Call me when you decide. Res: 937-5300." The restaurateur immediately had the patron arrested for theft of services. At trial, the cook admitted that whoever prepared the spaghetti did not wash and separate it to keep it from sticking. The customer was convicted in a bench trial, but the conviction was reversed on appeal. The appellate court stated,

> While the customer might be colored irritable and impatient and inconsiderate for not waiting to settle the dispute, we cannot conclude he "absconded" [an element of the crime in the state involved; meaning he intentionally left without paying]. He left his name, business address and telephone number of his business and residence. … [W]e cannot conclude that the evidence is sufficient to establish the requisite intent to commit the offense.

Fraudulent Payment

Additional statutes also protect the innkeeper and restaurateur from conniving patrons. Most states criminalize the act of knowingly issuing a bad check. A bad check is a check for which the maker has insufficient funds in the bank, or a check written on an account that has been closed. If a customer pays for dinner or a room with a bad check and knows the check is bad (the knowledge constitutes the required criminal mental state), the restaurant or hotel can pursue the patron on criminal charges. Although the statutes vary from state to state, the crime is typically a misdemeanor subjecting the customer to fines of up to $1,000 and a jail term of up to one year.

In addition, patrons who pay their bills with a credit card they know is stolen and who sign the card owner's name on the receipt are likely committing the crimes of possession of stolen property and forgery. The crime of **criminal possession of stolen property** is committed when a person knowingly possesses stolen property with intent to benefit herself or someone other than the owner. **Forgery** is the unauthorized alteration, completion, or making of a written instrument such as a credit card receipt or a check with intent to defraud or deceive. Most states designate forgery and criminal possession of stolen property as either high-level misdemeanors or felonies.

Hotels and restaurants may also be the victims of thefts of such items as hair dryers, courtesy bathrobes, ashtrays, silverware, glasses, towels, and the like. To avoid this type of theft, some hotels nail or otherwise affix the radios, televisions, and remote-control devices to the desks and dressers in guest rooms. If a guest does steal property, she is liable for the crime of larceny, which is either a misdemeanor or a felony depending on the state involved and the value of the goods stolen.

False Arrest

When a hotel or restaurant believes it is the victim of one of these crimes it should proceed cautiously. Overreaction can result in liability to the guest for **false arrest**—the tort of intentional and unprivileged detention or restraint of another person. If time permits, the restaurant or hotel manager should call the police rather than handling the matter in house. When officers arrive, the manager will explain the basis for believing a crime has occurred. The police will then assume the investigation.

A hotel was found not liable for false arrest where the front desk clerk called the police who detained the plaintiff for two hours. When the plaintiff registered at the hotel, the clerk observed that he was very rude and angry. She copied his driver's license, contrary to hotel policy. When he went to his room she called the police, concerned for the well-being of other guests. She shared the information on the license with the officers. His name, date of birth, and general description were identical to a man wanted for narcotics trafficking in Florida. The police came to the hotel, interviewed the plaintiff, handcuffed him, and detained him for two hours. Fingerprints eventually established that the plaintiff was not the wanted man. The plaintiff sued the hotel. The court dismissed the charges, holding that an inn is not liable for false arrest where its employees do not detain a guest but merely provide information to the police who thereafter detain the person.[16]

If, however, the suspect is likely to escape pending the arrival of police, the hotel or restaurant may want to act on its own. Again, prudence is advised. In many states hotels and restaurants will be liable for detaining a person unless that person has in fact committed a crime. A hotel with vacancies must provide accommodations for all who seek them with the limited exception of criminals, would-be guests who are intoxicated and disorderly, those who are unclean and unkempt, and people with easily spread contagious diseases. Therefore, hotel or restaurant management should not restrain a person unless the manager is quite sure the individual did in fact engage in criminal activity.

---

[16] *Roberts v. Essex Microtex*, 46 S.W.3d 205 (Tenn. 2001)

Key Terms

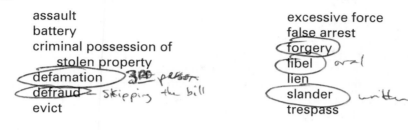

assault
battery
criminal possession of
    stolen property
defamation ~ 3rd person
defraud ~ skipping the bill
evict

excessive force
false arrest
forgery
libel) oral
lien
slander) written
trespass

Summary

The law gives the innkeeper numerous rights. Among them is the exclusive right to determine what room will be assigned to which guest, and, if necessary, to switch the room during the guest's stay at the hotel.

A restaurant can refuse to serve anyone for any reason except race, color, national origin, religion, gender, marital status, and disability. A hotel can evict guests who fail to pay their bill, are unruly, ill with contagious diseases, break house rules, or stay beyond their scheduled departure date. When evicting a guest, the hotel should attempt to avoid the use of force, but if force does become necessary, no more force should be used than is necessary to effect the eviction.

If a hotel guest fails to pay the bill, the hotel may be able to enforce an innkeeper's lien against the guest's property at the inn. If a restaurant patron or hotel guest attempts to leave without paying, the business can press criminal charges for theft of services or larceny. If the guest pays with a stolen credit card or bad check, the guest can be prosecuted for possession of stolen property, forgery, or issuing a bad check.

Preventive Law Tips for Managers

- *Do not refuse accommodations to a guest unless one of the permissible reasons for refusing accommodations exists.* The common law rule provides that a hotel may not refuse accommodations to a guest. With few exceptions, anyone seeking a room is entitled to one. A hotel can legally refuse to provide a room only if the prospective guest is unable to pay, intoxicated, disorderly, suffering from a contagious disease, unclean, a known criminal, accompanied by a pet (other than a service animal), or in possession of a firearm or explosives. The hotel can also deny accommodations if it has no vacancies. Absent one of these circumstances, the hotel must provide rooms for all who seek them.

- *Do not change a guest's room unless absolutely necessary, and then only after informing the guest and requesting cooperation.* The law allows an innkeeper to change a guest's room. Guests are foreseeably troubled and inconvenienced by such moves and so room changes should be avoided whenever possible. If a room change does become necessary, the best practice is to inform the guest and request cooperation. In addition to winning goodwill, such an approach can cushion anger generated by a surprise relocation.

■ *Do not enter a room assigned to a guest except for maintenance, imminent danger, nonpayment, or upon request.* When guests are assigned a room, they are the sole occupants for the duration of their stay; the innkeeper is not free to come and go in the room. The permissible reasons for hotel staff to enter are limited to cleaning, repairs, emergencies, or when requested by the guest, as when room service is called.

■ *Do not evict a guest unless the ground is one recognized by law: inability to pay, overstaying, bad reputation, disorderly, contagious disease, or breaking house rules.* Generally, once a guest is granted a room, she is entitled to occupy it during the scheduled stay and the hotel cannot expel her. A few exceptions exist, enumerated in italics. In those circumstances, a hotel can evict a guest. Eviction for any other reason can lead to liability.

■ *When evicting a patron, do not use any more force than is necessary.* When evicting a customer, the innkeeper or restaurateur should attempt to avoid the use of force. If appropriate, the patron should be invited to leave peaceably. If the patron refuses and repeated urging does not change his mind, and if circumstances permit, the innkeeper or restaurateur should summon the police. If circumstances do not permit, the patron can be physically removed from the premises, but the facility can use only that amount of force as is reasonably necessary. Use of a greater amount of force can result in liability for battery.

■ *When making an eviction, do not make derogatory remarks to the guest.* Insulting commentary during an eviction is inappropriate and serves only to worsen an already difficult situation. If the comments are false and overheard by passersby, the hotel may be liable for slander. If a guest wants to know why she is being evicted, she should be told the reasons without additional comment. Whenever possible, the encounter at which the innkeeper or restaurateur informs the guest of the eviction should occur in an office or private room where others cannot hear. The innkeeper will be well-advised to have an additional employee present who can testify later, if necessary, concerning the propriety of the eviction process.

■ *Hotels cannot evict long-term boarders who qualify as tenants without a court order.* To evict a tenant, the hotel/landlord must pursue a lawsuit for eviction. The law provides a summary (quick) proceeding for this purpose. Eviction without a court order violates a tenant's rights and may lead to liability.

■ *Restaurants should not refuse to serve a diner on the basis of race, national origin, color, religion, marital status, gender, or disability.* A restaurant, unlike a hotel, is not legally obligated to serve all who seek service. With the exceptions enumerated, the restaurant can refuse to serve anyone it chooses. Liability under civil rights laws will result if the restaurant discriminates on the prohibited grounds.

- *A hotel should not sell property subject to an innkeeper's lien without complying with the specific requirements of the relevant state law.* While the law in many states permits an innkeeper to sell property subject to an innkeeper's lien, each state has specific rules concerning the required method of sale, notice to the nonpaying guest, and related matters. Determine the applicable state law before selling guests' property and comply with it.

- *Train employees to detect stolen credit cards, forgeries, and bad checks.* Unfortunately, some hotel and restaurant patrons attempt to avoid payment by use of stolen credit cards, forgeries, bad checks, or simply failing to pay the bill. To help reduce the number of such incidents, employees should be trained to recognize these occurrences. Police are usually willing to address an employee training session on these issues.

- *Before pressing criminal charges, be sure the evidence supports a finding of a wrongful act and a criminal mental state.* To prove someone guilty of a crime involving fraud against a hotelier or restaurateur, the prosecutor must prove beyond a reasonable doubt that the defendant committed a wrongful act and had the required criminal mental state (intentionally or knowingly, depending on the crime). If the evidence suggests an innocent explanation for nonpayment, such as the patron's wallet was stolen while at the restaurant, criminal charges should be avoided. Wrongfully accusing someone of a crime can result in liability.

Review Questions

1. Under what circumstances can a hotel refuse to provide accommodations to someone seeking a room?

2. What precautions should a hotel take before moving a guest to another room?

3. Under what circumstances can an innkeeper enter a room assigned to a guest?

4. Can a hotel refuse to allow competing businesses to solicit its guests on its premises? Why or why not?

5. Name five legal grounds for eviction of a guest from a hotel.

6. How much force can a hotel use when evicting a guest?

7. What are the consequences to a hotel of using excessive force when evicting a guest?

8. Under what circumstances can a restaurant refuse to provide dinner to a would-be guest?

9. What is the difference between the torts of assault and battery?

10. What benefit does an innkeeper's lien provide to an innkeeper?

11. If a district attorney is prosecuting a defendant for theft of hotel services, what are the elements of the crime that the prosecutor must prove?

12. What acts constitute the crime of issuing a bad check?

Discussion Questions

1. Jan and Dave have dinner reservations at the Del Rio Restaurant for 7:30 P.M. They arrive at the restaurant at 8:15 P.M. Must the Del Rio honor their reservation?

2. Terry and Cindy, both waitresses at Hillary's Restaurant, were having a dispute. Terry made a gesture suggesting she was about to throw a plate at Cindy. Cindy was frightened and ran from the room. Has Terry committed any tort? If so, which one? What are the elements of that tort?

3. What is required of an innkeeper who is enforcing an innkeeper's lien?

4. What are the differences between a hotel's right to refuse to provide a room to a would-be guest and a restaurant's right to exclude?

5. Can a hotel adopt a house rule prohibiting pets on the premises? Where should the rule be posted? What right does a hotel have if a guest violates the rule and brings a dog to the room?

Application Questions

1. George was drinking at a hotel bar. He became intoxicated and left the bar around 10:00 P.M. While walking through the hotel lobby, he stopped a woman seated on a couch and tried to engage her in conversation. She requested that he leave, but he failed to go. This encounter was observed by a security guard. What action should the guard take? Discuss various possibilities.

2. Steve operates a restaurant. His girlfriend recently broke up with him for another man. The "other man" sought to eat dinner at the restaurant. Steve refused to seat him. Is Steve legally entitled to deny service to the man? Why or why not?

3. Tyrone and Jeff walked into a corner grocery store at 1:55 A.M. to buy beer. At 2:02 they took their selections to the cash register. The clerk refused to sell the beer because the law in the town prohibited alcoholic sales after 2:00 A.M. Tyrone, refusing to take no for an answer, left money on the counter and told the clerk, "Here's ten dollars for the beer and an extra $2 for your trouble. If there's any problem we're staying at the Polex Motel down the street, room 312." Based on their prior purchases of beer elsewhere, Tyrone and Jeff believed ten dollars was generous to cover the cost. Unknown to Tyrone and Jeff, the actual cost of the beer was $15.00. Have they committed the crime of larceny? Why or why not?

4. Several diners at the Olympia Restaurant have complained of stolen coats in the last few days. A regular customer known to the manager entered the store with a coat that resembled the description of one of the stolen coats. The

manager detained the customer pending an investigation. Was the manager's action in detaining the customer legal? Why or why not?

5. Barry is a guest at the Midway Inn. He paid his bill with a stolen credit card and signed his name on the receipt. Identify all the crimes that Barry has committed in this transaction.

Web Site

A Web site that will enhance your understanding of the material in this chapter includes:

http://www.ahma.com This is the site of the American Hotel and Lodging Association, a trade organization for the hotel and lodging industry. The site addresses numerous issues of interest to hotel proprietors and managers.

For additional resources, visit our Web site
www.hospitality-tourism.delmar.com

CHAPTER 10

Guests' Rights

INTRODUCTION

The law endows guests with a variety of rights. If an innkeeper violates any of these rights, liability can result.

Among the rights guests have are the following:

- The right to occupy hotel rooms without disruption
- The right to privacy in guest room, including the right to restrict access by the innkeeper, police, and others
- The right to be treated respectfully and not be insulted or humiliated by hotel staff
- The right to be free from false arrest or detention without cause
- The right to be free from credit card fraud by hotel staff
- The right to be informed of fees and charges before they are imposed
- The right to have hotel employees process guests' mail properly.

The extent of these rights will be discussed in this chapter.

Right to Occupy Assigned Room

A guest assigned a room in a hotel has the right to occupy the room without disruption from the innkeeper. An exception to this rule is where the innkeeper has legal grounds to remove the guest, as discussed in the previous chapter. An innkeeper who wrongfully excludes a guest from the room will be liable to the guest for damages.

The hotel in the following case violated a guest's right in this regard.

CASE EXAMPLE 10-1

Perrine v. Paulos
224 P.2d 41 (Cal. 1950)

Two young women were evicted by defendants from a hotel in Los Angeles. Returning from work one evening, they found padlocks on their rooms. They could not get to any of their personal belongings or clothing. They could not find other accommodations and had to sleep in their automobiles for three nights. Then, on demand of their counsel, they were permitted to again occupy their rooms.

The case was tried by the court, with judgment for plaintiffs for $500 each for general damages; and $500 more each, exemplary [punitive] damages. ...

The evidence establishes without contradiction that defendants owned the hotel and that plaintiffs were guests.

At common law, innkeepers were under a duty to furnish accommodations to all persons in the absence of some reasonable grounds. ...

An innkeeper who refuses accommodations without just cause is not only liable in damages, but is guilty of a misdemeanor. In such cases, exemplary damages may be assessed.

In this case, no showing whatever was made by defendants in excuse or in justification of their treatment of plaintiffs. They just locked them out.

Ruling of the Court: The judgment is affirmed. ...

Right to Privacy in Guest Room

A guest has the right to occupy the room without intrusion by the innkeeper or any unauthorized person. There are five exceptions when the innkeeper is authorized to enter the guest room. They are:

1. Normal maintenance (including housekeeping) and repair
2. Imminent danger
3. Nonpayment
4. When requested to enter by the guest, such as to respond to a guest's room-service order
5. When the rental period has expired and the guest has no basis to believe it has been extended.

In a case involving nonpayment, the hotel discovered on the second day of a guest's stay that the credit card the guest presented as her means of payment had been stolen. The manager went to the guest's room to resolve the issue and knocked several times. When the guest failed to respond, the manager opened the door with a master key and found her in the room. The guest objected to the intrusion on privacy grounds. The court held that an innkeeper who reasonably believes he has been defrauded relating to payment may enter a hotel room and ask the occupants to leave.[1]

In a case where the guest stayed beyond the end of the rental period, the guest had asked for a late departure. The hotel allowed her to remain an extra two hours. When the later time came and went, the guest was still packing. She became belligerent when the manager went to her room and advised her she needed to leave. The manager summoned the police who entered the room to confront the defendant and regain control of the room. While there, the officer observed drug paraphernalia and found forged checks in a search. The guest claimed this search violated her right of privacy and so the evidence should be suppressed. The court refused to exclude the evidence, holding that a guest's expectation of privacy normally ends upon the termination of rental period.[2]

The guest's right to privacy obligates the innkeeper to take steps to prevent, not only unauthorized employees from entering the guest's room, but also unauthorized would-be visitors. Without authorization from the guest, even the guest's spouse is not entitled to access. In the following case, the court affirmed the propriety of the hotel's caution in this regard.

CASE EXAMPLE 10-2

Campbell v. Womack
345 So.2d 96 (La. 1977)

Plaintiff, Elvin Campbell, is engaged in the sand and gravel business. Since the nature of his business often requires his absence from his home in St. Francisville, Mr. Campbell generally obtains temporary accommodations in the area in which he is working. For this purpose, Mr. Campbell rented a double room on a month-to-month basis at the Rodeway Inn in Morgan City, Louisiana. The room was registered in Mr. Campbell's name only.

From time to time, Mr. Campbell would share his room with certain of his employees; in fact, he obtained additional keys for the convenience of these employees. It also appears that Mr. Campbell was joined by his wife on some weekends and holidays, and that they jointly occupied his room on those occasions. However, Mrs. Campbell was not given a key to the motel room. On one such weekend, Mrs. Campbell, arriving while her husband was not at the motel, attempted to obtain the key to her husband's room from the desk clerk, Barbara Womack. This request was denied, since the desk clerk found that Mrs. Campbell was neither a registered guest for that room, nor had the registered guest, her husband, communicated to the motel management his authorization to release his room key to Mrs. Campbell. Plaintiffs allege that this refusal was in a loud, rude, and abusive manner. After a second request and refusal, Mrs. Campbell became distressed, left the Rodeway Inn, and obtained a room at another motel.

[1] *People v. Satz*, 71 Cal.Rptr.2d 433 (Cal. 1998)

[2] *State v. Loya*, 18 P.3d 1116 (Utah 2001)

Mr. Campbell later joined his wife at the other motel and allegedly spent the weekend consoling her. Shortly thereafter, suit was filed against the Rodeway Inn and desk clerk, Barbara Womack. ...

The motel clerk was under no duty to give Mrs. Campbell, a third party, the key to one of its guest's rooms. In fact, the motel had an affirmative duty, stemming from a guest's rights of privacy and peaceful possession, not to allow unregistered and unauthorized third parties to gain access to the rooms of its guest. ...

The additional fact that Mrs. Campbell offered proof of her identity and her marital relation with the room's registered occupant does not alter her third-party status; nor does it lessen the duty owed by the motel to its guest. The mere fact of marriage does not imply that the wife has full authorization from her husband at all times and as to all matters. ... Besides, how could Mrs. Campbell prove to the motel's satisfaction that the then present marital situation was amicable? This information is not susceptible of ready proof. ...

In another case the hotel was less diligent. A battered wife sought shelter in a Holiday Inn against her husband's abuse. Upon arrival, she informed the front desk that her husband had beaten her, requested that no calls be put through to her room, and no one be informed of her presence at the inn. Her husband, however, convinced the hotel manager not only to unlock her door for him, but also to cut the safety chain when she refused to unhook it. While in the presence of the manager, the husband stated he was going to kill his wife. Later that day, he beat her so severely she died in her sleep from her injuries. Her sister sued the hotel, among others. The hotel claimed it was not liable and sought summary judgment. The court denied the motion and referred the matter to a jury.[3] While the outcome of the jury trial is unreported and therefore unknown, this case illustrates that disregard of the innkeeper's duty to protect the privacy of its guests can have grave consequences and can result in liability on the hotel.

Not all states impose liability for disclosure of a guest's room number where harm by disclosing it is not foreseeable. In an Indiana case, the hotel gave a woman's room number to a man who represented himself to the front-desk clerk as the guest's brother who was seeking to help the guest with supposed car trouble. He was in fact her estranged husband. He went to her hotel room, found her there with a date, and attacked him. The court held the attack was unforeseeable and therefore the hotel was not liable for the resulting injuries.[4]

Peeping Toms

Another privacy issue involves employees creating peepholes through which they observe guests in their hotel rooms. Such conduct intrudes on guests' right to privacy. The following case, which received much media coverage, details how this phenomenon can occur.

---

[3] *Thetford v. City of Clanton*, 605 So.2d 835 (Ala. 1992)

[4] *Ellis v. Luxbury Hotels, Inc.*, 716 N.E.2d 359 (Ind. 1999)

CASE EXAMPLE 10-3

Carter v. Innisfree Hotel, Inc.
661 So.2d 1174 (Ala. 1995)

Paul Carter and Wendy Carter sued Innisfree Hotel, Inc. ("Innisfree") [a management corporation that managed the Travelodge Hotel] [and others] alleging various claims arising out of an alleged "peeping Tom" incident during their stay at the Birmingham Civic Center Travelodge Hotel. The trial court entered a summary judgment in favor of all defendants. The Carters appeal from the summary judgment as it relates to Innisfree. ...

On February 25, 1993 ... the Carters [traveled to attend a concert and] decided to rent a room for the night at the Birmingham Civic Center Travelodge. They checked into Room 221 that afternoon, and, after purchasing fast food, went back to their room to eat and relax. While in the room, they heard knocking and scratching sounds, which appeared to emanate from behind a wall near the bathroom; the wall was covered by a mirror. However, they assumed that the sounds were from a neighboring room. They conducted their private marital activities that afternoon, including sexual intercourse, without regard to the strange noises. Wendy was undressed in front of the mirror for nearly two hours that afternoon, while applying her makeup and fixing her hair in preparation for the concert. Before the concert, while Paul was brushing his teeth in front of the mirror, he noticed two scratches in the mirror at eye level. He did nothing about the scratches at that time. The Carters went to the concert as they had planned.

After the concert, Paul again looked into the mirror and saw the scratches. He then removed the mirror and found two round, dime-sized scratches on the back of the mirror. Upon closer inspection, Paul found a large hole in the wall behind where the scratches were placed on the mirror. There was a hollow space approximately 1.5 feet wide between the Carters' wall and the wall of the adjoining room, which allows for maintenance workers to repair wiring and plumbing pipes. After looking at the hole closely, the Carters noticed a hole in the wall of the adjoining room that was covered by the mirror in that room. There was black electrical tape stuck onto the mirror

of the other room; when Wendy pulled the tape off, the Carters discovered scratches on that mirror as well. ...

Paul then telephoned the police and asked them to investigate; they were not able to identify the alleged "peeping Tom." After the police left, the Carters checked out of the hotel and drove back to Huntsville. Paul testified that he has suffered chronic nervousness and sleeplessness since the incident. Wendy testified that she and Paul have had strains in their marriage resulting from nervousness and paranoia she has suffered due to the incident. ...

Nora Wood, a manager employed by Innisfree, stated that she inspects the Travelodge's rooms on a daily basis but said she did not know of the holes and scratches until the Carters complained about them.

The Travelodge customer who rented the adjoining room during the Carters' stay testified that he did not spy on the Carters. However, the record does not indicate whether he was absent from his room during the time the noises occurred. The record indicates that security guards, maintenance workers, housekeepers, and management personnel employed by Innisfree all have access to master keys that open the hotel rooms.

Invasion of Privacy

... Because the scratched mirror and the hole in the wall of Room 221 gave a secret viewing access into Room 221 from the adjoining room, a jury could find a wrongful intrusion into the Carters' right to privacy, and a jury could reasonably infer that the intrusion arose through the actions of Innisfree's agents, who have control over the hotel. The Carters need not prove the actual identity of the "peeping Tom," nor need they demonstrate actual use of the spying device, although, as we have already stated, a jury could reasonably infer from the evidence that the mirror and hole had been used to spy on them. There is no need for the Carters to establish that they saw another's eyes peering back at them through their mirror. ... There can be no doubt that the possible intrusion of foreign eyes into the private seclusion of a customer's hotel room is an invasion of that customer's privacy. ... Even if it is proven that a third party, someone other than an agent of Innisfree, caused the holes and scratches, Innisfree may be held liable for the invasion of the Carters' privacy. It had an affirmative duty, stemming from a guest's right of privacy and peaceful possession, not to allow unregistered and unauthorized third parties to gain access to the room of its guests. ...

Negligence/Breach of Contract

... A jury could reasonably conclude from the evidence that Innisfree, through reasonable inspections, could have prevented the scratched mirrors and the holes behind those mirrors. ...

The jury could conclude that Innisfree had a contractual obligation to the Carters, its customers, to provide them with security, which, at the least, would mean a room free from fear that they were being viewed through their mirror. The jury could also find that Innisfree negligently failed to fulfill this duty, by allowing viewing access to the Carters' room through its failure to inspect the wall and to replace the scratched mirror. The trial court erred in entering the summary judgment for Innisfree on these claims. ...

An important fact in *Carter* was that the hotel could have discovered the scratched mirrors through reasonable inspections of the hotel's premises. In another case involving "peeping Tom" holes discovered by guests in the bathroom mirror, no evidence existed that the hotel's employees knew or could have known of the installation or use of the spying device. The hotel was thus not liable for violating its duty of privacy.[5]

Protection Against Illegal Searches

Sometimes guests engage in illegal activity in a hotel room. For example, a guest might be hiding stolen property, storing drugs, harboring a kidnap victim, or committing rape. Or a guest might, while in his room, engage in conduct that is bothersome or threatening to other guests. Or the guest may confront a medical emergency while occupying the room. In these and related circumstances, a guest's right to privacy in his or her room may conflict with the interests of the innkeeper and police to enter and search a room as part of an investigation. The particular facts of each case determine whose rights and interests are given priority.

Report by Innkeeper of Illegal Activity

When a guest is assigned a room in a hotel, he has exclusive right to the room subject to the exceptions discussed in this chapter. The innkeeper and hotel employees are not permitted to enter a guest's room at will. Rather, they must have a legal basis to go in. Permissible grounds include cleaning the room, nonpayment, consent of the guest, when conduct in a room disturbs other guests, and in an emergency.

---

[5] *Cangiano v. Forte Hotels, Inc.,* 772 So.2d 879 (La. 2001)

If a hotel employee, in the course of legally entering a guest's room, finds evidence of illegal activity, what action should the hotel take? Permitting criminal activity to proceed unabated may endanger other guests in violation of the innkeeper's duty to exercise reasonable care to protect their safety. Tolerating illegal conduct may also jeopardize the hotel's license to carry on business, as we will discuss in Chapter 15.

The hotel should report the illegal activity to the police. Is the hotel violating any rights of the guest by informing the police? The answer is no, provided the hotel employee was legally in the guest's room when the wrongful conduct was discovered.

In *Engle v. State*, 391 So.2d 245 (Fla. 1980), a member of the hotel housekeeping crew discovered, while cleaning, automatic rifles under the bed and some marijuana in an ashtray. She reported her findings to her manager, who reported them to the police. The hotel did not violate any obligation owed to the guest by making the report to the police.

If a guest discards property in a wastebasket in the guestroom, the property is considered to have been abandoned and no privacy rights to that property remain. A hotel did not violate a guest's rights where housekeepers gave to police trash bags removed in the ordinary course of cleaning from a guest's room. The bag contained evidence of the crime of money laundering.[6]

A guest also loses privacy rights if he damages property in the guest room. An innkeeper can enter the room of a guest who is "smashing things" in the room without violating the guest's right to privacy.[7] Likewise, a guest who is engaging in loud and disruptive conduct in the room loses his expectation of privacy; the innkeeper can legally enter.[8] In these circumstances, the guest can anticipate that the hotelier will need to investigate to protect the interests of other guests and the hotel.

Search Warrant

Once the police are called, they cannot legally search a guest's room on the strength of permission given by the hotel manager or owner alone. The guest's right to privacy requires the guest's permission for the police to make a consental search. Without the *guest's* approval, the police must obtain a **search warrant**, which is an order from a judge commanding a police officer to search a designated place for evidence of criminal activity. If a search is made of a hotel room without the guest's permission and without a search warrant, the search invades the guest's privacy, subject to certain exceptions. Before issuing a search warrant, a judge must be satisfied that the police have probable cause to believe the search will uncover evidence of a crime. **Probable cause** consists of facts sufficient for a reasonably prudent person to believe that evidence of a crime is located in the place the police want to search. A suspicion or hunch is not enough.

---

[6] *Ohio v. Duncan*, 719 N.E.2d 608 (Ohio 1998)

[7] *McCary v. Commonwealth*, 548 S.E.2d 239 (Va. 2001)

[8] *State v. Perkins*, 588 N.W.2d 491 (Minn. 1999)

The warrant requirement provides a buffer between individuals and the police that helps ensure that people's privacy rights are not violated. The **exclusionary rule** holds that evidence obtained in a warrantless search will not be admissible in court; the prosecutor will not be able to use such evidence to help prove the defendant's guilt. In such a circumstance, the criminal charges placed against the defendant are customarily dismissed unless the police have other evidence.

In the *Engle* case, discussed previously, the police searched the hotel room for the weapons and the marijuana without first obtaining a search warrant. The defendant asked the court to suppress the evidence, and the court did so. Similarly, where a motel owner permitted police to search a hotel room occupied by a guest without the latter's permission and without a search warrant, "vines" of marijuana found in the room were suppressed and the criminal action against the guest was dismissed.[9]

Would the *innkeeper* be liable in either of these cases if the police, relying on information provided by a hotel employee, made an illegal search without a warrant? The answer is no. The hotel is not liable for the acts of the police; they are not employees or agents of the hotel. Thus, while the search without a warrant constitutes an invasion of the guest's privacy, the hotel cannot be held liable for that wrong.

Consent to Search

Consent is an exception to the requirement that the police must obtain a search warrant. If a guest voluntarily agrees to permit the police to enter the room and search it, the police are free to do so. Any evidence they find will not be suppressed.

For the consent to be valid, the person agreeing to the search must have the authority to give consent. Clearly, a guest has the authority to consent to a police search of his own room.

Suppose the guest is not in when the police arrive seeking permission to search. If they ask the innkeeper for approval and he consents, is the search valid? The answer is no. During the time a room is assigned to a guest, neither the innkeeper nor any employee of the hotel has the authority to consent to a search. If the police make a search of a guest's room relying only on consent granted by the innkeeper or a hotel employee, any evidence found will be suppressed. Will the hotel be liable to the guest? If the guest suffers a loss, a court would likely find the hotel liable for violating the guest's privacy.

Effect of Termination of Occupancy on Privacy Rights

As we have seen in this chapter, the guest's right to exclusive use of the room ends if the guest fails to pay as agreed or if the occupancy period expires. In these circumstances, the right to occupy the room reverts from the guest to the

---

[9]*People v. Greig*, 619 N.Y.S.2d 444 (1994)

innkeeper, who is then entitled to enter the room, remove any remaining property of the guest, and prepare it for the next guest.

Just as the guest's right to occupy the room ends, so too does the guest's expectation of privacy. A hotel guest has no reasonable expectation of privacy in a room after the rental period has expired. This rule applies even if the guest remained physically present in the room after checkout time. In a case where the guests had not vacated the room although checkout time had passed, housekeeping did not violate the guest's rights by alerting the police to the presence in the guest room of a handgun and loaded ammunition clip.[10] Similarly, a guest's privacy rights were not violated where the hotel notified police of drug paraphernalia discovered in the defendant's room after the designated check-out time.[11] Thus, if any evidence is found by hotel staff in the room while preparing it for the next guest and the police are called, they can search without a warrant and the evidence will not be suppressed. In *People v. Lerhinan*, 455 N.Y.S.2d 822 (1982), the guest was two weeks overdue in payments, so the innkeeper entered the room and removed the belongings. The hotel manager discovered liquor and tools that had been stolen from the hotel. He called the police, who investigated without a warrant. The guest was arrested the next day. His attempt to suppress the evidence was denied because, at the time the incriminating items were discovered, he no longer had the exclusive right to occupy the room and thus had no expectation of privacy.

Disturbing the Peace

Suppose a condition in a guest's room is disturbing to other guests. A hotel employee enters the room to quell the disruption and discovers evidence of a crime. Is this an illegal search requiring suppression of the evidence? The answer is no. The innkeeper has a duty to protect guests from interference by others. The innkeeper is thus entitled to enter the room where the disturbance is occurring. Any evidence in plain view found by the innkeeper while legally in the guest's room will not be suppressed. Further, when faced with conduct by one guest that is disturbing to others, the innkeeper can solicit the assistance of police who can in this circumstance enter a guest's room without the guest's permission and without a search warrant. This rule of law is explored in the following case.

CASE EXAMPLE 10-4

People v. Henning
96 Cal.Rptr. 294 (Cal. 1971)

Sometime after ten o'clock P.M. (the curfew hour), on the evening of December 25, 1969, the desk clerk of Hillside Inn called the police department asking assistance concerning a disturbance in one of its rooms. An officer responded. He was told that a guest had complained about a disturbance at room 109,

---

[10] *Commonwealth v. Brass*, 674 N.E.3d 1326 (Mass. 1997)

[11] *State v. Mitchell*, 20 S.W.3d 546 (Mo. 2000)

where a group of juveniles and adults were pounding on the door demanding admittance. The officer and a hotel employee went to the room. No one was then present in the outside hall, but inside "a very loud radio" was turned on. The officer knocked on the door repeatedly and called the name of the defendant Henning, to whom the room was registered. There was no response whatever, and there was no diminution of the radio's sound output. At the officer's request, the hotel employee unlocked the door. The officer again knocked on the door, with a similar lack of response within. The door was then pushed slightly ajar. The officer testified, "At that time I could see in, and I could see the lower half of a male's body extended in a prone position over the end of the bed fully clothed." The man was lying face down. Fearful that the man was in trouble, the officer entered to "check on his welfare." Upon the entry, in plain sight on the floor, on a table, and protruding from the prone man's pocket, the officer saw a portion of the narcotics and dangerous drugs that were later the subject of Henning's motion to suppress. The man partially on the bed was Henning, who appeared to be in a deep sleep.

From this evidence, it could reasonably be concluded that the officer entered Henning's room with consent of the hotel employee; that the initial purpose of the entry was to silence a loud radio that was annoying the hotel's guests; and that upon seeing Henning prone and in an unusual position on the bed, an additional purpose developed—concern for the man's safety. It may clearly be inferred that the officer at no time prior to the entry had a purpose to arrest anyone or to search the room. And he may reasonably be considered as an agent of the hotelman, who understandably did not wish, unattended, to risk a hostile confrontation in silencing a source of annoyance to the hotel's guests.

We have no hesitancy in concluding that a hotelkeeper himself may enter a rented, but presently unoccupied, room when reasonably necessary to quiet a "very loud radio" that is presenting a substantial annoyance to other guests. Indeed, it has been held that an innkeeper is under an obligation not to harbor persons dangerous to the peace and comfort of those for whose comfort he is bound to provide, ... to protect his patrons from annoyance, ... and to exercise proper care for the safety and tranquility of the guest.

It seems most reasonable for the hotel people to have called upon a police officer for assistance, rather than risk violence in pursuit of their duty of care for the nighttime comfort, tranquility and quiet of their guests. If so, then it was equally reasonable for the police officer, on request and with their consent and under the facts before us, to assist in such an undertaking.

The additional purpose of the officer, upon observing the condition of Henning within the room, was clearly without Fourth Amendment or other fault. Reason tells us, and valid authority holds, that an entry is proper when a police officer reasonably and in good faith believes such entry to be necessary in order to render aid to a person in distress. ...

[A] reasonable inference could be, and was, properly drawn by the court that the officer acted only in aid of the hotel management late at night to quell a disturbance—a loud radio—in the room. ...

[W]e must conclude that there was substantial evidence in support of the superior court's order denying Henning's motion to suppress evidence.

CASE QUESTION

1. If the radio had not been playing loudly, would the evidence have been suppressed?

Emergency Situation

Another circumstance under which an innkeeper is permitted to admit police into a guest's room is where reasonable grounds exist to believe that the guest is in distress and in need of assistance. If the police see evidence of a crime in plain view while in the room, it is admissible in court against the guest. In *State v. Wright*, 607 P.2d 19 (Ariz. 1980), the police were called to a hotel in response to a report of a disturbance. Guests in one room had been awakened by pounding on the door of the adjacent room. When the police arrived, two people were outside the room where the disturbance occurred. They explained they were trying to arouse their friend who had been drinking heavily earlier in the evening. No response was made to the officer's knocking. He obtained a key from the innkeeper and entered. The occupant was unconscious on the bed. His pulse was weak. An ambulance was called. The police found drugs in plain view on the table in the room. In the resulting criminal case charging the guest with possession of drugs, he claimed the police entry into the room was unauthorized and therefore the drugs should be suppressed. The court rejected this argument, holding that the police can enter the hotel room of a guest in an emergency where the occupant is in need of imminent aid or reasonably believed to be in such need.

Room Registered to Another

A person who is not a registered guest does not have a right of privacy in a hotel room. Similarly, a guest's right to privacy applies only to the room she occupies. In a case involving murder, the defendant was originally arrested for stealing his girlfriend's fur coat. When he was searched the police discovered a key to room 234 at a nearby hotel. The police obtained a search warrant for the room and found a corpse under the bed. The defendant's attempt to challenge the search was rebuffed by the court because, although he was a registered guest at the hotel, the room where the body was located was not the room registered to him.[12]

Search of Items Mislaid by Guests

A related privacy problem involves mislaid or forgotten luggage of a guest. Can an innkeeper who finds a guest's mislaid briefcase open it to help determine the true owner? The answer is yes. In such a case, the owner's right to privacy must yield to a reasonable search of the briefcase by the manager to determine the owner. If the innkeeper fails to verify ownership of the briefcase and by mistake gives it to someone other than the owner, the innkeeper will be liable for breach of its duty as bailee, as discussed in Chapter 8. The following case illustrates the various issues that can arise in this situation.

CASE EXAMPLE 10-5

Berger v. State
257 S.E.2d 8 (Ga. 1979)

The assistant manager of the Hyatt Regency Hotel was given a briefcase that had been found in the main lobby. It was closed but not locked. It was not an unusual occurrence to find several misplaced briefcases each day in the hotel. He opened the briefcase to find if it contained any identification of its owner. It

---

[12] *People v. Zappulla*, 724 N.Y.S.2d 433 (N.Y. 2001)

contained a wallet, a large amount of "business papers," and "bundles of money." Two men who inquired about the briefcase were directed to his office. One man, the defendant, stated that it was his briefcase. The manager asked him if he had any personal identification. The defendant told him his identification was in the wallet in the briefcase. The manager stated that it was hotel policy that identification must be made from the person and not from the lost object, and "if the person can't identify themselves, obviously we can't give it out." The manager was particularly concerned about this item because of the large amount of cash it contained. Both men were getting "agitated" and "a bit loud."

Police officers Derrick and Cochran were employed by the hotel as security personnel while they were off duty. Officer Derrick received a call over his "beeper" and was directed to report to the assistant manager's office. Officer Derrick testified that when he arrived, the assistant manager briefed him on the situation, and he identified himself to the defendant and asked him if the briefcase was his. The defendant stated that it was. Officer Derrick asked defendant if he had "any identification, driver's license or anything like that." The defendant said it was in the briefcase. ... According to Officer Derrick, the briefcase was unlocked and the top was mostly down. He opened up the case, pulled out the billfold and left the briefcase open. Officer Derrick asked the defendant to write out his signature for comparison purposes. "As I was looking at the signatures on the driver's license and ... the signature on the piece of paper, the case was right in front of me, and I noticed there was a bag of what I thought was marijuana inside the case in the back of it ... and [the defendant] saw me see the marijuana ... that's when he said ... "I don't want you to search the briefcase."...

The defendant testified that when he was asked for identification by the assistant manager, he took his wallet out of the briefcase

and told the manager what was in it, and at that time the officers came in. He stated the briefcase was closed and the wallet was in his hand. When asked for identification, he showed Officer Derrick his driver's license, and he signed his name to let the officer make a comparison. He testified that Officer Derrick said: "... yeah, that's you all right ... but that doesn't prove this is your briefcase. ... I am going to have to look in it. ... It was closed. ... I said I would prefer that you do not look in it." Although [the defendant] repeated his request not to look in the briefcase, the officer opened it and searched through the briefcase until he found the marijuana, cocaine, and $7,000 in cash. [Defendant tried to suppress the money and drugs on the ground that the search was illegal.] The court denied the motion to suppress. Defendant brings this appeal.

Defendant argues that ... [he] had a reasonable expectation of privacy in his briefcase that was protected by the Fourth Amendment. ...

Innkeepers of this state have a statutory liability to guests for property coming into their possession. ... It is not an unauthorized search for hotel management personnel, including security personnel, to open unlocked items found on their premises in an attempt to determine ownership so that the lost or misplaced property can be returned to its proper owner.

In the instant case, the incriminating evidence came into possession of the law enforcement authorities inadvertently and unmotivated by any desire to locate incriminating evidence. Assuming without deciding that Officer Derrick was acting as a police officer, we find nothing unlawful about a police officer opening an unlocked, lost, or misplaced item to determine ownership. The marijuana was then in plain view, and the officer was authorized to confiscate the contraband. ...

Ruling of the Court: Judgment affirmed. [The drugs found in the briefcase were admissible against the defendant in his trial for illegal possession of controlled substances.]

CASE QUESTION

1. Why was the search of the briefcase not a violation of the defendant's constitutional right against unreasonable searches?

Unclaimed Lost Property

What is the responsibility of an innkeeper or restaurateur when lost property is found and no one claims it? Many states have statutes that prescribe a procedure for disposing of such items. Typically, the proprietor is required to inform the police of the finding or deposit the property at the police station. When owners of lost property realize items are missing, they often do not know where they misplaced them. Police headquarters provide a central, easily located place for owners to pursue their property. Failure of the facility to notify the police or deposit the property may constitute a crime. See, for example, New York Personal Property Law § 252.

Protection Against Insults

Though the use of insulting and abusive language is objectional and can evoke anger, the courts have been slow to regard it as a basis of civil liability as between individuals. Most states do not recognize abusive language, without more, as a tort. However, if the language is beyond abusive and qualifies as outrageous, it may constitute the tort of intentional infliction of emotional stress. For this tort, the words must be "so extreme in degree, as to go beyond all possible bounds of decency and to be regarded as atrocious and utterly intolerable in a civilized community."[13] In addition, for a successful lawsuit, the plaintiff must have suffered severe or extreme emotional distress.

Some courts have allowed recovery for a lower threshold of abusive language in cases where an innkeeper and guest are involved. The reason is that the innkeeper, carrying on a business of a public nature, is expected to extend to guests respectful and decent treatment, and to refrain from conduct that would interfere with patrons' comfort or humiliate and distress them. *DeWolf v. Ford*, 86 N.E. 527 (N.Y., 1908), was one of the earliest cases on point. Here the court said,

> One of the things that a guest for hire at a public inn has the right to insist upon is respectful and decent treatment at the hands of the innkeeper and his servant, so that is an essential part of the contract, whether express or implied. This right of the guest necessarily implies an obligation on the part of the innkeeper that neither he nor his servants will abuse or insult the guest or indulge in any conduct or speech that may unnecessarily bring upon him physical discomfort or distress of mind.

No similar duty is owed to a nonguest. In *Jenkins v. Kentucky Hotel Co.*, 87 S.W.2d 951 (Ky. 1935), the plaintiff, who was not registered at the hotel, was waiting in the lobby for her brother, who was attending a banquet. The hotel detective approached the plaintiff and, in a rude and menacing manner, told her erroneously that no such meeting was going on in the hotel and ordered her to leave. Fearing bodily harm, she left. A few minutes later, she returned and went

---

[13] *Vinson v. Linn-Mar Community School District*, 360 N.W.2d 108 (Iowa 1984)

directly to the room where the meeting was in progress. The court ruled that although the detective's manners were rude and highly objectionable, "bad manners are not actionable." The court stated, "[A]ppellant was at most a mere licensee, [a status with less rights than a guest] and that if she had been requested in a proper manner to leave the lobby and had failed to do so, reasonable force could lawfully have been used to eject her."

In another nonguest case, the plaintiff, a patron of a lunch counter, was accused by the waitress of leaving without paying for his food when in fact he had paid. The court denied recovery, saying the waitress' statements were not so "outrageous or atrocious as to exceed all possible bounds of decency as is required."[14]

In *Jones v. City of Boston*, 738 F.Supp. 604 (Mass. 1990), the plaintiff, a black man, was a patron at the Sports Saloon in the Copley Square Hotel. After he spoke with a group of white women, the bartender allegedly said to them, "What did I tell you about talking to niggers?" Jones sued the hotel for his resulting emotional distress. In Massachusetts, to collect damages for emotional distress, the plaintiff's emotional injury must be severe. The court in this case held, "Although there is no question that referring to a person as a 'nigger' is outrageous," the plaintiff was unable to show that his distress was severe.

In another case, polite treatment of a guest helped to save the hotel from liability. A clerical error resulted in a hotel checking the plaintiff out of his room one day before his reservation was to expire. Another guest was soon thereafter given possession of the room. When the plaintiff returned to the hotel in the early morning hours, he was unable to occupy his room. He sued for "indignity, abuse and humiliation." According to the plaintif's testimony, the desk clerk was not discourteous or abusive. Said the court, "[I]t is difficult to find any degree of humiliation in an incident which unfolded in a deserted hotel lobby at 3:00 A.M. witnessed by a solitary and apologetic desk clerk. ... It is the publicity of abusive language] that causes the humiliation." The plaintiff's case was thus dismissed.[15]

Protection Against False Arrest

Neither a hotelkeeper nor a restaurateur is under any duty to prevent the arrest of a guest by police officers who are seemingly acting within their authority. However, if the arrest is due to a false statement by the hotel, restaurant, or their agents, the establishment could be liable. In *Nensen v. Barnett*, 134 N.W.2d 53 (Neb. 1965), a hotel employee falsely told a police officer that a guest had breached the peace, which led to her arrest. She successfully sued the hotel for **false arrest**, which is the unauthorized restraint of a person.

---

[14]*Henderson v. Ripperger*, 594 P.2d 251 (Kan. 1979). In accord is *Wallace v. Shoreham Hotel Corp.*

[15]*Pollock v. Holsa Corp.*, 454 N.Y.S.2d 582 (N.Y. 1982)

A hotel or restaurant commits the tort of false arrest or imprisonment when it detains a person illegally. *Only* if the person actually has committed a crime can the establishment legally detain him.

The plaintiff in *Jacques v. Childs Dining Hall Co.*, 138 N.E. 843 (Mass. 1923), accompanied by her aunt, entered the defendant's restaurant and proceeded through the crowded facility up one flight of stairs to the ladies' lounge. As the aunt did not desire anything to eat, the plaintiff went alone downstairs to the dining area and was served. Upon receiving her bill, she returned to her aunt and together they walked toward the door to leave. As they passed the cashier's desk, the plaintiff paid for the food she ate. As they started to leave the restaurant, the cashier called them back by ringing a bell and beckoning the plaintiff. The cashier questioned the plaintiff as to why the bill covered only one meal. She explained that her aunt had not eaten in the restaurant and again started to leave. The cashier commanded her to wait. The head waiter and then the manager were summoned. The plaintiff and her aunt were asked to accompany the headwaiter to the rear of the restaurant for questioning, where they were detained and questioned for some twenty-five minutes. The plaintiff's truthfulness was openly and repeatedly challenged, such that if the plaintiff had left the restaurant before being exonerated, "her departure might well have been interpreted by the lookers-on as an admission of guilt." Finally, the cashier approached the plaintiff, who was then with the manager, and said he (the cashier) had mistakenly mixed up the plaintiff's check with someone else's. The plaintiff was then allowed to leave.

Like many states, Massachusetts, the state in which the case occurred, authorizes a restaurant to detain a person if it has reasonable cause to believe she did not pay money owed, provided the detention lasts for only a reasonable amount of time and is carried out in a reasonable manner. If, however, the person is detained without reasonable cause or for an unreasonable amount of time or in an unreasonable manner, she is entitled to recover for damages. In the *Jacques* case, the court determined the detention was based on inattention and carelessness of the cashier, which falls short of the necessary standard of reasonable cause. Therefore, the restaurant was liable to the plaintiff.

This case underscores the principle that a hotel or restaurant cannot with impunity interfere with its patrons' freedom of movement or accuse them of illegal acts without good cause. To avoid liability, the hospitality facility needs reasonable grounds to believe the patron has acted illegally.

Protection Against Credit Card Fraud

Guests frequently pay their hotel and restaurant bills with a credit card. They expect employees with access to their credit card number to use it for official purposes only—to complete the payment transaction. Occasionally an employee misuses the information and makes unauthorized purchases charged to the customer's account. Or the employee might utilize the card number to engage in identity theft, meaning to obtain personal financial information about the credit-card holder and illegally use that information to transfer money from the customer's accounts to the employee.

Such unauthorized transactions constitute crimes and may subject the employee to civil liability for fraud, and criminal prosecution for larceny (theft), forgery, and criminal possession of stolen property. The hotel or restaurant employing the wrongdoer may also be liable if it failed to institute procedures designed to prevent such occurrences. Yet again, we see the importance of good management and supervision of employees.

Rights Concerning Rates and Fees

Legal mandates and good practice require that room rates and other fees be disclosed to guests before the costs are incurred. Further, a hotel cannot impose charges for services not provided.

Right to Advance Notice

Guests have a right to know, prior to contracting for a room, the fees and charges a hotel will impose. Many states require that rates be posted in each room and signs containing prices not be misleading.

Right to No Extraneous Fees

Guests also have the right not to be charged for services they did not receive. For example, a statute in New York provides that "no charge or sum shall be collected or received by any hotelkeeper for any service not actually rendered." Contrary to this statute, the Waldorf Astoria charged all guests a two percent fee for "sundries" (miscellaneous items), which covered messenger services that some guests used and others did not. The legality of the fee was successfully challenged by the New York State Attorney General, the chief legal officer of the state. The court's decision follows.

CASE EXAMPLE 10-6

State of New York v. Waldorf-Astoria
323 N.Y.S.2d 917 (1971)

Petitioner brings this special proceeding ... to permanently enjoin and restrain the respondents from conducting and transacting their business in a persistently fraudulent and illegal manner, and to direct restitution to all consumers of the amount charged for services not rendered ... pursuant to [statute]. ...

The General Business Law does require every hotel to post "a statement of the ... charges by the day and for meals furnished and for lodging." It further provides that "No charge or sum shall be collected or received by any such hotelkeeper or innkeeper for any service not actually rendered."

Between December 2, 1969 and May 21, 1970 the respondents did add to each bill of each customer a 2 percent charge for sundries. ...

Respondents argue that there was no violation of the General Business Law because it only prohibits charges "for any service not actually rendered" and that message services in fact were rendered. However, even respondents admit that all of their customers did not receive special, costly messenger service. They contend that 77 percent did receive such service but admit that 23 percent did not. None of their customers received any explanation or347itemization of the charge for sundries. All of them were charged this 2 percent during the period in question. ...

The business of an innkeeper is of a quasi public character, invested with many privileges and burdened with correspondingly great responsibilities. ... The charge for message services delineated as sundries was fraudulent and unconscionable. Accordingly, petitioner's application is granted to the extent that respondents are permanently enjoined from engaging in the fraudulent and illegal acts and practices complained of herein.

The amount of money to be refunded is admitted. The petitioner, by its Bureau of Consumer Frauds and Protection, investigated the records of the respondents and claims that the 2 percent charge for sundries during the period in question involved 64,338 customers and amounts to $113,202.83. Frank A. Banks, vice-president and manager of respondent, in an affidavit of June 10, 1971, states that during the period in question transient room sales amounted to $6,329,484. The 2 percent charge would therefore be over $126,000. However, the exact amount is not important, as the respondents are ordered to refund to each and every customer during the period in question all charges for unexplained sundries. These refunds are to be made within 60 days of the date of service of the judgment herein with notice of entry. Within 30 days thereafter canceled vouchers or copies thereof will be exhibited to the petitioner. ...

CASE QUESTION

1. What alternate arrangements for payment of the fee might the hotel have made to avoid liability for returning the money?

Hotels should ensure that they do not impose fees for services not actually rendered. If the hotel intends to charge for certain services, it should charge only those guests who utilize those services. If the demand for the service is insufficient to cover the costs, the hotel should reassess whether it wishes to continue offering that amenity.

As an alternative, a hotel can provide optional complementary services, such as breakfast, without charging the guest an additional fee. Instead, the cost to the hotel is incorporated into the room rate. The room fee remains constant regardless of whether the guest chooses to utilize the additional service. Since guests who do not use the service are not charged an extra fare, this arrangement is permissible.[16]

Telephone Charges

At one time, telephones in guest rooms were considered a courtesy offered by a hotel for the convenience of guests; there was no duty on the part of hoteliers to supply telephone services. Today, failure to provide a telephone in the room

---

[16]For an example of this type of pricing, see *Nashville Clubhouse Inn v. Johnson*, 27 S.W.3d 542 (Tenn. 2000).

may violate the innkeeper's duty to exercise reasonable care to protect guests' safety and to provide adequate security.

A telephone may be the only source of communication in an emergency situation. It might be used to give instructions to guests trapped in their rooms during a fire, or to summon help by a guest who suddenly takes ill and is unable to leave the room.

In the past, the charges that hotels could impose on guests for phone service were severely restricted by both state and federal regulation. Local and intrastate calls were regulated by state public utility commissions that allowed only a very small surcharge. Interstate and international calls were regulated by the Federal Communication Commission, which allowed no surcharge at all. As a result, hoteliers avoided installing elaborate telephone systems because they lost money on telephone services. More recently, however, most states have eliminated regulations that limited the surcharge that hotels may impose on local and intrastate calls, thus providing hotels with a source of revenue. In states where surcharge regulations still exist, innkeepers are bound to conform to them and may not impose a surcharge greater than that allowed by the state regulatory authority.

In states where the regulations have been withdrawn, only competition limits the fees charged. Many guests are irritated by the amount of the fee and the lack of uniformity in the amount; the charges vary significantly from hotel to hotel. Some states, including New York, now have a "truth-in-dialing act" that requires the hotel to display conspicuously a sign on or "in the immediate vicinity of" the phones in the room advising guests that the hotel will impose a fee when calls are made on the hotel's phone. The purpose of these laws is to protect hotel guests from surprise charges and secret surcharges.

Proper Handling of Mail and Packages

Hotel guests often receive mail and packages at the hotel. Sometimes mail arrives after guests depart. In either case, guests have a right to have the mail handled properly by the innkeeper. This right can be construed from the nature of the hotel business. The innkeeper can anticipate that mail will be sent to guests and should develop rules for processing letters and packages. The hotel may be liable to the intended recipient for negligent handling of the package if it is mistakenly delivered to the wrong person. An example of procedures that fulfill the hotel's responsibility to guests include the following:

1. When a package is received for a guest, a notice is placed in the guest's mailbox informing him of receipt by the hotel of the package.

2. The "call" light in the guest room is illuminated, alerting the guest to call the front desk.

3. The package is not released unless the person claiming it exhibits identification.

In a case where the hotel deviated from the above procedures, the claimant exhibited a room key instead of identification and the hotel gave the package to that person. The hotel later discovered that person was not the addressee. The facility will be liable to the intended recipient for negligent handling of the parcel.[17] A related issue involves facsimile communications. If the hotel provides a facsimile machine for guests to use, procedures should be established to ensure guests can send and receive faxed documents reliably.

The following case illustrates the problems a hotel can encounter if proper procedures are not followed. The innkeeper agreed to refuse delivery of a package expected by a departing guest. Unfortunately, a hotel employee accepted delivery and stored the package. The hotel was found to be a bailee (see discussion on bailments in Chapter 8) with a duty to exercise reasonable care.

CASE EXAMPLE 10-7

Berlow v. Sheraton Dallas Corp.
629 S.W.2d 818 (Tex. 1982)

Berlow, a designer and manufacturer of jewelry, frequently authorized her parents (the Soifers) to represent her in showing and selling jewelry to fashionable department stores. In January, 1978, Berlow authorized the Soifers to show ten pieces of jewelry in Dallas. Berlow arranged to have a package containing the jewelry delivered by United Parcel Service (UPS) to her parents at the hotel. The package was marked "insured" on the outside and showed Berlow's return address. The package did not arrive at the hotel during the four-day stay of the Soifers. During their stay, each of the Soifers asked frequently about it at the front desk and, before checking out, the Soifers informed front desk personnel that this was a very important package, although they deliberately refrained from telling them the contents or value of the package. They asked that the hotel refuse delivery of it, and personnel at the front desk agreed to refuse its delivery. Agreeing to and subsequently refusing delivery of packages upon the oral instructions of guests to front desk attendants was standard procedure for the hotel. Contrary to its agreement, however, when the package arrived the hotel took delivery of it, stored it at the front desk for a month, and then turned it over to the United

States Post Office (USPO) without postage, marked "Return to Sender." This, too, was standard procedure for the hotel in dealing with packages stored at the front desk. No attempt was made to determine if the Soifers had been recent guests at the hotel, nor to contact Berlow. The package was lost. At trial, Berlow testified that the fair market value of the jewelry was $10,231.

[T]he jury found that the hotel was negligent in its acceptance, care, and handling of the package, and that this negligence both increased the risk of loss of the package and was the proximate cause of the loss. The jury refused, however, to find the hotel grossly negligent. ... Additionally, the jury found that the hotel did not substantially perform its agreement to refuse delivery of the package by delivering it to USPO and that Berlow's loss was suffered because she relied on the hotel's promise to refuse the package. Finally, the jury found that the hotel, acting as a reasonable and prudent person, should have foreseen that the package contained property of substantial dollar value. The jury awarded Berlow $10,231, the fair market value of the jewelry. ...

The hotel argues that the bailment of the package was merely gratuitous and, as a gratuitous bailee, it can be held liable only for gross negligence. Because we find for reasons explained below that the bailment of the package was a bailment for mutual benefit and not

---

[17] *Bottoms & Tops International, Inc. v. United Parcel Service and Marco Polo, Inc.*, 610 N.Y.S.2d 439 (1994)

a gratuitous bailment, the hotel was liable for its ordinary negligence. ...

In order to constitute a bailment there must be a contract, express or implied, delivery of the property to the bailee, and acceptance of the property by the bailee. Uncontroverted evidence showed that the hotel, rather than refusing delivery, took possession of Berlow's package and stored it on the premises, under lock and key, for one month. Assuming custody of the package in this manner established an implied contract to bail the package. Delivery of the package and acceptance of it by the hotel were stipulated; thus bailment of the package was established as a matter of law.

That the bailment was one for mutual benefit and not merely gratuitous was also established as a matter of law. A bailment is for the mutual benefit of the parties, although nothing is paid directly by the bailor, where property of the bailor is delivered to and accepted by the bailee as an incident to a business in which the bailee makes a profit. The Soifers were paying guests at the hotel. It is not unusual for patrons to have packages delivered to them at a hotel, and, in this case, the evidence showed that the practice occurred frequently enough that the hotel developed standard procedures for dealing with packages. Although no direct charge was made, the price paid for the room also included the incidental services provided by the hotel. This provided consideration for the implied agreement to bail Berlow's package and established a bailment for mutual benefit as a matter of law.

Having entered into a bailment for mutual benefit, the hotel became liable for its ordinary negligence. The jury found that the hotel was negligent in its acceptance, care, and handling of the package, and there was some evidence to support this finding. The evidence showed that the hotel violated its own standard procedure, as well as its express agreement with the Soifers, to refuse delivery of packages when requested to do so. The evidence also showed that the package was stored for one month, during which the hotel made no attempt to contact the Soifers or Berlow, then delivered it to USPO without postage. This raises some evidence upon which the jury could find the hotel negligent.

[T]he hotel argues that, as a matter of law, it was not negligent. According to the hotel, because the package was delivered to USPO for return to Berlow, the liability for any loss rested with USPO as a subsequent bailee and not with the hotel. We do not agree. While the evidence showed that Berlow's package was lost while in the custody of USPO, it also showed that the hotel gave the package, which was insured when delivered to the hotel by UPS, to USPO without insurance or postage. This was evidence of negligence by the hotel, sufficiently strong to require submission of the issue to the jury. The hotel, therefore, did not establish its non-negligence as a matter of law.

There was also some evidence to support the jury's finding that the hotel's negligence was a proximate cause of Berlow's loss. ...[B]ecause the package was given to USPO without postage, the jury could find that the hotel should have reasonably foreseen that the package would never reach Berlow.

Likewise, there was some evidence to support the jury's finding that it was foreseeable that the package contained property of substantial dollar value. ... [T]he jury could find it reasonable for the hotel to foresee that guests would bring or deliver items of value to the hotel. ...

Because there was some evidence on each element of recovery on Berlow's theory that she and the hotel entered into a bailment for mutual benefit, the trial court erred in granting the hotel's motion for judgment notwithstanding the verdict; thus judgment should be rendered for Berlow. ...

[J]udgment rendered in favor of Berlow for $10,231.

CASE QUESTION

1. Assume that the hotel employee with whom the Soifers made arrangements for return of the package was not on duty when it arrived or had been terminated before it was delivered. What procedures might the hotel have instituted to ensure the Soifers' wishes were nonetheless honored?

Key Terms

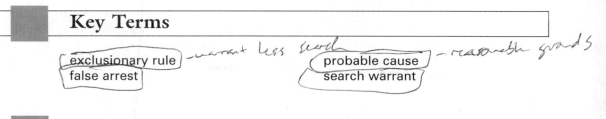

exclusionary rule   — warrant less search
false arrest

probable cause   — reasonable grounds
search warrant

Summary

Guests have a variety of rights, which innkeepers must honor or risk liability for their breach. Those rights include the right to occupy the guest room without disturbance; the right against unauthorized police searches; the right against insulting treatment by hotel employees; the right to be free from unlawful arrest or restraint by the hotel staff; the right to disclosure of information concerning fees and charges for the room, phone, and other services; and the right to proper handling of mail, facsimile transmissions, and incoming packages.

Preventive Law Tips for Managers

- *Do not disrupt a guest's occupancy of the room except for good and exceptional cause.* A guest has the right to occupy the hotel room without interference from the innkeeper. Once a room is assigned to a guest, the innkeeper can enter only for normal maintenance, imminent danger, nonpayment, disruption of other guests, and when requested by the guest. Entering the room at other times or forcing a guest out of a room without cause and without providing alternate accommodations violates this right and entitles the guest to damages from the hotel.

- *If police ask you for permission to search the room of a current guest who is not in arrears in payment, remind the officer that you do not have legal authority to consent to a search.* A police officer in pursuit of a defendant may not know or recall in the heat of an investigation that an innkeeper lacks authority to consent to a search of a guest's room. If police request authority to search an occupied room, ask to see the warrant. If they do not have one, remind them that by law an innkeeper does not have that authority to consent to a search (unless one of the exceptions apply) and any evidence obtained will be suppressed. In response, most officers will apply for a warrant.

- *Do not give lost or mislaid property to someone claiming to be the owner without verifying that person's identity and ownership.* An innkeeper has a duty to exercise reasonable care in tending to lost or mislaid property. The duty of reasonable care encompasses the return of the goods to its owner. If a hotel gives the merchandise to someone other than its rightful owner, the hotel may be liable to the owner. To avoid that happening, the innkeeper should require proof of ownership before giving the goods to anyone.

■ *Train employees to be polite and respectful of guests; stress the importance of avoiding insulting or abusive language.* Offensive or humiliating comments made by a hotel employee to a guest can result in liability for the hotel. Employees should be trained to address guests respectfully and avoid insulting comments.

■ *Train employees on how to handle a suspected theft properly.* Guests have the right not to be falsely accused of improper conduct by hotel staff. Employees should be taught proper procedures for handling suspicious activity. Those procedures might include any of the following, depending on the circumstances: contacting the manager or other supervisory employee; investigating further; and contacting the police.

■ *When investigating suspected criminal activity, do it confidentially, informing only those who need to know, and do it reasonably, with minimal disruption to the guest.* Conducting an investigation improperly can lead to liability. The investigation should be done within a reasonable amount of time from when suspicion arose. The treatment of the suspect during the investigation should be respectful and reasonable. The investigation should be no broader than necessary to determine the truth or falsity of the suspected activity.

■ *Do not impose any charge on a guest's bill for services not utilized by the guest.* A guest can legally be charged only for those services that he utilized while a guest at the hotel. Additional charges are not permitted. The hotel's billing procedures should be reviewed to ensure guests are not charged for unused services.

■ *Disclose information concerning the fees for in-room telephone use.* Most hotels charge a fee for the use of phones located in hotel rooms. The fees vary and guests are often uncertain as to the amount of the charges in a given hotel. Some states require that information identifying the charges be disclosed in writing near the phone. Compliance with these statutes is necessary to avoid fines. In states that do not statutorily require disclosure of this information, good practice calls for its disclosure. Unpleasant disagreements at check-out are thereby avoided.

■ *Develop procedures to ensure that mail addressed to guests and prior guests is properly handled, and follow those procedures carefully.* A hotel may be liable when mail or packages sent to guests or prior guests are not delivered to the addressee. The hotel should adopt procedures for handling the mail to ensure it reaches the intended recipient. Those procedures should include: (1) maintaining a record of the guest's home address; (2) determining the proper method of forwarding mail to a prior guest (United States mail, overnight mail service, etc.); (3) providing funds for postage and insurance; and (4) developing rules for proper handling during the period between receipt of the mail by the hotel and forwarding of it to the guest.

Review Questions

1. What obligation, if any, does a hotel have to refrain from using abusive or insulting language when addressing a guest?

2. Under what circumstances can an innkeeper enter a guest's room without consent?

3. What constitutional rights are at risk when the police search a hotel room for evidence?

4. If a police search violates a constitutional right, what happens to any evidence that is seized in the search?

5. Who issues a search warrant?

6. What must a police officer prove in order to obtain a search warrant?

7. Who has the authority to consent to a search of a hotel room that has been assigned to a guest? Who does not have that authority?

8. What restrictions does a hotel have concerning the fees it charges?

9. What obligation, if any, does a hotel have concerning mail, packages, and facsimile messages received by the hotel and addressed to guests?

Discussion Questions

1. According to the exclusionary rule, incriminating evidence found during an illegal search cannot be used against the defendant. Often, without that evidence, the defendant will be acquitted. What is your opinion about the exclusionary rule?

2. In what way does a guest's expectation of privacy vary depending on whether he is still a guest or has checked out? Why does the expectation of privacy vary in these two circumstances?

3. Why can a hotel employee look into a mislaid briefcase before returning it to a guest who claims ownership of it? Why does this not violate the owner's right of privacy?

4. You are the assistant manager of a hotel. You have been assigned the task of devising procedures for handling mail delivered to the hotel for guests, both current and past. What are the legal issues you will need to address and what procedures will you recommend?

Application Questions

1. Jan and Dean are friends and are both guests at the Morbury Hotel. While they were in the lobby after returning from a stroll through downtown, Jan called Dean insulting names. Dean was embarrassed and annoyed about the incident. Has the hotel violated any obligation owed to Dean? Why or why not?

2. Connor and his wife are guests at a hotel. During their stay and while Connor was supposed to be attending a business meeting, he was arrested for sale of illegal drugs. The police immediately went to the hotel and received from the innkeeper permission to search the room. During the search the police found illegal drugs and drug paraphernalia. Can they be used against Connor at trial? Why or why not? Does the hotel have any liability to Connor in this circumstance? Why or why not?

3. Elisha was a guest at the Billet Hotel. As she was checking out she discovered she was charged for various items she had thought were free. The hotel had not informed her previously that a fee would be imposed. She was angry and demanded to see the manager. Is the hotel legally entitled to collect these fees? What should the hotel have done to avoid this problem?

Web Sites

Web sites that will enhance your understanding of the material in this chapter include:

http://www.privacyrights.org   This site belongs to the Privacy Rights Clearinghouse and offers information about financial privacy of consumers.

http://www.cdt.org   This site is developed by the Center for Democracy and Technology. It gives information on the privacy of financial data.

The following sites contain the privacy statement of various hotels. A privacy statement explains the methods adopted to protect the privacy of information obtained about a guest:

http://www.holidayinnonthelane.com/privacy-statements.cfm

http://www.parkplace.com/claridge/atlanticcity/CorporatePages/privacystatement

http://www.nolo.com/lawcenter/faqs   Once on this site, click on *Consumer & Travel*, then scroll down to *Hotels and Other Accommodations FAQ*. Several questions and answers on this site address legal issues associated with rights of guests, including room selection and the right to privacy in guest rooms.

For additional resources, visit our Web site
www.hospitality-tourism.delmar.com

UNIT IV

■

Special Topics

■

CHAPTER 11

Liability and the Sale of Food

CHAPTER OUTLINE

Introduction

Adulterated Food

False Food Claims

Smoking Restrictions

Safety Concerns Particular to Food Preparation

Liability for Injuries to Patrons

INTRODUCTION

Studies suggest that one out of every three meals is eaten away from home. If restaurants serve unhealthy food, a serious health risk results. To encourage safe practices, the law imposes liability on restaurants that serve inedible food and requires that claims made about the food be truthful.

A restaurant has a duty to provide reasonably safe premises for its patrons. If a disturbance or attack is foreseeable, as where a belligerent patron remains on the premises or prior security incidents have occurred, the owner must take action to protect the customers from harm. Disregarding this duty can result in liability for damages.

This chapter will examine the laws applicable to the sale of food and the duty of a restaurant to protect the safety of its patrons.

Adulterated Food

A diner who is served food that causes illness has three possible grounds on which to sue: breach of warranty of merchantability, strict products liability, and negligence. A discussion of each of these causes of action follows.

Warranty of Merchantability

The **Uniform Commercial Code (UCC)** is a set of rules designed to simplify and modernize the law governing the sale of goods including food. Virtually all states and the District of Columbia have adopted the UCC. It imposes an implied warranty that goods are "merchantable" in all contracts for the sale of goods, including food, where the seller is a merchant.[1] A restaurant qualifies as a merchant for purposes of the warranty. **Merchantable** means the goods are at least of average quality and fit for their ordinary purpose. For example, if you buy a book bag and it tears when you put two books in it, the bag is not fit for its intended purpose and thus is not merchantable.

This warranty of merchantability is implied in all contracts for the sale of goods made by a merchant; it exists even if the parties never mention it in their negotiations. The warranty renders manufacturers and sellers of food virtual insurers that the food is edible and free from dangerous substances. The basis for imposing this liability is a public policy for protection of consumers.

Merchantable Food

Inappropriate objects in food will render it unmerchantable. Food, to be merchantable, must be fit for human consumption, that is, it will not make you ill when you eat it. To pass muster, food does not have to be nutritional or taste great; it merely must be eatable.

Objects in Food

A pizza served with a tack in it is not merchantable. The restaurant that served the pizza will be liable to a customer injured by the tack based on breach of the warranty of merchantability.

Foreign/Natural Test

In some states, whether an object found in food constitutes a breach of warranty is determined by the **foreign/natural substance test**. If the object is foreign—

---

[1]UCC 2-314. (This is a typical UCC citation. The numeral "2" identifies which of the UCC's nine articles is referenced. The number following the dash refers to a section within the referenced article.)

that is, unrelated to the components or ingredients of the product—the warranty is breached. If, however, the object is natural, the warranty is not breached.

An example of a foreign object is provided in *Deris v. Finest Foods, Inc.*, 198 So.2d 412 (La. 1967) where the plaintiff swallowed pieces of glass lodged in ice cream while eating a banana split. She successfully sued the restaurant that sold the ice cream. Other examples of foreign objects found in food include an unwrapped condom in a chicken salad[2] and grain and wood shavings in a "ready-to-cook" turkey carcass.[3]

A case illustrating the application of the foreign/natural test to a natural object is *Mix v. Ingersoll Candy Co.*, 59 P.2d 144 (Cal. 1936). The plaintiff was injured by a chicken bone while eating chicken pot pie in a restaurant. The court held the defendant was not liable. Although chicken bones are not expected in a pot pie, they are natural to chicken. Similarly, chicken-bone slivers in chicken soup and nutshell pieces in nut breads are natural substances and, under the foreign/natural test, do not violate the warranty of merchantability.

Reasonable Expectation Test

An alternate test applied by an increasing number of states is the **reasonable expectation test**, which examines whether an object found in food ought to have been anticipated by the consumer. This reasonable expectation test relies on "culturally defined, widely shared standards that food products ought to meet."[4] If the object should be expected, its presence in the food does not constitute a breach of the warranty. If, on the other hand, its presence is not reasonably anticipated, it does constitute a breach. Under this test, more circumstances are likely to constitute breach of the warranty than under the foreign/natural test because some objects may be natural but are nonetheless unexpected. Examples include the chicken bone in the chicken pot pie and the nutshell pieces in the nut bread. Other examples are a pit in a maraschino cherry used as a garnish on a dinner,[5] a piece of bone in a barbecue pork sandwich,[6] and a date pit contained in a date muffin.[7] The outcome of the application of the reasonable expectation test is not always clear because reasonable people might disagree about what should be reasonably anticipated. See if you agree with the judge's decision in the following case. *Note:* While most cases cite precedent as support for the judge's decision, you will enjoy the fact that this case cites the famed chef, Fanny Farmer.

---

[2] *Chambley v. Apple Restaurants, Inc.*, 504 S.E.2d 551 (Ga. 1998)

[3] *Ruggiero v. Perdue Poultry Company*, 1997 WL 811530 (N.Y. 1997)

[4] Restatement (Third) of Torts § 7

[5] *Williams v. Roche Brothers Supermarkets, Inc.*, 1999 WL 788509 (Me. 1999)

[6] *Norris v. Pig'n Whistle Sandwich Shop, Inc.* (Ga. 1949)

[7] *Phillips v. West Springfield*, 540 N.E.2d 1331 (Mass. 1989)

CASE EXAMPLE 11-1

Webster v. Blue Ship Tea Room, Inc. 198 N.E.2d 309 (Mass. 1964)

... On Saturday, April 25, 1959, about 1 P.M., the plaintiff, accompanied by her sister and her aunt, entered the Blue Ship Tea Room operated by the defendant. The group was seated at a table and supplied with menus.

This restaurant, which the plaintiff characterized as "quaint," was located in Boston on the third floor of an old building on T Wharf, which overlooks the ocean.

The plaintiff, who had been born and brought up in New England (a fact of some consequence), ordered clam chowder and crabmeat salad. Within a few minutes she received tidings to the effect that "there was no more clam chowder," whereupon she ordered a cup of fish chowder. Presently, there was set before her "a small bowl of fish chowder." She had previously enjoyed a breakfast about 9 A.M. that had given her no difficulty. The fish chowder contained haddock, potatoes, milk, water, and seasoning. The chowder was milky in color and not clear. The haddock and potatoes were in chunks (also a fact of consequence). She agitated it a little with the spoon and observed that it was a fairly full bowl. ... It was hot when she got it, she ... stirred it in an up and under motion. She denied that she did this because she was looking for something, but it was rather because she wanted an even distribution of fish and potatoes. She started to eat it, alternating between the chowder and crackers which were on the table with ... [some] rolls. She ate about 3 or 4 spoonfuls then stopped. She looked at the spoonfuls as she was eating. She saw equal parts of liquid, potato, and fish as she spooned it into her mouth. She did not see anything unusual about it. After 3 or 4 spoonfuls she was aware that something had lodged in her throat because she couldn't swallow and couldn't clear her throat by gulping and she could feel it. This misadventure led to two esophagoscopies at the Massachusetts General Hospital, in the second of which, on April 27, 1959, a fish bone was found and removed. The sequence of events produced injury to the plaintiff that was not insubstantial.

We must decide whether a fish bone lurking in a fish chowder, about the ingredients of which there is no other complaint, constitutes a breach of implied warranty under applicable provisions of the Uniform Commercial Code. ... As the judge put it in his charge, "Was the fish chowder fit to be eaten and wholesome? ... [N]obody is claiming that the fish itself wasn't wholesome. ... But the bone of contention here—I don't mean that for a pun—but was this fish bone a foreign substance that made the fish chowder unwholesome or not fit to be eaten?"

The plaintiff has vigorously reminded us of the high standards imposed by this court where the sale of food is involved ... and has made reference to cases involving stones in beans, ... trichinae in pork ... and to certain other cases, here and elsewhere, serving to bolster her contention of breach of warranty.

The defendant asserts that here was a native New Englander eating fish chowder in a "quaint" Boston dining place where she had been before; that [f]ish chowder, as it is served and enjoyed by New Englanders, is a hearty dish, originally designed to satisfy the appetites of our seamen and fishermen; that this court knows well that we are not talking of some insipid broth as is customarily served to convalescents. We are asked to rule in such fashion that no chef is forced "to reduce the pieces of fish in the chowder to minuscule size in an effort to ascertain if they contained any pieces of bone." "In so ruling," we are told (in the defendant's brief), "the court will not only uphold its reputation for legal knowledge and acumen, but will, as loyal sons of Massachusetts, save our world-renowned fish chowder from degenerating into an insipid broth containing the mere essence of its former stature as a culinary masterpiece." Notwithstanding these passionate entreaties we are bound to examine with detachment the nature of fish chowder and what might happen to it under varying interpretations of the Uniform Commercial Code.

Chowder is an ancient dish preexisting even the appetites of our seamen and fishermen. ... The word "chowder" comes from the French chaudiere meaning a "cauldron" or "pot." In the fishing villages of Brittany ... faire la chaudiere means to supply a cauldron in which is cooked a mess of fish and biscuit with some savoury condiments, a hodge-podge contributed by the fishermen themselves, each of whom in return receives his share of the prepared dish. The Breton fishermen probably carried the custom to Newfoundland, long famous for its chowder, whence it has spread to Nova Scotia, New Brunswick, and New England. ... Our literature over the years abounds in references not only to the delights of chowder but also to its manufacture. A namesake of the plaintiff, Daniel Webster, had a recipe for fish chowder that has survived into a number of modern cookbooks and in which the removal of fish bones is not mentioned at all. One old time recipe recited in the New English Dictionary study defines chowder as "A dish made of fresh fish (esp. cod) or clams, stewed with slices of pork or bacon, onions, and biscuit." Cider and champagne are sometimes added. Hawthorne speaks of "... [a] codfish of sixty pounds, caught in the bay, [which] had been dissolved into the rich liquid of a chowder." A chowder variant, cod "Muddle," was made in Plymouth in the 1890s by taking "a three or four pound codfish, head added. Season with salt and pepper and boil in just enough water to keep from burning. When cooked, add milk and piece of butter." The recitation of these ancient formulae suffices to indicate that in the construction of chowders in these parts in other years, worries about fish bones played no role whatsoever. This broad outlook on chowders has persisted in more modern cookbooks. "The chowder of today is much the same as the old chowder. ..." The all-embracing Fannie Farmer states in a portion of her recipe, fish chowder is made with a "fish skinned, but head and tail left on. Cut off head and tail and remove fish from backbone. Cut fish in 2-inch pieces and set aside. Put head, tail, and backbone broken in pieces, in stewpan; add 2 cups cold water and bring slowly to boiling point. ..." The liquor thus produced from the bones is added to the balance of the chowder. ...

Thus, we consider a dish that for many long years, if well made, has been made generally as outlined above. It is not too much to say that a person sitting down in New England to consume a good New England fish chowder embarks on a gustatory adventure which may entail the removal of some fish bones from his bowl as he proceeds. We are not inclined to tamper with age-old recipes by any amendment reflecting the plaintiff's view of the effect of the Uniform Commercial Code upon them. We are aware of the heavy body of case law involving foreign substances in food, but we sense a strong distinction between them and those relative to unwholesomeness of the food itself, e.g., tainted mackerel [on the one hand] ... and a fish bone in a fish chowder [on the other]. Certain Massachusetts cooks might cavil at the ingredients contained in the chowder in this case in that it lacked the heartening lift of salt port. In any event, we consider that the joys of life in New England include the ready availability of fresh fish chowder. We should be prepared to cope with the hazards of fish bones, the occasional presence of which in chowders is, it seems to us, to be anticipated, and which, in the light of a hallowed tradition, do not impair their fitness or merchantability ... We are most impressed by *Allen v. Grafton*, 170 Ohio St. 249, 164 N.E.2d 167, where in Ohio, the Midwest, in a case where the plaintiff was injured by a piece of oyster shell in an order of fried oysters. Mr. Justice Taft (now Chief Justice) in a majority opinion held that "the possible presence of a piece of oyster shell in or attached to an oyster is so well known to anyone who eats oysters that we can say as a matter of law that one who eats oysters can reasonably anticipate and guard against eating such a piece of shell ..."

Thus, while we sympathize with the plaintiff who has suffered a peculiarly New England injury. ...

Judgment for the defendant.

CASE QUESTION

1. The court's decision was based in part on its belief that people who eat fish chowder anticipate and expect that it will contain occasional bones. Do you agree? Do you think the decision would have been different if the plaintiff came from Nebraska?

In a similar case, the court, relying on *Webster*, ruled that an occasional piece of clam shell in a bowl of clam chowder should be reasonably expected. The court therefore decided in favor of a grocery store that sold a can of clam chowder to the plaintiff, who injured a molar when she bit down on a piece of shell while eating the soup.[8]

Trend Toward the Reasonable Expectation Test

In judging the merchantability of food, courts recently have been favoring the reasonable expectation rule over a strict application of the foreign/natural test. The reason for this is, at least in part, because even the presence of natural substances can sometimes render food unfit. A Florida court explained it well in *Zabner v. Howard Johnson's, Inc.*, 201 So.2d 824 (Fla. 1967):

> The reasoning applied in [the foreign/natural] test is fallacious because it assumes that all substances which are natural to the food in one stage or another of preparation are, in fact, anticipated by the average consumer in the final product served. It does not logically follow that every product which contains some chicken must as a matter of law be expected to contain occasionally or frequently chicken bones or chicken-bone slivers [just] because chicken bones are natural to chicken meat and both have a common origin. Categorizing a substance as foreign or natural is not determinative of what is unfit or harmful in fact for human consumption. A nutshell natural to nut meat can cause as much harm as a foreign substance, such as a pebble, piece of wire or glass. All are indigestible and likely to cause the injury.

The plaintiff in *Zabner*, while eating maple walnut ice cream, suffered punctured gums and fractured teeth from the presence of a walnut shell in the ice cream. The court held the shell, although a natural substance, could not be reasonably anticipated and thus its presence violated the warranty of merchantability.

In a case from the state of Washington, the plaintiff ordered a crab-melt open sandwich, which consisted of a toasted English muffin topped with shredded crab meat, melted cheese, and chopped parsley. The plaintiff bit into the sandwich and swallowed a one-inch piece of crab shell. Surgery was necessary to remove the shell from the plaintiff's esophagus. If Washington followed the foreign/natural test, the shell would have been deemed natural and the restaurant would not have been liable. But the state adopted the reasonable expectation rule. The court held that diners would not reasonably anticipate the presence of the shell and so its presence is a breach of the warranty of merchantability.[9]

In *Johnson v. C.F.M., Inc.*, 726 F.Supp. 1228 (Kan. 1989), the plaintiff purchased from a convenience store a cup of coffee that contained a considerable amount of coffee grounds. She became ill when she drank the beverage and inadvertently swallowed some of the grounds. She sued the store. Had the court applied the foreign/natural test, it would have dismissed the case. Instead,

---

[8] *Koperwas v. Publix Supermarkets, Inc.*, 534 So.2d 872 (Fla. 1988)
[9] *Jefferies v. Clark's Restaurant Enterprises, Inc.*, 580 P.2d 1103 (Wa. 1978)

the court applied the reasonable expectation test and referred the case to trial, leaving it up to a jury to decide whether the coffee grounds should reasonably have been anticipated.

In *Jackson v. Nestle-Beach, Inc.*, 589 N.E.2d 547 (Ill. 1992), the plaintiff bit into a Katydid, a chocolate-covered pecan-caramel candy, and broke a tooth on a hard pecan shell embedded in it. Again, had the court applied the foreign/natural test, the case would have been dismissed. Instead, the court applied the reasonable expectation test and referred the case to trial.

Consider a case in which the state applies the reasonable expectation test and the object found in the food is foreign. In most such cases, the object will be unexpected, so the food vendor will be liable for breach of warranty. For example, human blood would not be expected in biscuits and gravy purchased from a restaurant. A plaintiff found blood when she opened the styrofoam container in which her take-out breakfast was delivered. An investigation revealed that the preparer had not sufficiently bandaged a cut on her arm.[10] Likewise, two AA batteries would not be expected at the bottom of a Diet Coke can. Their presence constitutes a breach of the implied warranty of merchantability. A verdict in the consumer's favor in the amount of $554,000 was upheld on appeal.[11]

The following case also illustrates this point.

CASE EXAMPLE 11-2

Coulter v. American Bakeries Co.
530 So.2d 1009 (Fla. 1988)

... The uncontroverted evidence presented at trial revealed that appellant had purchased doughnuts manufactured by appellee and sealed in their original package. She opened the package in her automobile and in the course of driving to her destination consumed several pieces of one doughnut by breaking them off with her fingers and popping them into her mouth. Because of an abscessed tooth and sore jaw, instead of chewing the doughnut with her teeth, appellant would sip milk through a straw allowing the doughnut to dissolve in her mouth. In fact, it was the dissolving nature of the doughnut which had prompted appellant to purchase that particular product. Shortly after she began consuming the doughnut, she felt something stick in her throat and immediately ceased ingestion. It was later discovered through x-rays the same day that appellant had consumed a piece containing a metal wire and caused her subsequent injury.

A complaint was filed alleging breach of implied warranty in that the doughnuts were unfit for human consumption. ...

In a breach of an implied warranty action based on the presence of a harmful substance in food, the test of whether the presence of the harmful substance constitutes a breach of implied warranty is whether the consumer can reasonably expect to find the substance in the food as served. ...

Applying the foregoing to the instant case, there was simply no evidence that appellant could have expected to find a wire in the doughnut. ... [J]udgment in favor of appellant.

---

[10] *Flagstar Enterprises, Inc. v. Davis*, 1997 WL 564475 (Ala. 1997)

[11] *Vamos v. Coca-Cola Bottling Company of New York, Inc.*, 627 N.Y.S.2d 265 (N.Y. 1995)

Sometimes an object is not natural to a product but nonetheless is associated with that product. A court may determine such objects should be reasonably expected by the diner.

For example, in *Clime v. Dewey Beach Enterprises, Inc.*, 831 F.Supp. 341 (Del. 1993), the plaintiff suffered a serious illness from eating raw shellfish that contained bacteria. Expert testimony established that most people who eat that bacteria suffer only minor digestive-tract discomfort. However, if the diner has a compromised immune system or liver disease, he will suffer a more severe reaction. The plaintiff had a liver condition and sued the restaurant for breach of warranty of merchantability. Expert testimony established that the bacteria was common in the waters off North America and taken in by filter-feeding organisms such as clams. The court thus found that one who eats raw clams should expect the presence of substances that are indigenous to clams in their natural state, including the bacteria at issue in this case.

Another example is a pearl in oysters. A diner broke his tooth when he bit down on a pearl in an oyster poor-boy but was denied recovery in his lawsuit against the restaurant. The court, noting that a pearl "will occasionally" be found within an oyster, stated that the plaintiff should have reasonably anticipated the possible presence of the pearl.[12]

Other Grounds for Breach of Warranty of Merchantability

Foreign or unexpected objects in food are not the only basis for liability based on the sale of food. Other grounds include rancid or spoiled food, adulterated food, improper handling and preparation that result in unwholesome fare, or severely burned food. Thus, a restaurant was liable where a plaintiff bit into a cheeseburger that "splintered off [apparently due to it being greatly overcooked], causing a piece of severely burned cheeseburger to become lodged in his esophagus" requiring an emergency esophagoscopy to remove the burned burger.[13] If the food is unfit, regardless of the cause, the warranty of merchantability is breached.

Class Action

A restaurant's failure to properly handle or prepare food could result in not just one customer becoming ill, but in some cases many. If numerous people are made sick from the same unhealthy food, they may be able to ease the expense of the lawsuit by bringing a **class action**. This is a proceeding pursued on behalf of many people who are injured by the same cause, and whose cases raise common legal issues. Due to the decreased expense and relative ease of participating in a class action suit, potential plaintiffs who might not otherwise sue will assert their claim, thus expanding the liability exposure of the defendant. In *McFadden v. Staley*, 687 So.2d 357 (Fl. 1997), the complaint alleged that several hundred

---

[12]*Porteous v. St. Ann's Cafe & Deli*, 713 So.2d 454 (La. 1998)

[13]*Morin v. Troymac's, Inc.*, 2000 WL 670040 (Conn. 2000)

people contracted salmonella poisoning or other gastrointestinal ailments as a result of unsanitary and unsafe practices at the defendant's restaurant. The court authorized those who became ill to pursue the case against the restaurant as a class action.

Hot Beverages

Food establishments need to exercise caution when serving hot beverages. An elderly woman won a multimillion-dollar verdict against McDonald's after she was scalded by spilling hot coffee on her lap. A judge later reduced the amount of the verdict, but the fast-food restaurant nonetheless was forced to pay the plaintiff for her injuries. Numerous similar lawsuits followed involving not only coffee, but also hot tea and other hot beverages.

To avoid liability in this type of case, a restaurant should take several precautions. The temperature at which the drink is served should not be higher than industry standards. Cooler than near-boiling will suffice. Automatic tea and coffee makers can be preset to serve the drink at a safe-to-dispense temperature. Hot beverages served at a buffet should be capped when handed to customers. The caps should have a lift-off tab so customers can add sugar and cream without having to remove the cap. Wait personnel should avoid placing hot beverages near a child. Finally, if the drink is extremely hot, warn the customer either orally when the beverage is served, or in writing by placing a notice on the cup. McDonald's now places a warning on its cups that reads, "Caution: Contents Hot." Cups at Starbucks, the coffee chain, state, "Careful, the beverage you are about to enjoy is extremely hot." Both notices alert the customer to be cautious.

The following case illustrates a number of principles relevant to liability associated with hot beverages.

CASE EXAMPLE 11-3

Oubre v. E-Z Serve Corp.
713 So.2d 818 (La. 998)

... Plaintiff sued E-Z Serve [a convenience store] for burns she sustained from spilling in her lap, while riding in a car, a cup of hot coffee just purchased from E-Z Serve.

The record shows that plaintiff was a passenger in the back seat of a car driven by her husband. They stopped at an E-Z Serve in LaPlace where her husband and another passenger went inside to purchase breakfast. Plaintiff received a hotdog and a cup of coffee. The group left the E-Z Serve, driving a short distance away when, for unknown reasons, plaintiff spilled the coffee in her lap. She was wearing cotton sweat pants at the

time, which she alleged trapped the hot coffee and produced a serious second degree burn on her thigh.

Plaintiff alleged that the coffee was unreasonably hot, that E-Z Serve failed to warn consumers that the coffee was unreasonably hot, and other acts of negligence. ...

E-Z Serve's evidence included an affidavit from Glen Blackwell, who was employed by Standard Coffee Services as Manager of Field Services. He stated that he had sixteen years as a technician and supervisor in Standard's repair shop, and that he was familiar with the operation and repair of the Bunn-O-Matic, the same brand of machine that E-Z Serve used to brew and serve coffee. He stated that the brewing process starts with water being heated in a tank, controlled by a thermostat. The brewing water then exits a spray head at the top of the brewing funnel. Customarily, the temperature of the water at the time it exits the spray head is 195 degrees Fahrenheit, plus or minus 5 degrees. This is the temperature at which the oil and flavor is released from the coffee in the brewing funnel. The brewed coffee drips into a decanter or beaker through the bottom of the brewing funnel. Customarily the coffee has cooled approximately 5 degrees from the temperature of the water at the top of the spray head. Immediately after the coffee has finished dripping into the beaker and the brewing cycle is complete, its temperature is customarily between 175–185 degrees Fahrenheit. The warming plate under the coffee decanter maintains the coffee's temperature at approximately 175 degrees which is the temperature determined by the coffee industry as the one at which optimum flavor is retained. The temperature of the coffee will continue to decline over time stabilizing at approximately 155 degrees Fahrenheit. ...

E-Z Serve noted that it is customary to serve coffee hot, because the heat is needed to release the flavor from the beans, and consumers desire to purchase their coffee hot, not tepid. ...

The fact that the coffee was hot enough to cause injury if not properly handled does not mean that it was defective or negligently served. Where, as here, a product by its very nature had a dangerous attribute, liability is imposed only when the product has an attribute not reasonably contemplated by the purchaser or is unreasonably dangerous for its intended use. Since plaintiff clearly intended to purchase hot coffee, plaintiff must present evidenciary facts establishing that the coffee served by defendant was defective or unreasonably dangerous, or negligently served. ...

Plaintiff did not refute defendant's evidence of the accepted standard of coffee temperature, nor did she produce any evidence that her cup of coffee was superhot or hotter than normal. Moreover, the record shows that plaintiff was a frequent user of coffee, that she had purchased coffee from E-Z Serve before the incident, and has done so since.

Accordingly judgment for defendant.

CASE QUESTION

1. Given that the plaintiff was injured by the temperature of the coffee, why was the seller not liable?

Foodborne Illnesses

Restaurants must take precautions to protect against spreading foodborne illnesses—that is, bacteria found in the food. Usually proper handling will eliminate the risks. Failure of a restaurant to follow safeguards can result in liability if a diner becomes ill from eating improperly prepared food.

Salmonella is a type of bacteria that causes typhoid fever and other intestinal infections. It is often found in uncooked eggs, poultry, and meat. Proper sanitation and cooking will greatly reduce the risk of salmonella infection. E. coli, also a bacterium, is another risk in many foods, especially uncooked or undercooked beef.

Trichinosis is an illness caused by eating raw or undercooked pork and wild game products infected with the larvae of a species of worm called trichinella. Infection from pork was once quite common, but is now relatively rare due to strict legislation prohibiting the feeding of raw meat garbage to hogs and public awareness of the danger of eating raw or undercooked pork. Today, cases of trichinosis are more commonly associated with raw or undercooked game meats. Proper cooking eliminates the risk.

Restaurants should ensure that their chefs and kitchen staff have adequate training in food safety and that foods are properly prepared to protect diners' well-being.

Proof Problems Establishing Causation

A plaintiff in a breach of warranty action must prove that the food purchased at the defendant's establishment was the cause of an injury. If a person eats in a restaurant or buys take-out food and later becomes ill, is that sufficient proof that the food from the restaurant caused the illness? The answer, of course, is no. The food that made the plaintiff sick may have originated in the plaintiff's refrigerator. Likewise, the illness may have been caused by something other than bad food. To win the case, the plaintiff must prove that food purchased from the defendant's establishment was unwholesome and caused the illness. In the following case, the plaintiff failed to prove that the food was unfit for human consumption.

CASE EXAMPLE 11-4

Brown v. City Sam Restaurants, Inc.
666 N.Y.S.2d 409 (N.Y. 1998)

... We agree with the court [or original jurisdiction] that it is mere speculation to attribute plaintiff's flu-like symptoms to his consumption of unwholesome or contaminated lobster at defendant's restaurant where it is undisputed that plaintiff had eaten other foods earlier that day, that he had a known food allergy to some shellfish, that no one else in his dinner party became sick, and where his own medical evidence was inconclusive as to the cause of his symptoms. ... Plaintiff would not be able to prove that his symptoms were caused by his ingestion of contaminated lobster, such being an essential element to this lawsuit.

Complaint dismissed.

CASE QUESTIONS

1. What is the significance of the fact that the plaintiff had a known food allergy to some shellfish?

2. What is the significance of the fact that no one else in the plaintiff's dinner party became ill?

The following case explains in more depth the difficulty of proving a case based on adulterated food.

CASE EXAMPLE 11-5

Renna v. Bishop's Cafeteria Co. of Omaha
218 N.W.2d 246 (Neb. 1974)

Plaintiff seeks to recover damages as a result of being served food which was allegedly unwholesome, adulterated, and not fit for human consumption. ...

Plaintiff had breakfast at Bishop's Cafeteria in Omaha at approximately 9:20 A.M., October 25, 1968. Plaintiff, who was 63 years of age, had eaten a light lunch and a light evening meal the previous day and had nothing else to eat until this breakfast which consisted of several grapefruit sections, two fried eggs, hash browns, a roll, and a cup of coffee. He had eaten lightly the day before pursuant to his physician's instructions, preparatory for a cholesterol test which was made approximately an hour before his breakfast at Bishop's. Plaintiff testified the eggs were on the cool side and didn't taste just right. He began to experience stomach pains about 12:30 P.M. that day. These pains were mild at first but shortly became more severe and he began to feel nauseated, vomited, and experience diarrhea. He was admitted to the hospital at approximately 6 P.M. that day.

Doctor Maurice F. Stoner, who had been plaintiff's personal physician for a number of years, diagnosed plaintiff's affliction as acute pancreatitis, and stated his opinion that the precipitating cause was the food purchased at Bishop's Cafeteria. He found no evidence of either food poisoning or food infection in treating plaintiff, but the hospital did not look for such evidence. Doctor Stoner stated in regard to acute pancreatitis there is an underlying cause which no one understands and a precipitating cause. The precipitating cause could be alcohol, gallstones, emotional upset, or a hearty meal. The doctor felt the meal which plaintiff consumed at Bishop's Cafeteria was a hearty meal. It was his testimony that a wholesome meal could be the precipitating cause and could bring on the symptoms of pancreatitis. He also testified that fasting followed by a hearty meal could bring on symptoms of pancreatitis, whether the food was wholesome or otherwise. Plaintiff's doctor was unable to state with reasonable medical certainty that plaintiff consumed infected or poisoned food on October 25, 1968. He had no opinion as to whether plaintiff was suffering from food poisoning or food infection when he examined plaintiff at the hospital. He further testified that it would be speculation to say plaintiff had food poisoning or food infection.

A restaurateur engaged in serving food to paying guests for immediate consumption on the premises impliedly warrants that the food so served is wholesome and fit for human consumption and is liable for injuries to such person proximately caused by a breach thereof without proof of negligence. ... Before this rule becomes applicable, however, there must be proof that the food sold is unwholesome and not fit for human consumption. Plaintiff wholly failed to produce proof to sustain this issue.

True, plaintiff experienced difficulties approximately 3 hours after consuming his breakfast. His personal physician diagnosed his ailment as acute pancreatitis and testified the precipitating cause was the food consumed at Bishop's Cafeteria. However, he could not say that this meant the food was unwholesome, or tainted in any way. He testified a wholesome meal could have had the same effect. Doctor Stoner had no opinion as to whether plaintiff was suffering food poisoning or food infection when he examined him at the hospital. He further testified it would be speculation to say that food poisoning or food infection was present. The most plaintiff proved is he became ill following the ingestion of his breakfast at Bishop's. This, however, does not prove that the food eaten was unwholesome. His medical evidence indicates his condition could have been brought on because he ate a hearty breakfast after fasting.

The judgment [in favor of the cafeteria] is affirmed.

CASE QUESTIONS

1. How did the testimony of the plaintiff's doctor support the defendant's position?

2. Give two examples of facts that would have established that the food was unwholesome.

In a case in which the plaintiff alleged flu-like symptoms from the presence of a worm in a can of string beans purchased at a grocery store, the court dismissed the complaint due to the plaintiff's failure to prove the cause of her illness was the worm. Said the court, "The mere fact that the plaintiff became nauseous about one-half hour after consuming some of the contents of the can is insufficient [to avoid dismissal of the complaint]. There are many different causes of nausea, vomiting and stomach distress, which the plaintiff experienced. Moreover, the report of the plaintiff's own examining physician, in describing her visit to his office the day after the alleged incident, makes no reference to the incident." ...[14]

Similarly, a diner at a Kentucky Fried Chicken (KFC) noticed that his chicken "smelled kind of funny" and "didn't taste right." A day and several meals later, he developed severe abdominal pains. A doctor stated that his condition was consistent with improperly cooked poultry or meat but "chicken was at the top of the list" of culprits. The plaintiff had eaten bacon since his KFC meal. The trial court dismissed the case, ruling that the proof of proximate cause between the chicken and the illness was insufficient. The appellate court reversed and ordered that the case proceed to trial so that a jury could decide whether the evidence of proximate cause connecting the two was sufficient.[15]

Privity of Contract

Under common law, a direct contractual relationship was required between the plaintiff and the defendant in a breach of warranty action. The relationship between parties to a contract is called **privity of contract**. If you go into a store and purchase a can of corn and the corn is adulterated and makes you ill, you will be able to sue the store because you were in privity of contract with it. If, however, you ate the corn as a guest at a wedding reception held at a restaurant, you are not in privity of contract with the restaurant and so your right to sue the restaurant may be questioned.

All states have relaxed the requirement of privity to some extent. An example is provided by *Conklin v. Hotel Waldorf Astoria*, 161 N.Y.S.2d 205 (1957). A hotel guest invited a friend to lunch at the hotel. The friend was injured by a piece of glass in a roll. The bill for the meal was paid by the hotel guest. When the friend sued the hotel, it denied liability on the ground she was not in privity of contract

---

[14] *Valenti v. Great Atlantic & Pacific Tea Company*, 615 N.Y.S.2d 84 (N.Y. 1994)

[15] *McCarley v. West Quality Food Service*, 960 S.W.2d 585 (Tenn. 1998)

with the hotel. The court rejected this argument, holding that the hotel, by accepting the plaintiff's order, impliedly contracted with her even though she did not pay the bill. Another state with a more rigid approach to privity might have held against the plaintiff.

When the UCC was adopted, the states were in disagreement about how much to relax the privity rule. To accommodate all positions, the UCC contains three different rules concerning privity; each state selects the one it prefers. The most restrictive option limits the benefits of the warranty to the buyer, the buyer's family and the buyer's household guests. The broadest alternative covers any person who may reasonably be expected to consume the food. [16]

Strict Products Liability

To bypass the privity requirement, most states have adopted a related cause of action called **strict products liability** that is based in tort law rather than contracts; thus, privity is not required. To sue in strict products liability, a plaintiff must prove only three elements:

1. The defendant sold a product in a defective condition, such as food that was unhealthy.
2. The plaintiff was injured.
3. The injury was caused by the defect.

An example is a hamburger purchased at a restaurant that contained a hard piece of plastic, causing the customer to choke and become ill.[17]

While strict products liability may seem a lot like breach of warranty of merchantability, the former eliminates the requirement of privity and enhances a plaintiff's chances of success in a lawsuit based on defective food.

For example, a restaurant unknowingly bought eggs contaminated with salmonella. The presence of the salmonella deemed the eggs defective. An employee of the restaurant ate some of the eggs and became ill. The employee could sue the supplier for strict products liability although the employee was not in privity with the supplier.[18]

For the purposes of a lawsuit in strict products liability, food is defective if it is adulterated, contains foreign or unexpected objects, or is otherwise not fit for human consumption. If a diner becomes ill from food, but the cause is inherent in the food, poses no threat to most people, and the restaurant took precautionary measures to protect diners from the illness, the food will not be considered defective. For example, a patron of a Louisiana restaurant died from eating oysters that contained a rare bacteria that poses no threat to a healthy person but can be lethal to someone with a weakened immune system. His family sued the restaurant based on strict products liability. The evidence established that the bacteria was in the

---

[16]UCC § 2-318

[17]*Williams v. McDonald's of Torrington*, 1997 WL 276308 (Conn. 1997)

[18]*Bacci Restaurant v. Sunrise Produce Co.*, 1995 WL 774387 (Conn. 1995)

oysters when they were harvested from the sea and affected very few people. Also, the restaurant took many precautions to prevent contamination of the oysters. Restaurant employees carefully stocked and refrigerated the oysters, and restaurant personnel used approved sanitary procedures for shucking them. Similarly, the supplier followed state regulations, purchasing oysters only from licensed fishermen who harvested from state-approved oyster beds. Based on these facts, the court held the oysters were not defective and therefore the restaurant was not liable in strict products liability.[19]

Negligence

An additional basis for suing a restaurant that serves unhealthy food is negligence. In these cases an injured diner claims that the restaurant was careless while preparing the food and that inattentiveness led to the meal being tainted. For example, a restaurant that served a glass of water to a diner was liable for negligence where the water was contaminated with detergent due to an employee's carelessness and the guest became ill as a result.[20]

Choice of Action

A diner who is served defective food may have three bases on which to sue: breach of warranty, strict products liability, and negligence. How does the plaintiff determine on which basis to sue? Some states by statute limit the plaintiff to one cause of action. Absent such a statute, the plaintiff will usually include in the complaint all three hoping to prove at least one. For example, a restaurant diner who found a roach on his pizza sued the restaurant and referenced all three causes of action is his complaint.[21] The plaintiff will collect damages only once, even if she can prove more than one ground for recovery.

Customers with Allergies

Restaurant patrons frequently request that certain ingredients be eliminated from their food. These requests are often prompted by allergies. If the restaurant fails to honor the request and the customer suffers an allergic reaction from having eaten the offending food, the restaurant may be liable. In one case, a child's mother sent back a first serving of ice cream because it contained nuts, to which the child was allergic. The restaurant merely scraped off the nuts and squirted some fresh whipped cream on top and returned the ice cream to the customer. The child ate the ice cream and went into anaphylactic shock from the residue of the nuts.

---

[19] *Simeon v. The Sweet Pepper Grill*, 618 So.2d 848 (La. 1993)

[20] *Waddell v. Shoney's, Inc.*, 664 So.2d 1134 (Fl. 1995)

[21] *Cooke v. Pizza Hut, Inc.*, 1994 WL 680051 (Del. 1994)

When food is rejected by a patron due to allergies, wise policy mandates that substitute food be served and that it be presented on a clean dish. If only the offending ingredient is removed and the balance of the food is returned to the customer on the same plate, the residue although small in amount, may be sufficient to cause an allergic reaction.

Hazard Analysis Critical Control Point System

The Food and Drug Administration (FDA) is a federal agency that oversees the food industry. Its objectives include promoting public health by ensuring foods are safe, wholesome, sanitary, and properly labeled. Among the FDA's undertakings is a Food Code, which is a set of model ordinances that provides guidance on standards and practices for the achievement of food safety in restaurants and other segments of the food industry.

An important component of the Food Code is the Hazard Analysis Critical Control Point system (HACCP), a quality assurance scheme to identify and minimize spoilage and contamination problems during food manufacturing and service. Such a system requires food producers and servers to systematically look at hazards that can cause spoilage or contamination and identify how to avoid them. Among the control methods utilized are cooking, refrigeration, packaging, monitoring, and employee handwashing. The implementation of an HACCP quality control system is recognized as an essential element of managing the operations of a food-service facility. Adopting and complying with such a system helps prevent and mitigate legal liability for defective food.

Hand-Washing by Food Preparers

Employee hand-washing is a critical control point (CCP) in food safety and prevention plans. The reason is this: If food handlers (cooks and wait personnel) come to work when they are not well, their illness may be transferred to customers. One illness transferable in this way is hepatitis, which infects the liver. It can be spread by a food preparer inadequately washing his hands after using the restroom and before handling food. If an infected employee is discovered, county officials will likely become involved and a public announcement will be made to encourage at-risk patrons to seek treatment. In addition to harm caused a customer, the negative publicity to the eatery can seriously hurt its business. To safeguard against this, management should ensure that employees are knowledgeable about proper hand-washing procedures and compliant with them. Signs in bathrooms should remind employees to cleanse their hands properly after using the facilites.

False Food Claims

Restaurants often make various claims about the food they sell. These representations may refer to health or nutritional benefits, methods of preparation, or other attributes. The law requires that such representations be truthful. False claims can lead to prosecution.

Truth-in-Menu Laws

Both federal and state laws require accuracy in representations made by restaurants about the food they serve. Federal laws regulating menu descriptions apply only to items that are advertised with a nutrient or health claim such as "low fat" or "heart healthy." Despite these limited federal regulations, many restaurants strive for accurate menu descriptions out of concern for state laws, quality assurance, and consumer confidence. Most states have laws seeking to eliminate misleading food advertisements and labels. Some states have laws that specifically outlaw untruthful statements on menus. Other states have general statutes that bar "unfair trade practices" that have been interpreted to apply to fraudulent food claims. Controversies can result from omitting ingredients, mistaking a product's origin, misdescribing a dish, or inaccurately identifying the cooking method. For example, orange juice made from concentrate cannot be promoted as "fresh." Syrup promoted as "made in Vermont" must have been made in Vermont. This is because the public perceives that syrup from Vermont has attributes not available elsewhere that enhance the taste. Likewise, Maine lobster is considered sweeter and therefore is customarily more expensive than lobsters caught elsewhere. If a lobster was not caught in Maine, it cannot be advertised as Maine lobster. Sometimes when the name of a food product references a geographical place, that location does not denote place of origin and can be used regardless of where the food was made. For example, the word *swiss*, when used with cheese, describes the type of cheese and not the country in which it is made. Similarly the name *Kentucky Fried Chicken* does not suggest that the chicken was raised in Kentucky.

In a lawsuit involving another type of misleading food claim, Kentucky Fried Chicken was forced to rename its "Lite and Crispy" chicken to "Skinfree Crispy" and pay a fine of $25,000. Whereas the term *lite* usually suggests reduced calories, "Lite and Crispy" chicken was virtually identical to the alternative original recipe.

Fish or other products that have been frozen cannot be sold as "fresh."

Inaccurate cooking methods stated on a menu should be corrected. A fast-food chain was challenged by a consumer watchdog agency for using the word "grilled" to describe a chicken sandwich. In fact, the chicken patties were pre-cooked in a steam oven and the brown marks, which inferred searing of the meat on a grill, were applied by a machine called a heat-and-control rotary brander. The patties were then frozen and transported to restaurants, where they were thawed and cooked in a two-sided hot plate. In response to the inquiry the chain discontinued using the term "grilled" in connection with the product.

A growing number of people are vegetarians. Fast-food chains have attempted to attract these diners by providing vegetarian offerings. What constitutes "vegetarian" has been the subject of some dispute. One chain offered a Garden Veggie Pita labeled as a vegetarian meal in the company's nutritional brochure. The item was made with gelatin, a by-product of beef. When questioned, the chain explained that its suppliers had represented the product as vegetarian and so the misrepresentation was an "honest mistake." The chain removed the reference to vegetarian in the nutritional brochure.

To comply with the law and avoid customer displeasure, restaurants must pay close attention to accuracy in product descriptions.

Food Labeling

As the public has become more concerned about health issues, including cholesterol and saturated fat intake, health claims have become a significant factor in consumers' choice of food products. Food producers have tried to capitalize on customers' interests in healthy foods. Too frequently, manufacturers have stretched the truth or made claims they cannot substantiate.

An example of questionable claims is an advertisement for margarine, a product with a significant fat content, saying it was a "headstart to a healthier heart" and it "does your heart good." Similarly, advertisers have overused and misused words such as "light," "low-calorie," "low fat," and "low sodium."

A federal labeling law was passed in 1990 called the Nutrition Labeling and Education Act of 1990. The FDA has promulgated regulations to enforce the Act. Some applications apply to packaged foods only, and some to food served in restaurants. Both are discussed in the following sections.

Application to Packaged Foods

Mandatory nutritional labels are required for all packaged goods and they must contain the information specified in the following list, which enumerates what the Act requires.

1. Standardization of serving sizes. This is significant because information such as fat grams and calories are based on serving sizes. Before the effective date of the Act, food purveyors used varying serving sizes, making comparison shopping difficult. Companies often used an artificially small serving size, making the nutritional information such as calories and fat grams look unjustifiably appealing.

2. Regulation and standardization of words such as *light*, *cholesterol-free*, and *low calorie*.

3. Mandatory labeling of fat content by weight, specifying both total fat and saturated fat.

4. Mandatory labeling of fiber content by weight.

5. Mandatory labeling of the content of the following as percentages of the United States Recommended Daily Allowance (RDA): total fat, saturated fat, cholesterol, sodium, carbohydrates, and fiber.

6. Limitations on health claims. The statute specifies the permissible representation between foods and disease-avoidance. It permits only claims that the food "may" or "might" reduce the risk of disease and precludes statements that suggest a guaranteed reduction of risk.

Application to Restaurants

Many restaurants were exaggerating the nutritional value of their food items. To address this, special regulations were promulgated for restaurants. Whenever a restaurant makes a claim about the nutritional content (for example, "low sodium" or "light") or the healthfulness of a food product (for example, "fiber helps to prevent cancer"), the restaurant is required to provide to patrons upon their request the information required to be on a label of packaged food. As initially adopted, these regulations did not apply to health and nutritional-content claims made on menus, but rather only those made on signs, placards, or posters in the restaurant. The menu exclusion was challenged in court by a public-interest consumer group. It noted that almost half the American food dollar is spent on food consumed away from home, and argued that restaurant menus often contain misleading or false representations about the nutritional and health value of the food. The court held the exclusion of menus from the regulations was unauthorized. As a result, all restaurants that make health or nutritional-content claims on their menus must now provide the mandated nutritional information.[22]

However, the information is still not required to be included on the menu. Instead, the information need only be available "upon request." Some restaurants provide fliers, brochures, or handbooks with calorie, fat gram, and related information, even in the absence of a request. These are popular with some consumers. How do restaurants determine the nutritional content of their food? The regulations provide that restaurants can rely upon information from nutrient databases, cookbooks, and analyses, "or other reasonable bases that provide assurance that the food or meal meets the nutrient requirements for the claim."[23]

Further, if a restaurant uses as descriptors of its menu items any terms defined by the Act or regulations, the restaurant must comply with those definitions. Thus, if a restaurant promotes a menu item as "light," that item must meet the standard for that term as developed by the FDA.

Kosher Foods

Kosher food is a designation referring to food prepared consistent with Jewish religious requirements. For example, those mandates specify the method of slaughter of animals that produce meat and the time within which processing must occur following slaughter. The requirements also prohibit eating certain foods, regardless of method of slaughter or preparation, such as pork and seafood from water creatures that lack scales or fins. Thus, for example, lobster, crab, and scallops are prohibited.

The preparation of kosher food is supervised by a rabbi or a designee. Without the rabbi's verification that the food has been properly prepared to merit the designation of kosher, it cannot be advertised as such.

---

[22] *Public Citizen, Inc. v. Shalala*, 932 F.Supp. 13 (D.C. 1996)

[23] 21 C.F.R.§ 101.10

When food is labeled as kosher, the label suggests the food has been prepared in accordance with the requirements. People who "keep kosher"—that is, eat only food that is kosher—have a right to expect that a restaurant advertising kosher food will serve food prepared as required by applicable rules.

Laws in most states prohibit advertising food as kosher unless it is. Promoting non-kosher food as kosher violates these laws. Many states treat such conduct as criminal, subjecting wrongdoers to potential jail terms and fines.

Relationships Between Fast-Food Operations and Hotels

An expanded relationship has been developing between fast-food restaurants and hotels. Some hotels offer fast-foot selections such as Pizza Hut pizzas on their room-service menu. Brand-name food choices have proven to be popular items. The relationship between the hotel and the food company is a contractual one. According to the terms of the contract, the food is customarily prepared by hotel employees. For consistency and reputation purposes, the fast-food company has an interest in ensuring that hotel employees prepare the dishes in the same way they are made elsewhere. Therefore, the restaurant company customarily trains the hotel employees and determines the ingredients. In return for the training and the right to use the fast-food company's name, the hotel pays a licensing fee.

Suppose the food prepared by hotel employees is unwholesome in some way, perhaps because it contained a foreign object such as a nail, and a guest was injured while eating it. Who would be liable? The hotel? The fast-food company? Both? The answer is that the hotel will most likely be the only one liable, assuming the defect originated there. This is so because the hotel is not an agent of the food company nor are the employees of the hotel employees of the restaurant. The bases for the hotel's liability would be breach of warranty of merchantability, strict products liability, and possibly negligence in the preparation of the food.

In two circumstances, however, the food company might also be liable. If the flaw originated with the company, for example if it supplies the hotel with the cheese for pizza and the foreign object was in the cheese, both the food company and the hotel will be liable for breach of warranty of merchantability, strict products liability, and possibly negligence. The other circumstance in which the food company might be liable is where it failed to train hotel employees properly and the poor training led to the defect. The basis for the liability in this situation would be negligence. Absent these two situations, only the hotel will be liable.

Another relationship between fast-food companies and hotel chains exists. The economy hotels are a fast growing segment of the lodging industry, but few have restaurants. They often encourage family restaurant chains to open an outlet near their facilities. In these situations, the hotel and restaurant are two separate, unconnected businesses and, as long as they remain so, neither will be liable for the negligence or breach of warranty of the other. Likewise, the hotel would not be liable in strict products liability for food sold by the restaurant. While normally two separate businesses are not liable for each other's wrongful conduct, a guest who became ill from unwholesome food served by a local restaurant recommended by the hotel may claim the hotel was negligent for endorsing an allegedly substandard restaurant. To avoid this kind of liability, a hotel that refers guests to a restaurant not operated by the hotel should make periodic inspections of the restaurant to ensure proper operations. This will help avoid and defend against accusations of negligence.

Smoking Restrictions

Many states and localities have adopted laws that restrict or prohibit smoking in many public buildings, including restaurants. These laws are based on findings that breathing secondhand smoke, which contains carcinogens, is a significant health hazard for nonsmokers as well as smokers. Secondhand smoke consists of exhaled smoke from smokers and from smoldering cigarettes, cigars, or pipes. This smoke contains many of the same harmful chemicals that a smoker inhales. Secondhand smoke can both kill and cause irritation. It is estimated to cause approximately 3,000 lung-cancer deaths in nonsmokers annually. Secondhand smoke can cause heart disease, stroke, headaches, and nausea. It can exacerbate asthma and respiratory infections. The more a person is exposed to secondhand smoke, the greater is the risk. The danger applies to customers and even more so to service employees at bars and restaurants. The latter are customarily exposed to significant amounts of secondhand smoke throughout their work shifts.

Typically, laws that restrict but do not prohibit smoking require that a restaurant designate a nonsmoking area and allocate a certain percentage of seating capacity to it, such as 70 percent. Some prohibit smoking in the restaurant area, but permit it in an accessory bar. Some laws prohibit drifting of smoke from a designated smoking area into a nonsmoking area.[24] Some restaurants, upon being cited for violating a smoking regulation, have challenged their validity on constitutional grounds. Generally these statutes have been upheld as appropriate means to protect public health.[25]

In another case, a restaurant association (an organization of restaurant owners) successfully challenged a city ordinance that banned smoking altogether because the city ordinance was more restrictive than the related state statute. The state legislature had adopted a statute permitting smoking in a portion of dining areas in eateries. The court held that the state statute controlled and the conflicting local ordinance was unenforceable.[26]

In localities where smoking is permitted in a portion of a restaurant, the space is usually defined as a percentage of the dining area. Restaurants often want to maximize the permissible smoking section to accommodate their smoking patrons. Restaurant associations and individual restaurants charged with violations of the

[24]See, for example, Arizona Code § 11-19 (A)(5)

[25]See, for example, *Tucson v. Grezafel*, 23 P.3d 675 (Ariz. 2001)

[26]*Michigan Restaurant Association v. City of Marquette*, 626 N.W.2d 418 (Mich. 2001)

smoking ordinances have attempted to challenge the constitutionality of laws restricting or prohibiting smoking in restaurants. These efforts have generally not been successful. An issue in one case was whether a restaurant could include in the calculation of total square footage of the dining area a room designated for private parties and only intermittently available for public dining. If the room was included in the calculation, the permissible smoking area would be enlarged. The court held that such a room can be included.[27]

An avid cigar-smoker challenged New York City's anti-smoking law, one of the toughest in the nation as it relates to cigars. He claimed no reliable scientific study established that secondary cigar smoke was harmful. A court rejected his claim, finding sufficient basis for the belief that secondary cigar smoke subjected nonsmokers to health risks.[28]

Customers with illnesses such as asthma who find it particularly difficult to tolerate secondhand smoke have sued restaurants whose policies permit smoking. These cases have been limited in number because so many restaurants are now required by law to prohibit smoking. The cases that have been pursued are based on the Americans with Disabilities Act. They have been decided on a case-by-case basis and their outcome depends on the impact on the facility's business of prohibiting smoking. The greater the impact, the less likely the court will require that smoking be prohibited. See the Chapter 3 discussion on the Americans with Disabilities Act. Similarly, cases have been pursued by wait personnel whose health is impacted by customers smoking. Whether the restaurant is required to modify the smoking policy depends on the impact on its business a smoking prohibition would have. Again, see the Chapter 3 discussion on the Americans with Disabilities Act.

Generally, the enforcement mechanism for smoking regulations is the county board of health, and the penalty is a fine of several hundred dollars.

Safety Concerns Particular to Food Preparation

Some aspects of food service present particular safety risks to employees. The restaurateur has a duty to exercise reasonable care to minimize these risks.

Food Preparation

Kitchen areas are inherently dangerous. Most of the equipment can cause serious injuries if misused, such as meat cutters, grills, deep-fat fryers, knives, and stoves. In Chapter 6 we discussed the hazards associated with flaming foods, which can cause injury to employees and customers. Another danger is dropped food, which can result in slip-and-fall cases.

---

[27] *Bleiburg Restaurant, Inc. v. NYC Dept. of Health*, 658 N.Y.S.2d 574 (1997)

[28] *Beatie v. City of NY*, N.Y.L.J. (N.Y. Aug. 7, 1996)

A direct relationship exists between the quality of an accident-prevention program and the frequency and severity of accidents. Managers must devise policies to encourage safety in the food-preparation process. Employee training is imperative.

Risks Associated with Donated Foods

A restaurant with unused food may be motivated to give it to a charitable organization. Often food is donated because it is near the recommended last day of use or it is leftover from an event for which large amounts of food were prepared. In either circumstance, the donated food may be at risk for spoilage. Good intentions will not relieve the restaurant from liability for rancid or defective food. Food served beyond the recommended last date of use may be spoiled. Prepared food that has been displayed for awhile may have deteriorated without timely refrigeration or other preservation measures. Good managers will verify the condition of the food before it is donated to employees or people in need.

Liability for Injuries to Patrons

Restaurateurs and tavern keepers (referred to here collectively as restaurateurs) have a duty to protect a patron from injury caused by another customer when the injury is foreseeable. The duty is breached and liability results where a patron is disruptive and the restaurant fails to quiet or eject that customer. Restaurants have been held liable in several circumstances for failure to control activity on their premises. However, in circumstances where a fight or other security incident happens without warning and therefore could not have been anticipated, the bar will not be responsible.

Failure to Eject Quarrelsome Patron

If a patron is injured at a bar by a fight with another customer and the restaurant could reasonably have foreseen the coming attack, liability will result. Injury is foreseeable where a customer is rowdy, displays inappropriate conduct, or bothers others.

In *McFadden v. Bancroft Hotel Corp.*, 46 N.E.2d 573 (Mass. 1943), a military organization held its annual convention in the hotel operated by the defendant. The plaintiff, a conventioneer, was assaulted without provocation while in the grill room. The assailant had attracted attention prior to the attack on the plaintiff by hollering, loudly cursing, "swaying around," arguing with other patrons, and threatening to hit one of them. This conduct was observed by several hotel detectives. In the plaintiff's lawsuit against the hotel, the court held for the plaintiff, noting that the hotel had a duty to exercise reasonable care for the safety of its patrons. Because the hotel's agents had witnessed the assailant's erratic behavior prior to the attack, they should have foreseen an incident and removed him from the grill room before the assault occurred.

In *Shank v. Riker Restaurant Associates, Inc.*, 216 N.Y.S.2d 118, aff'd. 222 N.Y.S.2d 683 (1961), an unidentified "hoodlum" using abusive language had been creating a disturbance in the restaurant for over twenty minutes before the plaintiff's entry. At one point, he asked for a glass of water and then "drop kicked" it against the kitchen door, spreading water and pieces of glass over a wide area. Despite this conduct, he was not ejected by the manager. When the plaintiff arrived, the hoodlum first insulted her by calling her vile names, then knocked her to the floor and shoved a heavy, metal counter stool into her head, causing a severe fracture of her skull. The plaintiff won her case against the restaurant because it was negligent for not taking action to evict the ruffian when the disturbance began.

If restaurant employees are unable to remove a troublemaker, the police should be summoned. In *Dubak v. "Q" Lounge, Inc.*, 559 A.2d 424 (N.J. 1989), a bar was held liable for failing to call the police when the bouncers' repeated efforts to halt a fight were unsuccessful.

The restaurant's duty to intercede or call the police is a strict one. Failure to take remedial action can result in an award of punitive damages. The restaurant in the following case was ordered to pay punitive damages for its failure to intervene in a foreseeable disturbance, even though the plaintiff was found partially responsible for her injuries.

CASE EXAMPLE 11-6

Gould v. Taco Bell
722 P.2d 511 (Kan. 1986)

... Rosie Gould and her friend, Theresa Holmberg, ... drove to a Taco Bell restaurant. ... They arrived at the restaurant at approximately 11:30 P.M. There were six people who all sat together in the booth. After ordering their food, Gould and Holmberg sat down in a booth across from the group. Karen Brown was one of the individuals in that group.

Brown and her companions began engaging in loud, crude and vulgar conversation, designed to be overheard and to shock Gould and Holmberg. Neither Gould nor Holmberg made any comment to Brown or her companions during this conversation. At one point, a Taco Bell employee told the group to quiet down, but the conversation grew louder.

Eventually, the group got up to leave but prior to reaching the exit, Brown stopped and said, "Those two white bitches over there think they're hot shit." Gould was shocked and asked, "Are you talking to us?" When Brown responded, "Yes," Gould requested her to "please come over here and repeat yourself."

Brown responded by suddenly dashing to Gould's booth and striking her in the face with a clenched fist, knocking her sideways and bruising her face and nose. Gould, shocked, called Brown a "nigger." Brown then began hitting Gould with her fists with renewed effort. This beating continued for about thirty seconds until Holmberg intervened by moving between Gould and Brown. She told Brown, "We don't want any trouble." Gould and Holmberg began moving toward the door but Brown kept saying "Come on, hit me, bitch. Come on, I want to fight." Gould and Holmberg continued to insist they did not want to fight, but when they reached the door of the restaurant Brown began beating on Gould again.

During this second exchange, Mark Wills, the assistant manager at the restaurant, watched the altercation as he came out from behind the counter. Wills did not try to stop Brown because he did not want to get involved and for fear Brown would strike him for interfering. Nor did he call the police, since he didn't feel the situation warranted such action. However, Wills did tell Brown, "Why don't you just leave? You did this two weeks before in here."

[A fight in the parking lot ensued.] ... Holmberg screamed for someone to call the police. The Taco Bell employees did not respond. Holmberg was finally able to break away and ran inside to the food counter and asked Wills (who had followed her back inside) if she could use the phone to call the police. Wills advised her the phone was not for public use. Holmberg threatened to jump over the counter and use the phone. Wills finally reluctantly called the police. ...

This scared Brown and her companions and they got in their car and left.

Gould filed the present action against Taco Bell, alleging Taco Bell failed to provide security measures sufficient to protect Gould. ...

The jury found Gould 49% at fault and Taco Bell 51% at fault. They awarded Gould $500 in actual damages and $10,000 in punitive damages. Taco Bell appeals the jury's findings. ...

A proprietor of an inn, tavern, restaurant, or like business is liable for an assault upon a guest or patron by another guest or third party where the proprietor has reason to anticipate such an assault and fails to exercise reasonable care to forestall or prevent the same.

The duty of a proprietor of a tavern or inn to protect his patrons from injury does not arise until the impending danger becomes apparent to him, or the circumstances are such that a careful and prudent person would be put on notice of the potential danger. ...

It is not required that notice to the proprietor of such an establishment be long and continued in order that he be subject to liability; it is enough that there be a sequence of conduct sufficient to enable him to act on behalf of his patron's safety. ...

The evidence in this case was sufficient to establish such a "sequence of conduct." Thus, we hold the jury's verdict against Taco Bell for Gould's injuries is supported by the evidence. ...

Punitive damages are permitted whenever the elements of fraud, malice, gross negligence, or oppression mingle in the controversy. ...

Punitive damages are allowed not because of any special merit in the injured party's case, but are imposed to punish the wrongdoer for malicious, vindictive, or willful and wanton invasion of the injured party's rights, the purpose being to restrain and deter others from the commission of like wrongs. ...

Taco Bell argues its conduct could not be wanton because it had no reason to know that harm was imminent. This argument is not supported by the facts. The evidence at trial indicated that the shift manager, Mark Wills, saw Karen Brown strike the plaintiff while the plaintiff was still sitting in the booth, but he did nothing. As the parties moved toward the door, Wills came out from behind the food counter to an area within a few feet of the assailant and the plaintiff. He again failed to call the police or attempt to intervene, but instead observed a second attack upon Gould. It was not until Gould's friend, Theresa Holmberg, broke away from Karen Brown and ran inside and threatened to jump over the counter in order to phone the police that Wills finally called the police.

Evidence was also presented that Mark Wills believed Karen Brown had been the cause of a disturbance in the restaurant a couple of weeks before the present incident occurred, yet he failed to intervene or call the police when she began attacking Gould.

In addition, Mark Walters, the store manager, testified that since he became manager of the restaurant in August 1981, the late night patrons had been "destructive" and "uncontrollable." He stated that the late night business in Taco Bell originated in the neighboring bars and that the customers were rowdy and used loud, vulgar, and obscene language, and engaged in verbal fights and occasional physical fights. He also testified there was not sufficient help to handle such crowds and that Taco Bell's written policy was to call the police in case of disruptive customer behavior.

These facts indicate that Taco Bell was aware of the "imminence of danger" yet failed to intervene or warn plaintiff of such danger. There was substantial evidence to support the jury's award of punitive damages.

The judgment of the trial court is affirmed.

CASE QUESTIONS

1. In what three ways did Taco Bell fail to control the activity in its restaurant in this case?

2. Why was Taco Bell liable for punitive damages?

<u>Sudden, Unforseeable Attack</u>

Sometimes a fight occurs suddenly in a bar with no advance warning. In these circumstances, a fight and any resulting injuries are not foreseeable to the restaurant and thus the facility will not be liable. Numerous cases illustrate this point.

In *Griffin v. V&J Foods, Inc.*, 546 N.W.2d 579 (Wis. 1996), the court dismissed a lawsuit against a restaurant where the plaintiff was shot by a robber while waiting in a drive-through lane. The employee at the window testified that she knew the attacker and had never had trouble with him in the past. Further, the attack occurred "so suddenly that it could not have been prevented by additional security measures ... ."

In another case, the plaintiff was dancing on a crowded dance floor at a club when she was pushed from behind. She turned around and encountered a woman who said the plaintiff had stepped on her toe. While the plaintiff was apologizing, the woman hit the plaintiff in the jaw. The club's security personnel immediately removed the woman from the club. The plaintiff was taken to the hospital and underwent surgery for a broken jaw. The plaintiff's lawsuit against the bar was dismissed because the assault occurred without warning.[29]

In *Stevens v. Spec Inc.*, 637 N.Y.S.2d 979 (1996), the plaintiff, a nightclub patron, was struck in the face with a beer bottle by a member of the band during a dispute that started when the plaintiff failed to move from the stage area when requested. The plaintiff sued the nightclub, claiming it provided insufficient security for the safety of its customers. The court dismissed the case, finding that the altercation was spontaneous and unexpected. Although there had been "three or four" fights in the nightclub within a ten-month period prior to the evening in question, none was similar to the incident in which the plaintiff was hurt, and none involved the band member who struck the plaintiff.

In a related situation, a diner in a restaurant was paralyzed from the waist down in a drive-by shooting. The perpetrator was the estranged husband of a waitress on duty at the time of the shooting. Five months earlier, the husband had threatened to shoot a male employee who had been harassing the waitress. Restaurant management was aware of the prior incident. The paralyzed patron argued that the restaurant was on notice of the estranged husband's violent tendencies and had breached its duty to her by not providing better security. The court noted that the husband did not display a gun during the prior incident and the harassing employee had been fired, thereby eliminating the threat of such incident recurring. The court held the restaurant was not on notice that the estranged husband might attempt to kill his wife or act violently toward customers. The court therefore determined that the restaurant had not violated its duty to act reasonably to protect its patrons and dismissed the complaint.[30]

To review, if the restaurateur or bar owner cannot reasonably foresee injury to a patron, the owner's responsibility to take steps to prevent attacks is limited. If, however, circumstances suggest that customers are at risk of being accosted,

---

[29] *Murphy v. Second Street Corporation*, 48 S.W.3d 57 (Ky. 2001)
[30] *Hillcrest Foods, Inc. v. Kiritsy*, 489 S.E.2d 547 (Ga. 1997)

the restaurant or bar must take reasonable action to protect the patrons and prevent the attack.

Failure to Provide Adequate Security

A related circumstance in which a restaurant or bar may be liable to a patron for injuries caused by another customer is where the tavern keeper fails to provide a staff adequate to police the premises. Liability will turn on whether the restaurant took sufficient precautionary measures based on the foreseeability of the incident. If the restaurant is known to be the site of assaults, robberies, or similar incidents in the past, the owner is on notice that patrons may be in danger and has a duty to protect them.

In a South Carolina case, the defendant bar was located in a high crime area and failed to adopt commensurate security measures. It promoted an "End of Summer Bash" on a local radio station that broadcasted from the parking lot. Customers were offered prizes and music was played on loud speakers in the parking area. The plaintiff was injured when she was hit in the parking lot by an item that had been thrown. Said the court in reversing a directed verdict for the bar, "Despite these efforts to draw a large crowd in a dangerous area, the owner did not provide a door man or other security measures such as bouncers or wait staff."[31]

In *Early v. N.L.V. Casino Corp.*, 678 P.2d 683 (Nev. 1984), the plaintiff was attacked in the restroom of a casino restaurant and suffered physical and psychological injuries. The court found the attack was foreseeable, noting that the crime log books for the casino showed ninety-two crimes known to have been committed on the premises in the two years preceding the attack on the plaintiff. The court further found the casino took inadequate precautions to protect guests against foreseeable attacks. The security guards were given no formal training sessions, written materials, or security manuals. Few if any security staff meetings were held. On some occasions, no guards patrolled the casino entrance at night. The chief of security was unable to attend monthly hotel security chiefs' meetings because of low staffing. This was woefully inadequate for the risks involved.

In *Taco Bell, Inc. v. Lannon*, 744 P.2d 43 (Colo. 1987), the plaintiff was injured in the course of an armed robbery at a restaurant and suffered a gunshot wound. The restaurant argued that it could not have foreseen the particular incident because robberies occur randomly and without notice of the time or manner. The court rejected this argument, noting that the restaurant had experienced ten armed robberies during the prior three years. The court held that harm to customers was foreseeable and so the restaurant was required to institute security measures. Said the court,

> To establish that an incident is foreseeable, it is not necessary that an owner or occupier of land held open for business purposes be able to ascertain precisely when or how an incident will occur. Rather, foreseeability includes whenever it is likely enough in the setting of modern life that a reasonably thoughtful person would take account of it in guiding practical conduct.

---

[31]*Jeffords v. Lesesne*, 541 S.E.2d 847 (S.C. 2000)

The restaurant argued that security measures would be costly and create an economic burden. The court rejected this defense, saying,

> To be sure, such measures would result in some economic burden on Taco Bell and a predictable corresponding increase to customers in the cost of Taco Bell's food products. For the most part however, we believe that these potential measures—which, according to the evidence might include making sure the restaurant is well illuminated, installing highly visible video cameras, keeping [only] small amounts of cash in the registers, posting signs notifying potential robbers of the small amount of cash kept on the premises, training employees in methods for dealing with in-progress robberies, and locking non-public entrances during nighttime hours-are relatively inexpensive.

In the following case, shootings and fights frequently occurred at the defendant bar. The owner failed to take the steps necessary to protect the customers.

CASE EXAMPLE 11-7

Stevens v. Jefferson
436 So.2d 33 (Fla. 1983)

Earl Sidney Jefferson was shot and killed in a bar by a fellow patron. Stevens owned and operated the bar. Jefferson's widow alleged and proved that previously there had been numerous shootings and fights in the bar, that the owner had failed to train or equip employees to maintain order, and that no security personnel had been employed when the owner knew or should have known that his patrons were being exposed to risk of harm from fights or shootings by other patrons. In effect Mrs. Jefferson showed that Stevens either created a dangerous condition or allowed one to exist by the manner in which he ran his establishment. She did not allege, however, that Stevens knew of any dangerous propensities of Jefferson's assailant, and Stevens contends that Jefferson cannot prevail because of that lack of knowledge. We disagree.

The proprietor of a place of public entertainment owes his invitee a duty to use due care to maintain his premises in a reasonably safe condition commensurate with the activities conducted thereon. ... We have stated that the proprietor of a liquor saloon, although not an insurer of his patrons' safety, is bound to use every reasonable effort to maintain order among his patrons, employees, or those who come upon the premises and are

likely to produce disorder leading to the injury or inconvenience of patrons lawfully in his place of business. ... A determination as to whether this duty has been violated will, of necessity, depend upon a review of the facts of each individual case. Additionally, the risk of harm must be foreseeable. This foreseeability requirement has often been met by proving that the proprietor knew or should have known of the dangerous propensities of a particular patron. ... But specific knowledge of a dangerous individual is not the exclusive method of proving foreseeability. It can be shown by proving that a proprietor knew or should have known of a dangerous condition on his premises that was likely to cause harm to a patron. ...

To affix liability against a tavern owner for injuries to patrons intentionally inflicted by third parties, a risk of harm to his patrons must be reasonably foreseeable. ...

A tavern owner's actual or constructive knowledge, based upon past experience, that there is a likelihood of disorderly conduct by third persons in general which may endanger the safety of his patrons is also sufficient to establish foreseeability. ...

It is incumbent upon the plaintiff to prove legal causation. ... Mrs. Jefferson met her burden by showing that the bar was a "rough" place with a history of fights and gunplay and that the owner had terminated all security service and had left the premises in the charge

of a female employee who could not maintain order. Under these facts a jury could determine that a foreseeable risk of harm to patrons
existed, that the risk was either created or
tolerated by Stevens, that he could have
remedied the danger but failed to do so, and
that because of that failure to perform his
duties Jefferson was killed.

CASE QUESTIONS

1. What circumstances made violence at this establishment forseeable?

2. What action should a restaurant or bar owner take to protect patrons when the restaurant
   has been the site of many fights?

A bar did not owe a duty to provide security personnel where the defendant
facility is a "quiet, neighborhood bar whose typical patron is middle-aged or
older" and in the six months preceding the fight in which the plaintiff was injured
there was only one altercation on the premises and that was "non-physical."[32]

Attention to security issues is a must to avoid liability. A restaurant's protection plan should include thorough training of employees on how to handle a disturbance, and frequent assessments of the foreseeable risks and the precautionary
practices needed.

No Duty to Comply with Demands of Robber

In an unusual case, a patron at a fast-food restaurant who was held hostage by an
armed robber was injured when a restaurant worker failed to comply with the robber's demands for money. The customer sued the restaurant to recover for her injuries. The court held that a restaurateur has no duty to comply with a robber's
unlawful demands, even though compliance might lessen the danger to other persons on the premises.[33]

Key Terms

class action	privity of contract
foreign/natural substance test	reasonable expectation test
kosher	strict products liability
merchantable	Uniform Commercial Code (UCC)

---

[32] *Motuzick v. Yankee Restaurant, Inc.*, 2001 WL 400375 (Conn. 2001)

[33] *Kentucky Fried Chicken of California, Inc. v. Brown*, 927 P.2d 1260 (Ca. 1997)

Summary

Various laws protect patrons of restaurants against dangers of adulterated and mislabeled food. These laws include the implied warranty of merchantability, strict products liability, and negligence.

Claims made about food—including health or nutritional benefits, methods of preparation, and other attributes—must be accurate and comply with any statutory definitions.

Food preparation and service present particular safety issues that should be addressed. These include proper use of equipment, safegaurds related to service of hot beverages, adequate training on the preparation and service of flambé dishes, and precautions to avoid dropped food.

Assaults occasionally occur at food-service establishments. The proprietor must guard against forseeable risks to the safety of patrons. If the proprietor is aware of belligerent tendencies of a patron, the customer should be expelled. If fights or other security incidents have occurred in the past, precautions such as security personnel, bright illumination, and video cameras may be necessary.

Preventive Law Tips for Managers

- *Inspect food carefully before it is served to ensure it is fit for human consumption.* A restaurant that serves inedible food will be liable for breach of the warranty of merchantability. Liability will result, even if the restaurant is not aware that the food is unwholesome. To minimize the chances of serving unhealthy food, all food should be carefully inspected before it is used as an ingredient in a recipe and before it is served. Any unfit food should be removed, including adulterated food, foreign objects, and natural objects that a customer may not expect that can cause injury.

- *Cook pork thoroughly to destroy the parasite that causes trichinosis.* Uncooked pork often contains a parasite that can cause the life-threatening disease of trichinosis. The parasite is killed upon proper cooking of the pork. To ensure restaurant patrons are not exposed to the risk of the disease, all pork should be thoroughly cooked before serving.

- *Be sure all claims made about food offered at a restaurant are accurate.* The law requires that only truthful claims be made about food offered to restaurant patrons. Descriptions on menus such as "fresh," "made in Vermont," or "zero cholesterol" must be truthful. If a restaurant uses words that are standardized by regulations of the Food and Drug Administration (FDA) pursuant to the Nutrition Labeling and Education Act of 1990, such as *light* or *low-calorie*, the food item must meet the FDA standards. If food is promoted as kosher, it must meet the requirements mandated for that designation.

- *If a hotel recommends food from a restaurant not operated by the hotel, it should inspect the restaurant periodically to verify that sanitation, food preparation, and management standards are being met.* A guest injured by food from a restaurant promoted by a hotel may have a cause of action against the hotel if the latter has not assessed the operational practices of the restaurant on a regular basis. To protect itself from liability, a hotel that encourages its guests to dine in a particular restaurant should satisfy itself periodically that the restaurant is worthy of the endorsement.

■ *Comply with smoking restrictions imposed on hospitality facilities.* Most states and many localities have adopted smoking restrictions that require restaurants to either ban smoking, or set aside a certain percentage of seating capacity for use by nonsmoking diners. Know the law in your area and do whatever is necessary to comply.

■ *Attempt to reduce the effects of secondhand smoke.* Secondhand smoke can become an issue to customers and employees with respiratory illnesses or those with a general concern about their health. Lawsuits may be pursued under the Americans with Disabilities Act. Methods to reduce the effects of secondhand smoke, such as specially designed ventilation systems, should be investigated and seriously considered.

■ *Adopt procedures for use and maintenance of kitchen appliances to minimize injuries to employees.* Kitchens by necessity contain many potentially dangerous appliances and utensils including stoves, grills, meat cutters, knives, and deep-fat fryers. Procedures should be adopted for their use and maintenance to ensure maximum safety. Other components of a good risk-reduction plan are employee training and frequent monitoring of kitchen operations by managers.

■ *Eject patrons with known propensities for fighting.* A bar or restaurant may be liable if one patron causes injury to another in circumstances where the injury was foreseeable and adequate security measures were not taken. To reduce the possibility of injury, customers who are known to engage in fights should be denied entrance to the establishment.

■ *Immediately stop a fight that breaks out in a bar or restaurant and eject the participants.* If customers start fighting, the altercation should be stopped immediately and the participants ejected. Failure to end the brawl can result in liability. If the facility is unable to stop the fighting, the police should be called.

■ *Provide staff sufficient to address foreseeable problems.* A bar or restaurant must provide a staff sufficient to handle foreseeable difficulties. For example, if a large crowd is expected on a given day, or if the establishment has been the site of fighting in the past, the bar should have on duty personnel sufficient in size and training to handle associated problems. Failure to provide adequate staff can result in liability if one customer injures another.

■ *Come to the aid of a customer who has been injured.* If a customer is injured while on the premises, the bar or restaurant should aid the patron in obtaining help. The assistance required might include any of the following, depending on the circumstances: call the police; call an ambulance; call someone the customer requests you to call; allow the customer to use the phone; eject those who caused the injury.

■ *Develop and strictly follow a Hazard Analysis Critical Control Point System.* Such systems help to ensure that food served at restaurants is safe and wholesome by promoting development of prevention methods directed at hazards that can cause spoilage or contamination. Components of any such system for restaurants should include training and enforcement relating to good hand-washing procedures.

Review Questions

1. What states have adopted the Uniform Commercial Code?

2. What does the warranty of merchantability guarantee?

3. What is the difference between the foreign/natural test and the reasonable expectation test?

4. What disease can be contracted by eating uncooked pork?

5. What does "privity of contract" mean? How does it impact a lawsuit involving the warranty of merchantability?

6. What is strict products liability?

7. What is meant by "truth-in-menu"?

8. What impact does the 1990 Nutrition Education and Labeling Act have on restaurants?

9. What is kosher food?

10. Why do some states limit smoking in restaurants?

11. What is secondhand smoke?

12. What safety precautions are necessary to avoid injuries occurring to employees in a restaurant kitchen?

13. Under what circumstances is a restaurant liable when one patron injures another?

Discussion Questions

1. If you are the manager of a restaurant, would you prefer that the foreign/natural test or reasonable expectation test apply? Why?

2. Do you agree with the decision in *Webster v. Blue Ship Tea Room, Inc.* involving the bone in the fish chowder? Why or why not?

3. Dan ate breakfast at a restaurant known as Pam's Breakfast Shop. He later became ill. Are these facts sufficient to establish that Pam's Breakfast Shop sold unwholesome food? Why or why not? If not, what more is neded?

4. Must a plaintiff suing for breach of the warranty of merchantability show that the defendant was negligent? Why or why not?

5. What differentiates strict products liability from the warranty of merchantability?

6. What steps should a restaurant manager take to ensure that the menu contains no inaccurate statements?

7. Under what circumstances should a restaurateur foresee injuries to a patron?

Application Questions

1. Mandy, manager of a cafeteria at a large corporation, purchased a new freezer for the kitchen. It operated at a temperature a few degrees above the setting. Is the freezer merchantable? Why or why not?

2. A hotel chain and a well-known hamburger fast-food chain are negotiating a contract that would authorize the hotel to use the fast-food chain's name on the hotel's room-service menu to promote the sale of hamburgers. What terms will the hamburger company want to include in the contract? Why? What terms will the hotel want included? Why?

3. Jim owns a bar in an upscale part of town. It is patronized primarily by business people who stop in for a few drinks after work. No fights or disruptions have ever occurred and no patron has ever been unruly. One night a man started threatening other customers. Jim immediately approached the man and told him to leave. While Jim was escorting him to the door, the man punched another customer who suffered a broken nose. The patron sued Jim's bar for his injuries. Is the bar liable under these circumstances?

4. Look at a menu. Identify all the words whose meanings might be disputed by a diner who ordered the item and was disappointed.

5. An outdoor patio at a restaurant was the site of a post-football game party for the local high school. Anticipating many hungry fans, large quantities of picnic food (hot dogs, hamburgers, macaroni salad) were prepared and, at the appointed time, displayed buffet-style. Unfortunately, rain began in the middle of the game. As a result, many spectators left the game and so the crowd for the post-game party was much smaller than anticipated. Much of the buffet food was not eaten. The restaurant owner wants to donate the leftovers to a shelter for homeless people. What legal issues should the restaurant consider before making the donation?

Web Sites

Web sites that will enhance your understanding of the material in this chapter include:

http://www.FDA.gov This is the official site of the Food and Drug Administration, the federal agency that oversees food products. Included on the site is information about foodborne illnesses, allergy risks from undeclared ingredients of food products, and food labeling, to mention but a few.

http://www.restaurant.org This is the site of the National Restaurant Association, a trade organization for restaurant owners and managers. Among the issues addressed are food safety and handling and how to elect pro-restaurant legislators.

http://www.nraef.org This is the official site of the National Restaurant Association Educational Foundation. This site provides information and training on such topics as safe service of food and regulatory requirements for restaurant safety.

CHAPTER 12

■

Liability and the Sale
of Alcohol

INTRODUCTION

The government has long been concerned about the sale of alcohol. The driver of a vehicle who has been drinking has diminished abilities to operate and control the car. This leads to many fatal accidents. In recent years, more than 17,000 deaths and 285,000 injuries occurred annually as a result of alcohol-related traffic accidents. In an attempt to limit this type of bloodshed, each state highly regulates (restricts) the sale of liquor. Regulations include limitations on who can sell (a liquor license is required), who can buy, and even the days and times liquor can be sold.

Alcoholic Beverages and the Hospitality Industry

Restaurants and bars have various goals concerning the sale of alcohol, some of which are conflicting. On the one hand, hospitality facilities view liquor as a moneymaker. Many people regularly have one or more drinks and the income from those sales can be substantial. On the other hand, restaurants and bars also have significant motivation to moderate their promotion of alcohol. When enforcing liquor laws, the government shows no leniency; liquor laws are strictly enforced. Violation of liquor regulations can result in substantial liability. Potential consequences include revocation of the license to sell liquor, which may result in the business being forced to close; jail time; fines; and legal fees. With these penalties at stake, a liquor establishment is well-advised to strictly follow the law.

An additional concern for sellers of alcohol is that intoxicated persons are frequently belligerent and cause disturbances that interfere with other patrons. If injuries result, the bar or restaurant might be liable. See Chapter 11.

License to Sell Liquor

No business can sell alcohol without first obtaining a liquor license from the state.

To obtain a license to sell alcohol, a restaurant or hotel must apply to the appropriate government agency within the state. The agency will typically have a name like The Alcohol Beverage Control Board or Liquor Licenses and Control. In most states, to qualify for a license the applicant must prove he has not abused liquor in the past, whether as a consumer, a seller, a driver, or otherwise; has not been convicted of a felony; and is otherwise of good character and fitness.

A liquor license, once granted, may be revoked or suspended by the state if the licensee violates the liquor laws.

Illegal Sales

In most states, sales are prohibited to people under age 21, people who are visibly intoxicated, and known habitual drunkards.

You may think that the law imposes liability only on those people who wrongfully imbibe, for example the underage drinker. This is a misconception of the law. Because the effects of alcohol are potentially so dangerous, the law strives to motivate not just the consumer, but also the server to strictly comply with the law. Therefore, the restaurant or bar that wrongfully provides alcohol to a person not legally entitled to drink risks harsh penalties. Punishment can include suspension or revocation of a liquor license, civil liability for injuries caused by a patron who was wrongfully served, and, particularly in the case of serving a young person, criminal liability for which penalties include jail and a fine. Great care should be taken to avoid illegal sales.

Sales to Underage Patrons

Virtually every state outlaws serving alcohol to people under age 21. Individuals in this age range often try to finagle their way into a bar to be served. A licensee (a bar or restaurant with a liquor license) must develop and strictly enforce rules and procedures to ensure that proper proof of age is obtained before alcohol is served. It is the responsibility of the bar or restaurant to ask for an acceptable form of identification. Management must determine what type of identification will be acceptable. Among the recommended forms are a state-issued driver's license, a state-issued non-driver identification card, a military identification card, and a passport. To verify the identification, the bouncer should check the provided documentation for signs of tampering or alteration; check that the photo matches the patron and ensure that the patron matches the descriptive information provided such as color of hair, eyes, height, weight, and approximate age. The bouncer might also query would-be patrons about information on their identification documents. For example, the enforcer might ask patrons their middle name and see if it matches the one on the identification card.

Management should frequently reinforce to employees the importance of verifying age in the effort to minimize incidents of underage service. State statutes often provide a defense to a charge of serving someone under 21 where the young person displayed to the licensee an identification card with a photograph "apparently" issued by a governmental entity, and the licensee implemented a written policy requiring such identification. In many states it is illegal for people under 21 to misrepresent their age or present false identification. In such states, young people presenting false IDs or otherwise claiming to be older than they are face fines and, in some states, more serious penalties.

Sometimes a person of legal age purchases alcohol and gives it to someone underage. Is the licenses liable in these situations? The answer is—it depends. If the licensee had no reason to know that the underage person would gain access to the alcohol, the seller will not be liable. For example, in *Jones v. B.P. Oil, Inc.*, 632 So.2d 435 (Ala. 1994), a person bought beer from a convenience store. After exiting the store and proceeding beyond the sight of the sales clerk, he gave some of the beer to his underage friend who was driving. A car accident resulted, and the injured party sued the convenience store. The court held the store was not liable due to the absence of evidence that the store employees knew or should have known that the purchaser would share it with an underage person.

If, however, the circumstances are such that the licensee should have known that an adult purchased the beverages for a minor's use, the sale may be illegal. In one case, a minor asked his adult neighbor to purchase beer for him. The neighbor agreed and together the two went to a beer distributor. An employee of the distributor approached the car and the adult neighbor placed the order. After the beer was put in the car, the employee sought payment. The neighbor looked at the minor, who took money from a mug he was holding and handed it to the neighbor who in turn gave it to the employee. Apparently, the amount was insufficient because the employee returned to the car seeking additional money and again the neighbor looked to the minor, who withdrew additional money from the mug.

After leaving the store and consuming the beer, the minor climbed an electrical transmission tower, came into contact with a high-voltage line, was burned, and fell 100 feet to the ground, resulting in serious injury. He sued the beer distributor for his injuries. Pennsylvania, where the case occurred, renders a licensee liable to a minor if the minor is served alcohol and is injured as a result. The trial court dismissed the case, holding that the sale by the beer distributor was made to the neighbor and not the minor. On appeal, the case was referred to trial on the basis that a jury might determine that the beer distributor should have known the actual purchaser was the minor.[1]

This case instructs us that licensees must be alert to circumstances where an apparent purchase by an adult is in reality an illegal purchase by a minor. Failure to detect such unlawful buys can result in liability and loss of license. Bars and restaurants must always be vigilant.

Academic Exception

Often state laws that prohibit underage drinking include an exception for an academic course in which tasting alcohol is required for instructional purposes. Part of your curriculum may include such a course on bartending.

Sales to People Who Are Visibly Intoxicated

Sales of alcohol to people who are **visibly intoxicated** is illegal. For the sale to qualify as illegal, the person's appearance or actions must indicate he is intoxicated. Absent proof that a patron is noticeably intoxicated, service of alcohol to him is not illegal.[2] If proof of visible intoxication is presented and the bar or restaurant is unable to refute it, the bar will be responsible for the illegal sale.[3] A factual determination of intoxication cannot be made solely on the basis of how much alcohol a person has consumed, as the effects of alcohol differ greatly from person to person. Thus, the fact that a patron had four alcoholic drinks within an hour is alone insufficient to establish visible intoxication.[4] Where a driver in a car accident had a blood alcohol level two hours after the collision of .21, twice the legal limit, and the accident occurred soon after he left the bar, an expert witness extraploated that he was visibly intoxicated when he was at the bar.[5]

Although intoxication is sometimes difficult to detect, that may not be a defense to a charge of illegal sale. While the sale is illegal only if the customer is "noticeably" or "visibly" intoxicated, bartenders and wait personnel are expected to be familiar with indicia of intoxication. Servers must be trained to identify them. They include slurred speech, bloodshot and watery eyes, flushed face, and poor

---

[1] *Thomas v. Duquesne Light Co.*, 595 A.2d 56 (Penn. 1988)

[2] *Wilder v. Nickbert, Inc.*, 678 N.Y.S.2d 766 (N.Y. 1998)

[3] *Smith v. Blue Mountain Inn, Inc.*, 680 N.Y.S.2d 386 (N.Y. 1998)

[4] *Adamy v. Friday's*, 92 N.Y.2d 396 (N.Y. 1998)

[5] *Roy v. Volonino*, 694 N.Y.S.2d 399 (2nd Dept. 1999)

coordination, which is often evidenced by difficulty in performing such acts as making change or handling money, lighting a cigarette, standing without swaying, or walking without staggering or stumbling. Evidence of intoxication can also include being overly friendly, boisterous, loud, argumentative, aggressive, crude, and annoying to other customers, to mention only some.[6] Good training videotapes, developed by the National Restaurant Association and the American Hotel and Motel Association, are available to instruct bartenders and wait personnel on how to recognize intoxication. Training materials also cover such topics as how to manage the dispensing of alcoholic beverages, how to manage customers' consumption, how to prevent service to underage or intoxicated customers, how to prevent an intoxicated customer from driving, and what to do if those efforts fail. In addition to initial employee training, frequent refresher courses are an important component of alcohol-service training. Staff meetings provide a good opportunity to reinforce the message that alcohol must be served responsibly and to remind servers of the indicia of intoxication. Some states, for example Maryland, have laws that require all establishments that serve alcohol to be certified in an alcohol awareness training program.

Errors in who a licensee serves not only put at risk the license to sell alcohol, but also can lead to liability for injuries caused by the wrongly served patron, as will be discussed in the section of this chapter on the Dram Shop Act.

Proving Visible Intoxication

Visible or noticeable intoxication can be proved at trial in several ways. Various people may have observed the customer becoming intoxicated, including fellow revelers, the bartender, or servers. Expert witnesses may have relevant testimony in circumstances where a patron, after leaving the bar, is arrested for driving while intoxicated and submits to a breathalyzer test—a device that measures the amount of alcohol in one's system. If the amount of time between when the person left the bar and when the test occurred is known, expert witnesses can extrapolate backwards to determine the person's level of intoxication while still in the restaurant.[7] Also, officers at the crash scene may have observed indicia of intoxication, such as the smell of alcohol, bloodshot or watery eyes, slurred speech, and unsteadiness or staggering.[8]

Other factors that may aid in proving that a bar served a patron illegally include failure by the tavern to train its employees about alcohol consumption, absence of an employer policy about how much liquor can be served to a customer, and rotation of wait personnel so that no one server keeps track of the amount a particular patron drinks.[9]

---

[6] *Dollar v. O'Hearn*, 670 N.Y.S.2d 230 (N.Y. 1998)

[7] *Adamy v. Ziriakus*, 92 N.Y.2d 396 (N.Y. 1998)

[8] *McGee v. Alexander*, 2001 WL 1148126 (Ok. 2001)

[9] *Copeland v. Red Dog Saloon and Café*, 996 P.2d 931 (Ok. 1999)

Sales to Known Habitual Drunkards

Sale of alcohol to known habitual drunkards is prohibited. A habitual drunkard is someone who regularly imbibes alcohol and frequently becomes intoxicated. A licensee who serves a known habitual drunkard risks losing his license and may be liable for injuries caused by such person.

Proof of Visible Intoxication

In a lawsuit, intoxication is usually proved in one of two ways. The first is by showing the percent by weight of alcohol in the person's blood, called the BAC level. The BAC is determined by a device that analyses the blood, breath, urine, or saliva of the person believed to be intoxicated. The test must be done within a few hours of an arrest. In most states, if the percent by weight of alcohol is .10 or higher, the person is legally intoxicated. A growing trend is to reduce the level to .08. As the number of alcohol-related accidents increase, more states are considering lowering the percentage rates. Another impetus for lowering the BAC level is a federal law that provides a portion of federal highway-construction funds will be withheld from states that do not adopt a .08 standard by 2004. Currently 17 states utilize the .08 level for intoxication.

The second way intoxication can be proved is by the indicia of intoxication discussed previously in this chapter. Witnesses can include anyone who observed the patron in an intoxicated state, such as the bartender, wait staff, other customers, and the police.

Alcohol Vendors' Liability under Common Law

An issue that has long troubled liquor licensees is potential liability for injuries caused by a customer who was served alcohol illegally.

Under common law, in most states the licensee was not liable for damages caused when it served alcohol to someone who was under 21, visibly intoxicated, or a habitual drunkard and that person was injured or caused injury to another. Thus, if a wrongfully served customer left a bar, drove a car, and on the way home caused an accident in which the patron or someone else was injured, the bar was not liable. According to this common law rule, the cause of the injuries was the *consumption* and not the *sale* of the liquor. The injured person could sue only the drunk driver. The bar or restaurant that sold the alcohol to the driver was not liable.

As the number of alcohol-related accidents grew, most states found the common law rule unsatisfactory. Said one court, "With today's car of steel and speed it becomes a lethal weapon in the hands of a drunken imbiber. Accidents involving drunk drivers are commonplace. The resulting affliction of bodily injury to an unsuspecting public is also of common knowledge."[10]

---

[10]*Ohio Casualty Insurance Co. v. Todd*, 813 P.2d 508 (Ok. 1991)

The law came to recognize that a person able to prevent alcohol abuse is the licensee—that is, the bar or restaurant. The common law rule did nothing to encourage the server to prevent patrons from abusing alcohol.

Another weakness of the common law rule was that many intoxicated persons who cause injury have little money with which to compensate those they injure. The owner of a restaurant or bar is more likely to have insurance and assets.

Alcohol Vendors' Liability Greatly Increases under Dram Shop Act

Over time, public policy came to demand more responsibility on the dispenser of alcohol resulting in legislation in many states called **dram shop acts** (*dram shop* is an outdated term for a bar). These acts impose liability on a restaurant or bar for certain injuries resulting from illegal sales. The objectives of dram shop laws are to discourage proprietors from selling alcohol illegally and to afford compensation to victims whose injuries emanate from the unlawful sale of alcohol.

The potential liability is very significant. Some illegal sales have resulted in verdicts that have financially ruined the bar or restaurant involved.

The following quote from a decision in a case explains well the rationale for holding the bar or restaurant liable.

> When alcoholic beverages are sold by a tavern keeper to a minor or to an intoxicated person, the unreasonable risk of harm not only to the minor or the intoxicated person but also to members of the traveling public may readily be recognized and foreseen; this is particularly evident in current times when traveling by car to and from the tavern is so common-place and accidents resulting from drinking are so frequent. ...
>
> Today, the hazards of travel by automobiles on modern highways have become a national problem. The drunken driver is a threat to the safety of many. It is understandable that early cases did not recognize any duty of an innkeeper to the traveling public because a serious hazard did not exist. [Presumably because at one time cars were not yet invented, and once they were, initially they were not accessible to many people and did not have the speed potential of today's vehicles.] It is a well established, sound principle of legal philosophy that the common law is not static. Under the skillful interpretation of our courts, it has been adapted to changing times and conditions of our civilization. ...
>
> The increasing frequency of serious accidents caused by drivers who are intoxicated is a fact which must be well known to those who sell and dispense liquor. This lends support to those cases which have found the automobile accident to be "the reasonably foreseeable" result of furnishing liquor to the intoxicated driver.[11]

Liability of the bar or restaurant is not restricted to car accidents. Any injury caused by the wrongfully served patron will suffice, including, for example, those resulting from fights.

---

[11] *Rappaport v. Nichols*, 156 A.2d 1 (N.J. 1959)

Alcohol Vendor's Liability to the Patron

When a licensee makes an illegal sale and the person improperly served is injured (as distinct from a third person), is the licensee liable to the patron? The answer varies, depending on the state. In most states, dram shop acts do not impose liability for injuries to wrongfully served customers. In those states, the act imposes liability only for injuries to a third person. One court explained the reason as follows, "In our view, a rule which allows an intoxicated individual to hold a tavern owner liable without regard to his own actions in continuing to consume alcohol promotes irresponsibility and rewards drunk driving."[12] In the referenced case, a bar patron drank to excess and was injured in a car accident he caused while driving home. The court affirmed a jury verdict in favor of the bar. In *Jackson v. PKM Corp.*, 422 N.W.2d 657 (Mich. 1988), the plaintiff was injured in a single vehicle accident while driving home from the defendant's bar. She claimed that, prior to the accident, she was served alcohol even though she was visibly intoxicated. The court dismissed the case on the grounds that neither common law nor the state dram shop act imposed liability on a licensee for injuries to a wrongfully served patron.

In another case, the plaintiff was allegedly served at the defendant's bar after reaching a visibly intoxicated condition. While intoxicated, he fell from his stool and permanently injured his leg, requiring the use of a brace and crutches. His action against the bar was dismissed because neither Maryland's dram shop act nor common law permits the patron to sue the licensee.[13]

In *Cuevas v. Royal D'Ibervilee Hotel*, 498 So.2d 346 (Miss. 1986), the plaintiff was attending a medical technician's convention at the defendant hotel where she allegedly was served alcohol after becoming visibly intoxicated. She fell over a railing 30 feet to the lobby floor. Her action for damages against the hotel was likewise dismissed.

Minority Rule

A minority of states allow the wrongfully served patron to sue the licensee for resulting injuries, some based on dram shop liability and some based on negligence. An example of dram shop liability is provided by a Texas case in which the plaintiff was illegally served alcohol. While driving home she crashed into a telephone pole and was seriously injured. The bar was found liable.[14] In *Lyons v. Nasby*, 770 P.2d 1250 (Colo. 1989), the bar was held responsible on a negligence theory. The plaintiff, the decedent's relative, claimed the deceased was served at the defendant's restaurant when he was visibly intoxicated and then drove his car off a mountain road and was killed. In holding that the plaintiff could sue the restaurant, the court explained,

---

[12] *Tobias v. Sports Club, Inc.*, 474 S.E.2d 450 (S.C. 1996).

[13] *Fisher v. O'Connor's, Inc.*, 452 A.2d 1313 (Md. 1982).

[14] *Salzar v. Giorgio's*, 53 S.W.3d 412 (Tex. 2001).

We have stated before that a reasonable person would foresee that an inebriate will act without prudence, control or self-restraint ... We agree that voluntary [intoxication] is a self-indulgent act. We also note that a person who voluntarily consumes alcohol to the point of intoxication is at the very least partially responsible for his injuries. However, the fact that the patron has acted in an unacceptable manner should in no way lessen the equally unacceptable conduct of a tavern owner. One who stands behind a bar and serves drink after drink to a visibly intoxicated customer engages in behavior which is as opprobrious as that of the customer. ... Insulating tavern owners from liability does not send the message that they, as well as their patrons, must be accountable for their actions.

Note that the bar can assert the defense of comparative negligence (Chapter 5), thereby requiring the jury to allocate the relative liability for the accident between the tavern and the intoxicated patron.

Regardless of whether a particular state holds the bar liable to the patron, a licensee that makes an illegal sale of alcohol faces fines and license suspension.

Alcohol Vendor's Liability to Third Parties

Although licensees in most states will not be liable to a wrongfully served patron injured from the alcohol, the bar may be held liable to others who are injured from the patron's intoxication. For example, if a licensee serves a visibly intoxicated patron who, while driving home, hits another car causing injury to its driver, the licensee will be liable to that driver. In *Grayson Fraternal Order of Eagles v. Claywell*, 736 S.W.2d 328 (Ky. 1987), a visibly intoxicated patron drove from the premises of the licensee and collided with another car, killing one person and seriously injuring another. The court held that the licensee would be liable to the deceased's estate and the person injured. Similarly, if the wrongfully served patron leaves the bar, drives a boat, and causes an accident and injury to others, the bar may be liable.[15]

Another application of the dram shop act is the circumstance where a bar patron who was served too much alcohol engages in a fight and injures a third person. An example involves an intoxicated customer who threw an ashtray at the bartender but missed and instead hit another patron. Assuming proof that the contentious drinker was served while visibly intoxicated, the bar will be liable for the injuries caused by the ashtray based on dram shop liability.[16]

Dram shop liability also applied where numerous guests at a private function held at a hotel were wrongly served alcohol and thereafter, while dancing, they fell causing a "chain reaction." It ended with the plaintiff, who was involuntarily pulled onto the dance floor, being knocked down and suffering a broken wrist.[17]

The potential liability under dram shop acts is very significant. To protect against this liability, tavern keepers should do everything possible to avoid illegal alcohol sales. Employee training is critical. If an error is made and a patron is

---

[15] *Koehane v. Lakefront Pier Restaurant, Inc.*, 676 N.Y.S.2d 363 (N.Y. 1998)

[16] *Smith v. Blue Mountain Inn, Inc.*, 680 N.Y.S.2d 386 (1998)

[17] *Dollar v. O'Hearn*, 670 N.Y.S.2d 230 (N.Y. 1998)

wrongfully served, the barkeeper should discourage the customer from driving home. Many restaurants and bars today contract with companies that provide rides home to intoxicated patrons and in some circumstances drive the customer's car home as well.

The practice of managers overseeing service decisions made by bartenders and wait personnel can help to limit liability. In one case involving a proceeding to revoke a restaurant's liquor license, beer had allegedly been served to a visibly intoxicated customer. The manager observed the customer's condition and immediately removed the bottle of beer. Based on these facts, the court found for the restaurant. Similar action in a dram shop case might also save the licensee from liability.

Alcohol Vendor's Liability to Passengers in Patron's Car

Often when injury results from a car accident, the injured party is a passenger in the patron's car. If the passenger purchased alcohol for the driver or encouraged the latter to drink more than he could tolerate, most states will not impose dram shop liability. However, if the passenger did not contribute to the driver's intoxication, the bar or restaurant will be liable for the passenger's injuries. In the following case, the court discusses the circumstances under which a passenger's lawsuit against the licensee will and will not succeed.

CASE EXAMPLE 12-1

Goss v. Richmond
381 N.W.2d 776 (Mich. 1985)

Plaintiff alleged in his dram shop action that defendant Le-Rob, a licensed seller of alcoholic beverages, illegally sold intoxicating liquor to a visibly intoxicated person, defendant Robert Richmond. Richmond allegedly drove his automobile off the road and struck a tree. Plaintiff was a passenger in the Richmond automobile and suffered serious injuries.

Plaintiff testified that he and Richmond purchased pitchers of beer in "rounds," each taking turns buying pitchers. The trial court held that buying such "rounds" amount to buying drinks for defendant Richmond. The court held that, by doing so, plaintiff was a noninnocent party under the dram shop act and was thus precluded from proceeding under the act. ...

Plaintiff argues that his participation in bringing about the injury-producing intoxication should not bar recovery. ...

The objective of the Legislature in enacting the dram shop act was to discourage bars from selling intoxicating liquors to visibly intoxicated persons and minors and to provide for recovery under certain circumstances by those injured as a result of the sale of intoxicating liquor. ... To permit one who has been an intentional accessory to the illegality to shift the loss resulting from it to the tavern owner would lead to a result we believe the Legislature did not intend. A person who buys drinks for an obviously intoxicated person, or one whom he knows to be a minor, is at least as much the cause of the resulting or continued intoxication as the bartender who served the consumer illegally. In short, barring recovery by a wrongdoer by holding that the wrongdoer is not among those to whom the Legislature intended to provide a remedy advances both purposes of the act, to suppress illegal sales and to provide a remedy for those injured as a result of the illegality.

Plaintiff next argues that the "innocent party" doctrine as applied in this case denies him equal protection of the laws. Plaintiff claims that, because he could recover if he and defendant Richmond, instead of buying "rounds," would each have purchased their own pitchers and drank side by side, the "innocent party" doctrine as applied in this case creates an arbitrary distinction between persons of the same class. ...

The material question when a defendant claims a plaintiff is not an "innocent party" under the dram shop act is whether the plaintiff actively participated in the intoxicated person's inebriation. ...

We do not find the distinction between persons who purchase "rounds" and those who merely accompany the allegedly intoxicated person to be arbitrary. A person who purchases a pitcher of beer knowing that the allegedly intoxicated person will drink therefrom is a more direct participant in the other's intoxication and more directly encourages the other's intoxication than a mere drinking companion. Buying in "rounds" conceivably sets the pace at which the allegedly intoxicated person will consume alcohol and conceivably encourages the allegedly intoxicated person to consume his "fair share."

[Judgment for the licensee] Affirmed.

In another case, the intoxicated driver's passenger was killed when the car missed the entrance of a bridge and crashed into a wall. The passenger's estate was denied recovery against the bar in which the two had been drinking because the passenger had, on several occasions during the evening, obtained glasses of beer for the driver, and further, had purchased alcohol he and the driver drank while in the car.[18]

In *Prunty v. Keltie's Bum Steer*, 559 N.Y.S.2d 354 (N.Y. 1990), the plaintiff passenger had bought "at least one drink" for the driver. The one drink was found to be sufficient to preclude the plaintiff's dram shop action against the bar.

In *Griffin Motel Co. v. Strickland*, 479 S.E.2d 401 (Ga. 1997), the companion of an intoxicated driver was a passenger in the car and was killed in a one-car collision caused by the alcohol. No evidence was presented that the passenger had furnished alcohol to the driver. The passenger's estate was therefore able to sue the bar at which the driver had been served.

Interestingly, where a passenger who did not buy alcohol for the driver knew the driver was intoxicated, some states have determined that the act of riding with the inebriated driver is itself negligent, impacting recovery in the case. These states apply a comparative negligence apportionment of liability (discussed in Chapter 5) between the bar and the passenger. Thus, the passenger will have to absorb a percentage of his damages equal to the percentage of liability attributed to him.[19]

Two Licensees Serving One Patron

More than one bar or restaurant may be liable in a given case. For example, if a visibly intoxicated person is served first at one bar and then at a second one,

---

[18] *Pollard v. Village of Ovid*, 446 N.W.2d 574 (Mich. 1989)

[19] *Terwillinger v. Kitchen*, 781 A.2d 1201 (Pa. 2001)

both will be liable to a third person injured by the patron. The injured person cannot, however, recover twice for the same injuries. Instead, the liability will be allocated between the two bars. If, however, the drinker was not visibly intoxicated until he arrived at the second bar, the first bar will not be liable.

Apportionment of Liability Where Plaintiff Is Negligent

Where the person injured by the illegally served drinker negligently contributed to the cause of the accident, the injured person's recovery will be reduced accordingly. As in a comparative negligence case (see Chapter 5), the jury will allocate a percentage of the liability to the plaintiff. His recovery against the bar will be reduced by that percentage.[20]

States Without Dram Shop Acts

A few states do not have dram shop acts. Some have created a negligence cause of action for holding the licensee liable when an illegally served patron causes injury to a third party. Other states protect the tavern owner from liability for injuries caused by illegal sales. In these states, parties injured by a wrongfully served customer will not be able to collect from the liquor licensee for their injuries.

Liquor Liability Insurance

A licensee can purchase insurance to cover dram shop liability. This insurance is often called **liquor liability insurance** or dram shop insurance. The cost is based on numerous factors, including the volume of alcohol sold by the licensee, prior incidents of illegal sales, the nature of the establishment, and the hours it is open.

Some states require that liquor-license applicants have either liquor liability insurance or a liability bond to cover liability.

Emerging Liability

A developing area of potential liability involves companies that sponsor events at hotels or restaurants. An example is a corporation-sponsored holiday party, special-event reception, or retirement party held at a party house or restaurant. Some states hold the host company liable to someone injured by an illegally served attendee at the event. For example, in a Florida case, an employer that sponsored a meeting at a hotel was held liable for the employee's alcohol-related accident. The employee had numerous drinks throughout the evening at the hotel bar, including three purchased by the president of his company. The employee lived in the area and drove home following the evening's activities. The accident occurred on his way home and resulted in the death of two people in the other car. The

---

[20]*Steak and Ale of Texas, Inc. v. Borneman*, 2001 WL 1548958 (Tex. 2001)

family of one of the deceased sued the employer, alleging negligence. A jury trial resulted in a sizeable verdict against the employer. This case underscores yet again the importance of prudent alcohol service for all involved.

Other states relieve the sponsoring company from dram shop liability and hold liable only liquor licensees engaged in the commercial enterprise of selling and serving alcohol.[21]

Companies planning events at a restaurant or bar are well-advised to negotiate terms in their contracts obligating the licensee to supervise the liquor service, follow responsible alcohol dispensing procedures, serve alcohol only to those legally entitled to drink, and hold the company harmless (compensate the company) for any liability incurred as a result of alcohol at the function. Hospitality facilities may want to resist the "hold harmless" provision. The inclusion of such a term in a restaurant or bar's contract not only increases the facility's potential liability, but may also increases the facility's insurance premium.

Strategies to Avoid Liability

As we have seen, liability for illegal alcohol sales can lead to money verdicts against a bar or restaurant and revocation of the liquor license. This liability must be taken very seriously by all licensees. We have already discussed important steps to help reduce liability. These include employee training and refresher courses, oversight of sales by a supervisor, and providing transportation home to intoxicated customers. Other practices that can contribute to reduced risk of liability include the following:

- Adopt internal written policies and rules concerning alcohol sales and publish them in an employee newsletter, if the licensee has one, and near the employee lounge or the punch-in clock.

- Encourage groups of customers to select a designated driver. Provide free nonalcoholic drinks to that person.

- Have a written policy on what employees should do when confronted with a patron who has had too much alcohol. Require each employee to know the policy and have them sign a copy of it periodically to reinforce it.

- Post signs that inform customers of their responsibilities. Suggested wording is, "WARNING! No person shall sell or give away any alcoholic beverage to any person under age 21 or who is visibly intoxicated. WARNING! It is a violation punishable under law for any person under the age of 21 to present any written evidence of age that is false, fraudulent, altered, or not actually his own for the purpose of attempting to purchase alcohol.

- Post signs of the bar's willingness to drive patrons home.

- Educate employees about liquor liability laws and strategies for refusing service to visibly intoxicated patrons.

- Encourage responsible drinking in marketing and advertising.

---

[21] *McGee v. Alexander*, 2001 WL 1148126 (Ok. 2001)

■ Employ a system to determine the amount of alcohol served in each drink sold. Use premeasuring devices instead of free pouring.

■ Supervisors *must* support employees who discontinue service to a patron who is believed to be intoxicated.

■ Have a limit on the number of drinks that will be served to a patron during happy hour.

■ Promote alternatives to liquor, such as bottled waters and distinctive coffees and teas. Train service personnel to offer guests both a wine menu and a water/coffee/tea menu, or combine the two. Treat bottled waters as bottled wines in all aspects of sales and service. Consider the possibility of a special "house" water or other nonalcoholic drink carrying the licensee's name and logo.

■ Offer "minidrinks"—that is, drinks that contain less alcohol at a lower price. Frozen drinks with just a touch of alcohol can be fun and appealing with proper promotion.

■ Offer nonalcoholic wine and beer, which, as the name suggests, contain no alcohol.

■ For specialty drinks that contain more than the normally expected one to one-and-a-half ounces of liquor, state the quantity of alcohol on the beverage menu to alert customers.

■ As a last resort, if an intoxicated patron insists on driving home after being warned, call the police and inform them. An arrest of the customer will remove him from the road, prevent a possible accident, and save the bar from dram shop liability.

Alcohol Sales in Hotel Guest Rooms

Many hotel licensees sell alcohol through vending machines or other mechanical devices in guest rooms. Access to the liquor is restricted by means of a key or magnetic card. The prohibition against illegal sales applies to these devices. The innkeeper must not provide the key or magnetic card to anyone who is under 21, visibly intoxicated, or a habitual drunkard.

Miscellaneous Liquor Regulations

Various statutory mandates apply to licensees, depending on the state involved. States have gone to great lengths to control the sale of alcoholic beverages. The purpose of these laws is to foster and promote temperance in the consumption of alcohol, and respect for and compliance with the law. They are enforced by a state agency authorized to issue, suspend, and revoke liquor licenses. The name given to that agency varies from state to state, and will be referred to here as the liquor authority. The penalties for failing to abide by these laws include suspension or revocation of the liquor license and fines. Remember, these regulations vary from state to state.

Age of Alcohol Servers

Most states specify a minimum age (usually 18 or 19) for certain workers in establishments that serve alcoholic beverages. No one under that age can be on the wait staff or sell, dispense, or handle alcoholic beverages. Lower minimum-age requirements apply to dishwashers or busboys. The objective of these regulations is to limit the exposure to alcohol of young people.

Restrictions on Alcohol Sales on Sunday

In many locations, alcohol cannot be sold on Sunday before noon. Also, sales for off-premises consumption, such as purchases from a liquor store, may be prohibited all day. The objective of these laws is to further the recognition of a sabbath day.

Warnings to Pregnant Women

Licensees must display a sign close to where alcohol is dispensed stating the following: "Government Warning: According to the Surgeon General, women should not drink alcoholic beverages during pregnancy because of the risk of birth defects." The objective of this law is to caution pregnant women about the risks to the fetus from drinking alcohol.

Prohibition of Illegal Gambling

A licensee cannot permit the bar or restaurant to be used for illegal gambling. The objective of this law is to prevent illegal conduct from occurring where alcohol is sold.

Prohibition of Disorderly Conduct

A licensee cannot permit disorderly conduct, such as fighting, solicitation for purposes of prostitution, or lewd or indecent sexual acts or performances in the bar or restaurant. The objective of this law is to minimize the disorderly and illegal conduct that may occur where alcohol is served.

Maintenance of Prescribed Records

A licensee is required to maintain records of its suppliers, documenting the extent of its daily alcohol purchases and information about the vendor. The objective of this law is to permit the liquor authority to track liquor purchases and sales and determine the volume of sales of particular licensees.

Restrictions on the Type of Alcohol Sold

States usually offer various types of liquor licenses, including licenses for on-premises consumption, the type a restaurant would likely have; licenses for off-premises consumption, which a liquor store would have; licenses authorizing the sale of beer and wine only; licenses authorizing sales of alcohol for one day only; and other categories. A licensee with a limited right to sell must abide by the limitations. For example, a licensee with a wine and beer license cannot sell mixed drinks.

Limitations on Sales Promotions

The licensee may be restricted from utilizing specials such as "two for ones" and novelties such as gifts or prizes, in the sale of alcohol. The purpose of these laws is to encourage moderation in the intake of alcohol. For that reason, these practices should be discouraged even where legal. Under discrimination laws, bars are restricted from having a "ladies night" or "men's night" during which drinks are offered at a reduced price to one gender but not the other. Many bars disregard this prohibition.

Prohibition on Celebrity Endorsements

The licensee may be forbidden from displaying signs that suggest athletes or other celebrities recommend drinking alcohol. The purpose of this law is to discourage over-indulgence.

Proximity to School or Church

A licensee cannot be located within certain distances, such as 200 feet, from the entrance of a school or place of public worship. The objective is to protect the well-being of students, and the sanctity and tranquility of churches.

Sexually Explicit Entertainment

Some bars provide nude or sexually explicit dancers (sometimes called "adult entertainment"). Many municipalities and residents living nearby seek to discourage these businesses because of their impact on the community. Adult entertainment often attracts prostitutes, generates rowdiness, insults many people's morals, and discourages families from living nearby. The mechanisms used by governments to deter these establishments are regulations or ordinances that restrict these business' operations. Among regulations towns have adopted are prohibitions on total nudity; limitations on the hours of operation for sexually oriented businesses; prohibition of specific sexually explicit dance movements; and requirements that such businesses be located outside residential areas.

Courts have determined that nude or nearly-nude dancing is a form of speech that conveys eroticism. As such, it is entitled to some protection by the constitutional right to free speech. Adult entertainment businesses often challenge governmental restrictions, claiming they are unconstitutional and therefore void. To pass constitutional muster, the restrictions must further an important government interest unrelated to suppression of free expression (such as protecting public health and safety), and must not be broader than is necessary to achieve the stated government interest. Among permissible regulations are the requirement that dancers wear minimal clothing such as a G-string or panties; a limitation on the hours of operation, provided the limitation does not unreasonably confine the times the business can open; and restrictions on the geographical areas within the town an adult entertainment business can be located, provided locations exist where the adult entertainment business can operate.

Key Terms

dram shop act   visibly intoxicated
liquor liability insurance

Summary

Businesses that dispense alcohol must have a valid liquor license and should avoid sales to patrons who are visibly intoxicated, underage, or known habitual drunkards. Illegal sales can result in revocation of a liquor license, criminal sanctions, and dram shop liability, requiring the licensee to compensate a third person injured by the patron. In some states, the licensee might also be liable to compensate the illegally served patron.

Employee training programs addressing service of alcohol and identification of intoxicated drinkers are necessary to help limit liability and should be reinforced with frequent refresher courses. Dram shop insurance should also be considered.

Each state has adopted various regulations relating to the sale of alcohol. Liquor licensees should determine the applicable laws and strictly comply.

Preventive Law Tips for Managers

See Table 12-1 on pages 410–412 for a listing of additional alcohol-related laws by state.

- *Comply strictly with state restrictions on serving alcoholic beverages to avoid loss of a liquor license.* A restaurant or bar cannot serve alcohol without a license from the state. In most states, serving the following people is illegal: a visibly intoxicated person, someone under age 21, and a habitual drunkard. If a licensee does not strictly comply with these laws, the state can suspend or revoke the license. Most states are unyielding in their enforcement of the alcoholic beverage control laws. Stringent compliance is the only way to preserve a liquor license.

- *Another reason for avoiding illegal sales is dram shop liability.* Dram shop acts, adopted by most states, render a bar or restaurant liable when a person is injured by someone to whom the licensee sold alcohol illegally. To avoid this potentially financially devastating liability, the licensee should do all of the following: do not sell to persons in the prohibited categories; train employees on how to manage alcohol sales, how to detect if someone is intoxicated, and how to handle requests from customers who cannot legally be served; reinforce employee training regularly; offer alternatives to alcohol such as "minidrinks" containing less alcohol, bottled waters, and fancy coffees and teas; and provide a "ride-home" service for patrons who appear incapable of driving safely.

- *Train employees on detecting intoxicated drinkers.* Dram shop liability is based in part on serving customers who are already intoxicated. To assist employees in making the assessment of intoxication, training programs should be provided and regularly reenforced.

- *Train employees to identify underage patrons.* Serving customers who are too young to drink legally can result in revocation of a liquor license, criminal liability, and civil liability. To avoid errors by service staff in determining age, provide training on how to determine a customer's age and how to review identification documents for possible unauthorized alterations.

- *Underscore to employees the management's commitment to avoid serving alcohol illegally.* Employees will take the lead from management directives and attitudes. Supervisors, managers, and owners must evidence at all times a commitment to avoid service to those who are intoxicated, underage, or habitually drunk.

- *Develop a policy for dealing with customers who have been served too much alcohol.* Plan for the possibility of a customer becoming intoxicated at your bar by identifying methods you will use to assist the patron in getting home safely. Instruct your employees on how to handle such a customer.

- *Determine what additional regulations your state imposes on licensees and comply with them.* States have adopted various restrictions and regulations for its liquor licensees. Examples of such regulations include a minimum age for wait personnel in licensed restaurants and bars; required warnings to pregnant women about the effect of alcohol on the fetus; and prohibition of illegal gambling and disorderly conduct at the licensed premises.

Review Questions

1. The law prohibits the sale of alcohol to certain categories of people. Identify those categories. What penalties do states impose for illegal sales?

2. What is meant by dram shop liability?

3. When a patron who is visibly intoxicated continues to drink at two different licensees and then is in a two-car accident injuring the driver of the second car, which licensee is liable to the driver of the second car?

4. Identify three strategies for limiting dram shop liability.

5. What behaviors might alert wait service personnel that a patron is visibly intoxicated?

6. Identify five regulations some states impose on liquor licensees.

7. What factors determine the price of liquor liability insurance?

Discussion Questions

1. In most states, a patron who is illegally served alcohol and thereafter injured as a result cannot sue the licensee who made the illegal sale. A third person injured by the patron can sue the licensee. What is the rationale for distinguishing between the two?

2. Why does the law impose a minimum age for legal drinking of alcohol?

3. Raj was a waiter at a bar. A customer ordered a beer. Raj knew he had served the customer several beers already. What factors should Raj consider in determining whether to serve the customer another drink?

4. From the previous question, if Raj determines that the customer is intoxicated, how might Raj both refuse to provide another beer but nonetheless appease the patron?

5. Why might a municipality not want a business in town that provides adult entertainment?

Application Questions

1. Jerry had been drinking all evening at the Bonger Bar and became visibly intoxicated. The bartender continued to serve him. Thereafter, Jerry left the Bonger Bar and, still visibly intoxicated, went to Gordon's Restaurant, where he had another drink. While driving home from Gordon's, Jerry drove his car in the wrong lane and crashed head-on with another car. Both Jerry and the driver of the other car suffered serious injuries. Both sued Gordon's and Bonger Bar. Who is liable to whom?

2. A bartender at the Rascal Café, which is located in a state with a drinking age of 21 and a dram shop act, served a female who was 19 years old. She had only one drink. Due to the effects of the alcohol, she failed to stop at a red light and hit a pedestrian who was crossing the street. Is the Rascal Café liable to the pedestrian for the injuries? Why or why not?

3. Assume in the previous question that no one from the Café asked the patron for proof of age. What penalty might the Café face and why?

Table 12-1 Alcohol-related laws by state

States	Minimum BAC Consituting DWI***	Dram Shop Act	Mandatory Server Training	Sobriety Checkpoints Permitted*
Alabama	.08	yes	yes	yes
Alaska	.10	yes	yes	no
Arizona	.10	yes	no	yes
Arkansas	.10	no	no	yes
California	.08	**	no	yes
Colorado	.10	yes	no	yes
Connecticut	.10	yes	no	yes
Delaware	.10	no	yes	yes
District of Columbia	.10	yes	no	yes
Florida	.08	**	no	yes
Georgia	.10	**	no	yes
Hawaii	.08	yes	yes	yes
Idaho	.08	yes	no	no
Illinois	.08	yes	no	yes
Indiana	.08	yes	no	yes
Iowa	.10	yes	no	yes
Kansas	.08	no	no	yes
Kentucky	.10	yes	no	yes
Louisiana	.10	**	no	no
Maine	.08	yes	no	yes
Maryland	.10	no	yes	yes
Massachusetts	.08	yes	no	yes
Michigan	.10	yes	no	no

States	Minimum BAC Consituting DWI***	Dram Shop Act	Mandatory Server Training	Sobriety Checkpoints Permitted*
Minnesota	.10	yes	no	no
Mississippi	.10	yes	no	yes
Missouri	.10	**	no	yes
Montana	.10	yes	no	yes
Nebraska	.10	no	no	yes
Nevada	.10	no	no	yes
New Hampshire	.08	yes	no	no
New Jersey	.10	yes	yes	yes
New Mexico	.08	yes	yes	yes
New York	.08	yes	yes	yes
North Carolina	.08	yes	no	yes
North Dakota	.10	yes	no	yes
Ohio	.10	yes	no	yes
Oklahoma	.10	yes	no	yes
Oregon	.08	yes	yes	no
Pennsylvania	.10	yes	no	yes
Rhode Island	.10	yes	no	no
South Carolina	.08	yes	no	yes
South Dakota	.10	yes	no	yes
Tennessee	.10	**	yes	yes
Texas	.10	yes	no	no
Utah	.08	yes	yes	yes
Vermont	.08	yes	yes	yes
Virginia	.08	**	no	yes

States	Minimum BAC Consituting DWI***	Dram Shop Act	Mandatory Server Training	Sobriety Checkpoints Permitted*
Washington	.10	yes	yes	no
West Virginia	.10	yes	no	yes
Wisconsin	.10	**	yes	no
Wyoming	.10	**	no	yes

*	A sobriety checkpoint is a police roadblock requiring all vehicles traveling through the checkpoint to submit to momentary inspection by the police. If violations are discovered the motorist is typically ticketed. The police may observe indicia of intoxication when the driver is stopped for the checkpoint. An arrest for driving while intoxicated may result.
**	*Limited Application*. The state has a dram shop act but it application is limited. For example, it may apply to minors only.
***	States with a .10 BAC may soon legislate a change to .08 in response to a federal law that provides a portion of a state's federal highway funds will be withheld beginning in the fiscal year 2004 if the state has not adopted a .08 BAC.

Web Sites

Web sites that will enhance your understanding of the material in this chapter include:

http://www.azll.com   This is the site of the Arizona Department of Liquor, Licenses, and Control, the governmental agency that issues liquor licenses to appropriate applicants and monitors licensees' sales. Each state has a similar agency, which also has a Web site. Included in the Arizona site are state laws, information on the process to obtain a liquor license, advice on training servers, and frequently asked questions and their answers.

http://www.ncadd.com   This is the site of the National Commission against drunk driving, the successor organization to the Presidential Commission on drunk driving appointed by President Reagan in 1982. The organization's goal is to reduce impaired driving. Among the issues discussed are detecting impaired driving, preventing underage drinking, and sanctioning impaired drivers.

http://www.nhtsa.dot.gov   This is the site for the National Highway Safety Administration, a bureau of the United States Department of Transportation. The site contains information about all aspects of highway safety including much information about drinking and driving.

For additional resources, visit our Web site
www.hospitality-tourism.delmar.com

CHAPTER 13

■

Travel Agents and Airlines—
Rights and Liabilities

CHAPTER OUTLINE

■

INTRODUCTION

At one time the American travel industry catered primarily to three categories of travelers: the wealthy, business people, and government officials. This is no longer the case. United States citizens have developed one of the highest per capita incomes in the world. As a result, travel is now within the reach of many. As the travel industry has grown to serve more people, it has become more complex and the problems inherent in arranging travel also grow.

There was an Alka-Seltzer® television commercial in which a vacationing couple is seen sitting beside a swimming pool in a state of extreme agony. As the camera retreats, it becomes obvious that their vacation paradise is undergoing extensive construction and earth removal. The man shouts over the roar: "I asked the travel agent, 'Where can we go for a little peace and quiet?' He says, 'Mr. Fields, I've got just the place! A peaceful little cottage in the heart of the Mellow

Mountains.' " The sounds of construction increase. "My head ... my stomach ... I need some Alka-Seltzer." The travel industry felt so maligned by the ad that they pressured Alka Seltzer's advertising agency to change the commercial. But the picture it presented was not entirely fiction. Sometimes promised amenities do not materialize.

Travel agents do not just sell tickets; the travel agent also dispenses travel information and advice on all aspects of a trip including the best way to get there, where to stay, where to eat, and what to anticipate en route and upon arrival. Most travelers put their trust in the travel agent and expect to be notified of important information or risks affecting their trip. Unfortunately, that trust is sometimes misplaced.

The consumer rights movement has had a large impact on the travel industry. Travelers are very aware that they may be entitled to compensation when their travel plans go awry. Many disappointed travelers try to find that recompense in court via litigation against the travel agent or against one of the many third-party suppliers (for example, hotels and tour companies) that make up the travel industry.

This chapter discusses the rights of the traveler and the liabilities of the travel agent and the airlines when travel plans fail.

The Makeup of the Travel Industry

The travel industry generally is composed of the following four groups:

1. Suppliers of travel services, such as hotels, resorts, airlines and other types of transportation
2. Travel wholesalers that combine the services offered by suppliers into "package tours"
3. Travel agents who sell both package tours and services of individual suppliers
4. Travelers themselves.

To fully comprehend this chapter, you need to know a bit about two topics: agency law and tariffs. An introduction to each follows.

Agency Law

In some cases in this chapter, the issue arises whether the travel agent is a legal representative of the supplier of travel services (such as a hotel, airline, or bus company) or, in the alternative, a legal representative of the traveler. The legal term used for a legal representative is *agent*. The term is used in a more formal and legal way than the term *travel agent*. The latter term refers to an individual who advises travelers on most aspects of taking trips. While confusing, know that a travel agent sometimes is the legal representative (agent) of the traveler and sometimes is the legal representative (agent) of a travel service provider such as a hotel or airline. The outcome of a case against a travel agent or service provider is often determined by whether the travel agent acted as the agent (legal representative) of the traveler or of the service provider.

Agency is a related term that means a relationship in which one person acts for or represents another based on authority voluntarily given by that other person. Such relationships involve two parties: a principal and an agent. The **principal** is the person who authorizes someone else (an agent) to act on his behalf and who controls the method used by the agent to do the authorized tasks. The **agent** is the person so authorized, the one who represents or acts for the principal consistent with the principal's directions. A classic example of a principal/agent relationship is an employer (principal) and employee (agent). By using agents, a principal can conduct multiple business transactions simultaneously in different locations and thus greatly expand the principal's business.

When an agent acts on behalf of a principal and within the scope of the authority given by the principal, the latter is legally bound by (liable for) the agent's acts, and the agent is not. Thus, where a travel agent acts as an agent for an airline and arranges plane reservations for a traveler, the airline and not the agent is required to provide the air transportation.

When an agent acts outside the bounds of delegated authority, the principal is not bound and the agent may be liable for fraud (deception) for misrepresenting his authority. Thus, where a travel agent has not been authorized by an airline to sell its tickets, but the travel agent sells tickets on the airline's flights notwithstanding, the airline is not required to honor the tickets. The travel agent will be liable to the traveler for losses incurred.

Agency law requires that the agent disclose to the agent's client the identity of the principal so that the client can investigate the reputation or credit of the principal if the client is so inclined. Thus, where a travel agent is acting as an agent of a tour operator when selling a trip, the travel agent must inform the client of the tour operator's identity. If the agent fails to disclose either the identity of the principal or the fact that the agent is acting for another party, the client can legally assume the agent is acting on his own behalf. In this circumstance, the agent will be liable as a principal. A case in point is *Siegel v. Council of Long Island Educators, Inc.*, 348 N.Y.S.2d 816 (1973). Ten plaintiffs sued a travel agent in Small Claims Court for three days of lost touring time and other inconveniences suffered during a trip to Israel, caused by the agent's poor planning and failure to make reservations. When planning the trip, the travel agent disclosed that he was acting as an agent for a travel wholesaler, but did not disclose the latter's identity. The travel agent argued that, since he was acting as an agent of the wholesaler, the wholesaler and not the agent should be liable. The court held the travel agent was liable and the wholesaler was not because the travel agent failed to disclose the identity of the wholesaler to the plaintiffs.

Similarly, in *Van Rossem v. Penney Travel Service, Inc.*, 488 N.Y.S.2d 595 (N.Y. 1985), newlyweds were advised on their honeymoon departure day that the wholesaler of their trip had gone bankrupt. Fortunately, the wholesaler had paid for the couple's airline tickets. Unfortunately, the wholesaler had not paid for the hotel. The bride and groom opted to take the trip and pay anew for their accommodations. Upon their return, they sued the travel agency that arranged the trip. The agent claimed the wholesaler alone should be liable. The travel agency had not informed the couple that it was acting as an agent for a wholesaler or the identity of the wholesaler (the principal). As a result, the travel agency was liable.

An agency relationship must be distinguished from that of an independent contractor. Independent contractors may or may not be agents, depending on the facts. **Independent contractors** are people who contract to do work for someone else, but are engaged in an independent business for themselves. The only part of the work controlled by the party who hires an independent contractor is the outcome. Independent contractors furnish their own supplies and equipment, pay their own expenses, set their own hours of work, and are paid fees or commission, not salary. The acts of independent contractors who are not agents will not bind travel-service providers who hire the independent contractor to promote their services.

Tariffs

The tariff system is referenced in many cases in this chapter. A **tariff** is a rule or condition of air travel that binds the airline and passengers. Passengers are bound by tariffs even though they do not know about them and do not expressly agree to them. Tariffs are developed by the airlines and must be approved by a government agency. That agency was originally the Civil Aeronautics Board, which is no longer in existence. The relevant agency today is the Department of Transportation.

Tariffs on file with the Department of Transportation, if valid, control the services provided by the airline. Tariffs cover such items as limitations on the airline's liability for damaged baggage, procedures for filing a claim, rules for reservations and check-in times, limits on the airline's liability for schedule changes and flight delays, and personal injury liability limitations. Some of these tariffs contain very one-sided language favoring the airline. Copies of tariffs are available upon request at airports, although few passengers are aware of this and few ask to see them. Tariffs conclusively and exclusively govern the rights and liabilities between an airline and traveler.

The following case provides insights into the role of tariffs in travel law.

CASE EXAMPLE 13-1

Fontan-de-Maldonado v. Lineas Aereas Costarricenses
936 F.2d 630 (1st Cir. 1991)

The appellant, Ms. Enriqueta Fontan de Maldonado ("Fontan"), is an American citizen who lives in Puerto Rico. She planned a vacation in Costa Rica and booked a ticket, through a travel agent, to fly on a Costa Rican airline, Lineas Aereas Costarricenses, S.A. ("the Airline"). An employee of the Airline, she alleges, told her travel agent that she need take only her birth certificate, not her passport. But, because she did not take her passport, her return

journey became a nightmare, with officials in Panama (where she had intended a stop-over) refusing to accept her, the Airline shunting her from one country to another, and her eventually spending the night on the floor of a Venezuelan airport. She sued the Airline, claiming that its bad advice about the travel documents amounted to negligence. The Airline replied that the ticket says such documents are the traveler's, not the Airline's, responsibility and that its tariff holds it free of liability for bad advice about which documents are needed. ...

The relevant provision in the Airline's tariff says that passengers "shall comply with all ...

travel requirements of countries to be flown from, into, or over," and that the Airline "shall not be liable for any ... information given by any ... employee ... to any passenger in connection with obtaining necessary documents ... or for the consequences to any passenger resulting from his/her failure to obtain such documents. ..." As required by law ... the Airline has filed its tariff with the Department of Transportation, which regulates the rates and services of international airlines serving the United States. Fontan concedes that if this tariff provision is valid, she cannot prevail. Tariff provisions are binding on a passenger, even if the passenger did not actually know of them. ...

Remedies for Small Damages

The amount of damages suffered by a traveler whose plans have gone awry is not always large. The cost of a lawsuit may discourage such travelers from suing the party responsible for the disruption, whether that party was the travel agent, airline, or travel service supplier. Two developments reduce the cost of suing and therefore both encourage would-be plaintiffs to sue, thereby increasing liability exposure in the travel industry. These developments are Small Claims Court and class action lawsuits.

Small Claims Court

Many travel cases are brought in **Small Claims Court**, a forum that encourages people to act as their own advocates without a lawyer. To aid that process, Small Claims Court dispenses with formal rules of evidence and procedure that govern trials in other courts. The maximum amount of money a plaintiff can seek is relatively small and varies from state to state, but is typically around $3,000.

Because rules of procedure and evidence are relaxed, and because lawyers are not necessary, many plaintiffs who might be deterred from suing by the complexities and expense of a lawsuit decide instead to pursue their case in Small Claims Court. As a result, businesses, including those in the hospitality industry, have a much greater exposure for their shortcomings than if Small Claims Courts did not exist.

Class Action Suits

A *class action suit* is a legal device in which all people who have suffered losses from the same cause jointly sue the defendant. It is a financially attractive option for plaintiffs because the cost of the lawsuit is spread among many plaintiffs instead of just one. A class action was pursued on behalf of persons who purchased a vacation package from Club Med. The complaint alleged that the seller had promoted the accommodations as luxurious, but instead they lacked electricity, air conditioning, hot and cold running water, and operable toilets.[1] In *Guadago v. Diamond Tours*

---

[1] *King v. Club Med, Inc.*, 430 N.Y.S.2d 65 (1980)

and Travel, Inc., 392 N.Y.S.2d 783 (1976), the judge granted permission to five plaintiffs to represent a class action. The plaintiffs claimed that the defendants—Club Islandia, two Long Island travel agencies, a Long Island tour organizer, and a New York tour wholesaler—misrepresented the nature and quality of accommodations at a Jamaican resort and sued for fraudulent misrepresentation and breach of contract. The class was comprised of 400 people who took three separate charter tours during a three-week period. Said the court, "[C]lass action relief may well be necessary to vindicate the rights of members of the class, whose individual claims are otherwise too small (under $500) to warrant independent litigation against the impressive legal strength of the defendants."

This case is significant in the hospitality industry for a reason in addition to allowing the class to sue jointly rather than requiring each traveler to shoulder independently the cost of a lawsuit. By defining the class as including travelers on three separate charter tours, rather than limiting the class to just one, the potential liability for the travel industry defendant is increased.

The Rights of the Traveler

When travel plans do not turn out as represented and purchased, the law is quite supportive of the traveler and provides a remedy in many circumstances.

Baggage Claims—Domestic and International

A tariff provides that when travelers hand their baggage to an airline to have it transported to their destination, they are entering into a contract with the airline. This contract binds the airline to deliver the baggage to the destination and to restore it to the traveler upon arrival. If the airline fails to deliver the luggage at the destination, it has breached its contract. Under normal contractual circumstances, the traveler would be entitled to recover from the airline the value of the lost baggage and its contents. However, because of the frequency of loss or delayed delivery by the airlines, they would suffer a significant financial burden if travelers were able to recover the full value of lost property in every case. So tariffs have been adopted to protect the airline from unlimited liability.

While less than .10 percent of the luggage transported by airlines is misrouted, this number exceeds 350,000. The airlines report that 75 percent of those lost bags are reunited with their owners within twelve hours, and an additional 20 percent are delivered within five days. The remaining 5 percent still amounts to a significant number at 17,500. The concept of limiting the airline's liability for this lost luggage is similar to the limiting liability statutes applicable to innkeepers when guests' property is lost or stolen, as we saw in Chapter 8. One set of laws for limiting liability applies to international flights and another to domestic flights. Both will be reviewed in this chapter. In both, the passenger is entitled to compensation only for a portion of their lost property; compensation for emotional stress is not permitted, nor for punitive damages.

International Flights

International flights are governed by the **Warsaw Convention**, an international treaty that sets limits of liability for lost, stolen, damaged, or misdelivered baggage. Under the Convention, the limitation on liability for checked luggage on international flights is $9.07 per pound up to 44 pounds, or just about $400; the limit for carry-on baggage is $400. The passenger is informed of the limitation on the airline ticket. See Figure 13-1 for an example. In exchange for limited liability, the airline is presumed to be responsible when luggage is missing or lost. The airline can rebut this presumption if it can show it took all possible precautions to avoid the loss. Further, passengers have the option of purchasing insurance to cover loss in excess of the Convention's maximum.

ADVICE TO INTERNATIONAL PASSENGERS ON LIMITATION OF LIABILITY

Passengers on a journey involving an ultimate destination or a stop in a country other than the country of origin are advised that the provisions of a treaty known as the Warsaw Convention may be applicable to the entire journey, including any portion entirely within the country of origin or destination. For such passengers on a journey to, from, or with an agreed stopping place in the United States of America, the Convention and special contracts of carriage embodied in applicable tariffs provide that the liability of certain carriers, parties to such special contracts, for death of or personal injury to passengers is limited in most cases to proven damages not to exceed U.S. $75,000 per passenger, and that this liability up to such limit shall not depend on negligence on the part of the carrier. The limit of liability of U.S. $75,000 above is inclusive of legal fees and costs except that in case of a claim brought in a state where provision is made for separate award of legal fees and costs, the limit shall be the sum of U.S. $58,000 exclusive of legal fees and costs. For such passengers traveling by a carrier not a party to such special contracts or on a journey not to, from, or having an agreed stopping place in the United States of America, liability of the carrier for death or personal injury to passengers is limited in most cases to approximately U.S. $10,000 or U.S. $20,000.

The names of carriers, parties to such special contracts, are available at all ticket offices of such carriers and may be examined on request. Additional protection can usually be obtained by purchasing insurance from a private company. Such insurance is not affected by any limitation of the carrier's company. Such insurance is not affected by any limitation of the carrier's liability under the Warsaw Convention or such special contracts of carriage. For further information please consult your airline or insurance company representative.

NOTICE OF BAGGAGE LIABILITY LIMITATIONS

Liability for loss, delay, or damage to baggage is limited unless a higher value is declared in advance and additional charges are paid. For most international travel (including domestic portions of international journeys) the liability limit is approximately $9.07 per pound for checked baggage and $400 per passenger for unchecked baggage. For travel wholly between U.S. points federal rules require any limit on an airline's baggage liability to be at least $1250 per passenger. Excess valuation may be declared on certain types of articles. Some carriers assume no liability for fragile, valuable or perishable articles. Further information may be obtained from the carrier.

CARRIER RESERVES THE RIGHT TO REFUSE CARRIAGE TO ANY PERSON WHO HAS ACQUIRED A TICKET IN VIOLATION OF APPLICABLE LAW OR CARRIER'S TARIFFS, RULES OR REGULATIONS SUBJECT TO TARIFF REGULATIONS

Figure 13-1 Limitation of liability stated on the back of an airline ticket. (*Courtesy of United Airlines*)

The following case provides some background about the Warsaw Convention. In it, the traveler's lost property considerably exceeded the $400 maximum. As you read the case, note particularly the requirements the airline must follow to avail itself of the limited liability.

CASE EXAMPLE 13-2

Lourenco v. Trans World Airlines, Inc. 581 A.2d 532 (N.J. 1990)

... On January 24, 1988 plaintiffs and their two minor daughters were passengers on T.W.A. flight 33 from Nassau, Bahamas to J.F.K. Airport in New York City. The Flight was cancelled due to technical difficulties. The Lourencos and their children were later flown to Miami, Florida on Bahamas Air. The group then boarded a Pan American flight to J.F.K.

Their luggage, last seen in Nassau, was shipped separately and lost. It was delivered to plaintiff's home three days later. Plaintiffs allege the luggage was broken into and that $9,232.59 worth of jewelry and other valuables is missing.

Plaintiff, Mario Lourenco, is an employee of T.W.A. Neither he nor his wife made a special declaration of the value concerning the contents of their luggage. Plaintiffs did not request special handling of the baggage or purchase special insurance covering the full value of their possessions. ...

Defendant did not state the weight and number of pieces of luggage on plaintiffs' ticket or baggage check. The total weight of the items missing is stipulated as less than (50) fifty pounds.

T.W.A. argues that its liability is limited by the Warsaw Convention. ... The Convention is an international treaty that limits the liability of airlines for death, injury, property damage or loss and delay. It applies to all international transportation of persons, baggage or goods performed by aircraft for hire. The carrier is liable for loss or damage to any checked baggage occurring during transportation by air, including the period baggage is in the charge of the carrier whether in an airport or on an aircraft. Liability is limited to $9.07 per pound of lost baggage, except in cases of willful misconduct. The parties agree the baggage was in international flight and is governed by the Warsaw Convention.

In return for limited liability, the air carrier is presumed liable to a passenger unless the carrier can show that it had taken all necessary measures to avoid damages, or that it was impossible for it to take such measures.

The Convention permits an airline to limit its liability if the provisions of Article 4 are complied with. Article 4 of the Convention states:

1) For the transportation of baggage, other than small personal objects of which the passenger takes charge himself, the carrier must deliver a baggage check.

2) The baggage check shall be made out in duplicate, one part for the passenger and the other part for the carrier.

3) The baggage check shall contain the following particulars:

   (a) The place and date of issue;

   (b) The place of departure and of destination;

   (c) The name and address of the carrier or carriers;

   (d) The number of the passenger ticket;

   (e) A statement that delivery of the baggage will be made to the bearer of the baggage check;

   (f) The number and weight of the packages;

   (g) The amount of the value; ...

   (h) A statement that the transportation is subject to the rules relating to liability established by this convention.

4) The absence, irregularity, or loss of the baggage check shall not affect the existence or the validity of the contract of transportation which shall nonetheless be subject to the rules of this convention. Nevertheless, if the carrier accepts baggage without a baggage check having been delivered, or if the baggage check does not contain the particulars set out at (d), (f), and (h) above, the carrier shall not be entitled to avail himself of those provisions of the convention which exclude or limit his liability.

The Warsaw Convention is binding on a passenger if the passenger has notice of its provisions. Notice, ordinarily printed on the airline ticket, gives the passenger an opportunity to declare that the value of his baggage is in excess of standard limits. The passenger can then pay a supplementary fee to cover the excess and increase his potential recovery to the declared value. The passenger is also free to make a special contract with the airlines or purchase insurance.

Plaintiffs received written notice of the Convention's applicability. The defendant did not, however, write down on the baggage check the number of pieces or weight of plaintiffs' luggage as required by subsection (3)(f) of Art. 4. The parties agree that defendant complied with all other provisions of Art. 4.

What are the consequences to an airline if it does not strictly comply with subsection (3)(f) of Art. 4? The cases demonstrate a considerable split in authority.

The courts in the State of New York generally hold that when the claim check or ticket does not indicate the number and weight of the packages, the carrier cannot avail itself of the limitation [of liability].

The weight of federal authority, however, holds that the carrier's failure to record the number and weight of a passenger's luggage is a technical and insubstantial omission. ...

The economic interest of passengers to be adequately compensated for lost baggage competes with the airline's interest in controlling costs and curtailing litigation. The Convention's limits on liability have been criticized as unconscionably low. Nations in the Third World have complained that the limits of liability are too high. Compromises have been reached in setting the present limits; ... The economic policy choice, however, is not for this Court to make.

As an international treaty the Warsaw Convention remains "the supreme law of the land." It is not for Courts to "indulge in judicial treaty-making," or to decide if the U.S. Airline Industry, no longer in its infancy, still needs special protection. The Court's function is to construe the Convention, determine its meaning and apply it fairly. Whether the treaty is construed strictly or liberally the polestar should be to effectuate its evident purpose. There is populist appeal in subjecting the airlines to unlimited liability for lost baggage. This is not, however, the evident purpose of the Treaty. ...

This Court holds that the failure to record the weight and number of plaintiffs' luggage on the baggage check is a technical and insubstantial omission and should not deny defendant the benefit of the limitation of liability provisions of the Warsaw Convention. ...

The difficulty presented by the instant case is that the plaintiffs' luggage was lost, found and returned; with jewelry and other valuable items missing.

The Treaty bases damages on weight, not the actual value of the lost baggage. A pound of jewelry, or for that matter clothing, is obviously worth more than the $9.07 allowed. The plaintiffs were well aware of the worth of their jewelry, and the modest recovery permitted under the Convention for lost baggage, before they checked their luggage with the airline. They chose to run the risk of its loss without benefit of insurance or special declaration. Since the Court has decided that the Warsaw Convention's limitations of liability apply and the plaintiffs have stipulated that the missing items weighed fifty (50) pounds or less, it follows that defendant's liability is limited to a total of $453.50.

CASE QUESTION

1. On what principle did the court base its decision that the Warsaw Convention's limitation of liability applied?

The limitation of liability also applied in a case involving the lost luggage of a marketing director for a sporting goods company. The contents included 1500 T-shirts and 120 pairs of soccer shoes. The company sought damages in the amount of $15,728; the court held the company's recovery was restricted by the limitation of liability in the Warsaw Convention.[2]

Grounds for Loss of the Warsaw Convention's Limited Liability

Failure of the airlines to comply strictly with various provisions of the Convention can result in loss of the limited liability. A recent case followed the line of cases referenced in *Lourenco v. TransWorld Airlines, Inc.*, which cases hold that the airline, by failing to provide on the baggage claim stub the weight of a passenger's luggage, loses the Convention's limitation of liability. The case involved the loss of five pieces of luggage belonging to a family traveling from Washington, D.C. to Santo Domingo.[3]

The limitation of liability was likewise held inapplicable in *Schedlmayer v. Trans International Airlines, Inc.*, 416 N.Y.S.2d 461 (1979), a Small Claims Court case that turned on a different provision of the Warsaw Convention. The plaintiff, upon request, gave her hand luggage to a flight attendant for storage in the front of the plane during a charter flight from Austria to New York. After the plane was in flight, the plaintiff remembered that she had left a camera and $1,300 in currency in the bag. During a stopover, she asked the stewardess to retrieve her bag, but was told that she could not get it until the aircraft landed at its final destination in New York. Upon arrival in New York, the plaintiff retrieved her luggage and immediately discovered that, although the camera was still there, the currency was gone. The airline refused to reimburse her for the loss and the plaintiff sued. A threshold issue in the case was whether the Warsaw Convention applies to charter flights. The court held that it did. The determination of the extent of the airline's liability centered on a provision of the Convention (Article 4) that states: "If the carrier accepts baggage without a baggage check having been delivered ... the carrier shall not be entitled to avail himself of those provisions of the convention that limit his liability." The court held that when the flight attendant took the bag from the passenger, the airline took control of it so it then assumed the status of checked baggage. Since the stewardess failed to issue a claim check, as required by the Convention, the defendant airline could not take advantage of the limitations of the Convention and so was liable to the plaintiff for the full amount of her loss. The clear lesson for airline management is to comply strictly with the mandates of the Warsaw Convention, thereby avoiding loss of the benefits of limited liability.

Willful Misconduct

Another factor that will bar an airline from the advantages of the Convention's limited liability is "willful misconduct." The following case helps to define *willful misconduct* in reference to misplaced or damaged luggage on international flights. In *Compania De Aviacion Faucett v. Mulford*, 386 So.2d 300 (Fla. 1980), the Mulfords, who were touring Peru, boarded a flight on the defendant airline in

---

[2] *Abbaa v. Pan Am*, 673 F.Supp. 991 (Minn. 1987)

[3] *Rodriquez v. American Airlines*, 193 F.3d 526 (D.C. 1999)

Cuzco, Peru, with a destination of Lima, Peru. They were informed by the airline's employees that their luggage was on board the flight when in fact the luggage had been removed. It was not returned to the Mulfords until after they returned home. The court held that the airline had "deliberately or recklessly" given the Mulfords misinformation. The court thus held that the airline engaged in willful misconduct rendering the limiting liability provisions of the Warsaw Convention inapplicable. The airline was thus ordered to pay damages beyond the limits of the Convention.

Willful misconduct was also found in a case where plaintiffs exited a plane during a stopover in Rio de Janeiro, Brazil. The plane was continuing to New York. The plaintiffs' luggage was not unloaded. The plaintiffs, New York residents, were at the beginning of an 18-day trip and had with them only the clothes they were wearing. Despite the plaintiffs' urgent requests during the layover that airline personnel search the baggage compartment for the plaintiffs' suitcases, the airline refused. It claimed the search would have taken an hour and it did not want to delay the departure of the flight. The airline's lost-and-found agent assured the plaintiffs their luggage would be returned to Rio de Janeiro within two days. However, the plaintiffs' itinerary required they leave Rio de Janeiro the next day. The plaintiffs' luggage was never recovered. They sued for the full value of their belongings; the airline claimed the Warsaw Convention's limitation of liability applied. The court found the airline's refusal to attempt to locate the plaintiffs' luggage was willful misconduct and therefore the Convention's limitation of liability did not apply. Said the court, "[The lost and found agent's] callous disregard for plaintiffs' plight and willful renunciation of its contractual obligation to its passengers [to safely transport and deliver luggage] was motivated by selfish economic interest and justifies a finding of willful misconduct under the provisions of the Warsaw Convention." The court, however, rejected the plaintiffs' claim for damages based on physical inconvenience, discomfort, and mental anguish.[4]

Damaged Baggage

Occasionally, a traveler's luggage will be damaged during transport. To obtain recovery for damaged baggage requires that the traveler strictly follow the prerequisites identified in the tariffs. One such requirement is that notice be given to the airline within a specified number of days after receipt of damaged luggage. Failure to give timely notice is fatal to the lawsuit. In *Onyeanusi v. Pan Am*, 952 F.2d 788 (3rd Cir. 1992), Pan Am transported the plaintiff's mother's body from Pennsylvania to Nigeria. The casket arrived late; upon arrival the body and casket were damaged. Plaintiff complained to the airlines two months later, considerably in excess of the two-week notice period permitted by tariff. The plaintiff's lawsuit was thus dismissed.

Failure to comply with time requirements for written notice to the airlines will not result in dismissal of a case where the airlines misled the passenger about the required time limits. A disabled passenger on an international flight checked his

---

[4] *Cohen v. Varig Airlines*, 405 N.Y.S.2d 44 (1978)

wheelchair as baggage and it was damaged during the flight. While he gave prompt oral notice of the damage, his written notice was given beyond the applicable time period because the airline gave him incorrect information. Under the circumstances, although the notice was late, the lawsuit was not time-barred.[5]

Domestic Flights

The Warsaw Convention does not apply to domestic flights. Limits of liability for lost luggage on domestic flights are covered by tariffs, which, as we have seen, are developed by the airlines and approved by the Department of Transportation. By law, since 1987, the lowest maximum liability an airline can include in its tariff is $1,250. As with international flights, airlines must offer passengers the option of purchasing insurance coverage above the tariff's maximum.

Security Checkpoints

Before boarding a flight, passengers are required to pass through a security check in the airport consisting of metal detectors and x-rays of carry-on luggage. During the check, the passenger is separated from his bags as the carry-on luggage is placed on a conveyor belt and passed through x-ray detection equipment. An interesting case involved a passenger who grabbed the wrong hand baggage after proceeding through the security screening process. Upon discovering the mix-up, he reported it to the airlines, but his baggage was never returned. He sued the airline in Small Claims Court seeking the value of his lost goods. The airline claimed that, since it was required by law to perform the security checks, it should not be held liable for property lost during the process. The court determined the value of the passenger's lost property was $950 and ordered the airline to pay, stating that while the airlines are required to conduct security screenings they also have a duty to safeguard passengers' hand baggage during those checks.[6] Said the court,

> The traveling public is warned not to pack valuables in checked luggage which is stored within the aircraft's freight and luggage compartments during the flight's duration. Accordingly, valuables are encouraged to be packed in hand baggage intended to be carried aboard the plane to be kept within the passenger's view and control. Yet, the passenger and his hand baggage are separated as both go through the required security measures. The passenger, indeed, is placed in a catch-22 situation in need of a safe place to carry his travelers cheques, credit cards, travel and business documents, identification, airline tickets, eyeglasses and jewelry. ...
>
> Thus, the security system of an airline should operate in such a manner that it is accountable to the public for the return of hand baggage. ...

The airline in this case had hired an independent security company to perform the security checks. The airline's contract with the security company contained a

---

[5]*Dillon v. United Air Lines, Inc.*, 162 F.Supp.2d 380 (Pa. 2001)

[6]*Tremaroli v. Delta Airlines*, 458 N.Y.S.2d 159 (N.Y. 1983)

provision that required the latter to "indemnify and hold harmless" (compensate) the airline for any liability the latter incurred from the security checks. As a result, the security company was required to reimburse the airline for the $950. awarded to the plaintiff. Note the effectiveness of an "indemnity and hold harmless" clause in a contract.

In another factually similar case, but where the loss exceeded the maximum recovery permitted by tariff, the plaintiff's recovery was limited. The alarm sounded when the plaintiff went through the metal detector at the security checkpoint. She was "briefly inspected" and then permitted to continue to the airplane. By then, her handbag was no longer on the conveyor. A search was unsuccessful. She sued the airlines for the value of jewelry contained therein— $431,000. The court held the airline's liability was limited by its tariff amount of $1,250.[7] In a case involving an international flight, the plaintiff's carry-on bag likewise disappeared as she passed through the security checkpoint. She claimed it contained jewelry with a wholesale value of approximately $100,000. She was limited in her recovery to the $400 limitation of the Warsaw Convention.[8]

Other Applications of the Lost Baggage Tariff

Another plaintiff was likewise restricted to the maximum recovery stated in the tariff. The airline transported cremated remains from Georgia to Puerto Rico, and held them in its warehouse pending retrieval by the family. Prior to that time, the box containing the remains disappeared.[9]

Airplane Security

The surprise attack on September 11, 2001, on the Pentagon in Washington D.C. and the World Trade Center in New York City prompted significant expansion of airport security measures. Three hijacked commercial planes filled with passengers en route from New York and Boston to the West Coast were flown into the referenced landmark buildings by extremists on a suicide terrorist attack. Congress and the airline industry responded with increased security measures to help prevent further incidents. These enhanced precautions were directed at three areas of concern: (1) keeping terrorists away from airports; (2) at airports, detecting hijackers to prevent their access to planes; and (3) preventing unauthorized entry into cockpits.

Among the changes adopted or under consideration as this book goes to press include federal standards for airport security applicable throughout the country; federalization of airport baggage screeners and other security personnel; additional x-ray screenings of luggage; body pat-downs; multiple identification checks to occur at the ticket counter and the departure gates; security checkpoints throughout the airport; regular monitoring of all aspects of airport security systems

---

[7] *Wackenhut Corp. v. Lippert*, 609 So.2d 1304 (Fl. 1993)

[8] *Dazo v. Globe Airport Security Services*, 2001 WL 1197681 (Del. 2001)

[9] *Cubero Valderama v. Delta Air Lines, Inc.*, 931 F.Supp. 119 (P.R. 1996)

to ensure standards are being met; training for pilots on carrying guns and responding to attacks; enhanced training for flight attendants as first responders in on-board emergencies; prohibition of the following items in the passenger cabin, in carry-on luggage or on a traveler's person: knives, metal nail files, corkscrews, golf clubs, bats, pool cues, ski poles, hockey/lacrosse sticks, items of similar shape and hardness, instruments with retractable blades, scissors and other cutting or piercing instruments of any kind; hiring of federal marshals to fly on airlines at random to repel hijack attacks; installation of unpenetrable doors for the cockpit; and new training protocols for security personnel.

In addition, travelers are limited to one carry-on bag and one personal bag, such as a purse or briefcase. Further, only ticketed passengers are allowed beyond x-ray security checkpoints. Parents with children who will be traveling alone and certain attendants of disabled passengers can obtain a special pass from the ticket counter authorizing the caregiver to escort the child or handicapped person to the gate area.

All passengers 18 or over must carry government-issued photo-identification at all times in the airport and on the plane. Parking is now prohibited in a 300-foot zone around terminals. Due to these heightened security procedures, passengers are advised to arrive at the airport at least ninety minutes prior to the flight.

The breadth of these new safety measures and proposals evidence the heightened concern for safety aroused by the terrorist attacks.

Traveling with Animals

For purposes of determining an airline's liability for mishandling pets, animals are treated the same as suitcases. In *Young v. Delta Airlines, Inc.*, 432 N.Y.S.2d 390 (1980), the plaintiff's pet dog died while in the custody of the airline on a domestic flight. The plaintiff sued not only for the value of the dog (it was an expensive breed), but also for compensation for the emotional disturbance she suffered as a result of the dog's death and for punitive damages. The court dismissed the claims for mental suffering and punitive damages, noting that these types of damages are not recoverable where an airline mishandles a traveler's property. Concerning compensation for the value of the dog, the court held recovery was limited to $500 by applicable tariffs. The dog was classified as the plaintiff's personal property and, for compensation purposes, was the equivalent of an inanimate piece of luggage.

We have seen that a passenger can purchase insurance from the airlines to cover the value of property in excess of the maximum provided in the Warsaw Convention or the airline's tariffs. Could the dog owner have purchased insurance with the airline to cover the value of the dog so as to increase the amount of her recovery in the event of the animal's death? Must the airline sell such insurance? Based on the *Young* case, holding that the dog has the same status as luggage, it would follow that the airline would be obligated to sell insurance to cover the dog as it is for other baggage.

In *Gluckman v. American Airlines*, 844 F.Supp. 151 (N.Y. 1994), the plaintiff's golden retriever died as a result of heat stroke caused during a flight delay that resulted from mechanical difficulties. The delay was in Arizona on a June day when the temperature was 115 degrees fahrenheit. The dog had been maintained in the airplane's baggage compartment, which was unventilated. The court denied recovery to the plaintiff for emotional distress and loss of companionship of the pet. The plaintiff also sought recovery for pain and suffering *of the dog*. The facts established that, upon removal from the baggage compartment, "the [deceased] dog's face and paws were bloody; there was blood all over the crate; and the condition of the cage evidenced a panic effort to escape." Notwithstanding the dog's apparent distress, the court rejected this claim as well. The tariff restricted recovery to the value of the dog.

Personal Injury on Board International Flights

Accidents that occur on board a plane and cause physical injury to a passenger are covered by the Warsaw Convention. As with damage to or loss of luggage, the airline's liability for personal injury is limited by that Convention. The maximum amount recoverable is $75,000. Where a woman suffered personal injuries during a flight when a drink cart struck her knees while she slept, her recovery was limited by the Convention.[10]

Another case involved a disabled plaintiff who checked his motorized wheelchair as baggage during a flight. Upon arriving at his destination, the plaintiff discovered the chair had been damaged en route. Two days later the plaintiff was injured when the chair malfunctioned from the flight damage and hit a wall, causing personal injuries to the plaintiff. In the resulting lawsuit, the plaintiff argued that since he was not injured on board the aircraft, the limitations on liability of the Warsaw Convention were not applicable. The court held that the accident causing the injury (damage to the wheelchair) occurred on board and therefore the Warsaw Convention was applicable.[11]

Refunds on Tickets

Sometimes circumstances entitle a traveler to a refund on airline tickets, but getting that refund can be difficult.

In *Levine v. British Overseas Airways Corp.*, 322 N.Y.S.2d 119 (1971), the plaintiffs purchased round-trip tickets from the Comet Travel Agency for the itinerary of New York-London-Amsterdam-Copenhagen-Stockholm-London-New York. The plaintiffs paid Comet for the tickets and Comet in turn paid the airline, British Overseas Airway Corporation (BOAC). The airline thereafter cancelled the Stockholm leg of the trip. The plaintiffs returned their ticket directly to BOAC and sought a refund of $86, which the airline did not deny was due. However, consistent with a practice adopted by many airlines, BOAC sought to make refund payments directly to the travel agent (Comet) and deduct therefrom the travel agent's commission for the cancelled portion of the trip. The plaintiffs objected, seeking payment of the refund directly from BOAC.

---

[10] *Price v. KLM-Royal Dutch Airlines*, 107 F.Supp.2d 1365 (Ga. 2000)

[11] *Dillon v. United Air Lines, Inc.*, 162 F.Supp.2d 380 (Pa. 2001)

The court sided with the plaintiffs and stated that once the travel agent paid the fare to the carrier, the traveler has a valid claim for restitution against the carrier. While the travel agent was an agent for the plaintiffs when purchasing the tickets, once the travel agent had completed the ticket purchase, all authority to act for the customer ended. Therefore, Comet was not authorized to accept refund money on the plaintiffs' behalf, and so the court ordered the airline to pay the refund to the plaintiff directly.

In *Antar v. Trans World Airlines, Inc.*, 320 N.Y.S.2d 355 (1970), the plaintiff was the victim of fraud perpetrated by the travel agent, Peters. He sold the plaintiff a trip for six to Israel, which supposedly included air fare and hotel. The plaintiff paid the travel agent more than $8,000, in return for which Peters delivered to the plaintiff six TWA airline tickets issued on blank ticket forms. Thereafter, the travel agent disappeared without paying TWA for the tickets. The travel agent had been an authorized agent of TWA until two weeks prior to the plaintiff's ticket purchase, but then TWA had revoked the agency. The airline thus refused to honor the tickets. The plaintiff sued TWA. The court, noting that TWA was not a party to the fraud, held for the airline; the plaintiff was not entitled to a refund from TWA.

Remember, when an alleged agent is not authorized to act for the purported principal, that principal is not bound and the alleged agent is liable for fraud. Here the plaintiff could sue Peters for fraud. Unfortunately, the plaintiff will likely have difficulty finding him.

E-Tickets

A recent phenomenon in air travel eliminates the type of fraud committed by the travel agent in the *Antar v. TWA* case. **E-tickets**, also known as electronic tickets, are paperless tickets representing reservations that are recorded exclusively in computer files. The only paper produced in the transaction is a receipt for payment. An advantage to the airlines, in addition to avoiding the risk of theft applicable to paper-ticket stock, includes savings on costs associated with printing and handling paper tickets.

The popularity of e-tickets has grown rapidly. In 1999, 30 percent of all fliers used them; in 2002, 80 percent; and through mid-2003, 85 percent. Indeed, many airlines have imposed a surcharge on customers who insist on a paper ticket rather than an electronic one to increase the incentive to use e-tickets.

Advantages to passengers include avoidance of having to carry a ticket and worry about loss or theft; avoidance of lost ticket fees, which are approximately $75; and elimination of the need to pick up or arrange delivery of a ticket or a reissued ticket when itinerary changes become necessary, as e-tickets are issued instantly over the phone. Also, e-tickets permit passengers to use other e-services provided by the airlines, such as Internet check-in and self-service check-in at airport kiosks.

The advantage of electronic tickets to the airlines is significant cost savings. Expenses associated with paper tickets and not incurred with e-tickets include printing, auditing the printed tickets for accuracy, mailing, reprocessing collected paper tickets at the gates, and addressing problems associated with lost tickets.

Problems that existed, but have been significantly reduced as e-ticketing has evolved, include travelers arriving at the airport to discover their reservation is not in the computer; passengers having significant difficulty in changing their travel plans; and changing flights from one airline to another. More recently, the major airlines have developed agreements allowing travelers to trade e-tickets among their flights. This capability is called *ticket interlining* and gives passengers flexibility when needing to change travel plans.

Rights of Handicapped Travelers

Vinogradov, the great Russian philosopher, said that social change can only be made by legislating the change. In the United States, this maxim is constantly being proved. The school desegregation and other civil rights cases of the 1950s and 1960s stand as examples of this rather dismal truth. See Chapter 3 for a discussion of the civil rights laws as applied to hotels and restaurants. When we examine the transportation industry, we see that the airlines and other carriers were likewise slow to accommodate the disabled.

Until a short time ago, few laws impacted the decision of commercial airlines and other forms of transportation on whether to provide transportation to handicapped people. When a carrier decided to deny transportation, the reason usually given was simply that planes, trains, and buses were not equipped to transport the disabled.

The Americans with Disability Act (ADA) became effective in 1992, and The Air Carrier Access Act (ACAA) in 1986. The ADA is discussed at length in Chapter 3. The ACAA was adopted to prevent what Congress called the "humiliating and degrading" practices of airlines. It states that, "[N]o air carrier may discriminate against any otherwise qualified handicapped individual, by reason of such handicap, in the provision of air transportation." What effect do these statutes have on the approximately 43 million Americans who are disabled?

The law is quite clear that disabled people can use the airlines if they meet minimum requirements concerning mobility designed to ensure personal and public safety. Refusing service to handicapped people who meet these minimum criteria will result in liability, as evidenced in the following case.

CASE EXAMPLE 13-3

Tallarico v. Trans World Airlines, Inc.
881 F.2d 566 (8th Cir. 1989)

Polly Tallarico, who is fourteen years old, has cerebral palsy which impedes her ability to walk and talk. She generally uses a wheelchair, but is able to move about on her own by crawling. Although Polly is able to speak only short words, she is able to hear and understand the spoken word. She communicates by use of a variety of communication devices such as a communication board, a memo writer and a "Minispeak."

On November 25, 1986, the day before the Thanksgiving holiday, Polly arrived at Houston's Hobby Airport intending to fly to St. Louis, Missouri, unaccompanied. When the TWA ticket agent, Richard Wattleton, learned that Polly intended to fly alone he contacted Lynn Prothero, acting TWA station manager, and asked for directions as to how he should handle the situation. Wattleton had learned from the limousine driver assisting Polly that she could not speak or walk. Wattleton ... [informed Prothero] that Polly could communicate by use of a communications board. From this information, Prothero determined that Polly would not be allowed to fly unaccompanied and informed Wattleton of her decision. This decision was apparently made on the basis of Prothero's conclusion that Polly could not take care of herself in an emergency and could not exit the plane expeditiously. As a result of this decision, Polly's father had to fly to Houston to accompany Polly to St. Louis.

The Tallaricos brought suit alleging that TWA violated the ACAA by denying Polly the right to board the plane because of her physical handicaps. The jury found for the Tallaricos awarding damages in the amount of $80,000. The district court entered judgment notwithstanding the verdict on the issue of damages reducing the award to $1,350 which is equivalent to the Tallaricos' actual out-of-pocket expenses.

... The ACAA states that "[n]o air carrier may discriminate against any otherwise qualified handicapped individual, by reason of such handicap, in the provision of air transportation."...

[A] "qualified handicapped person" is a handicapped individual (1) who tenders payment for air transportation, (2) whose carriage will not violate Federal Aviation Administration regulations, and (3) who is willing and able to comply with reasonable safety requests of the airline personnel, or if unable to comply, who is accompanied by a responsible adult passenger who can ensure compliance with such a request. ...

The evidence at trial showed that Polly had tendered payment for air transportation, that her carriage would not violate any FAA regulations (in fact she had flown alone before), and that she was capable of complying with the reasonable safety requests of airline

personnel. The evidence demonstrated that Polly is able to crawl on her knees or her hands and knees, that she has normal intelligence, and that she is capable of communicating her needs. Polly has a variety of ways of communicating including the use of communication boards which contain the letters of the alphabet and some short phrases; a memo writer, an electronic typewriter-like device; and a "Minispeak," a portable computer with an electronic voice attached. Polly is able to fasten her own seat belt as well as put on an oxygen mask. In addition, Polly's mother testified that she was confident that Polly could crawl to the bathroom (and, presumably, an exit) on the plane if necessary. ...

The jury awarded the Tallaricos $80,000. The district court then granted judgment n.o.v. in favor of TWA as to $78,650 of the damages award. The court concluded that there was insufficient evidence to support the total award and that as a matter of law, the award was not sustainable. The court determined that $1,350 of the award was compensation for out-of-pocket damages as a result of TWA's refusal to allow Polly to board and the remainder was damages for emotional distress. ...

In this case the proof of the emotional distress which Polly suffered after TWA denied her boarding came from the testimony of her mother, her father, the assistant director for Polly's school and the driver who was with Polly when the incident occurred. Theodore Sherwood, the driver who took Polly to the airport, testified that Polly was with him when he was told she would not be allowed to board the aircraft. He stated he noticed that Polly was getting disturbed as she listened to his conversations with TWA employees. Sherwood also testified that he felt it necessary to call Polly's school to see if someone there could talk to Polly and calm her down because after the incident she was crying and upset about what had happened. Polly's father testified that Polly was very angry and upset about the incident. In addition, he stated that since the incident Polly has seemed more withdrawn, quiet and reserved. Polly's mother also testified that Polly was upset about what happened and that Polly was anxious about the situation and concerned about having to fly back to Houston after the Thanksgiving holiday. Susan Oldham, the assistant director of Polly's school, testified that prior to the incident Polly was very outgoing and socialized well with the other students. After the incident, Ms. Oldham testified, Polly seemed more withdrawn and would spend large amounts of time by herself in her room after school was over. Ms. Oldham stated that when she asked Polly if something about her trip home had upset her, Polly replied that what had happened had made her feel badly and had hurt her feelings.

We find that sufficient evidence was presented to support the jury's award of $80,000. Consequently, we reverse the district court's judgment n.o.v. ...

We agree with the district court that the Tallaricos failed to present sufficient evidence to support an award of punitive damages and similarly do not reach the question of whether punitive damages would be allowed under the ACAA.

CASE QUESTION

1. How could TWA have avoided the liability in this case? Include in your answer not just changes in their handling of the plaintiff's situation, but also steps to avoid liability in future cases involving disabled passengers.

If the airline has adopted a tariff requiring a companion for a disabled person and has a rational reason for that requirement, the tariff will be enforceable. In *DeGirolamo v. Alitalia-Linee Aeree Italiane*, 159 F.Supp.2d 764 (N.J. 2001), the plaintiff used a wheelchair for mobility. He sought to purchase a round-trip ticket from Alitalia Airlines from New Jersey to Italy. The airline refused to sell him a ticket for that flight unless he bought a second ticket for an attendant or companion to fly with him. Alitalia had a tariff requiring an attendant for passengers who use wheelchairs if the flight exceeds three hours. The rationale was that Alitalia wanted to ensure disabled passengers would be able to move expeditiously to an exit in the event of an emergency. The plaintiff purchased a more expensive ticket on another airline that permitted him to fly alone and sued Alitalia claiming damages and seeking a modification of the tariff. The court dismissed the plaintiff's case, concluding that the airline's policy sought to ensure the safety of passengers and thus "had a very real and rational relation to the services to be provided."

Other provisions of the ACAA include the following requirements: Air carriers must design new and renovated terminals to accommodate people with disabilities; airlines must provide fully accessible services in all existing airport facilities; airlines cannot require passengers with assistive devices to undergo special security procedures if the person using the aid clears the system without activating it, but airlines are entitled to examine assistive devices they believe may conceal a weapon; airlines must allow passengers with disabilities to store canes and other assistive devices close to their seat, and cannot count that equipment toward a person's limit of carry-on luggage; if space in the baggage compartment is insufficient to accommodate all travelers, priority must be given to wheelchairs and other assistive devices; and personal mobility equipment stored during flight in the airplane's baggage compartment must be among the first items removed from the compartment upon arrival at the destination.

Disclosing Need for Assistance

Handicapped travelers must make known their needs to the airlines. Travel providers need not guess what the needs of a disabled person are. In *Adiutori v. Sky Harbor International Airport*, 880 F.Supp. 696 (Ariz. 1995), the plaintiff had severe arthritis, which made walking very difficult and required the use of two canes. When his connecting flight was cancelled, he was rerouted, requiring him to change terminals, a distance of one-and-a-half miles. He requested a wheelchair and that was provided. A skycap pushed him in the chair from his plane to the bus stop where he would catch the bus to the new terminal. Upon arrival at the bus stop, the plaintiff was told, "This is where you get off. This is where the bus stop is." The plaintiff exited the chair without help and without request for further assistance. In the waiting area, all seats were occupied. The plaintiff stood in pain for twenty minutes while waiting for the bus. He refused the offer of an elderly woman to relinquish her seat to him. The bus that arrived was not handicapped accessible. He entered it with difficulty but without requesting assistance.

Soon thereafter, the plaintiff suffered a heart attack. He sued the airline, claiming the attack was caused by the lack of assistance in making the terminal change. The court held for the airline, noting that applicable laws and regulations "do not force air carriers to provide unrequested assistance to handicapped individuals. ... Furthermore, it is a violation of [applicable laws] to force handicapped individuals to accept services they do not request. ..." Addressing the requirements of the Americans with Disabilities Act, the court noted that the airport had two wheelchair-accessible shuttle vans available 24 hours a day, seven days a week. They could be summoned by passengers from special phones located at ground transportation areas or by airport personnel upon request by a disabled passenger. Because the plaintiff failed to request help, his claim against the airline was dismissed.

Travel Insurance

To protect against financial losses associated with trip cancellations, injuries, and other mishaps that can occur while on a trip, travelers can purchase **travel insurance**. The types of risks covered by travel insurance vary, but can include losses resulting from: (1) trip cancellations or interruptions due to war or terrorism, supplier default (for example, a hotel goes bankrupt and cancels room reservations), or sickness, injury, or death of the insured, an immediate family member, or a traveling companion; (2) trip delays due to natural disasters, quarantine, transportation cancellations (plane, train, bus, ship), injury, or stolen or lost passport, visa, or money; (3) medical expenses for an injury or illness incurred on a trip; or (4) loss or damage to baggage.

Travel insurance can be purchased through a travel or insurance agent. Given the significant costs of many trips, travelers are well advised to consider purchasing this insurance.

Special Rights of Airlines

Because of the nature of air travel, with the ever-present dangers associated with adverse weather conditions, hijacking, terrorism, and passenger safety, certain rules apply to airlines only.

Right of Airlines to Cancel Scheduled Flights

Many airline flights are cancelled each day, usually with a bona fide reason. Still, with each cancellation many travelers' schedules are disrupted. A great deal might depend on the traveler getting to her destination on time.

In normal contract situations, cancellation would constitute a breach of the airline's contractual duty to transport the passenger to the designated destination and liability would result. However, there are conditions under which the airline is not bound to fly. In such cases, cancellation of a flight will not result in liability for breach of contract. One of those conditions is mechanical problems with the aircraft; an airline will not be liable for breach of contract where it cancels a flight due to mechanical problems.[12] Another circumstance in which cancellation of a flight will not result in liability is poor weather. This is illustrated in the following case.

CASE EXAMPLE 13-4

Johnson v. Northwest Orient Airlines
642 P.2d 1067 (Mont. 1982)

On December 12, 1979, plaintiff bought a round trip Missoula-Billings ticket from Northwest. On December 22, 1979, plaintiff's scheduled return date, Northwest issued the plaintiff a boarding pass for the Billings-Great Falls-Missoula-Spokane flight. But weather conditions at take-off time, 9:50 A.M., prevented Northwest from landing in Missoula. Therefore, all Missoula passengers were placed on a Billings-Helena flight and were then taken by bus from Helena to Missoula. Plaintiff was offered a check for $29.70, the savings on his alternative transportation. The check was returned several months later, after this suit was initiated.

Plaintiff alleges he arrived home eight hours late because of the flight cancellation. He earned $153,000 in 1979, working 3,000 hours at $50 an hour. As an insurance agent, he claims his weekends are particularly lucrative, earning him more than $100 an hour for ten hours a day. He is seeking $1,000 damages for the loss of a ten-hour day and $122 refund for his plane fare. ...

The [lower] Court determined there were no material issues of fact and that Northwest was entitled to judgment as a matter of law.

Did weather conditions in Missoula prevent the plane from landing? Northwest needs three miles of visibility to land in Missoula. Common sense dictates that only the weather conditions existing prior to take-off, 9:50 A.M., are pertinent. In this case, plaintiff's own exhibit from the National Weather Service shows there was only one and one-half miles of visibility at 9:52 A.M. Therefore, weather clearly prevented Northwest from landing in Missoula.

Did Northwest have a legal right to cancel the Billings-Missoula flight in light of the poor weather? Civil Aeronautics Board regulations govern rights and liabilities between airlines

---

[12]*Cenzi v. Mall Airways, Inc.*, 531 N.Y.S.2d 743 (N.Y. 1988)

and passengers and cover this issue. Those regulations authorize airlines to cancel flights when necessary. Therefore, Northwest acted within its legal authority in canceling the Billings-Missoula flight.

Did Northwest have a right to refuse plaintiff a seat after a boarding pass had been issued? As noted above, the flight was properly cancelled due to adverse weather. [A] Civil Aeronautics Board Tariff does not require advance notice to be given of flight cancellations. Therefore, Northwest properly excluded plaintiff, even after a boarding pass had been issued.

[W]e believe there are no material issues of fact and that Northwest is entitled to judgment as a matter of law.

CASE QUESTION

1. Why do you think the law relieves an airline from liability for breach of contract when a flight is canceled due to weather conditions?

The fact that weather conditions or some other acceptable reason caused the cancellation is not the end of the inquiry. To avoid liability, the airline must assist passengers in locating alternate flights to reach their destination. Liability will result if the airline fails to adequately aid travelers in making other arrangements.

In a small claims case involving cancellation of a flight due to mechanical problems with the aircraft, the court held the airline was not liable for breach of contract. The airline had a tariff stating that where the airline deemed cancellation of a flight to be reasonably necessary for the safety of its passengers, it could cancel without liability. The airline thereafter provided the plaintiff with an alternative itinerary using scheduled flights of other airlines. Due to these circumstances, the original airline was not liable to the passenger when the second airline canceled the flight due to bad weather.[13]

Sometimes an airline's efforts to aid a passenger whose flight has been canceled or delayed are frustrated by the negligence of another airline. Liability in such a case may fall on the second airline and not the one that canceled the flight. Airlines are required to aid travelers whose flights with other airlines are canceled. In *Levy v. Eastern Airlines and Pan American Airlines*, 449 N.Y.S.2d 906 (1982), the plaintiff's family's flight on Eastern Airlines was delayed due to bad weather. Before he left home, the plaintiff was notified by phone of the delay and offered seats on a Pan American flight leaving 20 minutes earlier. He agreed and the Eastern representative confirmed the Pan American reservations. When the plaintiff and his family arrived at the airport, the Pan American representative denied knowledge of the reservations. The plaintiff contacted an Eastern representative who contacted Pan American by phone and again confirmed the reservations. The plaintiff's family went to the Pan American gate and again attempted to board. The Pan American ticket agent at the gate failed to check whether confirmed reservations existed for the plaintiff and summarily denied

---

[13] *Cenzi v. Mall Airways, Inc.*, 531 N.Y.S.2d 743 (N.Y. 1988)

them boarding. The plane left without the plaintiff and his family. The plaintiff sued both Eastern and Pan American. Concerning Pan American, the court held it had failed to satisfy its duty under an applicable tariff rule to assist passengers from other airlines' canceled flights. Pan American was thus liable.

The plaintiff also claimed that Eastern was liable. The court held Eastern complied with its obligation to assist in finding alternate travel arrangements. The plaintiff further argued that Pan American was acting as Eastern's agent and therefore Eastern should be liable to the plaintiff for Pan American's inappropriate actions. The court held no agency relationship existed between the two airlines, but rather Eastern was acting as an agent of the plaintiff. Therefore Eastern was not liable.

Rights of Airline Captains

Passengers in flight are confined in the aircraft for the duration of the trip. If anyone on the plane seeks to jeopardize the safety of the passengers—by hijacking, terrorist acts, assault, or otherwise—the option of calling the police is not available. The result is that the occupants of the plane can readily be placed at risk, as this country observed only too clearly when terrorists flew hijacked planes into the Pentagon and both towers of the World Trade Center in New York City. To address this peril, the law gives the pilot significant latitude in deciding to remove a ticketed passenger from the plane prior to takeoff.

The following case addresses the extent of the pilot's authority to remove travelers who are suspected of being hijackers.

CASE EXAMPLE 13-5

Zervigon v. Piedmont Aviation, Inc.
558 F.Supp. 1305 (N.Y. 1983),
aff'd w/out opinion,
742 F.2d 1433 (1983)

Eight plaintiffs, who were removed from an airplane owned and operated by defendant, Piedmont Aviation, Inc., ("Piedmont"), which was about to depart from Tampa, Florida, to New York City, were each awarded $7,500 damages by a jury. Piedmont now moves for judgment notwithstanding the verdict ("nov").

The Plaintiffs allege that their involuntary removal was discriminatory and in violation of [the law]. Piedmont justified its action upon the ground that in the opinion of the captain of the airplane plaintiffs' continued presence thereon (1) "would or might be inimical to the safety of [the] flight," and (2) presented the possibility that they "would cause disruption or serious impairment to the physical comfort or safety of other passengers or [the] carrier's employees," as provided under Piedmont's tariff filed with the Civil Aeronautics Board. ...

A trial court may correct a jury verdict only if after so viewing the evidence it is convinced that the evidence is so strong and overwhelming in favor of the prevailing party that reasonable and fair-minded persons, in the exercise of impartial judgment, could not render a verdict against it.

The issues must be considered against the totality of the facts as they existed at the time the captain took his action. His decision cannot be viewed in isolation separate from events that preceded it but in proper perspective as of the time of their occurrence and in relationship to one another. Whether a captain properly exercised the power to remove a passenger ... "rests upon the facts and circumstances of the case as known to the [captain] at the time [he] formed [his] opinion and made [his] decision and whether or not the opinion and decision were rational and reasonable and not capricious or arbitrary in the light of all those facts and circumstances." The fact that the safety and well being of many lives are dependent upon his judgment necessarily means that the captain is vested with wide discretion. "This is understandable when one considers that an airline usually must make such decisions on the spur of the moment, shortly before takeoff, without the benefit of complete and accurate information." Thus, "the reasonableness of the carrier's opinion ... is to be tested on the information available to the airline at the moment a decision is required. There is correspondingly no duty to conduct an in-depth investigation into a ticket-holder's potentially dangerous proclivities."

We thus consider the evidence against the applicable law. The eight plaintiffs and their band boy left LaGuardia Airport, New York City, on the morning of March 28, 1981, on a Piedmont airplane for Tampa, where they were to perform at a dance concert that evening. They were ticketed to return to New York the next morning at 7:05 on Piedmont Flight 372. After completing their performance, and following a brief stopoff in the early hours of the morning at a hotel, they arrived at the Tampa airport where they waited in an embarkation room preparatory to boarding the 7:05 A.M. plane. While there and waiting to enplane, the group, by their loud and boisterous manner, attracted the attention of Mr. Luis Ramos, another passenger. Mr. Ramos and his wife heard one of the group say to another in Spanish "when we arrive in the capital they will ask us for our experience on this flight," which Mr. Ramos regarded as unusual.

After the passengers were seated on the plane, it left the gate and readied for the takeoff. The members of the musical group were seated generally in the same area in the rear of the plane. However, before reaching the runway, the band boy assaulted a stewardess by grabbing her hand, twisting it and she

screamed. She was visibly shaken and reported the incident and her concern about the group to the captain, George Sturgil, who immediately called airport security and returned to the gate, where he ordered the band boy removed from the plane. Following the band boy's removal, the plane again taxied for the takeoff. It returned a second time to the gate, however, to remove a bass instrument that erroneously was thought to belong to the band boy.

While the plane was at the gate for the second time, Mr. Ramos, who had observed the band boy being taken off the plane by a police or security officer, said to a passenger seated next to him, Mr. Herbert Hill, that the band boy "belong[ed] to a group of musicians, like eight or ten, who were talking in the waiting room. And one of them said to another, 'when we arrive in the capital, they will ask us about our experience on this flight.' " Hill understood Ramos to say "[W]on't the people be surprised when we get to the capital with this aircraft." The use of the word "capital" suggested to Hill that the plane would not land as scheduled, and "rang a bell" in his head that it was Havana, Cuba, where the plane would be forced to land. Thereafter, Hill signalled a stewardess and at his request Ramos repeated the statement to her. She then apprised the captain of it, who immediately left the cockpit and went to where Hill and the Ramoses were sitting. Ramos then repeated his story to the captain. Captain Sturgil returned to the cockpit and ordered the removal of the plaintiffs. Mr. and Mrs. Ramos and Mr. Hill all testified that the overheard statement made them apprehensive that a highjacking to Cuba was in the making.

There can be no doubt that as a matter of law the captain's decision was reasonable and appropriate. The facts known to him provided a sufficient basis for concluding that plaintiffs' continued presence on the aircraft would or might be inimical to the safety of the flight. From the totality of circumstances, the captain was completely justified in believing that there existed a potential highjack threat. As commander of the aircraft, he was charged with the responsibility for the one hundred persons aboard: both passengers and crew alike. If he had decided otherwise, and continued the flight with the plaintiffs on board, his inaction might well have subjected the flight and passengers to grave danger. Indeed, with the information conveyed to him and the prior incident of an assault upon a crew member, if the captain had not taken the action he did he may well have faced a charge of dereliction of duty. Overall, his decision to remove the plaintiffs, therefore, was both reasonable and prudent. There is not the slightest basis to the charge that the action was not taken in good faith. The contention that he should have questioned each member of the group before ordering their removal is unrealistic. He had sufficient indicia of conduct centering about the members of the group that "would or might be inimical to the safety of [the] flight"

to warrant forthwith action. He did not have to tempt fate so that the prospect of highjacking became reality.

Moreover, the captain's action was justified under the terms of the tariff filed with the Civil Aeronautics Board. The information conveyed to him by the flight attendant as to the conduct of the group was sufficient to alert him to the "possibility ... that [the plaintiffs] would cause disruption or serious impairment to the physical comfort and safety of other passengers." Therefore, the Court grants defendant's motion and sets aside the jury's verdict. The complaint is dismissed and a verdict directed in favor of the defendant. So ordered.

CASE QUESTION

1. Why does a pilot need the authority to remove passengers from a flight?

In another case a pilot evicted from a plane the famous opera singer Jessye Norman. She had missed a connecting flight and boarded a later plane. She attempted to use an onboard phone to notify contacts of the change in her arrival time. She discovered that the telephone was out of order and so requested the flight attendant to ask the cockpit crew to call or radio her contact. The attendant informed Norman that such a call would be contrary to policy but he would inquire. When five minutes later he had not yet relayed her request to the crew, she became distraught and an angry exchange occurred. After a stopover the attendant refused to continue to work the flight unless Norman was ousted. The pilot ordered her removed based on the following: the attendant's description of her as unruly and therefore a safety threat, the unavailability of other attendants, a safety regulation barring the flight from flying without a minimum number of attendants, which the flight lacked without the attendant in question, and impending bad weather that jeopardized the flight if takeoff was further delayed. The court determined the pilot did not act arbitrarily in ordering Norman's eviction and dismissed her claim for damages.[14]

In review, the law gives the pilot considerable leeway in making decisions to remove passengers in order to protect the safety of passengers. Only if the decision is made arbitrarily or capriciously will the airlines face liability.

[14] *Norman v. Trans World Airlines, Inc.*, 2000 WL 1480367 (N.Y. 2000)

Overbooking

Because many people make airline reservations and then do not appear for the flight, airlines will frequently deliberately overbook a flight. This practice ensures that the plane will fly as close to capacity as possible. Airlines are not the only travel service suppliers that overbook; hotels also do it, as we discussed in Chapter 4.

A problem arises, of course, when there are fewer no-shows than expected. The result is insufficient seats on the plane (or rooms in a hotel) to accommodate everyone with a confirmed reservation. In such instances, the airline will "bump" some passengers, denying them transportation.

According to the Department of Transportation, for a three-month period, the airlines paid 127,500 passengers to give up their seats. In 2002 the 10 major airlines bumped involuntarily at the rate of .72 per 10,000 passengers, down from 1.01 for 2001.

Anytime an airline is forced to deny passage to a traveler with a confirmed reservation, the airline is well-advised to assist the customer in arranging alternate travel plans. By doing so, the airline may limit its liability.

Rights of Would-Be Passengers

What are the rights of the person who is bumped? An involuntarily bumped traveler may be entitled to damages for breach of contract and, in those cases where the carrier fails to assist the traveler in making alternate plans, to punitive damages.

In *Lopez v. Eastern Airlines, Inc.*, 677 F.Supp.181 (N.Y. 1988), Lopez, a lawyer, was bumped from an 8:00 P.M. flight on which he had confirmed reservations and rescheduled on a midnight flight, disrupting his plans by four hours. He sued the airline for $2,500; he was awarded $450 for breach of contract. The court determined the airline had breached its contract with him and so he was entitled to damages. He used his original ticket for the later flight so he suffered no out-of-pocket loss. The court based the award of $450 on the plaintiff's inconvenience, loss of time, anxiety, and frustration. In addition to the breach of contract claim, Lopez had also sued for the tort of fraudulent representation concerning his confirmed reservation. The court denied this claim on the ground that, "[T]he practice of overbooking in the air transportation industry was public information, openly discussed by the carriers, the Civil Aeronautics Board and publications of national circulation. Therefore the limitations of a 'confirmed' reservation should have been known by plaintiff."

If the airline has a tariff that permits the airline to overbook, it will not be liable to passengers who are unable to be seated. Thus, a passenger could not hold the airline liable even though he was rerouted due to overbooking where the airline had a tariff that authorized the carrier to accept reservations in excess of available space on board the aircraft. Nor was the airline liable for seating in the coach section a traveler with first class reservations where it overbooked first-class and a tariff provided that the airline does not guarantee assigned space within the aircraft.[15]

---

[15]*Guerrero v. American Airlines, Inc.*, 1998 WL 196199 (N.Y. 1998)

Priority Rules for Seating

When overbooking occurs, the law specifies how a determination will be made as to who will be denied seating. The airlines must first ask for volunteers who agree to wait for a later flight, usually in exchange for free airline tickets for a subsequent trip. Thereafter, the airline must apply its priority rules, which all airlines must develop and file with the Department of Transportation. This process is explained in the next case.

CASE EXAMPLE 13-6

Goranson v. Trans World Airlines
467 N.Y.S.2d 774 (1983)

This small claim is based on TWA's bumping of the plaintiff, Arlene Goranson, from her scheduled flight to London as part of a vacation tour for which she had contracted. The Court holds TWA liable for bumping as a common law breach of contract and awards compensatory damages in the amount of $1,500. ...

Plaintiff, Arlene Goranson, contracted with TWA for a flight to London as part of a tour to Great Britain and other places in Europe that was leaving on April 18, 1982. She is an intelligent woman having a genuine interest in gardening and is a member of various horticulture associations. She therefore had a special personal interest in visiting the Savill Gardens which was scheduled as part of the tour. She saved for this trip and waited many years before taking it. She selected TWA because of its representations as to reliability and responsibility. One of many such representations in TWA's brochures promoting the tour read:

Remove Uncertainties the TWA Way

Have you ever been stranded at an airport because you couldn't get on a plane? Have you ever had to travel miles out of your way to catch a "bargain" flight? If not, think about it. It's not the best way to begin a carefree vacation. Consider: *with TWA there are no charter risks, no standby blues or airport gambles. Every flight is scheduled, carrying with it the TWA reputation of reliability. You know in advance exactly where you'll fly from and when.* Maybe you'll pay a few dollars more for peace of mind, but don't you think it's worth it? [Emphasis by TWA]

When she arrived at JFK Airport on the evening of the scheduled departure date, TWA was unable to provide her with the previously confirmed space due to overbooking. Reliability and peace of mind, promised to her, vanished except for the printing in the advertisements.

She could not obtain transportation to London for two days and she arrived in London on the following Monday, missing the first two days of her tour which included the Savill Gardens. She asked permission from TWA during the tour to return to London at the end of the tour to see the places that she missed. However, TWA refused this proposal. She was required to return to the United States with the remaining passengers as scheduled. TWA offered to pay her $400 being the maximum set forth in the [Civil Aeronautics Board] regulations, but she refused and brought this small claim action for $1,500.

The two issues presented are: (1) whether TWA was liable because of overbooking and subsequent bumping as a simple common law breach of contract; and (2) whether the amount of damages is exclusively governed by, and cannot exceed that allowed by, CAB regulations.

In 1976, Justice Powell, in *Ralph Nader v. Allegheny Airlines, Inc.*, 426 U.S. 290, 294, 96 S.Ct. 1978, 1982, 48 L.Ed.2d 643 (1976), discussed the necessity of overbooking and the airlines contention that it was a desirable practice:

Such overbooking is a common industry practice, designed to ensure that each flight leaves with as few empty seats as possible despite the large number of "no-shows"—reservation-holding passengers who do not appear at flight time. By the use of statistical studies of no-show patterns on specific flights, the airlines attempt to predict the appropriate number of reservations necessary to fill each flight. In this way, they attempt to ensure the most efficient use of aircraft while preserving a flexible booking system. ... At times the practice of overbooking results in oversales, which occur when more reservation-holding passengers than can be accommodated actually appear to board the flight. When this occurs, some passengers must be denied boarding ("bumped"). The chance that any particular passenger will be bumped is so negligible that few prospective passengers aware of the possibility would give it a second thought. ...

The CAB's current policy embodied in its Oversales Regulations, however, is (1) to allow oversales, (2) to leave it to the carrier to ensure that bumping is minimized, (3) to provide a regulated amount or minimum compensation to the aggrieved passenger, and (4) to recognize the passengers optional right to recover damages in a court of law.

The inconsistency of the CAB's approval of the bumping practice, along with the implied recognition that it is a breach of contract, has proven to be troublesome.

Under CAB regulations, in the case of "deliberate overbooking," the airline must now follow a defined procedure. ... It must first request volunteers who are willing to relinquish their reserved space in return for compensation and second, it must arrange for comparable transportation for a passenger denied boarding.

The airline may then deny boarding to a passenger in accordance with its own boarding priority rules. The airline, however, must then provide compensation for those involuntarily denied boarding. The amount of this compensation as set forth in the tariff varies for each case, but the maximum is $400.

This Court now concludes that when TWA refused to provide plaintiff passage on the plane that she had tickets for—when she was "bumped," and when TWA did not provide plaintiff with the first two tour days she contracted for, in each instance, there was a common law breach of contract for which there is a traditional state court remedy.

Accordingly, TWA is liable for overbooking and bumping as simple common law breach of contract and plaintiff Arlene Goranson is awarded actual compensatory damages without regard to TWA's tariff or to any CAB regulation.

With respect to the damage issue, courts have held that damages may consist of a wide variety of elements, including expenses for substitute or alternate transportation, meals, compensation for humiliation, outrage and inconvenience. ...

Plaintiff's actual damages are related to her loss of two days of traveling and vacation in England where she had intended specifically to see the Savill Gardens and related attractions. She is therefore entitled to recoup these two days in England, with TWA paying her expenses as damages.

The Court therefore calculates her damages as the cost of round trip air transportation to London ($800), ground transportation to and from airports for the round trip ($100), hotel and meals for 3 days in England ($400) and tour expenses ($100). This totals $1400. Plaintiff is also entitled to recover for her extreme inconvenience, aggravated by TWA's refusal to allow her to return to England at the end of the tour to see the attraction she missed on her first 2 days. Since the Court's small claim jurisdiction is only $1500, only $100 additional can be allowed for inconvenience.

Judgment is therefore entered for Plaintiff for $1500 plus costs.

CASE QUESTION

1. What should the airline have done in this case to minimize the loss to the plaintiff?

In *Smith v. Piedmont Aviation, Inc.*, 567 F.2d 290 (5th Cir. 1978), the airline was liable for failing to follow its priority rules. The plaintiff was denied seating on his confirmed fight because it was overbooked. Piedmont used a first-come first-served basis to determine who would be bumped. However, Piedmont's tariff required priority be given based on the time and date the passenger booked the reservation. The boarding agent testified that had he abided by the airline's priority rule because the record check to ensure compliance with the tariff would have delayed the flight several hours. The plaintiff nonetheless won the case. The basis for the airline's liability was its disregard of its own priority rules. Clearly the airline needs to review the suitability of its regulation.

Punitive Damages for Overbooking

To avoid liability for punitive damages when a passenger is bumped, airlines should assist the traveler in arranging alternate transportation. The plaintiff in *Smith v. Piedmont* also sought punitive damages based on the following additional facts. The plaintiff originally rejected alternate flights offered by Piedmont because they would have caused him to miss a rehearsal for a wedding in which he was the best man. He thrice demanded a charter flight to his destination. The Piedmont agent finally responded, "I don't know when you're going to get it through your thick head we're not going to charter you a flight."

The court refused to award punitive damages, finding no malice on the part of Piedmont. Instead, the court termed the agent's statement "a reaction obviously provoked by [plaintiff's] repeated unreasonable requests for a charter flight." The court further noted, "Although he missed the rehearsal, plaintiff performed flawlessly as groomsman." An important point working in Piedmont's favor on the issue of punitive damages was that it assisted the plaintiff in securing alternate travel arrangements.

Punitive damages were awarded in *Bottenstein v. Connecticut American Bus Lines*, 509 N.Y.S.2d 248 (1986), involving bus transportation. The defendant bus company failed to honor the plaintiffs' confirmed bus tickets home from an overnight trip to Atlantic City because the bus was overbooked. The defendant also failed to help the plaintiffs find alternate means of transportation. The plaintiffs found a ride on Greyhound and sued the defendant for compensation for their expenses home, reimbursement for their ticket on the defendant's bus, and punitive damages. The court held for the plaintiffs on all counts, stating that the defendant's failure to assist the plaintiffs in "secur[ing] some safe alternative means of transportation is not to be countenanced, and shows a reckless and willful disregard towards the plaintiffs in derogation of their contract for safe passage."

Overbooking on International Flights

Overbooking on international flights is governed by the Warsaw Convention, discussed previously in this chapter. Bumping is covered by the Convention, which permits a maximum recovery of $400. Thus, a law student who missed the bar exam (the test a law student must pass to become a lawyer, which is given only twice a year) because she was not allowed seating on her flight from India, was awarded only $400.[16]

---

[16]*Minhas v. Biman Bangladesh Airlines*, 1999 WL 447445 (N.Y. 1999)

Punitive Damages on International Flights

A passenger who is refused seating on an oversubscribed international flight is not entitled to punitive damages due to the limitations of liability provided in the Warsaw Convention. The Convention was discussed previously in this chapter and governs international flights.[17]

Although protected from punitive damages, the airline is well-advised to assist the customer in arranging replacement travel plans.

Additional Legal Issues Involving Airlines

Airlines are occasionally sued on additional grounds, including failure to verify that international travelers possess the necessary documentation for entry into their country of destination, failure to advise such travelers of the needed documents, and in-flight acts of negligence.

Lack of Documentation for International Travel

When people travel to countries other than their place of residence, certain documents are often required for entry. These may include a passport and a visa. The airline tariffs provide that the traveler and not the airline is responsible for determining what documents are required and for securing them. Occasionally, a passenger who lacks the necessary documentation and is thus refused entry into the country of destination will attempt to blame the airline for not verifying that the traveler possessed the needed documentation. These cases uniformly result in a verdict for the airlines.

In one case, the plaintiff traveled from Taiwan to Atlanta, Georgia. Upon arrival at the international port of entry, the plaintiff was deported because he had not obtained an entry visa required by the United States. The plaintiff faulted the airline for permitting him to board without first assuring that he had obtained the proper documentation for entry into the United States. Applicable tariffs place the duty to ensure compliance with various international laws concerning entry solely on the passenger. The plaintiff's case was thus dismissed.[18]

In a similar case, a plaintiff was permitted to board a plane in Puerto Rico and flew to Turkey. Upon arrival, she was taken into custody by Turkish officials because she did not have the necessary visa to enter the country. Following her ordeal she sued the airline, claiming it should have informed her of the visa requirement. The airline's tariff places the requirement of securing the necessary travel documents on the passenger, and relieves the airline from advising the passenger concerning necessary documentation. Therefore, the case was decided in the airline's favor.[19]

---

[17] *Harpalani v. Air-India*, 634 F.Supp 797 (Ill. 1986)

[18] *Williams v. Airlines*, 163 F.Supp.2d 618 (N.C. 2001)

[19] *Aquasviva v. Iberia Lineas Aereas de Espana*, 902 F.Supp. 314 (P. R. 1995)

If the airline undertakes to verify proper documentation and refuses passage to a ticketed traveler who lacks a needed visa, the airline will not be liable for failure to provide transportation. In *Chukwu v. British Airways*, 915 F.Supp. 454 (Mass. 1996), the plaintiff, although ticketed, was not allowed to board his flight because he did not have the required visa. The airline refunded the cost of the ticket. The plaintiff sought damages for "unreasonable psychological traumatic experiences." The court dismissed the case, finding that the airline's tariff permitted it to deny boarding to a passenger whose travel documents were legally insufficient.

Wrong Destination

Passengers are responsible for ensuring their tickets accurately state their intended destination. A passenger seeking round-trip transportation to Brazzaville, Republic of Congo, accepted tickets printed with the destination of Douala, Cameroon. Rerouting was necessitated to reach Brazzaville, resulting in a late arrival and lost business. The traveler sued the airline, but the case was dismissed. The court held that the ticket evidences the parties' intent as to the transportation services to be provided by the airlines. If the destination is misidentified the traveler must initiate action to affect the necessary changes.[20]

Liability for Negligence

Airlines, like other hospitality businesses, are liable for negligence that causes injury to a guest. Examples of the type of negligent acts that can result in liability to an airline include: (1) failing to properly latch the door of a serving cart that swung open on takeoff and struck a passenger's knee; and (2) improper monitoring by flight attendants of overhead luggage racks, resulting in a suitcase falling on a passenger's head.[21]

Liabilities of Travel Agents and Charter Tour Companies

Travel agents play a key role in the travel industry, although their influence has decreased with the advent of home computers and the accessibility thereon to flight information and airline reservations. While in the past travel agents functioned as mere ticket dispensers, today they are information specialists on whose expertise much of the traveling public relies.

In this section we will examine the parameters of the retail travel agent's liability in day-to-day business conduct. This liability is based on the travel agent's own actions, those of the agent's employees, and under certain circumstances, those of third-party suppliers that a travel agent recommends to clients.

[20]*Fondo v. Delta Airlines, Inc.*, 2001 WL 604039 (N.Y. 2001)
[21]*Gee v. Southwest Airlines*, 110 F.3d 1400 (9th Cir. 1997)

Liability for Own Actions

A travel agent is not an insurer that all aspects of a trip are safe. Nor can the agent be expected to "divine and forewarn of an innumerable litany of tragedies and dangers inherent in foreign travel ... [A] travel agent cannot reasonably be expected to guarantee that a traveler will have a good time or will return home without having experienced an adverse adventure or harm."[22] However, like any other business person, the travel agent will be held liable to clients for wrongful acts, including torts such as negligence and fraud. The reason for this liability is that travel agents present themselves as experts in making travel arrangements and customers rely on that expertise. Travel agents must exercise reasonable care in making a client's travel arrangements and must not intentionally mislead a client.

Provide Accurate Information

If the travel agent gives false or incomplete information, the traveler may experience great inconvenience. In such a case the travel agent may be liable. In the next case, both the travel agent and the airline misled the plaintiff traveler. Both were required to compensate the plaintiff.

CASE EXAMPLE 13-7

Burnap v. Tribeca Travel
530 N.Y.S.2d 926 (N.Y. 1988)

In this small claims case, the court has been asked to decide when a ticket is a ticket. It all began when Mr. Boston and Ms. Burnap purchased two round-trip tickets from Tribeca Travel agency for Paris, back in August of 1987. The travel agency booked them on Continental Airlines departing on September 16, 1987 and returning from Paris on September 26, 1987.

Perhaps it did not bode well for their trip that the tickets did not arrive until September 15, 1987, but nevertheless they took off at the scheduled time on September 16, 1987.

Once in Paris they called to confirm their return flight three days before (Sept. 23) and they arrived at the airport on September 26, 1987 for their return flight in what they thought was a timely fashion, i.e., since the tickets indicated the departure time was 11:00 A.M. they arrived about 10 minutes before 10:00 and

were informed that the flight had been rescheduled for 10:00 A.M. and that given customs and security they could not make the flight. Since both Mr. Boston and Ms. Burnap had obligations in New York and Continental had no other flights that day, they purchased two one way tickets to New York on American Airlines.

Once back in New York, they wrote to Tribeca Travel requesting that they be reimbursed for the return tickets they had bought from American Airlines and Tribeca refused. Mr. Boston and Ms. Burnap sued Tribeca, and Tribeca in turn sued Sofa Travel (its agent) and Continental Airlines. ...

[T]hrough its president, Larry Handel, Tribeca Travel denied responsibility. Mr. Handel testified that the time of the return flight from Paris had been changed by Continental Airlines on September 5, 1987. Mr. Handel indicated that he wrote the ticket himself on September 4, 1987. He acknowledged however

---

[22] *Krautsack v. Anderson*, 768 N.E.2d 133 (Ill. 2002)

that the ticket was not delivered until September 15, 1987. When asked why the ticket was not altered to reflect the change in time between September 4 (when it was written) and September 15 (when it was hand delivered) Mr. Handel had a number of explanations which are presented here, not necessarily in the order argued. The first of those was that the change occurred over a holiday week-end (Labor Day). The second was that he did not have a computer on which to receive notice of the change. Third, he stated that the cost of the tickets ($440) was substantially less than the market price (over $1,200). Finally Mr. Handel argued that anyone who travels nowadays must count on delays and problems and that they must learn to take it in stride. Hence this decision since it seems clear to the Court that no monetary award alone will sufficiently indicate to the travel agent that while travel delays and hassles these days are more the rule than the exception, that he has some obligation to prevent them where he is responsible.

Following Mr. Handel's testimony Mr. Stuart Pollack, the General Manager of Continental Airlines, testified that Continental had rescheduled the time of the return flight from Paris to New York on September 4, 1987. As was their standard procedure for such changes (or "Ques" as they call them), the change was relayed by computer to Tribeca travel agents on September 5, 1987. He offered into evidence a computer printout with an accompanying explanation of the various codes contained in it which indicated that the information concerning the change in flights had been sent to the Continental Reservations Agents in Paris. When questioned about why Mr. Boston and Ms. Burnap had not been told of the time change when they called to reconfirm their flight in Paris, he responded that the code on the printout indicated that the travel agent had already been notified and therefore there was no need to tell them.

Neither the airline nor the travel agent acknowledge any responsibility for the failure to notify Boston and Burnap. Mr. Handel [president of Tribeca] implied that the purchase of a ticket at a bargain rate creates less of a contract than if it is purchased at full rate.

Mr. Handel seems to view the purchase of an airline ticket as no different from buying a subway token: Caveat emptor [let the buyer beware] and if the train comes, get on it quick! These arguments notwithstanding, the Courts have recognized that the purchase of an airline ticket creates a contract between the parties. Here the travel agent held himself out as being in the business of selling tickets. Both claimants responded and purchased tickets. Clearly part of the contract created by the purchase is being able to rely on the date and times of flight departures as they are given on the ticket.

The travel agent claims that he had no computer in his uptown office and therefore did not receive the transmission from Continental Airlines indicating that they had changed the time of departure. This is no defense since he had a computer in his other office and more importantly, he had an obligation to inform the passengers who purchased tickets and relied on him to provide them valid and proper tickets in exchange for the requested fare. Moreover, Sofa who worked for them and had provided the tickets in question acknowledged that they had a computer.

Nor can Continental Airlines be viewed as blameless. They sent the information to Paris and failed to notify Boston and Burnap when they called to confirm. Sofa on the other hand had no direct dealings with claimants. Tribeca, which sued Sofa, failed to establish any responsibility on [Sofa's] part for any of these occurrences.

However, Tribeca and Continental are both liable to claimants. Continental must pay claimants for the balance of the tickets paid for that were unused because claimants were not informed of the scheduled change. Judgment is awarded against Continental, in the amount of $440.

Tribeca Travel bears greater responsibility since it drew up the ticket but never corrected it to reflect the actual departure time. Since the claimants' return tickets cost $1,384 and Continental is liable for the unused half of the tickets, judgment is awarded against Tribeca Travel in the amount of $944. [The difference between the cost of the return tickets and the amount Continental was required to pay.]

CASE QUESTIONS

1. What should Tribeca Travel agency have done to avoid liability?

2. What could Continental Airlines have done to avoid liability?

3. Why do you think Tribeca Travel Agency was ordered to pay more than Continental Airlines?

In another case involving misfeasance by a travel agent, the latter issued airline tickets to a client for travel from New York City to Calcutta, India. The agent handwrote on the tickets "confirmed." In fact the travel agent knew the client was "wait listed" (on a waiting list without a confirmed reservation). When the client arrived for the flight he was denied a seat and sued the agent. The court held for the plaintiff, finding the agent had breached the duty of care and awarded the plaintiff both the cost of the tickets and money for emotional distress.[23]

Duty to Investigate Third-Party Suppliers

Travel agents have a duty to their customers to do the following vis-a-vis service providers (hotels, charter companies, tour operators, and so forth) they recommend: investigate their operations, locate material information about them that is reasonably available, and disclose that information to their customers. Travelers are legally entitled to expect that travel services recommended by a travel agent will be reliable and suitable. Failure of a travel agent to adequately investigate can lead to liability, as the agents in the following cases learned the hard way.

CASE EXAMPLE 13-8

Josephs v. Fuller (Club Dominicus)
451 A.2d 203 (N.J. 1982)

This is an action by John and Regina Josephs against a resort known as Club Dominicus and a travel agency known as Richard's Travel Service, brought because defendant's resort accommodations were substandard.

It is uncontested that defendant Richard's Travel Service (Richard's) recommended and arranged for plaintiffs to spend their vacations at Club Dominicus in the Dominican Republic, and that the accommodations provided by Club Dominicus were far below standard.

It appears, further, that Richard's is independent from Club Dominicus except for the commissions received for booking vacations.

Richard's moved for dismissal at the end of plaintiff's case on the ground that plaintiff had not proved any facts upon which liability of a travel agent could be based. (It should be noted that defendant Club Dominicus is not involved at this point of the litigation because it is in default for failing to answer the complaint.)

---

[23] *Das v. Royal Jordanian Airlines*, 766 F.Supp. 169 (N.Y. 1961)

Richard's argues that it was simply an agent for a disclosed principal and, as such, owed no duty to plaintiffs. The only party owing any duty to plaintiffs [according to Richard's] was the disclosed principal, Club Dominicus, and that party is the only one liable for a breach.

For the reasons enunciated herein, Richard's motion [to dismiss] is denied.

Defendant is mistaken in its contention that because it was paid by Club Dominicus it was the agent of Club Dominicus only, and since its principal was disclosed to the plaintiffs, it owed no duty to the plaintiffs. ...

Defendant's position is that, even if it was negligent in booking a vacation at a resort about which it knew nothing, it is not liable because it owed no duty to the plaintiffs. This is clearly wrong.

Since defendant's commissions were paid by Club Dominicus, those commissions would not be earned without plaintiff's patronage. The pecuniary benefit bestowed on defendant by plaintiff forms the basis of a legal duty.

As a travel agent, [defendant] owed a certain duty to [its customers]. A travel agent is a special agent, akin to a broker, which engages in a single business transaction with the principal.

[I]t would seem absurd to hold that defendant Richard's had no duty to acquire any knowledge of the facilities it was booking. Plaintiffs could well have made their own arrangements, choosing a resort at random. But rather than risk a substandard vacation, they took advantage of the service offered by defendant. As it turned out, defendant had little or no more knowledge than the plaintiffs.

This court, therefore, holds that when a traveler relies on the recommendations of a travel agent and suffers damage because of accommodations so totally unacceptable that any reasonable travel agent would have known not to make such recommendations, the travel agent is liable.

A travel agent was liable when a hotel he recommended to a customer was "closed, chained and guarded" upon the traveler's arrival. Said the court, "A travel agent has a duty to his customer to not only use reasonable care in making travel reservations, but also in confirming them prior to the date of the trip."[24] A travel agent who failed to investigate the viability of a tour operator was liable to a would-be traveler who paid for a trip to Israel that did not materialize because the operator went out of business.[25]

A travel agent was liable to his customer where the agent failed to confirm that a tour advertised as including two meals a day in fact included the meals. After the client paid $1,032 for two people and the agent sent the money to the tour operator minus the agent's commission, the agent learned the trip did not include the meals. Thereafter, upon the agent's representation to the customer that the trip could be canceled with a full refund, the customer chose to cancel rather than pay an additional $300 for the meals. In fact, the money already paid was not refundable, so the customer lost $1,032. He sued, and the court held that the travel agent was liable for this amount based on breach of contract and negligent performance of his duties. Said the court, "Defendant's contractual obligation included verifying and confirming that such tour with the enumerated components and at the stated price was actually available before he sold it."[26]

---

[24] *Barton v. Wonderful World of Travel, Inc.*, 502 N.E.2d 715 (Ohio 1986)

[25] *Grisby v. O.K. Travel*, 693 N.E.2d 1142 (Ohio 1997)

[26] *Pellegrini v. Landmark Travel Group*, 628 N.Y.S.2d 1003 (N.Y. 1995)

In another case, the travel agent was found liable for failing to have sufficiently investigated the status of a charter company with which he made reservations for the plaintiff and her four children. The plaintiff's trip to Puerto Rico occurred without incident. When she and her family arrived at the airport ready to board the flight home, she learned the air carrier had gone out of business. She sued the travel agent, seeking the cost of the tickets she purchased from another airline for the flight home. Said the court, "There was no testimony of efforts made [by the travel agent] to assure the performance [by the charter company] and no evidence that the travel agent provided the [traveler] with information about any risks associated [with a charter]." The court held the travel agent was liable for the cost of the return-flight tickets because it failed to ascertain the reliability of the charter company it recommended.[27]

Similarly, a travel agent was found liable for having insufficiently researched a tour operator it recommended. The tour company went bankrupt, resulting in the loss of a client's vacation money. The court ordered the travel agent to compensate the traveler for the loss.[28]

The clear lesson from these cases is that travel agents must investigate the third-party suppliers they recommend to ensure their continued existence and their ability to provide the contracted services. Failure to do so can result in liability.

Recommend Travel Insurance

Travel agents are well advised to suggest travel insurance to their customers. Such insurance compensates the would-be traveler for the cost paid for the vacation if the trip is canceled for certain reasons, including bankruptcy of the travel provider. Having recommended the purchase of travel insurance can assist a travel agent's defense when sued by a customer whose plans were frustrated by a defunct supplier. In *Creteau v. Liberty Travel, Inc.*, 600 N.Y.S.2d 576 (1993), the plaintiffs traveled to St. Croix. Partway through their two-week pre-paid vacation, both the airline and a subsidiary that made plaintiff's hotel arrangements went bankrupt. The plaintiffs had to pay anew for the hotel and their flight home. They sued the travel agent for the money they double-paid. The court held the travel agent was not liable to the plaintiff for the airline's bankruptcy. Facts in this case distinguish it from the two prior cases. The agent was aware that the financial condition of the airlines was questionable and had so informed the plaintiffs prior to booking the trip. They chose to continue their travel plans nonetheless. An additional factor noted by the court as a basis for finding no liability was the travel agent's repeated recommendation that the plaintiffs purchase travel insurance. The recommendation was included with a written confirmation the agent sent to the plaintiff of his itinerary, and again with the tickets.

[27] *Rodriguez v. Cardona Travel Agency*, 523 A.2d 281 (N.J. 1986)
[28] *Douglas v. Steel*, 816 P.2d (Ok. 1991)

Sometimes a travel agent will investigate recommended suppliers and find them in good order. Nonetheless, while the traveler is at the supplier's facility something unexpected occurs and the traveler's trip is disrupted. In these circumstances, the agent will not be liable. By researching the premises, agents satisfy their duty to their clients. In the following case, travelers accused a tour operator of failing to properly investigate the hotel accommodations provided on the tour. The tour operator, however, had researched the hotel, and so was not liable.

CASE EXAMPLE 13-9

Wilson v. American Trans Air, Inc.
874 F.2d 386 (7th Cir. 1989)

... American Trans Air (American) is a charter tour operator headquartered in Indianapolis, Indiana. It regularly plans and operates tours to the Cayman Islands. Participants in these tours are offered accommodations at the Holiday Inn Grand Cayman International Beach Resort (Holiday Inn Grand Cayman), operated by Humphreys (Cayman) Ltd, under a franchise agreement with Holiday Inns, Inc. American sometimes sponsors two or three trips to the Cayman Islands per month and has included, as an option, accommodations at the Humphreys hotel in its tours since at least 1976. One employee of American always accompanies the tours to the Caymans and stays with the tour group at the Humphreys hotel.

Mr. and Mrs. Wilson participated in an American tour to the Cayman Islands in October 1984. They chose to stay at the Humphreys hotel. On October 30, Mrs. Wilson was assaulted by an intruder entering her second floor hotel room through a balcony door while she was asleep. The intruder attempted to rob and rape Mrs. Wilson, and she suffered bodily injuries during the attack.

The majority of participants in these tours apparently do not choose to purchase an optional "ground package" that includes accommodations at a local hotel (in this case, Humphreys). However, promotional materials for this trip did include references to accommodations at the Holiday Inn Grand Cayman. In addition, brochures, rate cards, and other promotional material are provided to American by Humphreys at American's request. The

Wilsons also assert that, since 1978, American has published advertisements for 131 tours specifically offering accommodations at the Humphreys hotel.

American did conduct basic research regarding its tours. It attempted to gain information about the political stability and climate of the destination country. It apparently did not inquire into guest safety and security at the hotel. The Wilsons allege that there was substantial criminal activity involving guests at the Humphreys hotel in the months preceding the attack on Mrs. Wilson, but American disclaims any knowledge of such activity.

The Wilsons maintain that American is liable to them because it breached its duty as a charter tour operator to investigate proposed accommodations for safety and to warn prospective patrons of any dangerous conditions discovered during the investigation. The Wilsons submit that this duty arises out of contractual language contained in American's travel brochure, the federal regulations governing charter tour operators, and tort law.

The Wilsons ground their contract argument in the following language found in the advertising newsletter that American distributed to potential customers:

Responsibility of American Trans Air: This tour program is planned and operated by American Trans Air, Inc. ... as *principal* and tour operator ... American Trans Air is responsible for making all arrangements for transportation, provided that *in the absence of negligence on the part of American Trans Air*, the responsibility does not extend to any assumption of liability for any personal injury or property damage arising out of or caused by any negligent act on the part of any hotel, other air carrier or anyone rendering any of the services or accommodations being offered in connection with this Public Charter. ...

The Wilsons ... note that the contract states that American is the principal and is responsible for any negligent act of its own with respect to the accommodations offered in connection with the tour. The Wilsons assert that this duty required American to make some reasonable investigation into the safety of any accommodations that it promoted and recommended and to warn prospective patrons of any danger at the hotel that might affect them.

We cannot accept the Wilsons' contention. ...

[W]e note that a charter tour operator, as the principal responsible to tour participants for all the services and accommodations offered in connection with the charter tour, cannot disclaim liability for injuries arising out of its own negligence. A charter tour operator, as principal, employs independent contractors such as airlines and hotels to provide transportation and accommodation services to its patrons. Although a principal generally cannot be held liable for the torts of an independent contractor, [the] law does allow a principal to be held liable for the torts of a hired independent contractor when the consequences of the principal's own negligent failure to select a competent contractor caused the harm upon which the suit is based. This negligent selection theory would allow liability to be imposed upon American for its own negligence as principal, liability that it did not disclaim under

its contract and cannot disclaim under the applicable federal regulation.

Although the Wilsons' allegation that American breached a duty to investigate the safety and security of the hotel accommodations that it included in its tour package can be construed as a claim based on negligent selection theory, their claim cannot survive. American chose Humphreys to provide the hotel accommodations in its tour package. Humphreys operated a Holiday Inn. The hotel was located on Seven Mile Beach on Grand Cayman Island, British West Indies—a British Crown Colony. There is nothing in the record that indicates that the Holiday Inn Grand Cayman was located in a high-crime area, that the hotel experienced more safety and security problems than other resort hotels on the island, or that the level of criminal activity involving guests at the Holiday Inn Grand Cayman was unusually high for a large beach resort. In addition, American stated that, in considering guest safety and security at hotels included in its tour packages, it "rel[ied] on the general reputation" of the hotels involved. American also knew that Humphreys had security guards on the premises, and it had received no notice of any guest complaints regarding safety and security at the Holiday Inn Grand Cayman. An officer of American had visited the island and engaged in face-to-face negotiations over rates and payment policies with representatives of the hotel. Under such circumstances, American had no duty to make specific inquiries into guest safety or security at the Holiday Inn. ...

The judgment of the district court [in favor of American] is affirmed.

CASE QUESTIONS

1. On what principle did the court base its decision?

2. Based on the court's holding, how does the liability of a tour operator for a guest's safety compare with that of an innkeeper?

Security Incidents

If the travel agent is aware of security issues associated with a hotel or other service provider the agent recommends, the agent should disclose that information to the traveler. The latter can then make an informed decision on whether or not to utilize the service. Failure to reveal such information may expose the agent to liability. For example, vacationers in Jamaica were robbed and one was raped at gunpoint. Among the parties sued was the travel agent who made the arrangements for air travel and lodging. The court, noting that a travel agent is not an insurer or guarantor of its customers' safety, stated that the agent is not obligated to investigate safety factors of lodging accommodations unless requested by the customer to do so. However, the court also stated that "where the agent has knowledge of safety factors or where such information is readily available, a travel agent has the duty to inform the customer of those factors."[29] Based on the court's somewhat conflicting statements, travel agents would be well-advised to make inquiry of recommended destinations to ensure their relative safety.

The death of a college student on a Mexican party train led to a lawsuit by her parents against the tour operator that arranged the itinerary, transportation, and lodging. The deceased was killed on an unsafe platform when walking from one train car to another. Three prior deaths of college students had occurred on the party train, a fact known to the tour operator but not disclosed to the tour participants. The court refused to dismiss the lawsuit against the tour operator. While it noted that a travel agent or tour operator cannot be "reasonably expected to divine and forewarn of an innumerable litany of tragedies and dangers inherent in foreign travel," the court nonetheless found that the tour operator in this case may have violated its duty to disclose available information.[30]

Liability for Breach of Contract by Third-Party Service Suppliers

When a customer purchases a trip from a travel agent and the trip does not materialize as portrayed, the agent may be liable for breach of contract.

In the following case, the travel agent was found liable to a client for breach of contract where the client's vacation was spoiled by the wholesaler's failure to reserve hotel rooms.

CASE EXAMPLE 13-10

Odysseys Unlimited, Inc. v. Astrol Travel Service
354 N.Y.S.2d 88 (1974)

Following an earlier practice, in the summer of 1972 the Paterson and Majewski families began to plan a joint vacation over the Christmas holiday. In doing so they relied upon Astral Travel Service ("Astral") an agency with

which they had previously dealt. They looked forward to spending a few days with their five children in the Canary Islands, of course not anticipating the discomfort, inconvenience and disappointment they would suffer. ...

Astral (a retail travel agent) suggested to Dr. Paterson and Mr. Majewski a package tour prepared by Odysseys (a wholesale agency). The tour, entitled "Xmas Jet Set Sun Fun/Canary Isle," was scheduled to depart December 26,

---

[29] *Creteau v. Liberty Travel, Inc.*, 600 N.Y.S.2d 576 (N.Y. 1993)

[30] *Maurer v. Cerkvenik-Anderson Travel, Inc.*, 890 P.2d 69 (Ariz. 1994)

1972 by jet for Tenerife, Canary Isles, ... staying at the "delux Semiramis Hotel" and returning on January 1, 1973 by jet. Majewski and Paterson accepted this trip costing $1,375.90 and $1,076.80 respectively and made their down payments to Astral. Astral withheld its commission and forwarded the balance along with the reservations to Odysseys who in turn confirmed the reservations to Astral. ... An information sheet ... furnished details of the trip and referred to the accommodations at the "Five-Star Hotel Semiramis."

On December 26, 1972 the group flew off to the Canary Islands. They arrived at the airport in Tenerife at about dawn and waited about two hours ... before they were taken to the Hotel Semiramis. At this point the passengers had been en route some thirty hours. While at the airport they saw Mr. Newton, President of Odysseys, who accompanied the group tour. (The inference may reasonably be drawn that he went along because he anticipated the difficulties which were shortly to be encountered.) Two hundred fifty weary but expectant guests arrived at the Semiramis and were presented with a letter from the hotel ... advising them that there were no accommodations available to their group. Dr. Paterson confronted Mr. Newton with this letter and the latter acknowledged that there was no space available and that he was looking for others. For about four hours, two hundred fifty people (including baggage) were in the lobby of the Semiramis until they were divided into groups and directed to other [hotels]. The Paterson and Majewski families were brought to the Porto Playa Hotel which was not fully ready for occupancy because it was under construction and without the recreational facilities and conveniences available at the Hotel Semiramis. Portions of the Porto Playa Hotel were enclosed in scaffolding. Paterson and Majewski testified that work was done in their rooms, water supply uncertain, electric connections incomplete, etc., etc. throughout their stay.

The court is convinced that prior to the group's departure Mr. Newton was aware that there were no reservations at the Semiramis Hotel for his charges. He testified that on either December 18th or 19th, 1972 he knew of the overbooking at the hotel. ... In his letter of January 12, 1973 addressed to tour members, Mr. Newton confirms the fact that he had been aware of some "problem with overbooking by that hotel" (Semiramis Hotel) and states that his agent "had the foresight to have arranged for alternate accommodations". ... [T]he reservations for the tour were not confirmed and, therefore, the hotel was not obligated to accommodate the members of the group. ...

Majewski and Paterson sue in contract and negligence seeking recovery of their payments for their trip and for their ordeal. Their claims spring from a breach of contract by Astral for its failure to furnish the hotel accommodations agreed upon. Majewski and Paterson are entitled to recover from Astral for the breach of contract. Damages in the usual breach of contract action should indemnify a party for the gains prevented and losses sustained by the breach; to leave him in no worse, but put him in no better, position than he would have been had the breach not occurred. ... However, when a passenger sues a carrier for a breach of their agreement concerning accommodations the [i]nconviences and discomforts which a passenger suffers ... are to be considered in the assessment of the damages. ...

The agent should be held responsible to: (a) verify or confirm the reservations and (b) use reasonable diligence in ascertaining the responsibility of any intervening 'wholesaler' or tour organizer. Because the contract was violated and the accommodations contracted for not furnished, a more realistic view for awarding damages to Majewski and Paterson would include not only the difference in the cost of the accommodations but also compensation for their inconvenience, discomfort, humiliation and annoyance.

Odysseys attempted to mitigate the damages to Majewski and Paterson by offering proof as to the difference in value between what they received (at a four-star hotel) and what was agreed upon (a five-star [hotel]). However, this evidence is without force because the hotel at which they stayed was under construction, its recreational facilities were non-existent and its location was not nearly as desirable as that of the Semiramis. The proverbial expression about a picture being worth a thousand words has particular application to Exhibits [presented by plaintiffs] to reveal what Majewski and Paterson expected and what they found. Paterson and

---

Majewski are entitled to the return of the total sum each paid for the trip as damages to them and their family for the inconvenience and discomfort they endured. ...

On Astral's cross-claim against Odysseys for breach of contract, concerning the Majewski and Paterson claims ... Astral is entitled to a judgment against Odysseys in the amount of $2,452.70 less $308.30 which Astral retained as its commission, because Odysseys failed to perform its contract and it was Odysseys which was responsible for the fate which befell Majewski and Paterson.

At first it may seem unfair that the travel agent is liable to the client for the dereliction of the wholesaler. But remember, the party who dealt face-to-face with the client and who arranged the travel itinerary was the travel agent; the client likely had no direct dealings with the wholesaler and may not even know how to contact the wholesaler. Also, imposing liability on the travel agent will motivate the agent to verify that the travel wholesaler is making the necessary plans and reservations for the booked tour. Further, the travel agent is not without a remedy. Note in the last paragraph of the case, the judge said that the travel agent was able to collect from the wholesaler the money the agent was required by the court to pay the client. Thus, the liability ultimately rests with the party at fault, the wholesaler. However, if the wholesaler goes bankrupt or has discontinued business and cannot be located, the travel agent will bear the loss.

Not every traveler makes arrangements through a travel agent or airline office. Some travelers use charter companies that offer reduced rates for those who do not mind traveling without a lot of frills. The charter company is liable if it breaches its contract to provide transportation.

CASE EXAMPLE 13-11

Musso v. Tourlite International, Inc. 500 N.Y.S.2d 969 (1986)

When Thomas Wolfe wrote *You Can't Go Home Again* it is clear he had no reference to Mr. Musso, the plaintiff in this case. On the other hand, given what happened to Mr. Musso, he undoubtedly felt the sentiments of Wolfe's title during the events.

Mr. Musso's travels began with his decision to purchase charter airline tickets from Tourlite Inc. to pay a visit to Italy, from whence he came. He bought round trip tickets for himself and his wife and they flew to Rome with no incident.

Mr. Musso was aware of the rules of the charter which required a confirmation of the return flight at least 72 hours prior to departure (which he complied with and there is no dispute as to the fact that this was done). He was also required to arrive at the airport three hours in advance of the flight.

Mr. Musso testified that he and his wife arrived at the airport for their return flight on August 3, 1985 at 10 A.M. The flight was scheduled to depart at 1 P.M., but when he inquired at the information counter, Mr. Musso was informed that the flight was delayed until 3 P.M. The person at the booth instructed him to get on line at about 1:30 P.M. Mr. Musso remained at the airport and joined the line at 1:30 as he had been instructed. There was only one line for charter flights. When he finally arrived at the front he was told by the person behind the counter that while they had his reconfirmed reservation, the plane was full and that it was ready to leave, and that he would therefore not be able to board it. Later, he was told by a representative of the charter company (Tourlite) that he might be able to catch the following week's charter. Upon hearing that Mr. Musso, who from his description remained calm in the face of being told that he had no flight home, decided that he would make other arrangements. He rented a car, drove into Rome where he checked into a hotel overnight, and bought two Alitalia tickets to New York for the following day.

Once he returned to New York, Mr. Musso sued Tourlite, the charter company, in Small Claims Court for the cost of the airline tickets. ...

The rights of an airline passenger are provided for in Civil Aeronautics Board regulations, which establishes the obligations of airlines. While the flight here was not on a scheduled airline, and was booked through the charter company, it is clear that the purchase of airline tickets creates a contract between the purchaser and the provider of service. Tourlite agreed to bring Mr. Musso and his wife to Italy and back providing they complied with certain conditions. As the facts indicate Mr. Musso fulfilled his end of the bargain—he reconfirmed, he appeared promptly for departure, but was told there was no room for him on the plane.

Tourlite, in its defense, offered the testimony of the Director of Customer Service, Hans Elsevier. Mr. Elsevier, who was not present in Rome at the time these events occurred, testified that on the day in question, the flight manifest [a list of a plane's passengers] indicated twenty-seven vacant seats. He stated that while Tourlite had a representative present, the seating for the plane is done by a "handling agent." The manifest also indicated that the Mussos were confirmed on the flight in question. He said that a representative of Tourlite was stationed in front of the counter to assist passengers with difficulties. However, Mr. Musso testified that he had not encountered any such person although he had looked for someone. Mr. Elsevier admitted that he had no idea why Mr. Musso had not been permitted to board the plane.

None of the arguments advanced by defendant Tourlite relieves it of its contractual responsibility to the plaintiff here. The testimony indicated Mr. Musso complied with his part of the contract by reconfirming. He appeared at the airport, and waited on line. Since Mr. Elsevier was not present at the time of these events it is difficult to accept his hearsay testimony that a representative of Tourlite was there and was assisting those on line.

Mr. Musso is therefore entitled to recover from Tourlite the cost of his Alitalia airline tickets ($1100) and the additional cost for the rental car ($55) that he needed to go back into Rome to spend the night, together with interest from August 1985.

No Liability for Third-Party Suppliers' Negligence

Travel agents and tour operators are not guarantors that third-party suppliers will act without negligence. Rather, agents and tour operators are not liable to travelers when the latter are injured at recommended facilities due to the supplier's carelessness.

Travel Agents

Travel agents are not liable for the negligence of a hotel, resort, or other service provider booked by the agent for a client. Thus, the agent who made reservations for a customer at a Club Med resort was not liable to the vacationer who suffered injuries due to the resort's negligence.[31] Likewise, a bed-and-breakfast reservation service was not liable to a customer who fell at a facility because the steps lacked railings.[32] Similarly, where a traveler on a European bus tour sustained injuries due to the negligence of the bus company, the travel agency that arranged the tour was not liable for the injuries.[33]

Tour Operators

Tour operators, like travel agents, are not liable for negligence of third-party suppliers. While touring Morocco a plaintiff's bus stopped to permit tourists to observe camels wandering about the desert. As the plaintiff stepped from the bus to the ground she slipped on loose sand causing a broken ankle. She sued the tour operator and bus company claiming they were both negligent for not having disclosed to her the danger of exiting the bus. The tour operator denied liability because it did not own the bus, did not employ any of the tour personnel who served the plaintiff in Morocco (the bus company owned the bus and employed the guides), and did not possess knowledge of the existence of the alleged dangerous condition. The court agreed and dismissed the claim against the tour operator for the reasons stated.[34] In another case, the plaintiff was injured when the jet ski he rented from his hotel malfunctioned. His claims of negligence against the tour operator and the travel agent were dismissed since neither owned or controlled the skis or the rental personnel.[35] The proper defendant would be the hotel, which managed the ski rental operation and hired the staff. Likewise, neither the travel agent nor the tour operator were liable when customers vacationing in Cancun, Mexico, fell 15 feet because their hotel-room balcony collapsed without warning due to the hotel's negligence.[36]

Tour operators are also not liable for suppliers' contract breaches. Thus, where a tour operator organized a tour that included a charter flight and the flight was canceled for unexplained reasons, the tour operator was not liable.[37]

Tour operators also are not liable for the negligence of independent contractors that provide services to those on a tour. Thus, a tour operator responsible for coordinating transportation, hotel accommodations, and certain special events was not liable when a tour participant took a "booze cruise" and was served too much alcohol, which caused him to leap overboard to his death.[38]

---

[31] *Stein v. Club Med Sales, Inc.*, 658 N.Y.S.2d 639 (N.Y. 1997)

[32] *Manes v. Coats*, 941 P.2d 120 (Alaska 1997)

[33] *Dorkin v. American Express Co.*, 351 N.Y.S.2d 190 (N.Y. 1974)

[34] *Davies v. General Tours, Inc.*, 774 A.2d 1063 (Conn. 2001)

[35] *Chimenti v. Apple Vacations*, 2000 WL 33401822 (Mi. 2000)

[36] *DiBiase v. Oasis International*, 2001 WL 1200324 (Conn. 2001)

[37] *Saachi v. TNT Vacations*, 2001 WL 291950 (N.H. 2001)

[38] *Smith v. West Rochelle Travel Agency, Inc.*, 656 N.Y.S.2d 340 (N.H. 1997)

Nor are tour operators generally liable when a tour participant is injured during sightseeing at an attraction on the tour, assuming the sight is not under the control of the tour operator. In *Loeb v. Tauk Tours*, 793 F.Supp 431 (N.Y. 1992), the plaintiff, while a member of a tour offered by the defendant, fell near her lodge while visiting the Grand Teton National Park in Moran, Wyoming. The tour operator claimed it was not responsible for any dangerous condition on which the plaintiff tripped, nor did it have control over the area surrounding the inn and therefore it should not be liable. The plaintiff argued that since the tour operator selected the tour sites and provided supervision, it had a duty to warn of foreseeable risks such as rocky slopes and steep trails. The court rejected the plaintiff's position and held that a tour operator has no duty to warn or protect tour participants from a possible hazardous condition that may exist on the property of others.

Disclaimers by the Travel Agent

Travel agents frequently insert disclaimers in their written materials. A **disclaimer** is a term in a contract that attempts to avoid all liability on the part of one party to the contract. The effectiveness of disclaimers in limiting the liability of travel agents is questionable. The courts have not looked favorably on attempts by travel agents to relieve themselves from liability for negligence or other wrongful conduct and have usually limited the enforceability of disclaimers. Such clauses are often invalidated under various legal theories, including insufficient notice to the customer, lack of specificity in the language, inequality of bargaining power, and, perhaps most important, offensiveness to public policy.

A travel agent, rather than inserting a disclaimer in contracts with clients, should use instead information that defines the relationship between all the parties involved and properly sets out what liabilities attach to each. In this way travel agents can make clear to clients that suppliers of travel services are not agents of the travel agent and so the travel agent generally is not liable if the supplier is negligent or breaches a contract or otherwise disrupts the client's travel plans. Such explanatory material enhances the client's understanding of the relationships involved and may aid the travel agent in avoiding a lawsuit.

Know that providing information about liability will not relieve travel agents from their own negligence or wrongful conduct.

Errors and Omissions Insurance for Travel Agents

Mistakes and poor judgment can happen in any business, although with good management their occurrence should be limited. A travel agent or travel wholesaler can purchase **errors and omissions insurance** to cover its loss when mistakes are made. The objective of insurance is to minimize for the agent or wholesaler the financial effects of errors made by travel agents and their staffs.

While many types of insurance coverage are available, "errors and omissions" covers the cost of defending a lawsuit and any adverse judgment resulting from the travel agent's failure to fulfill its obligation to a client. Insurance, however, should not be used as an excuse for poor management techniques or shoddy business practices. Clients are entitled to better, and with each lawsuit the travel agent's reputation and business will suffer and the cost of the insurance is likely to escalate.

Credit Card Fraud

Many sales of airline tickets are made over the Internet or on the phone. Facilitated by e-tickets, such transactions can be completed without the need for the agent and buyer to ever meet face-to-face. These long-distance transactions, while good for business volume, provide ample opportunity for unscrupulous customers to commit **credit card fraud**. Travel agents must be vigilant to avoid being victims.

If the credit card used in a ticket transaction is stolen or its use is otherwise unauthorized and the true cardholder denies the charges after reviewing the monthly bill, the travel agent may be financially responsible for the sale. In a typical travel fraud scheme, the buyer orders airline tickets by phone and is quite willing upon request of the agent to send by fax or mail any identification documents requested—for example, copies of credit cards, a passport, authorizations, or a birth certificate. They all appear real, but the travel agent has no way to authenticate them. When the documents later turn out to be counterfeit or used without authority and the true owner denies liability, the travel agent has no way to locate the supposed customer and may be liable for the cost of the ticket.

The way to protect against liability when the true cardholder refuses payment is to have an imprint of the actual credit card and the cardholder's signature. While Internet and phone transactions are consummated regularly in commercial transactions without an imprint or signature, travel agents accepting credit cards without in-person contact must be aware of the risks and act cautiously to avoid being the target of fraud.

Rental Cars

The car-rental business is an important component of the travel industry, as it provides travelers with mobility and relieves them from reliance on public transportation. However, car rentals present potential problems for travelers and the rental companies, including overbooking issues and liability for accidents.

Overbooking

A traveler who flies into a strange city expecting a car to be waiting and discovers the rental company cannot fill the reservation will not be happy. A few states have enacted consumer protection laws that deal with unfilled car-rental reservations. These laws state that if a company fails to provide a car to a customer with a confirmed reservation, the company may be subject to a fine. Each rental company has a contingency plan for unfilled reservations. Most have adopted a compensation policy for travelers whose car reservations cannot be filled and who rent a car from another company at a higher price. The amount the rental companies will pay is the difference between their contract price and the higher price the customer pays to the other company.

Accidents in Rental Cars

When a rental car is involved in an accident while a customer is driving, questions arise as to whether the rental company is liable to people injured. Generally, the rental company is not liable. An exception is the circumstance where it negligently entrusts the vehicle to a lessee. **Negligent entrustment** means providing a product (in this circumstance, a car) for use by another person knowing that person is likely to use the car in a dangerous manner. A car-rental company is liable for negligent entrustment only when it has reason to know the lessee is incompetent to drive the car. If it has such knowledge and the lessee is in an accident, the car-rental company may be liable for the damages. As the following case illustrates, the law gives considerable leeway to the rental company.

CASE EXAMPLE 13-12

Drummond v. Walker
643 F.Supp. 190 (D.C. 1986),
aff'd 861 F.2d 303 (1988)

This action arises out of a car accident which occurred early in the morning on August 6, 1984. Plaintiff alleges that defendant Kenneth Scott, while driving a car rented from defendant Americar, fell asleep at the wheel and struck a guardrail on Route 70 near Hagerstown, Maryland. Plaintiff, a passenger in the car, suffered facial injuries in the accident.

Scott did not actually execute the rental agreement for the car. Defendant Charlene Walker rented the car for Scott on August 2, 1984, because Scott lacked the appropriate identification and credit necessary to rent the car. When Walker rented the car, the Americar manager gave the keys to Scott, who drove the car away from the Americar lot. Walker never took possession of the car.

In ... her complaint, plaintiff alleges that Americar is liable for her injuries by virtue of Americar's negligent entrustment of the car to Scott. She contends that the entrustment was negligent because Scott lacked proper identification and did not possess a credit card. Plaintiff further suggests that Americar was negligent in entrusting the car to Scott whom they knew to be slightly under 21 years of age. Americar has a policy of not renting to drivers under 21 years.

Even if Americar's employees knew that Scott would be driving the car, that he lacked proper identification and credit, and that he was under 21 years of age, such knowledge would still be insufficient to establish a prima facie case of negligent entrustment. One liable for negligent entrustment is:

[o]ne who supplies, directly or through a third person, a chattel for the use of another, whom the supplier knows or has reason to know to be likely because of his youth, inexperience, or otherwise, to use it in a manner involving unreasonable risk of physical harm to himself and others ...

Generally, negligent entrustment of a vehicle to an incompetent driver is imposed only where the owner entrusts the vehicle to one whose appearance or conduct is such as to indicate his incompetency or inability to operate the vehicle with care. In order to impose liability in other cases, where the incompetency of the driver is not apparent to the owner of the vehicle at the time of entrustment, it must be affirmatively shown that the owner had at that time knowledge of facts and circumstances which established the incompetency of the driver.

The negligent entrustment rule is considered a harsh rule because it imposes liability on an owner for the negligence of a driver over whose conduct the owner is unable to exercise the slightest degree of supervision or control. Its application has, therefore, been held limited to situations where the owner had knowledge that the driver did not know how to drive, was physically or mentally incapable of operating a motor vehicle, was intoxicated or who had the habit of becoming intoxicated, or was a minor with a record of reckless driving.

In order for defendant American to be liable for negligent entrustment it would have to be established that defendant Scott belonged "to a class which is notoriously incompetent to use [cars] safely" and that his incompetency was the proximate cause of plaintiff's injury. None of the facts presented by plaintiff, even if known by American, would indicate that Scott belonged to a notoriously incompetent class. The fact that Scott was under the age of 21, or lacked adequate identification or credit does not reflect directly on his ability to operate a car competently. American would not be on notice by virtue of these facts that Scott was not a safe driver. Therefore, [the cause of action based on negligent entrustment] must be dismissed. ...

Consequently, this action is dismissed.

CASE QUESTION

1. Why was the car-rental company able to avoid liability in this case?

A similar issue arose in *Nielson v. Ono and Dollar Rent-A-Car*, 750 F.Supp. 439 (Hi. 1990). Here, too, the court held the rental company had not negligently entrusted the vehicle. Yoshiko Ono, a Japanese national with a valid Japanese driver's license, rented a car from the defendant, Dollar-Rent-A-Car. While driving the car, she lost control of it and struck the plaintiff's vehicle. The plaintiff sued Dollar, claiming it negligently entrusted the vehicle to Ono, arguing that Ono, as a foreign citizen, was presumably unfamiliar with local driving and traffic laws. The court rejected the plaintiff's claim and held for Dollar. In the opinion, the court identified the types of circumstances that constitute negligent entrustment. Said the court,

Plaintiff does not allege Ono was intoxicated or otherwise physically or mentally impaired when Dollar turned the car over to her. Additionally, there is no proof that she appeared unusually young or inexperienced. Finally, plaintiff has made no showing that Ono rented cars from Dollar on other occasions, thereby putting Dollar on notice of her alleged incompetence as a driver ... [F]oreign citizenship alone cannot constitute notice of a driver's incompetence.

Renting to a person under age 25, without more, does not constitute negligent entrustment.[39] Nor does negligent entrustment apply where a car-rental company had intended but failed to place the renter on a "Do Not Rent" list. The reason the company intended to restrict her rental privileges was that she had

---

[39] *Smith v. Hertz*, 722 So.2d 231 (Fl. 1998)

a record of returning cars late and not making timely rental payments. She was inadvertently permitted to rent and the car was in an accident. Since the late returns and nonpayment do not bear on competency to drive, renting the car to her did not constitute negligent entrustment.[40]

Rental of a Car Known to Be Defective

Another circumstance that can give rise to liability on the part of the car-rental company is knowingly renting a vehicle that has mechanical problems. In *Betancourt v. Manhattan Ford Lincoln Mercury, Inc.*, N.Y.L.J. Feb. 18, 1994, p.1, the plaintiff was forced to make an emergency stop on the side of a busy unlighted highway because the car he rented malfunctioned. While so situated, he was hit and killed by a passing truck. The rental company was aware at the time it rented the car to the plaintiff that it had a history of overheating and leaking engine coolant. The court refused to dismiss the case and instead referred it for a jury trial.

Unauthorized Drivers

A problem that car-rental companies often confront is use of the rented vehicle by unauthorized drivers. Authorized operators include the lessee and anyone else the rental company approves in writing. Everyone else is an unauthorized driver. Virtually all car-rental contracts include a provision forbidding operation of the rental car by an unauthorized driver, as well as a provision stating that insurance coverage applies only to authorized drivers. If a traveler rents a car and allows a friend to drive who has not been approved by the rental company, the friend is an unauthorized driver. If the friend is in an accident with the car, the rental company will not be liable for resulting injuries and the rental company's insurance will not cover the collision. The traveler who rented the car will be liable to the rental company for damage to the car. The traveler, in turn, may be able to recover from the friend. Travelers who rent cars can avoid these problems by ensuring the rental cars are driven only by authorized drivers.

In the following case, a question arose whether the driver was authorized. Take note of the court's unwillingness to interpret the contract to include an implied (unwritten) term that would allow as permissible drivers people who are not expressly authorized by the rental company but who are granted permission to drive by an authorized driver. Thus, a valet was not an authorized driver even though he parked a rental car with the permission of the authorized driver.

CASE EXAMPLE 13-13

Travelers v. Budget Rent-a-Car Systems, Inc. 901 F.2d 765 (9th Cir. 1990)

The facts are not in dispute. In October 1985, while vacationing on the island of Maui in Hawaii, Albert Mellon rented a car from Budget Rent-A-Car. The rental agreement stated that

---

[40] *Francis v. Crawford*, 732 So.2d 152 (La. 1999)

Budget would provide liability insurance for Mellon and any other authorized driver. Budget was self insured.

Several days after renting the car, Mellon and his wife drove to Mama's Fish House, a local restaurant of some renown. On arrival, Mellon turned the rental car over to Brent Jones, a valet parker in Mama's employ. The Mellons partook of piscine fare; Mr. Mellon had the mahi-mahi, Mrs. Mellon the shrimp.

After a satisfying dinner, Mellon dispatched Jones to retrieve the car. Jones drove the car to the restaurant entrance, where while still seated behind the wheel—he opened the passenger side door for Mrs. Mellon. As Mrs. Mellon stood beside the open door, Jones got out of the car. The car lurched backward. The open door struck Mrs. Mellon, dragged her along the ground and caused numerous injuries.

The Mellons filed suit against Mama's and Jones. That suit was settled when Travelers Insurance, Mama's insurer, tendered its full policy limit of $300,000. Budget, as owner and insurer of the car that struck Mrs. Mellon, also paid her $15,000 pursuant to Hawaii's no-fault insurance statute. Travelers then instituted the present suit seeking a declaration that Budget must also indemnify [reimburse] Travelers ... because the valet used the car with Mellon's permission.

... The district court held that, because Jones did not have Budget's permission to drive the car, he was not insured by Budget. Consequently, the court granted ... judgment in Budget's favor.

Travelers appeals. ...

To allow Travelers to recover from Budget on the basis of the rental agreement would require an act of interpretive legerdemain [trickery or magic]; the language of the contract could not be clearer. The rental agreement provides liability coverage "only for Renter and any Authorized Driver ... for bodily injury ... arising from use or operation of Vehicle as permitted by this Agreement." As to what is permitted by the agreement, it states explicitly that the:

> Vehicle shall not, under any circumstances, be used or operated by any person: (a) Other than Renter or any Authorized Driver which shall by definition include only the Additional Driver shown on the reverse side hereof, and any driver who is a member of Renter's immediate family, his employer, his employee, or his partner provided such driver has Renter's prior permission and is a qualified, licensed driver of at least 21 years of age, ...

Brent Jones is neither the Renter nor an Authorized Driver as provided by the rental agreement. Under the plain terms of the contract Budget provides no coverage for the accident at Mama's Fish House. ...

Travelers ... asks us to read into the rental agreement an implied term providing liability coverage to anyone who drove the car with Mellon's permission. The company points to cases from other jurisdictions that have found such an implied term. ...

For one thing, an implied term providing liability coverage to anyone other than the renter or an authorized driver would be directly contrary to the express language of the contract. It is elementary contract law that a court will only supply a term where the contract does not address the dispute between the parties. ... Where the language of a contract is clear and addresses the issue before the court, the court may not interpret the contract by supplying an implied term. ... The Budget-Mellon rental agreement is definite and unambiguous on this point; the contract excludes insurance coverage for the events at Mama's parking lot. There is no occasion to supply an implied term, and that should be the end of the matter as far as Hawaii contract law is concerned.

Travelers nonetheless points to cases from other jurisdictions ... According to these courts, car rental companies must expect that some renters will allow other people to drive the rental car in violation of the agreement. Therefore, the rental companies are deemed to have consented to the breach. ...

To recite such reasoning is to criticize it. The idea that a party may not rely on a contract term because the other side can be expected to violate it cuts at the very heart of contract law. Contracts enable parties to define their mutual rights and responsibilities; they are useful only insofar as each side can count on being able to hold the other to the terms of the agreement. If a contract provides anything at all, then, it is the reasonable expectation that the parties will fulfill their obligations, either voluntarily or under judicial compulsion. For a court to deny enforcement of a contract term because breach is foreseeable defeats the purpose of having a contract, effectively withdrawing that particular issue from regulation by mutual assent. ...

The rule Travelers advocates is also dangerous because it adds a heaping measure of uncertainty where certainty is essential. Insurance companies, like other commercial actors, need predictability; they write their contracts in precise language for that reason, and they calculate their premiums accordingly. When insurance contracts no longer mean what they say, it becomes exceedingly difficult to calculate risks. Insurance companies can predict with a fair degree of accuracy the risks involved when a car "may only be used or operated by an Authorized Driver." Just how many other risks will some court find foreseeable and inevitable? Increasing uncertainty through judicial meddling raises insurers' costs of doing business; inevitably those costs are passed on to customers. ... [Judgment for Budget] Affirmed.

CASE QUESTION

1. Why was the court so adamant in the penultimate paragraph not to read into the rental contract an implied provision that would extend coverage of the car-rental company's insurance to unauthorized drivers?

In another unauthorized-driver case, the 17-year-old brother of the car renter took the vehicle without permission. He was at the time intoxicated. He caused an accident that killed his passenger. The family sued the car-rental company claiming negligent entrustment. The court denied recovery on the grounds that the rental company did not entrust the car to the brother, and further the company could not foresee that the brother would gain access to the car or be in an intoxicated state.[41]

Age Discrimination with Car Rentals

Many car-rental companies have refused to rent a car to a person who is under age 25. The reasons given for the refusal are high accident rates and high insurance premiums for this age group. The law in some states upholds the right of a rental company to refuse to rent to people under 25.[42] The law in other states prevents car-rental companies from refusing to rent a car to someone who is at least 18 years of age, provided insurance coverage is available. Most such states provide that any additional insurance costs imposed because of the age of the driver can be passed on to the driver. While some car-rental companies continue to resist rentals to those under 25, a case in New York upheld the state law requiring rentals to customers who are at least 18.[43]

---

[41] *Fleming v. Enterprise Leasing Company*, 2001 WL 1090411 (Ill. 2001)

[42] *Lazar v. Hertz*, 82 Cal.Rptr.2d 368 (Ca. 1999)

[43] *People v. Alamo Rent A Car*, N.Y.L.J. 1 (N.Y. 1997)

Key Terms

agency
agent
credit card fraud
disclaimer
errors and omissions insurance
e-tickets
independent contractors

negligent entrustment
principal
Small Claims Court
tariff
travel insurance
Warsaw Convention

Summary

Airline travelers have certain rights when they travel, including the right to compensation, albeit limited, when an airline loses luggage the right to rerouting assistance from an airline when flights are canceled, and the right of handicapped travelers to access planes for transportation.

Travel agents must exercise reasonable care in making a client's travel arrangements and must not intentionally mislead. A travel agent may be liable for giving false or incomplete information and for failing to investigate third-party suppliers for financial viability and for suitability of facilities. A travel agent will not generally be liable for the negligence of third-party suppliers such as hotels, tour guides, and restaurants.

A tour operator is generally not liable for the negligence of a third-party provider over whom the operator has no supervisory control. A tour operator may be liable when third-party suppliers fail to provide promised accommodations.

Car-rental companies provide an important service to travelers. These companies are liable if they negligently entrust a car to a driver they know or should know is incompetent or if they rent a car they know or should know is not roadworthy. A car-rental company will not be liable for an accident caused by an unauthorized driver of the rented vehicle.

Preventive Law Tips for Managers

■ *If employed by an airline, regularly review your company's system of baggage control to minimize the number of suitcases that are misrouted.* Failure to deliver luggage to a passenger's destination breaches the airline's contract with the traveler to transport the luggage, as well as the passenger, to the destination. Although the law provides limited liability, thereby sparing airlines from the need to compensate passengers for the full value of their loss, reimbursement at the limited liability rates can be costly. Further, loss of passengers' luggage generates bad will and may cause loss of future business. Taking precautions to minimize the incidents of misrouted luggage will save the company from unnecessary lawsuits and liability.

■ *If employed by an airline, regularly review your company's baggage-check proce-dures to ensure compliance with the Warsaw Convention for international flights.* Lack of compliance can result in loss of limited liability. The Convention requires that the airlines do the following for international flights: (1) prepare a baggage check receipt in duplicate, giving the passenger one copy and retaining the other; and (2) include on the receipt the following information: place and date of issue, place of departure and destination, name and address of the carrier(s), the number of the passenger ticket, a statement that delivery of the suitcases will be made to the bearer of the baggage check, the number and weight of packages, the value of the contents, and a statement that trans-port of the luggage is subject to the rules relating to liability established by the Warsaw Convention.

■ *If employed by an airline, do not mislead passengers concerning the whereabouts of lost luggage.* Intentionally giving passengers false information about the whereabouts of their suitcases can lead to loss of limited liability. Be truthful and accommodating when passengers inquire about misplaced baggage.

■ *If employed by an airline, be sure your company's rules and facilities for transporting pets protect the well-being of the animal.* An airline may be liable for injury to pets in flight. While critters are considered the equivalent of baggage for airline liability purposes, thus entitling the airlines to limited liability, animals have needs that suitcases do not. Those needs should be met to the fullest extent possible.

■ *If a flight is canceled, the airline should offer assistance to passengers in making alternate arrangements.* The law recognizes that bad weather and other circumstances can present safety issues for air travel, and the airline will not be liable for breach of contract where circumstances dictate cancelation of a flight. However, the law also recognizes that passengers' travel plans will be disrupted by the cancelation and so imposes on the airlines a duty to aid passengers in locating alternate flights. Failure to assist displaced passengers can lead to liability.

■ *If employed by an airline or as a travel agent, accord handicapped patrons the rights provided under the Americans with Disabilities Act and the Air Carrier Access Act.* These Acts generally require that handicapped persons be given access to places of public accommodation, including travel agents' offices and air transportation. The law also requires that airlines make necessary accom-modations for disabled passengers, provided they are able to travel without presenting a risk to themselves or others.

■ *In the event of overbooking, the airline should offer assistance to passengers in making alternate arrangements to reach their destinations.* The law recognizes that overbooking will occur on occasion as a result of the airlines' attempts to run their business as efficiently as possible. To avoid liability to bumped passengers, the airlines should assist them in finding alternate transporta-tion. Also, when determining who to bump, the airline should follow its priority rules and tariffs.

- *If engaged as a travel agent, double-check the times of your clients' flights and give them accurate information.* If a travel agent gives incorrect information about the times of a flight or fails to update a client about a change in departure time, the travel agent may be liable for the clients' inconvenience and costs for alternate travel. Diligence in verifying information can avoid this problem.

- *If engaged as a travel agent, do not misrepresent a client's status on a flight.* If a travel agent informs a client that he has a confirmed seat, when in fact the client is on the waiting list, the travel agent may be liable for inconvenience and the added expense caused to the client by the misrepresentation. The travel agent should always give the client only truthful information.

- *If engaged as a travel agent, investigate thoroughly any travel wholesaler you recommend to a client.* A travel agent may be liable to clients for the failure of a travel wholesaler to provide the intended trip if the agent did not adequately investigate the wholesaler. The agent may also be liable to the client on breach of contract theory when the wholesaler fails to perform in whole or part. Although in such cases the travel agent may be able to obtain compensation from the wholesaler, bad will is generated by the unhappy clients. Further, if the wholesaler has gone out of business, compensation may not be obtainable. A thorough check into the wholesaler's business operations, experience, financial status, and past tours can help ensure reliability by the wholesaler and freedom from liability for the travel agent.

- *If engaged as a travel agent, investigate thoroughly any travel services you recommend to a client.* A travel agent may be liable to clients for the nonperformance or substandard performance of any travel service or accommodation recommended by the agent. Before recommending a hotel, bus, train, limousine service, sightseeing tour, or other service, the agent should familiarize himself with the company's services and reliability to ensure they are suitable for the client.

- *If employed in the car-rental business, regularly review your procedures to ensure the number of unfilled reservations is kept to a minimum.* When a car-rental company overbooks its fleet and is unable to accommodate customers with reservations, it is in breach of contract and liability will follow. To minimize this occurrence, frequent review of procedures should be undertaken.

- *If employed in the car-rental business, do not rent a car to someone who is obviously incompetent to drive.* A car-rental company will be liable for negligent entrustment where it rents a car to someone who obviously is incapable of driving lawfully. The car-rental company should require a valid driver's license. If the would-be renter appears intoxicated or high on drugs, the rental company should investigate further. If it rents to someone it should have known was not qualified and that person is in an accident with the car, the rental company may be liable for resulting injuries.

- *If employed in the car-rental business, inspect your fleet of cars regularly for mechanical problems.* If a car develops a mechanical problem, remove it from service until the matter is fully repaired. A car-rental company that rents a vehicle known to contain mechanical problems may be liable if an accident results. To avoid this liability, inspect the cars regularly and repair any problems found to exist.

Review Questions

1. Name the four groups that compose the travel industry.

2. What differentiates Small Claims Court from other courts?

3. If an agent acts with authority for a principal, who is legally bound by the acts of the agent?

4. What is the difference between an agent and an independent contractor?

5. What is a tariff?

6. What is an airline's responsibility when it takes custody of a passenger's luggage?

7. What should be included on the baggage check an airline gives to a client on an international flight?

8. What treaty binds the United States and other countries on matters involving international plane flights?

9. Why should a travel agent be familiar with the places he recommends?

10. What is a disclaimer and how do the courts treat them?

11. What obligation, if any, does an airline have to passengers when it cancels a flight due to bad weather?

12. Under what circumstances can a pilot remove a person from a plane and refuse to provide her transportation?

13. What is the consequence of a person representing himself as an authorized agent when in fact the "agent" has not been authorized by the principal to act?

14. What is errors and omissions insurance?

15. What laws protect the rights of disabled passengers?

16. What is negligent entrustment?

Discussion Questions

1. How does Small Claims Court increase the potential liability of the travel industry?

2. How does one distinguish between an agent and an independent contractor?

3. Why does the Warsaw Convention require that a passenger have notice of its provisions?

4. A travel agent has made arrangements through a travel wholesaler for a client's tour. The wholesaler fails to make hotel reservations and as a result the client must stay in an inferior hotel. Is the travel agent liable? Why or why not?

5. How might airport security checks be modified to ensure that passengers and their carry-on luggage do not become separated?

6. Identify at least five enhanced safety precautions airlines have recently adopted.

Application Questions

1. Theresa is a pilot for ABC Airlines. Does either Theresa or the airline qualify as a principal or an agent? If so, which qualifies as which? Why?

2. Melanie contracted with a travel agent for the purchase of a charter trip to England. The travel agent made the necessary arrangements with the charter company and recommended a one-day side trip, which the client agreed to purchase. While the client was on the side trip, she was injured because a step on the company's bus was rusted. Further, the airline over-booked the client's return flight, which resulted in a two-day delay in the client's arrival home. What potential liability, if any, does the travel agent have in these circumstances?

3. Salvatore had confirmed reservations on a flight from New York City to Boston. The airline overbooked the flight. How should the airline determine whether or not Salvatore will get bumped? Why should it use that method?

4. Tyrone was struck by a car while rollerblading on the sidewalk. The car was a rental car. Under what theory might Tyrone attempt to hold the car-rental company liable for his injuries? What would he need to prove to establish his case? How could he prove that?

5. Ariel and Jeremy were passengers on a plane that was about to take off. They were loud and rowdy, and were overheard to say "This is the big one." Passengers in adjoining rows became alarmed and summoned the flight attendant. She asked Ariel and Jeremy to settle down and they became angry and more boisterous. What rights do the attendant and the pilot have in this circumstance? Why?

Web Sites

Web sites that will enhance your understanding of the material in this chapter include:

http://www.faa.gov This is the official site of the Federal Aviation Administration. Topics covered include general aviation safety, cabin safety, and security tips for air travelers.

http://www.wld.com This site offers information on many legal topics, including various airline issues.

http://www.restaurant.org This is the site of the National Restaurant Association, a trade organization for restaurant owners and managers. One of the issues addressed on the site is class action reform.

http://www.ftc.gov/bcp/conline/pubs/tmarkg/trvlfrd.htm This site contains information about telemarketing travel fraud. ("Hello. You have been specially selected to receive our SPECTACULAR LUXURY DREAM VACATION offer.")

CHAPTER 14

■

Employment

INTRODUCTION

The employer-employee relationship is fertile ground for lawsuits against the employer. These cases seek to enforce employment laws and can take one of two forms, either a lawsuit by the employee against an employer or an action brought by the government.

Employment law is far-reaching and affects employees' wages; prohibits discrimination on the grounds of race, religion, color, national origin, gender, pregnancy, age, and disability; and requires the employer to verify worker eligibility for employment in the United States. We will study each of these topics in this chapter.

Fair Labor Standards Act

The **Fair Labor Standards Act (FLSA)** is a federal law adopted in 1938 to eliminate unfair methods of compensation and labor conditions injurious to the health and efficiency of workers. It mandates minimum wages, one-and-one-half pay for overtime work, equal pay for equal work, and restrictions on child labor. The Act has been amended and updated numerous times since its original passage.

Minimum Wage

The FLSA requires that, with few exceptions, employers involved in interstate commerce pay employees at least the minimum wage set by Congress. The minimum wage is increased from time to time as Congress sees fit. As of June, 2003, the minimum wage is $5.15 an hour. States may specify a minimum wage higher than Congress. If so, employers in those states must pay the higher amount set by the state.

Low Sales Exception to Minimum-Wage Requirement

Excepted from the minimum-wage requirement are employers with less than $500,000 in annual sales. In the following case, the court had to decide whether a hotel and adjacent restaurant were two separate businesses, each of which fell below the threshold amount for FLSA coverage (then $362,500 in annual sales), or one business subject to the Act.

CASE EXAMPLE 14-1

Brock v. Best Western Sundown Motel, Inc.
883 F.2d 51 (8th Cir. 1989)

Ronald and Beverly Halling appeal the District Court's determination that their motel and restaurant business violated the minimum wage provisions of the Fair Labor Standards Act (FLSA). The Hallings do not dispute that their business has paid some of its employees less than the federal minimum wage, and has failed to pay the required overtime premium of one and one-half times the federal minimum wage for work in excess of 40 hours a week. The only issue in dispute is whether the Hallings' business is exempt from the provisions of the FLSA.

Ronald Halling owns the Best Western Sundown Motel, which generates an approximate annual sales volume of $265,000. Beverly Halling owns an adjoining restaurant, Grandmother's House, which generates an approximate annual sales volume of $190,000. If the motel and the restaurant are taken to be separate enterprises, both would be exempt from the operation of the FLSA, in that both have an annual sales volume of less than $362,500, the minimum required for application of the FLSA. The Secretary of Labor contends that the motel and restaurant form a single enterprise (with a total income over the $362,500 threshold) ... in that they are related activities performed through unified operation and common control for a common business purpose.

The District Court held for the Secretary. The Court found that the motel and restaurant are physically connected, that each business operates without regular payment of rent on property owned jointly by the Hallings, and that the establishments share a telephone, laundry facilities, and advertising. The Court further found that Ronald often did work in the restaurant and once signed the restaurant's income-tax return, while Beverly frequently did work at the motel. The Court also found the Hallings jointly hired a couple to manage the motel and restaurant together. ...

The Hallings' arguments generally dispute the District Court's interpretation and construction of testimony, but they provide [no basis to conclude] that the District Court committed error. On the facts found by the District Court, we have little trouble affirming its legal conclusion that the Hallings' motel and restaurant constitute a single enterprise under the FLSA. ... [T]he Hallings' establishments are clearly under the common control of the same owners, with substantially overlapping operations. ... [Thus the income of the two businesses should be considered together for purposes of determining whether the business is subject to the Fair Labor Standards Act.]

Affirmed.

If the two businesses are not in close proximity, but rather separated by several miles, the outcome is different. A case involved two ski resorts separated by six miles. The two resorts had a common owner, marketed their operations as one enterprise, and shared accounting, management, and other personnel. Said the court, "Common ownership and a close functional and economic relationship between physically separated units of a business are not sufficient to make such combined units a single establishment, particularly where, as here, the geographic separation is substantial."[1]

Tips Exception to Minimum-Wage Requirement

Another exception to the minimum-wage requirement applies to employees who routinely receive at least $30 per month in tips on the job. For those employees, an employer can credit a percentage of the tips against the hourly minimum-wage requirement. As of June, 2003, up to 59 percent of the minimum wage can be replaced by tips. For example, a restaurant owner could pay a waiter $2.13 (41 percent of the minimum wage) rather than $5.15 an hour. However, the credit cannot exceed the tips actually received by the employee. Thus, for the restaurant to take advantage of the tip credit and pay the waiter only $2.13 per hour, the waiter must receive a minimum of $3.02 per hour in tips. In those states that have adopted higher minimum-wage laws, the amount the employer will have to pay after applying the tip credit will be higher. Under federal law, tip pooling among tipped employees, including wait personnel, counter help, bus help, and bartenders is permitted for purposes of the employer utilizing the tip credit to reduce an employee's pay below minimum wage. Several states have passed laws that prohibit employers from reducing an employee's pay based on tip pooling.

---

[1] *Chessin v. Keystone Resort Management, Inc.*, 184 F.3d 1188 (Co. 1999)

Training Wage Exception to Minimum-Wage Requirement

An employer can pay a specified training wage below minimum wage to a limited class of employees. The training wage is 85 percent of the federal $5.15 per hour minimum wage, which as of June, 2003 is $4.38 per hour. The application of this exception is limited. The only employees to whom this wage applies are workers between the ages of 16 and 19 who are entering the workforce for the first time. The employer can pay the training wage in lieu of minimum wage for a maximum of 90 days. Thereafter, the employer must pay minimum wage. Employers are prohibited from displacing employees to hire young people at the training wage.

Overtime Pay

The FLSA requires that certain employees who are paid on an hourly basis and who work more than 40 hours in one week be paid at least one-and-one-half times their regular pay for the hours in excess of 40. For example, if a receptionist at a restaurant is paid $6 per hour and works 45 hours in one week, the employer must pay $9 per hour for the last 5 of those hours.

Exempt Employees

The statute contains an exemption to the overtime and minimum-wage requirements for executive, administrative, and professional employees. Employers often seek to avoid overtime pay for employees believed to be within the exempt categories. Employees denied overtime pay may contest their classification. A discussion of the exemptions follow. Two general rules apply: (1) to qualify, an employee must pass a salary test and a duties test, and (2) employees paid an hourly wage are nonexempt regardless of their duties.

Executive Employees

To qualify for the executive exemption, the employee must meet a duties test and a salary test. To qualify as an executive, the employee's duties must include managing the business or part of it and regularly directing the work of two or more employees. In addition, the employee must either: (a) be paid a salary (as opposed to an hourly wage) of at least $250 per week, or (b) have the authority to hire, fire, or promote and be paid a salary of at least $155 per week.

The issue of whether an employee's job responsibilities satisfy the executive employee test is not strictly a question of how much time is allocated to managerial duties as opposed to other tasks. Rather, the court will also evaluate such factors as the importance of the managerial duties as opposed to other responsibilities, the frequency with which the employee exercises discretion, and his relative freedom from supervision.

A chain restaurant claimed its lowest-level manager, whose job title was Associate Manager, was an executive position and therefore exempt from overtime pay. The job, an entry-level position, included work that regular crew members do (preparing pizzas, salads, and other food, running the cash register, waiting on customers, cleaning), tasks described by the company as "learning by doing," and studying company manuals to prepare for management tests. Associate Managers perform little or no supervision of other employees, are not in charge of a restaurant, and do not supervise shifts. Not surprisingly, the court held that the position of Associate Manager was not an executive position.[2]

Concerning the salary test, for an employee to qualify for the exemption from minimum and overtime pay, his compensation must be a predetermined amount and cannot be based on the number of hours worked. The amount of pay must not be reduced for variations in the quantity or quality of work performed. Thus, a salaried employee is not exempt from overtime pay if his pay is reduced when he works fewer hours than anticipated or when his work product does not meet expectations.[3]

Administrative and Professional Employees

In addition to executive employees, also exempt from the overtime and minimum-wage requirements of the FLSA are administrative and professional employees. To qualify as administrative employees, workers must generally exhibit discretion and independent judgment, spend at least 50 percent of their time at work on office or nonmanual work relating to management policies or general business operations, and earn a salary of at least $250 per week. The test for professionals is similar, except the 50 percent criteria applies to performing work requiring specialized study. The duties and salary tests also apply to these employees.

Miscellaneous Exemption

Another category of employees is exempt from the overtime provisions, but not the minimum-wage requirement. Often called the "miscellaneous exemption," this grouping includes seasonal workers, camp employees, domestic workers, movie-theater workers, agricultural employees, taxi drivers, and amusement workers.

Time Worked

The FLSA identifies what constitutes time worked for purposes of determining the number of hours for which an employee is entitled to hourly pay and for determining whether an employee has worked overtime. In addition to time spent on job-related tasks, the following are counted as time worked: coffee and snack breaks; meetings to discuss daily operations problems; rest periods of 20 minutes or less; travel from job site to job site or to customers; required training; and clearing a cash register or totaling receipts after regular work hours.

An employer is legally obligated to pay employees for the time they work. Likewise, an employer is not required to pay for time the employee does not

---

[2] *Dole v. Papa Gino's of America, Inc.*, 712 F.Supp. 1038 (Mass. 1989)

[3] *Martin v. Malcolm Pirnie, Inc.*, 949 F.2d 611 (N.Y. 1991)

work. Therefore, an employee with a split shift (for example, a server who works lunch and dinner with a few hours off in the middle of the afternoon) is entitled to payment only for the hours worked and not for the hours off in the middle of the split shift. Similarly, if an employee is sent home partway through a shift because of lack of work, the employee is not entitled to payment for the time he did not work.

Equal Pay for Equal Work

A 1963 amendment to the FLSA, called the Equal Pay Act (EPA), requires that men and women who do the same job, or jobs that require equal skill, effort, and responsibility, be paid the same or according to the same pay schedule, a practice known as **equal pay for equal work**. An issue that often arises is whether jobs are the same. The test is whether they have a "common core" of tasks; or, stated otherwise, whether "a significant portion" of the two jobs is identical. In one case, the court found two jobs to be substantially equal even though one but not the other required some travel and minor additional responsibilities.[4] While the Act protects both men and women, most lawsuits invoking the EPA have involved situations where a woman was paid less than a man.

Comparable Worth

The EPA applies only when two people are doing the same job, or jobs that require the same skills and responsibility. Sometimes men and women work at jobs that are quite different and one is paid more than the other, yet the value of their work to the employer is more or less equal. **Comparable worth** refers to jobs requiring different skills and responsibilities that have equal value to the employer. Courts have rejected the argument that comparable worth requires equal pay. If adopted, courts would be required to evaluate the worth of different jobs and rank them according to their relative values, something courts seem ill-equipped and unwilling to do. Advocates of equal pay for jobs of comparable worth argue that the concept would address the undervaluation of jobs traditionally associated with women, a circumstance that is not addressed by the EPA.

In 1989, comparable worth was again rejected in *International Union v. Michigan*, 886 F.2d 766 (6th Cir. 1989). In that case, the employer (the State of Michigan) had done its own market studies and was aware of wage disparities in its pay system between jobs predominantly filled by males and different jobs of comparable worth filled by females. The plaintiffs, female state employees, claimed that by perpetuating such a system the employer discriminated against female workers. In denying the plaintiffs' claims, the court stated,

[Laws prohibiting unequal pay are] not a substitute for the free market, which historically determines labor rates. ... Mere failure to rectify traditional wage disparities that exist in the marketplace between predominantly male and predominantly female jobs is not actionable.

---

[4] *Fallon v. Illinois*, 882 F.2d 1206 (Ill. 1989)

Given this precedent, few comparable-worth cases have been brought since 1989.

Retaliatory Discharge

If an employee believes she is being paid unfairly and complains or commences a lawsuit under the FLSA, the employer is often irritated and sometimes antagonistic toward her. The EPA addresses this circumstance by prohibiting an employer from discharging or otherwise discriminating against such an employee.[5] Thus, where a restaurant discharged a manager for complaining about the restaurant's break policy and nonpayment of overtime compensation, the discharge was retaliatory and violated the FLSA. The court awarded the terminated manager in excess of $52,000 for unpaid overtime, back pay, and other compensatory damages.[6]

Restrictions on Child Labor

Many employees in hotels and restaurants are young, often high-school or even junior-high students. The FLSA provides a minimum age for employees, restricts the number of hours younger employees can work, and limits the tasks they can perform. The goal of the Act is to provide young people with non-hazardous working conditions and hours that do not interfere with their schooling or health.

The minimum work age is 14; an employer cannot legally hire a person younger than that. During the school year, an employee who is 14 or 15 cannot work more than 18 hours a week and not more than 3 hours on a school day. During the school year, these employees cannot begin work earlier than 7:00 A.M. or end later than 7:00 P.M. During vacation, that same employee can work up to 8 hours a day and cannot exceed 40 hours a week. The workday cannot begin earlier than 7:00 A.M. or end later than 9:00 P.M. No federal law restricts the number of hours a 16- or 17-year-old can work.

Some states have additional, stricter rules that further limit the hours young people can work. For example, in New York, 16- and 17-year-olds are limited to 4 hours of work per day except for Fridays, Saturdays, and Sundays when they can work 8 hours. The maximum number of hours a week they can work while school is in session is 28, and if the employer wants them to work beyond 10:00 P.M., parental permission is necessary, as is verification from the school that the employee's academic standing is satisfactory.

The federal law as well as some state laws limit the types of work young employees can do. These limitations are intended to protect young people's safety. For example, under the FLSA a worker under the age of 18 cannot operate meat grinders, meat-slicing machines, meat and bone cutting saws, or power-driven knives used for meat processing. Also prohibited are dough mixers, batter mixers,

[5] 29 U.S.C. § 215(a)(3)

[6] *Brown v. Pizza Hut of America, Inc.,* 113 F.3d 1245 (Ok. 1997)

bread-slicing and wrapping machines, and cake-cutting band saws. The young worker is also barred from driving a motor vehicle on the job and delivering messages, food, or other goods (room service) between the hours of 10:00 P.M. and 5:00 A.M. As an example of a related state law, an employee in New York under age 16 cannot operate a slicing machine or paint the exterior of a building.

Enforcement of the FLSA

An employee whose rights under the FLSA have been violated has two options in pursuing the case: (1) file a claim with the Wage and Hour Division of the United States Department of Labor, an agency charged with overseeing enforcement of laws that protect employees; or, (2) commence a lawsuit against the employer seeking damages and attorney fees. If the employer's actions are willful, the employer can be criminally prosecuted by the United States Justice Department, a branch of government charged with prosecuting federal crimes. Penalties include fines and jail.

The maximum fine for violations of the child labor provisions is $10,000 for each employee who was the subject of a violation. The same fine applies to retaliatory discharges. Employers who willfully or repeatedly violate the minimum-wage or overtime pay provisions may be required to compensate the wronged employee for twice the amount of unpaid back pay, plus attorney's fees and court costs, and are subject to a civil penalty of up to $1,000 for each violation.

Family and Medical Leave Act

The Family and Medical Leave Act (FMLA) addresses a problem that employees often face—obtaining time off from work to care for sick children or other family members. The FMLA, effective in 1993, entitles eligible employees to take up to 12 weeks of unpaid leave per year for childbirth, adoption, foster placement, or to care for a child, spouse, or parent who has a serious health condition, or for the employee's own serious health situation. To be eligible, an employee must have been employed for at least 12 months before the leave commences and have worked at least 1,250 hours during the 12-month period prior to the leave. Employers covered by the FMLA are those who carry on their payroll 50 or more employees for each working day for each of 20 or more weeks in the year.

Upon returning from the leave, an employee must be reinstated to the position held before the leave or to a comparable position with equivalent pay, benefits, and other terms of employment.

At-Will Employment

In many states, employment arrangements between employers and employees are considered "at-will." **At-will employment** means the employment contract between an employer and an employee is indefinite in duration and can be terminated by either party for any reason or no reason at any time without liability.

If, however, a written employment contract exists between the employer and employee, and if the contract contains a provision stating that an employment arrangement will exist for a specified period of time, early termination can result in liability. In *Parker v. John Q. Hammons Hotels, Inc.*, 914 F.Supp. 467 (N.M. 1994), a management trainee was terminated for making a profane statement to a fellow employee and for other misconduct. He sued the hotel claiming breach of his employment contract. That contract did not contain a provision stating his employment would last for a specific time period. The court held that the employment relationship was at-will, enabling the hotel to terminate it at any time without obligation to the trainee. His lawsuit was thus dismissed.

Illegal Job Discrimination

Notwithstanding an employer's right to terminate an employment contract based on the at-will doctrine, an employer cannot discriminate against workers on the basis of race, skin color, religion, gender, national origin, disability, age if the employee is at least 40 years old, or pregnancy. These categories are called **protected classes**. In some locales, discrimination on the basis of sexual orientation is likewise illegal.

Discrimination in employment is the basis for many lawsuits. These cases are based on the Civil Rights Act of 1964, the Civil Rights Act of 1991, and the Americans with Disabilities Act, all of which have enhanced employees' rights. These lawsuits underscore the need to treat all employees and applicants fairly.

Other statutes we will study in this chapter also prohibit discrimination. For example, just as discrimination against people with disabilities is prohibited by the Americans with Disabilities Act, and discrimination against United States citizens employed abroad by United States companies is prohibited by the Civil Rights Act of 1991, so too is discrimination on the basis of age prohibited by the Age Discrimination in Employment Act. The referenced acts are federal laws. State statutes prohibit discrimination on grounds similar to the federal statutes. Many encompass additional protected classes including martial status, arrest and conviction record, and in some locales, sexual orientation.

Title VII of The Civil Rights Act of 1964

The statute that outlaws most grounds for discrimination is Title VII of the federal Civil Rights Act of 1964. It reads, in relevant part, as follows:

> It shall be an unlawful employment practice for an employer (1) to fail or refuse to hire or to discharge any individual or otherwise discriminate against any individual with respect to his compensation, terms, conditions, or privileges of employment, because of such individual's race, color, religion, sex, or national origin.[7]

---

[7] 42 U.S.C. § 2000e-2(a)

For example, a restaurant violates Title VII by hiring only males as wait personnel and refusing to hire females, as would a hotel that refuses to hire anyone who is Norwegian or any other specific nationality. Often acts of discrimination are not as obvious as these examples. Instead, the discrimination can be very subtle and therefore difficult to detect as well as prove. Title VII outlaws both **disparate treatment** discrimination, which is intentional discrimination based on considerations of race, color, religion, gender or national origin, as well as **disparate impact** discrimination, which involves neutral practices that result, often unintentionally, in unequal treatment. For example, an employer's no-beard policy was found to discriminate against black males because they suffer in substantially greater numbers than white males from a skin disorder that makes shaving difficult. In enforcing the no-beard policy, the employer had not intended to restrict employment opportunities for black males, but the effect of the rule was to do exactly that.[8]

Title VII covers employers with 20 or more employees. It created the **Equal Employment Opportunity Commission (EEOC),** a federal government agency that is charged with enforcing Title VII's mandates.

Filing a Complaint

Before a Title VII action can be brought in federal court, a discrimination charge must be filed with the EEOC, which has regional offices throughout the country. The reason for the requirement of initial recourse to the EEOC is Congress' intention that the principal administrative mechanism to resolve employment discrimination claims is that agency. The EEOC has specific rules and procedures for filing and strict time limits within which cases must be pursued. Generally, an employee must file a claim with the agency within 180 days after the alleged discriminatory act. Thereafter, an EEOC staff attorney or investigator will meet with the employee and make an initial assessment of whether the case is justified and should proceed. If the EEOC determines there is no reasonable basis to believe the charges are true, the agency will decline to pursue the claim. The employee can nonetheless proceed with a lawsuit in court against the employer. If the EEOC finds grounds to prosecute the claim, it will prepare a complaint, forward it to the employer, and then meet with the employer in an effort to reach a resolution.

Due to a large caseload, the EEOC has a sizeable backlog and cannot fully pursue every claim. If the agency fails to act on a claim within 180 days of filing, the employee can request a right-to-sue letter authorizing the worker to file a lawsuit in federal court against the employer notwithstanding inaction by the EEOC. Once the employee receives a right-to-sue letter, he has only 90 days to file the lawsuit.

---

[8]*Bradley v Domino's Pizza*, 939 F.2d 610 (Neb. 1991)

Remedies

The remedies available to a successful plaintiff in a Title VII case are substantial and were recently expanded. Until 1991, the remedies were limited to the following:

- An injunction, which is a court order precluding the employer from continuing the offending conduct
- A court order requiring the employer to adopt a policy forbidding discrimination and mandating implementation of the policy
- Attorney's fees, thereby relieving the plaintiff of this substantial expense
- Back pay where the plaintiff suffered a loss of income due to the discrimination.

Back pay refers to the difference between (a) the amount of money the plaintiff would have earned in the absence of discrimination, which might include increased salary that would have accompanied a promotion that he was denied or salary that was lost due to wrongful termination, and (b) the amount of money the plaintiff earned as the victim of discrimination. This might include his salary without the raise he should have received, or pay earned in alternate employment, or if the plaintiff did not seek another job, what he could reasonably have earned had he looked for employment.

Prior to 1991, compensatory and punitive damages were available in discrimination cases only for plaintiffs who could prove *intentional* job discrimination based on race or skin color. Compensatory damages include in addition to back pay, future monetary losses, emotional pain and suffering, mental anguish, and other nonmonetary losses.

The categories of plaintiffs to whom a judge can award compensatory or punitive damages in a Title VII case was greatly expanded by the Civil Rights Act of 1991, although intentional discrimination remains a prerequisite, (as opposed to disparate impact). The Act authorizes compensatory and punitive damages as a remedy for plaintiffs seeking redress, not only from intentional discrimination based on race or skin color, but also those victimized by intentional discrimination based on gender, religion, and national origin. Note that age discrimination is not included; a plaintiff in such a case is still not entitled to compensatory or punitive damages.

Plaintiffs in cases involving intentional discrimination on the basis of race and skin color can collect unlimited damages. The Civil Rights Act of 1991 places a cap on the amount an employer will be obligated to pay (exclusive of back pay) in any one suit involving gender, religion, or national origin. The amount is based on the number of employees an employer has. For employers with 15 to 100 employees, the maximum is $50,000; for those with 101 to 200 employees, $100,000; 201 to 500, $200,000; and for those with more than 500, the maximum is $300,000. These caps do not apply to back pay awards; those are limited only by the amount of pay lost.

Punitive damages can be awarded only in those circumstances in which the employee can show that the employer engaged in illegal discrimination "with malice or with reckless indifference to the federally protected rights" of the employee.

Expert Witness Fees

Another remedy authorized by the Civil Rights Act of 1991 is compensation for expert witness fees. This is an important addition because most discrimination cases require one or more expert witnesses, such as a specialist on gender stereotyping in a gender discrimination case. Each expert witness must spend time reviewing the case, researching particular issues, preparing for trial with the plaintiff's attorney, and testifying. As a result, their fees are typically quite high.

Defense of Bona Fide Occupational Qualification

A **bona fide occupational qualification** (BFOQ) relieves an employer from liability for disparate treatment (intentional) discrimination where selection of an employee based on gender, religion, age, or national origin is reasonably necessary for the normal operation of the employer's business. This defense is construed narrowly by the courts. To qualify, two elements are necessary: (1) the job in issue must require a worker of a particular gender, religion, age, or national origin; and (2) such requirement must be necessary to the essence of the business' operation. An example of a BFOQ is hiring only women to model women's makeup or women's bathing suits.

Another example of a BFOQ is a rule promulgated by the Federal Aviation Administration that requires pilots who reach age 60 to retire. In an age discrimination lawsuit brought by a 60-year-old pilot who wished to continue flying for Federal Express, the court determined that, "At some age everyone reaches a level of infirmity or unreliability that is unacceptable in a pilot in air transportation. That age will vary from person to person but cannot yet be predicted in a specific individual." The court thus determined that being 60 or younger was a BFOQ for pilots and did not constitute discrimination based on age.[9] In a job where safety is not as significant an issue, as with pilots, a mandatory retirement age of 60 does not constitute a BFOQ and will likely constitute illegal discrimination. See, for example, *EEOC v. Johnson & Higgins*, 887 F.Supp. 682 (N.Y. 1995), in which a mandatory retirement age of 62 for directors of an employee-benefits consulting firm was found to constitute age discrimination and not to qualify as a BFOQ.

Note that BFOQ is *not* a defense to a claim of racial discrimination.

Defense of Business Necessity

Business necessity may relieve an employer of liability for disparate impact (unintentional) discrimination. If a neutral selection criterion has a disparate impact on a protected class, but constitutes a business necessity, the requirement will not violate the Civil Rights Act of 1964. **Business necessity** means that the criterion has an obvious relationship to job performance. An example of a business necessity is speaking fluent English for a person with a job requiring communication with English-speaking people. Some job applicants from countries other than the

---

[9]*Coupe v. Federal Express Corporation*, 121 F.3d 1022 (Tenn. 1997)

United States may not meet this job requirement. They can for that reason be excluded from consideration. Like BFOQs, business necessity is defined narrowly, thereby minimizing the number of potential employees who can be eliminated from consideration.

Prohibited and Permitted Interview Questions

To help ensure that employers do not discriminate against protected classes in the hiring process, the law bars employers from asking certain questions at employment interviews. Permissible questions relate to the job the candidate is seeking. Prohibited questions seek information relating to a candidate's potential membership in a protected class. The ban applies to all aspects of the hiring process, including the application form, the interview, and questions contained in any testing materials the employer may utilize.

Prohibited Questions

National Origin
What is your nationality?
What country are you from?
What is your native language?
Your name is unusual. Where is it from?
Citizenship
Are you a United States citizen?
Where are you a citizen?
Age
How old are you?
What is your date of birth?
When did you graduate high school?
Marital Status
Are you married? Engaged? Divorced?
With whom do you live?
Children
Are you using birth control?
Are you pregnant?
Do you plan to have a family? If so, when?
Do you have children? How many?
What childcare arrangements have you made?
Religion
What religion do you practice?
Disabilities or Medical Conditions
Do you have any disabilities?
Have you ever been hospitalized?

Have you had a major illness in the last five years?

How many days were you absent from work because of illness last year?

Have you ever been treated for a mental condition?

Are you taking any prescribed medication?

Have you ever been treated for drug addiction or alcoholism?

(If a person is blind) When did you lose your eyesight? How?

Arrest Record

Have you ever been arrested?

Permissible Questions

National Origin/Citizenship

Are you authorized to work in the United States?

Age

Can you meet the minimum age requirements for this job as set by law?

Are you over the age of 18?

Marital Status

Would you be willing to relocate?

Would you be willing to travel as needed for the job?

Would you be willing to work overtime if necessary?

Religion

We often work holidays and weekends. Is there anything that would prevent you from doing so?

Disability

Are you able to lift a 50-pound weight and carry it 100 yards, which is required by this job?

Are you able to perform the essential functions of the job? (This question assumes the interviewer has thoroughly described the job.)

Can you demonstrate how you would perform the following job-related functions: ...?

Arrest Record

Have you been convicted of any of the following crimes? (The crimes listed must be reasonably related to the job.)

Race

As we have seen, race is one of the grounds on which Title VII outlaws discrimination. The statute's main objective concerning race was to eliminate discrimination against blacks. Sadly, racism pervaded our society and mandated this remedial legislation. Its application, however, is not restricted to any one racial or minority group. In the words of the United States Supreme Court, the prohibition against discrimination in employment on the basis of race bars "discriminatory preference for any racial group, minority or majority." Additional examples of racial groups include Caucasian, Hispanic, Asian, Native American, and Eskimo.

The outlawed discrimination includes not only refusals to hire, resistance to promote, and unjustified firings, but also all other types of discrimination, such as refusal to allow an employee to wear an Afro-American hairstyle and terminating a white employee for associating with a black colleague.

An interesting application of Title VII is found in *Vaughn v. Texaco*, 918 F.2d 517 (5th Cir. 1990). The plaintiff was a black attorney. Her supervisor, while unhappy with her work, was advised by the department manager not to relay his dissatisfaction to her but rather to "let it ride" to avoid charges of racial discrimination. The plaintiff thereby missed the opportunity to improve her performance through constructive criticism and counseling from her supervisor. The plaintiff was terminated when the department manager, in a cost-cutting effort, was forced to terminate the two lowest-rated employees. The court held that the employer's failure to provide feedback and develop the plaintiff was motivated by race and violated Title VII.

An employer can defend against a claim of discriminatory firing by establishing a legitimate, nondiscriminatory reason for the termination. A charge of discrimination made by a caucasian dining-room supervisor was dismissed in the following case because the employer could establish misconduct on the employee's part, thus justifying the termination.

CASE EXAMPLE 14-2

Singh v. Shoney's, Inc.
64 F.3d 217 (5th Cir. 1995)

Delores Singh (Singh) filed a complaint against her former employer Shoney's, Inc. (Shoney's), alleging that she was fired because of her race. ... The district court granted summary judgment in favor of Shoney's. We affirm.

Singh, a white female, was hired by Shoney's in September 1981. At the time of her termination in January 1993, Singh held the position of Dining Room Supervisor in a Shoney's restaurant in New Orleans, Louisiana. Her duties included hiring, firing, supervising, disciplining, and training the hostesses, waitresses, and salad bar attendants who worked in the restaurant.

In January, 1993, defendant's corporate office received a "petition" signed by 36 workers employed at the same restaurant as Singh. The petition alleged that Singh had been engaging in offensive, racially-discriminatory conduct toward subordinate employees. Shoney's responded to the petition by sending its Vice-President of Personnel, John Southerland, and its Equal Employment Opportunity Manager, Juanita Presley (both of whom are black), to New Orleans to investigate the allegations. Southerland and Presley interviewed 44 employees at the restaurant, including Singh. Based on these interviews, Shoney's concluded that Singh had engaged in offensive, inappropriate conduct in the workplace, and terminated her employment.

During the course of the investigation, it came to Shoney's attention that the manager of the restaurant, Terry Dumars, a black male, had also engaged in inappropriate conduct in the workplace, and he was terminated. Dumars was replaced with a white male, and Singh was replaced with another white female.

... In order to make out a prima facie case of discrimination, a plaintiff alleging discriminatory discharge must show (1) that she is a member of a protected group; (2) that she was qualified for the job that she formerly held [and performing her job at a level that met the employer's legitimate expectations]; (3) that she was discharged; and (4) that after her discharge, the position she held was filled by someone not within her protected class [or the discharge occurred under circumstances giving rise to an inference of discrimination based on plaintiff being part of a protected class]. Once the plaintiff establishes a prima facie case of discrimination, the defendant must articulate a legitimate, nondiscriminatory reason for the discharge. If the defendant states a legitimate reason, the plaintiff must show, by a preponderance of the evidence, that the reason provided by the defendant was a pretext for discrimination. ...

Singh failed to make out a prima facie case of racial discrimination on this record, because she was replaced by a white female. Moreover, Shoney's has stated a legitimate nondiscriminatory reason for discharging Singh. ... Shoney's reasonably believed the allegation contained in the petition, and acted on it in good faith.

CASE QUESTION

1. Why is it necessary for a terminated employee seeking to establish discrimination to show she was replaced by someone not within her protected class?

In another case, a bartender at the Adams Mark Hotel in Philadelphia proved a prima facie case. He was black; he was employed for six years and received good reviews, thus establishing that he was qualified for the position; he was discharged and replaced by someone who was caucasian. If the hotel failed to present any evidence seeking to justify the termination, the plaintiff would win. The hotel did respond and claimed the firing was due to the plaintiff misappropriating hotel property by providing a "free drink" to a former hotel employee in violation of a well-established hotel policy. If the hotel can prove those allegations, it will have successfully rebutted the plaintiff's prima facie case. To win the case thereafter, the plaintiff must present evidence showing that the hotel's proffered explanation is a pretext, meaning either it is untrue or not the motivating factor for the discharge.[10]

One way a plaintiff can show that the employer's claimed explanation for the termination was not in fact the reason is by showing that other employees who committed similar violations were retained. For example, assume the plaintiff in the previous case could show that other bartenders violated the same rule and were nonetheless retained. The hotel's justification for the plaintiff's termination would thus be exposed as pretextual. In a New Jersey case, an African-American casino dealer was terminated for rude and discourteous treatment of a customer. He was able to show a few individual cases of white employees who were not terminated for similar infractions. In response, the hotel established that of fifteen employees terminated within five years of the plaintiff, twelve were for inappropriate conduct toward a patron. Eight of those were caucasian employees. The court determined that the plaintiff's discharge was justified and for nondiscriminatory reasons.[11]

---

[10] *Williams v. Adam's Mark Hotel*, 51 F.Supp.2d 637 (Pa. 1999)

[11] *Jason v. Showboat Hotel & Casino*, 747 A.2d 802 (N.J. 2000)

An African-American manager of McDonald's established a prima facie case of race discrimination by showing that she was denied a pay raise while four white managers of stores owned by the same proprietor were given increases. The owner rebutted the claim by showing that the plaintiff's overall work rating was "needs improvement," while the others given a raise were rated "good." This would constitute a good defense to the discrimination charge. However, the plaintiff claimed that the employer's argument was a pretext because the nonminority managers also underperformed on most or all of their goals and still received a "good" rating and a salary increase. If the plaintiff is able to prove this allegation, she will have established that the employer's explanation is pretextual and the real reason for the difference in treatment is racial discrimination.[12]

Racially Hostile Work Environment

Also constituting discrimination based on race is the creation or tolerance by an employer of a racially hostile work environment. An employment atmosphere that permits racially derogatory comments, jokes, and conduct has been determined to significantly and adversely affect the psychological well-being of an employee.

In *Schwapp v. Town of Avon*, 118 F.3d 106 (2nd Cir. 1997), a police officer alleged a hostile work environment based on twelve racially hostile comments and jokes made during his twenty-month tenure. The incidents included a comment by his supervisor that the plaintiff officer had to accept the fact that he was working with racists and should not be so sensitive. In the officer's lawsuit against the police department, the court determined these incidents would amount to a hostile environment and denied summary judgment to the police department.

A racially hostile environment was found in a case in which an African-American plaintiff established numerous incidents of racial slurs including: an instructor in a stress-management session at the employer's facility offered an example of a stressful situation as being in a bar patronized mainly by blacks; one of the plaintiff's supervisors stated in the plaintiff's presence that certain African-American murder suspects looked like "apes or baboons" and another supervisor was present and laughed; on Halloween, a co-worker said to the plaintiff and others, "all you spooks have a nice Halloween" and plaintiff's co-workers turned to look at her when the remark was made; during a training seminar, one co-worker made repeated references to "Arnold Schwarzenigger" and another commented that an unidentified Caucasian had "some nerve bringing his brown-skinned wife to the party"; a co-worker called the plaintiff "nigger"; two co-workers distributed a copy of a racially offensive joke that included use of the word "nigger".[13]

The lesson from these two cases is that employers have an obligation to ensure the workplace is tolerant and accepting of all races.

To escape liability for permitting a hostile work environment, it is not enough for an employer to have on record a policy prohibiting such conduct. The employer must take steps to train employees about the policy and must enforce it.

---

[12] *Cotter v. McDonald's Restaurants*, 35 F.Supp.2d 824 (Kan. 1999)

[13] *Richardson v. NY State*, 180 F.3d 426 (N.Y. 1999)

National Origin

National origin, another protected class, refers to the country where people were born or from which their ancestors came. A refusal to hire workers of, for example, Spanish ancestry violates Title VII. The law also protects "hyphenated-Americans," such as Italian-Americans, Polish-Americans, and Mexican-Americans. National origin discrimination was established in a case involving the Westin Tucson Hotel. The plaintiff was a Nigerian-born black man who was employed in the hotel's laundry. He tried six times unsuccessfully to transfer to other jobs for which he was qualified, primarily in the accounting department. When he asked about his status, he was told by the head of housekeeping, "Go back to Africa where you came from. We don't have any job for you here"; and by the Director of Human Services, you "should go to a black business to find a job." The court awarded the plaintiff employment in the accounting department of the hotel, back pay, and attorney's fees.[14]

If a plaintiff is unable to prove national origin prejudice on the part of the employer, the employee will likely not win a discrimination lawsuit. A Puerto Rican credit manager at a newly-opened hotel was terminated soon after receiving a raise and a letter of commendation. She claimed the basis for her discharge was discrimination based on national origin. The hotel countered that the termination was due to poor job performance. The court decided the case for the hotel. In its reasoning, the court identified various circumstances that suggest national origin discrimination. The court stated, "Here plaintiff offers no evidence that [the hotel] fired Puerto Ricans in greater proportion than non-Puerto Ricans, engaged in a pattern of firing Puerto Ricans and replacing them with non-Puerto Ricans, or adopted corporate policies discriminatory toward Puerto Ricans. There is no evidence of statements by [the hotel's] management or officers indicating a bias against Puerto Ricans, and no evidence that [the hotel's] evaluation of her performance was infected by stereotyped thinking or other types of unconscious national-origin bias."[15]

A Nigerian employee who was terminated claimed the basis was national origin discrimination. As evidence of discrimination he referenced numerous statements by the employer including: (1) "Provide proof of your legal residence in the United States" and (2) "You are difficult to understand, particularly when you become excited." The court found neither of these statements sufficient to establish evidence of discrimination. Concerning the first, an employer is required by federal law to obtain proof of legal residence. (See the discussion on the Immigration Reform and Control Act later in this chapter.) The meaning and intent statement is unclear and could refer to the plaintiff's speed, tone, or volume of speech. Absent further evidence to suggest the comment was a veiled reference to the plaintiff's national origin, it does not support an inference of discrimination. See *Okumabuo v. McKinley Community Services, Inc.*, 2001 WL 709457 (Ill. 2001).

---

[14] *Odima v. Westin Tucson Hotel*, 53 F.3d 1484 (Ariz. 1994)

[15] *Feliciano de La Cruz v. El Conquistador Resort*, 218 F.3d 1 (P.R. 2000)

Employer tolerance of ethnic slurs or jokes by employees or supervisors also constitutes discrimination based on national origin.

Fluency in English

Employers often prefer to hire an employee who is fluent in English. People from other countries may not speak or understand English well. Refusal to hire someone whose English is faltering may constitute illegal discrimination on the basis of national origin. However, as discussed earlier in this chapter, if the ability to speak English is a business necessity for the job, an employer who refuses to hire an applicant not well-versed in English is not discriminating illegally. An example of English fluency being a business necessity is a job that requires communication with English-speaking patrons, such as wait personnel in restaurants or a hotel concierge.

In *Stephen v. PGA Sheraton Resort, Ltd.*, 873 F.2d 276 (11th Cir. 1989), the plaintiff, a black male of Haitian origin, was a purchasing clerk for a Sheraton Resort. His duties included delivering supplies to many of the departments at the resort. His inability to understand English resulted in misdelivery of supplies and at least one employee having to obtain her own supplies. The plaintiff was terminated from the clerk position and offered a lesser-paying job in housekeeping. He sued the hotel, claiming national origin discrimination. The court held for the Sheraton, determining that the plaintiff's termination "rested on proper concerns of business necessity. ... [T]he employer took the contested employment action for a legitimate non-discriminatory reason."

If fluency in English is not required for the job, as is the case for housekeeping personnel at a hotel or dishwashers at a restaurant, refusal to hire based on poor language skills would be illegal.

In the following case, the hotel refused to promote a Hispanic employee because of her limited capacity to speak English. The court denied her claim of illegal discrimination, finding the hotel's requirement of fluent English was a business necessity.

CASE EXAMPLE 14-3

Mejia v. New York Sheraton Hotel
459 F.Supp. 375 (N.Y. 1978)

This is an employment discrimination case pursuant to Title VII of the Civil Rights Act of 1964. ...

Plaintiff alleges in her complaint that she was discharged on June 24, 1975 from her position as a chambermaid with the Sheraton Hotel on account of her Spanish surname and the fact that her primary language was Spanish and that two years earlier she was denied a promotion to a front office cashier position for the same reasons.

The defendants deny any discriminatory purpose or effect of their conduct and assert that ... the reason why plaintiff was not promoted to the front office cashier position which she sought was that she was not qualified by reason of the paucity of her English language ability and her lack of familiarity with office procedures.

The facts established herein are the following.

Plaintiff is a female Dominican national who came to the United States in about 1970 as the holder of a visa entitling her to become employed in this country. Her education and schooling occurred abroad in a Spanish school and she never had any education in the English language until she arrived in this country. The plaintiff was employed as a chambermaid in the housekeeping department of the Sheraton Hotel from on or about October 29, 1970 to on or about June 24, 1975. During her employment, whatever ability she possessed to understand, speak and write English she acquired through courses that she had taken in English at New York University during a period of three months after her arrival here.

The defendant [is] New York Sheraton Hotel. ...

Commencing in April 1973 the plaintiff enrolled in an Industry Training Program, a program jointly sponsored by plaintiff's Union and the city's hotel industry to train hotel employees for positions within the hotel industry. ... A week after her training she applied for a position as a front office cashier. Such a job was never tendered to her. ...

In 1974 there was an opening in the cashier's department and plaintiff spoke to the manager but she was told that she would have to learn to speak better English because the position required a greater aptitude than the plaintiff possessed. ... The management found that the plaintiff's language barrier was a stumbling block to a front office post for the plaintiff, a post that would necessarily bring her in contact and communication with the guests of the hotel. ...

Following her discharge, plaintiff resorted to the EEOC charging that she was discriminated against because ... of her national origin and was not promoted because she was Spanish. ...

The evidence in the case established beyond peradventure of doubt a serious past and current inability on the plaintiff's part to articulate clearly or coherently and to make herself adequately understood in the English language. She continued taking English courses after her discharge in the summers of 1975, 1976 and 1977 with minimal improvement. Her instructor's latest report card for the 1977 session recites that she was a poor student and definitely should not go on to [the next] level as she could not do the written work and that pronunciation was also a problem. ... Plaintiff's exhibition on the witness stand emphasized the current existence of an English language deficiency that made it quite difficult for the Court, the reporter and counsel to understand what she was saying in her testimonial responses.

The requirement of the hotel for greater English proficiency than the plaintiff can exhibit was significantly related to successful job performance and did not operate to exclude minority applicants at a higher rate than applicants who are not of that minority group. There is no doubt that the plaintiff was not sufficiently qualified to be placed in a position in the front office cashier's department. The defendants found her not acceptable for such employment in a legitimate, nondiscriminatory manner. ... Plaintiff's Hispanic origin ... formed no part of defendant's refusal to place her in the front office cashier's department. Business necessities precluded a person of plaintiff's qualifications from being placed in the front office cashier type occupation in a large public hotel. The Sheraton Hotel employs about 650 persons, more than a third of whom are of Hispanic origin. ... Although plaintiff cannot be faulted for her eagerness to advance from the position of a chambermaid to the front office of the hotel, the evidence conclusively shows that she was never sufficiently qualified and therefore was not eligible for the position she sought in the defendant's front office. ...

Accordingly, the complaint herein is dismissed. ... Judgment for defendant.

CASE QUESTION

1. Why was fluency in English important in the job the plaintiff sought? Why was it less important for her job as a chambermaid?

National Origin and Accent Discrimination

A person from another country may be knowledgeable about English but speak with an accent. Said one court, "Accent and national origin are inextricably intertwined." The law in this area is very important to managers in the accommodations industry, where so many employees are foreign-born.

A plaintiff who has been discriminated against solely because of his accent is a victim of illegal discrimination based on national origin. An employer can, however, refuse to hire a job applicant based on an accent if it materially interferes with job performance. A professor was denied tenure (a permanent teaching position) because students complained her accent was difficult to understand. She sued the school district, claiming discrimination on the basis of national origin. The court found for the school district stating, "Unlawful discrimination does not occur when a plaintiff's accent affects his ability to perform the job effectively."[16] Similarly, where the accent of a Vietnamese mailroom clerk was so strong that other employees could not understand her and organizational productivity was diminished, her termination was justified and did not constitute illegal discrimination based on national origin.[17]

But if the accent does not interfere with the ability to perform the job, the employer cannot refuse to hire or promote or otherwise discriminate on that basis. A bank employee was denied a promotion to Loan Officer because of his accent. The court determined that his accent would not have interfered materially with his performance. The judgment in the plaintiff's favor, which was upheld on appeal, included back pay, lost future pay, expert witness fees, attorney's fees, compensation for emotional distress, and expenses for medical and psychiatric treatment necessitated by the discrimination.[18]

Religion

An employer cannot discriminate against a person based on religion, including all aspects of religious observance and practice. This rule can sometimes present difficulties for employers. For example, some workers celebrate sabbath in such a way that work is precluded. Some celebrate it on Saturday and others on Sunday. Accommodating religion-based requests for days off can complicate an employer's work schedule. Must an employer oblige employees' requests for days off to celebrate religious holidays? An employer has an affirmative duty to attempt to accommodate the religious observances and practices of its employees. If, however, the employer can demonstrate that such an accommodation would cause undue hardship to the business, it can refuse to grant the days off. Stated differently, an employer who is unable to reasonably satisfy the religious needs of an employee can escape liability if it can show it made a good-faith attempt to accommodate those needs or that to do so would cause undue hardship.

---

[16] *Forsythe v. Board of Education, Hays, Kansas*, 956 F.Supp. 927 (Kan. 1997)

[17] *Bishop v. Hazel & Thomas*, 151 F.3d 1028 (Va. 1998)

[18] *Xieng v. People's National Bank of Washington*, 844 P.2d 389 (Wa. 1993)

Reasonable accommodation requires an employer to give unpaid time off for religious holidays if the employee's services are not needed at work on the days in question. Further, if paid leave is allowed for other purposes, unpaid leave for religious holidays may not qualify as a reasonable accommodation. An employer is required to accept schedule changes prompted by religious observance and arranged by the employees unless there is a good reason not to permit the substitution, as where the alternate worker lacks necessary skills to do the job. Another reasonable accommodation an employer might provide is a means of communication among employees to facilitate their finding substitutes, such as a bulletin board in the employee break room.

Before an employer is required to make a reasonable accommodation of an employee's religious practices, the employee must establish that the religious foundation for the requested accommodation is bona fide. A Muslim banquet waiter who had been employed by a hotel for 14 years appeared for work one evening with a one-eighth inch beard (two to five days' growth) in violation of the hotel's rules. When asked by a supervisor about the facial hair, the waiter responded, "It is part of my religion." The hotel, concerned about its reputation, refused to let the waiter work. Three months later, the waiter shaved his beard. He sued the hotel claiming religious discrimination. The court rejected his claim, finding that his assertion that an accommodation of his beard was mandated by his religious beliefs was not made in good faith. The court noted that the waiter had worked without a beard for 14 years, he did not explain why he had not worn a beard previously (for example, he might have claimed he was a recent convert), and the fact of his shaving the beard three months later undercut his claim of religious necessity.[19]

In another case, a store salesperson took an unauthorized leave to go on a religious pilgrimage in late October. The employer had a policy prohibiting all leaves during the two-month busy season immediately prior to Christmas, including the period of the plaintiff's religious sojourn. She explained the timing of her trip by saying, "I felt from deep in my heart that I was called. I had to be there at that time." Upon her return, she was terminated. She sued claiming religious discrimination. The court ruled for the employer, stating that, to claim she is entitled to an accommodation, she needed to establish that the timing was part of a bona fide religious belief. Said the court, "Title VII does not protect secular preferences."[20]

A manicurist and a skin specialist sought a day off without pay to observe Yom Kippur, a Jewish holy day, which fell on a Saturday, the busiest day in the salon business. The employer, noting that the employees already had customers booked for appointments on the day in question, denied the request. Neither employee came to work on Yom Kippur and both were terminated from their jobs. They sued claiming discrimination based on religion. The employer was unable to show that it tried to accommodate the employees' religious practices or that it would suffer an undue hardship by granting the day off. The employer was thus liable for religious discrimination.[21]

---

[19] *Hussein v. Waldorf-Astoria Hotel*, 134 F.Supp.2d 591 (N.Y. 2001)

[20] *Tiano v. Dillard Department Stores*, 139 F.3d 679 (Ariz. 1998)

[21] *EEOC v. Ilona of Hungary, Inc.*, 108 F.3d 1569 (Ill. 1997)

In the hospitality industry, Saturdays and Sundays, the days on which many religious observances fall, are busy and therefore important business days. Accommodating employees who need these days off on a regular basis may cause a hardship to employers. Factors that can support a claim of undue hardship by an employer include lack of availability of substitute employees, lost efficiency to the operation caused by the absence of the observant employee's skills, costs necessarily incurred by employers such as paying a premium to encourage other employees to work on the weekend, and lost patronage.

Gender

Title VII outlaws discrimination in employment on the basis of gender. An employer cannot refuse to grant women or men a benefit of employment based on their gender. For example, paying men more than women for the same job responsibilities, based only on gender, constitutes illegal discrimination.

Hiring only one gender for a particular job generally constitutes discrimination. For example, a restaurant cannot hire only males as wait personnel. The EEOC brought a discrimination action against Joe's Stone Crab Restaurant, a well-known Florida eatery that did exactly that. In a lawsuit brought by the EEOC, the court stated, "While women have predominated among Joe's owner/managers, as well as among the laundering, cashiering and take away staff, women have systematically been excluded from the most lucrative entry level position, that of server." The court thus held the restaurant's hiring practices violated Title VII.[22] Now both men and women fill the ranks of servers at the restaurant.

A related case involved Hooters, a 330-restaurant chain in 43 states and several countries with a theme of scantily clad women performing most jobs involving customer interaction including wait personnel, bartenders, and receptionists. Males were hired only as managers or kitchen help. The company was charged with gender discrimination in a class action lawsuit brought by males who had applied for wait jobs and had either been refused on the basis of their gender or hired to work in lesser-paid kitchen jobs. The case was settled for $3.75 million and a commitment by Hooters to hire males as bartender assistants, greeters at the door, and in a new "staff position," which involves clearing tables and bringing condiments to the table. As part of the settlement, the staff position will earn more than what bussers customarily make and will share in tips. In exchange for expanding job opportunities for males, the principal server position remains female-only. Had the case proceeded to court, Hooters would likely have been directed to modify its theme to permit male waiters.

In another case, a hotel that refused to hire women as bartenders "patently offended" Title VII.[23]

---

[22] *EEOC v. Joe's Stone Crab, Inc.*, 136 F.Supp 1311 (Fl. 2001)

[23] *Krause v. Sacramento Inn*, 479 F.2d 988 (Ca. 1973)

An airline that required women flight attendants to be single but hired married men for the same position acted illegally.[24]

An employer cannot use the argument that a particular job is dangerous as a basis to hire only men. An objective of Title VII is to permit each woman to make the decision for herself whether she chooses to incur the risks associated with certain jobs. The United States Supreme Court held that an employer discriminated illegally when it excluded women of child-bearing age, but not men of a similar age, from jobs requiring exposure to lead, which had the potential to damage both male and female reproductive systems.[25]

The protection against gender discrimination is not limited to females, but also protects males. A male guest-service agent at a Pennsylvania Sheraton Hotel had a basis to sue when he was able to show that his reassignment to a phone operator position was motivated by considerations of gender.[26]

Proving that an employer's discriminatory acts are based on gender can sometimes be difficult. Statements made by management that women in general are simply not competent to perform a particular job are classic examples of evidence that helps to establish a gender discrimination case. The following comments, made by an employer who was hiring for the position of collections manager, helped to prove a case of gender discrimination: "Women cannot get tough enough with customers and collect the money," and "This job requires a man to do it."[27]

In another case, a discharged female sales representative attempted unsuccessfully to establish that her termination was due to gender discrimination. One of the circumstances she cited as establishing discrimination was her supervisor's scheduling a lunch meeting at Hooters restaurant. The court, while referring to the meeting site as "grossly unprofessional" found the meeting locale insufficient to support a discrimination verdict.[28]

Competency Required

To establish a case of discrimination for failing to hire or promote based on gender, plaintiffs must establish that they are qualified for the position they seek. An employer can refuse to hire or promote a person who lacks the skills necessary to perform a job adequately. In *EEOC v. Marion Motel Associates*, 763 F.Supp. 1334 (N.C. 1991), the plaintiff, the assistant general manager of the defendant motel, sought promotion to general manager. When the position was assigned to a man, she sued for gender discrimination. The court decided the case in favor of the hotel, finding that the plaintiff was not qualified for the position. In making that determination, the court referenced testimony that established that the plaintiff

---

[24] *Sprogis v. United Air Lines, Inc.*, 444 F.2d 1194 (Ill. 1971)

[25] *International Union, United Automobile Workers v. Johnson Controls, Inc.*, 117 S.Ct. 1196 (1991)

[26] *Davis v. Sheraton Society Hill Hotel,* 907 F.Supp. 896 (Pa. 1995)

[27] *Haynes v. W.C. Caye & Co.*, 52 F.3d 929 (Ga. 1995)

[28] *Ray v. Tandem Computers, Inc.*, 63 F.3d 429 (Tex. 1995)

was occasionally tardy for work, failed to alert off-site management of excessive absences of the general manager, and "was reluctant to perform tasks over and above her regular job duties."

Gender-Differentiated Grooming Standards

A number of cases involve male employees who were fired for failing to comply with grooming standards imposed on men but not women. The plaintiffs in these lawsuits claim the personal appearance regulations discriminate on the basis of gender. The law is now clear that minor differences in an employer's appearance rules for men and women that reflect customary modes of grooming for one sex but not the other do not violate Title VII. The objective of Title VII is to equalize employment opportunities. Discrimination based on gender characteristics that are unchangeable is prohibited, but discrimination based on factors of personal preference that an employee can modify does not illegally restrict employment opportunities. Thus, requiring that male employees have short hair but imposing no similar restriction on female employees is not gender discrimination. A male employee who was terminated for violating such a hair policy has no basis on which to successfully sue his former employer.[29] Likewise, a prohibition against men wearing earrings while women are permitted to do so does not violate the discrimination laws.[30] Said the court, "[A]n employer is permitted to exercise legitimate concern for the business image created by the appearance of its employees."

An employer cannot require one sex to wear a uniform and not the other where both are doing the same job. A bank that required female tellers as well as office and managerial employees to wear uniforms while permitting men to work in customary business attire was liable for sex discrimination. The court explained the defendant had several options: permit women to wear "appropriate business attire"; require the male employees to wear uniforms; or make uniforms optional for both men and women. Said the court, "Title VII does not require that uniforms be abolished but that defendant's similarly situated employees be treated in an equal manner."[31]

Sexual Harassment

Sexual harassment is a form of sexual discrimination and constitutes a violation of Title VII. Sexual harassment includes two types of illegal action: (1) unwelcome sexual advances or requests for sexual favors in return for job benefits and (2) verbal or physical conduct of a sexual nature that creates an intimidating, hostile, or offensive work environment. The former is called **quid pro quo sexual harassment**; the latter, **hostile environment sexual harassment**.

[29] *Tavora v. New York Mercantile Exchange*, 101 F.3d 907 (N.Y. 1996)

[30] *Capaldo v. Pan American Federal Credit Union*, 43 E.P.D. § 37,016 (N.Y. 1987)

[31] *Carroll v. Talman Federal Savings & Loan Association*, 604 F.2d 1028 (Ill. 1979)

Quid Pro Quo Sexual Harassment

Examples of quid pro quo sexual harassment include firing a female worker who rejects her supervisor's sexual advances;[32] promising to promote an employee who agrees to perform sexually;[33] denying a woman a promotion and/or training opportunities because she rejects her boss' advances;[34] threatening to write disparaging reviews concerning an employee's job performance unless she engaged in sexual intercourse;[35] demoting a female employee for the same reason;[36] and conditioning the grant of a two-week leave of absence for a female employee on her performing oral sex on her supervisor.[37]

Hostile Environment Sexual Harassment

An example of a hostile work environment is one in which female employees are exposed to persistent lewd remarks and ubiquitous pinups.[38] Said the court, "Pornography on an employer's wall or desk communicates a message about the way he views women, a view strikingly at odds with the way women wish to be viewed in the workplace." Another example of a hostile work environment includes a situation in which an employee was confronted with unwelcome sexual advances on five separate occasions.[39] In *Splunge v. Shoney's, Inc.*, 97 F.3d 488 (11th Cir. 1996), the following clearly constituted a hostile environment: Male employees grabbed at the female plaintiffs, commented extensively on their physical attributes, showed them pornographic photos and videotapes, offered them money for sex, favored other employees who had affairs with them, and speculated aloud as to the plaintiffs' sexual prowess.

The actions enumerated are typical of the types of conduct that underlie sexual harassment hostile environment claims. Also constituting hostile environment sexual harassment is the following circumstance: A waitress' supervisor, on at least a dozen occasions, bumped into her from behind and rubbed against her or ran his hands over her buttocks at the pie cooler or in other behind-the-counter spaces; he inquired about her sex life; and he led other employees to believe he was having an affair with her.[40]

The types of activity that can constitute sexual harassment are many and include insults, pressure for sexual activity, repeatedly asking someone out on a date when the invitee has indicated a lack of interest, suggestive sounds, obscene

---

[32] *Sparks v. Pilot Freight Carriers, Inc.*, 830 F.2d 1554 (Ga. 1987)

[33] *Wu v. Best Western Lighthouse Hotel*, 2001 WL 492475 (Ca. 2001)

[34] *Henson v. City of Dundee*, 682 F.2d 897 (Fl. 1982)

[35] *Virgo v. Sheraton Ocean Inn*, 2001 WL 1136052 (Tenn. 2001)

[36] *Carrero v. New York City Housing Authority*, 890 F.2d 569 (N.Y. 1989)

[37] *Nichols v. Frank*, 42 F.3d 503 (Or. 1994)

[38] *Robinson v. Jacksonville Shipyards, Inc.*, 760 F.Supp. 1486 (Fl. 1991)

[39] *Phillips v. Taco Bill Corp.*, 83 F.Supp.2d 1029 (Mo. 2000)

[40] *Knabe v. Big Boy East*, 114 F.3d 407 (Tenn. 1997)

gestures, lewd pictures, touching, pinching, grabbing, brushing against someone, coerced sexual intercourse, and giving personal gifts. Cases have established common patterns of victims' reactions to sexual harassment, including distraction, inability to work, anger, anxiety, depression, sleeping problems, and other physical ailments.

Casual or isolated incidents of discriminatory conduct such as a few sexual comments or slurs will not constitute a hostile environment. However, conduct less severe than that in *Splunge v. Shoney's, Inc.* will cross the threshold and result in liability. Factors to consider include the frequency of the harassing conduct, its severity, whether it is an offensive utterance or is physically threatening or humiliating, and whether it unreasonably interferes with an employee's work performance.

Frequency of Offending Conduct

Customarily, the objectionable conduct in hostile environment cases occurs repeatedly over a period of time. However, one incident can qualify if it is sufficiently hostile and abusive. Thus, sexual harassment occurred where a male supervisor traveling for business with a female subordinate engaged in sexual conversation, appeared at her hotel door barely clothed, entered the room uninvited, sat on her bed, touched her thigh, and attempted to kiss her, all of whch was unwelcome.[41]

Same Gender Sexual Harassment

In many cases alleging sexual harassment, the offending employee is male and the victim is female. That fact notwithstanding, sexual harassment can also be perpetrated by a female against a male. Prior to 1995, a question existed whether sexual harassment could occur between two males or two females. The United States Supreme Court resolved the issue in *Oncale v. Sundowner Offshore Services, Inc.*, 523 U.S. 75, 118 S.Ct. 998 (1998), holding that sexual harassment can occur between two people of the same gender.

The complainant in *Oncale*, a male, was working with a drilling crew of eight men on an oil platform in the Gulf of Mexico. On several occasions, he was forcibly subjected to "sex-related, humiliating actions" by a male supervisor in the presence of the all-male crew. Complainant was also physically assaulted and threatened with rape. Protests to other supervisory employees prompted no remedial action. He sued and two courts dismissed his lawsuit holding that same gender sexual harassment is not actionable. The high court reversed those decisions, stating, "When the workplace is permeated with discriminatory intimidation, ridicule, and insult that is sufficiently severe or pervasive to alter the conditions of the victim's employment and create an abusive working environment, Title VII is violated." The gender of the perpetrator and of the victim is without significance.

---

[41] *Moring v. Arkansas Department of Correction*, 243 F.2d 452 (Ark. 2001)

Unwelcomed Conduct

A critical factor for sexual harassment is that the activity be unwelcome by the employee and this fact is known by the harasser. If the conduct is desired, it is not harassment.

Consent alone does not establish that the conduct is welcome. An employee may begrudgingly consent to unwelcome acts because of fear of losing a job or promotion. In *Meritor Savings Bank v. Vinson*, 477 U.S. 57, 106 S.Ct. 2399 (1986) a bank employee agreed to have sexual relations with a bank vice-president because she feared losing her job if she refused. The encounters continued for a period of years. She later sued the bank for sexual harassment. The bank defended in part by claiming the relationship was voluntary. The court responded, "The correct inquiry is whether respondent by her conduct indicated that the alleged sexual advances were unwelcome, not whether her actual participation in sexual intercourse was voluntary." The appellate court referred the case back to the court with original jurisdiction to determine whether the acts were unwelcome. Note that the court did not rule that the long-term aspect of the relationship merited a presumption or inference that the sexual conduct was welcome. Rather, a sexual relationship between a supervisor and a subordinate employee is suspect for being unwelcome.

In some circumstances, the unwelcome nature of the conduct can be implied from the nature of the activity, such as coerced (nonvoluntary) sexual intercourse. In other circumstances, the conduct's offensiveness will be less clear and the employee must relay that it is not appreciated. If a supervisor asks an employee out on a date for the first time, the request is normally not sexual harassment, even if the employee refuses. If, following the refusal, the supervisor continues to invite that employee on dates, the repeated requests may constitute sexual harassment.

An employee need not verbalize the unwelcome nature of sexually suggestive conduct; consistent demonstration through action is sufficient notification. In *Chamberlin v. 101 Realty, Inc.*, 915 F.2d 777 (1st Cir. 1990), the court held an employee adequately relayed the unwelcomed nature of her boss' advances where, on several different occasions, she failed to respond to his sexual innuendos, changed the subject when he suggested intimacy between them, and pulled her hands away when he reached for them across a restaurant table at lunch.

Employer Liability

Employers such as hotels and restaurants often attempt to avoid liability by claiming that a supervisor's harassing conduct should not be attributable to the employer. The liability of an employer depends in part on the type of sexual harassment involved. For quid pro quo sexual harassment (where a supervisor conditions a job, job benefits, or the absence of a job detriment on an employee's submission to sexual conduct), the harasser's employer is liable. The theory of the employer's liability is respondeat superior—that is, the employer is liable for the wrongful acts of an employee (the supervisor) done in furtherance of the employee's job responsibilities (granting job benefits or detriments).

In a case where a supervisor creates a hostile environment, the employer is presumed liable but an affirmative defense exists. The employer can escape liability if it satisfies three elements constituting the defense: (1) no adverse employment action was taken against the employee (for example, the worker was not fired or demoted); (2) the employer exercised reasonable care to prevent and correct promptly any sexually harassing behavior (for example, the employer has in place an anti-harassment policy with a complaint procedure); and (3) the plaintiff unreasonably failed to take advantage of preventive or corrective opportunities provided by the employer to avoid harm (for example, the employee did not report the harassing conduct to the company representative designated to receive such complaints).[42]

The following case illustrates appropriate response by an employer to a sexual harassment complaint. As a result, the employer escaped liability.

CASE EXAMPLE 14-4

Gregg v. Hay-Adams Hotel
942 F.Supp. 1 (D.C. 1996)

... Plaintiff Debra Denise Gregg is currently employed as an Assistant Pastry Chef at the Hay-Adams Hotel in Washington, D.C. She was hired as such in June of 1993 and has remained in this position since that time. She alleges that within a few months of her hiring, the Executive Chef of the Hotel, Patrick Clark, began to make suggestive remarks toward her, culminating in unwelcome physical contact. ...

On April 14, 1994, some eight months after the harassment allegedly began, Gregg complained about Clark to Payroll/Personnel Assistant Toya Roberts. Independently, another coworker, Victoria Dade, also complained about Clark to Roberts that very day. There had never been a sexual harassment complaint by any hotel employee prior to this date.

Still on April 14, 1994, Roberts reported the complaints to Human Resources Director Jeffrey Lea, who instructed Roberts to prepare a memorandum regarding the charges—which she delivered to him the next day. In the memo, Roberts reported, among other things, that she told Gregg she would assist her and urged Gregg to take down notes concerning the events.

On Friday morning, April 15, 1994, Lea met with Urs Aeby, the General Manager of the hotel who then ordered an immediate investigation of the complaints. Aeby then met with each of the two women to inform them that all appropriate steps would be taken to provide them a harassment-free workplace, and he further assured them that they would not be subject to retribution. Statements were taken from Gregg, Dade, and several other employees who might have knowledge of the events. Clark was told generally about the allegations but not about who had made them.

On April 26, 1994, less than two weeks after the complaints, Aeby issued Clark a "formal and final written warning." The letter stated that the investigation revealed behavior "verging on harassment" and that even with respect to unsubstantiated allegations, Clark had "shown a serious lack of judgment." The letter further warned him that any retributive acts could be punishable by termination of employment.

There have been no subsequent sexual harassment accusations since the April 14, 1994 charges. ...

Gregg attempts to place liability on the employer by arguing that the hotel "violated its expressed company policy regarding sexual harassment to refrain from sexually

---

[42]*Burlington Industries v. Ellereth*, 524 U.S. 742, 118 S.Ct. 2270 (1998) and *Faragher v. Boca Raton*, 524 U.S. 775, 118 S.Ct. 2275 (1998)

discriminating against plaintiff by allowing its agents and employees to make sexual advances towards plaintiff and by creating an intimidating hostile and offensive work environment." Gregg neither alleges, nor has evidence to suggest, that the employer actually knew or had reason to know of the harassment [prior to Gregg's complaint], nor that the Hotel approved of it. ... When a company, once informed of allegations of sexual harassment, takes prompt remedial action to protect the claimant, the company may avoid Title VII liability.

Turning to the issue of whether the hotel actually did respond in an appropriate and timely fashion to Gregg's complaint, the court finds that defendant did so, and to a degree which would remove it from any Title VII liability.

It is undisputed that the Hotel took the following actions:

1. When Gregg reported her complaints to the Payroll/Personnel Assistant, Sonya Roberts, she immediately carried the news to the Human Resources director.

2. Gregg (and another woman who complained) was assured that she would be helped.

3. Within a week of the allegations, four interviews, plus statements by complainants were taken to confirm or disaffirm the charges.

4. The General Manager of the Hotel notified Clark of the allegations, and personally assured Gregg that sexual harassment would not be tolerated.

5. Clark was issued a "formal and final warning," placed in his personnel file, on April 26, 1994, less than two weeks after the complaint was made.

6. The warning to Clark stated that further behavior would result in the immediate termination of his employment.

7. Clark was also threatened with termination should he retaliate against those who complained about him.

8. Clark apologized to Gregg.

9. The Hotel re-issued its sexual harassment policy, ran seminars on sexual harassment (with mandatory attendance for all employees), and Gregg was told to report any further harassment or retaliation directly to the Human Resources Director or the General Manager.

10. A new Human Resources Director, Graciela Lewis, made several visits to the kitchen to ensure the working environment was comfortable there.

11. Gregg admits there was no further harassment after April 14, the date of her first and only complaint to the hotel.

These steps are substantial enough both in action and effect to negate Title VII liability. ...

CASE QUESTION

1. What is the lesson of this case concerning on how an employer who receives a sexual harassment complaint should respond?

Importance of Remedial Action

An employer who fails to take appropriate and effective remedial action will face liability. In a case involving an Adam's Mark Hotel, the banquet manager reported to the general manager incidents of sexual harassment by a supervisor. The general manager issued a warning to the supervisor, but the harassing conduct continued. The banquet manager then complained to the Director of Personnel who took no action. The banquet manager next complained to the Director of Food and Beverages who told her to "get over it" and "work around" the supervisor. Two other employees also complained about sexually harassing conduct by the same supervisor, but no corrective action resulted. The banquet manager ultimately quit her job and sued the hotel for sexual harassment. She won her case and was awarded $400,000 in compensatory damages, $55,000 in back pay, and $187,000 for attorney's fees and litigation expenses. The hotel's indifference led to this avoidable expensive result.[43] The moral of this case is that an employer should promptly address all sexual harassment complaints by investigating the charges and taking appropriate remedial action.

Sexual Harassment by Co-Workers

An employer may be liable for sexual harassment, not only when supervisors initiate the harassment, but also when co-workers harass an employee. For an employer to be liable for sexual harassment administered by nonsupervisory co-workers, the employer must be aware of the harassment, as where it is occurring openly and blatantly, or where the harassed employee reports it to a superior.

Sexual Harassment by Customers

An employer who condones or tolerates a sexually hostile work environment created, not by supervisors or co-workers, but by customers, may also be liable to the employee. The reasoning for this rule is that the employer ultimately controls the conditions of the work environment and has a duty to protect employees from abuse. Thus, a Pizza Hut restaurant was liable where the manager denied a waitress' request not to be assigned to customers who made sexual comments when she served them previously. After she seated them, one grabbed her hair and she again asked her supervisor to be relieved of their table. When he refused and she served them beer, one pulled her to him, grabbed her breast and put his mouth on it. She was awarded compensatory damages and attorneys fees. To avoid liability, the manager should have honored her request to be reassigned, insisted that the customers cease their abusive conduct, or require that they leave the restaurant.[44]

In another case involving sexual harassment by patrons, a Las Vegas casino cocktail waitress reported harassing comments by customers to her boss who did nothing in response. The casino defended its inaction by claiming that inappropriate comments, sexual or otherwise, by patrons is inevitable in a job that requires constant contact with the public, particularly in a city that is a "fun" destination where people sometimes drink to excess and often lose more money than they should. The court clearly rejected this defense. Said the court, "[E]mployers are liable for failing to remedy or prevent a hostile or offensive work environment of which management-level employees knew or in the exercise of reasonable care should have known."[45]

---

[43]*Ellis v. Adam's Mark Hotel,* 229 F.3d 1151 (Tenn. 2000)

[44]*Lockard v. Pizza Hut, Inc.,* 162 F.3d 1062 (Ok. 1998)

[45]*Powell v. Las Vegas Hilton Hotel & Casino,* 841 F.Supp. 1024 (Nev. 1992)

An employer that takes prompt and substantial action to protect employees from customer harassment will avoid liability. In one such case, a professional mime performed for Circus Circus Casino in the character of a life-size children's wind-up toy. She was sufficiently convincing in this role that casino patrons occasionally tried to touch her to determine if she was human. When the mime discussed her concerns about this circumstance with her supervisor, he assigned a large man dressed in a clown costume to accompany her when she performed. Further, a sign was prepared for her to wear that read, "Stop: Do not touch." Further, other casino employees were alerted to call security if they saw that she was being harassed and to direct customers not to touch her. Thereafter, a customer touched the mime despite another employee warning the customer three times not to do so. The mime sued the casino, claiming it did not take sufficient precautions to protect her. The court disagreed, finding the casino took reasonable and sufficient steps to protect the mime from customer harassment.[46]

In another case involving harassment by customers, an employer was held liable where it forced an employee to wear a sexually provocative uniform that the employer could reasonably forsee would subject the employee to sexual harassment by customers.[47] Indeed, it did subject her to such conduct. Employers such as bars and casinos, who require waitresses to wear short skirts and low-cut tops, may incur liability when the scant clothing foreseeably provokes harassing behavior by the clientele.

Policies and Complaint Procedures

To limit occurrences of sexual harassment, employers should develop a company policy clearly establishing that sexual harassment will not be tolerated. The policy should be posted and published to all employees. It should include a complaint procedure that authorizes employees to file complaints with a high-level employee *not* in their line of supervision. Complaints should be treated seriously and investigated thoroughly. When warranted, appropriate and prompt remedial action should be taken, including the following:

- In a quid pro quo case, changing the work site of the harasser, terminating the harasser, and denying him or her a promotion and raise

- In a hostile environment case, mandating that the objectionable conduct stop (such as requiring that pinups be removed and lewd comments cease), penalizing those who caused the hostile environment through adverse job action, and requiring employee training about sexual harassment.

Pregnancy

Female workers who become pregnant have historically been subject to termination, even though they are able to perform their job responsibilities. Pregnant employees now have legal protection against discrimination on the basis of

---

[46] *Folkerson v. Circus Circus Hotel & Casino*, 107 F.3d 754 (Nev. 1997)

[47] *EEOC v. Sage Realty Corp.*, 507 F.Supp. 599 (N.Y. 1981)

pregnancy. Part of Title VII, called the Pregnancy Discrimination Act, makes it unlawful for an employer to treat medical conditions relating to pregnancy and childbirth less favorably than other disabilities, unless justified by business necessity.[48] The basic principle of the Act is that women who are pregnant or affected by related conditions must be treated the same as other applicants and employees; adverse job action can only be based on the inability to work. A woman is therefore protected against such practices as being fired or forced to take a leave of absence because she is pregnant. Pregnancy discrimination includes reneging on a promised promotion from Manager of Catering to Director of Catering and Sales because the employee became pregnant.[49] Women who are pregnant and able to work must be permitted to work on the same conditions as other employees.

If the pregnancy becomes disabling and the woman is not able to work for medical reasons, she must be accorded the same rights, privileges, and other benefits as other workers who are disabled. An employer could not terminate a pregnant woman whose doctor requires her not to work if the employer allows workers with other disabilities to take a leave of absence. This is an important right for a pregnant worker since, with a leave of absence, the employee preserves her right to the job, seniority, and benefits. If the employee is terminated and later rehired, she loses the seniority and benefits she accumulated prior to the termination.

If an employer is imposing adverse job action on all employees, the employer can include the pregnant woman among those affected. For example, if the pregnancy coincides with a slowdown in the employer's business during which the employer is cutting hours of all employees—as, for example, a summer resort in the fall—the employer can legally cut the pregnant employee's hours as well.

Business Necessity

If an employer can show that a business necessity renders pregnant employees unfit, the employer can require pregnant employees to take a leave of absence pending wellness following birth.

In a case involving business necessity, an airline's policy of removing flight attendants as soon as their pregnancy became known was challenged by a pregnant stewardess. The court upheld the airline's policy, noting that fatigue and nausea often accompany pregnancy and could render a flight attendant unable to perform job responsibilities in an emergency, thus risking the safety of passengers. Although different women have different physical reactions to pregnancy, the airline would not be able to predict which pregnant stewardesses would suffer from ailments and which would not. Therefore, the policy of not allowing pregnant stewardesses to work satisfied the business necessity exception and did not constitute illegal discrimination.[50]

---

[48] 42 U.S.C. § 2000e

[49] *Newman v. Deer Path Inn*, 1999 WL 1129105 (Ill. 1999)

[50] *Levin v. Delta Air Lines, Inc.*, 730 F.2d 994 (Tex. 1984)

Reinstatement after Giving Birth

Reinstatement policies for employees returning to work after giving birth must be the same as for employees returning to work after absences due to other temporary disabilities. The EEOC has declared that an employer cannot prohibit an employee from returning to work during a specified length of time after childbirth. Instead, individualized determinations of the time needed for recovery should be made in the same manner adopted for other disabilities.

Abortion Issue

An issue of abortion rights was raised in a case involving a busser at a Holiday Inn who became pregnant and so informed her manager and fellow staff members. She also discussed with them that she had not ruled out the possibility of an abortion. According to the Food and Beverage Director, "We have a very Christian staff in that restaurant who were very offended by [the busser's discussion of a possible abortion]." The busser was disciplined for creating an "uproar" among the staff and advised if she spoke of an abortion again at work she would be terminated. She ultimately was fired based on her "pondered abortion." The court held that discharging an employee on the basis of a statement that she is considering an abortion, has had one, or intends to have one, constitutes illegal pregnancy discrimination. The court also determined that the busser had adequately presented a claim of religious discrimination since her belief that abortion was morally permissible, as opposed to the Christian employees who objected to abortion, was identified as the cause of staff uproar and contributed to her termination.[51]

Age

As medical developments have expanded life expectancy, the American work force has aged and issues of age discrimination arise with greater frequency and take on heightened importance. An employer may prefer a 25-year-old for a wait job over a 60-year-old. Can the employer fire or refuse to hire the older person? The answer is no; if an employer opts not to hire or fires the older worker because of age, the employer will be liable for age discrimination. A federal law called the Age Discrimination in Employment Act (ADEA), 29 U.S.C. §§ 621–634, bars an employer from discriminating against an employee on the basis of being 40 years of age or older. The ADEA makes it unlawful for an employer to refuse to hire, discharge, or otherwise discriminate with respect to compensation or conditions of employment because of a person's age. The purpose of the ADEA is "to promote employment of older persons based on their ability rather than age; to prohibit arbitrary age discrimination in employment; and to help employers and workers find ways of meeting problems arising from the impact of age on employment."

The ADEA attempts to balance the needs of seasoned workers with those of the business community. As with all the discrimination laws, the ADEA does not mandate that an employer hire a person over 40. Rather, it requires the employer

---

[51] *Turic v. Holiday Inn*, 85 F.3d 1211 (Mi. 1996)

to make employment decisions based on legitimate reasons other than age, such as qualifications. Also, an employer can refuse to hire older workers if it can show that youth is a legitimate business necessity. An example would be hiring young males to model fashions that are popular with teens only.

A plaintiff, age 67, an assistant manager of a Brew Burger restaurant in New York City, proved discrimination based on age where he was terminated when the restaurant closed and he was not rehired when it reopened under the same ownership. He was the oldest employee at the restaurant and the only one not rehired or reassigned to another restaurant owned by the defendant. The plaintiff was replaced by a man eight years his junior.[52]

In the following case, two hotel employees claimed that they were fired because they were each over 40 years old. A want ad placed by the restaurant and comments made by the owner established illegal age discrimination.

CASE EXAMPLE 14-5

EEOC v. Marion Motel Associates 763 F.Supp. 1338 (N.C. 1991) aff'd 961 F.2d 211 (1992)

... The Plaintiff, on behalf of claimants Aileen Peterson and Effie C. Petersen, alleged that the Defendant ... terminated their employment on the basis of their ages. ...

The evidence established that both claimants were over 40 years of age during their employment by the Defendant. Gary F. Hewitt, owner and manager of the Defendant Park Inn, testified that he was satisfied with the work of claimant Effie C. Petersen. While there was some testimony as to claimant Aileen Peterson's tardiness in reporting to work, it appears that she also generally met the legitimate expectations of Defendant. Moreover, the evidence was that Hewitt expressed his desire to replace claimants Aileen Peterson and Effie C. Petersen with younger employees. According to the testimony, although Hewitt was an experienced businessman, he caused an unlawful advertisement to be published in The McDowell News which announced vacancies in all supervisory and desk clerk positions and urged "young, energetic persons" to apply for employment at the Park Inn. Hewitt testified that when claimant Effie

Petersen offered to learn additional tasks for the second shift, he replied, "You can't teach an old dog new tricks." The evidence further established that the job application used by the Defendant contained a notice regarding prohibitions under the Age Discrimination in Employment Act (hereinafter "the Act"). ...

The Court sent the issues covering the age discrimination claim of Aileen Peterson and Effie Petersen to the jury. The jury responded in the affirmative to the question, "[D]id the Defendant ... terminate the employment of claimant Aileen Peterson and claimant Effie C. Petersen because of their age?"

The evidence was that Hewitt was an experienced businessman with knowledge of the Act. Hewitt used job application forms at the Park Inn that contained a notice regarding the Act's prohibitions. As stated above, Hewitt placed an advertisement in The McDowell News, that was in violation of federal law. Moreover, the Court heard the testimony about Hewitt's age-biased comment to Effie Petersen and the circumstances regarding her departure. The Court finds that the totality of the evidence establishes a course of conduct [establishing violation of the Act]. ...

[Judgment for plaintiff affirmed.]

---

[52] *Tarshis v. Riese Organization*, 211 F.3d 30 (N.Y. 2000)

Retaliatory Discharge

It is illegal for an employer to retaliate against an employee who files a complaint with the EEOC or otherwise objects to or protests an employer's violation of civil rights laws. Retaliation often takes the form of terminating the employee. Such an unlawful discharge is called a **retaliatory discharge**. In *Brady v. Sam's Town Hotel & Gambling Center*, 110 F.3d 67 (Nev. 1997), the plaintiff had been employed by the defendant as a poker dealer until June 1991. Thereafter, he testified against the defendant in a discrimination lawsuit brought by another employee. Subsequently, the plaintiff re-applied for a poker dealer's position at the defendant's casino. The defendant normally followed a policy of rehiring dealers who had previously worked at its casino before hiring new dealers. The plaintiff was told by the poker room manager that "I don't even know if they're gonna want to hire you back because of the involvement with the [discrimination case]." The defendant thereafter twice hired new dealers rather than the defendant. The court held these facts support a finding of retaliatory discharge.

Another form of prohibited retaliations is writing a negative job reference for someone who files a discrimination complaint. In *Hashimoto v. Secretary of the Navy*, 118 F.3d 671 (9th Cir. 1997), a budget analyst for the Navy filed a complaint against her immediate supervisor alleging race and gender discrimination. She thereafter sought a position with the Army and asked the supervisor for a reference. He provided one but it was not flattering. The court concluded that the negative reference was motivated by "retaliatory animus" and thus violated Title VII.

Mixed Types of Discrimination

Sometimes an employer will discriminate against a worker on more than one illegal ground. As you read the following case, see how many illegal bases for discrimination you can find. While the case is quite long, it provides an excellent review of many of the discrimination topics we have discussed.

CASE EXAMPLE 14-6

EEOC v. Hacienda Hotel
881 F.2d 1504 (9th Cir. 1989)

On May 30, 1986, the Equal Employment Opportunity Commission ("EEOC" or "the Commission") initiated this employment discrimination action against appellant defendant Hacienda Hotel ("Hacienda" or "the Hotel"), in El Segundo, California. The Commission alleged that the Hacienda, its General Manager (Frank Godoy), its Executive Housekeeper (Alicia Castro), and its Chief of Engineering (William Nusbaum), had engaged in unlawful employment practices against female employees in the Hacienda housekeeping department by sexually harassing them, terminating them when they became pregnant, failing to accommodate their religious beliefs, and retaliating against them for opposing Hacienda's discriminatory practices. Relief was sought and obtained on behalf of five current and former Hacienda maids, all but one of whom were undocumented aliens, who were alleged to have been victims of appellant's discriminatory employment practices during 1982 and 1983. We affirm.

[Facts of the case involving Teodora Castro:]

The Hotel hired Teodora Castro in June 1980. Teodora became pregnant in late 1981 and continued to work for defendant. During the course of her pregnancy, both Alicia Castro and Nusbaum made numerous crude and disparaging remarks regarding her pregnancy. Nusbaum, for example, told Teodora that "that's what you get for sleeping without your underwear;" he also asked why she was pregnant by another man and made comments about her "ass." Nusbaum often subjected her to sexually offensive remarks in the presence of Alicia Castro, who merely laughed. Alicia Castro herself told Teodora that she did not like "stupid women who have kids," and on many occasions called her a "dog" or a "whore" or a "slut."

In late 1981 and early 1982, Teodora Castro complained to Frank Godoy and Jose Ortiz, the union representative, about Nusbaum's and Alicia Castro's comments, but the situation did not improve. On June 30, 1982, Teodora Castro was terminated, as Alicia Castro admitted in her deposition and at trial, because of her pregnancy. She was rehired in November 1982, following the birth of her child.

Teodora Castro is also a Seventh Day Adventist who observes the Sabbath on Saturdays. Prior to her termination, she had been given Saturdays off. After she was rehired in November 1982, however, Alicia Castro informed her that she would have to work Saturdays. Teodora reminded the Executive Housekeeper that she needed Saturdays off in order to observe her Sabbath, but Alicia Castro denied her request. On December 17, 1982, Alicia Castro terminated Teodora for refusing to work on her Sabbath. During this time period, another maid in the Housekeeping Department, who was less senior than Teodora, was permitted to have both Saturdays and Sundays off after she had been attacked on the way home from work while waiting for public transportation, which was inadequate on weekends.

Following her termination, Teodora immediately sought employment [without immediate success]. After another pregnancy, she finally secured new employment at another hotel in May 1984. Between May 1984 and the date of the trial, Teodora Castro earned less than she would have earned had she remained employed by the Hacienda.

[Facts of the case involving Maria Elana Gonzales:]

Maria Elana Gonzalez was a maid in the Hacienda Housekeeping Department from October 27, 1980, to September 21, 1982. Gonzalez is a Jehovah's Witness and observes her Sabbath on Sundays. In early September 1982, Gonzalez requested that she be given Sundays off in order to observe the Sabbath. Alicia Castro initially granted Gonzalez's request; two days later she changed her mind and told Gonzalez that she had to work Sundays or quit.

Gonzalez filed a union grievance complaining of Castro's refusal to accommodate her religious beliefs. Gonzalez also informed the General Manager of the Hacienda Hotel, Frank Godoy, of Alicia Castro's refusal to adjust her schedule. Godoy told Gonzalez that he would speak with Castro regarding her request. Alicia Castro subsequently told Gonzalez that because she had complained to Godoy, she would never have Sundays off and that she should be grateful that she had a job. Castro also told Gonzalez that she [Castro] was going to "make life so difficult for her that she [Gonzalez] would not know her head from her feet."

During the month of September 1982, Castro issued four disciplinary warnings to Gonzalez and terminated her on September 21, 1982. Following her termination, Gonzalez sought other comparable employment.

[Facts of the case involving Flora Villalobos:]

The Hotel hired Flora Villalobos in April of 1980. After she became pregnant in early 1982, she was regularly subjected to sexually offensive remarks from Alicia Castro and Nusbaum. Castro often called her a "dog" or a "whore," and Nusbaum told her that women "get pregnant because they like to suck men's dicks." On many occasions, Nusbaum threatened to have her fired if she did not submit to his sexual advances. Castro witnessed some of Nusbaum's behavior and laughed at his sexual remarks. On October 31, 1982, when Villalobos was approximately seven months pregnant and still able and willing to work, Castro terminated her employment because of her pregnancy. Villalobos had obtained a statement from her doctor indicating that she was able to continue working until two or three weeks before her estimated delivery date of December 28, 1982.

On February 9, 1983, Villalobos provided Castro a written statement from her doctor indicating that she was able to return to work immediately. Villalobos was not rehired until April 8, 1983. The Hotel hired two maids, one rehire and one new employee, while Villalobos was awaiting rehire.

[Facts of the case involving Leticia Cardona:]

Leticia Cardona was employed by the Hotel from May 15, 1981, to September 28, 1982. After she became pregnant in early 1982, she was subjected to sexually offensive comments by Alicia Castro and Nusbaum. In September 1982, when Cardona was six months pregnant, Castro told her that she was too fat to clean rooms and fired her on September 28, 1982. Although at trial Castro testified that Cardona was terminated for poor work performance, Castro had previously admitted in a deposition that she terminated Cardona pursuant to her practice of terminating pregnant employees. Cardona's notice of termination form, which was completed by Castro, states that she was terminated because of her pregnancy.

In December 1982, after the birth of her baby, Cardona returned to the Hotel and requested her job back, but Castro refused. Castro testified that Cardona was not rehired because she was a poor worker.

[Facts of the case involving Mercedes Flores:]

Throughout her term of employment from October 8, 1978, to March 10, 1983, William Nusbaum made sexual advances and offensive sexual comments to Mercedes Flores. Nusbaum regularly offered, for example, to give her money from his paycheck and an apartment to live in if she would "give him [her] body." He also assured her that she would never be fired if she would have sex with him. Flores claimed to have heard Nusbaum make offensive sexual comments to other maids, including complainants Cardona, Castro, and Villalobos. On one occasion, for example, she heard him say to Villalobos: "You have such a fine ass. It's a nice ass to stick a nice dick into. How many dicks have you eaten?" ...

[Pregnancy Discrimination]

Alicia Castro admitted that it was her practice to terminate pregnant employees rather than permit them to take temporary leaves of absence, although she did not terminate other employees who were similarly temporarily disabled because of illness or injury. Alicia Castro specifically admitted that she terminated claimants Castro, Villalobos, and Cardona because of pregnancy.

Appellant argues that it should not be held liable for pregnancy discrimination because no one suffered any "damage" as a result of an application of the discriminatory policy. In particular, appellant contends that Teodora Castro and Villalobos were rehired following their pregnancies without loss of seniority or other benefits, while Cardona would not have been reinstated in any event because of her poor work performance. ...

Even if no employee suffered a "tangible loss" of an "economic nature," i.e., a loss of seniority or wages or other monetarily quantifiable employment benefit, appellant's implementation of a policy or practice under which pregnant employees were treated differently from other temporarily-disabled employees with similar capacity for work would still be a violation of both the letter and spirit of Title VII's prohibition against pregnancy discrimination. Appellant overlooks, moreover, the district court's ultimate determination that at least one of the pregnancy discrimination claimants, Flora Villalobos, actually did lose wages because of appellant's discriminatory policy. ...

[Religious Discrimination]

The district court found that Teodora Castro and Marie Elena Gonzalez informed Alicia Castro of their religious beliefs and requested that their schedules be adjusted such that they would have a day off on their Sabbath, that their supervisor, Alicia Castro, denied their requests, threatening them with discharge if they did not work on their Sabbath, and that Teodora Castro was actually dismissed for refusing to work on her Sabbath. These findings are clearly sufficient to establish appellees' prima facie case of religious discrimination. ...

[The] Hacienda made no effort whatsoever to accommodate the religious beliefs of both these women. Alicia Castro admitted that she never asked any maid if they would volunteer to work nor did she make any effort to rearrange the schedule of the maids according to the religious needs of the employees within the housekeeping department. The record also reflects that there was at least one voluntary substitute, Teodora's sister, who was willing to work for her. ...

[T]he Hacienda failed reasonably to accommodate the religious practices of Teodora Castro and Maria Elena Gonzalez, and it terminated Teodora Castro because of her religion, in violation of Title VII. ...

[Retaliatory Discharge]

The district court found that Maria Elena Gonzalez established a prima facie case of retaliation. When Alicia Castro found out that Gonzalez had spoken with Frank Godoy, she told Gonzalez that now she would never have Sundays off and threatened to make her life very difficult. Within less than a month of her complaint to Godoy, Castro issued three written warnings to Gonzalez and fired her.

Appellant contends, however, that Gonzalez was fired for poor work performance and not for any retaliatory reasons. ... [D]uring trial, Alicia Castro testified that she fired Gonzalez for poor work performance. The court below, however, explicitly found that Alicia Castro was not a credible witness. ...

[Sexual Harassment Claim]

Hacienda argues that the sexually harassing conduct in which Castro and Nusbaum were proven to have engaged was not sufficiently severe or pervasive to be actionable. Appellant also contends that it could not be held liable for the acts of Nusbaum and Castro of which it had no notice. Finally, Hacienda argues that its policy against discrimination and its internal grievance procedures should shield it from liability for sexual harassment. We consider each of Hacienda's contentions in turn.

There is no dispute in this case that the acts of sexual harassment complained of occurred, and that they were unwelcome. The contested issue is whether the harassment was sufficiently "severe or pervasive" to alter the terms and conditions of the claimants' employment and to create a sexually hostile work environment. As the record reveals, Nusbaum repeatedly engaged in vulgarities, made sexual remarks, and requested sexual favors from the complainants. The complainants' direct supervisor, Alicia Castro, also frequently witnessed,

laughed at, and herself made these types of comments. Castro had direct authority to hire, discharge, and discipline housekeeping employees, and Nusbaum threatened at least one of the claimants that he would have Castro fire her if she did not submit to his sexual advances. ... [W]e agree with the district court's conclusion that the complainants were subjected to severe and pervasive sexual harassment that "seriously tainted" the working environment and altered the terms and conditions of their employment. ... [that is, attempts to resolve disagreements in-house without going to court. Internal remedies might include discussion, negotiations, mediation, or arbitration.]

Appellant's remaining argument, that the complainants failed to pursue internal remedies under appellant's general nondiscrimination policy, can be disposed of quickly. ... Where, as here, the employer's discrimination policy does not specifically proscribe sexual harassment, and its internal procedures require initial resort to a supervisor who is accused of engaging in or condoning the harassment of which the employee complains, it would be plainly unreasonable to require discrimination claimants to exhaust such procedures as a predicate to suit. In any event, this court has held that a Title VII plaintiff need not exhaust her employer's internal remedies.

[Undocumented Aliens]

Appellant argues that the district court erred in awarding back pay to Teodora Castro, Flora Villalobos, and Maria Elena Gonzales, all of whom were undocumented alien workers [meaning an immigrant who lacks necessary immigration documents to prove they have the legal right to be employed in this country; see Mandatory Verification of Employment Status, later in this chapter] when they were subjected to appellant's discriminatory employment practices. The Hacienda also challenges the district court's calculation of the back pay awards. ...

The district court in this case assumed that Title VII, including its remedial provisions, applied to the undocumented aliens who were subjected by appellant to various forms of employment discrimination. It is basically undisputed that all of the employees who were awarded back pay for the Title VII violations in this case were in the United States, were not subjected to deportation proceedings, and were available for employment throughout the back pay period that could readily be calculated with certainty. Under our existing case law, then, the district court did not err in concluding that Castro, Villalobos, and Gonzalez were entitled to back pay in this case despite their status as undocumented aliens.

[Back Pay]

We turn now to appellant's arguments that the district court abused its discretion in calculating the back pay awards in this case. ... In awarding back pay, the district court is required to attempt to make victims of discrimination whole by restoring them to the position in which they would have been absent the discrimination. Title VII also requires mitigation of damages, however, by providing that "amounts earnable with reasonable diligence [by the employee]" be deducted from a back pay award. The back pay award in this case was well within the court's discretion. ...

[Injunctive Relief]

Appellant's final arguments challenge the district court's decision permanently to enjoin [forbid] appellant from "engaging in any employment practice which discriminates on the basis of sex, religion [or otherwise violates employment laws]." ... Appellant contends that injunctive relief ... was an inappropriate and unneeded sanction because there is no reasonable expectation that the alleged violations will recur. ...

Even if the individual complainants have been made whole by the [monetary] relief awarded by the district court, this court has recognized that the EEOC has a right of action [for an injunction] that is independent of the employees' private rights of action. This is because the EEOC is not merely a proxy for the victims of discrimination, but acts also "to vindicate the public interest in preventing employment discrimination." By seeking injunctive relief, the EEOC not only deters future unlawful discrimination but also seeks to protect aggrieved employees and others similarly situated from the fear of retaliation for filing Title VII charges. ...

An employer that takes curative actions only after it has been sued fails to provide sufficient assurances that it will not repeat the violation to justify denying an injunction. Appellant's recent efforts to train managerial employees regarding discrimination problems and the absence of further EEOC charges in recent times are encouraging and laudable; however, the district court did not abuse its discretion by awarding permanent injunctive relief on the facts of this case.

For all of the foregoing reasons, the judgment of the district court is AFFIRMED.

The Civil Rights Act of 1991

We have already seen that the Civil Rights Act of 1991 (CRA91) contained some significant changes to discrimination law. It increased the categories of discrimination for which a plaintiff can be awarded compensatory and punitive damages. It permits a successful plaintiff to collect expert witness fees from the defendant. Many businesses opposed CRA91 because these factors motivate victims of discrimination to pursue lawsuits.

CRA91 provides plaintiffs with other benefits as well. These additional advantages affect United States citizens employed abroad, mixed motive cases, burden of proof in discrimination cases, and "glass ceilings."

United States Citizens Employed Abroad

Prior to the CRA91, protection against discrimination did not apply to citizens of this country employed abroad by an American company. In *EEOC v. Arabian*

American Oil Co., 111 S.Ct. 1227 (1991), decided before the adoption of CRA91, a United States citizen working in Saudi Arabia for an American Company was denied protection of Title VII. CRA91 effectively reverses that decision and extends the Civil Rights Act of 1964, including Title VII, to those citizens. An exception is provided for the circumstance where compliance would violate the law of the foreign country. For example, if a United States employer is doing business in a country that prohibits women from working more than a certain number of hours per week, the employer could not be faulted for discriminating against women when hiring for a job requiring more than that number of hours.

Mixed Motive Cases

Not infrequently, acts of discrimination are motivated by more than one factor, only one of which is illegal. Prior to the CRA91, an employer could avoid liability for discrimination by proving that it would have made the same adverse decision concerning the employee's work status even if the illegal consideration, such as gender, had not played a role. The CRA91 significantly modifies this rule. Now, if a termination or other adverse employment action is motivated even in part by illegal discrimination, the action is illegal. The opportunity for the employer to escape liability by showing the same decision would have been made regardless of the illegal consideration has been eliminated. CRA91 provides, "An unlawful employment practice is established when the complaining party demonstrates that race, color, religion, sex, or national origin was a motivating factor for any employment practice, *even though other factors also motivated the practice.*" (Emphasis added.)

A successful plaintiff in a mixed motive case is not entitled to compensatory or punitive damages or back pay. The remedies are limited to injunction, declaratory judgment, attorney's fees, and court costs.

Glass Ceiling

Glass Ceiling refers to artificial barriers that have held women and minorities back from promotion to management and decision-making positions in business. To address the underrepresentation of women and minorities, CRA91 established a Glass Ceiling Commission to study the manner in which businesses fill management positions.

The report, issued in 1995 and still relevant today, concluded that substantial barriers exist for women and minorities at the highest levels of business. The Commission found that white males hold 96 percent of all senior-management positions at the level of vice president or higher. Major contributors to this circumstance include persistent bias, negative stereotypes, prejudice concerning women and racial minorities, and inadequate laws. Among the Commission's recommendations for removing these barriers are the following:

1. Chief executive officers must demonstrate commitment to diversity.
2. Affirmative action should be used as a tool to ensure equal opportunity to compete for upper-management positions. Affirmative action refers to employment programs designed to remedy discriminatory practices in hiring.

3. Senior managers and directors should be sought from nontraditional sources and backgrounds.

4. Businesses should prepare minorities and women for senior positions (for example, provide training, and mentoring.)

5. Businesses should provide training to sensitize employees about gender, racial, ethnic, and cultural differences.

6. Recognizing that women are still primarily responsible for home and family, companies should adopt policies that accommodate the balance between work and family.

Companies should review their policies and practices, and modify them where needed to facilitate the achievement of diversity and the advancement of all segments of the workforce.

Americans with Disabilities Act

The Americans with Disabilities Act (ADA), which became effective in 1992, is an uncompromising proclamation of this country's commitment to equal opportunity for the disabled. The impact of this law can be understood from estimates that put the number of Americans with disabilities at 43 million. Prior to the adoption of the ADA, many employers declined to hire people with disabilities because of fears that they would be unable to perform the job or would be absent frequently or would require a lot of assistance. Such fears are based on stereotypes and should not be the basis for employment decisions. The ADA seeks to eliminate the barrier of those stereotypes for disabled persons who are able to perform on the job.

We saw in Chapter 3 the ADA's provisions requiring accessibility to places of public accommodation. In this chapter we study the Act's employment provisions. They apply to all phases of employment including hiring, advancement, discharge, compensation, and training. To the hospitality industry, the ADA has effectuated fundamental changes in personnel policies.

In short, the ADA provides that an employer cannot refuse to hire or otherwise discriminate against a disabled person who can, with reasonable accommodation, perform the essential functions of a job. A **disability** is defined as a physical or mental impairment that substantially limits a person's ability to walk, see, hear, perform manual tasks, learn, work, or care for themselves. **Essential functions** are the core responsibilities of a job as distinguished from marginal or incidental assignments. The ADA applies to employers with a minimum of 15 employees; it does not apply to employers with less than 15 workers.

Essential Functions

In determining what functions are essential to a job, a court will consider the following: the employer's judgment as to which functions are essential; written job descriptions drafted before the job was advertised or interviewing began;

and the amount of time on the job allocated to performing the function. Examples of essential functions in the job of a server are lifting, carrying, and lowering heavy trays.

The following are circumstances that may render a job function essential: the reason the position exists is to perform that function; only a limited number of employees are available who can perform the task; the function may be highly specialized and the reason for hiring a particular person is her expertise or ability to perform that duty.

In *Polesnak v. R. H. Management Systems, Inc.*, 1997 WL 109245 (Tenn. 1997), a general manager of a Burger King was terminated due to obesity (he weighed 600 pounds), which qualified as a disability. He had always received excellent reviews evidencing that his weight did not prevent him from performing the essential functions of the job. The employer thus violated the ADA and was liable to pay the plaintiff back and future wages that the plaintiff lost due to the illegal discharge.

Reasonable Accommodation

If an employee with a disability is able to perform the essential functions of the job with a reasonable accommodation, the employer may be obligated to make the adjustment. What constitutes a reasonable accommodation depends on the facts of each individual case. The ADA may require an employer to do any of the following: restructure the job; modify facilities to make them accessible, such as enlarging doors to make them negotiable in a wheelchair; modify work schedules; acquire equipment, such as magnifiers for the visually impaired; or modify exams and training programs for the visually impaired or learning disabled. While employers have expressed concerns about the cost of accommodations, studies have concluded that over 70 percent of accommodations cost less than $500 and 50 percent cost less than $50. Some tax incentives are available for providing accommodations. Employers are not required to provide personal use items such as hearing aids or eyeglasses.

The employer's duty to provide reasonable modifications applies not only to applicants for employment, but also to employees already on staff who are or become disabled and cannot perform their original jobs. Reasonable accommodation in these circumstances can include, in addition to the accommodations listed above, reassigning employees to a vacant job for which they are qualified. If accommodations are unavailing and no alternate job is available, the employer is not required to continue the employment.

Undue Hardship

If the accommodations required to enable the employee to perform the essential job functions are not reasonable, but rather impose an undue hardship on the business, the employer can legally refuse to extend employment to the disabled person. An **undue hardship** refers to an accommodation that requires significant difficulty or expense on the part of the employer, or major modification of the employer's business, taking into account such factors as the nature of the business, cost of the accommodation, and the business' resources. For example, a night club that features live music need not discontinue the music to accommodate a would-be waiter who is hearing impaired and unable to hear customers' beverage and food orders over the sound of a band. To eliminate music would change the format of the business and thus constitute an undue hardship.

Preference Not Required

An employer is not required to give preference to a disabled person, but can instead hire the most qualified applicant. For example, two people apply for a typing job in the corporate offices of a hotel chain. Speed is needed to perform the job duties successfully. One applicant has a disability and types 50 words a minute. The other has no disability and types 60 words a minute. The employer can hire the faster typist because he has the best qualifications.

If the fastest typist is the one with the disability, the employer cannot decline to hire him because of the handicap. If, to enable the employee to do the job, the employer would need to make an accommodation, the employer must do so absent proof that the accommodation creates an undue hardship. For example, assume that the disability prevents the employee from driving and public transportation results in the typist arriving at work a half hour after the beginning of the business day. The employer would need to modify the hours of the position unless the altered schedule presented an undue hardship for the employer.

An employer cannot make employment decisions based on inability to perform *nonessential* functions of the job, which are marginal tasks that do not qualify as essential functions. Change the facts of the typing example a bit: a nonessential function of the job is occasionally answering the phone; the disabled person, who is the fastest typist, is unable to hear and so cannot answer the phone. Can the employer hire the other applicant because of the disabled person's inability to answer the phone? The answer is no because answering the phone is not an essential job responsibility.

ADA Impacts on Application Process

The ADA permeates all aspects of the hiring decision. At the preemployment interview an employer cannot ask job applicants about the nature of a disability. Prohibited questions include: Do you have a disability? How severe is your disability? What medications are you taking? Have you been hospitalized recently? The employer can inquire whether the applicant can perform the essential functions of the job and can ask the applicant to demonstrate ability to perform those tasks. Depending on the job, permissible questions might include: Can you lift and carry a 20-pound tray? Will you please demonstrate your ability to do this?

An employer cannot require that an applicant submit to a medical exam prior to extending a job offer. However, the offer can be conditioned on the results of a medical exam, but only if all incoming employees in the same job title are required to be examined regardless of disability. The information obtained from the test must be kept confidential and in a file *separate* from the employee's employment file. The only people entitled to see the medical report are first-aid personnel, supervisors who need the information to determine necessary restrictions and accommodations, and government officials investigating compliance with the ADA.

Drugs and Illnesses

Drug tests are treated differently from medical exams. An employer can require a test to detect illegal use of drugs as part of the application process. An applicant for employment who uses illegal drugs is not protected by the ADA. An employer can discriminate against such a person when making employment decisions. However, if a would-be employee abused drugs in the past, but has since been rehabilitated or is enrolled in a supervised rehabilitation program and does not currently use them, she qualifies as a person with a disability and cannot be denied a benefit of employment on that ground.

The Act does not require a restaurateur to hire as a food handler a person with an infectious or communicable disease that is transmitted to others through food handling. For a disease to qualify, it must be on a list developed by the Secretary of Health and Human Services (hereinafter, the Secretary) that is required to be updated annually. Diseases that are on the list include Hepatitis A, salmonella typhi, staphylococcus aureus, and staphylococcus pyogenes. An employer can refuse to hire a would-be food handler who has these illnesses. With the list, the Secretary publishes symptoms that may indicate the presence of one of the listed diseases. The symptoms include diarrhea, vomiting, open skin sores, boils, fever, dark urine, and jaundice. AIDS is not transmitted through food handling and is not on the list. Persons afflicted with AIDS and people who are HIV positive are considered disabled for purposes of protection under the ADA. A restaurant that refuses to hire a food handler with AIDS because of the disease violates the ADA

Past Disabilities and Caregivers

The ADA protects not only people with disabilities, but also those with a past disability. For example, an employer cannot refuse to hire a recovered cancer patient. Also protected are those people who have a relationship with or are caregivers for a disabled person, such as a spouse or parent. Although the employer may fear that an applicant with a disabled child might be absent frequently, that relationship cannot be used as a reason for rejecting the applicant. If the applicant is hired and does take excessive leave, she can be terminated for that reason.

Pursuing an ADA Case

The ADA encourages would-be plaintiffs to resolve their complaints through mediation rather than litigation. A person wishing to pursue a claim under the ADA can file a complaint with the Equal Employment Opportunity Commission or pursue the case in court. The potential liability a defendant faces in a lawsuit is significant and includes the following:

1. Compensatory damages, including emotional pain and suffering, mental anguish, and loss of enjoyment of life
2. Punitive damages
3. Attorney's fees
4. Expert witness fees
5. Reinstatement where an employee was wrongly terminated
6. Back pay.

The ADA encourages employers to attempt reasonable accommodation by relieving them from liability for compensatory damages where they made a good-faith effort in consultation with the disabled person to identify and make a reasonable accommodation. For a plaintiff to win punitive damages, she must prove that the employer acted with malice or reckless indifference to the rights guaranteed under the ADA.

Inability to Perform Essential Elements

The responsibilities of employers to disabled employees and job applicants are triggered only when the disabled person is able to perform the essential functions of the job with or without reasonable accommodations. The Act does not protect an applicant or employee who cannot perform the essential components of a job. Thus, the termination of a food server did not violate the ADA where the server suffered from panic attacks when the restaurant became crowded causing a "complete inability to function." In those circumstances, she was unable to serve food. The attacks occurred notwithstanding an accommodation made by the employer assigning the server to the least-busy workstation.[53]

Another case involved a kitchen worker who, due to a back injury, was no longer able to clean oven hoods, stock various products, change oil in the fryers, sweep and mop floors, pick up and carry chicken, move continuously to work the grill during peak hours, and wash windows, several of which were essential elements of his job. The only accommodation that would have enabled the plaintiff to retain his job was for the restaurant to hire an additional employee to perform the tasks the plaintiff could not, or to exempt the plaintiff from performing many of his essential functions. Neither of these accommodations is reasonable and thus they are not required by the ADA.[54]

A manager at Pizza Hut faced a similar situation. Her job required that she perform tasks done by supervised employees when they were late or absent. Due to inflammatory arthritis, she was unable to lift more than twenty pounds and could not do repetitive motions with her arms. Her doctor advised that for her to

---

[53] *Johnston v. Morrison, Inc.*, 849 F.Supp. 777 (Ala. 1994)

[54] *Clement v. Bojangles' Restaurants, Inc.*, 2001 WL 66317 (N.C. 2001)

continue work, the restaurant would need to hire a new employee to perform the functions of truant employees that the plaintiff was unable to perform. The court held this was not a reasonable accommodation and therefore the employer did not violate the ADA by terminating her employment.[55]

Similarly, a slot attendant at a casino suffered a neck injury deeming him unable to carry heavy items. An essential function of his job was to carry bags of coins. Termination of his employment was therefore not discrimination under the ADA.[56]

Mandatory Verification of Employment Status

Not everyone in our country is legally entitled to work here. Citizens from other countries must have proper authorization to be legally employed in the United States. The necessary documentation proving authorization must be verified by employers.

Entrance to this country is restricted by law. While tourists are permitted to come in large numbers, only a limited number of people can enter each year for other purposes. To immigrate to the United States to attend school, work, or otherwise live here requires permission from the Immigration and Naturalization Service (INS), the government agency responsible for overseeing the immigration laws. An **immigrant** in the United States is a citizen of another country who enters this country with authorization from the INS. One who enters without the necessary approval is an **illegal alien.**

Immigration Reform and Control Act

The Immigration Reform and Control Act (IRCA), 8 U.S.C. §§ 1324a and 1324b, is a federal law passed in 1986 that enlists employers in the effort to prevent illegal aliens from working in this country. The IRCA requires employers to verify the employment status of workers they hire. An employer must complete and retain a form called the Employment Eligibility Verification Form, commonly referred to as Form I-9. The primary purpose of this form is to verify that the individual is authorized to work in the United States. The employee must present identification and proof that he has permission from the INS to work here. The employer is required to examine the document(s) to determine if, in the words of the statute, it "reasonably appears on its face to be genuine." No later than three days following the date of hire, the employer must sign Form I-9, stating under penalty of perjury that the employer has verified that the individual is not an unauthorized alien. The employee must also sign attesting to legal status. The employer must retain the form for three years following the date of hire or until one year after the employee leaves, whichever is longer. Form I-9 is shown as Figure 14-1 on pages 516 and 517.

---

[55] *Burnett v. Pizza Hut of America, Inc.*, 92 F.Supp.2d 1142 (Kan. 2000)
[56] *Van de Pol v. Caesars Hotel Casino*, 979 F.Supp. 308 (N.J. 1997)

U.S. Department of Justice
Immigration and Naturalization Service

OMB No. 1115-0136

Employment Eligibility Verification

Please read instructions carefully before completing this form. The instructions must be available during completion of this form. ANTI-DISCRIMINATION NOTICE: It is illegal to discriminate against work eligible individuals. Employers CANNOT specify which document(s) they will accept from an employee. The refusal to hire an individual because of a future expiration date may also constitute illegal discrimination.

Section 1. Employee Information and Verification. To be completed and signed by employee at the time employment begins.

Print Name: Last	First	Middle Initial	Maiden Name

Address (Street Name and Number)		Apt. #	Date of Birth (month/day/year)

City	State	Zip Code	Social Security #

I am aware that federal law provides for imprisonment and/or fines for false statements or use of false documents in connection with the completion of this form.

I attest, under penalty of perjury, that I am (check one of the following):
- [ ] A citizen or national of the United States
- [ ] A Lawful Permanent Resident (Alien # A_____)
- [ ] An alien authorized to work until ___/___/___
  (Alien # or Admission #) _____

Employee's Signature	Date (month/day/year)

Preparer and/or Translator Certification. *(To be completed and signed if Section 1 is prepared by a person other than the employee.) I attest, under penalty of perjury, that I have assisted in the completion of this form and that to the best of my knowledge the information is true and correct.*

Preparer's/Translator's Signature	Print Name

Address (Street Name and Number, City, State, Zip Code)	Date (month/day/year)

Section 2. Employer Review and Verification. To be completed and signed by employer. Examine one document from List A OR examine one document from List B and one from List C, as listed on the reverse of this form, and record the title, number and expiration date, if any, of the document(s)

List A	OR	List B	AND	List C
Document title:_____		_____		_____
Issuing authority: _____		_____		_____
Document #: _____		_____		_____
Expiration Date (if any): ___/___/___		___/___/___		___/___/___
Document #: _____				
Expiration Date (if any): ___/___/___				

CERTIFICATION - I attest, under penalty of perjury, that I have examined the document(s) presented by the above-named employee, that the above-listed document(s) appear to be genuine and to relate to the employee named, that the employee began employment on *(month/day/year)* ___/___/___ **and that to the best of my knowledge the employee is eligible to work in the United States. (State employment agencies may omit the date the employee began employment.)**

Signature of Employer or Authorized Representative	Print Name	Title

Business or Organization Name	Address (Street Name and Number, City, State, Zip Code)	Date (month/day/year)

Section 3. Updating and Reverification. To be completed and signed by employer.

A. New Name (if applicable)	B. Date of rehire (month/day/year) (if applicable)

C. If employee's previous grant of work authorization has expired, provide the information below for the document that establishes current employment eligibility.

Document Title:_____ Document #: _____ Expiration Date (if any): ___/___/___

I attest, under penalty of perjury, that to the best of my knowledge, this employee is eligible to work in the United States, and if the employee presented document(s), the document(s) I have examined appear to be genuine and to relate to the individual.

Signature of Employer or Authorized Representative	Date (month/day/year)

Form I-9 (Rev. 11-21-91)N Page 2

FIGURE 14-1 Employment Eligibility Verification Form, commonly referred to as Form I-9

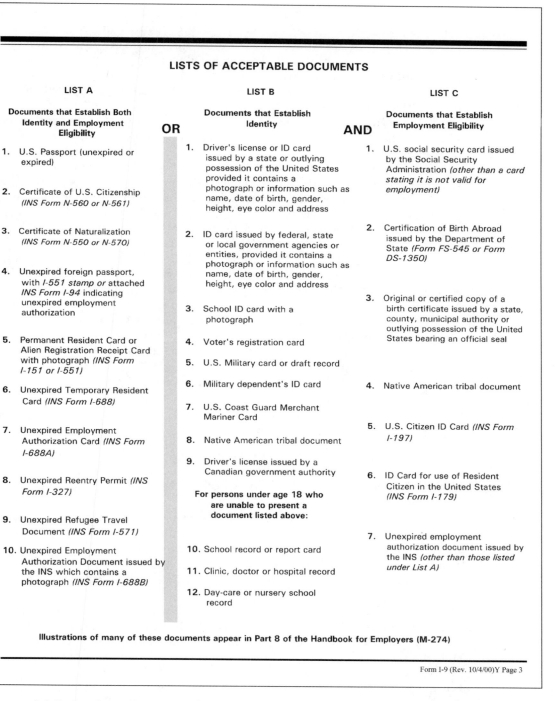

LISTS OF ACCEPTABLE DOCUMENTS

LIST A		LIST B		LIST C
Documents that Establish Both Identity and Employment Eligibility	**OR**	Documents that Establish Identity	**AND**	Documents that Establish Employment Eligibility

LIST A — Documents that Establish Both Identity and Employment Eligibility

1. U.S. Passport (unexpired or expired)

2. Certificate of U.S. Citizenship *(INS Form N-560 or N-561)*

3. Certificate of Naturalization *(INS Form N-550 or N-570)*

4. Unexpired foreign passport, with *I-551 stamp or* attached *INS Form I-94* indicating unexpired employment authorization

5. Permanent Resident Card or Alien Registration Receipt Card with photograph *(INS Form I-151 or I-551)*

6. Unexpired Temporary Resident Card *(INS Form I-688)*

7. Unexpired Employment Authorization Card *(INS Form I-688A)*

8. Unexpired Reentry Permit *(INS Form I-327)*

9. Unexpired Refugee Travel Document *(INS Form I-571)*

10. Unexpired Employment Authorization Document issued by the INS which contains a photograph *(INS Form I-688B)*

LIST B — Documents that Establish Identity

1. Driver's license or ID card issued by a state or outlying possession of the United States provided it contains a photograph or information such as name, date of birth, gender, height, eye color and address

2. ID card issued by federal, state or local government agencies or entities, provided it contains a photograph or information such as name, date of birth, gender, height, eye color and address

3. School ID card with a photograph

4. Voter's registration card

5. U.S. Military card or draft record

6. Military dependent's ID card

7. U.S. Coast Guard Merchant Mariner Card

8. Native American tribal document

9. Driver's license issued by a Canadian government authority

For persons under age 18 who are unable to present a document listed above:

10. School record or report card

11. Clinic, doctor or hospital record

12. Day-care or nursery school record

LIST C — Documents that Establish Employment Eligibility

1. U.S. social security card issued by the Social Security Administration *(other than a card stating it is not valid for employment)*

2. Certification of Birth Abroad issued by the Department of State *(Form FS-545 or Form DS-1350)*

3. Original or certified copy of a birth certificate issued by a state, county, municipal authority or outlying possession of the United States bearing an official seal

4. Native American tribal document

5. U.S. Citizen ID Card *(INS Form I-197)*

6. ID Card for use of Resident Citizen in the United States *(INS Form I-179)*

7. Unexpired employment authorization document issued by the INS *(other than those listed under List A)*

Illustrations of many of these documents appear in Part 8 of the Handbook for Employers (M-274)

Form I-9 (Rev. 10/4/00)Y Page 3

FIGURE 14-1 Employment Eligibility Verification Form, commonly referred to as Form I-9 *(continued)*

If the employee is unable to locate the necessary documents, the employer may allow 21 days for the employee to secure them. If the employee has not produced them by the end of the 21 days, the employer must terminate that worker. Failure to sever the employee will subject the employer to a penalty up to $1,000, even if the employee's legal status is later confirmed. If an employer illustrates a pattern of disregard for the required verifications, the penalty increases to $3,000 for each offense.

When reviewing documents to satisfy the IRCA, it is the employer's responsibility to check the expiration dates. An expired document is not adequate proof of a person's status.

The penalty for hiring an illegal alien is a cease and desist order, which requires the employer to terminate the employee, and a fine that ranges from $250 to $2,000 for each unauthorized alien for a first offense. Fines can range up to $5,000 per illegal worker for a second offense, and up to $10,000 per illegal worker for a third offense. The law intentionally makes repeated offenses prohibitively expensive.

When the IRCA was under consideration by Congress, various minority groups feared that employers would attempt to avoid liability by refusing to hire all aliens. While the Civil Rights Act outlaws discrimination based on national origin, it does not include noncitizens as a protected class. To prevent discrimination against immigrants who are authorized to work, the IRCA prohibits discrimination in employment based on citizenship status, which means an employer cannot refuse to hire, based on lack of citizenship, a qualified alien authorized to work. Interestingly, the IRCA provides a preference in hiring and recruiting for a United States citizen over an alien "if the two individuals are equally qualified."

Résumé Fraud

Misrepresentations contained in a résumé are termed *résumé fraud* or *credentials fraud*. The untruths can relate to the college attended, degrees received, prior employers, prior job responsibilities, salary history, certifications earned, and virtually any other factor contained in a vita.

The Internet expands the opportunities for résumé fraud because it provides easy access to fake degrees, authentic-looking diplomas, and even fill-in-the-blank transcript templates. Credential falsification creates dilemmas for employers because it increases the difficulty of finding the best candidates for openings. Résumé fraud is likewise costly to employers because it results in higher employee turnover and increased training time.

Some employers are addressing the problem by utilizing in the hiring process intensive one-on-one, in-person testing of candidates for each skill required by the job and also for communication proficiencies. Also helpful in detecting embellishments of an applicant's background are thorough reference checks.

Another precaution employers should consider is including a statement at the bottom of the application form stating that the would-be employee swears to the truth of the information provided. If any data is later discovered to be false, this statement lays the foundation for a civil case in fraud or a criminal prosecution for perjury. Penalties for perjury include jail, fines, and probation. Consequences for civil fraud include reimbursement to the employer of expenses incurred as a result of the untruthful information.

Occupational Safety and Health Administration

The Occupational Safety and Health Administration, a federal agency known by its acronym OSHA, is a federal agency whose mission is to ensure safe and healthy workplaces in the United States. It enforces laws passed by Congress and regulations adopted by OSHA that mandate safe conditions at work sites. Additionally, some states have adopted their own safety standards, which are at least equal to OSHA's and may be more stringent.

Examples of the thousands of OSHA regulations include proper labeling and storing of hazardous materials (such materials may be present in cleaning solvents and pesticides used in restaurants or hotels), mandated safety devices for meat-cutting machinery, procedures to reduce the spread of such diseases as Hepatitis B and the HIV virus through bloodborne pathogens, proper storage and placement of portable fire extinguishers, and maintenance of specified first-aid devices.

The agency hires and trains inspectors who visit workplaces to investigate whether employers are complying with applicable safety rules. In addition to routine safety audits, inspections occur in response to accidents, complaints by employees or customers, and referrals from other government agencies. All employers are required to post information for employees about their safety and health rights and how to contact OSHA if they observe violations. Restaurant and hotel trade associations provide training and awareness materials to assist members in identifying risks, preventing accidents, and complying with OSHA regulations.

Hospitality facilities need to be aware of federal and state workplace safety rules. Violations can result in substantial fines and other penalties.

Unions

Unions are organizations of workers whose mission includes negotiating for higher wages, better benefits, greater job stability, and safer workplaces. These goals are achieved in significant part by **collective bargaining**, which is the process whereby representatives of the union negotiate with representatives of management (the owners and operators of a company) on terms of employment such as hours, wages, benefits, vacations, and working conditions. The resulting contract between workers and management is called a **collective bargaining agreement.**

Union membership customarily enhances the bargaining power of workers because unions are acting on behalf of not just an individual but rather groups of employees. The collective bargaining agreement typically secures rights greater than provided to employees by law. For example, we have studied that the law provides that employment is customarily at-will, meaning the employer can terminate for any reason except illegal discrimination. Contrast that with the terms of a collective bargaining agreement, which customarily restrict the employer's right to terminate absent good cause. Management, not surprisingly, usually prefers a nonunionized workplace where its control is unbridled by a union.

National Labor Relations Act

The National Labor Relations Act (NLRA), a federal law enacted in 1935, protects employees' right to form, join, or assist a union. Congressional findings that led to the passage of the Act include the following: "Experience has proved that protection by law of the right of employees to organize and bargain collectively safeguards commerce from … interruption by removing certain recognized sources of industrial strife and unrest by encouraging practices fundamental to the friendly adjustment of industrial disputes arising out of differences as to wages, hours, or other working conditions, and by restoring equality of bargaining power between employers and employees."

Union membership is a protected class for purposes of discrimination. An employer violates the NLRA if it refuses to hire an applicant because of union activity or retaliates against a union activist by, for example, demoting, transferring, or terminating that person.

National Labor Relations Board

Enforcement of the NLRA is done by the National Labor Relations Board (NLRB) which, among other powers, has the authority to prevent employers from engaging in unfair labor practices. Such prohibited acts include threats, warnings, and orders to refrain from protected union action; discrimination against employees who participate in union activities; retaliation for filing a charge of an unfair labor practice with the NLRB; and refusal to negotiate in good faith with union representatives over conditions of employment.

Key Terms

at-will employment
back pay
bona fide occupational
    qualification (BFOQ)
business necessity
collective bargaining
collective bargaining agreement
comparable worth
disability
disparate impact

disparate treatment
Equal Employment Opportunity
    Commission (EEOC)
equal pay for equal work
essential functions
Fair Labor Standards Act
glass ceiling
hostile environment sexual
    harassment
illegal alien

immigrant
protected classes
quid pro quo sexual harassment

retaliatory discharge
sexual harassment
undue hardship

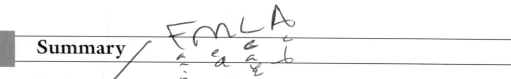

Summary

Employment laws cover virtually every aspect of the employer-employee relationship. The Fair Labor Standards Act mandates minimum wages, one-and-one-half pay for overtime work, equal pay for equal work, and restrictions on child labor. The Family and Medical Leave Act entitles qualified employees to unpaid leave to care for a child, spouse, or parent, or for the employee's own illness.

The Civil Rights Act of 1964, Title VII, prohibits discrimination on the basis of race, color, religion, gender, and national origin. Other laws prohibit discrimination on the basis of pregnancy, age (over 40), disability, marital status, arrest record, lack of citizenship, and union activity.

The Immigration Reform and Control Act requires employers to verify the employment status of employees, primarily to prevent illegal aliens from working in this country.

Employers are also required to follow safety regulations to help protect employees from workplace injuries.

Preventive Law Tips for Managers

- *Unless your business is exempt, pay your employees the applicable minimum wage.* The Fair Labor Standards Act (FLSA) imposes an obligation on employers to pay a minimum wage. Effective September 1, 1997, the federal minimum wage is $5.15. State governments can increase the minimum wage. Some exceptions to the federal minimum wage apply, including employers whose annual sales are less than $500,000, and employees who receive part of their pay in tips.

- *Pay employees one-and-one-half times their hourly wage for hours they work in excess of 40 per week.* The FLSA requires time-and-a-half pay for time worked in excess of 40 hours in any given week. This rule does not apply to qualifying managerial, administrative, or professional employees.

- *Utilize the same pay scales and ranges for male and female employees who perform the same job.* The Equal Pay Act, a provision of the FLSA, requires equal treatment in pay for men and women who do the same jobs.

- *Do not hire anyone under age 14.* The FLSA prohibits the employment of young people under age 14.

- *If you hire young workers, review the applicable restrictions on their hours and duties and abide by them.* The FLSA and laws in many states restrict both the hours certain teenage employees can work and the types of tasks they can perform. Do not assign these workers to illegal hours or prohibited responsibilities. Determining permissible working hours can be confusing because they differ by age groups and change for school days, weekends, and holidays. Careful attention to the various restrictions is required to avoid fines and unwanted negative publicity.

- *Do not discriminate on the basis of race.* Race is a protected class. Employees should not be treated differently because of their race. Racial groups include African-Americans, Caucasians, Asians, Native Americans, Eskimos, and Native Hawaiians.

- *Do not discriminate on the basis of national origin.* National origin is a protected class. Employees should not be treated differently because of their country of origin.

- *Do not discriminate on the basis of accent or inability to speak English unless mastery of the language is a job necessity.* Generally, discrimination against a person who cannot speak English well or who speaks with an accent constitutes discrimination on the basis of national origin. If, however, performance of the job requires knowledge of English and the ability to speak it well, someone who cannot understand it or who cannot be understood is not qualified, and so failure to hire that person would not be illegal discrimination.

- *Do not discriminate on the basis of religion.* Religion is a protected class. Employees should not be treated differently because of their religion. If an employee needs a modified work schedule to comply with religious observances, the employer is required to make a reasonable effort to accommodate the employee. If accommodation would cause the employer undue hardship, the employer can refuse to oblige the employee's religious needs and will not be liable for religious discrimination.

- *Do not discriminate on the basis of gender.* Gender is a protected class. Employees should not be treated differently because of their gender.

- *Do not tolerate sexual harassment.* Sexual harassment is a form of gender discrimination. Managers should be vigilant to prevent quid pro quo and hostile environment sexual harassment.

- *Do not treat pregnancy or childbirth differently from any other disability.* The Pregnancy Discrimination Act, which is part of Title VII, requires that pregnant employees be treated the same as other employees. An employer cannot treat pregnant employees differently from employees with other temporary disabilities in regard to opportunities to continue to work, make leave arrangements, or be reinstated after a leave.

- *Take steps to ensure your work site is free from illegal discrimination.* Develop and strictly enforce an antidiscrimination policy. Sponsor training sessions for all employees on what constitutes illegal discrimination and underscore the company's intolerance of it. Identify one or more persons to whom complaints can be made and include someone outside the line of employees' supervision such as a representative of the personnel department. When a complaint is made, react to it promptly by investigating thoroughly and taking appropriate corrective action. Consult the employee who complained before initiating remedial action.

■ *If you employ United States citizens abroad, do not discriminate on the basis of race, skin color, religion, gender, or pregnancy.* The Civil Rights Act of 1991 outlaws discrimination against United States citizens working abroad for American companies.

■ *Do not discriminate against employees because they are 40 years of age or older.* The Age Discrimination in Employment Act (ADEA) renders people age 40 or older a protected class. An employer cannot treat them differently because of their age. A preference for youth is an illegal basis on which to make job decisions unless youth is a business necessity.

■ *Abide by the Americans with Disabilities Act (ADA).* Do not discriminate on the basis of disability. The ADA outlaws discrimination against disabled applicants or employees who are able, with or without accommodations, to perform the essential functions of the job. Examples of reasonable accommodations include enlarging doors to accommodate wheelchairs and modifying schedules to coincide with public transportation. People protected by the ADA include not only those with disabilities, but also those with a past disability and those responsible for the care of a disabled person.

■ *Do not make employment decisions based on nonessential functions of a job.* An employer who refuses to hire a qualified disabled person because that person is unable to perform nonessential job functions has violated the ADA.

■ *Accurately write job descriptions so they include all essential functions of the job.* Job descriptions are one source of information for identifying what the essential functions of a job are. To ensure applicants are qualified with or without accommodations to perform the essential functions, and to ensure applicants are not excluded because of inflated descriptions of job responsibilities, the job description should accurately describe the duties of the job.

■ *When interviewing a job applicant, do not ask questions about the person's medical condition or disability.* The employer can inquire whether an applicant can perform the essential functions of the job and can ask that she demonstrate the ability to do so. Questions about the person's medical condition, disability, medication, or hospital stays violate the ADA.

■ *If employees become disabled, attempt to find them other jobs within the company that they are qualified to perform.* The ADA requires that employers attempt to reassign an employee who becomes disabled while employed.

■ *Do not require an applicant to submit to a medical exam prior to offering that person a job.* The ADA precludes an employer from mandating a pre-offer medical exam. An offer, once made, can be conditional on the results of a medical exam provided all incoming employees are required to submit to such exam.

- *Keep information obtained from a medical exam confidential.* This information cannot be kept in an employee's employment file, but instead must be kept in a separate file. The only people entitled to review it are first-aid personnel, supervisors who need the information to determine necessary restrictions and accommodations, and government officials investigating compliance with the ADA.

- *If your business is accused by an employee of illegal discrimination or if it is investigated for illegal discrimination by the EEOC or a state agency, take prompt remedial action.* Whenever a complaint or investigation is made, your attorney should be consulted on how best to handle it. Prompt corrective action may rectify the illegal discrimination and mitigate the outcome.

- *Do not discharge employees or take other adverse job action against them because they complained about illegal discrimination or filed a complaint with the EEOC.* Such a discharge or adverse action is retaliatory and is itself illegal discrimination.

- *Verify the employment status of each employee you hire within three days of the date of employment.* The Immigration Reform and Control Act (IRCA) seeks to minimize the number of illegal aliens employed in this country. Employers are required to examine their worker's employment documents to verify authorization to work in the United States. Any employee who cannot produce the necessary proof within 21 days of employment must be terminated.

- *Do not discriminate against immigrants who are authorized to work in this country.* The IRCA prohibits an employer from refusing to hire a qualified alien on the ground she is not a citizen.

Review Questions

1. What statute imposes a minimum-wage requirement on employers?

2. Name two exceptions to the minimum-wage requirement.

3. How much is an employee entitled to be paid for working in excess of 40 hours a week?

4. Name five protected classes for employment purposes.

5. What is Title VII?

6. To what do the initials EEOC refer?

7. Name four remedies available for a Title VII violation.

8. What must a plaintiff prove to establish a retaliatory discharge?

9. Name two racial groups other than African-Americans and Caucasians.

10. Under what circumstance can an employer refuse to hire an applicant who speaks only minimal English?

11. In the category of age, who is included within the protected class under federal law?

12. What are the two types of sexual harassment? Provide an example of each.

13. Name five types of activity that can constitute sexual harassment.

14. In what ways can an employee relay the unwelcome nature of sexually harassing conduct?

15. What type of discrimination against a pregnant worker is prohibited by the Pregnancy Discrimination Act?

16. What is the "glass ceiling"? What has Congress done about it?

17. To what aspects of employment does the Americans with Disabilities Act apply?

18. What is the difference between essential functions of a job and nonessential functions?

19. Who can an employer require to submit to a medical exam before making a job offer?

20. What does the Immigration Reform and Control Act require of an employer? What is the penalty if the employer fails to comply?

Discussion Questions

1. What is the difference between the legal concepts of equal pay and comparable worth?

2. What do you think prompted the laws that impose a minimum age for employment and restrict the hours an employee under specified ages can work?

3. Why do you think Congress placed a cap in the Civil Rights Act of 1991 on the amount of compensatory damages a court can award to a plaintiff in most civil rights cases?

4. Why are minor differences in grooming rules for male and female employees acceptable?

5. The dining room manager of a restaurant is hiring wait personnel. A person who walks with a limp applies. The manager is concerned about the applicant's ability to handle the physical demands of the job. What can the manager ask the applicant during the interview, and what can the manager not ask?

Application Questions

1. An employer has an aversion to red hair. She refuses to hire anyone with that color hair. Is this illegal discrimination? Why or why not?

2. Lee is opening a Thai restaurant. He refuses to hire anyone who was not born in Thailand as chef, dishwashers, and wait personnel. Is this illegal discrimination against applicants of other nationalities? Why or why not?

3. Marti is an observant Jew and celebrates eight religious holidays that do not coincide with legal holidays. Does Title VII require that her employer give her time off for these holidays? Why or why not?

4. Allison's boss continually makes sexually suggestive comments to her and often brushes against her when she is in his office. She has asked him to stop but he continues. She reported his conduct to the vice president for personnel. He felt she was exaggerating the facts and did not investigate or take any action.
   A. What should the vice president have done?
   B. Is the company Allison works for liable for sexual harassment under these circumstances? Why or why not?

5. Kyle, who is deaf, has applied for a job as a bookkeeper at the Brookside Hotel. The bookkeeper is required to maintain financial records of the business and prepare financial reports for management. The information is obtained primarily from guest invoices, bills, and receipts. Most of the required reports are submitted in written form. The bookkeeper is also required to attend two staff meetings a week at which the general manager orally informs the staff of developments at the hotel. The general manager frequently consults informally with the bookkeeper concerning financial matters.
   A. What accommodations could the hotel make to enable Kyle to handle the job responsibilities?
   B. Will the hotel be obligated to make those accommodations or can it refuse to hire Kyle because of his disability? Why?

6. The Bystone Restaurant, a 25-table family restaurant with a strong business of take-out ice cream, has advertised for a manager. Among the applicants are a woman in a wheelchair with a bachelor's degree in restaurant management and two year's experience as an assistant manager at a similar restaurant, and a man with a master's degree in restaurant management and five year's experience, three as an assistant manager and two as a manager. What is the employer's obligation to the disabled applicant?

7. The Nimark Hotel is hiring a business manager. Of all the applicants, the two most qualified are a citizen of the United States and a citizen of France legally authorized to work in this country. According to the Immigration Reform and Control Act, if the two are equally qualified, which one should be offered the job? Why?

Web Sites

Web sites that will enhance your understanding of the material in this chapter include:

http://www.dol.gov This is the Department of Labor's site. It contains information on a variety of labor-related issues, including minimum pay, overtime pay, tips, occupational safety and health regulations, the Family and Medical Leave Act, and workplace injuries. The site also contains a list of state labor departments and their addresses, phone numbers, and Web sites.

http://www.ahma.com This is the site of the American Hotel and Lodging Association, a trade organization for the hotel and lodging industry. The site addresses numerous topics of interest to the hotel industry, including employment.

http://www.restaurant.org This is the site of the National Restaurant Association, a trade organization for restaurant owners and managers. Among the employment issues it addresses are tip reporting, new legislation impacting rights of workers, and career information.

http://www.eeoc.gov This is the official site of the Equal Employment Opportunity Commission, the federal agency that enforces discrimination laws. Among its features are access to federal laws that prohibit job discrimination and information on how to file a claim and use of mediation to settle claims.

http://www.allaboutosha.com This is the site of a company offering products designed to enable employers to comply with OSHA regulations, reduce on-the-job accidents, and thereby lower insurance rates. The site also provides information about OSHA regulations.

http://www.oshadefenseleague.com This is the site of a full-service independent safety and regulatory consulting firm. The business provides services in the area of OSHA compliance, loss control, and workers' compensation claims reduction. The site contains compliance guides, safety plans, and information about compliance products.

http://www.findlaw.com This site contains updates on legal news and links to sites covering many legal topics, including immigration laws and rights of employers and employees.

http://www.wld.com This site offers information on a variety of legal topics relevant to employment, including sexual harassment, disabled workers, labor unions, and collective bargaining.

CHAPTER 15

■

Regulation and Licensing

CHAPTER OUTLINE

■

Introduction

Regulation of the Marketplace

Franchising

Regulation of Hotel and
Restaurant Internal Affairs

Licensing and Zoning

INTRODUCTION

The law regulates various aspects of the hotel and restaurant business. Throughout this book we have seen numerous circumstances in which the law significantly impacts the manner in which a hotel or restaurant is operated. In this chapter we will see even more examples, including the law of trademarks, copyrights, anticompetitive activities, franchising, registration of guests, rates charged for rooms, recycling, licensing requirements, and zoning.

Regulation of the Marketplace

Numerous regulatory laws impact the marketplace in which hospitality establishments do business. These laws apply to trademarks, copyrights, antitrust concerns, and franchising.

Trademarks and Service Marks

Various aspects of successful businesses are sometimes emulated by other companies desiring to trade on the familiar name, style, and image portrayed to the public. The reason for this is obvious. If you decided to open a fast-food restaurant specializing in hamburgers, you would probably make considerably more money if you called it McDonald's rather than, say, Sue's Hamburgers. However, the name McDonald's, when used in the fast-food industry, is a trademark, which means the owner has the exclusive right to its use. If you use the name without the owner's permission, you will be illegally infringing on McDonald's trademark.

A **trademark** is any word, name, symbol (such as the Nike "swoosh"), or device adopted and used by a manufacturer or merchant to identify its goods and distinguish them from products sold or manufactured by others. A **service mark** is similar to a trademark except that it identifies services rather than goods. A company can obtain a trademark or service mark in its name or logo simply by using it in connection with its business. The company can also register the mark with the federal Patent and Trademark Office located in Washington, D.C., which notifies other potential users that the name has been appropriated. The ownership of the mark, however, is acquired by use alone and is unaffected by failure to register. When two companies are using the same name, the test to determine who has the rights to the name is who used it first.

Someone who uses another's trademark or service mark in connection with a similar product or service in the same market area without permission will be liable for trademark infringement. For example, Burger King has a trademark on the name "Chicken Tenders" for battered and fried chicken-breast pieces. A defendant who sold a chicken-breast meat product under the same name was thereby liable for trademark infringement.[1]

An infringement occurs not only when a second company uses the identical name, but also when another company uses a similar name that is likely to confuse consumers and divert business from the trademark owner. For example, a federal court found that a restaurant was imitating Howard Johnson's trade name by using the name "Henry Johnson's." The court enjoined (prohibited) Henry Johnson's from using that name.[2]

---

[1] *Burger King Corporation v. Pilgrim's Pride Corporation*, 934 F.Supp. 425 (Fl. 1996)

[2] *Howard Johnson Co. v. Henry Johnson's Restaurant*, Civil Case 1258 U.S.D.C. (N.C. 1964)

The law on trademarks and service marks is found in the Lanham Act, a federal statute that prohibits the passing off of services by one person under the guise that they are the services of another. The statute states:

> any person who shall affix, apply, or annex, or use in connection with any ... services ... a false designation of origin, or any false description or representation, including words or other symbols tending falsely to describe or represent the same ... shall be liable to a civil action by any person ... who believes that he is or is likely to be damaged by the use of any such false description or representation.[3]

Proving Infringement

To prove a trademark infringement case, the plaintiff must show two things: (1) ownership of a distinctive mark or name and (2) defendant's use of a similar mark or name that is likely to cause confusion as to the source of the products or services. The test for infringement is whether the second user's adoption of the name is confusingly similar to the original user—that is, will consumers be diverted from the first user and do business with the second because they were misled by the trade name? The more similar the names and products being offered by the two companies, the more likely a trademark infringement will exist. Similarity in names and services was the basis for a finding of infringement in *In Re Dixie Restaurants, Inc.*, 105 F.3d 1405 (1997). The trademark owner used the name "Delta" in its hotel, motel, and restaurant business. A new restaurant sought to use the name "The Delta Café." The court noted the similarity of the services offered by each party (restaurant operation) and also that the dominant element in the cafe's name (Delta) was identical to the trademark owner's name.

Another infringement lawsuit was brought against a restaurant named "Cafe Renaissance" that opened in the same city as an existing cafe with the exact name. The court found infringement notwithstanding the plaintiff cafe was open only for breakfast and lunch, occupied only 240 square feet, and had a large take-out service, whereas the defendant was a 4000 square-foot dinner-only restaurant that also provided entertainment.[4] On the other hand, a court rejected Econo Lodge's infringement claim brought against a hotel located directly across the street from an Econo Lodge named "Econotel."[5]

Even the script used to promote a name can add to the likelihood of confusion. In the case of *Tisch Hotels, Inc., v. Americana Inn, Inc.*, 350 F.2d 609 (7th Cir. 1965), the court ruled illegal the use of the word *Americana* by a Chicago hotel company that adopted that name without permission from a luxury hotel that had a trademark on the same name. Said the court, "Not only did the defendant pirate the name, but it also adopted plaintiff's fanciful presentation of the name in all details, namely, 'americana' all in lowercase letters with a white line extending through the first "a" and a five-point star as the dot over the i."

---

[3] 15 VSC 1125(a)

[4] *Cicone v. Cafe Renaissance, Inc.*, 2000 WL 1725483 (R.I. 2000)

[5] *Choice Hotels v. Kaushik*, 147 F.Supp.2d 1242 (Al. 2000)

Likelihood of Confusion

The required element of likelihood of confusion can be proven by showing actual confusion—that is, customers who were misled. While actual confusion is not essential, it provides the court or jury with positive proof of the required element of substantial likelihood of confusion.

Penalties

Penalties for infringing a trademark include an injunction prohibiting further infringement; return of profits diverted from the trademark owner, and fines. The effects of an injunction are illustrated in *Gas Town, Inc. of Delaware v. Gas Town*, 331 F.Supp. 626 (Conn. 1971). The Marathon Oil Company of Ohio had registered the name "Gas Town" as a trademark. Eighteen months later, a corporation with 200 service stations in New England, New York, and Louisiana used "Gas Town" as the name for its stations. The Marathon Oil Company sued for trademark infringement. A federal court issued an injunction barring the second corporation from using the name and ordered it to remove the Gas Town signs from its 200 stations. The infringer thus had to pay for new signs and for advertising to introduce the public to its new name—no small expense.

Prior to adopting a trade name, a business can and should conduct a trademark search on a registry maintained by the United States Copyright and Trademark Office. The registry, accessible by computer, will disclose whether the desired name is already in use.

The following case illustrates the application of many of these rules.

CASE EXAMPLE 15-1

Gilbert/Robinson, Inc. v. Carrie Beverage-Missouri, Inc. 758 F.Supp. 512 (Mo. 1991)

Plaintiff Gilbert/Robinson, owner of HOULIHAN'S restaurants, initiated this action alleging service mark infringement ... based on defendants ... use of the service mark MIKE HOULIHAN'S on their bars.

... In April 1972, plaintiff began to use the service mark HOULIHAN'S OLD PLACE to identify its bar and restaurant located in Kansas City, Missouri. ...

Since April 1972, plaintiff has opened establishments under the name HOULIHAN'S or HOULIHAN'S OLD PLACE in 22 different states. Currently, these establishments number 55, including three in metropolitan St. Louis. There

are also 10 franchise HOULIHAN'S locations in the United States. In approximately 1983, plaintiff discontinued the use of OLD PLACE in its signs and advertising for the company-owned HOULIHAN'S because the majority of its customers refer to the establishments simply as HOULIHAN'S. ...

Since 1972, plaintiff has spent nearly $27 million in advertising and promoting its HOULIHAN'S establishments nationwide and those establishments have yielded nationwide sales in excess of $1 billion during that time. Advertisements for HOULIHAN'S bars and restaurants have appeared on television, radio and in newspapers and magazines throughout the United States.

In 1982, defendant Carrie Beverage Incorporated opened a bar which it operates in the Grand Avenue shopping mall in downtown

Milwaukee, Wisconsin under the service mark MIKE HOULIHAN'S. The names in the service mark MIKE HOULIHAN'S refer to Michael Heyer and John Houlihan, who are the sole shareholders of defendant Carrie Beverage, Inc. ...

During the fall of 1984, plaintiff announced that it would open another HOULIHAN'S in St. Louis Union Station in December 1985. In August 1985, plaintiff learned of defendant's plans to open a MIKE HOULIHAN'S in the St. Louis Centre shopping mall in downtown St. Louis, Missouri. Plaintiff ... informed defendants of plaintiff's rights in the HOULIHAN'S marks and insisted that defendants change their mark. ...

Five months after [defendant] had opened its MIKE HOULIHAN'S bar in St. Louis, plaintiff opened its restaurant utilizing the service mark HOULIHAN'S and HOULIHAN'S OLD PLACE in the Union Station complex in St. Louis, Missouri.

Plaintiff presented strong evidence of a nationwide reputation. Plaintiff's expert, Marshall Scott, testified that HOULIHAN'S is a well-known name inside and outside the restaurant industry and across the country. ... To customers seeking food and beverage services in Missouri and across the nation, HOULIHAN'S means plaintiff's HOULIHAN'S.

Substantial actual confusion resulted from defendants' use of the name MIKE HOULIHAN'S in St. Louis Centre. Both plaintiff's and defendants' establishments experienced instances of actual confusion by customers and vendors, including misdirected telephone calls, misdirected vendor deliveries, and misdirected service calls. ... Although the frequency of actual confusion has diminished over time, it continued up through the time of trial.

HOULIHAN'S is the distinctive word in the HOULIHAN'S marks as well as in the name MIKE HOULIHAN'S. The HOULIHAN'S marks are displayed in standard block lettering. MIKE HOULIHAN'S is also displayed in block lettering, which is slightly scripted. The HOULIHAN'S and MIKE HOULIHAN'S marks are similar in appearance.

HOULIHAN'S and MIKE HOULIHAN'S are in direct competition for bar revenues. The bar is a very important part of plaintiff's business. ...

A survey was conducted at plaintiff's request to determine the likelihood of confusion of customers with respect to whether HOULIHAN'S and MIKE HOULIHAN'S are part of the same operation. The survey was conducted by a firm which specializes in consumer surveys. The survey was conducted in an unbiased and scientific manner, utilizing generally accepted survey techniques. Impartial interviewers drew responses from a relevant pool of potential consumers. The questions posed were not leading, misleading or biased, and the recordation was handled in an unbiased manner. ...

Of the 200 respondents interviewed, more than two-thirds, 67.5%, believed that both establishments were owned or affiliated with the same company. Moreover, more than four out of five respondents who said they think that both establishments are owned by or affiliated with the same company cited the name as the reason they came to that conclusion. ...

Specifically, the ultimate issue is whether defendant's design so resembles plaintiff's mark that it is likely to cause confusion among consumers as to whether plaintiff has sponsored, endorsed or is otherwise affiliated with the defendant. ...

In order to claim ownership of a distinctive mark or name, a party must demonstrate that his use of the mark has been of such a quality and for such a duration that it has come to identify goods bearing it as originating from that party. ...

The exclusive right to use the mark belongs to the first person who appropriates it and uses it in connection with a particular business. Any doubts as to confusion are to be decided against the newcomer. ...

In order to constitute an infringement, it is not necessary that the trademark be literally copied. Neither is it necessary that every word be appropriated. There may be infringement where the substantial and distinctive part of the trademark is copied or imitated. ... The similarity of marks is to be determined by looking at the total effect of designation rather than by comparing individual features. ...

Although names are not identical, similarity will deceive almost as much as precise identity. Nice and careful discrimination between the names cannot be expected from a busy public.

The right to operate under one's own name is not unlimited: The first user of the name is entitled to protection. A family name cannot be used to appropriate the business of another. ...

It is true that there are some minor differences between the two marks. Defendants' mark is in a slight script. Further, defendants use the word MIKE in front of the word HOULIHAN'S. However, the use of a modifying word is not sufficient to dispel the likelihood of confusion, when the most prominent word in the name appears in both.

[T]he similarity and competitive proximity of the products is an important factor in determining likelihood of confusion. The greater the similarity, the greater the likelihood of confusion. ...

In this case, both plaintiff and defendant operate facilities with bars ... and the two facilities are located within one mile from each other. ...

Surveys are often used to demonstrate actual consumer confusion. Courts frequently give substantial weight to properly conducted surveys, unless they are seriously flawed. ...

In this action, the Court finds that the survey is valid and was properly conducted. The survey demonstrated that more than two-thirds of those persons polled believe that HOULIHAN'S and MIKE HOULIHAN'S were affiliated in some manner... this factor weighs strongly in favor of finding trademark infringement on the part of defendant. ...

Plaintiff has proven uncontroverted evidence that in 1972 it appropriated the name HOULI-HAN'S for its restaurant and has since used the name continuously. Plaintiff's appropriation and use of the name was prior to that of defendants, who first began use of the name in 1982. Therefore, plaintiff has acquired trademark rights in that name. It is further the conclusion of this Court that plaintiff has established that defendants' use of the mark MIKE HOULIHAN'S is likely to cause confusion as to the source of the products sold by defendants. ... Therefore plaintiff is entitled to relief.

JUDGMENT AND ORDER

... [D]efendant is permanently enjoined [barred] from using his trademark MIKE HOULIHAN'S ... effective ninety days from the date of this judgment.

CASE QUESTION

1. Explain what the court meant when it said in the eighteenth paragraph, "Although names are not identical, similarity will deceive almost as much as precise identity. Nice and careful discrimination between the names cannot be expected from a busy public."

You may wonder why the court did not order the defendant to stop using the name "Mike Houlihan's" immediately rather than in ninety days. The reason for the delay is to allow the defendant time to adopt a new name and make necessary arrangements to change its signs, menus, advertising materials, and any other items on which the restaurant promotes its name.

Geographic Proximity

Remember, the test for infringement is likelihood of confusion. Absent a likelihood of confusion, no infringement exists. If the trademark owner and second user do not compete in the same markets, the public is unlikely to confuse one for the other. In such circumstances the use of the mark by the newcomer may not be illegal. In *Steak & Brew, Inc., v. Beef & Brew Restaurant, Inc.*, 370 F.Supp. 1030 (Ill. 1974), the plaintiff, which operated a chain of restaurants under the name "Steak & Brew," attempted to prevent the defendant, which operated a restaurant named "Beef & Brew," from using the word *Brew* in its name. The defendant operated only one restaurant, which was in Rock Island, Illinois; the closest restaurant in the plaintiff's chain was 100 miles away. The facts in the case established that the defendant had innocently adopted the name without knowledge of the plaintiff's use, and "Steak & Brew" was unknown in the Rock Island, Illinois area. The court stated that ordinarily the use and registration of a trademark will bar a subsequent business from using the same name. However, when two parties employ the same mark on goods of the same class, but they operate in remote and separate markets, the second user may legally continue to use the name. An exception to this rule is where it appears that the second adopter has selected the mark to benefit from the reputation of the first user or to forestall the expansion of the first user's business.

Similarly, two companies independently and concurrently developed several restaurants under the name "John Q's." The plaintiff, with a restaurant in Cleveland, could not prevent the defendant from opening one in Cincinnati, 240 miles away. The plaintiff failed to present evidence that the restaurant in Cincinnati would be patronized by customers of the Cleveland restaurant or any other evidence that confusion would result. Further, there was no evidence that the defendant attempted to deceive the public or capitalize on the plaintiff's name.[6]

Descriptive Terms

Another reason the court found no infringement in the Steak & Brew case is that the word *brew* is descriptive and in common use. Therefore, it is not subject to exclusive appropriation. Ordinarily a company cannot gain trademark rights in a word that is part of the English language and commonly used. Such a word could achieve trademark protection only upon proof that it attained a secondary meaning, that is, the public identifies the term or phrase with the company using it. Thus, for example, Kentucky Fried Chicken cannot prevent another restaurant from using the word *chicken* or *fried chicken* in its name. However, the public has come to recognize the phrase *Kentucky Fried Chicken* as the name of a chain of fast-food restaurants. Therefore, no other company could name itself Kentucky Fried Chicken. On this basis also, the court ruled there were no grounds for a finding that the defendant's use of the name "Beef & Brew" violated the plaintiff's trademark—*Steak & Brew*. The defendant was allowed to continue using the name but only for the one restaurant in Rock Island.

Public Domain

According to trademark law, a valuable trademark may be lost if the word becomes a part of the language—that is, used in common speech. When this happens, the word becomes part of **public domain**, meaning it has become so commonly used that it loses its trademark protection. Over the years, this has happened to such notable trademarks as Aspirin, Frisbee, Rollerblade, Mimeograph, Linoleum, Dry Ice, Escalator, Cellophane, and Kerosene. In each instance, what began as a trademark ended as a frequently used word in normal parlance. Doubtless, the English language has been enriched, but the manufacturer is the poorer—penalized, ironically, because its product became too popular.

---

[6]*Stouffer Corp. v. Winegardner & Hammons, Inc.*, 502 F.Supp. 232 (Ohio 1980)

How does the law determine that a trademark has gone into the public domain? While the point in time is rarely clear, the main prerequisite is that the public has come to consider the word as the generic name for the thing itself, rather than as an indication of a specific manufacturer or that manufacturer's specific product. For example, a court held that "Toll House," at one time a trademark for a cookie made by Nestle, was no longer entitled to trademark protection because so many consumers used that term to describe a kind of cookie rather than one specific maker of the cookie.[7] For the same reason, "Shredded Wheat" lost its status as a trademark.[8]

Trademark Registration

We have seen that a trademark can be registered with the federal Patent and Trademark Office. Although registration is not necessary for trademark protection since rights accrue from mere use of a name, registration helps to discourage unauthorized use and makes a trademark infringement case easier to prove. It helps to protect the mark from infringement nationwide.

The process of registration includes: submission of various documents to the Patent and Trademark Office; publication of the proposed mark by that office to alert others with similar names; opportunity for objection to registration by others who might already be using the same or a similar name; and, if there is no objection or if there is and the applicant wins, issuance of a registration certificate that completes the registration process.

Once a trademark is registered, the owner should include with the name, usually after the last letter, the following insignia: ® (the capital letter "R" in a circle). This alerts the public that the word is a registered trademark and cannot be used by others. Most states have registration procedures that protect a business' name on a state-wide basis. The process is easier and less expensive than federal registration. Which registration is appropriate depends on the geographical area in which the business anticipates using the name. If the business owners foresee opening other similar businesses with the same name in more than one state, or if they anticipate franchising the operation, (see discussion later in this chapter on franchising) federal registration should be pursued.

One case that encompasses many trademark principles is *Holiday Inns, Inc. v. Holiday Inn*. The defendant was the first user of the name "Holiday Inn" in Myrtle Beach, South Carolina. It undertook a course of action calculated to associate itself in the public eye with the plaintiff, the owner of the trademark in the remainder of the country, intentionally misleading the traveling public. The case presents historical background on a giant of the hotel industry, states the test of what constitutes trademark infringement, and discusses the rights of the traveling public not to be deceived. As the case suggests, the plaintiff Holiday Inn chain was, at the time of the case, one of the biggest and most prominent hotel chains in the industry.

---

[7] *Nestle Co., Inc. v. Chester's Market, Inc.*, 571 F.Supp. 763 (Conn. 1983) rev'd on other grounds, 756 F.2d 280 (1985)

[8] *Kellogg Co. v. National Biscuit Co.*, 305 U.S. 111, 59 S.Ct. 109 (1988)

CASE EXAMPLE 15-2

Holiday Inns, Inc. v. Holiday Inn
364 F.Supp. 775 (S.C. 1973)

This action is brought by the plaintiff, Holiday Inns, Inc., ... the largest company in the restaurant and lodging business in the United States, hereinafter referred to as "the Chain." The suit is for ... service mark infringement against the defendant Holiday Inn, a South Carolina corporation that operates a motel and restaurant at Myrtle Beach, South Carolina, under the name of Holiday Inn. This defendant has counterclaimed, alleging [trademark] infringement and unfair competition, and seeks cancellation of certain of plaintiff's [trademark] registrations. ...

This matter was heard before the court without a jury ... [T]he court makes the following finding of facts:

1. The plaintiff Holiday Inns, Inc., ... is a corporation ... founded in 1952 and since that time has grown to the point that it is now the largest factor in the restaurant and lodging business in the United States. ... The Plaintiff's principal business is providing restaurant and lodging services operating under the name Holiday Inn. These services are provided either through company owned facilities or facilities franchised by the Chain. At present the Chain has a facility in almost every major city in the United States, including 33 in the State of South Carolina. The Chain presently owns or franchises approximately 1,300 facilities in the United States.

2. The Chain's original concept was to establish a network of motels and restaurants spanning the entire country upon which the traveling public could rely in obtaining satisfactory services. The facilities affiliated with the Chain are readily recognizable, with quality controls exercised by the Chain and many similar services available at all facilities, such as free use of baby cribs, no charge for children under 12 when sleeping in the room with the parent, kennels for pets, etc.

3. The Chain had developed and prominently displays on each facility a large sign, generally referred to as the "great sign." This sign is one of the major features by which travelers generally identify a motel as belonging to or affiliated with the Chain. This sign is quite large, but in some cities smaller versions are used in order to comply with local zoning restrictions. The sign has a green background with the name HOLIDAY INN in large distinctive script lettering, a large star at the top and smaller stars by the name HOLIDAY INN, a large orange arrow starting at the bottom of the sign and running in a sort of semicircle with the point indicating the location of the facility. There is always an attraction panel near the bottom of the sign. ...

5. In the promotion of its services, the plaintiff also uses certain slogans, one of which is YOUR HOST FROM COAST TO COAST. ...

7. The above registered service marks of plaintiff are well known to the American traveling public. They have been extensively used and advertised in promoting plaintiff's services and the services of its franchisees. Numerous advertisements have appeared in magazines, newspapers, on radio and television and billboards, as well as a house magazine and a directory of member facilities of which more than ten million are printed and distributed each year. ...

8. The defendant Holiday Inn was incorporated in 1960 (Emphasis Added). ...

10. The defendant's facility grew over the years to its present 87 units. ...

12. The plaintiff first learned of defendant's facility in 1956 when a franchisee of plaintiff, who was constructing a motel facility in Myrtle Beach, received a letter from defendant's lawyer objecting to the proposed usage of HOLIDAY INN within the Myrtle Beach area. Plaintiff's franchisee obtained permission from plaintiff to operate the facility within the plaintiff's system under the name HOLIDAY LODGE. This facility has been operated continuously since 1956. ... A great sign was erected in front of the facility presenting the words HOLIDAY LODGE in large script lettering above the words HOLIDAY INNS OF AMERICA SYSTEM. ...

15. In 1968 the defendant's general manager ordered a sign constructed and placed in its parking lot immediately across the street from

its facility. He requested the sign maker to design a sign which would resemble, but not exactly duplicate, the plaintiff's "great sign" and delivered to the sign maker one of plaintiff's brochures to use as a guide. ... [T]he signs are so similar that the traveling public would be easily confused and upon seeing defendant's sign would conclude that it was a franchisee of plaintiff or affiliated with it. The colors of the two signs are almost identical. The use of stars, the big arrow, the attraction panel, and the script of Holiday Inn are so similar that the court can only conclude that defendant erected his sign with the intent and purpose of infringing the rights of the plaintiff and unfairly competing with it. ...

23. Confusion has developed as a result of the similarity of names and there have been mix-ups in bills, letters, reservations, deliveries, etc. ...

26. ... [C]onfusion has been deliberately and systematically nurtured by the defendant in an effort to profit from the national recognition and goodwill of the plaintiff. ...

Conclusions of Law

2. Upon review of the evidence the court is compelled to conclude that the defendant's course of conduct proves it guilty of ... service mark infringement. ...

3. The test for trademark infringement ... is whether ... imitation of the registered mark is "likely to cause confusion, or to cause mistake, or to deceive." The test is to be applied with regard to the effect of the marks on an ordinary purchaser having an indefinite recollection of the mark to which he has been exposed on a previous occasion. [T]he sign erected by the defendant in 1968 is substantially identical to the plaintiff's "great sign" and although differences are obvious when pictures of the two signs are compared side by side, the effect of the defendant's sign was obvious and was likely to cause confusion, mistake or to deceive the public. ...

4. The script form in which defendant presents its name Holiday Inn is substantially identical to the distinctive script used by plaintiff. ... Although there may be slight differences in the location of the stars, the overall effect is such as is likely to cause confusion, mistake and to deceive the public.

5. Defendant's slogan, YOUR HOST ON THE COAST and YOUR HOST WHILE AT MYRTLE BEACH, differs from the plaintiff's slogan, YOUR HOST FROM COAST TO COAST, and if these slogans alone were the basis of the plaintiff's complaint, this court would not find them to be an infringement. However, when considered with the other acts of the defendant, ... the court must conclude that the use of these slogans by the defendant was an effort to trade upon the goodwill of the plaintiff and represent an infringement of its protected mark, YOUR HOST FROM COAST TO COAST.

6. Although intent is not a necessary element of trademark infringement, there can be no question of defendant's intent to infringe upon the plaintiff's marks. ...

7. The plaintiff's [trade]marks are famous throughout the United States and are becoming well known in many other countries. Great effort and expenditure of funds by the plaintiff have not only built up its successful business but have created in the mind of the public strong recognition of its name and service marks. ... These property rights of the plaintiff are entitled to broad protection. ...

10. The defendant has asserted and this court finds that it is the prior user of the name Holiday Inn in Myrtle Beach, South Carolina. ... The defendant is entitled to continue the use of the name Holiday Inn within the city limits of Myrtle Beach, South Carolina, but this court will not prevent the plaintiff from operating its facilities now known as Holiday Lodge ... in Myrtle Beach. ...

Now, Therefore, It Is Ordered, Adjudged and Decreed:

1. The defendant [is] hereby perpetually enjoined and restrained from:

    a. Using either directly or indirectly a script identical to or any colorable imitation of plaintiff's script Holiday Inn on the outside of its building, on any billboards or on any advertising material.

    b. Using directly or indirectly its version of plaintiff's "great sign" or any colorable imitation thereof.

    c. Using directly or indirectly the slogan YOUR HOST WHILE AT MYRTLE BEACH or YOUR HOST ON THE COAST or any colorable imitation thereof.

d. Using directly or indirectly any sign, script, slogan or star design, color combination or other indicia of plaintiff that suggests or tends to suggest a connection with the plaintiff.

2. The defendant shall have ninety (90) days from the date of this order to comply and defendant's attorney within such time shall submit to the court evidence of compliance.

3. The defendant has the right to continue using the name Holiday Inn within the town of Myrtle Beach, South Carolina. ...

And it is so ordered.

Copyright Basics

A **copyright** is the exclusive right of an author or other copyright owner to reproduce and license (authorize) the reproduction of literature, art, music, drama, sculpture, motion pictures, computer software, and other audiovisual works including broadcasts of sporting events.

Generally, the copyright is initially owned by the creator of the work. The rights associated with a copyright are separate from the work itself. Indeed, the artist can sell the work but retain the copyright. For example, a restaurant owner who purchases a copyrighted painting can display it but cannot reproduce it onto placemats without permission of the copyright owner. Normally, the copyright owner will charge a fee for the permission, thus enabling the owner to benefit repeatedly from the creative talent utilized in the work. If, however, the artist sells the copyright, the purchaser becomes the copyright owner and can reproduce the work without further authorization.

A copyright comes into existence automatically when the work is created. Prior to March 1, 1989, the law required the copyright owner to place a copyright notice on the work when it was first made available to the public in order to retain the copyright. Failure to include the notice resulted in loss of the copyright. The required notice consisted of three parts: (1) the letter "c" in a circle—©, (2) the name of the copyright owner, and (3) the year of first publication. Due to a change in the law, the copyright notice is no longer necessary, although it is strongly recommended to discourage unauthorized copying.

Illegal Satellite Reception

An area of copyright law that has been the subject of litigation in the hospitality field is the use of satellite dishes to receive and exhibit audiovisual programming without the permission of the program's copyright owner. Such use infringes on the copyright of the programs. In one case, a Holiday Inn was sued for copyright infringement by various cable stations including Home Box Office, Inc. (HBO), ESPN, Showtime, and The Movie Channel, Inc. The hotel had installed a satellite system enabling it to receive copyrighted programming without paying for it. The

Holiday Inn in turn offered to its guests the opportunity to view the programming in their rooms for a fee. No part of the proceeds was paid to the cable stations. The stations claimed the interception and exhibition of the copyrighted programs without their permission constituted copyright infringement. The court agreed and issued an injunction against the hotel requiring it to stop.[9]

Another case involved the satellite interception by several bars of a blacked-out football game. The National Football League (NFL) customarily contracts with the television networks for the broadcast of its games. The contract states that if a game is not sold out seventy-two hours before the start, it cannot be broadcast within seventy-five miles of the home team's field. The defendant bar owners used satellite dishes to receive transmissions of the blacked-out games without the approval of the NFL, which owned the copyright. The bar owners were thus able to exhibit the blacked-out games to their patrons. The NFL sued the bars. The court held the unapproved exhibition of the copyrighted games constituted an unauthorized reproduction of the work and a copyright infringement. The court issued an injunction against the bars.[10]

Another basis on which to pursue a business that exhibits television programming without authority is the Communications Act, a federal law that prohibits the interception of cable or satellite transmissions without authority from the sender of the transmission.

Pay-for-view programming requires viewers to pay a fee to obtain access to a show. As illustrated in the following case, a bar or restaurant that receives access without payment of the fee views and displays the show illegally in violation of the Communications Act.

CASE EXAMPLE 15-3

Cablevision Systems Corp. v. 45 Midland Enterprises, Inc. 858 F.Supp. 42 (N.Y. 1994)

Plaintiff has a franchise to provide cable television in Port Chester. Defendant operates a tavern/restaurant, which intercepted the Home Box Office ("HBO") signals for the February 6, 1993, boxing match between Riddick Bowe and Michael Dokes without having paid the required fee. ...

Defendant subscribed to and was authorized to receive basic service, which did not include HBO signals. To authorize receipt of the HBO signal, plaintiff provides a decoder box to the customer. The box unscrambles the signal. Plaintiff related that a market exists for unscrambling devices, which are not authorized by plaintiff and which will however permit reception of HBO signals, and explained that a subscriber to basic channels, who was displaying a premium channel such as HBO, was employing an unauthorized converter-decoder device to gain access to the premium channel.

Robert Weber, plaintiff's audit investigator, visited [defendant] on the evening of February 6, 1993. Fifty-six (56) individuals were present along with two (2) television sets. The televisions were displaying the introductions of the boxers to the Bowe-Dokes match, which was

---

[9] *Home Box Office, Inc. v. Corinth Motel, Inc.*, 647 F.Supp. 1186 (Miss. 1986)
[10] *National Football League v. McBee and Bruno's, Inc.*, 792 F.2d 726 (Mo. 1986)

scheduled for live broadcast that evening. Weber noted that the sets were tuned to channel 6, which is the HBO channel in Port Chester. He also observed what he described as a cable television converter-decoder device near the television in the area of the bar. This device was not of the type and color which plaintiff provided to authorized subscribers. ...

The evidence was sufficiently convincing to persuade me that defendant violated the statue by unauthorized interception of a cable television signal on February 3, 1993. ...

In a related factual situation, a bar that had not paid a required pay-for-view fee exhibited a videotape of a restricted boxing match that had been made and brought to the bar by a patron who apparently had paid to view the match at home. The tavern was sued for violation of the Communications Act and found liable.[11]

We learn from these cases that companies in the business of selling pay-for-view rights regularly send investigators to bars and restaurants at the time restricted programming is broadcast to determine if the business is illegally exhibiting the limited-access show. A sports bar or like establishment seeking to attract customers by showing restricted events must first obtain the necessary license and pay appropriate fees. Failure to do so will likely result in liability leading to payment of damages, fines, attorney's fees for the opposing party (in addition to one's own), and an injunction.

In several cases, an investigator visited a bar during a pay-for-view boxing match, violations were discovered, lawsuits were commenced, and the defendant taverns failed to serve an answer. As we learned in Chapter 2, the result was a default judgment against the bars rendering the plaintiff automatically entitled to damages. It is likely the defendants' delinquency was related to the absence of justification for their actions.[12]

Music Performances

Many restaurants and hotels offer musical entertainment. The music may be live, on a juke box, or presented by a disc jockey. Live presentations may involve a single performer on weekends only, a band that plays every night of the week, or any combination thereof. Most music is copyrighted. The performer(s) may, during any performance, play the music of many different copyright owners. How does the restaurant or hotel know from whom permission must be obtained and how can it manage the many different authorizations that may be required? While at first it may appear that obtaining permissions can be very complicated, a system has been developed that streamlines the process.

---

[11] *Kingvision Pay Per View, Ltd., v. 900 Club*, 1996 WL 496600 (Ill. 1996)

[12] For example, see *Kingvision Pay-Per-View v. Tito's Bar and Grill*, 2001 WL 682205 (Tex. 2001)

Most owners of copyrights on musical compositions belong to one of three associations that collect copyright fees for its members. Hotels and restaurants need only deal with these organizations and not with each composer individually. The two main organizations are the American Society of Composers, Authors, and Publishers (**ASCAP**), and Broadcast Music, Inc. (**BMI**). Both license (grant for a fee), on a nonexclusive basis, the public performance rights of its members' copyrighted works. A hotel or restaurant must have a license from these organizations to use the works in their collection. Since an establishment cannot easily restrict its musical offerings to the works controlled by one organization or the other, in most circumstances hotels or restaurants will need a license from both.

ASCAP and BMI distribute the receipts from license fees, minus overhead, to their members as royalties for the use of their compositions. The allocation of the money among members is based on detailed, weighted formulas.

ASCAP

The license fees charged to hotels and restaurants, bars, and clubs by ASCAP are not based on the songs actually performed. Rather, they are based on a combination of factors that include the number of nights a week the establishment offers music, seating capacity, and whether admission is charged.

ASCAP controls such a large part of the performance rights of the music industry that it could exercise monopoly power. To avoid this, the law has imposed restrictions on its ability to dictate fees. The process for determining the license fee a user must pay is as follows: The hotel or restaurant submits a written application to ASCAP. It responds in writing, advising the business of the proposed fee. A sixty-day negotiation period follows in which the restaurant or hotel can object to the fee; the parties can then attempt to reach a mutually agreeable compromise. If they are unsuccessful, the hotel or restaurant can apply to a federal district court for a determination of a reasonable license fee. The mandated negotiation period and the right of the music user to seek a court determination of a reasonable fee substantially lessens ASCAP's ability to wield its potentially controlling bargaining power.

BMI

License fees charged by BMI are determined through negotiations between BMI officials and established trade associations such as the National Restaurant Association. For hotels and restaurants, the fees are determined based on annual expenditures for musicians and entertainers. For concert halls, fees are determined by seating capacity. For other establishments such as ballrooms and clubs, fees are based on a percentage of gross annual income.

Consequence of Performing Music Without a License

If a restaurant or hotel fails to obtain the necessary licenses for musical performances, it will be liable for copyright infringement. Remedies include the following:

1. An injunction requiring the infringer to stop.

2. Damages in an amount equal to the copyright owner's actual loss and the profits the infringer made or, in the alternative, the copyright owner can opt for statutory damages, an amount of money determined by the court of not less than $750 or more than $30,000, depending on the circumstances.

3. Reimbursement for the plaintiff's attorney's fees.

4. Reimbursement for other costs associated with the lawsuit.

Before bringing a lawsuit, ASCAP or BMI will inform the facility that a license is necessary and encourage its purchase. If the owner refuses to pay and continues to provide musical entertainment, a lawsuit by ASCAP or BMI against the hotel or restaurant is likely. Both organizations are zealous in pursuing their members' rights.

BMI discovered that a restaurant, without cost to customers, was playing its members' music on a jukebox to enhance the dining experience. The restaurant did not have a license to do so. BMI attempted to remedy the circumstance without a lawsuit by making "repeated written and telephonic requests, as well as one personal visit, to urge Blueberry Hill Restaurant to enter into a licensing agreement and to warn of the consequences of failing to do so." Because the defendant failed to respond to these numerous entreaties, BMI filed a lawsuit. The court ordered the restaurant to discontinue playing protected music without a license and to pay damages to BMI.[13]

In another case, ASCAP suspected that the Cheetah Lounge was playing copyrighted music without having paid for a license to do so. Despite numerous attempts by ASCAP to contact the lounge by phone and letter, the Cheetah failed to reply or comply. To prove its case, ASCAP sent an investigator to the facility. He spent four hours there making contemporaneous notes of the songs he heard performed. The list was then compared with the list of music ASCAP protected. Five songs were on both lists. ASCAP sued the lounge for copyright infringement and the Cheetah was found liable. Penalties included an injunction, statutory damages in the amount of $10,000 ($2000 per song infringed), attorney's fees, and court costs. The amount of statutory damages would likely have been smaller had the lounge been less resistant to the mandates of copyright law.[14]

Amplified Radio Music

Not infrequently, a restaurant will play the radio as background music for its diners' enjoyment. The music played on the radio is copyrighted. Radio stations customarily have a license with BMI and ASCAP to play protected songs. The following case addresses the circumstances in which a restaurant may violate the copyright laws for using radio music in this way.

---

[13] *BMI v. Blueberry Hill Family Restaurants, Inc.*, 899 F.Supp. 474 (Nev. 1995)

[14] *MLE Music v. Kimble, Inc.*, 109 F.Supp.2d 469 (W.V. 2000)

CASE EXAMPLE 15-4

Cass County Music Company v. Port Town Family Restaurant
55 F.3d 263 (7th Cir. 1995)

The plaintiffs ... own copyrights to six songs that are the subject of this suit. The defendant was the owner of the Port Town Family Restaurant located in Racine, Wisconsin. The restaurant is a free-standing building accommodating up to 128 patrons with a public dining area of approximately 1500 square feet. The restaurant is equipped with a "radio-over-speaker" sound system that provides a consistent level of background music throughout the dining area.

On the night of March 13, 1992, two investigators employed by ASCAP had dinner in the Port Town Family Restaurant . While dining, the investigators heard some of the plaintiffs' songs played over the restaurant's sound system. The source of the music was a radio broadcast of WMYX-FM, a Milwaukee station. The radio station is an ASCAP licensee. The license between ASCAP and WMYX-FM prohibits retransmissions of the station's broadcasts. ...

The ASCAP licensing fee for establishments that play music four to seven nights a week and seat between 76 and 150 patrons is $327 per year. From May, 1985, until December 1991, ASCAP repeatedly and unsuccessfully approached the Port Town Family Restaurant about the need for the restaurant to obtain an ASCAP license in order to continue legally to play background music.

The plaintiffs subsequently brought this action against the restaurant owner. They allege copyright infringement on the basis of the public performance of the six copyrighted musical compositions. The plaintiffs requested an injunction prohibiting further performances, $1000 damages for each infringement, and costs including reasonable attorneys' fees. ...

The Copyright Act contains an exemption that allows the use of ordinary ["home-type"] radios and television sets for the incidental entertainment of patrons in small businesses or other professional establishments, such as taverns, lunch counters, hairdressers, dry cleaners, doctors' offices, etc. ...

There are two ways in which an establishment could fall outside the exemption. First, if any non-home-type components are used, then the entire system must be considered a non-home-type system. Second, if the establishment has configured the home-type equipment in a way not commonly used in a home, the exemption is lost. The critical factors are the type and sophistication of the equipment used, the size of the area in which the broadcast is audible, and whether the equipment has been altered, augmented, or integrated in some fashion. ...

The Port Town Family Restaurant's music system utilizes, in addition to a Radio Shack receiver, a separate control panel containing five selector switches, nine speakers recessed into the dropped acoustic tile ceiling, and concealed wiring. Each speaker consists of an aluminum grille, an 8" loudspeaker, and a 70-volt (70-V) loudspeaker line matching transformer. Without the addition of the transformers, the receiver is designed to drive only four speakers over moderate lengths of speaker cable. However, with the 70-V transformer attached to each speaker, ... the receiver effectively can power up to forty speakers wired in parallel, thirty-six speakers more than the receiver was designed to handle without overloading. ... The restaurant's nine speakers are evenly spaced within the 1500 square-foot dining area. ... The set up ... provides background music that is consistent and evenly audible throughout the public seating area.

The system at issue here cannot be characterized fairly as "homestyle," that is, commonly found in homes. The receiver clearly is used beyond the normal limits of its capabilities. Accordingly, the Port Town Family Restaurant is not exempt from compliance with the Copyright Act.

Artwork

As discussed previously, copyright law also protects artwork. To merit copyright protection, the work must reflect the artistic creativity of the artist. For example, with photographs such creativity can be reflected in the posing of the subjects, lighting, angle, and other variants.

In a case involving menu design, the defendant, a company that designed and printed restaurant menus, incorporated photographs taken by the plaintiff, a printer specializing in preparing and printing Chinese restaurant menus. The plaintiff sued, claiming copyright infringement. The court noted that the pictures in question depicted Chinese dishes common in take-out menus including sweet and sour chicken, barbecue spare ribs, pu pu platter, and Peking duck. The pattern of the food on the plates was "extremely common," reflecting Chinese tradition. Neither the lighting nor the angles were notable. The court concluded the pictures lacked creativity and instead "serve a purely utilitarian purpose; to identify for restaurant customers the appearance and ingredients of certain dishes on the menu." Lacking the necessary inventiveness, the photos were not copyrightable.[15]

Antitrust Problems

The economic system of the United States is based on free and open competition. It seeks to ensure new businesses can enter the market and all businesses can compete on a more or less equal basis. The reason for promoting competition is the belief that it motivates producers both to make better products and to sell them at lower prices, thereby benefiting consumers. Certain laws, called **antitrust laws**, attempt to ensure that open competition is preserved.

An important federal antitrust law is the Sherman Antitrust Act, passed in 1890 and supplemented by a second Act in 1914 called the Clayton Act. These remain the two key federal antitrust laws. The United States Supreme Court described the objective of the Sherman Act as follows:

> The Sherman Act was designed to be a comprehensive charter of economic liberty aimed at preserving free and unfettered competition as the rule of trade. It rests on the premise that the unrestrained interaction of competitive forces will yield the best allocation of our economic resources, the lowest prices, the highest quality and the greatest material progress, while at the same time providing an environment conducive to the preservation of our democratic, political, and social institutions. But even were that premise open to question, the policy unequivocally laid down by the act is competition.[16]

The Sherman Act states the following:

> Every contract, combination ... or conspiracy, in restraint of trade or commerce among the several states ... is hereby declared illegal. ... Every person who shall monopolize any part of the trade or commerce among the several states ... shall be

[15] *Oriental Art Printing v. Goldstar Printing*, 2001 WL 460950 (N.Y. 2001)

[16] *Northern Pacific Railroad v. United States*, 356 U.S. 1, 78 S.Ct. 514 (1968)

deemed guilty of a felony, and, on conviction thereof, shall be punished by a fine [and/or imprisonment] ...[17]

The specific activities that restrain competition and are addressed by the antitrust laws are listed below. Some are **per se violations**, which means they are always illegal. Others are subject to the **rule of reason**: they are not always illegal, but rather their benefits (such as economic efficiency) are balanced against their anticompetitive effects in a particular case. If the benefits outweigh the drawbacks, the activity will be permitted. If the anticompetitive impact is too great, the activity will be outlawed.

Penalties

Penalties for violation of antitrust laws are significant and include **dissolution**, which means a business is ordered to terminate its operations; **divestiture**, which means a business is required to terminate *part* of its operations; criminal penalties, including jail and substantial fines; and **treble damages**, or mandated payment of three times the loss suffered by an injured plaintiff.

Application of the Per Se Rule

The following is a list of activities that restrain competition and are per se violations of antitrust laws.

- **Price-fixing agreements**, in which competitors agree among themselves to sell goods at a certain price and not lower.
- **Vertical price-fixing**, in which a manufacturer establishes minimum prices at which lower-level dealers in a distribution system can sell a product.
- **Territorial division agreements**, in which competitors assign to each other a territory and agree not to compete in the others' territories, thereby each obtaining a territorial monopoly.
- **Group boycott**, in which two or more sellers refuse to do business with a particular person or company, intending thereby to eliminate competition or block entry to a market.
- **Resale price-maintenance agreements**, in which a manufacturer determines the price at which retailers must sell.
- **Price discrimination**, where a seller of goods charges different prices to different buyers for the same product (not applicable to services).
- **Exclusive dealing contracts**, in which a seller (usually a wholesaler) forbids a buyer (usually a retailer) from purchasing the products of the seller's competitors.

An example of the per se violation of price fixing is provided by a case in which four hotel firms and the Hawaii Hotel Association (a trade association of hotel

---

[17]15 U.S.C. §§ 1,2

owners) were charged with violations of price-fixing laws. All pled no contest, an alternative plea to guilty or not guilty that is allowed in some states. This plea means that the defendant, while not admitting guilt, declines to dispute the charges. Defendants Sheraton Hawaii Corporation and Hilton Hotels were fined $50,000 each, and Cinerama Hawaii Hotels and Flagship International were each ordered to pay $25,000, while the trade group was fined $10,000.

The following case is an example of the application of the Sherman Act and the per se rule to a group boycott situation. We learn from this case that avoidance of antitrust liability requires a hotel or restaurant to do more than just give detailed directives to its employees about what conduct is unacceptable. The hotel must also conduct follow-up checks to ensure employees are abiding by the orders.

CASE EXAMPLE 15-5

United States v. Hilton Hotels Corporation
467 F.2d 1000 (Or. 1972)

This is an appeal from a conviction under an indictment charging a violation of section 1 of the Sherman Act.

Operators of hotels, restaurants, hotel and restaurant supply companies, and other businesses in Portland, Oregon, organized an association to attract conventions to their city. To finance the association, members were asked to make contributions in predetermined amounts. Companies selling supplies to hotels were asked to contribute an amount equal to one percent of their sales to hotel members. To aid collections, hotel members, including [Hilton Hotels Corporation] agreed to give preferential treatment to suppliers who paid their assessments, and to curtail purchases from those who did not.

The jury was instructed that such an agreement by the hotel members, if proven, would be a per se violation of the Sherman Act. [Hilton Hotels Corporation] argues that this was error. ...

[T]he conduct involved here was of the kind long held to be forbidden. ... "Throughout the history of the Sherman Act, the courts have had little difficulty in finding unreasonable restraints of trade in agreements among competitors, at any level of distribution, designed to coerce those subject to a boycott to accede

to the action or inaction desired by the group or to exclude them from competition."

[T]he necessary and direct consequence of defendants' scheme was to deprive uncooperative suppliers of the opportunity to sell to defendant hotels in free and open competition with other suppliers, and to deprive defendant hotels of the opportunity to buy supplies from such suppliers in accordance with the individual judgment of each hotel, at prices and on terms and conditions of sale determined by free competition. ...

The primary purpose and direct effect of defendants' agreement was to bring the combined economic power of the hotels to bear upon those suppliers who failed to pay. The exclusion of uncooperative suppliers from the portion of the market represented by the supply requirements of the defendant hotels was the object of the agreement, not merely its incidental consequence.

[Hilton Hotel Corporation's] president testified that it would be contrary to the policy of the corporation for the manager of one of its hotels to condition purchases upon payment of a contribution to a local association by the supplier. The manager of [Hilton's] Portland hotel and his assistant testified that it was the hotel's policy to purchase supplies solely on the basis of price, quality, and service. They also testified that on two occasions they told the hotel's purchasing agent that he was to take no part in the boycott. The purchasing agent confirmed the receipt of these instructions, but admitted that, despite them, he had threatened a supplier with loss of the hotel's business unless the supplier paid the association assessment. He testified that he violated his instructions because of anger and personal pique toward the individual representing the supplier. ...

The court instructed the jury that a corporation is liable for the acts and statements of its agents "within the scope of their employment," defined to mean "in the corporation's behalf in performance of the agent's general line of work," including "not only that which has been authorized by the corporation, but also that which outsiders could reasonably assume the agent would have authority to do." The court added:

A corporation is responsible for acts and statements of its agents, done or made within the scope of their employment, even though their conduct may be contrary to their actual instructions or contrary to the corporation's stated policies.

[Hilton] objects only to the court's concluding statement.

Congress may constitutionally impose criminal liability upon a business entity for acts or omissions of its agents within the scope of their employment. Such liability may attach ... even though [the conduct] may have been contrary to express instructions. ...

In enacting the Sherman Act, Congress was passing drastic legislation to remedy a threatening danger to the public welfare. ... The statute was designed to be a comprehensive charter of economic liberty aimed at preserving free and unfettered competition as the rule of trade. It rests on the premise that the unrestrained interaction of competitive forces will yield the best allocation of our economic resources, the lowest prices, the highest quality and the greatest material progress, while at the same time providing an environment conducive to the preservation of our democratic, political and social institutions.

With such important public interests at stake, it is reasonable to assume that Congress intended to impose liability upon business entities for the acts of those to whom they choose to delegate the conduct of their affairs, thus stimulating a maximum effort by owners and managers to assure adherence by such agents to the requirements of the Act. ...

Violations of the Sherman Act are a likely consequence of the pressure to maximize profits that is commonly imposed by corporate owners upon managing agents and, in turn, upon lesser employees. In the face of that pressure, generalized directions to obey the Sherman Act, with the probable effect of foregoing profits, are the least likely to be taken seriously. And if a violation of the Sherman Act occurs, the corporation, and not the individual agents, will have realized the profits from the illegal activity. ...

For these reasons we conclude that as a general rule a corporation is liable under the Sherman Act for the acts of its agents in the scope of their employment, even though contrary to general corporate policy and express instructions to the agent. ...

The purchasing agent was authorized to buy all of appellant's supplies. Purchases were made on the basis of specifications, but the purchasing agent exercised complete authority as to source. He was in a unique position to add the corporation's buying power to the force of the boycott. [Hilton] could not gain exculpation [freedom from liability] by issuing general instructions without undertaking to enforce those instructions by means commensurate with the obvious risks. ...

Ruling of the Court: [Conviction of Hilton for violating the Sherman Act] Affirmed.

CASE QUESTIONS

1. In what way does a group boycott such as the one in this case restrict competition?

2. Why was the hotel liable for the conduct of an employee who was acting contrary to his supervisor's directives?

An example of vertical price-fixing, another per se violation, is a wholesaler who sells to a distributor chicken-wing sauce intended for restaurants and the sale is conditioned upon the distributor's agreement not to resell the sauce below a specified price.[18]

Application of the Rule of Reason

The following is a list of activities that may restrain competition and are judged according to the rule of reason:

- **Territorial restrictions**, in which a manufacturer restricts the territory in which dealers can sell, thereby preventing other dealers from competing in a given territory.

- **Monopoly**, in which one firm controls the market for a particular product with the intent of excluding competitors.

- **Tying arrangements**, in which a seller conditions the sale of a product on the buyer's agreement to purchase some other product produced or distributed by the seller.

- **Mergers**, in which two businesses are combined into one, resulting in a reduction of competition.

A case in which the rule of reason was applied in a tying arrangement was *Martino v. McDonald's System, Inc.*, 625 F.Supp. 356 (Ill. 1985). McDonald's, the fast-food hamburger operation, required its franchisees (owners of individual restaurants; see discussion later in this chapter) to sell Coca-Cola and no other cola drink as a condition for allowing the franchisees to use the McDonald's name. The reason for the requirement was McDonald's interest in a standard menu at all its restaurants for purposes of uniformity, and in a linkage with a product known and popular among consumers. Some franchisees wanted to sell Pepsi because they could buy it for less. They sued McDonald's, seeking to have the Coca-Cola requirement declared an illegal tying arrangement. The court held the restriction was *legal* based on the rule of reason. The court noted that McDonald's is by no means a monopoly in the fast-food industry; McDonald's does not dominate the cola market; competition was not substantially lessened by McDonald's Coca-Cola requirement; McDonald's does not have a financial interest in the profits of the Coca-Cola Company; and its reasons for imposing the restriction (including uniformity among franchises) were reasonable.

The following case explores restrictions against monopolies. We discussed in Chapter 10 that a hotel can prohibit from its premises businesses that compete with the services the hotel offers; the resulting exclusive right to sell to hotel guests is not considered an illegal monopoly. Similarly, a sports stadium can prohibit spectators from bringing in food from outside sources. Such a prohibition does not violate the antitrust laws although it gives the stadium the exclusive right during the event to sell food to those in attendance. The reason why this mini-monopoly is not illegal is discussed in the following case.

---

[18] *Prince Heaton Enterprises, Inc. v. Buffalo's Franchise Concepts, Inc.*, 117 F.Supp. 1357 (Ga. 2000)

CASE EXAMPLE 15-6

Elliott v. The United Center
126 F.3d 1003 (1997)

Millions of spectators have attended games and other events at the United Center, home of the world-famous Chicago Bulls, as well as the Chicago Blackhawks, circuses, ice shows, concerts, and in 1996 the Democratic National Convention. But ever since the United Center opened, it has had a policy that prohibits all patrons of the center from bringing food into the arena. This, according to Thornton Elliott and his co-plaintiffs, has given a "monopoly" on food sales to the Center. Elliott [the plaintiff] and his colleagues are licensed peanut vendors who, up until the time the United Center imposed this policy, turned a respectable profit selling peanuts outside the stadium. They brought this suit under section 2 of the Sherman Act, claiming that the United Center's food policy constitutes an illegal attempt to monopolize food sales inside the arena and in the surrounding geographic area. The district court was unpersuaded and dismissed the case. We agree. ...

According to the complaint, ever since the United Center implemented its food policy in September 1994, patrons are inspected for food when they enter the stadium, and if any is found, it is confiscated by stadium security. If a fan buys a bag of peanuts from Elliott, therefore, she must consume it before she enters the United Center, unless she wants to risk contributing it to the "illegal food" stash collected by the security personnel. Worse yet, if she has a hankering for peanuts during the Bull's game, her desires will go unfulfilled because the United Center does not offer peanuts for sale in the stadium (except little bags of peanuts for the circus elephants). This policy has cost Elliott dearly ... the average sales of peanuts have dropped to approximately one-fifth of sales in previous years. Predictably, some vendors have gone out of business, and the remaining ones are struggling to survive. ...

[Plaintiffs] conceded that the United Center might have had a legitimate business reason to prohibit certain kinds of food, such as cans, bottles, or alcoholic beverages in general, in the interest of maintaining order in the facility, but plaintiffs claim that no such reason could be advanced for the blanket food ban. The complaint points out the United Center's monopoly over the presentation of live National Basketball Association games and live National Hockey League games in the Chicago market, and implicitly argues that the Center is, through the food policy, attempting to extend its monopoly to the alleged food concession market. ... Plaintiffs claim the fewer the food concessions, the higher the price the United Center can charge for food its patrons consume, and the more consumers will suffer. ...

The United Center can recoup the cost of putting on an event in any of a number of ways. It can charge very high ticket prices, and allow unlimited numbers of food concessions in and around the stadium, or it can charge somewhat lower ticket prices and restrict the number of concessions (thereby earning some of its profits from food sales.) ... The United Center is obviously not monopolizing the market for peanuts: it is staying strictly out of the peanut business. Prices and output of peanuts in the area are totally unaffected by the United Center's policies.

The logic of Elliott's argument would mean that exclusive restaurants could no longer require customers to purchase their wines only at the establishment, because the restaurant would be "monopolizing" the sale of wine within its interior. Movie theaters, which traditionally (and notoriously) earn a substantial profit of their revenue from the sales of candies, popcorn, and soda, would be required by the antitrust laws to allow patrons to bring their own food. ... Elliott's principal point is that the customer knows that once he is ready to walk through the entry gate, he may not have with him any "outside" food. The same could be said of any of the establishments we have just mentioned: once inside a restaurant, or a movie theater, the customer is at the mercy of the place he has chosen. The price of the refreshments or the wine is just one part of the price of the evening out.

[The facts here do not present a] violation of the antitrust laws. ... We therefore conclude that the district court correctly dismissed Elliott's complaint. ... Affirmed.

Franchising

Towns and cities look more and more alike as each have hotels, restaurants, and stores with the same names. This phenomenon is based in significant part on franchising. A **franchise** is an arrangement in which the owner of a trademark, service mark, or copyright licenses others, under specified conditions, to use the mark or copyright in the sale of goods or services. As we have seen, use of another's service mark, trademark, or copyright without permission constitutes infringement.

There are two parties in a franchise arrangement. The **franchisor** is the owner of the mark or copyright; the **franchisee** is the party who receives the right to use it. Examples of franchises include Wendy's, Dunkin' Donuts, Tony Roma's, Day's Inn, and Super 8 Motels.

Nature of the Franchise Relationship

The relationship between the franchisor and the franchisee is contractual. By contract, the franchisor authorizes the franchisee to utilize the trademark, service mark, or copyright. In return, the franchisee customarily agrees to pay the franchisor an initial sum of money plus a percentage of profits on an ongoing basis. The better known the business name is, the higher will be the fees paid by the franchisee. The contract customarily requires the franchisee to maintain certain standards and the franchisor to provide various kinds of technical assistance.

Because the relationship is a contractual one and not an employment relationship or a principal/agent relationship, the franchisor customarily is not liable for the acts of a franchisee. Thus, if a fast-foot franchisee negligently prepares a meal in such a way that a customer is injured, generally the franchisor will not be liable; only the franchisee is legally responsible. The reason is that the franchisee and not the franchisor is the owner and operator of the business. This principle is illustrated in *Choice Hotels International, Inc. v. Palm-Aire Oceanside, Inc.*, 95 F.3d 41 (4th Cir. 1996). A hotel franchisee was negligent in the maintenance of a balcony railing. A two-year-old guest fell seventy feet to the ground when deterioration caused the railing to give way. The guest sued both the franchisee and the franchisor. The court held the franchisor was not liable.

The franchisor would be liable only if the franchisor's agents participated in the day-to-day operations and management of the business or, where a patron is injured by a product, if the franchisor made or sold the item that caused the injury.

Benefits to the Franchisee

The franchisee stands to benefit from a franchise relationship in several ways. The use of the franchised name is usually valuable because it is known to customers. In addition, the franchisor is typically required to provide technical help to the franchisee, including the following: market research to decide where to locate the business, advice on layout and design of the building, employee training, recipes, accounting methods, information on suppliers, and other assistance that may be needed. Another important benefit is group advertising. Each franchisee contributes a sum of money for promotions, and the franchisor prepares print and broadcast advertisements. The individual franchisee thus receives the benefit of an expensive advertising campaign for a fraction of the cost.

Benefits to the Franchisor

The franchisor benefits financially from the fees paid by franchisees. The franchisor also benefits from the additional exposure of the name resulting from the franchisee's use. The more the name is known and accepted by the public the more valuable it is, and the greater the franchise fee the franchisor can command from subsequent franchisees. The value of the name is preserved in part by contract provisions requiring the franchisee to maintain certain standards including specifications of products sold, size of building, interior and exterior design, and cleanliness. These requirements provide consistency, and therefore the foundation for public acceptance of a franchise operation. For example, although each McDonald's restaurant is individually owned, we have a certain expectation of what we will find if we visit one, and at whichever outlet we choose we will likely find what we expect.

Exclusive Territory

An exclusive territory is very valuable to a franchisee because it protects the business from competition from a nearby franchisee. If a franchisee receives an exclusive territory, it will be stated in the contract. A franchisee is well-advised to attempt to negotiate a provision in the franchise agreement granting an exclusive territory. Without it, the franchisee's patronage may be invaded by a like business, resulting in a considerable loss in income. In *Payne v. McDonald's Corp.*, 957 F.Supp. 749 (Md. 1997), a McDonald's franchisee was frustrated when the franchisor authorized two additional restaurants within two miles of his eatery. He sued the franchisor for breach of contract. The court stated, "The problem faced by plaintiffs in claiming a breach of contract by McDonald's is their inability to point to any provision in the express and unambiguous agreement between the parties which has been breached by McDonald's." A provision in the contract stated, "[N]o exclusive, protected or other territorial rights in the contiguous market area of the restaurant is hereby granted or inferred." The franchisee's case was dismissed.

Fraud and Breach of Contract by the Franchisor

If a franchisee pays the franchise fees and the franchisor fails to promote the name, provide technical assistance, or otherwise comply with its contractual obligations, the franchisee may be the victim of fraud and/or breach of contract. To reduce the chances of this happening, a would-be franchisee should thoroughly investigate a franchisor before investing in a franchise.

Disclosure Requirements for Franchisors

When the concept of franchising first began, unscrupulous franchisors often took money from unsuspecting franchisees and failed to provide the promised services. To protect franchisees against this occurrence, both federal and state laws require franchisors to disclose detailed information about their business at least ten days before accepting any money from the franchisee.

The information typically required to be disclosed includes:

- The name and address of the franchisor
- The business experience of persons affiliated with the franchisor
- Whether any such person has been convicted of a felony
- The length of time the franchisor has conducted a business of the type to be operated by the franchisee
- The franchisor's most recent financial statement, and information about any material changes in the finances since the statement was prepared
- An explanation of all fees imposed on the franchisee
- A copy of the franchise contract typically used by the franchisor
- A statement of all fees that the franchisee will be required to pay
- The proposed application of the fees by the franchisor
- Whether any franchisees have sued the franchisor
- Circumstances under which the franchise agreement can be terminated
- The number of franchises already sold and the number proposed to be sold in the future
- The responsibilities of the franchisor and the franchisee
- A statement whether the franchisee will receive an exclusive territory.

The document in which this information is presented is called a *prospectus*. A franchisor that provides false information in the prospectus faces both civil and criminal penalties including compensation for damages, jail, and fines.

The required ten-day waiting period between disclosure and acceptance of money by the franchisor is intended to give the franchisee opportunity to review the information and discuss it with advisors such as a lawyer and an accountant.

Tying Arrangements in Franchises as an Antitrust Issue

A franchisor often wants its franchisees to purchase supplies and equipment from the franchisor. This arrangement ensures the franchisor of both a market for its products and the uniformity that is so important to franchise operations. If its trademark is sufficiently valuable, franchisees may be willing to agree to buy from the franchisor exclusively in return for the right to use the name. From an antitrust point of view, this is a tying arrangement—that is, the obligation to purchase products from the franchisor is tied to the grant of the franchise. As a result, the franchisor is spared from competition by other suppliers and they in turn are denied access to franchisees as potential customers.

As we have seen, tying arrangements are not per se violations of antitrust laws, but rather are subject to the rule of reason. In determining whether a particular tying arrangement is legal or not, the court will examine several factors, including the amount of commerce affected and whether some special justification exists for the tying arrangement. The greater the impact on competition and the less compelling the justification is, the more likely the tying arrangement will be unenforceable. For example, franchisees of Mr. Softee, a soft ice-cream seller, objected to a franchise agreement provision requiring that they purchase all of their ice-cream mix from the franchisor. Claiming it was an illegal tying arrangement, the franchisees sued. The court held that the franchisor's requirements were reasonable so as to ensure that the consumer always receives a consistent product and because the trademark Mr. Softee and the particular ice-cream mix sold by the franchisor are inseparable.[19] The desire by a franchisor to maintain uniformity and quality standards does not always qualify as sufficient justification.

In the following case, franchisees of Domino's Pizza alleged that the franchisor violated antitrust laws by requiring that franchisees purchase ingredients and dough from the franchisor. The court disagreed and dismissed the case.

CASE EXAMPLE 15-7

Queens City Pizza, Inc. v. Domino's Pizza, Inc.
124 F.3d 430 (3rd Cir. 1997)

Domino's Pizza, Inc. is a fast-food service company that sells pizza through a national network of over 4200 stores. Domino's Pizza owns and operates approximately 700 of these stores. Independent franchisees own and operate the remaining 3500. Domino's Pizza, Inc. is the second largest pizza company in the United States, with revenues in excess of $1.8 billion per year.

A franchisee joins the Domino's System by executing a standard franchise agreement with Domino's Pizza, Inc. Under the franchise agreement, the franchisee receives the right to sell pizza under the "Domino's" name and format. In return, Domino's Pizza receives franchise fees and royalties.

The essence of a successful nationwide fast-food chain is product uniformity and con-sistency. Uniformity benefits franchisees because customers can purchase pizza from any Domino's store and be certain the pizza will taste exactly like the Domino's Pizza with which they are familiar. This means that individual franchisees need not build up their own good will. Uniformity also benefits the franchisor. It ensures the brand name will continue to attract and hold customers, increasing franchise fees and royalties.

For these reasons, section 12.2 of the Domino's Pizza standard franchise agreement requires that all pizza ingredients, beverages, and packaging materials used by a Domino's franchisee conform to the standards set by Domino's Pizza Inc. Section 12.2 also provides that Domino's Pizza, Inc. may "in our sole discretion require that ingredients, supplies and materials used in the preparation, packaging and delivery of pizza be purchased exclusively from us or from approved suppliers or distributors." Domino's Pizza reserves the right to "impose reasonable limitations on

[19] *Tserpelis v. Mister Softee*, 106 F.Supp.2d 423 (N.Y. 1999)

the number of approved suppliers or distributors of any product." To enforce these rights, Domino's Pizza, Inc. retains the power to inspect franchisee stores and to test materials and ingredients. Section 12.2 is subject to a reasonableness clause providing that Domino's Pizza, Inc. must "exercise reasonable judgment with respect to all determinations to be made by us under the terms of this Agreement." Under the standard franchise agreement, Domino's Pizza, Inc. sells approximately 90% of the $500 million in ingredients and supplies used by Domino's franchisees. These sales, worth some $450 million per year, form a significant part of Domino's Pizza, Inc.'s profits. Franchisees purchase only 10% of their ingredients and supplies from outside sources. With the exception of fresh dough, Domino's Pizza, Inc. does not manufacture the products it sells to franchisees. Instead, it purchases these products from approved suppliers and then resells them to the franchisees at a markup.

The plaintiffs in this case are eleven Domino's franchisees and the International Franchise Advisory Council, Inc. (IFAC), a Michigan corporation consisting of approximately 40% of the Domino's franchisees in the United States, formed to promote their common interests. The plaintiffs contend that Domino's Pizza, Inc. has a monopoly in "the $500 million aftermarket for sales of supplies to Domino's franchisees" and has used its monopoly power to unreasonably restrain trade, limit competition, and extract supracompetitive profits.

First, plaintiffs allege that Domino's Pizza, Inc. has restricted their ability to purchase competitively priced dough. Most franchisees purchase all of their fresh dough from Domino's Pizza, Inc. Plaintiffs here attempted to lower costs by making fresh pizza dough on site. They contend that in response, Domino's Pizza, Inc. increased processing fees and altered quality standards and inspection practices for store-produced dough, which eliminated all potential savings and financial incentives to make their own dough.

Plaintiffs also allege Domino's Pizza, Inc. prohibited stores that produce dough from selling their dough to other franchisees, even though the dough-producing stores were willing to sell dough at a price 25% to 40% below Domino's Pizza, Inc.'s price.

Next, plaintiffs object to efforts by Domino's Pizza, Inc. to block IFAC's attempt to buy less expensive ingredients and supplies from other sources. ...

Plaintiffs also allege Domino's Pizza entered into exclusive dealing arrangements with several franchisees in order to deny [alternate purveyors] access to a pool of potential buyers sufficiently large to make an alternative purchasing scheme economically feasible. In addition, plaintiffs contend Domino's Pizza, Inc. commenced anti-competitive predatory pricing to shut other suppliers out of the market. For example, they maintain that Domino's Pizza, Inc. lowered prices on many ingredients and supplies to a level competitive with [others'] prices and then recouped lost profits by raising the price on fresh dough, which [competitors] could not supply.

As a result of these and other alleged practices, plaintiffs maintain that each franchisee store now pays between $3000 and $10,000 more per year for ingredients and supplies than it would in a competitive market. Plaintiffs allege these costs are passed on to consumers. ...

Courts and legal commentators have long recognized that franchise tying contracts are an essential and important aspect of the franchise form of business organization because they reduce agency costs and prevent franchisees from freeriding-offering products of sub-standard quality insufficient to maintain the reputational value of the franchise product while benefitting from the quality control efforts of other actors in the franchise system. Franchising is a bedrock of the American economy. More than one-third of all dollars spent in retailing transactions in the United States are paid to franchise outlets. We do not believe the antitrust laws were designed to erect a serious barrier to this form of business organization. ...

Here, plaintiffs' acceptance of a franchise package that included purchase requirements and contractual restrictions is consistent with the existence of a competitive market in which franchises are valued, in part, according to the terms of the proposed franchise agreement and the availability of alternative franchise opportunities. Plaintiffs need not have become Domino's franchisees. If the contractual restrictions in section 12.2 of the general franchise agreement were viewed as overly burdensome or risky at the time they were proposed, plaintiffs could have purchased a different form of restaurant, or made some alternative investment. They chose not to do so. Plaintiffs must purchase products from Domino's Pizza not because of Domino's market power ... but because they are bound by contract to do so. If Domino's Pizza, Inc. acted unreasonably when, under the franchise agreement, it restricted plaintiffs' ability to purchase supplies from other sources, plaintiffs' remedy, if any, is in contract, not under antitrust laws. ...

CASE QUESTION

1. Explain what the court meant when it said, "Plaintiffs must purchase products from Domino's Pizza not because of Domino's market power ... but because they are bound by contract to do so." What effect did this statement have on the decision?

Termination of a Franchise

Many abuses have occurred surrounding terminations of franchises. Once a franchisee has invested money, time, and energy in developing the franchise business, courts are reluctant to allow the franchisor to terminate the franchise without good cause. Many states have passed statutes limiting the circumstances under which a franchisor can withdraw the franchise. Typical is the Indiana statute, which bars a franchisor from terminating a franchise "without good cause or in bad faith."[20] Sufficient grounds for termination include repeated failures by a franchise restaurant to pay franchise fees.[21] and failure by the franchisee to satisfy the franchisor's cleanliness standards as identified in the contract (dirty restrooms, trash on the floor and "other generally unsanitary conditions") coupled with failure to purchase insurance as required by the contract.[22]

Once a franchise agreement expires or is terminated, the franchisee's right to use the franchisor's trademark terminates. Continued use of the name by the franchisee constitutes trademark infringement. Thus, where a Burger King franchise expired and was not renewed, and the franchisee continued to operate the business under the name Burger King, the franchisee was liable for trademark infringement. The franchisee's claim of wrongful termination was not a defense to the trademark infringement action. The remedy for the alleged wrongful termination was a lawsuit seeking money damages based on breach of contract.[23] Where a Dunkin' Donuts franchisee failed to pay franchise and advertising fees, triggering a contractual termination of the franchise agreement, the continued use of the Dunkin' Donuts name constituted trademark infringement.[24] Similarly, where a

[20]Ind. Code §§ 23-2-2.7-1(7) and (8)

[21]*McDonald's v. Kristina Denise Enterprises*, 189 F.3d 461 (N.Y. 1999)

[22]*Zeidler v. A&W Restaurants*, 2001 WL 62571 (Ill. 2001)

[23]*Burger King Corp. v. Agad*, 911 F.Supp. 1499 (Fl. 1995)

[24]*Dunkin' Donuts, Inc. v. Towns Family, Inc.*, 1996 WL 328018 (Ill. 1996)

Ramada franchise was terminated due to the franchisee's failure to upgrade its property and pay franchise fees, continued use of the Ramada name constituted trademark infringement.[25]

Regulation of Hotel and Restaurant Internal Affairs

Numerous regulatory laws impact the operation of hospitality establishments. These laws apply to maintenance of guest registers, posting of rates, and recycling.

Guest Register

Most cities and states have passed ordinances that require motels and similar businesses to maintain a register containing guests' names and addresses. The government's interest in a guest register includes, for example, the register's use to verify residence for long-term guests whose right to vote is challenged on residency grounds and in criminal investigations. In one case, a defendant charged with a crime sought to use his signature in an out-of-town motel's guest register to substantiate his alibi defense.[26] The register can also aid authorities in locating lost or stolen automobiles and finding wanted persons.

Another example of using the register for police investigations is provided by a case involving a man charged with endangering the welfare of a minor. A hotel register confirmed his whereabouts on critical dates. He was thirty-seven years old and developed a sexually explicit online relationship with a thirteen-year-old. On two occasions he made arrangements to travel from his home to see the girl, staying both times at a hotel. When the relationship was discovered by the girl's mother and reported to the police, the man denied the encounters. The hotel registration documents constituted important evidence to establish his presence in her town on the dates identified by the girl.[27]

Many states have regulations making it unlawful for a hotelkeeper to knowingly accept as a guest a person who has registered under a pseudonym. Falsification of a guest's name frustrates the use of the register as a law-enforcement aide. The innkeeper should not permit a guest to register under a name the innkeeper knows is not the guest's true name.

Innkeepers should familiarize themselves with the laws concerning guest registers in their state. In the case of *Commonwealth v. Blinn*, 503 N.E.2d 25 (Mass. 1987), a state trooper wanted to inspect the guest register of a Howard Johnson Motor Lodge. The manager refused, believing such an examination constituted an illegal search. However, the applicable state statute clearly stated that law-enforcement officers were allowed to inspect motel registers to determine if someone who was the target of a criminal investigation had registered. The trooper

---

[25] *Ramada v. Jacobcart, Inc.*, 2001 WL 540213 (Tex. 2001)

[26] *Norris v. State*, 469 S.E.2d 214 (Ga. 1996)

[27] *Pierce v. State*, 2001 WL 1097728 (Ga. 2001)

charged the innkeeper with violation of the law and the manager was successfully prosecuted. If the manager had been informed about the law, much time, money, and embarrassment would have been saved.

Many states require that the register be retained for a period of several years. The statutes usually specify that the register can be kept on microfilm, electronic imaging, or other like storage process. Again, innkeepers should familiarize themselves with locally applicable laws.

Rates

Many states or localities have statutes requiring hotels to make known the price charged for each room by posting the rates at the hotel. The purpose of these statutes is to eliminate price gouging in the industry. As the court in *State v. Norval Hotel Co.*, 133 N.E. 75 (Ohio 1921), observed,

> It is a matter of common knowledge that at times when large numbers of the public meet in cities or towns for conventions, or similar gatherings, the capacity of hotels and places for public accommodation is overtaxed and opportunity is thereby given for the exaction of exorbitant or unfair charges.

The prices are set by the hotel; legislatures do not attempt to fix the price of any room in a hotel, nor do they require that a hotel offer accommodations or services at any particular rate. But when a law has been duly adopted requiring posting of rates, the hotel must post its room charges and abide by the posted prices. Such statutes do not prevent the hotel from raising its rates, but they do require that the hotel post new rate schedules within specified time limits.

A hotel can charge different guests different rates provided the different rates are not the result of illegal discrimination. Varying rates would constitute illegal discrimination if based upon gender, race, color, religion, national origin, marital status, or disability. For further discussion on illegal discrimination, see Chapter 3. Issues associated with charging different rates were addressed in the following case.

CASE EXAMPLE 15-8

**Archibald v. Cinerama Hotels
140 Cal.Rptr. 599 (1977)**

[Plaintiff is a resident of California who stayed at the defendant's hotel in Hawaii.]

It is alleged in the first cause of action that the rates charged plaintiff and members of her class are higher than those charged to residents of the State of Hawaii. It is not alleged that the rates charged Californians are different than the rates charged any person or class of persons from anywhere else in the world, nor is it alleged that the rates charged plaintiff are unreasonable or excessive. While the complaint categorizes the rate charged her and other nonresidents as a "surcharge" which is "discriminatory," the "preferential treatment" described in the complaint consists of ... an unspecified rate presumably lower than the regular rate paid by all nonresidents and is illustrated by advertisement in the yellow pages of the telephone book placed by certain hotels such as "Ask about our [local resident] rates or [local resident] discounts."

Plaintiff has based her case in large part on the common law pertaining to innkeepers. She asserts there was, and is, a duty to charge exactly the same rates to everyone. Reliance is placed by plaintiff principally on textbook authority that innkeepers must provide lodging for all at a reasonable price and that all should be served equally and without discrimination. However, looking at plaintiff's authorities, ... we observe that the concern of the common law was and is limited to assuring each traveler freedom from unreasonably high rates. Since travel upon the highway at night was hazardous and there was little choice of lodging for the night, the common law approved restrictions upon innkeepers to [e]nsure a charge of "reasonable value" for services, to prevent them from extorting exorbitant rates.

We have found no authority holding that the offering of a discount to certain clients, patrons or customers based on an attempt to attract their business is unlawful under the common law, whether the discount be for salesmen, clergymen, armed services personnel, or local residents. In fact it has been indicated in court decisions that even the common law duty to charge reasonable value for services is inapplicable where the guest is not one who might be stranded on a road in the nighttime or might otherwise be at the mercy of a single innkeeper. ...

We do not perceive that the common law is concerned with rates as such, except that they not be unreasonable; nor is it concerned with charges lower than reasonable charges, or discounts to induce patronage from certain groups or classes. ...

Our research has disclosed no California statute, rule or policy which requires a hotel to charge a uniform rate to all its guests. ... Insofar as policy or rules are concerned, an innkeeper has a duty to receive and accommodate all persons at a reasonable charge.

The judgment [dismissing the complaint] is affirmed.

CASE QUESTION

1. Can a motel that is the only inn within a twenty-five mile radius charge whatever rates it chooses? Why or why not?

Mandatory Recycling

Most states and localities have adopted laws requiring businesses and individuals to recycle some of their waste products. The purpose of recycling is to save natural resources, reduce pollution, and decrease the amount of waste that goes into landfills. For example, up to seventeen trees are needed to make a ton of paper; when paper is recycled, less new paper is needed and so fewer trees are harvested.

Recycling laws vary from state to state and locality to locality, but basically they require that businesses and individuals separate recyclable waste from the rest of the garbage, and waste haulers are required to deliver the recyclable waste to recycling centers. Food service businesses are typically required to separate certain food and beverage containers, such as wine bottles, metal and aluminum containers, and certain types of plastic containers. The law may require that the containers be cleaned, that the glass containers be separated from other recycleables, that each color of glass containers be separated from other colors, and that tops and caps be removed. All businesses are typically required to recycle office paper and corrugated cardboard. Penalties for noncompliance are usually fines ranging in amount from $50 to $1,000 per infraction.

Restaurants and hotels have found a variety of additional ways to further the environment. These include installing water-saving shower heads in guest rooms, offering guests the option of less-than-daily washing of sheets and towels, and donating used furniture and linens to charitable organizations.

Licensing and Zoning

Prerequisites to operating a hotel, restaurant, or bar include securing required licenses and permits and compliance with relevant zoning laws. The next sections of this chapter discuss license application, renewal, and revocation processes, and the mandates of zoning laws.

Licensing

The state or government may require that the owner of an inn, hotel, restaurant, or similar establishment obtain various licenses and permits before opening for business. The goal of licensing requirements is to prevent hospitality establishments from becoming menaces to the public welfare by requiring licensed businesses to maintain proper operation, sanitation, construction, and fire protection. The authority of government to license and regulate is based on the power of government to adopt laws that further public health, safety, and welfare. This power is referred to as the **police power**.

When a government licenses a business or grants a permit, the license or permit confers the right to do something that would otherwise be prohibited. A license is a special privilege rather than a right common to all. For example, you cannot drive a car without a license. Only people who have proven their ability to pilot a motor vehicle are entitled to a driver's license. The operation of hotels and restaurants is likewise subject to legislative authority to regulate and license because, like driving, those businesses affect the public welfare.

A considerable body of law has been developed concerning the granting and revoking of licenses. These laws seek to balance the concerns of the licensing body and the interests of the licensed party or party seeking a license or permit.

Principles for Granting Licenses and Permits

Hotel and restaurant owners must obtain all necessary licenses and permits before opening their businesses. Those required vary from locality to locality and may include a hotel operator's license, a restaurant operator's license, a liquor license, health and fire code permits, and zoning permits. Determination of what licenses and permits are required and what prerequisites are necessary to qualify for them usually requires considerable research and the aid of an attorney.

Sample Licensing Experience

Every state and county has a health department whose mission is to ensure the health of residents. These health departments engage in a multi-faceted approach to eliminating foodborne disease. The various components include mandatory plan reviews for all new and remodeled food establishments, mandatory health permits for restaurants, inspections to ensure compliance with health and sanitation rules, prompt investigations of consumer complaints, mandatory food manager training, and litigation against repeat violators of the health code.

Before a restaurant can operate it must obtain a permit from the health department (in addition to other licenses and permits). Prior to issuing the permit, the health department will send an inspector to investigate the premises to determine if it complies with all health and sanitation rules, in addition to any other applicable regulations. If the establishment passes inspection, a permit will be issued. Thereafter, the facility will be subject to periodic announced and unannounced inspections. The frequency of inspections will be accelerated if the health department receives complaints from customers or employees about the health or sanitation conditions at the facility. The purpose of the inspections is to reduce risk factors that contribute to foodborne illness and to avert adulteration of food products.

The health department inspectors are typically trained public-health professionals. They are given various titles depending on the locality, including environmental health specialist, health inspector, and sanitarian.

When they visit an eatery, inspectors will examine the following: how employees receive, process, and store food; the temperatures at which food is cooked, held, and reheated; washing procedures for food and dishes; employee practices such as hair restraints and hand washing; the condition of cooking equipment and how it is shelved; adequacy of the ventilation and heating systems; sewage and waste disposal; whether walls, ceilings, and floors are clean, made of proper materials, and in reasonable condition; the bathroom facilities; how hazardous materials (for example, cleaning fluids, insect repellents) are labeled and stored; whether evidence of vermin exists; whether ingredients are properly disclosed to diners (truth-in-menu issues); whether required signs and notices are posted (for example, mandated warnings about alcohol and pregnancy, and most localities require restaurants to post their public health permit and business license).

Also, during an inspection the inspector may ask an employee to demonstrate a procedure—such as the use of a sanitizer during dish washing—to determine if it is being done correctly.

As a result of an inspection, the health department may issue to the restaurant citations, which are accusations of health or sanition code violations. Owners have the opportunity to dispute the alleged violations at a hearing. If serious or repeated violations are discovered the health department will suspend or revoke the restaurant's permit, thereby forcing it to close.

Examples of violations restaurants might be cited for include: employees not practicing "good hygiene"; insufficient hand-washing facilities; toxic items improperly stored, labeled, or used; food not meeting temperature requirements during service (or storage); presence of insects or rodents; broken self-closer on back door allowing rodents in; hand-washing facilities not accessible; hand sink missing shields thereby permitting splashing onto clean dishes; and evidence of cigarette smoking in food-preparation area.

Violations are customarily categorized. The most serious relate directly to the protection of the public from foodborne illness and, if found, must be corrected immediately. A second tier of violations include cleanliness issues.

Many local health departments are now posting inspection results on the Internet to allow consumers to make informed decisions regarding patronage of food establishments. On some sites, to help consumers understand the significance of a violation, the consumer can click on an infraction for which a restaurant was cited and read the public health reasons for the rule.

Compliance with Laws

To qualify for a license, the applicant must prove that he will abide by all applicable laws. In the following case, an applicant was denied a hotel license because the government entity charged with issuing the license believed the applicant would permit immoral activity.

CASE EXAMPLE 15-9

Hertenberger v. City of Texarkana
272 S.W.2d 435 (Ark. 1954)

The applicant [E]velyn Hertenberger applied to the City of Texarkana for a license to operate a hotel. The [City] council, after considering the application, refused to issue the license. [She appealed the decision of the City Council.]

Ordinance B-439 of the City of Texarkana pertains to the licensing of rooming houses and hotels, and provides: "such license shall not be granted unless it shall appear probable to the Council that such applicant will not rent rooms for immoral purposes or allow prostitutes or pimps to remain on such premises or permit gambling or the sale, storage or keeping of intoxicating liquor on such premises." ...

Without going into detail as to the evidence, suffice it to say that the council was justified in reaching the conclusion that if Mrs. Hertenberger was granted a license, in all probability the hotel rooms would be rented for immoral purposes; and Ordinance B-439 specifically provides that the license shall not be granted in such circumstances.

Although the right to operate a hotel is a property right, this fact does not preclude the city council from refusing to issue a license where the issuance of such license would be in violation of a valid ordinance. ...

We have reached the conclusion that the ordinance is valid and none of the applicant's constitutional rights were violated in refusing her a license to operate a hotel in Texarkana.

CASE QUESTIONS

1. Why would the City of Texarkana want to ensure that a hotel or boarding house owner would not permit gambling, prostitution, and other illegal activities on the premises?

2. What evidence do you think was presented to convince the city council that Hertenberger would have permitted immoral activity at her hotel?

Grounds for Denial of a License

To deny a license, the licensing body must have a reasonable basis; it cannot deny the license on arbitrary, capricious, or unreasonable grounds. In making its determination, a licensing authority may take into account a wide range of factors such as traffic, noise, size, community sentiment, the type of business conducted by the applicant, and the applicant's reputation. In *Hertenberger*, the court held that the city council's concern about immoral activity was reasonable, probably based on prior incidents in which Hertenberger was found guilty of prostitution, gambling, or illegal sales of alcohol.

Residents in the vicinity of a proposed new restaurant, hotel, or bar may oppose the new establishment for fear of noise, traffic, congestion, or crime. Organized community resistance to the granting of a license is a legitimate consideration when a board is reviewing a license application. In one case, an applicant sought a license to open a liquor store. Fifty-three residents signed a petition urging the town board to deny the application for the following reasons: two other liquor stores existed within a quarter mile in each direction and the area around the proposed location was across from the community church and "presents the wrong message to children who attend the church." The town board denied the license based in considerable part on the townspeople's resistance. The applicant appealed, claiming that denial of a license based on community opposition is arbitrary and capricious. The court upheld the board's decision, ruling that reliance on residents' opposition is not arbitrary.[28]

Adequate parking is another legitimate concern of a board reviewing a license application. For example, a sports bar applied for a liquor license. A town prerequisite was a specified minimum number of parking spaces. The applicant was able to meet the minimum requirement but only by counting off-site parking that was "remote and not conveniently accessible." This, coupled with a location across the street from homes, schools, and parks was ground for denial of the license.[29]

In an instructive case, McDonald's, the fast-food hamburger company, was denied a **victualer's** (restaurateur's) license for a proposed restaurant in a shopping center, in part because of inadequate parking and in part because of concerns about increased traffic endangering students in a nearby high school. McDonald's appealed and the court ruled the denial of the license was arbitrary and capricious, and McDonald's was entitled to the license. The court noted the following: the proposed McDonald's location was in a relatively empty corner of the shopping center, peak hours at the restaurant did not coincide with the arrival and departure of school buses, and police were assigned to traffic duty at times the school buses operate. Further, the shopping center was not close to a major highway; therefore, the restaurant was likely to attract only those customers already in the immediate area on other business. The court also held the board had incorrectly interpreted a town parking ordinance that required businesses located on a separate lot, as the proposed McDonald's would be, to have adequate parking on that lot, which

---

[28] *Thompson v. Lake Edward Township*, 2000 WL 1869565 (Minn. 2000)

[29] *Woods v. Trussville City Council*, 795 So.2d 725 (Ala. 2001)

McDonald's did not. However, according to the terms of the lease, McDonald's was entitled to use the mall's common parking lot, which contained sufficient parking space. The court thus held that adequate parking was available.[30]

In the following case, also involving McDonald's, we learn that the licensing body, when deciding whether to grant a license, can consider the number of similar licenses already granted, the need for another like business, and public sentiment. Note the conflict-of-interest issue discussed near the end of the decision.

CASE EXAMPLE 15-10

McDonald's Corp. v. Town of East Longmeadow
506 N.E.2d 172 (Mass. 1987)

[McDonald's Corp. appeals the denial of a victualler's license.] ... In denying the license the board [of Selectmen, which is the equivalent of a Town Council] gave the reasons set forth in the margin.[1] McDonald's claims that the board considered factors which are not connected with the preparation and delivery of food, and that the reasons were not supported by evidence. It urges, for example, that the number of twenty-two licenses deemed sufficient was determined arbitrarily and without any studies. We agree with the trial judge that McDonald's has not shown the decision was arbitrary or capricious. ...

The breadth of discretion which local authorities enjoy in granting or denying licenses varies. In the case of common victualler licenses ... for example, town and city boards may exercise judgment about public convenience and public good that is very broad indeed. ... There is no question that the board may consider the number of licenses already granted in determining the public good. ... The board was not required to make studies to determine the number of licenses to be issued. The board members, local residents of the town, were aware of local patron needs, took a view, and noted that there were fifteen restaurants along route 83. The board also properly considered the proximity of another McDonald's.

In particular, McDonald's challenges the board's consideration of public sentiment, traffic, and litter. There was widespread opposition to the grant of the license at the board's hearing. This was in large part because of the "traffic danger to children in the nearby park." ...

While the board's decision appears to be based primarily on the lack of a need for an additional license, the board also took these other considerations into account ... These "ancillary and contributing reasons," even if not sufficient in themselves to warrant a denial of license to McDonald's, did not vitiate the action of the [board]. ...

The licensing authorities are not ... required to grant any licenses to common victuallers. Whether any such licenses shall be granted and, if any, the number to be granted rest in the sound judgment of the licensing board as to the demands of the public welfare in the respective communities. ... There was here no basis on the record to disturb the board's decision.

One of the selectmen disqualified himself from voting because he was employed by Friendly's Corporation. McDonald's, a competitor of Friendly's, asserts that the selectman's participation in speaking against the application and chairing the board's meetings was a [conflict of interest]. Although such participation may have been inappropriate, ... the trial judge, on the basis of the testimony of the other two selectmen, concluded that the facts did not warrant a finding that the selectman's affiliation with Friendly Corporation constitutes a conflict of interest which tainted the ... decision. That finding was not clearly erroneous and is consonant with applicable law. ...

Judgment [denying the license] affirmed.

---

[30] *McDonald's Corporation v. Board of Selectmen of Randolph*, 399 N.E.2d 38 (Mass. 1980)

[1] The applicant has offered no evidence of the need for the new establishment on North Main Street, or that the good of the Town of East Longmeadow requires it, and the Board finds that the need does not exist, and the License and Permit would not be for the good of the town.

An expression of protest of the restaurant is reflected in the petition bearing 600 names, and delivered to the Selectmen. The Board finds that with regards to need, there are already 22 Common Victualler's Licenses in this small town. The Springfield McDonald's is but a short distance away.

In making its decision the Selectmen have also considered the potential for increased traffic particularly during peak hours on North Main Street which is the town's main thoroughfare, and the immediacy of the proposed location to the public park and the resulting negative concerns as to pedestrian safety and adequate disposal of waste.

Past Use of the Property

Another factor the licensing body will consider is the prior use of the property. For example, a junior college applied for a license to operate as dormitories certain buildings it owned. Although the buildings had previously been used as dorms by another college, the neighbors staged an intense protest to the proposed use based on fears of congestion, inadequate parking, and noise. The license was initially denied but granted on appeal. The court held the denial was not based on a reasonable basis and noted that the buildings had previously been used as dormitories with no complaints by neighbors. The court also noted that the junior college applicant was an accredited institution and no unfavorable evidence was presented about its capacity to operate the dorms or about the character of its officers.[31]

Administrative Procedure

Licenses are often issued by a government agency—that is, a governmental subdivision managed by directors appointed by elected officials responsible for administering particular laws. When a licensee fails to abide by the applicable rules, the agency is responsible for prosecuting the violation. Until now, most of the cases we have discussed in the book have been pursued in court. When a government agency is involved, the initial forum for the case is usually the agency rather than a court. If the matter is appealed, the first appeal is often still within the agency. If it is appealed again it will be heard by a court.

Before a matter that is within the jurisdiction of a government agency can be heard in a court, the *administrative remedies must be exhausted*. This means all appeals available within the agency must have been utilized before the case is heard.

License Fees

Licensees often complain that the cost of a license is high. A municipality can require a reasonable fee to be paid for a license intended to protect the public. Many licenses must be renewed annually with a fee imposed for each renewal. If

---

[31] *Newberry Junior College v. Town of Brookline*, 472 N.E.2d 1373 (Mass. 1985)

the fee covers the municipality's costs to administer the license—including the cost to prepare and distribute applications, inspect licensed and would-be licensed premises, and pursue violators—and does not generate significant additional money, the fee is reasonable and valid. Governments cannot use licensing fees as a revenue-raising device. If a license fee produces a significant profit above the costs of administration, the fee will be considered unreasonable and subject to modification. In a ruling more than 100 years old, which remains the law today, a court said,

> The amount the municipality has a right to demand for such fee depends upon the extent and expense of the municipal supervision made necessary by the business in the city or town that issues the licenses. A fee sufficient to cover the expense of issuing the license, and to pay the expenses which may be incurred in the enforcement of such police inspection or superintendence as may be lawfully exercised over the business, may be required. It is obvious that the actual amount necessary to meet such expenses cannot, in all cases, be ascertained in advance, and that it would be futile to require anything of the kind. The result is, if the fee required is not plainly unreasonable, the courts ought not to interfere with the discretion exercised by the [legislature] in fixing it; and, unless the contrary appears on the face of the ordinance requiring it, or is established by proper evidence, they should presume it to be reasonable.[32]

Consequences of Operating Without a License

Failure to obtain a required license can lead to unpleasant consequences, as can failure to obtain a license renewal, which is customarily required at regular intervals, often annually.

Penalties and Fines

If a business fails to qualify for or otherwise obtain a necessary license, the government can bar it from opening or, in the case of an existing business that fails to obtain a renewal, force the business to close. In addition, fines may be imposed. In some states including Florida, the innkeeper or restaurateur may be required to attend "at personal expense, an educational program sponsored by the Hospitality Education Program."[33]

Loss of Protection of Law

Depending on the type of license, another consequence of operating without it may be that the business is unable to enforce its contracts. If the purpose of the license is to protect the public, as is the case of a license to operate a restaurant, the absence of the license will in some states bar the restaurant from enforcing its contracts in court. For example, if a restaurant is not properly licensed and a diner fails to pay, the restaurant may be unable to enforce the guest's contractual duty to do

---

[32] *City of Fayetteville v. Carter*, 12 S.W. 573 (Ark. 1889)
[33] Florida Statutes § 509.261(a)(b)

so. This should be sufficient motivation for restaurateurs and innkeepers to abide by the applicable licensing laws. Where, however, the purpose of the license is to raise revenue (income for the government) and is unrelated to protection of the public, the ability of a business lacking the license to enforce its contracts will not be affected.

Revocation or Suspension of a License

As we have discussed, a license is a privilege, not a right. A licensee must establish it is worthy of the license; there is no automatic entitlement to it. If a licensee fails to continuously meet the requirements of the license, it can be suspended (withdrawn temporarily) or revoked (withdrawn permanently) by the licensing body, which is usually a government agency.

Cause for Revocation or Suspension

The legislature empowers a licensing board to revoke a license when it is satisfied that the licensee is unfit to engage in a business authorized by the license. For example, licensed innkeepers who allow illegal or objectionable activity on the premises, such as illicit gambling or drinking by minors, may be found unfit to keep the license.

In the following case, a restaurant was found to have tolerated numerous safety violations, resulting in a denial of its application for renewal of its liquor license. Take note of the breadth of reasons in the relevant statute that justify denial of a license.

CASE EXAMPLE 15-11

**Oronoka Restaurant, Inc. v.
Maine State Liquor Commission
532 A.2d 1043 (Me. 1987)**

... On January 8, 1986, Oronoka Restaurant (Oronoka) applied for the renewal of its liquor license. On February 10, 1986, the municipal officers of the Town of Orono [in which the restaurant was located] conducted a public hearing on the application and voted unanimously to deny the application for renewal. The Town based its decision on sewage discharge violations, numerous fire code violations, and the failure of the applicant to allow the Town's code enforcement officer access to the premises to inspect for code or ordinance violations. Oronoka filed a timely appeal with the Maine State Liquor Commission (Commission). The Commission ruled that the fire code violations constituted health and safety hazards and thus were valid grounds to deny the application for renewal. ...

Under the [applicable state statute] the Commission may consider all of the following as grounds to deny a liquor license:

A. Conviction of the applicant of any [of a specified level of crime];

B. Noncompliance of the licensed premise with any local zoning ordinance or other land use ordinance not directly related to liquor control;

C. Conditions of record such as waste disposal violations, health or safety violations, or repeated parking or traffic violations on or in the vicinity of the licensed premises and caused by persons patronizing or employed by the licensed premises or other such conditions caused by persons patronizing or employed by the licensed premises which unreasonably disturb, interfere with or affect the ability of persons or businesses residing or located in the vicinity of the licensed premises to use their property in a reasonable manner;

D. Repeated incidents or record of breaches of the peace, disorderly conduct, vandalism or other violations of law on or in the vicinity of the licensed premises and caused by persons patronizing or employed by the licensed premises; and

E. A violation of any [of the liquor sales laws]. ...

The Commission heard extensive and very specific testimony concerning the fire code violations from the Town's fire chief and its code enforcement officer. Of particular concern was an unlicensed, unapproved and illegally installed solid fuel unit or "wood burning boiler." Witnesses testified that the unit lacked appropriate safety systems and could possibly explode. Despite repeated warnings by Town officials that the boiler failed to meet applicable safety standards, Oronoka's owner, as of the time of the Town hearing, had not brought the unit into compliance and had not obtained the necessary approval for its use.

The hazardous solid fuel unit and Oronoka's other fire code violations fall within the grounds specified [by the state statue] upon which a town may deny a liquor license renewal. ... We affirm the judgment.

CASE QUESTION

1. Why are safety violations relevant to the renewal of a liquor license?

A license might also be suspended if the licensee provided false information on the application. Thus, where a restaurant obtained a license to operate a family-style eatery, but instead offered nude dancing and the "hottest adult entertainment to hit the Northeast," its license was suspended.[34]

A victualer's license can be revoked where criminal conduct occurs on the premises. Thus, a good cause for nonrenewal of a restaurant license existed where drug dealing was happening in the facility even without involvement of owners or employees. "Every business is responsible for illegal activity on its premises."[35]

Similarly, a license to operate a grocery store can be revoked where the owner failed to prevent or "meaningfully control" an ongoing pattern of loitering and drug dealing both inside and outside the store's front entrance.[36]

Due Process

The licensee is entitled to **due process**, the right not to be deprived of property (including a license) without a fair hearing. This means that before a license can be revoked, the licensee is entitled to reasonable notice of the grounds for revocation, an opportunity to prepare a defense, a hearing, the opportunity to obtain an attorney, an impartial decision-maker, and a decision based solely on the record—the evidence presented at the hearing.

In the notice, the licensee is entitled to information identifying the specific conduct attributable to him that allegedly violates the rules relating to the license.

---

[34]*D.H.L. Associates, Inc. v. Krussel*, 1996 WL 754910 (Mass. 1996)

[35]*Hard Times Cafe, Inc. v. City of Minneapolis*, 625 S.W.2d 165 (Minn. 2001)

[36]*CUP Foods, Inc. v. City of Minneapolis*, 633 N.W.2d 557 (Minn. 2001)

The reason for this requirement is to provide sufficient information to enable the licensee to address the allegations and prepare a defense. Clearly, a notice of revocation that does not state the grounds is not sufficiently specific. In *Manchester v. Selectmen of Nantucket*, 293 S.W.2d 631 (Ky. 1956), the licensee was charged with operating a hotel improperly. The licensing body gave Manchester the following notice:

> You are herewith advised that ... a hearing will be held at 10 A.M. Wednesday, August 24, 1955, at the Selectmen's Rooms, 17 Federal Street, on complaints received by the board as regards your operation of the premises known as "Nantucket New Ocean House."

The court held that this notice did not adequately inform the license holder of the charges she faced, and thus violated her due process rights.

To satisfy due process rights, not only the notice of the grounds for revocation, but also the date of the hearing must be given by the licensee far enough in advance to enable the licensee to prepare a defense. In another case, a lounge was licensed to provide live entertainment, including exotic dancing. One night it presented male dancers rather than the usual females. The crowd exceeded permissible building capacity. Two days later the town Board of Selectmen, the body that issues and revokes entertainment licenses, notified the owner of the lounge at 5:30 P.M. that a special meeting would be held that evening at 7:00 P.M. to consider revoking his license. This short notice violated the owner's due process rights.[37]

Where a licensee receives a notice to appear before the licensing board and believes the notice is inadequate, the licensee should request additional information concerning the charges or additional time to prepare a defense, as the case may be. Failure to object may result in a waiver of any due process defects in the notice.

Decision Based on Record

Due process requires that decisions concerning a business' license be made based exclusively on evidence presented on the record at the hearing. Due process would be violated if members of a city council, while deciding whether to revoke a restaurant license, considered information not presented at the hearing and made up their minds before the hearing was completed. If these circumstances were proven, the due process violations would require a new hearing on the issue of the license revocation.[38]

Zoning

Zoning is a process by which local governments can restrict the ways property owners can use their land. For example, a zoning ordinance may limit use of property to residential purposes and preclude commercial and industrial uses, or may provide a maximum height for a building—for example, five stories—or may

---

[37] *Konstantopoulos v. Town of Whately*, 424 N.E.2d 210 (Mass. 1981)

[38] *Hard Times Cafe, Inc. v. City of Minneapolis*, 625 S.W.2d 165 (Minn. 2001)

restrict the size and type of sign a business can display on its property to advertise its services—for example, flashing neon signs may be prohibited.

For the would-be innkeeper or restaurateur, zoning laws may ban development of the business. For example, a commercial establishment will not be permitted in an area zoned exclusively residential. Before any resources are committed to a new business, the owner should investigate the applicable zoning restrictions.

The purpose of zoning laws is to achieve balanced development, preserve the residential quality of residential neighborhoods, and minimize adverse effects resulting from inappropriate location, use, or design of certain buildings or businesses. A Connecticut case further clarifies the objectives of zoning. It involved a zoning district in the town of Stratford in which only single-family residences were permitted. The owners of one of the homes operated a rooming house with ten boarders. The zoning enforcement officer ordered the owners to terminate the boarding house. The owners, wanting to continue its operation, challenged the law. The court upheld it, stating,

> [Local governments are empowered] to lay out zones where family values, youth values, and the blessings of quiet seclusion and clean air make the area a sanctuary for people ... [b]oarding houses ... present urban problems. More people occupy a given space; more cars rather continuously pass by; more cars are parked; noise travels with crowds.[39]

The rooming house was thus forced to close.

Some localities have zoning ordinances that prohibit drive-thru windows as a means to restrict traffic congestion. These rules effectively bar the utilization of this sales device within the locality to which the ordinance applies. Not surprisingly, these regulations are a bane to fast food restaurants.[40]

Another zoning ordinance requires that at least sixty percent of a restaurant's total sales be from food rather than alcohol. The city sent a warning notice to a restaurant believed to be in violation. The eatery was told it needed to rectify the problem or its license to operate would be canceled following a hearing. The restaurant failed to rectify the issue, and a hearing was held. The council concluded that although the restaurant claimed to be in compliance, its method for allocating its sales to food or alcohol was a "subterfuge" and it was not complying with the ordinance. The license was thus canceled. The ordinance and revocation were upheld on appeal.[41]

Another typical zoning ordinance requires a minimum number of parking spaces for various land uses based on factors such as the type of business involved, the number of employees, and the square footage of the facility. A license to operate will not be granted without the proper number of parking spots being available. Sometimes, after a license has been issued, the number of parking spaces is reduced perhaps due to development, deterioration, or otherwise. If the remaining number of parking spots is insufficient to satisfy the zoning rules, the business will be required to address the problem or face revocation of its license.[42]

---

[39] *Dinan v. Board of Zoning Appeals of the Town of Stratford*, 595 A.2d 864 (Conn. 1991)

[40] *Renaissance v. Zoning Board*, 2001 WL 770847 (R.I. 2001)

[41] *West End Pinck v. City*, 2001 WL 1329242 (Tex. 2001)

[42] *American Condominium Association v. Benson*, 2001 WL 1452781 (R.I. 2001)

In the following case, a bar violated a local zoning ordinance and as a result was required to discontinue its business.

CASE EXAMPLE 15-12

Schleuter v. City of Fort Worth
947 S.W.2d 920 (Tex. 1997)

... In an attempt to mitigate the negative secondary effects of sexually oriented businesses, the City of Fort Worth added sections to its Comprehensive Zoning Ordinance (CZO). A person violates the CZO if he or she operates a "sexually oriented business" within 1000 feet of residentially zoned property. "Sexually oriented business" is defined as "any commercial venture whose operations include the 'providing, featuring or offering of employees or entertainment personnel who appear on the premises while in a state of nudity or simulated nudity.' "...

On May 11, 1995, Sports Fantasy opened for business in Fort Worth. Sports Fantasy is a "sports bar" ... described by the owner as an "upscale sports bar ... catering to gentlemen clientele." Sports Fantasy featured entertainment in the form of "state dancing" by female entertainers. While dancing, the female entertainers would strip their clothing off to the point where they would only be wearing "T-back" bottoms and latex pasties covering only the areola of their breasts. Sports Fantasy was located within 1000 feet of residentially zoned property.

After a bench trial the trial court entered a permanent injunction against Fantasy Sports [prohibiting it from carrying on a sexually oriented business].

[On appeal, the sports bar raised various arguments seeking to have the zoning ordinance declared invalid and unenforceable. The court rejected these arguments and determined the ordinance was valid and enforceable and affirmed the injunction.]

In circumstances where zoning laws prohibit a desired use or development, the land owner can seek a **variance**, which is permission from the local government to deviate from the restrictions. Variances are given sparingly and only when the deviation will not have a significantly negative impact on the goals sought by the zoning law in issue.

A variance was granted to a hotel seeking relief from a zoning ordinance that limited hotels in a particular district to two stories and thirty-five feet in height. The hotel seeking the variance wanted to build a five-story, forty-five-foot high hotel. The local planning board granted the variance and the town appealed. The court upheld the variance for three reasons: (1) office buildings in the district were permitted to be six stories and ninety feet high; (2) the facade of the proposed hotel was designed to resemble the nearby offices; and (3) the hotel was targeted to commercial travelers and so would complement the surrounding commercial area. The court thus concluded that granting a variance for the hotel's height was consistent with commercial development in the area and had "positive relevance to the town's planned economic development."[43]

---

[43]*Commercial Realty & Resources Corp. v. First Atlantic Properties Co.*, 585 A.2d 928 (N.J. 1991)

Key Terms

ASCAP
antitrust laws
BMI
copyright
dissolution
divestiture
due process
exclusive dealing contracts
franchise
franchisee
franchisor
group boycott
merger
monopoly
per se violations
police power

price discrimination
price-fixing agreements
public domain
resale price maintenance
   agreement
rule of reason
service mark
territorial division agreements
territorial restrictions
trademark
treble damages
tying arrangement
variance
vertical price-fixing
victualer
zoning

Summary

The business of operating a hotel or restaurant is highly regulated. The owner must be aware of applicable laws to avoid liability for their violation.

Businesses are prohibited from using another's trademark or service mark, as well as copyrighted works, without the permission of the owner. One arrangement where permission is granted to use a trademark or service mark is franchising. The relationship between a franchisor and franchisee is contractual. The parties should include in their agreement all terms relevant to their relationship.

To encourage competition, the law prohibits certain practices that restrain competition. The laws that ban these practices are called antitrust laws.

A hotel is required to maintain a guest register including some or all of the following information, depending on the laws of each particular state: names; addresses; make and model of car; license number; room assignment; and date and hour of arrival. The innkeeper may also be required to post notices of the rates charged for rooms.

Concerns about protecting our environment have engendered laws mandating recycling. While the particular requirements vary from state to state, the purpose of these laws is to save natural resources, reduce pollution, and reduce the amount of waste that goes into landfills.

An innkeeper or restaurateur must obtain all necessary licenses. Operating a business without the required licenses can result in forced closure, fines, and unenforceable contracts. Zoning laws restrict the permissible uses of land. For example, a business cannot be built in an area that is zoned exclusively residential.

Preventive Law Tips for Managers

■ *Do a trademark search before adopting a name for your hotel or restaurant.* Use of another's trademark or service mark can result in forced discontinuance of a name in which you have invested money to advertise and promote. This can be avoided by undertaking a trademark search prior to adopting the name. The search is customarily done by a trademark attorney. It reveals the names of any other businesses that are using the same or similar name you propose to use. If someone else is already using it for a similar product, you can save promotion money and an infringement lawsuit by selecting an alternative.

■ *Do not intercept and transmit copyrighted television programs without the permission of the copyright owner.* Use of a satellite dish to intercept copyrighted programming without the permission of the copyright owners constitutes copyright infringement and can lead to a lawsuit. If you want to offer your guests the opportunity to watch cable television in their rooms or to view limited-access sports events in a bar or restaurant, make the necessary arrangements with the cable stations to receive cable programming through legal means.

■ *Do not offer musical entertainment without first obtaining licenses from ASCAP and BMI.* Providing music for the enjoyment of a hotel or restaurant's patrons without purchasing the required copyright licenses constitutes copyright infringement. To comply with the law and avoid a lawsuit, make the necessary arrangements with the organizations that represent the owners of copyrights in musical compositions and recordings.

■ *Review the operating practices of your hotel or restaurant to be sure you are not in violation of antitrust laws.* Failure to comply with antitrust laws results in criminal liability and steep damage awards (treble damages) in civil cases. Initiate regular reviews of the practices of your hotel or restaurant—including pricing, purchasing, selling, advertising, and relationships with other hotels—to ensure the hotel is not engaging in antitrust violations. Use for this purpose the checklist of illegal activities contained in this chapter.

■ *If you buy a franchise, carefully review the disclosure documents and discuss them with your attorney and accountant before making a decision to buy.* By law, a franchisor is required to disclose in writing detailed information about the franchise operation at least ten days prior to accepting any money from a franchisee. Review this information carefully and ask your lawyer and accountant to do the same. The purpose for the disclosure requirement is to give a potential franchisee time to absorb and evaluate all relevant information. Take advantage of the law.

■ *If you buy a franchise, be sure all agreements are embodied in the contractual agreement.* The contract between the franchisor and franchisee should be in writing and should contain all agreements of the parties. Read the contract carefully before signing to ensure the terms are as expected and all agreements are included.

■ *As a manager, keep fully apprised of your employees' actions and practices.* As seen in *United States v. Hilton Hotels Corp.* on page 547, an employer may be liable for the acts of its employees even when the employee is violating the employer's policies. To avoid liability on this ground, keep close tabs on your employees. Inquire often about methods they are using to fulfill job responsibilities, watch them work, review their outgoing mail, and meet with them frequently to discuss the job.

■ *Keep a register of guests' names and other information required by law.* Laws in most states require an innkeeper to keep a record of information about all registered guests at the hotel and to preserve the record for a specified period of time. The type of information required varies from state to state, but customarily includes the guest's name and address; make, model, and license number of any car parked at the hotel; date and time of arrival; and room number assigned. Failure to maintain the register or failure to show the register to an inquiring law-enforcement officer violates the law and leads to penalties. Be sure to obtain the necessary information from your guests, preserve the register for the time period required by state law, and provide it to those legally entitled to access.

■ *File and post room rates.* Laws in many states require innkeepers to post the rates at the hotel in a place where they will easily be seen. Whenever the rates are changed, the new rates must likewise be posted.

■ *Comply with recycling laws applicable in the locality where your business is located.* Laws requiring businesses to recycle parts of their waste have been adopted in most states and localities. These laws typically require a restaurant to recycle glass, metal, aluminum, and some plastic containers. Failure to comply can result in fines plus damage to the environment.

■ *Determine the necessary licenses and permits needed for your business and take the appropriate steps to obtain them.* Failure to obtain required licenses and permits can result in the government forcing you to close your business, fines, and refusal by the courts to enforce your contracts. The types of licenses needed for a particular business vary from locality to locality. Check with your lawyer to ensure you are aware of all the licenses and permits you will need. Thereafter, contact the relevant government officials to determine what conditions must be met to qualify for the licenses, and then satisfy those conditions.

■ *Determine whether and when your licenses must be renewed and take the necessary steps to extend them.* Failure to renew a license or permit within the allotted time can result in the same penalties applicable to failure to obtain a license when you first open your business. Check with your lawyer or the governmental entity responsible for administering the licenses to determine when they must be renewed and the process you must follow. Take the necessary steps to ensure your licenses do not expire without obtaining a renewal.

■ *Stay current on all requirements contained in the health and sanitation codes, and closely monitor your facility's compliance.* Health department inspectors will make announced and unannounced visits to determine if the establishment is conforming to the mandates in these codes. Violations can result in a variety of consequences, including fines, public embarrassment by Internet or newspaper posting of violations and, for serious infractions, forced closure.

■ *When planning to build or expand a hotel or restaurant, comply with the zoning laws or seek a variance.* Zoning laws restrict the ways in which land and buildings can be used. Planning a construction project without verifying that the proposed use and resulting facility comply with applicable zoning laws can result in having to abandon or scale down a project. Advance research of the zoning laws will enable you to plan within zoning restrictions and avoid unwanted and costly surprises.

Review Questions

1. What interest does a city have in requiring a hotel to maintain a register containing guests' names, addresses, type of car, and license plate numbers?

2. What is the objective of the antitrust laws?

3. Name and define three examples of per se violations of the antitrust laws.

4. Name and define three examples of antitrust violations subject to the rule of reason.

5. Must a business register its name to obtain trademark protection? If not, how else is protection obtained?

6. What constitutes a trademark infringement?

7. What is a franchise?

8. What information must a franchisor disclose to a franchisee?

9. What is a copyright? Give three examples of copyrighted works.

10. What are the objectives of recycling laws?

11. What is the purpose of zoning laws?

12. If zoning laws negatively impact you, what remedy can you seek?

13. What is the basis for the government's authority to require hotels and restaurants to obtain a license before opening for business?

14. What penalties can be imposed on a business that operates without the necessary licenses?

15. Name five things that a health department will look at when inspecting the restaurant.

16. If the government wants to revoke a liquor license, what rights, if any, does the licensee have?

Discussion Questions

1. What is the policy reason behind the requirement that licensees must be given due process rights before a license can be revoked?

2. Why are some violations of the antitrust laws subject to the rule of reason while others are violations per se?

3. In the *Holiday Inn* trademark case, Findings of Fact, paragraph 3, the judge, while talking about the great sign, said that in some localities the Holiday Inn chain uses smaller versions to comply with local zoning laws. What governmental objective of a locality would be fulfilled by limiting the size of business signs?

4. Buy a soda and look at the can. How many copyright and trademark notices do you see? What aspect of the soda can is copyrighted?

5. Xerox Corporation, known for its copiers and other office machines, has expressed concern that it may lose its trademark on the name Xerox. Indeed, it has advertised in various trade journals that Xerox has two "R's" in it. Why is the trademark in jeopardy, and what is meant when the company says there are two "R's" in Xerox?

6. In what ways do the disclosure requirements imposed on franchisors help franchisees to avoid becoming victims of dishonest franchisors?

Application Questions

1. Sharina is a franchisee of Burger King. She has an exclusive territory with a five-mile radius in which Burger King cannot authorize anyone else to open a Burger King restaurant. Why is she fortunate to have this? Does this agreement violate the antitrust laws? Why or why not?

2. You are licensed to operate a hotel in a summer tourist area. You receive a notice from the town council, which has the authority to issue and revoke licenses, that your license may be revoked because of illegal activity occurring at your hotel. What rights do you have concerning the revocation proceeding? What action should you take in response to this notice? What will happen if you take no action?

3. Tamika opened a restaurant in California and named it "The Best in the West." The nationwide hotel chain of Best Western brought a trademark action against Tamika. What factors will the judge consider in deciding whether or not Tamika has violated the Best Western trademark? How would you rule on the issue? Why?

4. Samantha bought a taco at a Mexican food franchise restaurant. When she bit into the food, she discovered a piece of glass in it. The glass injured her gums. What additional information would you need to know to determine if the

franchisor is liable to Samantha for her injuries? Why is this information needed?

5. Joshua Sears has decided to initiate a franchised chain of bars to be called Sears' Cheers and Beers. The well-known department store is disturbed that its name will be used in conjunction with a bar. Sears Roebuck & Company thus commences a trademark action against Joshua. What is the department store's likelihood of success and why?

Web Sites

Web sites that will enhance your understanding of the material in this chapter include:

http://www.loc.gov/copyright This is the official site of the United States Copyright Office. It includes information about copyright basics, how to register a copyright, fees, and frequently asked questions.

http://www.cybercrime.com This site was created by the Department of Justice, a federal agency. It explores online crimes involving copyrights and trademarks.

http://www.privacyrights.org This site provides information about protecting copyrighted information in cyberspace.

http://www.ftc.gov This is the official site of the Federal Trade Commission, a federal agency that monitors consumer safety, including consumers of franchises and business opportunities. The site contains various guides and articles on issues associated with purchasing a franchise.

http://www.franchising.org This site provides information about pitfalls for the franchisor and franchisee.

:http://www.hotelbusiness.com This site provides a wealth of business information about recent occurrences in the hotel industry. Among the legal topics covered is franchising.

http://real-estate-law.freeadvice.com/zoning This site contains a wealth of information on zoning matters.

For additional resources, visit our Web site
www.hospitality-tourism.delmar.com

CHAPTER 16

■

The Developing Law of
Casinos

CHAPTER OUTLINE

■

INTRODUCTION

An exciting development in the hospitality industry is the increased numbers of casinos and casino resorts. Just as these facilities present unique management challenges, they also create specialized legal issues and applications. This chapter will look at the developing law of casinos. While reading the chapter you will reacquaint yourself with some areas of law we have studied in other sections of this book, but the application here will be limited to casinos. You will also learn about laws we have not yet studied that are applicable exclusively to casinos.

A Short History of Gambling

Contrary to conventional wisdom, **gambling** is not a recent phenomenon. The Chinese, Japanese, Greeks, Romans, and Egyptians played games of skill and chance for amusement as early as 2300 B.C. In the United States, both European colonists and Native Americans brought a history of gambling from their own cultures. Native Americans believed that their gods determined fate and chance.

British colonization of America was partly financed through lottery proceeds. Lotteries were viewed in England as a popular form of voluntary taxation and became fashionable in America as European settlers arrived here. A half-dozen lotteries sponsored by prominent individuals such as Ben Franklin, John Hancock, and George Washington operated in each of the thirteen colonies to raise funds for building projects. In the late 1700s, Massachusetts authorized lotteries to help build and equip Harvard College. Many other educational institutions were funded through lotteries, including Yale and Columbia. Even the financing for the American Revolution benefited from a lottery.

Attitudes changed, albeit temporarily, and the states outlawed virtually all types of gambling by 1910. Two decades later, the pendulum was swinging back. By 1931 Nevada legalized casinos. In the 1930s, twenty-one states legalized racetrack gambling, and many states authorized low-stakes charity bingo. During the 1940s and 1950s, most states modified their laws to allow pari-mutuel betting. **Pari-mutuel** means a betting system in which winners share the total stakes minus a percentage paid to the management. Examples of pari-mutuel betting include horse racing and greyhound dog racing. With a pari-mutuel system, the track does not care which horse wins because, unlike other gambling, the money used to pay the winners is not the track's, but rather that of the people holding the losing tickets.

In 1978 the first casino opened in Atlantic City, New Jersey. In 1987 two events occurred that stimulated the proliferation of Indian casinos in this country. The two events, discussed in more detail later in this chapter, include the United States Supreme Court decision of *California v. Cabazon Band of Mission Indians*, 480 U.S. 202, 107 S.Ct. 1083, which affirmed the right of Indian tribes to self-regulate high-stakes versions of all betting games not prohibited by state law, and the adoption of the Indian Gaming Regulatory Act.

In 1990 riverboat casinos became popular. These are ships carrying casino facilities that take patrons out to sea where state gambling prohibitions are not applicable.

Pari-mutuel betting facilities have suffered with the proliferation of casinos. A phenomenon that is compensating somewhat for pari-mutuel's loss of popularity is simulcast wagering—that is, broadcasting races over a television network enabling bettors at other tracks and locations around the country not only to watch the live races via television and place their bets, but also to cash in their winning tickets as if the race were being held at their location.

Gambling Today

Gambling today is a thriving industry. Eleven states host 432 commercial casinos[1] (243 of those are in Nevada), 23 states have casinos on Indian reservations, and 5 have racetrack casinos. Forty states plus the District of Columbia sponsor lotteries. Pari-mutuel wagering is legal in some form in 41 states, and charitable gaming is legal in 47 states plus the District of Columbia. Gaming taxes ranked first as a source of tax revenue in Nevada, were within the top 5 revenue sources in Louisiana and Mississippi, and were among the top 10 in Indiana and New Jersey. During the past decade, the casino workforce has increased more than 79 percent.

Casinos are second only to the lottery as the most popular form of gaming entertainment in the United States. More than one-quarter of the over-age-21 population of this country participate in casino gaming.

Tribal gaming now plays a major role in the gaming industry. There are more than 87 Native American gaming enterprises operating in 23 states, and those numbers continue to grow.

Also popular is online gambling, which includes Web sites at which players can place their bets. Begun in 1995 with the development of the Internet, this realm of gambling has seen explosive growth.

Gambling is highly regulated by government with the objective of protecting the betting public against potential fraudulent practices and preventing infiltration of the gambling industry by organized crime. State sponsored gambling commissions oversee casinos operations. Among the responsibilities of these commissions are the following: process gambling license applications including financial background checks and criminal history checks; conduct inspections of gambling facilities to ensure compliance with relevant laws; investigate reports of illegal gambling activities; test gambling equipment for compliance and integrity; and in some states with tribal casinos, enforce and regulate the tribal-state compacts. This will be discussed later in the chapter.

Gaming Issues

Several legal issues are peculiar to casinos. These include the role of state gaming commissions in the resolution of disputes involving wagering outcomes, blackjack players who are card counters, malfunctioning slot machines, casinos granting credit to players, and compulsive gamblers. These issues are addressed in the next several sections of this chapter.

Resolution of Gaming Issues

States with legalized gambling have created **gambling commissions** for the resolution of disputes involving gaming debts and alleged winnings. These

---

[1]The states with commercial gambling are Colorado, Illinois, Indiana, Iowa, Louisiana, Michigan, Mississippi, Missouri, Nevada, New Jersey, and South Dakota.

commissions have jurisdiction to the exclusion of the courts. An example is Mississippi, in which the body is called the Mississippi Gaming Commission. In a case where a casino patron playing mini-baccarat claimed the dealer refused to allow him to increase his "flat" bet although the amount he sought to wager was within the table limits, the only forum with jurisdiction to hear the dispute was the Gaming Commission.[2]

Casino Owes No Duty to Inform Patrons of Laws Relevant to Gambling

In a number of cases, patrons who have been arrested for violating gaming laws asserted a duty on the casino to inform them of the law. The courts have rejected the existence of such a duty. Thus, where a patron was arrested for accepting gaming chips on credit without a marker, he sued the casino for negligence, claiming it should have warned him that his conduct was illegal. The court dismissed the case, finding no such duty existed.[3]

Similarly, a casino whose employees were aware that a slot machine was out of adjustment, resulting in more frequent payoffs, did not owe a gambler the duty to inform him that use of the machine was illegal. When the player was arrested and thereafter sued the hotel for nondisclosure, the hotel would not be liable.[4] And a casino was not responsible for informing a keno player who found a winning ticket in a wastebasket that redemption of a keno ticket without having paid for it is illegal. Thus, the casino was not liable for his subsequent arrest.[5]

Exclusion of Card Counters Permissible

A **card counter** is someone who keeps track of the cards played in blackjack, also known as "21", in the course of a shoe (a shoe is a round of play defined by the number of decks of cards included in the round). A card counter has an advantage in blackjack play because, as the cards in the shoe decrease, the likelihood of cards not yet played coming up is increased. Thus, the card counter secures an advantage in the odds. A casino can legally exclude counters from playing blackjack.[6]

To counter the counting advantage, a growing number of casinos utilize a device that, on a continuing basis, automatically shuffles the cards that have been played and uses them to resupply the cards from which the dealer draws. This

---

[2] *Grand Casino Tunica v. Shindler*, 772 So.2d 1036 (Mi. 2000) (concerning the final decision, the commission did not believe the gambler attempted to increase the bet).

[3] *Vinci v. Las Vegas Sands, Inc.*, 984 D.2d 750 (Nev. 1999)

[4] *El Dorado Hotel, Inc. v. Brown*, 691 P.2d 436 (Nev. 1984)

[5] *Hazelwood v. Harrah's*, 862 P.2d 1189 (Nev. 1993)

[6] *Ziglin v. Player's Island Casino*, 36 S.W.3d 786 (Mo. 2001)

eliminates the ability of a counter to anticipate cards not yet played, thereby eliminating the problem of card counters.

Slot Machines

Slot machines are very popular casino gaming devices. Sometimes these devices malfunction, resulting in an apparent but not real win for a customer. This was the circumstance in a Mississippi case that is instructive about preserving evidence, the role of gambling commissions in payout disputes, and the mechanical aspects of slot machines.

A slot player claimed he was entitled to a $2,700,000 progressive jackpot. He sued the casino when it refused to pay him. He described the circumstances in this way: "I began playing Cool Millions slot machine number 2947 at approximately 11:00 P.M. playing three coins at a time. After playing for a brief period, the machine locked up and began to make noises. Whistles were blowing, bells sounded, and to my left a light flashed white on top and blue on the bottom. At this time "three animals" were lined up across the pay line." According to [the plaintiff] the three symbols that were lined up on the pay line looked like frogs, which matched the combination that was indicated on the top of the machine to be the winning combination for the highest jackpot. The casino slot supervisor was called and he investigated.

The casino claimed that the plaintiff was putting coins into the slot before the reels had stopped spinning so that the coin did not register. Therefore, when the plaintiff pulled the handle the reels would not spin and this resulted in the appearance of the three matching frogs. The casino also claimed that the winning combination was three ducks, not frogs. The slot supervisor of the casino testified that he had opened the machine and cleared a coin jam. The assistant slot manager on the night in question testified that he was called to the machine and performed a last-game recall test, which indicated the plaintiff had not won the jackpot. The assistant manager also performed a calibration test, which established that the machine was working properly.

The casino had a policy presumably adopted by many casinos requiring that when a patron is involved in a disputed claim and the slot supervisor determines the casino should not pay it, the slot surveillance department should be notified to focus the cameras on the machine in question. The casino unfortunately failed to follow its policy in this case. Had it been able to capture the circumstance on camera, the pictures would have provided important evidence.

The court ultimately held that the player was not entitled to the jackpot because the slot machine was working properly at the time and did not indicate a jackpot had been won, based on the calibration and recall tests. However, the casino was chastised by the court for failing to initiate contact with the Gambling Commission immediately upon the occurrence of the dispute as required by law. The casino was likely fined for this violation.[7]

---

[7] *Thomas v. Isle of Capri Casino*, 781 So.2d 125 (Miss. 2001)

Contracts and Gambling Debts

Many casino patrons who bet large amounts of money will establish credit with the casino. The transaction is a contractual one, not unlike seeking credit on a Visa or MasterCard. To reacquaint yourself with rules of contract law, see the discussion in Chapter 4. In a credit transaction, the casino agrees to extend credit to the patron to enable her to gamble. In return, the customer agrees to repay the casino for the amount borrowed plus interest. The patron hopes to make money on gambling, in which case reimbursement to the casino is easy. Unfortunately, a gambler often loses. If the patron fails to repay the casino, it will likely pursue payment in court. The lawsuit is based on contract. As in any contract case, the gambler can assert any applicable contract defenses, including incapacity (underage, mentally incompetent, or very intoxicated), duress (threats of harm) and unconscionability (grossly unfair, resulting from unequal bargaining power).

In one case in which a casino sought payment on a credit contract, the gambler incurred over $165,000 in gambling debts in a 24-hour period. He alleged he was a compulsive gambler and offered as evidence of this condition the following: at various casinos he was abusive, cursed the dealers, accused them of cheating him, threw cards, smashed an ashtray, and made a spectacle of himself. He asserted that because he was a compulsive gambler, it was unconscionable of the casino to have extended him credit. The court rejected the defense of compulsive gambling, stating, "This court finds no support in legislation or case law that the disorder of compulsive gambling should, in and of itself, be recognized as a defense to capacity to contract which will render a contract void."[8] Thus we learn that the circumstance of being a compulsive gambler will not relieve the borrower from liability to repay a gambling debt.

Compulsive Gamblers

Unfortunately, some people suffer from a recognized disorder called **pathological gambler** or compulsive gambler—that is, an inability to refrain from gambling. It is a recognized illness in the field of psychology. Just as some people can become addicted to alcohol or drugs, it is possible for a person to have an uncontrollable urge to gamble. The casino industry has addressed this problem in certain ways. For example, in Atlantic City, a person who knows he is a compulsive gambler can initiate placement of his name on a list of persons to whom the extension of credit by a casino is prohibited. The list is kept by the Casino Control Commission, an agency that regulates casinos, which is required to provide the list to the credit departments of each casino.[9] The Nevada Council on Problem Gambling maintains a Problem Gamblers Helpline available twenty-four hours a day, seven days a week, to answer questions and offer confidential assistance.

Congress created the National Gambling Impact and Policy Commission to conduct a study of the social and economic impact of gambling at all levels of our

---

[8]*Lomonaco v. Sands Hotel Casino and Country Club*, 614 A.2d 634 (Superior Court 1992)
[9]N.J.S.A. 5:12-101(j)

society. Among the issues the Commission reviewed is, "pathological or problem gambling and its impact on society." The Commission recommended that the government support studies to determine the prevalence of problem and pathological gambling among casino patrons and employees, generally, and also among specific "major subpopulations" including youth, women, elderly, Native American, and other minority group gamblers. The proposed studies would also examine gambling's effect on divorce, domestic violence, child abuse, suicide, bankruptcies, and crime. An additional topic recommended was, "The extent to which the practices of some gambling facilities to provide free alcohol to customers while gambling, the placement of cash advance credit machines close to the gambling area, and the offer of similar inducements" magnify a gambling disorder. The resulting data is being used for the development of future legislation dealing with gaming.

Torts Involving Casinos

Negligence

The rules of negligence applicable to hotels and restaurants are also applicable to casinos. See the discussion of negligence in Chapter 5. Like other hospitality facilities, casinos are not insurers of their guests' safety. They are, however, obligated to act reasonably to safeguard the well-being of their patrons.

In one case a plaintiff was playing nickel poker in a slot machine at the Grand Casino in Golfport, Mississippi. She noticed a chair to her immediate right. While putting money in the machine she reached back to pull the chair to her and began to sit. Unfortunately, in the short interim the chair had been moved. When she started to sit she lost her balance and fell to the floor. She sued the casino claiming it had provided an insufficient number of chairs to accommodate the players. The casino established that it provided one seat for each slot machine and that virtually all slot machines are designed to be played by only one patron at a time. The court, deciding in favor of the casino, held that the plaintiff was negligent for attempting to sit on the chair before she made certain she had a place to sit. Said the court, "Plaintiff's inattentiveness resulted in her fall, not an unsafe condition of the casino."[10] If the number of chairs in the slot machine area had been less than one per machine, the casino would likely have been at least partially liable. Management should ensure that seating is adequate in the casino playing area.

In another case, the injured party was a change attendant on a riverboat casino. Her duties included selling customers slot machine tokens, which she carried in a velcro change belt tied around her waist. Depending on the amount of tokens in the belt, it could weigh as much as 50 pounds. All change attendants had their own storage container known as a change bank, which was stocked with buckets of tokens delivered on a mobile change cart. When the plaintiff's change

---

[10]*Greco v. Grand Casinos of Mississippi*, 1996 WL 617401 (La. 1996)

bank ran low, she ordered additional tokens from a slot attendant who brought the token order to her in buckets on a mobile change cart. The buckets had handles and weighed approximately five to ten pounds. All change attendants were required to lift the buckets from the change cart to their individual change bank. They then replenished the change belt from the change bank. One day, while lifting the buckets, she suffered a back pain for which she sought treatment. It was diagnosed as a dorsal spine sprain and required physical therapy. She was permanently restricted from lifting more than thirty-five to forty pounds.

The plaintiff sought compensation from the casino for her back injury, claiming it was negligent for requiring her to carry such heavy loads in the course of her job. The casino moved to dismiss the case on the ground it had done nothing illegal. The court refused to dismiss the case, holding that a reasonable jury could find that the employer failed to use reasonable care in providing the plaintiff with safe equipment to perform the job. For example, the jury might conclude that the employer should have provided the plaintiff with a mobile cart to carry the change rather than wearing a heavy change belt and lifting buckets of tokens.[11]

Note: while in most states lawsuits by employees against employers are controlled by Workers' Compensation Laws, which would have barred the change attendant's lawsuit, different rules apply when the employee is injured at sea. See the discussion of the Jones Act later in this chapter.

The following case addresses the duty of a casino to a guest having a medical emergency while gambling. The rules of law reviewed in this decision apply equally to hotels and restaurants. Note the efficient emergency response system in place by the casino.

CASE EXAMPLE 16-1

Lundy v. Adamar of New Jersey, Inc. t/a Trop World
34 F.3d 1173 (3rd Cir. 1994)

Appellant Sidney Lundy suffered a heart attack while a patron at appellee's casino, TropWorld Casino ("TropWorld"), in Atlantic City, New Jersey. While he survived, Lundy was left with permanent disabilities. ...

On August 3, 1989, Lundy, a 66-year-old man with a history of coronary artery disease, was patronizing TropWorld Casino. While Lundy was gambling at a blackjack table, he suffered cardiac arrest and fell to the ground unconscious. Three other patrons [including a critical nurse, a surgeon and a Dr. Geenberg, a pulmonary specialist] quickly ran to Lundy and began to assist him. ...

Meanwhile, the blackjack dealer at the table where Lundy had been gambling pushed an emergency "call" button at his table which alerted TropWorld's Security Command Post that a problem existed. The Security Command Post is electronically designed to designate the location from which such alarms are triggered and record the time that the alarm is sounded. The alarm was recorded as being received at 10:57 P.M. Noting that the source of the alarm was "Pit 3," a Security Command Post employee notified by phone the security post located on the casino floor near where Lundy had suffered his cardiac arrest. At 10:59 P.M., the Security Command Post employee sent radio directions to all of the guards on the casino floor requesting that they each go to Lundy's location.

---

[11] *Watson v. Hollywood Casino-Aurora, Inc.*, 1996 WL 559960 (Ill. 1996)

A sergeant in TropWorld's security force and a TropWorld security guard arrived at the blackjack table apparently within fifteen seconds of their receiving the radio message from the Security Command Post. [The three patrons] were already assisting Lundy. Upon arriving, the security guard called the Security Command Post on her hand-held radio and requested that someone contact the casino medical station, which was located one floor above the casino. Several witnesses agree that Nurse Margaret Slusher ("Nurse Slusher"), the nurse who was on duty at the casino medical station at the time, arrived on the scene within a minute or two of being summoned. As soon as Nurse Slusher arrived, she instructed the security guards to call for an ambulance. TropWorld's records indicate that an ambulance was summoned at 11:00 P.M.

Nurse Slusher brought with her an ambu-bag, oxygen, and an airway. She did not, however, bring an intubation kit [a tube inserted into one's trachea to help restore the ability to breath] to the scene. Dr. Greenberg testified that he asked Nurse Slusher for one and she told him that it was TropWorld's "policy" not to have an intubation kit on the premises. ... Nurse Slusher testified that some of the equipment normally found in an intubation kit was stocked in TropWorld's medical center, but that she did not bring this equipment with her because she was not qualified to use it.

Nurse Slusher proceeded to assist the three patrons in performing CPR on Lundy. Specifically, Nurse Slusher placed the ambu-bag over Lundy's face while the others took turns doing chest compressions. ... Dr. Greenberg testified that he was sure that air was entering Lundy's respiratory system and that Lundy was being adequately oxygenated during the period when he was receiving both CPR treatment and air through the ambu-bag. Dr. Greenberg went on to say that the only reason he had requested an intubation kit was "to establish an airway and subsequently provide oxygen in a more efficient manner."

... [A]n Emergency Medical Technician ("EMT") unit arrived at TropWorld by ambulance at approximately 11:03 P.M. A technician, with the help of the two doctor patrons, attempted to intubate Lundy using an intubation kit brought by the EMT unit. Dr. Greenberg claimed that, due to Lundy's stout physique and rigid muscle tone, it was a very difficult intubation, and that there were at least a half dozen failed attempts before the procedure was successfully completed. After intubation, Lundy regained a pulse and his color improved. According to EMT reports, the ambulance departed from TropWorld with Lundy at 11:27 P.M. ...

TropWorld had a contract with Dr. Carlino providing that he would run an in-house medical station to supply medical services for TropWorld's employees, guests, and patrons in cases of work-related injuries and injuries or sicknesses occurring on the premises. The contract required that Dr. Carlino provide a licensed physician on the casino premises for five hours each day, and a physician "on-call" for the rest of the day. ... Furthermore, Dr. Carlino was obligated to have a registered nurse present in the medical station during the hours that the casino was open. ... In August of 1989, Nurse Slusher was a registered, licensed nurse . ...

The District Court held that TropWorld had fulfilled its duty to Lundy ...

Generally, a bystander has no duty to provide affirmative aid to an injured person, even if the bystander has the ability to help. New Jersey courts have recognized, however, that the existence of a relationship between the victim and one in a position to render aid may create a duty to render assistance. ... .

The Restatement of Torts [a compilation of rules used for guidance by courts] provides that an innkeeper is under a duty to its guests "to take reasonable action to protect them against unreasonable risk of physical harm and to give them first aid after it knows or has reason to know that they are ill or injured, and to care for them until they can be cared for by others ... ." The duty does not extend to providing all medical care that the innkeeper could reasonably foresee might be needed by a patron.

Nurse Slusher was a registered, licensed nurse who had been trained in emergency care and who had fifteen years of nursing experience. Despite this training and experience, she was not competent to perform an intubation. The Lundys claim the casino was obligated to provide full-time on-site capability to perform intubations. Certainly, maintaining on a full-time basis the capability of performing an intubation goes far beyond any "first aid" contemplated by the Restatement of Torts. ...

We understand Lundy's contention to be that Nurse Slusher should have returned to the medical center and retrieved the intubation tube for Dr. Greenberg's use, and TropWorld is liable for her failure to do so. We reject the notion that TropWorld, by contracting with Dr. Carlino, voluntarily assumed a duty to Mr. Lundy it would not otherwise have had. ...

The duty owed to Mr. Lundy was a duty limited to summoning aid and, in the interim, taking reasonable first aid measures. It did not include the duty to provide medical equipment and personnel necessary to perform an intubation. ...

The judgment of the district court [granting summary judgment to the casino] will be affirmed.

CASE QUESTIONS

1. How big a role did the casino emergency alarm system play in the court's decision?

2. Why do the Restatement of Torts and the courts impose a duty on the casino to provide first aid to a patron in distress?

Criminal Activity at Casinos

The large sums of money that flow in casinos unfortunately attract criminal activity. See the discussion of crimes in Chapter 10. One vivid example is the kidnapping of the daughter of Stephen Wynn, the chief executive officer of Mirage Resorts, Inc., which owns several large, upscale casinos in Las Vegas and elsewhere. Mr. Wynn paid $1.45 million in ransom money, after which Ms. Wynn was safely returned. The perpetrators were later arrested and convicted. One was sentenced to 24 years in jail; the other to 19 years.[12]

One scam involves the manufacture and sale of fraudulent slot-machine tokens. When discovered, casinos will alter the machines so that they reject the fraudulent tokens.[13] Another illegal scheme promoted by organized crime involved the game of blackjack and consisted of "capping"—increasing the amount of winning bets after the cards are dealt. The rules of the game forbid players from altering their bets once the dealer begins to distribute the cards. Therefore, this scheme requires the participation of the dealer. In one instance in Massachusetts, dishonest gamblers paid the dealers 25 percent of the proceeds. They regularly met the players at a secret location to split the take. Before the conspiracy was caught on surveillance cameras, it went on for 5 months, 5 days a week, with an average nightly profit of $10,000.

Casino Patron as Crime Victim

The casino owes its customers the same duty of care owed by hotels and restaurants—use reasonable care to protect patrons' safety. There is no general duty to

---

[12] *United States. v. Sherwood*, 98 F.3d 402 (Nev. 1996)

[13] *United States v. Joost*, 92 F.3d 7 (R.I. 1996)

protect customers from criminal conduct of third persons. That duty arises only where such incidents have occurred in the past and are thus foreseeable.

A casino patron on a gambling vessel was attacked in the bathroom. He sued the casino, claiming it was negligent because its security was inadequate. The injured customer argued that "a gambling establishment provides a fertile environment for criminal conduct," and thus the casino should owe a duty to protect its customers throughout the facility. The court rejected this argument, saying that "courts have focused on the frequency and similarity of prior criminal acts on the premises, rather than the nature of the [business transacted at the] particular premises in determining foreseeability." In this case, no other incidents of criminal activity had occurred in the casino's restrooms and the casino had experienced virtually no violent criminal activity on its premises. The court refused to find the ship negligent and dismissed the case.[14]

Would-be robbers seeking a target with a lot of money can easily spot the ideal victim in a casino by watching for gamblers with many chips. In *State of Louisiana v. Timon*, 683 So.2d 315 (La. 1996), the robbers' target won $20,000 at a blackjack table. He was escorted to his car by casino security. The robbers followed him on an expressway and, in a remote area, shot his tires, causing a flat that forced him to stop, thus creating the opportunity for the robbery. Like hotels and restaurants, casinos must exercise reasonable care to protect the safety of their guests. In this case, in addition to the parking-lot escort, the casino provided surveillance cameras at the gambling tables and cashier's stand. These reasonable efforts to protect patrons proved unavailing in this case to stop the criminal act. These precautions will, however, protect the casino from civil liability for negligence in the event a crime victim sues the casino for the loss.

Duty Owed to Intoxicated Patrons Who Become Crime Victims

Virtually every casino has numerous bars, and free alcohol is frequently provided to gamblers. As a result, overindulgence is a recurrent problem. Intoxication can lead to disorderly conduct, which may cause the casino to physically evict the person from the premises. Recognizing that inebriated customers may not be able to care for themselves, a legal obligation to exercise reasonable care is imposed on the casino when ejecting a customer. This legal duty applies likewise to hotels and restaurants.

In one case, a patron (the plaintiff) was drinking heavily (the court described her condition as "extremely intoxicated") while her husband was betting. She began talking with another customer (the defendant) and they had numerous drinks together. She then became confrontational with several employees and a guard removed her to the security office. The defendant followed. He informed the guard that he would take care of her and urged the security officer not to arrest her. Ultimately the guard drove the plaintiff and the defendant to the defendant's hotel and left the plaintiff with the defendant. She awoke the next day naked in bed with the defendant and began to scream. The defendant hit her and told her

---

[14]*Marmer v. Queen of New Orleans at the Hilton*, 787 So.2d 1115 (La. 2001)

to shut up. He then raped her repeatedly. He later was arrested, pled guilty to rape, and was sentenced to prison.

The plaintiff sued the casino; it claimed it did not have any reason to know an assault was about to occur and therefore it did not owe her any duty. The court found that the casino did owe a duty, since it voluntarily took charge of the plaintiff, a patron, in an obviously intoxicated state. The casino owed a duty to take reasonable steps to ensure that she was not left in a worse position than when it found her.[15]

The lesson from this case is to exercise care for the well-being of patrons a casino takes into custody who are not able to care for themselves due to intoxication or otherwise.

False Imprisonment

False imprisonment occurs when a person is restrained against his will without justification . See the discussion of false imprisonment in Chapter 11. Occasionally, a facility believes a patron has engaged in criminal activity and wants to detain the person during an investigation. A potential problem exists: If the investigation reveals that the patron has done nothing illegal, the facility may be liable for false imprisonment. To save casinos from this liability, some states have adopted a defense for this type of claim specifically for gambling establishments. The defense authorizes the casino to detain a person if it has probable cause to believe the patron is engaging in criminal activity. "Probable cause" means sufficient evidence to lead a reasonable person to conclude that the individual detained was committing a crime. Probable cause is to be distinguished from speculation, a whim or guess.

Trademark Infringement

A trademark is a name or logo that identifies the source of a product or service. See the discussion of trademarks in Chapter 15. A well-known trademark has considerable value in attracting customers. For example, if you decide to have a hamburger for lunch, you would be more apt to stop at McDonald's, Wendy's, or Burger King than a place called Karen's Hamburgers. The reason is that you are familiar with the former, but not the latter. Rather than take a chance on something new, many people will go where they know the product.

As a result, a trademark of a popular product can be very valuable. Occasionally, competing companies will adopt a trademark similar to the leading company in the field. Their purpose may be to divert customers to their establishment. This is unfair to the owner of the well-received trademark and to the misled patrons. To help prevent this, the law makes illegal the use of a trademark that is confusingly similar to another mark when used by a business selling a similar or related product. An example of such a circumstance is provided in the following case. Note the extensive remedies awarded to the plaintiff by the court.

---

[15] *Atkinson v. Stateline Hotel Casino & Resort*, 21 P.3d 667 (Utah 2001)

CASE EXAMPLE 16-2

Aztar Corporation v. MGM Casino
2001 WL 939070 (Va. 2001)

... Plaintiff operates hotels and casinos under the TROPICANA mark in Las Vegas and Atlantic City as well as riverboat gambling enterprises in Indiana and Missouri. Plaintiff's TROPICANA mark is prominently displayed in signs, in advertising and promotional materials, and on collateral goods [for example, towels and napkins] used in plaintiff's casinos and hotels. The popularity and recognition of the TROPICANA mark has made it an asset of extraordinary value to Plaintiff.

Plaintiff also has used its TROPICANA mark to establish a significant presence on the internet. Specifically, Plaintiff maintains several Web sites including "tropicanaresort.com," "tropicanalasvegas.com" and tropicana.net" that describe its casinos, products, and services. Plaintiff's long-standing use of the TROPICANA mark and variations thereof have caused the public to expect that domain names and Web sites incorporating TROPICANA or variations thereof, are owned by Plaintiff.

Defendant MGM Casino ("MGM") is a foreign corporation with its principal place of business in St. John's Antigua. Defendant operates an interactive gambling Web site under the name "Tropicana Casino" and uses the domain name "tropicanacasino.com" to divert the public to that Web site. In addition, Defendant uses the Tropicana mark as a metatag to ensure that its Web site will appear when an internet user enters the word TROPICANA into an internet search engine. Defendant's use of the Tropicana mark occurred long after Plaintiff's use of that mark had made it famous and distinctive. ...

Plaintiff has established itself as the owner of the famous incontestable, federally registered TROPICANA mark. The existence of defendant's Tropicana casino Web site with the "tropicanacasino.com" domain name is certain to cause confusion among consumers. Defendant's Web site uses Plaintiff's mark in its entirety in connection with the identical services provided by Plaintiff, namely Internet gambling...

In the instant case, the Court finds that Plaintiff has made the requisite showing for [a case of trademark infringement]. ... Internet users quite instinctively would assume that a Web site that offers internet gambling under the title "Tropicana Casino" with the domain name "tropicanacasino.com" is connected to the world famous Aztar Tropicana Casinos. The consumer's perceived connection of defendant's site with plaintiff's mark is reinforced by the fact that defendant has used the TROPICANA mark as a metatag in its Web site which causes defendant's Web site to appear in the results of an internet search engine inquiry made for the word "tropicana." Internet users using search engines to locate plaintiff's Web sites would likely be diverted to defendant's Web site mistakenly believing that defendant's Web site is affiliated with plaintiff. ...

Relief to plaintiff is granted as follows.

1) Entry of a judgment that defendant has engaged in trademark and service infringement.

3) Entry of an injunction restraining and enjoining defendant and its employees from making any present or future use of TROPICANA or any other marks or names confusingly similar thereto, or domain name, Web site content, or metatag.

4) Entry of an order directing that the domain name "tropicanacasino.com" be transferred to plaintiff.

5) Entry of an order directing defendant to pay plaintiff $100,000 in statutory damages.

6) Entry of an order directing defendant to pay plaintiff's attorneys fees and costs.

7) Entry of an order directing defendant to disseminate, within 20 days, corrective advertisements in a form approved by the court to acknowledge its violations and to ameliorate the false and deceptive impressions produced by such violations.

In another case, plaintiff owned and operated a casino in Paradise Island called "Paradise Island." The defendant owned the Sands Hotel Casino in Atlantic City. The defendant opened a lounge in the casino called "Paradise Isle." The court determined that the defendant infringed on the plaintiff's trademark because the two names were alike and the services offered by both parties were similar.[16]

Copyright Infringement

A **copyright** is the exclusive right to reproduce creative work such as artwork, writings (books, poetry, essays, and so forth), music, and software. One who creates such a work is entitled to the exclusive right to reproduce it. See the discussion of copyrights in Chapter 15. If another party wishes to reproduce copyrighted work, such as a restaurant owner who would like to copy a painting onto paper placemats, the restaurateur must first obtain the permission of the artist. Customarily, the artist will charge a fee for that permission. Copying without permission constitutes copyright infringement, a tort. A person whose copyrighted work has been reproduced without permission can sue to force the infringer to "cease and desist" from further copying and to compensate the copyright owner for any losses resulting from the unauthorized duplication.

A copyright dispute over casino advertising led to a lawsuit in *Le Moine d/b/a Le Moine Studios v. Empress River Casino Corp.*, 1996 WL 332688 (Ill. 1996). The plaintiff was hired by the defendant's advertising company to create concepts for billboard advertising for the defendant riverboat gambling company. The concepts were rejected by Empress' senior director of marketing and public relations. Thereafter, Empress developed an advertising campaign for outdoor billboards, radio, and television. The plaintiff claimed the advertisements copied his compositions and therefore infringed his copyright. Empress conceded that both Le Moine's work and the advertising campaign the casino adopted emphasized the excitement of the casinos, but denied that the works were sufficiently similar to constitute copyright infringement. The court noted the following similarities: both incorporate the Empress logo; both express the idea of boredom (from which the casino can supposedly save the observer) with a front-loading washing machine; and both represent Empress Casinos with a slot machine.

The court found the works were not substantially similar and therefore awarded judgment to Empress. The court stated,

> [T]here are only a few stereotyped means to represent the idea of a casino. Le Moine's use of a slot machine was more or less dictated by the idea of a casino, or at least standard to the treatment of casinos ... the similar appearance of the two works stems only from the individual elements they share, not from a substantially similar total concept and feel arising from the creative arrangement and interaction of common elements. Accordingly, as a matter of law, an ordinary observer could not conclude that Le Moine's compositions and Empress' advertising campaign evoke a substantially similar total concept and feel.

---

[16]*Resorts International, Inc. v. Great Bay Hotel and Casino, Inc.*, 22 U.S.P.Q.2d 1740 (N.J. 1992)

Sexual Harassment Occurring at Casinos

Sexual harassment laws protect employees from harassing conduct of a sexual nature in the workplace. For a detailed discussion of sexual harassment, see Chapter 14. A good example of a hostile environment sexual harassment case in a casino setting is provided by the following case. The facts of the case furnish insight into the practice of "comping," whereby certain gamblers who bet large sums of money are offered free meals, rooms, and even air transportation as an inducement to secure their patronage at a particular casino.

CASE EXAMPLE 16-3

Steiner v. Showboat Hotel & Casino
25 F.3d 1459 (9th Cir. 1994)

... Showboat hired Barbara Steiner to work as a blackjack dealer at Showboat Hotel and Casino in March of 1986. Two months later she was promoted to be the casino's first female "floorperson." Her supervisor was Jack Trenkle, a Showboat vice-president.

In 1987 Steiner complained to Showboat management that Trenkle was calling her offensive names based on her gender, such as "dumb fucking broad," "cunt," and "fucking cunt." Trenkle was not reprimanded; rather, Steiner was moved to a different shift so that she would not have to be in contact with him. After about one month, however, she decided the new shift was too inconvenient and moved back to her old shift.

On December 19, 1989, Trenkle learned that Steiner had "comped" (offered a free meal to players betting high stakes) a breakfast for two men who had been playing Blackjack at her table. He confronted Steiner in front of customers and other employees, expressing his disapproval of her decision in the following words: "You are not a fucking floor man [her job]. You are a fucking casino host. You comp every fucking fleabag that walks through the door." She claims he moved toward her in a threatening manner during this tirade. By his own admission, he then yelled, "Why don't you go in the restaurant and suck their dicks while you are at it if you want to comp them so bad?"

She claims he repeated this two or three times, laughed, and walked off with a grin on his face. Her version is corroborated by the deposition of a cocktail waitress who overheard the exchange.

Steiner complained to Showboat's manager the next day, and Trenkle was told to apologize. He did, although Steiner claims it was in a rude and sarcastic manner. Unsatisfied with this response, Steiner filed a complaint with the Nevada Equal Rights Commission. Once aware of her complaint, Showboat conducted a more serious investigation, in which numerous Showboat employees were questioned about Trenkle's treatment of Steiner and of women generally. Their statements establish that Trenkle was abusive to men and women alike; however, his abusive treatment and remarks to women were of a sexual or gender-specific nature.

As a result of its investigation, Showboat sent a written reprimand to Trenkle for "sexually harassing" Steiner. Trenkle was told that if he ever again used sexual or derogatory language to or about any employee, he would be fired. Trenkle's shift was changed so that he and Steiner would no longer be at work during the same hours. ...

In November, Trenkle was fired because he broke the terms of his disciplinary letter. Specifically, he denied a female employee's request to leave early by saying, "I wouldn't want you to lose your job either because you have got big boobs. I'd hate to terminate someone with big boobs." ...

Steiner's claim relies upon the hostile or offensive work environment theory of liability for sexual harassment. ... [W]hile coworkers' occasional annoying or "merely offensive" comments do not constitute sexual harassment, [illegal conduct] comes into play before the harassing conduct leads to a nervous breakdown. It is enough, rather, if such hostile conduct pollutes the victim's workplace, making it more difficult for her to do her job, to take pride in her work, and to desire to stay on in her position.

Steiner has established without contradiction that Trenkle habitually referred to her and to other female employees in a derogatory fashion using sexually explicit and offensive terms. Moreover, Trenkle's ongoing comments and conduct were sexually explicit, offensive, highly derogatory, and publicly made. Steiner has made her case unless Showboat can demonstrate that it took adequate remedial and disciplinary action. ...

Showboat claims in defense that Trenkle harassed everyone, male and female alike, and therefore his harassment of Steiner was not based on her gender. ...

[While] Trenkle was indeed abusive to men, his abuse of women was different. It relied on sexual epithets, offensive, explicit references to women's bodies and sexual conduct. While Trenkle may have referred to men as "assholes," he referred to women as "dumb fucking broads" and "fucking cunts," and when angry at Steiner, suggested that she have sex with customers. And while his abuse of men in no way related to their gender, his abuse of female employees, especially Steiner, centered on the fact that they were females. It is one thing to call a woman "worthless," and another to call her a "worthless broad."

Furthermore, even if Trenkle used sexual epithets equal in intensity and in an equally degrading manner against male employees, he cannot thereby "cure" his conduct toward women. ... We do not rule out the possibility that both men and women working at Showboat have viable claims against Trenkle for sexual harassment.

[Concerning whether Showboat took adequate remedial action], The evidence suggests that Showboat was consistently slow to react to Steiner's claims, and did not seriously investigate them or strongly reprimand Trenkle until after Steiner had filed her complaint with the Nevada Equal Rights Commission. Moreover, Showboat [originally] changed Steiner's shift rather than changing his shift or work area within the casino or, indeed, firing him outright and early on. A victim of sexual harassment should not have to work in a less desirable location [or time] as a result of the employer's remedial plan.

We reverse the district court's grant of summary judgment in Showboat's favor ... it would seem that on remand Steiner herself may be entitled to summary judgment on her claim of sexual harassment.

CASE QUESTIONS

1. Why did the court object to the casino changing Steiner's work schedule as a method to curb the sexual harassment?

2. To avoid liability for sexual harassment, what should an employer do when addressing a claim of sexual harassment?

An employer can avoid liability for sexual harassment if it takes appropriate remedial action. To be appropriate, the response must be prompt and reasonably calculated to end the harassment. In *Klutch v. Grand Victoria Casino*, 1996 WL 465393 (Ill. 1996), a female coat check attendant at the casino filed a complaint against an employee in the engineering department alleging that the latter continually made inappropriate sexual remarks to her. The day after the complaint was filed, the general manager placed the alleged offender on a three-day investigative suspension. The plaintiff quit during the three-day period. The offender was allowed to return to work, but a written warning was placed in his file directing him to refrain from sexually harassing conduct and advising him that any further complaints would result in immediate termination. The court determined this was an appropriate response by the casino and therefore dismissed the plaintiff's case.

In a contrasting circumstance, the court found a casino was too slow to respond to an employee's complaints of sexual harassment. The plaintiff was a fry cook in the Garden Cafe at Harrah's Las Vegas Casino. Her fellow male workers repeatedly asked her to have sex with them, one used a sausage to simulate a male body part in front of the plaintiff, others hit her in the buttocks, another popped her bra strap and put his hands around her waist, and many subjected her to a variety of sexually explicit comments and references to her menstrual cycle. Despite the plaintiff's continued complaints, management took no corrective action for fifteen months until the plaintiff reported the circumstances to the Equal Employment Opportunity Commission. Due to the casino's inaction, the court denied Harrah's motion to dismiss plaintiff's claim.[17]

Casinos and the Dram Shop Act

The Dram Shop Act is a statute that imposes liability on establishments that sell alcohol for certain injuries resulting from illegal sales (the patron was visibly intoxicated when served, was underage, or was a known alcoholic). See the discussion on this topic in Chapter 12. In most states, the liability applies only to a third party injured by the illegally served patron. Some states, including New Jersey, allow the illegally served patron to recover for at least a portion of his damages. An interesting attempt was made to extend dram shop liability to a uniquely casino application. Most casinos offer their guests free drinks while they are gambling. The plaintiffs in several lawsuits were given free drinks by a casino after becoming intoxicated. They then incurred significant gambling debts owed to the casino. They sued the casino claiming that the debt constituted damages resulting from illegal alcohol service and therefore they should be relieved from their debt.

The complaint in one of these cases described this practice as follows:

> The Casino [Taj Mahal in Atlantic City] continuously provided [plaintiff] with complementary 4–5 ounce gin martinis during the entire period he was gambling and the casino continued to provide this stream of alcohol to plaintiff beyond the point when he was visibly and substantially intoxicated. Because defendant allowed plaintiff to continue gambling while visibly intoxicated, including extending him additional credit by permitting him to draw markers against his credit account while intoxicated, he allegedly sustained gambling losses in excess of $2,000,000 while visibly intoxicated.[18]

---

[17] *Burns v. Mayer*, 2001 WL 1557459 (Nev. 2001)

[18] *Hakimoglu v. Trump Taj Mahal, Inc.*, 876 F.Supp. 625, 625 (N.J. 1994), aff'd, 70 F.3d 291 (3rd Cir. 1995)

The court rejected this argument and held for the casino. Among the reasons were the following:

1. Dram shop liability had not previously been extended beyond injuries related to driving while intoxicated, barroom accidents, and barroom brawls.

2. The casino industry is very highly regulated. Had New Jersey intended to impose liability on casinos for allowing intoxicated patrons to gamble, a statute to that effect would likely have been adopted.

3. Extension of dram shop liability to gambling debts would present difficult questions of proximate cause, as sober gamblers can play well and nonetheless suffer significant losses, intoxicated gamblers can win big, and under the prevailing rules and house odds, the house will win and the gamblers will lose in the typical transaction.

4. Even if we assume that alcohol will affect the gambler's judgment, many casino games require no skill and instead are determined by the draw of a card, a throw of the dice, or the random appearance of pictures on a slot machine.

5. Proof of intoxication could be more easily fabricated in a gambling case than in the typical dram shop situation, which is a car accident. In the latter case, the occurrence of the accident is a specific event marked by police and accident reports. Reliable evidence of alcohol in a person's body is usually obtained as part of the accident investigation. None of this occurs in the gambling scenario. A gambler's loss at the gambling table is not cause for investigation, nor is a casino dealer likely to recall it at a later date.

For these reasons, the dram shop act does not apply to a gambler who is served alcohol by a casino after becoming visibly intoxicated and who continues to place bets and thereby incurs a gambling debt. The bettor is not entitled to reimbursement of his loss from the casino.

Riverboat Casinos and the Jones Act

Many cities bordering on waterways have adopted **riverboat casinos**. The proliferation of this type of casino is the result of laws that prohibit gambling on shore but do not apply at sea. In some states, a riverboat located dockside but totally in a body of water can legally house gaming. In other states, a boat must travel a certain distance off shore before it can validly permit gambling.

Numerous federal laws affect events occurring on boats on the waterways of the United States. These laws are referred to as **maritime laws**. Sometimes the outcome of a case can depend on whether maritime law or a state law applies. Litigation has resulted to determine which laws apply to riverboat casinos. One issue that varies greatly depending on which law applies is the appropriate remedy when an employee on a riverboat casino is injured while on duty. According to state law, any monetary recovery from the employer in this circumstance will be limited by workers' compensation laws. Such laws produce a relatively prompt resolution of the case outside of court, but restrict the amount of compensation an employee will receive. For example, under workers' compensation laws, an employee cannot recover damages for pain and suffering, a measure of damages that compensates an injured person for the physical pain and mental anguish that she may have endured because of an injury.

The Jones Act

Contrasted with state workers' compensation laws is a federal maritime law known as the **Jones Act**, which enables employees injured while on a boat to sue in court for the full value of their injury, including pain and suffering. For the Jones Act to apply, the boat on which the injury occurred must qualify as a "vessel in navigation." What constitutes such a vessel has been the subject of several cases.

The application of the Jones Act was at issue in *Pavone v. Mississippi Riverboat Amusement Corporation*, 52 F.3d 560 (5th Cir. 1995). A bartender stepped on a screw that penetrated his shoe and injured his foot while he was working on a dockside casino in Biloxi, Mississippi. The casino, named the Biloxi Belle, sat on a barge that was moored to shore by lines tied to sunken steel pylons that were filled with concrete. Shoreside utility lines were permanently connected. A continual standby towing contract existed for the barge and casino to tow them to sheltered waters in the event potentially damaging weather was forecast. The Biloxi Belle had no engine, no captain, no navigational aids, no crewquarters, and no lifesaving equipment. For visual effects only, it had a decorative pilot house, which contained no operating parts other than a single light switch. It also had a motorized but nonfunctional paddle wheel, which rested permanently above the water level and served no propulsion function.

The barge had not been built to transport passengers, cargo, or equipment and had never been used for that purpose. The Biloxi Belle did not employ a crew for navigation or nautical purposes. All employees were engaged solely in connection with the casino business.

The court determined, not surprisingly, that the casino and barge were not "vessels in navigation" for purposes of the Jones Act. Therefore, the employee's remedy for his injuries was limited by workers' compensation laws.

In another case, a waitress was injured on a riverboat casino in Illinois and she sued. The casino/employer sought a dismissal of the case on the ground that the ship was not a vessel and therefore the waitress' only remedy was through workers' compensation and not the Jones Act. The casino boat, called the Northern Star, was constructed in New Orleans and had traveled to Illinois up the Mississippi River on its own power. It has an engine, a captain, lifesaving equipment, crew quarters, and fulltime marine operations department employees. Equipped as such, the court held the boat was a vessel in navigation and the waitress could sue under the Jones Act.[19]

---

[19] *Wiora v. Harrah's Joliet Casino*, 68 F.Supp.2d 988 (Il. 1999)

Casinos on Native American Reservations

In recent times, many casinos have been built on Indian reservations. This phenomenon was a natural outgrowth of two circumstances. First, the laws in most states prohibit gambling. Second, the law accords to Native American reservations sovereign authority, which means the governing bodies of the Native American tribes have the supreme authority to govern the reservation and its inhabitants independent of state and federal laws. Therefore, although the law of the state in which the reservation is located may outlaw gambling, that fact does not preclude the reservation's governing body from determining that gambling will be permitted on the reservation. However, as the following discussion reveals, some limitations do apply.

Sovereign Authority

Native American tribes exercise **sovereign authority** over their members and territories. This means tribes are separate from our federal and state governments and have the power to regulate their internal affairs by making their own substantive law. The power to enforce that law rests with their tribal courts and not federal courts. Tribal sovereignty is subordinate only to the federal government. As sovereigns, tribes are immune from lawsuits unless they specifically waive that immunity. These concepts are illustrated in the following cases.

Lawsuits Against Native American Tribes

A decisive application of the tribal sovereignty rule occurred in 1987 in a California case. Two Native American tribes in that state were engaging in various forms of gambling. The state sought to force the tribes to comply with state gambling regulations. Resistance by the tribes led to a lawsuit that ultimately was decided by the United States Supreme Court. The justices held the state did not have authority to enforce its gambling laws on the Native American reservation[20]. That case led Congress to pass the **Indian Gaming Regulatory Act** (hereinafter "IGRA") in 1988, which to some extent restricts a tribe's ability to conduct gambling activities. Before gaming can legally occur on a reservation, the tribe must comply with IGRA. One of IGRA's goals was to balance the states' interest in regulating high stakes gambling within their borders and the Native Americans' resistance to state intrusions on their sovereignty. IGRA is discussed in more detail in the next section of this chapter.

In another case, a table game operator who had been employed at a Native American casino claimed he was wrongfully terminated. He commenced a lawsuit in federal district court against the casino. The tribe that owned the facility moved to dismiss the case claiming the proper forum was the Tribal Court. The federal court held that, as a sovereign power, the tribe was entitled to sovereign immunity

---

[20]*California v. Cabazon Band of Mission Indians*, 480 U.S. 202, 107 S.Ct. 1083 (1987)

and it had not waived that entitlement. Accordingly, the court lacked jurisdiction and dismissed the case.[21]

In *Romanella v. The Mashantucket Pequoz Tribal Nation*, 993 F.Supp. 163 (Conn. 1996), a pit cashier at Foxwoods Resort & Casino fell in a nearby parking lot used by casino patrons. Her fall resulted from an accumulation of snow and ice. The lot was not on the reservation but was owned and maintained by the tribe. The cashier sued in federal court the Native American tribe that operates Foxwoods. The court, noting that Native American tribes are independent domestic nations, held that the defendant tribe was immune from lawsuits in federal court involving events occurring on tribal territory. The federal court case was thus dismissed. The plaintiff could pursue her case in the tribal court. Similarly, a plaintiff who fell on a wet, slippery floor at the Mohegan Sun Casino in Connecticut was foreclosed from suing the casino in a state court. Instead, the case was referred to a tribunal created by the tribe to resolve legal disputes arising at the casino. Appropriately, that forum was named the Gaming Disputes Court.[22]

Lawsuits Against Casino Employees

While tribes are entitled to sovereign immunity from negligence liability, states differ on whether individuals associated with the tribe are. Some states hold that individual tribal officers as well as tribal employees acting in their representative capacity and within the scope of their authority are entitled to the immunity. Some states have held otherwise. For example, a casino patron in California suffered a broken hip and shattered elbow when he was knocked down by a participant in a parking lot fight while the plaintiff was en route to his car. He sued various casino employees, claiming they did not exercise sufficient precautions for his safety. The court held that when the casino employees designed the facility's security plan, they were working in their capacities as tribal representatives and were therefore protected by sovereign immunity.[23]

A Connecticut court found otherwise, holding that employees of the tribe, as distinguished from tribal officials, are not entitled to immunity. A woman was injured on the premises of Mohegan Sun Casino, run by the Mohegan tribe. She sued for negligence two employees of the tribe, the director of facilities operations and another "building official." Neither was involved in the operations of the tribal government. The court therefore held they were not entitled to immunity. Said the court, "[T]he mere employment relationship of the defendants with the Mohegan Tribe does not grant them the right to assert the Tribe's sovereign immunity."[24]

Not infrequently, Native American tribes will transfer the management of casinos to a corporate entity separate from the tribe. These entities are normally

---

[21] *Barker v. Menominee Nation Casino*, 897 F.Supp. 389 (Wis. 1995)

[22] *Paszkowski v. Chapman*, 2001 WL 118765 (Conn. 2001)

[23] *Trudgeon v. Fantasy Springs Casino*, 84 Cal.Rptr.2d 65 (Ca. 1999)

[24] *Kizis v. Morse Diesel International, Inc.*, 2000 WL 1281816 (Conn. 2000)

named as a defendant when a casino patron is injured and sues. The question arises whether these entities are entitled to immunity. Customarily they are.[25]

Another example of the limitation on Native American sovereignty is provided by *Reich v. Mashantucket Sand & Gravel*, 95 F.3d 174 (2nd Cir. 1996). The issue in this case was whether a construction company maintained by a Native American tribe and used to construct additions to a casino was subject to the federal Occupational Safety and Health Act ("OSHA"). That Act imposes many safety requirements on employers to help ensure the well-being of workers. Federal OSHA inspectors entered the casino and found four safety violations that threatened the health of the construction workers. For these violations, the construction company was fined $4,000. The tribe challenged the imposition of the fine, claiming OSHA did not apply to it due to the tribe's sovereignty. The federal court ruled that the sovereignty of a tribe is limited, not unlike the sovereignty of a state. A tribe's sovereignty applies only to the power needed to control internal matters of the reservation. The construction work, although it occurred entirely on the reservation, has a much broader impact than just within the reservation. The company employed non-Native Americans, and the construction project involved a resort and casino that serves a multi-state clientele, much broader than just residents of the reservation. For these reasons, the court held that the tribe was bound by OSHA.

Dram Shop Act

Tribal immunity is not a bar to a lawsuit arising from the wrongful sale of alcohol at a Native American casino. The reason is states' concern for the protection of the safety of its residents.[26]

Indian Gaming Regulatory Act

The federal government has maintained some oversight of gaming conducted on reservations. Its authority is embodied in the Indian Gaming Regulatory Act, IGRA, 25 U.S.C. § 2701 *et seq*, which was adopted by Congress in 1988. IGRA provides a comprehensive design for regulating gaming activities on Native American lands. One of IGRA's objectives is "to provide a statutory basis for the operation of gaming by Indian tribes as a means of promoting tribal economic development, self-sufficiency, and strong tribal governments."

IGRA divides gaming into three classifications, each subject to differing degrees of tribal, state, and federal jurisdiction and regulation. The class most highly regulated is known as Class III and includes blackjack, craps and related dice games, wheel games, roulette, electronic games of chance, slot machines, card games in which the players play against the house, and keno. For a casino on a reservation to host these types of games, IGRA mandates the following four

---

[25]See, for example, *Trudgeon v. Fantasy Springs Casino*, 84 Cal.Rptr.2d 65 (Ca. 1999)

[26]*Schram v. Ohar*, 1998 WL 811393 (Conn. 1998)

requirements: (1) the gaming must be authorized by an ordinance or resolution adopted by the governing body of the Indian tribe having jurisdiction over the land; (2) the type of gaming involved must be permitted by the state for some purpose by some person or organization (such as for charitable purposes); (3) the gaming must be approved by the chairperson of the National Indian Gaming Commission, which was established by Congress to develop and oversee rules and regulations relating to IGRA; and (4) the gaming must be conducted consistent with a Tribal-State treaty entered into by the Native American tribe and the state. Such a treaty is initiated by the tribe requesting the state in which the lands are located to negotiate for the purpose of entering into an agreement governing such gaming. These treaties, called **compacts**, are written agreements between a state and an individual tribe, and they govern the operation of casino gaming on Native American lands. Examples of terms that are included in a state-tribal compact are the types of games allowed, hours of operation, number of gambling stations authorized, maximum bets, background investigations of people working in the casino, and minimal standards for internal management and financial controls.

Where tribes have undertaken gaming operations without satisfying these prerequisites, the federal government is authorized to obtain search warrants and seize slot machines and related gambling devices and paraphernalia from the casinos. Further, the managers and operators of a Native American casino operating illegally are subject to federal prosecution for the violation. For example, in *United States v. E.C. Investments, Inc.*, 77 F.3d 327 (9th Cir. 1996), the managers of a California Native American casino were prosecuted for providing slot machines without first entering a compact with the state. Additionally, the United States government can seek injunctive relief against the casino to prevent it from operating.[27]

Internet Gambling

Since the advent of the Internet in 1995, online gambling has exploded in popularity. The number of gambling Web sites is estimated at 1,400, and they are predicted to collect more than $6.5 billion annually. Online casinos, using catchy names such as Virtual Vegas, High Card Casino, and BigCat Internet Casino, feature nearly every game available in a brick-and-mortar facility. These include blackjack, roulette, poker, keno, slot machines, sports wagering, lotteries, and bingo.

To qualify to play, customers open an account with the site by providing certain information. Funds for betting must then be deposited by using a credit card, electronic withdrawal from a bank account, certified check, money order, or wire transfer. Once the account is open the user is able to place bets.

Unlike online gambling, land-based casinos in the United States represent one of the most heavily regulated industries in the nation. Laws impacting the

[27] *U.S. v. Santee Sioux Tribe of Nebraska*, F.Supp.2d, 2001 WL 1561104 (Neb. 2001)

gambling industry address such matters as licensing, fraud, crimes, additional consumer protection measures, and taxation of earnings made by casinos and gamblers. Operators of online casinos based outside this country are not subject to any of these regulations, a matter of considerable concern to state and federal governments and the commercial casino industry. Some states prohibit online gambling within the state. Congress is considering a law that would ban Internet wagering. Additional developments on the issues of the legality and regulation of online gambling are anticipated in the near future.

Key Terms

card counter
compacts
copyright
false imprisonment
gambling
gambling commissions
Indian Gaming Regulatory Act
(IGRA)

Jones Act
maritime laws
pari-mutuel betting
pathological gambler
riverboat casinos
sovereign authority

Summary

Casinos are rapidly growing in popularity, and in response their numbers are quickly increasing. This phenomenon offers new opportunities for workers in the hospitality field. The legal challenges associated with this relatively new entity include some known to hospitality law and others unique to casinos.

Just as hotels and restaurants need to take appropriate precautions to protect the safety and well-being of their guests, casinos must do the same. Laws dealing with negligence, false imprisonment, trademarks, and copyrights are equally applicable to gaming facilities. The Dram Shop Act and the law of contracts are likewise binding on casinos.

Casinos have new venues not normally associated with hotels and restaurants. These include riverboats and Native American reservations. Both of these sites are the subject of laws that are not applicable elsewhere. A thorough study of the law of casinos requires exposure to maritime law and Native American law.

Preventive Law Tips for Managers

■ *Anticipate circumstances that may cause injury to patrons and take the necessary action to eliminate the risks.* Casinos are obligated to use reasonable care to protect their patrons from injury. Failure to do so will result in liability. Managers and employees should always be alert to conditions on the premises that may present risks. Upon discovery of any such conditions, take the necessary action to eliminate them.

■ *Aid patrons who evidence signs of physical distress.* While the law does not generally require that people come to the aid of someone in danger, where a special relationship exists—such as a casino and the people it invites to its premises—a duty does exist to exercise reasonable care to provide first aid to an ill or injured patron. The casino should develop an emergency response system and thoroughly train its employees concerning the system.

■ *Do not detain a patron without probable cause to believe the customer has engaged in illegal conduct.* Detaining a patron on suspicion of engaging in criminal conduct without having probable cause can lead to liability for false imprisonment. Unfortunately, casinos can be victims of criminal conduct that can cause considerable loss to the casino or its clientele. However, the casino must balance its interest in preventing crime against the interest of its customers who have a right not to be detained without probable cause.

■ *Do not adopt a trademark that is confusingly similar to another mark used in the gaming industry.* If a casino uses a name that is confusingly similar to a competitor's, the casino may be forced to discontinue use of that name regardless of money spent to advertise and promote it. To avoid this, employ marks that are unique and not likely to be confused with other trademarks already in use.

■ *Use only original material in advertising.* If your advertising or promotional materials are copied from another marketing campaign or other source, you may be liable for copyright infringement. When designing advertising, use original ideas and elements. If you wish to utilize someone else's materials, obtain their authorization first.

■ *Take precautions to protect your customers from criminal activity.* Successful gamblers are attractive targets for criminals. Adopt procedures to protect your customers. Such procedures might include providing a security escort to patrons' cars; surveillance cameras; a well-trained security force; training all employees to detect and prevent criminal activity; maintaining contact with security personnel in other nearby casinos to learn of the latest schemes in your area; and maintaining a close relationship with the local police for ongoing security assistance.

■ *Do not sell alcohol illegally.* Dram Shop Acts render a casino liable when a person is injured by someone who was illegally served alcohol. To avoid this type of liability, do not sell alcohol to prohibited classes of people; train employees on how to detect if a customer is intoxicated or underage; and reinforce that training regularly.

■ *For casinos on Native American reservations, comply fully with the Indian Gaming Regulatory Act.* The Indian Gaming Regulatory Act (IGRA) contains the prerequisites a casino on a reservation must meet to legally provide gambling on its premises. Failure to comply can result in government seizure of gaming devices and criminal prosecution of the casino's officers and managers. To ensure compliance with this specialized area of law, consult with an attorney knowledgeable about the IGRA.

Review Questions

1. What defenses are available to a gambler who has incurred a sizeable loss while betting on credit?

2. What is a pathological gambler?

3. What duty of care is owed by a casino to its patrons?

4. What is the Jones Act and what is its relevance to casinos?

5. What is "probable cause" and how does it apply to the tort of false imprisonment?

6. What led to the proliferation of riverboat casinos?

7. What led to the proliferation of casinos on Native American reservations?

8. What is the Indian Gaming Regulatory Act?

9. What is the meaning of the term *sovereign authority*?

10. What laws regulate online gambling?

Discussion Questions

1. Describe several criminal schemes to which casinos may be vulnerable. How can casinos protect themselves?

2. What determines whether the Jones Act applies to a water-based casino? What attributes of the casino will be considered by a court in determining whether the Jones Act applies?

3. What factors will a court consider when deciding whethere the name of a casino constitutes trademark infringement?

4. In *Le Moine v. Empress River Casino, Corp.*, concerning an allegation of copyright infringement relating to advertising adopted by the Empress Riverboat Casino, both the plaintiff's proposed advertising campaign and the one adopted by Empress represented the casino pictorially with a slot machine. Why was this not significant evidence of copyright infringement?

5. Why have the courts not applied dram shop liability to gambling debts?

6. Explain the hostile work environment theory of sexual harassment and identify why it is illegal.

7. What must a Native American tribe wishing to initiate gambling do to comply with the Indian Gaming Regulatory Act? What are the consequences if it offers gaming without complying with the Act?

8. What do gambling commissions regulate and why?

Application Questions

1. Latasha was a security employee at a casino. Her boss, who was male, often made demeaning comments to her related to her gender. She felt humiliated and distressed as a result. Latasha filed a complaint with the personnel office of the casino.
   A. What legal wrong did Latasha's boss commit?
   B. What action should the casino take to limit its liability?

2. Eduardo was gambling at a casino. Luck was with him and he won almost $10,000. What security precautions should the casino have in effect to protect Eduardo and other customers from criminal activity?

3. Barry was a security guard at a casino. He took a fifteen-minute break in the middle of his shift. When he returned, he noticed a player at a blackjack table who had not been there when he left. Barry also noticed the player had a large number of betting chips. Barry suspected foul play and detained the player. While Barry undertook further investigation he later learned that the player had done nothing wrong. The player then sued the casino for false imprisonment. Would the casino be able to utilize the defense of probable cause? Why or why not?

4. Sarina was playing the slot machines at a casino for several hours. A waitress periodically approached her and offered her free drinks. After drinking ten beers she became angry and violent when the player next to her won a major jackpot. Security was called and she was taken to the security office. Security personnel determined that she was very intoxicated. What duty does the casino owe to Sarina under these circumstances?

Web Sites

Web sites that will enhance your understanding of the material in this chapter include:

http://www.indiangamingnews.com/legalforum.htm This site contains numerous articles addressing myriad legal issues associated with Native American gaming.

http://www.gamblingcommission.com This is the site of the Gambling Commission, an independent organization created to regulate online gaming organizations, discourage corrupt online gaming operations, and provide for gamblers "a closely monitored, safe online gaming environment."

http://www.americangaming.org This is the site of the American Gaming Association, a trade association of the "commercial casino entertainment industry." It provides up-to-date information on the gaming industry, including issues associated with responsible gaming.

http://www.michigangaming.com This site contains abundant legal information about Native American casinos and gaming in the state of Michigan.

For additional resources, visit our Web site
www.hospitality-tourism.delmar.com

APPENDIX A

■

Limiting Liability Statutes

All fifty states, Washington, D.C., Puerto Rico, the Virgin Islands, and Guam place statutory limits on the liability of hotels for loss or damage to guests' property. To qualify for this protection in any of these jurisdictions, hotels must provide a safe for guests' valuables and post notice of its availability and the hotel's limited liability in strict accord with the state law. The statutes and liability limitations are as follows. The statute references are to the particular title within each state's statutory scheme that addresses hotels. That title is variously referred to as Hotels, Commerce, Business Regulations, or General Business Law.

State	Statutory Limitation	Statute Section
Alabama	$300	34-15-13
Alaska	$1,000	08.56.050
Arizona	$500	33-302
Arkansas	$300	20-26-302
California	$500	1860
Colorado	value declared by guest	12-44-105
Connecticut	$500	44-1
Delaware	none stated	15-1502
Florida	$1,000	509.111
Georgia	$750	43-21-10
Guam	$250	41402
Hawaii	$500	486K-4
Idaho	$1,000	39-1804
Illinois	$500	90/1
Indiana	$600	32-33-7-2
Iowa	$100	671.1
Kansas	$250	36-402
Kentucky	$300	306.020
Louisiana	$500	2971

State	Statutory Limitation	Statute Section
Maine	$300	3851
Maryland	$300	15-103
Massachusetts	$1,000	140 §10
Michigan	$250	427.102
Minnesota	$1,000	327.71
Mississippi	$500	75-73-5
Missouri	$0	419.020
Montana	$0	70-6-504
Nebraska	$500	41-208
Nevada	$750	651.010
New Hampshire	$1,000	353:1
New Jersey	$5,000	29:2-2
New Mexico	$0	57-6-1
New York	$1,500	12-200
North Carolina	$500	72-3
North Dakota	$300	60-01-29
Ohio	$500	4721.02
Oklahoma	$250	15-503a and b
Oregon	$300	699.010
Pennsylvania	$300	37-61
Puerto Rico	$1,000	10-712
Rhode Island	$500	5-14-1
South Carolina	$2,000	45-1-40
South Dakota	$300	43-40-1
Tennessee	$300	62-7-104
Texas	$50	13-2155-052
Utah	$250	29-1-2
Vermont	none stated	9-3141
Virginia	$500	35.1-28
Virgin Islands	$200	27-402
Washington	$1,000	19.48.030
Washington, D.C.	$1,000	30-101
West Virginia	$250	16-6-22
Wisconsin	$300	254.80
Wyoming	$0	33-17-101

APPENDIX B

Guidelines on Discrimination Based on Gender

(From the Code of Federal Regulations, Vol. 29, § 1604.11)

SEXUAL HARASSMENT

(a) Harassment on the basis of sex is a violation of Sec. 703 of Title VII. Unwelcome sexual advances, requests for sexual favors, and other verbal or physical conduct of a sexual nature constitute sexual harassment when (1) submission to such conduct is made either explicitly or implicitly a term or condition of an individual's employment, (2) submission to or rejection of such conduct by an individual is used as a basis for employment decisions affecting such individual, or (3) such conduct has the purpose or effect of unreasonably interfering with an individual's work performance or creating an intimidating, hostile or offensive working environment.

(b) In determining whether alleged conduct constitutes sexual harassment, the Commission will look at the record as a whole and at the totality of the circumstances, such as the nature of the sexual advances and the context in which the alleged incidents occurred. The determination of the legality of a particular action will be made from the facts, on a case by case basis.

(c) [Reserved}

(d) With respect to conduct between fellow employees, an employer is responsible for acts of sexual harassment in the workplace where the employer (or its agents or supervisory employees) knows or should have known of the conduct, unless it can show that it took immediate and appropriate corrective action.

(e) An employer may also be responsible for the acts of nonemployees, with respect to sexual harassment of employees in the workplace, where the employer (or its agents or supervisory employees) knows or should have known of the conduct and fails to take immediate and appropriate corrective action.

In reviewing these cases the Commission will consider the extent of the employer's control and any other legal responsibility which the employer may have with respect to the conduct of such nonemployees.

(f) Prevention is the best tool for the elimination of sexual harassment. An employer should take all steps necessary to prevent sexual harassment from occurring, such as affirmatively raising the subject, expressing strong disapproval, developing appropriate sanctions, informing employees of their right to raise and how to raise the issue of harassment under Title VII, and developing methods to sensitize all concerned.

(g) Other related practices: Where employment opportunities or benefits are granted because of an individual's submission to the employer's sexual advances or requests for sexual favors, the employer may be held liable for unlawful sex discrimination against other persons who were qualified for but denied that employment opportunity or benefit.

APPENDIX C

The Americans with Disabilities Act

TITLE I—EMPLOYMENT

§ 101. DEFINITIONS. As used in this title:

(1) COMMISSION.—The term "Commission" means the Equal Employment Opportunity Commission. ...

(2) COVERED ENTITY.—The term "covered entity" means an employer, ...

(3) DIRECT THREAT.—The term "direct threat" means a significant risk to the health or safety of others that cannot be eliminated by reasonable accommodation.

(4) Employee.—The term "employee" means an individual employed by an employer.

(5) EMPLOYER.—

(A) IN GENERAL.—The term "employer" means a person engaged in an industry affecting commerce who has 15 or more employees for each working day in each of 20 or more calendar weeks in the current or preceding calendar year, ...

(8) QUALIFIED INDIVIDUAL WITH A DISABILITY.—The term "qualified individual with a disability" means an individual with a disability who, with or without reasonable accommodation, can perform the essential functions of the employment position that such individual holds or desires. For the purposes of this title, consideration shall be given to the employer's judgment as to what functions of a job are essential, and if an employer has prepared a written description before advertising or interviewing applicants for the job, this description shall be considered evidence of the essential functions of the job.

(9) REASONABLE ACCOMMODATION.—The term "reasonable accommodation" may include—

(A) making existing facilities used by employees readily accessible to and usable by individuals with disabilities; and

(B) job restructuring, part-time or modified work schedules, reassignment to a vacant position, acquisition or modification of equipment or devices, appropriate adjustment or modifications of examinations, training materials or policies, the provision of qualified readers or interpreters, and other similar accommodations for individuals with disabilities.

(10) UNDUE HARDSHIP.—

    (A) IN GENERAL.—The term "undue hardship" means an action requiring significant difficulty or expense, when considered in light of the factors set forth in subparagraph (B).

    (B) FACTORS TO BE CONSIDERED.—In determining whether an accommodation would impose an undue hardship on a covered entity, factors to be considered include—

        (i) the nature and cost of the accommodation needed under this Act;

        (ii) the overall financial resources of the facility or facilities involved in the provision of the reasonable accommodation; the number of persons employed at such facility; the effect on expenses and resources, or the impact otherwise of such accommodation upon the operation of the facility;

        (iii) the overall financial resources of the covered entity; the overall size of the business of a covered entity with respect to the number of its employees; the number, type, and location of its facilities; and

        (iv) the type of operation or operations of the covered entity, including the composition, structure, and functions of the workforce of such entity; the geographic separateness, administrative, or fiscal relationship of the facility or facilities in question to the covered entity.

§ 102. DISCRIMINATION

    (a)   GENERAL RULE.—No covered entity shall discriminate against a qualified individual with a disability because of the disability of such individual in regard to job application procedures, the hiring, advancement, or discharge of employees, employee compensation, job training, and other terms, conditions, and privileges of employment.

    (b)   CONSTRUCTION.—As used in subsection (a), the term "discriminate" includes—

    (1) limiting, segregating, or classifying a job applicant or employee in a way that adversely affects the opportunities or status of such applicant or employee because of the disability of such applicant or employee;

    (2) participating in a contractual or other arrangement or relationship that has the effect of subjecting a covered entity's qualified applicant or employee with a disability to the discrimination prohibited by this title (such relationship includes a relationship with an employment or referral agency, labor union, ... an organization providing fringe benefits to an employee of the covered entity, or an organization providing training and apprenticeship programs);

    (3) utilizing standards, criteria, or methods of administration—

        (A) that have the effect of discrimination on the basis of disability; or

        (B) that perpetuate the discrimination of others who are subject to common administrative control;

    (4) excluding or otherwise denying equal jobs or benefits to a qualified individual because of the known disability of an individual with whom the qualified individual is known to have a relationship or association;

(5) (A) not making reasonable accommodations to the known physical or mental limitations of an otherwise qualified individual with a disability who is an applicant or employee, unless such covered entity can demonstrate that the accommodation would impose an undue hardship on the operation of the business of such covered entity; or

(B) denying employment opportunities to a job applicant or employee who is an otherwise qualified individual with a disability, if such denial is based on the need of such covered entity to make reasonable accommodation to the physical and mental impairments of the employee or applicant;

(6) using qualification standards, employment tests or other selection criteria that screen out or tend to screen out an individual with a disability or a class of individuals with disabilities unless the standard, test or other selection criteria, as used by the covered entity, is shown to be job-related for the position in question and is consistent with business necessity; and

(7) failing to select and administer tests concerning employment in the most effective manner to ensure that, when such test is administered to a job applicant or employee who has a disability that impairs sensory, manual, or speaking skills, such test results accurately reflect the skills, aptitude, or whatever other factors of such applicant or employee that such test purports to measure, rather than reflecting the impaired sensory, manual or speaking skills of such employee or applicant (except where such skills are the factors that the test purports to measure).

(c) MEDICAL EXAMINATIONS AND INQUIRIES.—...

(A) PROHIBITED EXAMINATIONS OR INQUIRY.—... [A] covered entity shall not conduct a medical examination or make inquiries of a job applicant as to whether such applicant is an individual with a disability or as to the nature or severity of such disability.

(B) ACCEPTABLE INQUIRY.—A covered entity may make pre-employment inquiries into the ability of an applicant to perform job-related functions. ...

(4) EXAMINATION AND INQUIRY—

(A) PROHIBITED EXAMINATIONS AND INQUIRIES.—A covered entity shall not ... make inquiries of an employee as to whether such employee is an individual with a disability or as to the nature or severity of the disability, unless such examination or inquiry is shown to be job-related and consistent with business necessity.

(B) ACCEPTABLE EXAMINATIONS AND INQUIRIES.—... A covered entity may make inquiries into the ability of an employee to perform job-related functions. ...

§ 103. DEFENSES

(a) IN GENERAL.—It may be a defense to a charge of discrimination under this Act that an alleged application of qualification standards, tests, or selection criteria that screen out or tend to screen out or otherwise deny a job or benefit to an individual with a disability has been shown to be job-related and consistent with business necessity, and such performance cannot be accomplished by reasonable accommodation, as required under this title.

(b) QUALIFICATION STANDARDS.—The term "qualification standards" may include a requirement that an individual shall not pose a direct threat to the health or safety of other individuals in the workplace. ...

(d) LIST OF INFECTIOUS AND COMMUNICABLE DISEASES.—

(1) IN GENERAL.—The Secretary of Health and Human Services, shall ...

(B) publish a list of infectious and communicable diseases which are transmitted through handling the food supply; ...

Such list shall be updated annually.

(2) APPLICATIONS.—In any case in which an individual has an infectious or communicable disease that is transmitted to others through the handling of food, that is included on the list developed by the Secretary of Health and Human Services ... and which cannot be eliminated by reasonable accommodation, a covered entity may refuse to assign or continue to assign such individual to a job involving food handling. ...

§ 104. ILLEGAL USE OF DRUGS AND ALCOHOL

(a) QUALIFIED INDIVIDUAL WITH A DISABILITY.—For purposes of this title, the term "qualified individual with a disability" shall not include any employee or applicant who is currently engaging in the illegal use of drugs, when the covered entity acts on the basis of such use.

(b) RULES OF CONSTRUCTION.—Nothing in subsection (a) shall be construed to exclude as a qualified individual with a disability an individual who—

(1) has successfully completed a supervised drug rehabilitation program and is no longer engaging in the illegal use of drugs, or has otherwise been rehabilitated successfully and is no longer engaging in such use;

(2) is participating in a supervised rehabilitation program and is no longer engaging in such use; or

(3) is erroneously regarded as engaging in such use, but is not engaging in such use; except that it shall not be a violation of this Act for a covered entity to adopt or administer reasonable policies or procedures, including but not limited to drug testing, designed to ensure that an individual described in paragraph (1) or (2) is no longer engaging in the illegal use of drugs.

(c) AUTHORITY OF COVERED ENTITY.—A covered entity—

(1) may prohibit the illegal use of drugs and the use of alcohol at the workplace by all employees;

(2) may require that employees shall not be under the influence of alcohol or be engaging in the illegal use of drugs at the workplace; ...

§ 105. POSTING NOTICES

Every employer, employment agency, labor organization, or joint labor-management committee covered under this title shall post notices in an accessible format to applicants, employees, and members describing the applicable provisions of this Act, ...

TITLE III—PUBLIC ACCOMMODATIONS AND SERVICES OPERATED BY PRIVATE ENTITIES

§ 301. DEFINITIONS. As used in this title:

(7)   PUBLIC ACCOMMODATION.—The following private entities are considered public accommodations for purposes of this title, if the operations of such entities affect commerce—

(A) an inn, hotel, motel, or other place of lodging, except for an establishment located within a building that contains not more than five rooms for rent or hire and that is actually occupied by the proprietor of such establishment as the residence of such proprietor;

(B) a restaurant, bar, or other establishment serving food or drink;

(C) a motion picture house, theater, concert hall, stadium, or other place of exhibition or entertainment;

(D) an auditorium, convention center, lecture hall, or other place of public gathering; ...

  (I) a park, zoo, amusement park, or other place of recreation; ...

  (L) a gymnasium, health spa, bowling alley, golf course, or other place of exercise or recreation.

(9)   READILY ACHIEVABLE.—The term "readily achievable" means easily accomplishable and able to be carried out without much difficulty or expense. In determining whether an action is readily achievable, factors to be considered include—

(A) the nature and cost of the action needed under this Act;

(B) the overall financial resources of the facility or facilities involved in the action; the number of persons employed at such facility; the effect on expenses and resources, or the impact otherwise of such action upon the operation of the facility;

(C) the overall financial resources of the covered entity; the overall size of the business of a covered entity with respect to the number of its employees; the number, type, and location of its facilities; and

(D) the type of operation or operations of the covered entity, including the composition, structure, and functions of the work force of such entity; the geographic separateness, administrative or fiscal relationship of the facility or facilities in question to the covered entity. ...

§ 302. PROHIBITION OF DISCRIMINATION BY PUBLIC ACCOMMODATIONS

(a)   GENERAL RULE.—No individual shall be discriminated on the basis of disability in the full and equal enjoyment of the goods, services, facilities, privileges, advantages, or accommodations of any place of public accommodation by any person who owns, leases (or leases to), or operates a place of public accommodation.

(b) CONSTRUCTION ...

(i) DENIAL OF PARTICIPATION.—It shall be discriminatory to subject an individual or class of individuals on the basis of a disability or disabilities of such individual or class, directly, or through contractual, licensing, or other arrangements, to a denial of the opportunity of the individual or class to participate in or benefit from the goods, services, facilities, privileges, advantages, or accommodations of an entity.

(ii) PARTICIPATION IN UNEQUAL BENEFIT.—It shall be discriminatory to afford an individual or class of individuals, on the basis of a disability or disabilities of such individual or class, directly, or through contractual, licensing, or other arrangements with the opportunity to participate in or benefit from a good, service, facility, privilege, advantage, or accommodation that is not equal to that afforded to other individuals.

(iii) SEPARATE BENEFIT.—It shall be discriminatory to provide an individual or class of individuals, on the basis of a disability or disabilities of such individual or class, directly or through contractual, licensing, or other arrangements with a good, service, facility, privilege, advantage, or accommodation that is different or separate from that provided to other individuals, unless such action is necessary to provide the individual or class of individuals with a good, service, facility, privilege, advantage, or accommodation, or other opportunity that is as effective as that provided to others. ...

(B) INTEGRATED SETTINGS.—Goods, services, facilities, privileges, advantages, and accommodations shall be afforded to an individual with a disability in the most integrated setting appropriate to the needs of the individual. ...

(D) ADMINISTRATIVE METHODS.—An individual or entity shall not, directly or through contractual or other arrangements, utilize standards, or criteria or methods of administration—

(i) that have the effect of discriminating on the basis of disability; or

(ii) that perpetuate the discrimination of others who are subject to common administrative control.

(E) ASSOCIATION.—It shall be discriminatory to exclude or otherwise deny equal goods, services, facilities, privileges, advantages, accommodations, or other opportunities to an individual or entity because of the known disability of an individual with whom the individual or entity is known to have a relationship or association.

(2) SPECIFIC PROHIBITIONS.

(A) DISCRIMINATION.—For purposes of subsection (a), discrimination includes—

(i) the imposition or application of eligibility criteria that screen out or tend to screen out an individual with a disability or any class of individuals with disabilities from fully and equally enjoying any goods, services, facilities, privileges, advantages, or accommodations, unless such criteria can be shown to be necessary for the provision of the goods, services, facilities, privileges, advantages, or accommodations being offered;

(ii) a failure to make reasonable modifications in policies, practices, or procedures, when such modifications are necessary to afford such goods, services, facilities, privileges, advantages, or accommodations to individuals with disabilities, unless the entity can demonstrate that making such modifications would fundamentally alter the nature of such goods, services, facilities, privileges, advantages, or accommodations;

(iii) a failure to take such steps as may be necessary to ensure that no individual with a disability is excluded, denied services, segregated or otherwise treated differently than other individuals because of the absence of auxiliary aids and services, unless the entity can demonstrate that taking such steps would fundamentally alter the nature of the good, service, facility, privilege, advantage, or accommodation being offered or would result in an undue burden;

(iv) a failure to remove architectural barriers, and communication barriers that are structural in nature, in existing facilities, and transportation barriers in existing vehicles and rail passenger cars used by an establishment for transporting individuals (not including barriers that can only be removed through the retrofitting of vehicles or rail passenger cars by the installation of a hydraulic or other lift), where such removal is readily achievable; and

(v) where an entity can demonstrate that the removal of a barrier under clause (iv) is not readily achievable, a failure to make such goods, service, facilities, privileges, advantages, or accommodations available through alternative methods if such methods are readily achievable. ...

(C) DEMAND RESPONSIVE SYSTEM.—For purposes of subsection (a), discrimination includes ...

(ii) the purchase or lease by [a private entity] that provides transportation on an as-needed basis and not along a prescribed route with a fixed schedule for use on such system of a vehicle with a seating capacity in excess of 16 passengers (including the driver), ... that is not readily accessible to and usable by individuals with disabilities (including individuals who use wheelchairs) unless such entity can demonstrate that such system, when viewed in its entirety, provides a level of service to individuals with disabilities equivalent to that provided to individuals without disabilities.

§ 303. NEW CONSTRUCTION AND ALTERATIONS IN PUBLIC ACCOMMODATIONS AND COMMERCIAL FACILITIES

(a) APPLICATION OF TERM.—...[D]iscrimination for purposes of section 302(a) includes—

(1) a failure to design and construct [new] facilities ... that are readily accessible to and usable by individuals with disabilities, except where an entity can demonstrate that it is structurally impracticable to meet the requirements of such subsection in accordance with standards set forth or incorporated by reference in regulations issued under this title; and

(2) with respect to a facility or part thereof that is altered by, on behalf of, or for the use of an establishment in a manner that affects or could affect the usability of the facility or part thereof, a failure to make alterations in such a manner that, to the maximum extent feasible, the altered portions of the facility are readily accessible to and usable by individuals with disabilities, including individuals who use wheelchairs. Where the entity is undertaking an alteration that affects or could affect usability of or access to an area of the facility containing a primary function, the entity shall also make the alterations in such a manner that, to the maximum extent feasible, the path of travel to the altered area and the bathrooms, telephones, and drinking fountains serving the altered area, are readily accessible to and usable by individuals with disabilities where such alterations to the path of travel or the bathrooms, telephones, and drinking fountains serving the altered area are not disproportionate to the overall alterations in terms of cost and scope (as determined under criteria established by the Attorney General).

(b) ELEVATOR.—Subsection (a) shall not be construed to require the installation of an elevator for facilities that are less than three stories or have less than 3,000 square feet per story unless the building is a shopping center, a shopping mall, or the professional office of a health care provider or unless the Attorney General determines that a particular category of such facilities requires the installation of elevators based on the usage of such facilities. ...

§ 307. EXEMPTIONS FOR PRIVATE CLUBS AND RELIGIOUS ORGANIZATIONS

The provisions of this title shall not apply to private clubs or establishments exempted from coverage under ... the Civil Rights Act of 1964 or to religious organizations or entities controlled by religious organizations, including places of worship.

§ 308. ENFORCEMENT

(a) IN GENERAL.—...

(2) INJUNCTIVE RELIEF.—In the case of violations of sections 302(b)(2)(A)(iv) and section 303(a), injunctive relief shall include an order to alter facilities to make such facilities readily accessible to and usable by individuals with disabilities to the extent required by this title. Where appropriate, injunctive relief shall also include requiring the provision of an auxiliary aid or service, modification of a policy, or provision of alternative methods, to the extent required by this title.

(b) ENFORCEMENT BY THE ATTORNEY GENERAL.—

    (i) IN GENERAL.—The Attorney General shall investigate alleged violations of this title, and shall undertake periodic reviews of compliance of covered entities under this title.

    (B) POTENTIAL VIOLATION.—If the Attorney General has reasonable cause to believe that

        (i) any person or group of persons is engaged in a pattern or practice of discrimination under this title; or

        (ii) any person or group of persons has been discriminated against under this title and such discrimination raises an issue of general public importance, the Attorney General may commence a civil action in any appropriate United States district court.

(2) AUTHORITY OF COURT.—In a civil action under paragraph (1)(B), the court—

    (A) may grant any equitable relief that such court considers to be appropriate, including to the extent required by this title—

        (i) granting temporary, preliminary, or permanent relief—

        (ii) providing an auxiliary aid or service, modification of policy, practice, or procedure, or alternative method; and

        (iii) making facilities readily accessible to and usable by individuals with disabilities.

    (B) may award such other relief as the court considers to be appropriate, including monetary damages to persons aggrieved when requested by the Attorney General; and

    (C) may, to vindicate the public interest, assess a civil penalty against the entity in an amount—

        (i) not exceeding $50,000 for a first violation; and

        (ii) not exceeding $100,000 for any subsequent violation ...

(4) PUNITIVE DAMAGES.—For purposes of subsection (b)(2)(B), the term "monetary damages" and "such other relief" does not include punitive damages.

(5) JUDICIAL CONSIDERATION.—In a civil action under paragraph (1)(B), the court, when considering what amount of civil penalty, if any, is appropriate, shall give consideration to any good faith effort or attempt to comply with this Act by the entity. In evaluating good faith, the court shall consider, among other factors it deems relevant, whether the entity could have reasonably anticipated the need for an appropriate type of auxiliary aid needed to accommodate the unique needs of a particular individual with a disability. ...

APPENDIX D

■

Immigration Reform and Control Act

[EXCERPTS]

Unlawful Employment of Aliens

§ 274A. (a) "8 U.S.C. 1324a" MAKING EMPLOYMENT OF UNAUTHORIZED ALIENS UNLAWFUL.—

(1) IN GENERAL.—It is unlawful for a person or other entity to hire, or to recruit or refer for a fee, for employment in the United States—

(A) an alien knowing the alien is an unauthorized alien (as defined in subsection (h)(3)) with respect to such employment, or

(B) an individual without complying with the requirements of subsection (b).

(2) CONTINUING EMPLOYMENT.—It is unlawful for a person or other entity, after hiring an alien for employment in accordance with paragraph (1), to continue to employ the alien in the United States knowing the alien is (or has become) an unauthorized alien with respect to such employment.

(3) DEFENSE.—A person or entity that establishes that it has complied in good faith with the requirements of subsection (b) with respect to the hiring, recruiting, or referral for employment of an alien in the United States has established an affirmative defense that the person or entity has not violated paragraph (1)(A) with respect to such hiring, recruiting, or referral.

(4) USE OF LABOR THROUGH CONTRACT.—For purposes of this section, a person or other entity who uses a contract, subcontract, or exchange, entered into, renegotiated, or extended after the date of the enactment of this section, to obtain the labor of an alien in the United States knowing that the alien is an unauthorized alien with respect to performing such labor, shall be considered to have hired the alien for employment in the United States in violation of paragraph (1)(A).

***

(b) EMPLOYMENT VERIFICATION SYSTEM.—The requirements referred to in paragraphs (1)(B) and (3) of subsection (a) are, in the case of a person or other entity hiring, recruiting, or referring an individual for employment in the United States, the requirements specified in the following three paragraphs:

(1) ATTESTATION AFTER EXAMINATION OF DOCUMENT.—
(A) IN GENERAL.—The person or entity must attest, under penalty of perjury and on a form designated or established by the Attorney General by regulation, that it has verified that the individual is not an unauthorized alien by examining
  (i) a document described in subparagraph (B), or
  (ii) a document described in subparagraph (C) and a document described in subparagraph (D).
  A person or entity has complied with the requirement of this paragraph with respect to examination of a document if the document reasonably appears on its face to be genuine. If an individual provides a document or combination of documents that reasonably appears on its face to be genuine and that is sufficient to meet the requirements of such sentence, nothing in this paragraph shall be construed as requiring the person or entity to solicit the production of any other document or as requiring the individual to produce such another document.
(B) DOCUMENTS ESTABLISHING BOTH EMPLOYMENT AUTHORIZATION AND IDENTITY.—A document described in this subparagraph is an individual's—
  (i) United States passport;
  (ii) certificate of United States citizenship;
  (iii) certificate of naturalization;
  (iv) unexpired foreign passport, if the passport has an appropriate, unexpired endorsement of the Attorney General authorizing the individual's employment in the United States; or
  (v) resident alien card or other alien registration card, if the card—
    (I) contains a photograph of the individual and such other personal identifying information relating to the individual as the Attorney General finds, by regulation, sufficient for purposes of this subsection, and
    (II) is evidence of authorization of employment in the United States.
(C) DOCUMENTS EVIDENCING EMPLOYMENT AUTHORIZATION.—A document described in this subparagraph is an individual's—
  (i) social security account number card (other than such a card which specifies on the face that the issuance of the card does not authorize employment in the United States);

       (ii) certificate of birth in the United States or establishing United States nationality at birth, which certificate the Attorney General finds, by regulation, to be acceptable for purposes of this section; or

      (iii) other documentation evidencing authorization of employment in the United States which the Attorney General finds, by regulation, to be acceptable for purposes of this section.

  (D) DOCUMENTS ESTABLISHING IDENTITY OF INDIVIDUAL.— A document described in this subparagraph is an individual's—

      (i) driver's license or similar document issued for the purpose of identification by a State, if it contains a photograph of the individual or such other personal identifying information relating to the individual as the Attorney General finds, by regulation, sufficient for purposes of this section; or

      (ii) in the case of individuals under 16 years of age or in a State which does not provide for issuance of an identification document (other than a driver's license) referred to in clause (ii), documentation of personal identity of such other type as the Attorney General finds, by regulation, provides a reliable means of identification.

(2) INDIVIDUAL ATTESTATION OF EMPLOYMENT AUTHORIZATION.— The individual must attest, under penalty of perjury on the form designated or established for purposes of paragraph (1), that the individual is a citizen or national of the United States, an alien lawfully admitted for permanent residence, or an alien who is authorized under this Act or by the Attorney General to be hired, recruited, or referred for such employment.

(3) RETENTION OF VERIFICATION FORM.—After completion of such form in accordance with paragraphs (1) and (2), the person or entity must retain the form and make it available for inspection by officers of the Service or the Department of Labor during a period beginning on the date of the hiring, recruiting, or referral of the individual and ending—

  (A) in the case of the recruiting or referral for a fee (without hiring) of an individual, three years after the date of the recruiting or referral, and

  (B) in the case of the hiring of an individual—

      (i) three years after the date of such hiring, or

      (ii) one year after the date the individual's employment is terminated, whichever is later.

APPENDIX E

■

Family and Medical Leave Act

[INFORMATION]

(From Title 29, Code of Federal Regulations § 825.100)

§ 825.100 What is the Family and Medical Leave Act?

(a) The Family and Medical Leave Act of 1993 (FMLA or Act) allows "eligible" employees of a covered employer to take job-protected, unpaid leave, or to substitute appropriate paid leave if the employee has earned or accrued it, for up to a total of 12 workweeks in any 12 months because of the birth of a child and to care for the newborn child, because of the placement of a child with the employee for adoption or foster care, because the employee is needed to care for a family member (child, spouse, or parent) with a serious health condition, or because the employee's own serious health condition makes the employee unable to perform the functions of his or her job (see § 825.306(b)(4)). In certain cases, this leave may be taken on an intermittent basis rather than all at once, or the employee may work a part-time schedule.

(b) An employee on FMLA leave is also entitled to have health benefits maintained while on leave as if the employee had continued to work instead of taking the leave. If an employee was paying all or part of the premium payments prior to leave, the employee would continue to pay his or her share during the leave period. The employer may recover its share only if the employee does not return to work for a reason other than the serious health condition of the employee or the employee's immediate family member, or another reason beyond the employee's control.

(c) An employee generally has a right to return to the same position or an equivalent position with equivalent pay, benefits and working conditions at the conclusion of the leave. The taking of FMLA leave cannot result in the loss of any benefit that accrued prior to the start of the leave.

(d) The employer has a right to 30 days advance notice from the employee where practicable. In addition, the employer may require an employee to submit certification from a health care provider to substantiate that the leave is due to the serious health condition of the employee or the employee's immediate family member. Failure to comply with these requirements may result in a delay in the start of FMLA leave. Pursuant to a uniformly applied policy, the employer may also require that an employee present a certification of fitness to return to work when the absence was caused by the employee's serious health condition (see § 825.311(c)). The employer may delay restoring the employee to employment without such certificate relating to the health condition which caused the employee's absence.

APPENDIX F

Minimum Wage Law in the United States

The federal minimum wage is $5.15 per hour. If a state minimum-wage rate differs from the federal minimum, the higher amount applies. The following details minimum wage's by state.

State	State Minimum Wage	Comparison with Federal Minimum Wage
Alabama	No state minimum-wage law	
Alaska	$5.65*	Higher
Arizona	No state minimum-wage law	
Arkansas	$5.15	Same
California	$6.75	Higher
Colorado	$5.15	Same
Connecticut	$6.70	Higher
Delaware	$6.15	Higher
Florida	No state minimum-wage law	
Georgia	$5.15	Same
Guam	$5.15**	Same
Hawaii	$6.25	Higher
Idaho	$5.15	Same
Illinois	$5.15**	Same
Indiana	$5.15	Same
Iowa	$5.15	Same
Kansas	$2.65	Lower
Kentucky	$5.15**	Same
Louisiana	No state minimum-wage law	
Maine	$6.25	Higher
Maryland	$5.15**	Same
Massachusetts	$6.75	Higher
Michigan	$5.15	Same

State	State Minimum Wage	Comparison with Federal Minimum Wage
Minnesota	$5.15	Same
Mississippi	No state minimum-wage law	
Missouri	$5.15**	Same
Montana	$5.15**	Same
Nebraska	$5.15	Same
Nevada	$5.15**	Same
New Hampshire	$5.15	Same
New Jersey	$5.15**	Same
New Mexico	$4.25	Lower
New York	$5.15	Same
North Carolina	$5.15**	Same
North Dakota	$5.15	Same
Ohio	$4.25	Lower
Oklahoma	$5.15**	Same
Oregon	$6.50	Higher
Pennsylvania	$5.15**	Same
Puerto Rico	$3.61—$5.15	Lower to same
Rhode Island	$6.15	Higher
South Carolina	No state minimum-wage law	
South Dakota	$5.15	Same
Tennessee	No state minimum-wage law	
Texas	$5.15**	Same
Utah	$5.15**	Same
Vermont	$6.25	Higher
Virginia	$5.15**	Same
Virgin Islands	$4.65	Lower
Washington	$6.90	Higher
Washington, DC	$6.15***	Higher
West Virginia	$5.15	Same
Wisconsin	$5.15	Same
Wyoming	$5.15	Same

   * The Alaskan minimum wage is automatically set at 50 cents above the federal minimum.
  ** This state (or territory) adopts the federal minimum-wage rate.
*** The minimum wage of Washington, DC, is automatically set at one dollar above the federal minimum.

GLOSSARY

A

ab initio "From the beginning" (Latin).

abrogate The destruction, ending, or annulling of a former law.

absolute contractual obligation A commitment in a contract, the breach of which will render the promising party liable for breach of contract.

absolute liability *See* strict liability.

acceptance An expression of agreement by the offeree to the terms of an offer.

accessory A person who had some part in a crime without being present.

accessory before the fact A person who, without being present, encourages or helps someone commit a crime.

accessory after the fact A person who condones a crime by concealing it or the criminal.

accord and satisfaction Agreement to settle or compromise a claim and satisfactory payment of the amount agreed upon.

action A lawsuit.

action ex delicto "Action arising out of a tort" (Latin).

act of God A happening not controlled by the power of humans, but rather from the direct, immediate, and exclusive operations of the forces of nature.

actual notice Notice expressly and directly given to a person.

additur An increase provided by the courts to an award of damages to the plaintiff.

adduce To offer an example or a reason.

adjudication The legal process of resolving a dispute.

administrative agency A governmental subdivision charged with administering legislation that applies to a particular industry.

administrative law Laws that impact administrative agencies.

admissible evidence Evidence that is allowed to be used by the triers of fact in a court proceeding.

adversary system Any system similar to that of the United States, Canada, or England where the judge makes the decisions between opposing parties.

adverse Opposed to or against one's position or interest.

affidavit A written statement that has been sworn to before an officer who is permitted by law to administer such an oath.

affirmative defense A defense that introduces new matters that, even if the plaintiff's contentions are true, constitute a defense to the complaint.

a fortiori With a greater force; said of a conclusion that, as compared with some other, is even more certain or necessary.

agency A relationship in which one person (the agent) acts for another (the principal) based on authority voluntarily given.

agent A person authorized by a principal to act on the principal's behalf under the principal's direction.

agreement not to compete In the sale of a business, a contractual provision barring the seller from competing with the buyer in the geographical area where the business is located for a specified period of time.

allegation In pleading, that which a person will attempt to prove; an unproven assertion.

allege To assert before proving.

alternative pleading Alleges claims that constitute conflicting courses of action.

ambience Atmosphere or environment; the mood or sentiment evoked by a place.

amicus curiae "Friends of the court" (Latin); usually one who is not a party to the lawsuit but who is permitted to give the court information that is in doubt or would not otherwise be considered by the court, or to advise the court in respect to some matter of law that directly affects the case in question.

annul To cancel a relationship as if it never was.

anticipatory breach A breach committed before the arrival of the actual time of required performance.

antitrust laws Laws that attempt to ensure that open competition is preserved.

appeal A review by one court of the decision of another court, initiated by the party who lost in the prior court; a complaint made by a litigant to a superior court that a trial judge committed an error, and a request that the superior court correct the error.

appearance The coming into court as a party plaintiff or defendant to a lawsuit.

appellant The party involved in an appeal that initiated the appeal.

appellate court A court with the authority to review the handling and decisions of a case tried in a lower court.

appellee The party involved in an appeal that did not initiate the appeal.

appreciation An increase in value.

appurtenance Attached to something else.

arbitration The process of dispute resolution by an arbitrator chosen by the parties to decide the case.

arbitrator An objective third party chosen by litigants to decide their dispute out of court.

arguendo Purely for the sake of argument; the parties assume something as true, whether or not it is.

arraigned To be brought before a court to hear and assume the charges and to plead guilty or not guilty.

arrest Deprive a person of liberty because of criminal charges or detain a person for some reason that may involve force.

arrogate Claim or take something without having any right to it; to usurp or appropriate as one's own.

assault The tort of intentionally putting someone in fear of harmful physical contact, such as making a fist in a way suggestive of an imminent punch. (Compare to battery.) Also, the crime of intentionally causing physical injury to another person.

assumpsit An action of equitable character founded upon contract.

attachment A writ to seize (take and hold) by legal procedure.

attempt to commit An intent to commit an act combined with some action that moves beyond mere preparation.

attractive nuisance A potentially dangerous object or condition of exceptional interest to young people.

attrition clause In reference to a room reservation contract between an association hosting a convention and a hotel, a contractual provision obligating the organization to compensate the hotel if less than a specified number of rooms are rented by conventioneers.

aver Allege, assert, verify, or justify as in a formal complaint.

averment A statement of the allegations.

B

baggage That which a person travels with while on a journey of either short or long duration.

bail Valuables, usually money or property, that are put up for release of a person in jail.

bailee The person receiving possession of goods or personal property.

bailment A transfer of possession of goods or personal property from a person in possession of the property to another with the understanding that the property will be returned.

bailor The owner of goods or personal property who transfers such property to a bailee.

battery The tort of causing harmful physical contact to a person, such as punching someone. (Compare assault.)

beneficiary The receiver of some benefit or advantage.

best evidence rule A rule of evidence that requires the most persuasive evidence be used; original documents, not copies, must be made.

bill of exceptions A written statement submitted to a trial court stating all objections made to the rulings of or instructions given by the trial judge.

blue laws A law that forbids certain activities, such as the sale of certain goods, on Sunday.

boiler plate forms A preprinted form for a document that is usually sold commercially and that is standardized without tailoring to individual legal problems.

bona fide "In ood faith" (Latin).

bone fide occupational qualification (BFOQ) A job qualification that legally discriminates on the basis of race, religion, national origin, or gender because (1) excluded classes cannot perform the job effectively, (2) such inability is factually supported, and (3) the job classification is reasonably necessary for the normal operation of the business.

breach The failure of performance by a party of some contracted-for or agreed-upon act.

brief A written statement of a person's case to be submitted to a court, usually including a summary of the law involved in the case; a condensed statement of facts, and arguments regarding how the law applies to the facts.

burden of proof The required amount of evidence for the plaintiff to win a lawsuit. In civil cases, the proof required is a preponderance of the evidence; in criminal cases, the proof must be beyond a reasonable doubt.

burglary Entering a building unlawfully with the intent to commit a crime therein.

business judgment rule The principle that bad results—if made in an honest, careful manner by corporate powers—will not be interfered with by the courts.

"but for" rule Primarily refers to the question, Would the accident or happening have occurred "but for" the negligence involved?

C

capacity to contract The ability to understand the terms of a contract and to understand also that failure to perform its terms can lead to legal liability.

case books Books in which decisions are published.

case decision An interpretation of the law applied by a judge to a set of facts in a given case.

case method or system The study of actual cases (opinion of the court) and the drawing of a general legal principal based on other similar cases.

cases Written decisions by judges.

cashier check A prepaid check issued by a bank that authorizes on-demand payment to the payee of the stipulated sum of the check.

cause of action The legal basis on which to bring a lawsuit.

caveat "Let him beware" (Latin); usually used with another word such as *emptor* ("buyer"). Expresses the general idea that the buyer purchased at his or her peril, and no warranties (expressed or implied) are included by the seller.

certified check A check containing a certification that funds are available for the amount of the check.

certiorari An appeal to a higher court, but one that the court need not accept.

chattel Any property other than land; includes personal property and animals.

check A draft upon a bank and payable on demand, signed by the maker as an unconditional promise to pay a stated amount to the order of the payee.

citation A reference to a legal authority such as a court decision, statute, or treatise.

citator A set of books (such as *Shepard's Citator*) that traces the history of a statute or case since it was passed or ruled on.

civil action A lawsuit brought by one person against another, usually seeking monetary damages.

civil contempt Usually the failure to do something that the court orders done for the benefit of another party.

civil rights Personal rights that derive primarily from the Constitution, for example, equal protection, free speech, freedom of contract, privacy, and due process.

claim A demand for a remedy, usually money, to compensate for a perceived wrong.

class action A lawsuit brought by a group of persons who are similarly situated.

clean hands doctrine A doctrine that will not allow equitable relief to a person bringing a lawsuit who has been guilty of impropriety in the case.

code A compilation of laws such as the Uniform Commercial Code.

cognizance Right of a court to take action.

cohabitation Living together; often refers to an unmarried couple living together and having sexual intercourse.

collusion Action by two or more persons together for the purpose of committing a fraud.

common carrier One who transports for hire.

common law Legal rules that evolved in England from decisions of judges and from customs and practices that were intended to be common or uniform for the entire English kingdom obtained their authority from the test of time. Also refers to judges' decisions as opposed to statutory law.

common law marriage A marriage created by a couple publicly living together as married for a time period sufficient to create a legal marriage.

common victualler A keeper of a restaurant.

comparable worth The concept that two jobs requiring different skills and responsibilities have equal value to the employer. Courts have rejected the concept that comparable worth requires equal pay.

comparative negligence The rule followed in some states apportioning damages according to the comparative contribution of the negligence of the parties. A jury will allocate the liability between the plaintiff and the defendant depending on their degree of culpability based on a total of 100 percent.

compensatory damages Out-of-pocket expenses including doctor bills and lost wages, and compensation for pain and suffering, loss of enjoyment of life, loss of consortium, and loss of services.

complainant The originator of a lawsuit; the plaintiff.

complaint The initial pleading filed in court in a civil lawsuit consisting of a statement of the wrong or harm allegedly done to the plaintiff by the defendant and a request for specific help from the court.

conclusion of law Application of a rule of law to a set of facts.

condition An event on which a contractual duty is contingent.

condition precedent A right or obligation *created* if a certain future event happens.

condition subsequent A right or obligation *ended* if a certain future event happens.

condominium A form of separate ownership of individual units in a multiunit development where parts of the development are owned as tenants in common.

confession of judgment A method of permitting a judgment to be entered by consent against a person in advance of his default on his debt, for a stipulated sum, without the formality, time, or expense of an ordinary legal proceeding.

conflicts of law Variations that exist between different laws of the same state or sovereignty upon the same subject matter; when a choice exists between laws of more than one state, in which case the judge makes the decision as to applicable law.

Congress The primary law-making body of the federal government.

consanguinity Blood relationship, kinship.

consent To agree.

consideration Something of value exchanged for something else of value.

consortium The right of a married couple to each other's love and services.

conspicuous Out in the open; easily seen.

constitutional law The law embodied in the federal constitution, prescribing the organization and powers of the federal government, and defining rights of the people.

constructive The opposite of actual, wherein a law is accepted as a substitute for what is otherwise required.

constructive bailment Bailment created by law rather than by the parties agreeing.

constructive notice Information or knowledge of a fact imputed to a person by law because he or she could have discovered the fact by proper diligence or because the situation was such as to put upon such person the duty of inquiry.

contempt Any action by a person or persons to obstruct a court's work or lessen the dignity of the court—for example, disobeying a court order or an official of the court.

contract An agreement between two or more people that is enforceable in court.

contract (voidable) A contract that may be canceled at the option of one party.

contributory negligence The rule followed in some states that prevents a plaintiff from collecting damages if the plaintiff's negligence contributed to the injury.

conversion Action that deprives owners of the property that legally belongs to them.

copyright The exclusive right of a creator or other copyright owner to reproduce and license (authorize) the reproduction of the following: literature, art, music, drama, sculpture, choreography, motion pictures, computer software, and other audiovisual works including broadcasts of sporting events.

corporate veil An assumption that all action by the corporation is not that of the owners and therefore not impugned to the corporate officers.

corporation An organization that is formed under state or federal law and exists, for legal purposes, as a separate being or an "artificial person."

corpus delicti "Body of the crime" (Latin); facts that prove a crime has been committed.

counteroffer A response to an offer that modifies one or more of its provisions.

court The place where judges work; also refers to the judge.

criminal contempt Acts of disrespect of the courts or its processes.

criminal possession of stolen property Act of knowingly taking possession of stolen property with intent to benefit someone other than the owner.

D

damages The remedy sought by the injured party in a civil case.

declaratory relief Establishes the rights of the parties or expresses the opinion of the court on a question of law without ordering anything to be done.

decree A judgment by a court as to its decision on the facts of the case; the power of the court derived from its equity jurisdiction.

defamation The tort of making false written statements about someone to a third person when those statements subject the former to ridicule or scorn.

defendant The party who is sued in a lawsuit by the plaintiff.

defraud To cheat or trick, intentionally misrepresenting an important fact intending for someone to rely on the misrepresentation and thereby suffer damages.

delegated powers Those powers expressly allocated to the federal government in the Constitution.

demeanor Physical appearance and behavior.

de minimus Insignificant, minute, or frivolous.

demise A term used to describe a conveyance of an estate in real property.

demurrer A method of pleading that asserts that the allegations in the complaint are insufficient to constitute a cause of action.

derogation Partial taking away of the effectiveness of a law; to repeal partially or abolish a law.

disability (as defined by the Americans with Disabilities Act) A physical or mental impairment that substantially limits a person's ability to walk, see, hear, perform manual tasks, learn, work, or care for him/herself.

disclaimer A term in a contract that attempts to avoid all liability on the part of one party.

discrimination The act of treating some people different from and less favorably than others.

disparate impact Neutral employment practices that unintentionally result in unequal treatment.

disparate treatment Intentional discrimination based on race, color, religion, gender, or national origin.

discovery The process by which each side obtains evidence known to the other side.

dissolution The termination of business operations, sometimes applied as a penalty for antitrust violations.

diversity of citizenship Takes place in a federal court when the plaintiff is a resident of one state and the defendant is a resident of another.

divestiture The act of giving up part of a business operation, sometimes imposed as a penalty for antitrust violations.

doctrine of apparent authority Authority granted by legal principals to agents to act in their behalf.

due process The right not to be deprived of life, liberty, or property without a fair hearing. With respect to licenses and regulations, this means that proprietors are entitled to reasonable notice of the grounds for any proposed legal action, an opportunity to prepare a defense, and a hearing.

duty A responsibility imposed by law, the disregard for which can lead to liability.

E

effects Personal property; in hotel law usually refers to a traveler's baggage.

enjoin Require or command; a court's issuing of an injunction directing a person or persons to do, or more likely, to refrain from doing certain acts; to restrain.

entity A real being; a separate existence.

equitable estoppel A legal principle that precludes a person from claiming a right or benefit that might otherwise have existed because that person made a false representation to a person who relied on it to his or her detriment.

equitable relief A remedy in a court of equity that is just, fair, and right for a particular situation.

equity court A court having authority over cases involving various rights or matters of equity rather than matters of the written laws or statutes.

eschew To abstain from or shun as something wrong or distasteful.

escrow A written instrument deposited with a neutral third party.

essential job functions (as defined by the Americans with Disabilities Act) The core responsibilities of a job as distinguished from marginal or incidental assignments.

estoppel A bar to alleging or denying a fact because of one's previous actions or words to the contrary.

estray Anything out of its normal place.

exclusionary rule The rule that holds evidence obtained in consequence of a warrantless search is not admissible in court.

ex contractu "From" or "out of a contract" (Latin).

exemplary damages The terms *exemplary, punitive,* and *vindictive damages* are synonymous and are awarded when the wrong done to a plaintiff is aggravated by circumstances of violence, oppression, malice, fraud, or wanton conduct.

ex parte "With only one side present" (Latin).

F

feasance Performing a duty; doing an act.

felony A crime that has a sentence of more than one year; a serious crime.

forbearance Refraining from doing something you have a legal right to do.

foreign/natural substance test A test that holds that the presence of an object natural to a food product does not breach the warranty implied in its sale. (The presence of a foreign object is a breach of warranty.)

forgery The unauthorized alteration, completion, or making of a written instrument with intent to defraud or deceive.

forum "Court" (Latin).

forum non conveniens "Inconvenient court" (Latin).

franchise An arrangement in which the owner of a trademark, service mark, or copyright licenses others, under specified conditions, to use the mark or copyright in the sale of goods or services.

franchisee The party who receives the right to use a trademark, service mark, or copyright in connection with the sale of goods or services.

franchisor The owner of a trademark, service mark, or copyright who has licensed another to use it in connection with the sale of goods or services.

fraud An intentional untruthful statement made to induce reliance by another person or for the purpose of misleading someone, usually for personal gain.

full faith and credit The constitutional requirement that each state must treat as valid, and enforce where appropriate, the laws and court decisions of other states.

G

goodwill A favorable reputation producing an expectation of future business.

government agency A government subdivision, usually appointed by elected officials, responsible for administering particular laws.

gratuities Something given voluntarily or without obligation.

gravamen The essence of a complaint.

guest room The rooms in a hotel assigned to guests for overnight stays.

guest A person who contracts for an overnight room at a hotel.

H

hospitality law Law applicable to hotels, restaurants, travel agents, airlines, and places of entertainment.

hotel, inn, motel Terms used interchangeably to refer to places that provide overnight accommodations to transients.

hung jury A jury so irreconcilably divided that it cannot reach a verdict.

I

illegal alien One who enters the United States without the necessary authorization.

illusory A contractual term that fails to contain a firm commitment; a promise that is so indefinite that the party making it has not in fact committed to do anything.

impute To assign to a person or other entity the legal responsibility for the act of another, because of the relationship between the person so made liable and the actor, rather than because of actual participation in or knowledge of the act.

in accordance with In agreement with or following a specific rule or act.

independent contractor One who contracts to do work for another, but who maintains control of the method of accomplishing the work. Also, someone hired by another to perform a given task according to methods and procedures that are independent from the control of the hiring party.

infra "Below," "beneath" (Latin); refers to something appearing subsequently in a text.

infra hospitium Meaning "within the inn." This doctrine states that under common law hotels were liable as insurers for guests' property on the hotel premises.

injunction A court order forbidding a party to a lawsuit from engaging in specified acts.

innkeepers, hoteliers, hotelkeepers Terms used interchangeably to refer to the operator or manager of a hotel.

innocent misrepresentation An untruthful statement that the speaker believes is accurate.

insurer One who is generally obligated to compensate another for losses.

inter alia "Among other things" (Latin).

interstate commerce Business affecting more than one state, as opposed to business done between two parties in the same state.

in toto "In entirety," "in total" (Latin).

invitee One who comes to an establishment for its business purpose; that is, for a purpose directly or indirectly connected with that business.

ipso facto "By the fact itself," "in and of itself" (Latin).

J

joint tenancy A single estate in property, real or personal, owned by two or more persons (under one legal paper) who have equal rights in everything during their lives.

jurisdiction The authority of a court to hear a case, as determined by the legislature.

L

landmark A court decision that sets a precedent marking a turning point in the interpretation of law.

larceny Stealing of any kind; petit larceny is usually under $1000; grand larceny over $1000.

law Rules, enforceable in court, requiring people to meet certain standards of conduct.

law court A court that administers justice according to the rules and practice of the common law and statutes, but that has no powers dealing with equitable problems.

legislative process The process by which the federal government, as well as other units of government, adopts laws.

legislators The elected members of the legislature.

legislature A law-making body whose members are elected to office by the citizenry.

lessee A person who leases or rents something from someone; a tenant.

lessor Person who leases or rents land or a building to another person.

liability Culpability; responsibility for a legal wrong obligating the wrongdoer to compensate an injured party for the consequences of the wrongful conduct.

libel Written defamation.

licensee In cases of negligence, one who does not qualify as an invitee but who has been given permission by the owner or occupier to enter or remain on the property. Also, a person who has been granted a license to engage in certain conduct, such as the sale of alcohol.

lien A charge or obligation due or owing against real or personal property for the satisfaction of a debt.

limiting liability statutes Laws that restrict an innkeepers' liability for property loss in exchange for strict statutory compliance by the innkeeper. Also called *limiting statutes.*

litigants The parties to a lawsuit.

long-arm statute A state law that allows the courts of that state to claim jurisdiction over persons or property outside the state.

M

magistrate A judge with limited power.

malfeasance Wrongdoing; sometimes doing an illegal act by a public official.

mediation The process in which litigants settle their dispute out of court by mutual agreement with the aid of a mediator.

mediator An objective third party chosen by litigants to facilitate discussion and negotiations between the parties toward settlement of the dispute out of court.

minor A person under the legal age (usually under 18).

misdemeanor A criminal offense, less than a felony, that is usually punishable by under one year in jail.

misfeasance Doing something wrong.

Mrs. Murphy's boarding house clause A stipulation that an establishment that has five or fewer rooms for rent and that is actually occupied by the proprietor is excluded from the Civil Rights Act of 1964.

mutuality of contract A principle of law that says each side must do something or promise to do something to make a contract binding and valid.

mutual mistake A mistake made by both parties.

N

negligence Breach of a legal duty to act reasonably that is the direct (or proximate) cause of injury to another.

negligence per se When a defendant has violated a law or ordinance designed to protect the safety of the public.

negligent entrustment Providing a product for use by another, knowing that person is likely to use the product in a dangerous manner.

no-cause termination clause A contract term that permits either party to terminate the contract for any or no reason.

nondelegable duty A duty that cannot be assigned (or delegated) to another.

nonfeasance Failure to perform a required duty.

novation The substitution of another party for one of the original parties to a contract with the consent of the remaining party.

nuisance Anything that unreasonably annoys or disturbs one's right to enjoy one's property, or violates the public health, safety, or standards of decency of others.

O

offer A proposal to do or give something in exchange for something else.

offeree The person to whom an offer is made.

offeror The person who makes an offer.

ordinance A law adopted by a local governmental body.

P

parol Oral or spoken.

parol evidence rule What prevents the parties from successfully modifying a complete written contract with evidence of oral agreements made prior to signing the writing.

parties The individuals in conflict in a lawsuit; also referred to as litigants. A party may be a person, a business or other private organization, or a governmental body.

patron A customer of a hotel or restaurant, including but not limited to a guest.

Peeping Tom A person who finagles access to observe activities of others that are intended to be private.

per se "In and of itself," "by itself" (Latin).

per se violations (of antitrust laws) Activities that are always considered illegal under antitrust legislation.

personal service of process The direct hand-to-hand delivery of a summons to the person being summoned.

persona non grata A person not acceptable.

petitioner One who starts an equity procedure or appeals a case.

plain view doctrine Doctrine that the observation of objects in plain view, as opposed to a search to find those objects, does not constitute an illegal search.

plaintiff The party who commences a lawsuit seeking a remedy for an injury or loss that is the responsibility of another party, the defendant.

pleadings The complaint, the answer, and the reply.

preamble Introductory comments explaining why a document was written.

precedent A court decision that becomes a basis for deciding future cases.

preventive law An approach to the study of law that has as its objective the prevention of lawsuits.

prima facie Such evidence as will suffice to establish a cause of action until contradicted and overcome by other evidence.

prima facie liability rule A rule that states that hotelkeepers are liable for property loss only if the loss occurs through their negligence; if the loss results from some other cause, the innkeeper is not liable.

principal A person who authorizes an agent to act on his or her behalf and controls or directs the method used by the agent in performing authorized tasks.

privity Private or inside knowledge or a close, direct financial relationship.

privity of contract A contractual relationship that exists between two parties.

probable cause A reasonable ground for belief in certain alleged facts; facts sufficient for a reasonably intelligent and prudent person to believe the defendant committed a crime or that evidence of a crime is located in the place the police want to search.

probation A system whereby criminal offenders remain out of jail but are supervised by a probation officer.

procedural law Rules for carrying out the lawsuit; the way to enforce rights in court such as laws of pleading, evidence, and jurisdiction.

promulgate publish; to announce officially.

proximate cause The direct and immediate foreseeable connection between a breach of duty and a resulting injury.

public domain Belonging to the general public and not subject to patent or trademark protection.

punitive damages Also called exemplary damages, money awarded to a plaintiff over and above compensatory damages, to punish or make an example of the defendant. They are awarded only in cases where the defendant's wrongful acts are aggravated by violence, malice, or fraud.

pursuant In accordance with.

R

rabbi The official leader of a Jewish congregation; similar to a minister or priest.

rape Sexual intercourse that is against the victim's will.

ratification Confirmation of a previous act.

readily achievable Easily accomplishable without great difficulty or expense.

reasonable Not excessive or extreme.

reasonable expectation test A test that examines whether an object found in food ought to have been anticipated by the consumer. If so, its presence in the food does not constitute a breach of the warranty.

rebuttal presumption A conclusion that will be drawn unless facts or arguments are raised to counter it.

register In a hotel, to make oneself known by putting down one's name; a book or cards used to keep track of guests.

regulations Laws adopted by administrative agencies.

res ipsa loquitur "The thing speaks for itself" (Latin). The doctrine that frees the plaintiff from the burden of proving the specific breach of duty committed by the defendant. It applies where an accident would not normally happen without

negligence and the instrumentality causing the injury was in the defendant's exclusive control.

reinstate To put a case back on the calendar.

remand To send back; a higher court might remand a case to a lower court for action.

remedial statute A law, the purpose of which is to correct an existing law that is not working or that has caused harm instead of good.

remuneration To pay for; to be recompensed.

replevin An action in law to get back personal property that is in the hands of another person.

reprisal To take action against.

res judicata "A thing decided" (Latin). When a case is decided by the courts, the subject of that case is finally decided between the persons involved in the suit; therefore, no further lawsuit on the same subject may be brought by the persons involved.

respondeat superior "Let the master (employer) answer" (Latin). The liability of the employer for the acts of its employees.

restaurateur The operator, owner, or manager of a restaurant.

revocation To end; to withdraw power or authority.

riparian rights Rights of a person owning land bordering a body of water.

rule of reason (applied to antitrust laws) The balancing by the court of the economic benefits and drawbacks in determining the legality of a particular business practice as it affects open competition.

S

search warrant An order from a judge commanding a police officer to search a designated place for evidence of criminal activity.

secular day A nonreligious day.

service mark Any word, name, symbol, or device adopted and used by an organization to identify its services and distinguish them from services provided by others. Compare to *trademark*.

service of process Formally notifying the defendant of the impending lawsuit by the plaintiff.

sexual harassment (1) *Quid pro quo* sexual harassment: unwelcome sexual advances or requests for sexual favors in return for job benefits. (2) *hostile environment* sexual harassment: verbal or physical conduct of a sexual nature that creates an intimidating, hostile or offensive work environment.

shepardization A method by which statutes or legal cases are updated to see whether they have been modified or overruled by court decisions or legislature; discovering the present status of statutory law, court decisions, or administrative decisions.

slander The tort of making defamatory statements orally, as opposed to in writing.

stare decisis "The matter stands decided" (Latin). The principle that courts will follow precedents when they are applicable.

statute A law adopted by the federal or state legislature.

statutory law Law passed by legislatures.

strict liability Also called *absolute liability;* the doctrine that imposes all the risks of an ultra-hazardous activity upon those who engage in it.

strict products liability The doctrine that imposes liability on the seller of a defective product without regard to negligence.

subpoena An order by a court for a person to appear in court to testify in a case.

substantive law The basic law of rights and duties as opposed to procedural law; for example, contract law, criminal law, negligence, and liquor liability.

subterfuge Deception; to evade.

summary judgment A procedural device available for prompt and expeditious disposition of a case where there is no genuine issue of fact and the moving party is entitled to win as a matter of law.

summary jury trial A trial heard by a jury without witnesses; sometimes used in federal courts to save time and money. The jury renders a nonbinding decision and the law requires the parties to negotiate their dispute after the jury rules.

supra "Above" (Latin). In a written work, refers readers to a previous section.

surety One who undertakes or guarantees to pay the debt of another in the event the debt is not paid.

surrogate A judicial officer of limited jurisdiction in probate and in some adoptions; one who acts for another.

T

tariff A rule or condition of air travel that binds the airline and passengers. Tariffs are developed by airlines and approved by the federal Department of Transportation.

tavern A place where alcoholic beverages are sold to be consumed on the premises.

tenancy A person's right to possess or hold an estate, whether by lease or by title.

tenancy at suffrage A tenancy whereby one is originally in lawful possession of a lease and subsequently holds over beyond the end of one's expired lease without lawful authority.

tenancy at will A right of possession that arises by an express contract or by implication for an indefinite time.

tenancy by the entirety Ownership by husband and wife.

tenancy in common The possession of property by two or more people wherein each party possesses an undivided interest in the entire property.

time sharing A joint ownership of property that unites in unity of interest or liability, is participated in or used by two or more people, and is held or shared in common.

theft of services A crime consisting of the use of services, such as a hotel room or a restaurant meal, with the intent of avoiding payment and the act of failing to pay.

tort A violation of a legal duty (a wrongful act) by one person that injures another. (Breaches of contractual duties are not considered torts, however.)

tortious Wrongful.

trade usage Practices or modes of dealing that are generally adhered to in a particular industry, such that an expectation arises that they will be honored in a given transaction.

trademark Any word, name, symbol, or device adopted and used by a manufacturer or merchant to identify its goods and distinguish them from goods sold or manufactured by others (such as McDonald's yellow arches).

trademark infringement Use of another company's business name or logo without permission.

transient A person who seeks a room at an inn on a temporary rather than a permanent basis.

treble damages The award of three times the loss suffered by an injured plaintiff.

trespasser One who enters a place without permission of the owner or occupier.

U

under seal A signed document that attests it was made in a formal manner by a particular insignia attached that imports consideration as a necessary part of a valid contract.

Uniform Commercial Code (UCC) A set of rules designed to simplify and modernize the law governing the sale of goods.

uniform standard Regular; even; applying generally to all equally.

unilateral mistake An error made by one party to a contract as to the terms or performance expected.

unitary rule The rule enforcing the Civil Rights Act when a covered facility is located within a noncovered business; both the covered and noncovered businesses are subject to the Act.

unjust enrichment An inequitable profit at someone else's expense.

V

variance Permission from the local government to deviate from a zoning restriction.

victualler A keeper of a restaurant.

violation Not in accordance with.

vitiate Destroy the legal effect or binding force of something.

void contract A contract that is unenforceable in court.

W

will The expression of a person's wishes concerning disposition of property after death.

withhold To hold back; refrain.

writ of attachment The act of taking or seizing the property of an individual in order to bring him or her under the control of the court.

Z

zoning The process by which local governments can restrict the manner in which property owners can use their land.

INDEX